Teacher's Calendar

PARENT-TEACHER COLLECTION

1999-2000

The Day-by-Day Directory to Holidays, Historic Events, Birthdays and Special Days, Weeks and Months

Compiled by Sandy Whiteley

With Kim Summers and Sally Walker

CONTEMPORARY BOOKS

☆ *The Teacher's Calendar, 1999–2000* ☆

NTC/CONTEMPORARY PUBLISHING GROUP, INC.
A TRIBUNE EDUCATION COMPANY
4255 WEST TOUHY AVENUE
LINCOLNWOOD, ILLINOIS 60646-1975
FAX: (847) 679-6388
PHONE: (847) 679-5500

Printed in USA

— NOTICE —

Events listed herein are not necessarily endorsed by the editors or publisher. Every effort has been made to assure the correctness of all entries, but neither the authors nor the publisher can warrant their accuracy. IT IS IMPERATIVE, IF FINANCIAL PLANS ARE TO BE MADE IN CONNECTION WITH DATES OR EVENTS LISTED HEREIN, THAT PRINCIPALS BE CONSULTED FOR FINAL INFORMATION.

GRAPHIC IMAGES

The interior illustrations were created for this book by Dan Krovatin.

Library of Congress Cataloging-in-Publication Data

Whiteley, Sandra, 1943–
    The teacher's calendar, 1999–2000 : the day-by-day directory to holidays, special days, weeks and months, festivals, historic events, and birthdays / compiled by Sandy Whiteley with Kim Summers and Sally Walker.
        p.   cm.
    Includes bibliographical references and index.
    ISBN 0-8092-2662-6
    1. Holidays.   2. Birthdays.   3. Anniversaries.   4. Festivals.
5. Schedules, School.   I. Summers, Kim (Kim A.)   II. Walker, Sally M.   III. Title.   IV. Title: Teacher's calendar.
LB3525.W55   1999
371.2′3—dc21   99-13240
                                                                          CIP

☆ *The Teacher's Calendar, 1999–2000* ☆

TABLE OF CONTENTS

★ in text indicates Presidential Proclamations

☆ *The Teacher's Calendar, 1999–2000* ☆

WELCOME TO *THE TEACHER'S CALENDAR*

Welcome to The Teacher's Calendar

This first edition of *The Teacher's Calendar* contains about 3,900 events that you can use in planning the school calendar, creating bulletin boards and developing lesson plans. Many of the entries were taken from the 1999 edition of *Chase's Calendar of Events*, a reference book which for 42 years has provided librarians and the media with events arranged day-by-day. Several hundred entries were written especially for *The Teacher's Calendar*. For example, among the Birthdays Today entries are birthdays for hundreds of authors of children's books. We've also added the dates of national professional meetings for teachers, children's book conferences and other events of interest to professional educators.

Types of Events

National Holidays and State Days: Public holidays of other nations are gleaned from United Nations documents and from information from tourism agencies. Technically, the United States has no national holidays. Those holidays proclaimed by the president apply only to federal employees and to the District of Columbia. Governors of the states proclaim holidays for their states. In practice, federal holidays are usually proclaimed as state holidays as well. Some governors also proclaim holidays unique to their state but not all state holidays are commemorated with the closing of schools and offices.

Religious Observances: Principal observances of the Christian, Jewish and Muslim faiths are presented with background information from their respective calendars. We use anticipated dates for Muslim holidays. There is no single Hindu calendar and different Hindu sects define the Hindu lunar month differently. There is no single lunar calendar that serves as a model for all Buddhists either. Therefore, we are able to provide only a limited number of religious holidays for these faiths.

Historic Events and Birth Anniversaries: Dates for these entries have been gathered from a wide range of reference books. Most birthdays here are for people who are deceased. Birthdays of living people are usually listed under Birthdays Today.

Astronomical Phenomena: Information about eclipses, equinoxes and solstices, and moon phases is calculated from the annual publication, *Astronomical Phenomena*, from the US Naval Observatory. Dates for these events in *Astronomical Phenomena* are given in Universal Time (i.e., Greenwich Mean Time). We convert these dates and times into Eastern Standard or Eastern Daylight Time.

Sponsored Events: We obtain information on these events directly from their sponsors and provide contact information for the sponsoring organization.

Presidential Proclamations: We have included in the day-by-day chronology proclamations that have continuing authority with a formula for calculating the dates of observance. The most recent proclamations can be found on the World Wide Web at the Federal Register Online: www.access.gpo.gov.

Other Special Days, Weeks and Months: Information on these events is also obtained from their sponsors.

Process for Declaring Special Observances

How do special days, weeks and months get created? The president of the United States has the authority to declare a commemorative event by proclamation, but this is done infrequently. In 1998, for example, the president issued about 100 proclamations. Many of these, such as Mother's Day and Bill of Rights Week, were proclamations for which there was legislation giving continuing authority for a proclamation to be issued each year.

Until 1995, Congress was active in seeing that special observances were commemorated. Members of the Senate and House could introduce legislation for a special observance to commemorate people, events and other activities they thought worthy of national recognition. Because these bills took up a lot of time on the part of members of Congress, when Congress met in January 1995 to reform its rules and procedures, it was decided to discontinue this practice. Today, the Senate passes resolutions commemorating special days, weeks and months but these resolutions do not have the force of law.

It is not necessary to have the president or a senator declare a special day, week or month; many of the events in *The Teacher's Calendar* have been declared only by their sponsoring organizations.

Websites

Web addresses have been provided when relevant. These URLs were checked the first week in December, 1998. Although we have tried to select sites maintained by the government, universities and other stable organizations, some of these sites undoubtedly will have disappeared by the time you try and look at them.

Curriculum Connections

These sidebars were written by Sally Walker, an author of children's books and a children's literature consultant, to give teachers ideas for integrating some of the events in *The Teacher's Calendar* into the classroom.

Acknowledgements

Thanks to the many people who helped in the process of compiling this first edition of *The Teacher's Calendar*: the staff at the Evanston and Skokie public libraries and the Northwestern University Library. Special thanks to our colleagues at NTC/Contemporary Publishing: Michael Brown, Phil Elliott, Gigi Grajdura, Beth Broadrup Lieberman, Richard Spears, Terry Stone and Jeanette Wojtyla. And now Assistant Editor Kim Summers and I invite you to join us in the celebration of the coming school year.

January 1999   Sandy Whiteley, MLS, Editor

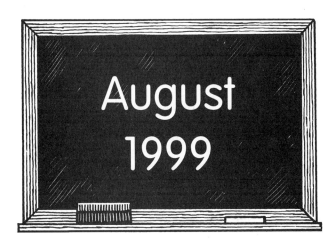

August 1999

AUGUST 1 — SUNDAY
Day 213 — 152 Remaining

AMERICAN FAMILY DAY IN ARIZONA. Aug 1. Commemorated on the first Sunday in August.

AMERICAN HISTORY ESSAY CONTEST. Aug 1. American History Committee activities are promoted throughout the year with the essay contest conducted in grades 5–8 beginning in August and concluding when the national winners are announced in April at the DAR Continental Congress. Events vary, but include programs, displays, spot announcements and recognition of essay writers. For info: Natl Soc Daughters of the American Revolution, Historian-General, Admin Bldg, 1776 D St NW, Washington, DC 20006-5392. Phone: (202) 628-1776.

BENIN, PEOPLE'S REPUBLIC OF: NATIONAL DAY. Aug 1. Public holiday. Commemorates independence from France in 1960. Benin at that time was known as Dahomey.

BURK, MARTHA (CALAMITY JANE): DEATH ANNIVERSARY. Aug 1, 1903. Known as a frontierswoman and companion to Wild Bill Hickock, Calamity Jane Burk was born Martha Jane Canary at Princeton, MO, in May 1852. As a young girl living in Montana, she became an excellent markswoman. She went to the Black Hills of South Dakota as a scout for a geological expedition in 1875. Several opposing traditions account for her nickname, one springing from her kindness to the less fortunate, while another attributes it to the harsh warnings she would give men who offended her. She died Aug 1, 1903, at Terry, SD, and was buried at Deadwood, SD, next to Wild Bill Hickock.

CHILDREN'S VISION AND LEARNING MONTH. Aug 1–31. A month-long campaign encouraging parents to have their children's vision examined by an eye-care professional prior to the start of the new school year. For info: Huck Roberts, Exec Dir, American Foundation for Vision Awareness (AFVA), 243 N Lindbergh Blvd, St. Louis, MO 63141. Phone: (800) 927-AFVA. Fax: (314) 991-4101. E-mail: afva@aol.com.

DIARY OF ANNE FRANK: THE LAST ENTRY: 55th ANNIVERSARY. Aug 1, 1944. To escape deportation to concentration camps, the Jewish family of Otto Frank hid for two years in the warehouse of his food products business at Amsterdam. Gentile friends smuggled in food and other supplies during their confinement. Thirteen-year-old Anne Frank, who kept a journal during the time of their hiding, penned her last entry in the diary Aug 1, 1944: "[I] keep on trying to find a way of becoming what I would like to be, and what I could be, if . . . there weren't any other people living in the world." Three days later (Aug 4, 1944)

Grüne Polizei raided the "Secret Annex" where the Frank family was hidden. Anne and her sister were sent to Bergen-Belsen concentration camp where Anne died at age 15, two months before the liberation of Holland. Young Anne's diary, later found in the family's hiding place, has been translated into 30 languages and has become a symbol of the indomitable strength of the human spirit. See also: "Frank, Anne: Birth Anniversary" (June 12).

EMANCIPATION OF 500: ANNIVERSARY. Aug 1, 1791. Virginia planter Robert Carter III confounded his family and friends by filing a deed of emancipation for his 500 slaves. One of the wealthiest men in the state, Carter owned 60,000 acres over 18 plantations. The deed included the following words: "I have for some time past been convinced that to retain them in Slavery is contrary to the true principles of Religion and Justice and therefore it is my duty to manumit them." The document established a schedule by which 15 slaves would be freed each Jan 1, over a 21-year period, plus slave children would be freed at age 18 for females and 21 for males. It is believed this was the largest act of emancipation in US history and predated the Emancipation Proclamation by 70 years.

FIRST US CENSUS: ANNIVERSARY. Aug 1, 1790. The first census revealed that there were 3,939,326 citizens in the 16 states and the Ohio Territory. The US has taken a census every 10 years since 1790. The next one will be in 2000. For the exact population of the US today, calculated to the second, go to www.census.gov/main/www/popclock.html.

MITCHELL, MARIA: BIRTH ANNIVERSARY. Aug 1, 1818. An interest in her father's hobby and an ability for mathematics resulted in Maria Mitchell's becoming the first female professional astronomer. In 1847, while assisting her father in a survey of the sky for the US Coast Guard, Mitchell discovered a new comet and determined its orbit. She received many honors because of this, including being elected to the American Academy of Arts and Sciences—its first woman. Mitchell joined the staff at Vassar Female College in 1865—the first US female professor of astronomy—and in 1873 was a cofounder of the Association for the Advancement of Women. Born at Nantucket, MA, Mitchell died June 28, 1889, at Lynn, MA.

NATIONAL BACK-TO-SCHOOL MONTH. Aug 1–31. Grassroots community effort to help at-risk children prepare mentally, emotionally and physically for the upcoming school year. A key component of the Back-To-School program is insuring that children have the proper clothes and supplies they need to feel good about going to school. For info: Donna Strout, Operation Blessings Intl, 977 Centerville Turnpike, Virginia Beach, VA 23463. Phone: (757) 226-2443. Fax: (757) 226-6183. E-mail: donna.strout @OB.ORG.

NATIONAL INVENTORS' MONTH. Aug 1–31. To educate the American public about the value of creativity and inventiveness and the importance of inventions and inventors to the quality of our lives. This will be accomplished through the placement of media stories about living inventors in most of the top national, local and trade publications, as well as through the electronic media. Sponsored by the United Inventors Association of the USA (UIA-USA), the Academy of Applied Science and *Inventors' Digest*. See Curriculum Connection. For info: Joanne Hayes-Rines, Inventors' Digest. Phone: (617) 367-4540. Fax: (617) 723-6988. Or Julia Schopick. Phone: (708) 848-4788. Fax: (708) 848-4769. Web: www.inventorsdigest.com/.

OAK RIDGE ATOMIC PLANT BEGUN: ANNIVERSARY. Aug 1, 1943. Ground was broken at Oak Ridge, TN, for the first plant built to manufacture the uranium 235 needed to build an

AUGUST 1–31
NATIONAL INVENTORS MONTH

Student inventiveness and imagination are perfect tie-ins to National Inventors Month. Start by defining the term "invention." Then, have students list inventions they see in the classroom. Don't forget the small things like pens, paper, erasers and staplers. Move on to more elaborate inventions they use at home and in other places. Inventions may be grouped into categories with headings like Entertainment, Medicine or Making Work Easier. Then, turn your students into inventors—with artwork and writing projects. You may want to make up an "Invention Criteria Sheet" to steer the activity toward practical, rather than fanciful, inventions. If your students explore this subject in-depth, they can make prototypes of their inventions. A collection of inventions could become an Invention Fair.

Students should be encouraged to produce supportive documentation for inventions, including assembly instructions, owners' manuals or warranties. Encourage students to bring in examples of such documentation from home. Together, you can discuss the advantages of the booklets (safety and use) and the drawbacks (too long or too hard to understand).

Additional topics for older students include: patents, packaging and marketing. Advertising campaigns and marketing slogans breathe life and fun into the new inventions.

Related books that students will enjoy are: *Accidents May Happen: 50 Inventions Discovered by Mistake*, by Charlotte Jones (Bantam, 0-385-32240-2, $10.95 Gr. 2–8); *Brainstorm!: The Stories of Twenty American Kid Inventors*, by Tom Tucker (Farrar, Straus, 0-374-40928-5, $6.95 Gr. 3–8); and *Inventors*, by Martin W. Sandler (HarperCollins, 0-06-024923-4, $21.95 Gr. 4 & up).

atomic bomb. The plant was largely completed by July of 1944 at a final cost of $280 million. By August 1945 the total cost for development of the A-bomb ran to $1 billion.

PRESIDENT'S ENVIRONMENTAL YOUTH AWARD NATIONAL COMPETITION. Aug 1–July 31, 2000. Young people in all 50 states are invited to participate in the President's Environmental Youth Awards program, which offers them, individually and collectively, an opportunity to become an environmental force with their community. The program encourages individuals, school classes, schools, summer camps and youth organizations to promote local environmental awareness and positive community involvement. For info: Doris Gillispie, Environmental Education Coord, US Environmental Protection Agency, 401 M St, #1707, Washington, DC 20460. Phone: (202) 260-8749. Fax: (202) 260-0790.

PUPPETEERS OF AMERICA NATIONAL FESTIVAL. Aug 1–7. University of Washington, Seattle, WA. Festival of the Millennium. Celebrate a millennium of puppetry with an intense week of performances, workshops, panels and parties. For info: Puppeteers of America, #5 Cricklewood Path, Pasadena, CA 91107-1002. E-mail: PoAFest99@aol.com. Web: www.puppeteers .org/1999natl/default.htm.

August 1999	S	M	T	W	T	F	S
	1	2	3	4	5	6	7
	8	9	10	11	12	13	14
	15	16	17	18	19	20	21
	22	23	24	25	26	27	28
	29	30	31				

SISTERS' DAY. Aug 1. Celebrating the spirit of sisterhood—sisters nationwide show appreciation and give recognition to one another for the special relationship they share. Send a card, make a phone call, share memories, photos, flowers, candy, etc. Sisters may include biological sisters, sisterly friends, etc. Annually, the first Sunday in August each year. For info: Tricia Eleogram, 666 Hawthorne, Memphis, TN 38107. Phone: (901) 725-5190 or (901) 7550751. Fax: (901) 754-9923. E-mail: sistersday@aol.com.

SWITZERLAND: NATIONAL DAY. Aug 1. Anniversary of the founding of the Swiss Confederation. Commemorates a pact made in 1291. Parades, patriotic gatherings, bonfires and fireworks. Young citizens' coming-of-age ceremonies. Observed since 600th anniversary of Swiss Confederation was celebrated in 1891.

TRINIDAD AND TOBAGO: EMANCIPATION DAY. Aug 1. Public holiday.

BIRTHDAYS TODAY

Gail Gibbons, 55, author and illustrator (*Catch the Wind: All About Kites*), born Oak Park, IL, Aug 1, 1944.

AUGUST 2 — MONDAY
Day 214 — 151 Remaining

ALBERT EINSTEIN'S ATOMIC BOMB LETTER: ANNIVERSARY. Aug 2, 1939. Albert Einstein, world-famous scientist, a refugee from Nazi Germany, wrote a letter to US President Franklin D. Roosevelt, first mentioning a possible "new phenomenon . . . chain reactions . . . vast amounts of power" and "the construction of bombs." "A single bomb of this type," he wrote, "carried by boat and exploded in a port, might very well destroy the whole port together with some of the surrounding territory." An historic letter that marked the beginning of atomic weaponry. Six years and four days later, Aug 6, 1945, the Japanese port of Hiroshima was destroyed by the first atomic bombing of a populated place.

ANTIGUA AND BARBUDA: AUGUST MONDAY. Aug 2–3. The first Monday in August and the day following form the August Monday public holiday in this Caribbean nation.

AUSTRALIA: PICNIC DAY. Aug 2. The first Monday in August is a bank holiday in New South Wales and Picnic Day in Northern Territory, Australia.

BAHAMAS: EMANCIPATION DAY. Aug 2. Public holiday in Bahamas. Annually, the first Monday in August. Commemorates the emancipation of slaves by the British in 1834.

CANADA: CIVIC HOLIDAY. Aug 2. The first Monday in August is observed as a holiday in seven of Canada's 10 provinces. Civic Holiday in Manitoba, New Brunswick, Northwest Territories, Ontario and Saskatchewan, British Columbia Day in British Columbia and Heritage Day in Alberta.

COLORADO: ADMISSION DAY: ANNIVERSARY. Aug 2. Colorado. Annually, the first Monday in August. Commemorates Admission Day when Colorado became the 38th state in 1876.

DECLARATION OF INDEPENDENCE: OFFICIAL SIGNING ANNIVERSARY. Aug 2, 1776. Contrary to widespread misconceptions, the 56 signers did not sign as a group and did not do so July 4, 1776. John Hancock and Charles Thompson signed only draft copies that day, the official day the Declaration was adopted by Congress. The signing of the official declaration occurred Aug 2, 1776, when 50 men probably took part. Later that year, five more apparently signed separately and one added his name in a subsequent year. (From "Signers of the Declaration . . ." US Dept of the Interior, 1975.) See also: "Declaration of Independence" (July 4).

DISABILITY DAY IN KENTUCKY. Aug 2.

GRENADA: EMANCIPATION DAY. Aug 2. Grenada observes public holiday annually on the first Monday in August. Commemorates the emancipation of slaves by the British in 1834.

ICELAND: SHOP AND OFFICE WORKERS' HOLIDAY. Aug 2. In Iceland an annual holiday for shop and office workers is observed on the first Monday in August.

JAMAICA: INDEPENDENCE DAY. Aug 2. National holiday observing achievement of Jamaican independence from Britain Aug 6, 1962. Annually, the first Monday in August.

L'ENFANT, PIERRE CHARLES: BIRTH ANNIVERSARY. Aug 2, 1754. The architect, engineer and Revolutionary War officer who designed the plan for the city of Washington, DC, Pierre Charles L'Enfant was born at Paris, France. He died at Prince Georges County, MD, June 14, 1825.

MACEDONIA, FORMER YUGOSLAV REPUBLIC OF: NATIONAL DAY. Aug 2. Commemorates the nationalist uprising against the Ottoman Empire in 1903. Also known as St. Elias Day, the most sacred and celebrated day of the Macedonian people.

US GIRLS' JUNIOR (GOLF) CHAMPIONSHIP. Aug 2–7. Green Spring Valley Hunt Club, Owings Mills, MD. For info: US Golf Assn, Golf House, Championship Dept, Far Hills, NJ 07931. Phone: (908) 234-2300. Fax: (908) 234-9687. E-mail: usga@ixnetcom.com. Web: www.usga.org.

ZAMBIA: YOUTH DAY. Aug 2. National holiday. Focal point is Lusaka's Independence Stadium. Annually, the first Monday in August.

BIRTHDAYS TODAY

James Howe, 53, author (the Bunnicula series), born Oneida, NY, Aug 2, 1946.

AUGUST 3 — TUESDAY
Day 215 — 150 Remaining

COLUMBUS SAILS FOR THE NEW WORLD: ANNIVERSARY. Aug 3, 1492. Christopher Columbus, "Admiral of the Ocean Sea," set sail half an hour before sunrise from Palos, Spain. With three ships, *Niña*, *Pinta* and *Santa Maria*, and a crew of 90, he sailed "for Cathay" but found instead a New World of the Americas, first landing at Guanahani (San Salvador Island in the Bahamas) Oct 12. See also: "Columbus Day" (Oct 12).

GUINEA-BISSAU: COLONIZATION MARTYR'S DAY. Aug 3. National holiday is observed.

NATIONAL NIGHT OUT. Aug 3. Designed to heighten crime prevention awareness and to promote police-community partnerships. Annually, the first Tuesday in August. For info: Matt A. Peskin, Dir, Natl Assn of Town Watch, PO Box 303, Wynnewood, PA 19096. Phone: (610) 649-7055 or (800)648-3688. Web: www.natw.org.

NEW JERSEY STATE FAIR. Aug 3–13. Cherry Hill, NJ. Reithoffer Shows, book fair, various types of music entertainment, circus, food booths and sports events. Est attendance: 206,000. For info: New Jersey State Fair, 406 Richard Rd, Rockledge, FL 32955. Phone: (407) 633-4028. Fax: (407) 633-6930.

NIGER: INDEPENDENCE DAY. Aug 3. Commemorates the independence of this West African nation from France on this date in 1960.

SCOPES, JOHN T.: BIRTH ANNIVERSARY. Aug 3, 1900. Central figure in a cause célèbre (the "Scopes Trial" or the "Monkey Trial"), John Thomas Scopes was born at Paducah, KY. An obscure 24-year-old schoolteacher at the Dayton, TN, high school in 1925, he became the focus of world attention. Scopes never uttered a word at his trial, which was a contest between two of America's best-known lawyers (William Jennings Bryan and Clarence Darrow). The trial, July 10–21, 1925, resulted in Scopes's conviction "for teaching evolution" in Tennessee. He was fined $100. The verdict was upset on a technicality and the statute he was accused of breaching was repealed in 1967. Scopes died at Shreveport, LA, Oct 21, 1970.

BIRTHDAYS TODAY

Mary Calhoun, 73, author (*High-Wire Henry*), born Keokuk, IA, Aug 3, 1926.

AUGUST 4 — WEDNESDAY
Day 216 — 149 Remaining

COAST GUARD DAY. Aug 4. Celebrates anniversary of founding of the US Coast Guard in 1790.

MANDELA, NELSON: ARREST ANNIVERSARY. Aug 4, 1962. Nelson Rolihlahla Mandela, charismatic black South African leader, was born in 1918, the son of the Tembu tribal chief, at Umtata, Transkei territory of South Africa. A lawyer and political activist, Mandela, who in 1952 established the first black law partnership in South Africa, had been in conflict with the white government there much of his life. Acquitted of a treason charge after a trial that lasted from 1956 to 1961, he was apprehended again by security police, Aug 4, 1962. The subsequent trial, widely viewed as an indictment of white domination, resulted in Mandela's being sentenced to five years in prison. In 1963 he was taken from the Pretoria prison to face a new trial—for sabotage, high treason and conspiracy to overthrow the government—and in June 1964 he was sentenced to life in prison. See also: "Mandela, Nelson: Prison Release Anniversary" (Feb 11).

MOON PHASE: LAST QUARTER. Aug 4. Moon enters Last Quarter phase at 1:27 PM, EDT.

SCHUMAN, WILLIAM HOWARD: BIRTH ANNIVERSARY. Aug 4, 1910. American composer who won the first Pulitzer Prize for composition and founded the Juilliard School of Music, was born at New York. His compositions include *American Festival Overture*, *New England Triptych*, the baseball opera *The Mighty Casey* and *On Freedom's Ground*, written for the centennial of the Statue of Liberty in 1986. He was instrumental in the conception of the Lincoln Center for the Performing Arts and served as its first president. In 1985 he was awarded a special Pulitzer Prize for his contributions. He also received a National Medal of Arts in 1985 and a Kennedy Center Honor in 1989. Schuman died at New York City, Feb 15, 1992.

SCOTLAND: ABERDEEN INTERNATIONAL YOUTH FESTIVAL. Aug 4–14. Aberdeen, Scotland. Talented young people from all areas of the performing arts come from around the world to participate in this festival. Est attendance: 30,000. For info: Nicola Wallis, 3 Nuborn House, Clifton Rd, London, England SW19 4QT. Phone: (44) (181) 946-2995. Fax: (44) (181) 944-6507.

BIRTHDAYS TODAY

Yasser Arafat, 70, president of the Palestinian National Authority, born Jerusalem, Aug 4, 1929.

Roger Clemens, 37, baseball player, born Dayton, OH, Aug 4, 1962.

Jeff Gordon, 28, race car driver, born Pittsboro, IN, Aug 4, 1971.

AUGUST 5 — THURSDAY

Day 217 — 148 Remaining

BATTLE OF MOBILE BAY: ANNIVERSARY. Aug 5, 1864. A Union fleet under Admiral David Farragut attempted to run past three Confederate forts into Mobile Bay, AL. After coming under fire, the Union fleet headed into a maze of underwater mines, known at that time as torpedoes. The ironclad *Tecumseh* was sunk by a torpedo, after which Farragut is said to have exclaimed, "Damn the torpedoes, full steam ahead." The Union fleet was successful and Mobile Bay was secured.

BURKINA FASO: REPUBLIC DAY. Aug 5. Burkina Faso (formerly Upper Volta) gained autonomy from France in 1960.

ELIOT, JOHN: BIRTH ANNIVERSARY. Aug 5, 1604. American "Apostle to the Indians," translator of the Bible into an Indian tongue (the first Bible to be printed in America), was born at Hertfordshire, England. He died at Roxbury, MA, May 21, 1690.

FIRST ENGLISH COLONY IN NORTH AMERICA: FOUNDING ANNIVERSARY. Aug 5, 1583. Sir Humphrey Gilbert, English navigator and explorer, aboard his sailing ship, the *Squirrel*, sighted the Newfoundland coast and took possession of the area around St. John's harbor in the name of the Queen, thus establishing the first English colony in North America. Gilbert was lost at sea, in a storm off the Azores, on his return trip to England.

LYNCH, THOMAS: 250th BIRTH ANNIVERSARY. Aug 5, 1749. Signer, Declaration of Independence, born Prince George's Parish, SC. Died 1779 (lost at sea, exact date of death unknown).

WALLENBERG, RAOUL: BIRTH ANNIVERSARY. Aug 5, 1912. Swedish architect Raoul Gustaf Wallenberg was born at Stockholm, Sweden. He was the second person in history (Winston Churchill was the first) to be voted honorary American citizenship (US House of Representatives 396–2, Sept 22, 1981). He

is credited with saving 100,000 Hungarian Jews from almost certain death at the hands of the Nazis during WWII. Wallenberg was arrested by Soviet troops at Budapest, Hungary, Jan 17, 1945, and, according to the official Soviet press agency Tass, died in prison at Moscow, July 17, 1947.

WHOLE LANGUAGE UMBRELLA CONFERENCE. Aug 5–8. Rochester, NY. Affiliated with the National Council of Teachers of English, this conference presents children's authors speaking about their books. For info: Olga Vaughn, Conference Chair. Phone: (716) 266-0991. E-mail: nev27@aol.com.

WISCONSIN STATE FAIR. Aug 5–15. State Fair Park, Milwaukee, WI. Wisconsin celebrates its rural heritage at the state's most popular and most historic annual event. Features giant midway, concessions, livestock, food and flower judging and top-name entertainment. [Call 24-hour recorded information line at (414) 266-7188 for performance times and dates.] Est attendance: 930,000. For info: PR Dept, Wisconsin State Fair Park, PO Box 14990, West Allis, WI 53214-0990. Phone: (414) 266-7060. Fax: (414) 266-7007. E-mail: wsfp@mail.state.wi.us. Web: www.wsfp.state.wi.us.

BIRTHDAYS TODAY

Neil Alden Armstrong, 69, former astronaut (first man to walk on moon), born Wapakoneta, OH, Aug 5, 1930.

Patrick Aloysius Ewing, 37, basketball player, born Kingston, Jamaica, Aug 5, 1962.

AUGUST 6 — FRIDAY

Day 218 — 147 Remaining

ATOMIC BOMB DROPPED ON HIROSHIMA: ANNIVERSARY. Aug 6, 1945. At 8:15 AM, local time, an American B-29 bomber, the *Enola Gay*, dropped an atomic bomb named "Little Boy" over the center of the city of Hiroshima, Japan. The bomb exploded about 1,800 ft above the ground, killing more than 105,000 civilians and destroying the city. It is estimated that another 100,000 persons were injured and died subsequently as a direct result of the bomb and the radiation it produced. This was the first time in history that such a devastating weapon had been used by any nation.

BOLIVIA: INDEPENDENCE DAY. Aug 6. National holiday. Gained freedom from Spain in 1825. Named after Simon Bolivar.

FIRST WOMAN SWIMS THE ENGLISH CHANNEL: ANNIVERSARY. Aug 6, 1926. The first woman to swim the English Channel was 19-year-old Gertrude Ederle of New York, NY. Her swim was completed in 14 hours and 31 minutes.

FLEMING, ALEXANDER: BIRTH ANNIVERSARY. Aug 6, 1881. Sir Alexander Fleming, Scottish bacteriologist, discoverer

August 1999	S	M	T	W	T	F	S
	1	2	3	4	5	6	7
	8	9	10	11	12	13	14
	15	16	17	18	19	20	21
	22	23	24	25	26	27	28
	29	30	31				

of penicillin and 1954 Nobel Prize recipient, was born at Lochfield, Scotland. He died at London, England, Mar 11, 1955.

"GREAT DEBATE": ANNIVERSARY. Aug 6–Sept 10, 1787. The Constitutional Convention engaged in the "Great Debate" over the draft constitution, during which it determined that Congress should have the right to regulate foreign trade and interstate commerce, established a four-year term of office for the president and appointed a five-man committee to prepare a final draft of the Constitution.

HIROSHIMA DAY. Aug 6. There are memorial observances in many places for victims of the first atomic bombing of a populated place, which occurred at Hiroshima, Japan, in 1945, when an American B-29 bomber dropped an atomic bomb over the center of the city. More than 205,000 civilians died either immediately in the explosion or subsequently of radiation. A peace festival is held annually at Peace Memorial Park at Hiroshima in memory of the victims of the bombing.

JAMAICA: INDEPENDENCE ACHIEVED: ANNIVERSARY. Aug 6, 1962. Jamaica attained its independence after centuries of British rule. Sir Alexander Bustamante became the first Jamaican Prime Minister.

OHIO STATE FAIR. Aug 6–22. Columbus, OH. Family fun, amusement rides, games, food booths, parades, entertainment, rodeos, circus, auto thrill show and tractor pulls. Est attendance: 900,000. For info: Ohio State Fair, 717 E 17th Ave, Columbus, OH 43211. Phone: (614) 644-4000. Fax: (614) 644-4031.

ROOSEVELT, EDITH KERMIT CAROW: BIRTH ANNIVERSARY. Aug 6, 1861. Second wife of Theodore Roosevelt, 26th president of the US, whom she married in 1886. Born at Norwich, CT, she died at Long Island, NY, Sept 30, 1948.

VOTING RIGHTS ACT OF 1965 SIGNED: ANNIVERSARY. Aug 6, 1965. Signed into law by President Lyndon Johnson, the Voting Rights Act of 1965 was designed to thwart attempts to discriminate against minorities at the polls. The act suspended literacy and other disqualifying tests, authorized appointment of federal voting examiners and provided for judicial relief on the federal level to bar discriminatory poll taxes. Congress voted to extend the Act in 1975, 1984 and 1991.

BIRTHDAYS TODAY

Frank Asch, 53, author and illustrator (*Mooncake*), born Somerville, NJ, Aug 6, 1946.

Barbara Cooney, 82, illustrator and author (Caldecott for *The Ox-Cart Man, Chanticleer and the Fox*), born Brooklyn, NY, Aug 6, 1917.

David Robinson, 34, basketball player, born Key West, FL, Aug 6, 1965.

AUGUST 7 - SATURDAY

Day 219 — 146 Remaining

BUNCHE, RALPH JOHNSON: 95th BIRTH ANNIVERSARY. Aug 7, 1904. American statesman, UN official, Nobel Peace Prize recipient (the first black to win the award), born at Detroit, MI. Died Dec 9, 1971, at New York, NY.

CHILDREN'S LAWN PARTY. Aug 7 (Aug 8 rain date). Roseland Cottage, Bowen House, Woodstock, CT. Popular Victorian games from the 1800s such as hoop rolling, games of graces, ninepins and bilboquet along with croquet, spinning tops, marbles and jacks will delight young and old. The original peanut hunt will also be held and a hat-making table for children to create their own hats to wear during the day will be available. Roseland Cot-

tage is owned and operated by the Society for the Preservation of New England Antiquities and is a National Historic Landmark. Annually, the first Saturday in August. Est attendance: 200. For info: Pam Russo, Site Mgr, Roseland Cottage, PO Box 186, Woodstock, CT 06281. Phone: (860) 928-4074. Fax: (860) 963-2208.

COTE D'IVOIRE: NATIONAL DAY. Aug 7. Commemorates the independence of the Ivory Coast from France in 1960.

DESERT SHIELD: ANNIVERSARY. Aug 7, 1990. Five days after the Iraqi invasion of Kuwait, US President George Bush ordered the military buildup that would become known as Desert Shield, to prevent further Iraqi advances. In January 1991, this would lead to the Persian Gulf War or Desert Storm.

FIRST PICTURE OF EARTH FROM SPACE: 40th ANNIVERSARY. Aug 7, 1959. US satellite *Explorer VI* transmitted the first picture of Earth from space. For the first time we had a likeness of our planet based on more than projections and conjectures.

HALFWAY POINT OF SUMMER. Aug 7. At 11:40 AM, EDT, Aug 7, 1999, 46 days, 19 hours and 51 minutes will have elapsed and the equivalent will remain before 7:31 AM, EDT, Sept 23, 1999, the autumnal equinox and the beginning of autumn.

NATIONAL MUSTARD DAY. Aug 7. Mustard lovers across the nation pay tribute to the king of condiments by slathering their favorite mustard on hot dogs, pretzels, licorice and even ice cream (an acquired taste)! The Mount Horeb Mustard Museum contains the world's largest collection of prepared mustards and mustard memorabilia. Celebration festivities include free hot dogs, mustard games and mustard squirting. Annually, the first Saturday in August. Est attendance: 1,000. For info: Barry M. Levenson, Curator, The Mount Horeb Mustard Museum, 109 E Main St, Mount Horeb, WI 53572. Phone: (608) 437-3986. Fax: (608) 437-4018. E-mail: curator@mustardweb.com. Web: www.mustardweb.com.

PURPLE HEART: ANNIVERSARY. Aug 7, 1782. At Newburgh, NY, General George Washington ordered the creation of a Badge of Military Merit. The badge consisted of a purple cloth heart with silver braided edge. Only three are known to have been awarded during the Revolutionary War. The award was reinstituted on the bicentennial of Washington's birth, Feb 22, 1932, and recognizes those wounded in action.

US WAR DEPARTMENT ESTABLISHED: ANNIVERSARY. Aug 7, 1789. The second presidential cabinet department, the War Department, was established by Congress.

BIRTHDAYS TODAY

Betsy Byars, 71, author (*The Summer of the Swans*, the Bingo Brown series), born Charlotte, NC, Aug 7, 1928.

AUGUST 8 - SUNDAY

Day 220 — 145 Remaining

BHUTAN: NATIONAL DAY. Aug 8. National holiday observed commemorating independence from India in 1949.

BONZA BOTTLER DAY™. Aug 8. To celebrate when the number of the day is the same as the number of the month. Bonza Bottler Day™ is an excuse to have a party at least once a month. For info: Gail M. Berger, 109 Matthew Ave, Poca, WV 25159. Phone: (304) 776-7746. E-mail: gberger5@aol.com.

DON'T WAIT—CELEBRATE! WEEK. Aug 8–14. To encourage frequent festivities acknowledging small but significant accomplishments such as team wins, good grades, completed projects, new neighbors, braces off, balanced checkbooks. Gathering for these minigalas will enhance and nurture relationships while raising the self-esteem of the honorees. Annually, the second full week in August. For info: Patty Sachs, Celebration Creations, 4520 Excelsior Blvd, Minneapolis, MN 55416. Phone: (612) 879-4592. E-mail: partysachs@internetmci.com. Web: www.geocities.com/~partyexpert/Dontwait.html.

FAMILY DAY. Aug 8. To focus attention on family solidarity and its potential as the best teacher of basic beliefs and values. Annually, the second Sunday in August. For info: Kiwanis Intl, Program Dvmt Dept, 3636 Woodview Trace, Indianapolis, IN 46268. E-mail: kiwanismail@kiwanis.org. Web: www.kiwanis.org.

HENSON, MATTHEW A.: BIRTH ANNIVERSARY. Aug 8, 1866. American black explorer, born at Charles County, MD. He met Robert E. Peary while working in a Washington, DC, store in 1888 and was hired to be Peary's valet. He accompanied Peary on his seven subsequent Arctic expeditions. During the successful 1908–09 expedition to the North Pole, Henson and two of the four Eskimo guides reached their destination on Apr 6, 1909. Peary arrived minutes later and verified the location. Henson's account of the expedition, *A Negro Explorer at the North Pole*, was published in 1912. In addition to the Congressional medal awarded all members of the North Pole expedition, Henson received the Gold Medal of the Geographical Society of Chicago and, at 81, was made an honorary member of the Explorers Club at New York, NY. Died Mar 9, 1955, at New York, NY.

MONTANAFAIR. Aug 8–15. MetraPark, Billings, MT. Montana's biggest event featuring exhibits, livestock events, carnival, rodeo and entertainment. Est attendance: 240,000. For info: MetraPark, PO Box 2514, Billings, MT 59103. Phone: (406) 256-2400.

ODIE: BIRTHDAY. Aug 8, 1978. Commemorates the birthday of Odie, Garfield's sidekick, who first appeared in the Garfield comic strip in 1978. For info: Kim Campbell, Paws, Inc, 5440 E Co Rd, 450 N, Albany, IN 47320. Web: www.garfield.com.

RAWLINGS, MARJORIE KINNAN: BIRTH ANNIVERSARY. Aug 8, 1896. American short-story writer and novelist (*The Yearling*), born at Washington, DC. Rawlings died at St. Augustine, FL, Dec 14, 1953.

BIRTHDAYS TODAY

Tipper Gore, 51, Second Lady, wife of Vice-President Al Gore, born Mary Elizabeth Aitcheson, Washington, DC, Aug 8, 1948.

Jane Dee Hull, 64, Governor of Arizona (R), born Kansas City, MO, Aug 8, 1935.

Edward T. Schafer, 53, Governor of North Dakota (R), born Bismarck, ND, Aug 8, 1946.

		S	M	T	W	T	F	S
August		1	2	3	4	5	6	7
1999		8	9	10	11	12	13	14
		15	16	17	18	19	20	21
		22	23	24	25	26	27	28
		29	30	31				

AUGUST 9 — MONDAY
Day 221 — 144 Remaining

ATOMIC BOMB DROPPED ON NAGASAKI: ANNIVERSARY. Aug 9, 1945. Three days after the atomic bombing of Hiroshima, an American B-29 bomber named *Bock's Car* left its base on Tinian Island carrying a plutonium bomb nicknamed "Fat Man." Its target was the Japanese city of Kokura, but because of clouds and poor visibility the bomber headed for a secondary target, Nagasaki, where at 11:02 AM, local time, it dropped the bomb, killing an estimated 70,000 persons and destroying about half the city. The next day the Japanese government surrendered, bringing WWII to an end.

COCHRAN, JACQUELINE: DEATH ANNIVERSARY. Aug 9, 1980. American pilot Jacqueline Cochran was born at Pensacola, FL, in 1910. She began flying in 1932 and by the time of her death she had set more distance, speed and altitude records than any other pilot, male or female. She was founder and head of the WASPs (Women's Air Force Service Pilots) during WWII; she won the Distinguished Service Medal in 1945 and the US Air Force Distinguished Flying Cross in 1969. She died at Indio, CA.

NIXON RESIGNS: 25th ANNIVERSARY. Aug 9, 1974. Richard Milhous Nixon's resignation from the presidency of the US, which he had announced in a speech to the American people on Thursday evening, Aug 8, became effective at noon. Nixon, under threat of impeachment as a result of the Watergate scandal, became the first person to resign the presidency. He was succeeded by Vice President Gerald Rudolph Ford, the first person to serve as vice president and president without having been elected to either office. Ford granted Nixon "full, free and absolute pardon" Sept 8, 1974. Although Nixon was the first US president to resign, two vice presidents had resigned: John C. Calhoun, Dec 18, 1832, and Spiro T. Agnew, Oct 10, 1973.

PIAGET, JEAN: BIRTH ANNIVERSARY. Aug 9, 1896. Born at Neuchatel, Switzerland, Piaget is the major figure in developmental psychology. His theory of cognitive development still influences educators today. Piaget died at Geneva, Switzerland, Sept 16, 1980.

PERSEID METEOR SHOWERS. Aug 9–13. Among the best-known and most spectacular meteor showers are the Perseids, peaking about Aug 10–12. As many as 50–100 may be seen in a single night. Wish upon a "falling star"!

SINGAPORE: INDEPENDENCE DAY. Aug 9, 1965. Most festivals in Singapore are Chinese, Indian or Malay, but celebration of national day is shared by all to commemorate the withdrawal of Singapore from Malaysia and its becoming an independent state in 1965. Music, parades, dancing.

SOUTH AFRICA: NATIONAL WOMEN'S DAY. Aug 9. National holiday. Commemorates the march of women in Pretoria to protest the pass laws in 1956.

TRAVERS, P(AMELA) L.: BIRTH ANNIVERSARY. Aug 9, 1899. Famous for her Mary Poppins series, P.L. Travers was born at Maryborough, Queensland, Australia. *Mary Poppins* was made into a movie by Disney in 1964. Travers died at London, England, Apr 23, 1996.

UNITED NATIONS: INTERNATIONAL DAY OF THE WORLD'S INDIGENOUS PEOPLE. Aug 9. On Dec 23, 1994, the General Assembly decided that the International Day of the World's Indigenous People shall be observed every year during the International Decade of the World's Indigenous People (1994–2004) (Res 49/214). The date marks the anniversary of the first day of the meeting in 1992 of the Working Group on Indigenous Populations of the Subcommission on Prevention of Discrimination and Protection of Minorities. For info: United Nations, Dept of Public Info, Public Inquiries Unit, RM GA-57, New York, NY 10017. Phone: (212) 963-4475. Fax: (212) 963-0071. E-mail: inquiries@un.org.

VEEP DAY. Aug 9. Commemorates the day in 1974 when Richard Nixon's resignation let Gerald Ford succeed to the presidency of the US. This was the first time the new Constitutional provisions for presidential succession in the Twenty-Fifth Amendment of 1967 were used. For info: c/o Bob Birch, The Puns Corps, PO Box 2364, Falls Church, VA 22042-0364. Phone: (703) 533-3668.

WEBSTER-ASHBURTON TREATY SIGNED: ANNIVERSARY. Aug 9, 1842. The treaty delimiting the eastern section of the Canadian-American border was negotiated by the US Secretary of State, Daniel Webster, and Alexander Baring, president of the British Board of Trade. The treaty established the boundaries between the St. Croix and Connecticut rivers, between Lake Superior and the Lake of the Woods and between Lakes Huron and Superior. The treaty was signed at Washington, DC.

BIRTHDAYS TODAY

William Daley, 51, US Secretary of Commerce (Clinton administration), born Chicago, IL, Aug 9, 1948.

Whitney Houston, 36, singer ("And I Will Always Love You"), actress (*Waiting to Exhale*), born Newark, NJ, Aug 9, 1963.

Brett Hull, 35, hockey player, born Belleville, Ontario, Canada, Aug 9, 1964.

Ashley Johnson, 16, actress ("Growing Pains," voice of Gretchen on "Recess"), born Camarillo, CA, Aug 9, 1983.

Patricia McKissack, 55, author, with her husband Fredrick (*Christmas in the Big House*), born Nashville, TN, Aug 9, 1944.

Deion Sanders, 32, football and baseball player, born Ft Meyers, FL, Aug 9, 1967.

Seymour Simon, 68, author (*Earthquakes, The Universe*), born New York, NY, Aug 9, 1931.

AUGUST 10 — TUESDAY
Day 222 — 143 Remaining

ECUADOR: INDEPENDENCE DAY. Aug 10. National holiday. Celebrates declaration of independence in 1809. Freedom from Spain attained May 24, 1822.

GINSBURG SWORN IN AS 107th JUSTICE: ANNIVERSARY. Aug 10, 1993. One week after her confirmation by the Senate, Judge Ruth Bader Ginsburg was sworn in as the 107th Supreme Court justice. Ginsburg, a former leading women's-rights advocate, became the court's second woman justice.

HOOVER, HERBERT CLARK: 125th BIRTH ANNIVERSARY. Aug 10, 1874. The 31st president of the US was born at West Branch, IA. Hoover was the first president born west of the Mississippi River and the first to have a telephone on his desk (installed Mar 27, 1929). "Older men declare war. But it is youth that must fight and die," he said at Chicago, IL, at the Republican National Convention, June 27, 1944. Hoover died at New York, NY, Oct 20, 1964. The Sunday nearest Aug 10th is observed in Iowa as Herbert Hoover Day.

JAPAN'S UNCONDITIONAL SURRENDER: ANNIVERSARY. Aug 10, 1945. A gathering to discuss surrender terms took place in Emperor Hirohito's bomb shelter; the participants were stalemated. Hirohito settled the question, believing continuation of the war would only result in further loss of Japanese lives. A message was transmitted to Japanese ambassadors in Switzerland

and Sweden to accept the terms issued at Potsdam July 26, 1945, except that the Japanese emperor's sovereignty must be maintained. The Allies devised a plan under which the emperor and the Japanese government would administer under the rule of the Supreme Commander of the Allied Powers and the Japanese surrendered.

MISSOURI: ADMISSION DAY: ANNIVERSARY. Aug 10. Became 24th state in 1821.

SMITHSONIAN INSTITUTION FOUNDED: ANNIVERSARY. Aug 10, 1846. Founding of the Smithsonian Institution at Washington, DC. It was designed to hold the many scientific, historical and cultural collections that belong to the US. The National Museum of Natural History, the National Zoo, the National Museum of American Art, the National Air and Space Museum and the National Gallery of Art are among the museums in the Smithsonian Institution. For info for teachers from the Smithsonian: educate.si.edu. For info: Smithsonian Institution, 900 Jefferson Dr SW, Washington, DC 20560. Phone: (202) 357-2700.

BIRTHDAYS TODAY

Thomas J. Dygard, 68, author of sports books (*Game Plan*), born Little Rock, AR, Aug 10, 1931.

AUGUST 11 — WEDNESDAY
Day 223 — 142 Remaining

ATCHISON, DAVID R.: BIRTH ANNIVERSARY. Aug 11, 1807. Missouri legislator who was president of the US for one day. Born at Frogtown, KY, Atchison's strong pro-slavery opinions made his name prominent in legislative debates. He served as president pro tempore of the Senate a number of times, and he became president of the US for one day—Sunday, Mar 4, 1849—pending the swearing in of President-elect Zachary Taylor, Mar 5, 1849. The city of Atchison, KS, and the county of Atchison, MO, are named for him. He died at Gower, MO, Jan 26, 1886.

CHAD: INDEPENDENCE DAY. Aug 11. National holiday. Commemorates independence from France in 1960.

FREDERICK DOUGLASS SPEAKS: ANNIVERSARY. Aug 11, 1841. Having escaped from slavery only three years earlier, Frederick Douglass was legally a fugitive when he first spoke before an audience. At an antislavery convention on Nantucket Island, Douglass spoke simply but eloquently about his life as a slave. His words were so moving that he was asked to become a full-time lecturer for the Massachusetts Anti-Slavery Society. Douglass became a brilliant orator, writer and abolitionist who championed the rights of blacks as well as the rights of all humankind.

FREEMAN, DON: BIRTH ANNIVERSARY. Aug 11, 1908. Author and illustrator (*Corduroy*), born at San Diego, CA. Died Feb 1, 1978.

HALEY, ALEX PALMER: BIRTH ANNIVERSARY. Aug 11, 1921. Born at Ithaca, NY, Alex Palmer Haley was raised by his grandmother at Henning, TN. In 1939 he entered the US Coast Guard and served as a cook, but eventually he became a writer and college professor. His first book, *The Autobiography of Malcolm X*, sold six million copies and was translated into eight languages. *Roots*, his Pulitzer Prize–winning novel published in 1976, sold millions, was translated into 37 languages and was made into an eight-part TV miniseries in 1977. The story generated an enormous interest in family ancestry. Haley died at Seattle, WA, Feb 13, 1992.

INDIANA STATE FAIR. Aug 11–22. Indiana State Fairgrounds Event Center, Indianapolis, IN. Top-rated livestock exhibition, world-class harness racing, top country music, giant midway and Pioneer Village. Est attendance: 700,000. For info: Jeff Fites, Publicity Coord, Indiana State Fair, 1202 E 38th St, Indianapolis, IN 46205-2869. Phone: (317) 927-7500. Fax: (317) 927-7578. Web: www.state.in.us/statefair/

MOON PHASE: NEW MOON. Aug 11. Moon enters New Moon phase at 7:08 AM, EDT.

"RUGRATS" PREMIERE: ANNIVERSARY. Aug 11, 1991. This animated cartoon features the toddler children of a trio of suburban families. One-year-old Tommy Pickles and his dog Spike play with 15-month-old twins Phil and Lil DeVille. Other characters include two-year-old Chuckie and three-year-old Angelica. Created by the animators of "The Simpsons." A Rugrats movie was released in 1998.

SAINT CLARE OF ASSISI: FEAST DAY. Aug 11, 1253. Chiara Favorone di Offreduccio, a religious leader inspired by St. Francis of Assisi, was the first woman to write her own religious order rule. Born at Assisi, Italy, July 16, 1194, she died there Aug 11, 1253. A "Privilege of Poverty" freed her order from any constraint to accept material security, making the "Poor Clares" totally dependent on God.

SOLAR ECLIPSE. Aug 11. Total eclipse of the sun. Eclipse begins at 4:26 AM, EDT, reaches greatest eclipse at 6:51 AM, EDT and ends at 9:40 AM, EDT. Visible in northeastern parts of US, eastern Canada, North Atlantic Ocean, Europe (including British Isles), North Africa, Asia except eastern part, North Indian Ocean.

BIRTHDAYS TODAY

Joanna Cole, 55, author (The Magic School Bus series), born Newark, NJ, Aug 11, 1944.

Will Friedle, 23, actor ("Boy Meets World"), born Hartford, CT, Aug 11, 1976.

Hulk Hogan (born Terry Gene Bollea), 46, wrestler, actor, born Augusta, GA, Aug 11, 1953.

Tim Hutchinson, 50, US Senator (R, Arkansas), born Gravette, AR, Aug 11, 1949.

Stephen Wozniak, 49, Apple computer co-founder, born Sunnyvale, CA, Aug 11, 1950.

AUGUST 12 — THURSDAY
Day 224 — 141 Remaining

IOWA STATE FAIR. Aug 12–22. Iowa State Fairgrounds, Des Moines, IA. One of America's oldest and largest state fairs with one of the world's largest livestock shows. Ten-acre carnival, superstar grandstand stage shows, track events, spectacular free entertainment. 160-acre campgrounds. Est attendance: 900,000. For info: Kathie Swift, Mktg Dir, Iowa State Fair, Statehouse, 400 E 14th St, Des Moines, IA 50319-0198. Phone: (515) 262-3111. Fax: (515) 262-6906. Web: iowastatefair.org.

KING PHILIP ASSASSINATION: ANNIVERSARY. Aug 12, 1676. Native American, Philip, son of Massasoit, chief of the Wampanog tribe, was killed near Mt Hope, RI, by a renegade Indian of his own tribe, bringing to an end the first and bloodiest war between American Indians and white settlers of New England, a war that had raged for nearly two years and was known as King Philip's War.

MISSOURI STATE FAIR. Aug 12–22. Sedalia, MO. Livestock shows, commercial and competitive exhibits, horse show, car races, tractor pulls, carnival and headline musical entertainment. Economical family entertainment. Est attendance: 350,000. For info: Kimberly Allen, PR Dir, Missouri State Fair, 2503 W 16th, Sedalia, MO 65301. Phone: (816) 530-5600. Fax: (816) 530-5609.

SPACE MILESTONE: *ECHO I* (US). Aug 12, 1960. First successful communications satellite in Earth's orbit launched, used to relay voice and TV signals from one ground station to another.

THAILAND: BIRTHDAY OF THE QUEEN. Aug 12. The entire kingdom of Thailand celebrates the birthday of Queen Sirikit.

BIRTHDAYS TODAY

Mary Ann Hoberman, 69, author (*One of Each*), born Stamford, CT, Aug 12, 1930.

Ann Martin, 44, author (The Baby-Sitter's Club series), born Princeton, NJ, Aug 12, 1955.

Fredrick McKissack, 60, author, with his wife Patricia (*Christmas in the Big House*), born Nashville, TN, Aug 12, 1939.

Walter Dean Myers, 62, author (*Slam!*), born Martinsburg, WV, Aug 12, 1937.

Pete Sampras, 28, tennis player, born Washington, DC, Aug 12, 1971.

Antoine Walker, 23, basketball player, born Chicago, IL, Aug 12, 1976.

AUGUST 13 — FRIDAY
Day 225 — 140 Remaining

BERLIN WALL ERECTED: ANNIVERSARY. Aug 13, 1961. Early in the morning, the East German government closed the border between east and west sectors of Berlin with barbed wire fence to discourage further population movement to the west. Telephone and postal services were interrupted, and, later in the week, a concrete wall was built to strengthen the barrier between official crossing points. The dismantling of the wall began Nov 9, 1989. See also: "Berlin Wall: Dismantling Anniversary" (Nov 9).

CAXTON, WILLIAM: BIRTH ANNIVERSARY. Aug 13, 1422. First English printer, born at Kent, England. Died at London,

August 1999	S	M	T	W	T	F	S
	1	2	3	4	5	6	7
	8	9	10	11	12	13	14
	15	16	17	18	19	20	21
	22	23	24	25	26	27	28
	29	30	31				

England, 1491. Caxton produced first book printed in English (while working for a printer at Bruges, Belgium), the *Recuyell of the Histories of Troy*, in 1476, and in the autumn of 1476 set up a print shop at Westminster, becoming the first printer in England.

CENTRAL AFRICAN REPUBLIC: INDEPENDENCE DAY. Aug 13. Commemorates Proclamation of Independence from France of the Central African Republic in 1960.

FRIDAY THE THIRTEENTH. Aug 13. Variously believed to be a lucky or unlucky day. Every year has at least one Friday the 13th, but never more than three. One Friday in 1999 falls on the 13th day, in August. One Friday in 2000 falls on the 13th, in October. Fear of the number 13 is known as triskaidekaphobia.

INTERNATIONAL LEFT-HANDERS DAY. Aug 13. To recognize the needs and frustrations of left-handers and celebrate the good life of left-handedness. For info: Lefthanders Intl, Box 8249, Topeka, KS 66608. Phone: (913) 234-2177. Fax: (913) 232-3999.

OAKLEY, ANNIE: BIRTH ANNIVERSARY. Aug 13, 1860. Annie Oakley was born at Darke County, OH. She developed an eye as a markswoman early as a child, becoming so proficient that she was able to pay off the mortgage on her family farm by selling the game she killed. A few years after defeating vaudeville marksman Frank Butler in a shooting match, she married him and they toured as a team until joining Buffalo Bill's Wild West Show in 1885. She was one of the star attractions for 17 years. She died Nov 3, 1926, at Greenville, OH.

STONE, LUCY: BIRTH ANNIVERSARY. Aug 13, 1818. American women's rights pioneer, born near West Brookfield, MA, Lucy Stone dedicated her life to the abolition of slavery and the emancipation of women. A graduate of Oberlin College, she had to finance her education by teaching for nine years because her father did not favor college education for women. An eloquent speaker for her causes, she headed the list of 89 men and women who signed the call to the first national Woman's Rights Convention, held at Worcester, MA, October 1850. On May 1, 1855, she married Henry Blackwell. She and her husband aided in the founding of the American Suffrage Association, taking part in numerous referendum campaigns to win suffrage amendments to state constitutions. She died Oct 18, 1893, at Dorchester, MA.

TUNISIA: WOMEN'S DAY. Aug 13. General holiday. Celebration of independence of women.

BIRTHDAYS TODAY

Fidel Castro, 72, President of Cuba, born Mayari, Cuba, Aug 13, 1927.

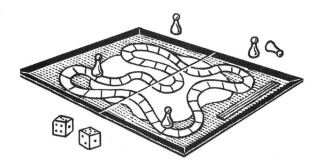

AUGUST 14 — SATURDAY
Day 226 — 139 Remaining

ATLANTIC CHARTER SIGNING: ANNIVERSARY. Aug 14, 1941. The charter grew out of a three-day conference aboard ship in the Atlantic Ocean, off the Newfoundland coast, and stated policies and goals for the postwar world. The eight-point agreement was signed by US President Franklin D. Roosevelt and British Prime Minister Winston S. Churchill.

BUD BILLIKEN PARADE. Aug 14. Chicago, IL. A parade especially for children begun in 1929 by Robert S. Abbott. The second largest parade in the US, it features bands, floats, drill teams and celebrities. Annually, the second Saturday in August. For info: Michael Brown, PR Dir, Chicago Defender Charities, 2400 S Michigan, Chicago, IL 60616. Phone: (312) 225-2400. Fax: (312) 255-9231.

SOCIAL SECURITY ACT: ANNIVERSARY. Aug 14, 1935. The Congress approved the Social Security Act, which contained provisions for the establishment of a Social Security Board to administer federal old-age and survivors' insurance in the US. By signing the bill into law, President Franklin D. Roosevelt was fulfilling a 1932 campaign promise.

V-J DAY. Aug 14, 1945. Anniversary of President Truman's announcement that Japan had surrendered to the Allies, setting off celebrations across the nation. Official ratification of surrender occurred aboard the USS *Missouri* at Tokyo Bay, Sept 2 (Far Eastern time).

BIRTHDAYS TODAY

Earvin ("Magic") Johnson, Jr, 40, former basketball player, born Lansing, MI, Aug 14, 1959.

Gary Larson, 49, cartoonist ("The Far Side"), born Tacoma, WA, Aug 14, 1950.

Alice Provensen, 81, author and illustrator, with her husband Martin (Caldecott for *The Glorious Flight: Across the Channel with Louis Bleriot*), born Chicago, IL, Aug 14, 1918.

AUGUST 15 — SUNDAY
Day 227 — 138 Remaining

ASSUMPTION OF THE VIRGIN MARY. Aug 15. Greek and Roman Catholic churches celebrate Mary's ascent to Heaven.

BONAPARTE, NAPOLEON: BIRTH ANNIVERSARY. Aug 15, 1769. Anniversary of birth of French emperor Napoleon Bonaparte on the island of Corsica. He died in exile May 5, 1821, on the island of St. Helena. Public holiday at Corsica, France.

CHAUVIN DAY. Aug 15. A day named for Nicholas Chauvin, French soldier from Rochefort, France, who idolized Napoleon and who eventually became a subject of ridicule because of his blind loyalty and dedication to anything French. Originally referring to bellicose patriotism, chauvinism has come to mean blind or absurdly intense attachment to any cause. Observed on Napoleon's birth anniversary because Chauvin's birth date is unknown.

CHILDREN'S LITERATURE NEW ENGLAND. Aug 15–21. Radcliffe College, Cambridge, MA. The topic of this summer institute is "Pathfinders." For info: Martha Walke, Children's Literature New England, PO Box 1422, Pepperell, MA 01463. Phone: (978) 433-1911. E-mail: Martha_Walke@Pike.pvt.k12.ma.us.

CONGO (BRAZZAVILLE): NATIONAL HOLIDAY. Aug 15. National day of the People's Republic of the Congo. Commemorates independence from France in 1960.

HARDING, FLORENCE KLING DeWOLFE: BIRTH ANNIVERSARY. Aug 15. Wife of Warren Gamaliel Harding, 29th president of the US, born at Marion, OH, Aug 15, 1860. Died at Marion, OH, Nov 21, 1924.

INDIA: INDEPENDENCE DAY. Aug 15. National holiday. Anniversary of Indian independence from Britain in 1947.

KOREA, REPUBLIC OF: LIBERATION DAY. Aug 15. National holiday commemorates acceptance by Japan of Allied terms of surrender in 1945, thereby freeing Korea from 36 years of Japanese domination. Also marks formal proclamation of the Republic of Korea in 1948. Military parades and ceremonies throughout country.

LIECHTENSTEIN: NATIONAL DAY. Aug 15. Public holiday.

TRANSCONTINENTAL US RAILWAY COMPLETION: ANNIVERSARY. Aug 15, 1870. The Golden Spike ceremony at Promontory Point, UT, May 10, 1869, was long regarded as the final link in a transcontinental railroad track reaching from an Atlantic port to a Pacific port. In fact, that link occurred unceremoniously on another date in another state. Diaries of engineers working at the site establish "the completion of a transcontinental track at a point 928 feet east of today's milepost 602, or 3,812 feet east of the present Union Pacific depot building at Strasburg (formerly Comanche)," CO. The final link was made at 2:53 PM, Aug 15, 1870. Annual celebration at Strasburg, CO, on a weekend in August. See also: "Golden Spike Driving: Anniversary" (May 10).

BIRTHDAYS TODAY

Stephen G. Breyer, 61, Associate Justice of the Supreme Court, born San Francisco, CA, Aug 15, 1938.

Linda Ellerbee, 55, journalist, host of "Nick News," born Bryan, TX, Aug 15, 1944.

AUGUST 16 — MONDAY

Day 228 — 137 Remaining

BENNINGTON BATTLE DAY: ANNIVERSARY. Aug 16, 1777. Anniversary of this Revolutionary War battle is a legal holiday in Vermont.

CANADA: YUKON DISCOVERY DAY: ANNIVERSARY. Aug 16. In the Klondike region of the Yukon, at Bonanza Creek (formerly known as Rabbit Creek), George Washington Carmack discovered gold Aug 16 or 17, 1896. During the following year more than 30,000 people joined the gold rush to the area. Anniversary is celebrated as a holiday (Discovery Day) in the Yukon, on nearest Monday.

August 1999	S	M	T	W	T	F	S
	1	2	3	4	5	6	7
	8	9	10	11	12	13	14
	15	16	17	18	19	20	21
	22	23	24	25	26	27	28
	29	30	31				

DOMINICAN REPUBLIC: RESTORATION OF THE REPUBLIC. Aug 16. The anniversary of the Restoration of the Republic is celebrated as an official public holiday.

LAWRENCE (OF ARABIA), T. E.: BIRTH ANNIVERSARY. Aug 16, 1888. British soldier, archaeologist and writer, born at Tremadoc, North Wales. During WWI, led the Arab revolt against the Turks and served as a spy for the British. His book, *Seven Pillars of Wisdom*, is a personal account of the Arab revolt. He was killed in a motorcycle accident at Dorset, England, May 19, 1935.

WYOMING STATE FAIR. Aug 16–21. Douglas, WY. Recognizing the products, achievements and cultural heritage of the people of Wyoming. Bringing together rural and urban citizens for an inexpensive, entertaining and educational experience. Features Livestock show for beef, swine, sheep and horses; Junior Livestock show for beef, swine, sheep, horses, dogs and rabbits; competitions and displays for culinary arts, needlework, visual arts and floriculture; 4-H and FFA County Chapters State qualifications competitions; Youth Talent Show; Demo Derby; live entertainment; midway; rodeos and an All Girl Rodeo (rough stock). Est attendance: 82,000. For info: Wyoming State Fair, Drawer 10, Douglas, WY 82633. Phone: (307) 358-2398. Fax: (307) 358-6030. E-mail: wystfair@coffey.com.

BIRTHDAYS TODAY

Matt Christopher, 82, author of sports books (*On the Court With . . . Michael Jordan*), born Bath, PA, Aug 16, 1917.

Reginald VelJohnson, 47, actor ("Family Matters"), born Raleigh, NC, Aug 16, 1952.

AUGUST 17 — TUESDAY

Day 229 — 136 Remaining

BALLOON CROSSING OF ATLANTIC OCEAN: ANNIVERSARY. Aug 17, 1978. Three Americans—Max Anderson, 44, Ben Abruzzo, 48, and Larry Newman, 31—all of Albuquerque, NM, became first to complete transatlantic trip in a balloon. Starting from Presque Isle, ME, Aug 11, they traveled some 3,200 miles in 137 hours, 18 minutes, landing at Miserey, France (about 60 miles west of Paris), in their craft, named the *Double Eagle II*.

CROCKETT, DAVID "DAVY": BIRTH ANNIVERSARY. Aug 17, 1786. American frontiersman, adventurer and soldier, born at Hawkins County, TN. Died during final heroic defense of the Alamo, Mar 6, 1836, at San Antonio, TX. In his *Autobiography* (1834), Crockett wrote, "I leave this rule for others when I'm dead, Be always sure you're right—then go ahead."

FORT SUMTER SHELLED BY NORTHERN FORCES: ANNIVERSARY. Aug 17, 1863. In what would become a long siege, Union forces began shelling Fort Sumter at Charleston, SC. The site of the first shots fired during the Civil War, Sumter endured the siege for a year and a half before being returned to Union hands.

FULTON SAILS STEAMBOAT: ANNIVERSARY. Aug 17, 1807. Robert Fulton began the first American steamboat trip between Albany and New York, NY, on a boat later called the *Clermont*. After years of promoting submarine warfare, Fulton engaged in a partnership with Robert R. Livingston, the US minister to France, allowing Fulton to design and construct a steamboat. His first success came in August 1803 when he launched a steam-powered vessel on the Seine. That same year the US Congress granted Livingston and Fulton exclusive rights to operate steamboats on New York waters during the next 20 years. The first Albany-to-New York trip took 32 hours to travel the 150-mile course.

Although his efforts were labeled "Fulton's Folly" by his detractors, his success allowed the partnership to begin commercial service the next year, Sept 4, 1808.

GABON: NATIONAL DAY. Aug 17. National holiday. Commemorates independence from France in 1960.

INDONESIA: INDEPENDENCE DAY. Aug 17. National holiday. Republic proclaimed in 1945. It was only after several years of fighting, however, that Indonesia was formally granted its independence by the Netherlands, Dec 27, 1949.

BIRTHDAYS TODAY

Christian Laettner, 30, NBA forward, member of the Dream team in the 1992 Olympics, born Angola, NY, Aug 17, 1969.

Myra Cohn Livingston, 73, poet (*Sky Songs, Space Songs*), born Omaha, NE, Aug 17, 1926.

AUGUST 18 — WEDNESDAY
Day 230 — 135 Remaining

CLEMENTE, ROBERTO: 65th BIRTH ANNIVERSARY. Aug 18, 1934. National League baseball player, born at Carolina, Puerto Rico. Drafted by the Pittsburgh Pirates in 1954, he played his entire major league career with them. Clemente died in a plane crash Dec 31, 1972, while on a mission of mercy to Nicaragua to deliver supplies he had collected for survivors of an earthquake. He was elected to the Baseball Hall of Fame in 1973.

DARE, VIRGINIA: BIRTH ANNIVERSARY. Aug 18, 1587. Virginia Dare, the first child of English parents to be born in the New World, was born to Ellinor and Ananias Dare, at Roanoke Island, NC, Aug 18, 1587. When a ship arrived to replenish their supplies in 1591, the settlers (including Virginia Dare) had vanished, without leaving a trace of the settlement.

LEWIS, MERIWETHER: 225TH BIRTH ANNIVERSARY. Aug 18, 1774. American explorer (of Lewis and Clark expedition), born at Albemarle County, VA. Died Oct 11, 1809, near Nashville, TN.

MAIL-ORDER CATALOG: ANNIVERSARY. Aug 18, 1872. The first mail-order catalog was published by Montgomery Ward. It was only a single sheet of paper. By 1904, the Montgomery Ward catalog weighed four pounds.

MOON PHASE: FIRST QUARTER. Aug 18. Moon enters First Quarter phase at 9:47 PM, EDT.

NINETEENTH AMENDMENT TO US CONSTITUTION RATIFIED: ANNIVERSARY. Aug 18, 1920. The 19th Amendment extended the right to vote to women.

BIRTHDAYS TODAY

Rosalynn (Eleanor) Smith Carter, 72, former First Lady, wife of President Jimmy Carter, 39th president of the US, born Plains, GA, Aug 18, 1927.

Paula Danziger, 55, author (*The Cat Ate My Gymsuit, Amber Brown Is Not a Crayon*), born Washington, DC, Aug 18, 1944.

Mike Johanns, 49, Governor of Nebraska (R), born Osage, IA, Aug 18, 1950.

Martin Mull, 56, actor ("Sabrina, the Teenage Witch"), born Chicago, IL, Aug 18, 1943.

AUGUST 19 — THURSDAY
Day 231 — 134 Remaining

AFGHANISTAN: INDEPENDENCE DAY. Aug 19. National day. Commemorates independence from British control over foreign affairs in 1919.

CLINTON, WILLIAM JEFFERSON (BILL): BIRTHDAY. Aug 19, 1946. The 42nd US President, born at Hope, AR. Re-elected to a second term in 1996.

KENTUCKY STATE FAIR (WITH WORLD CHAMPIONSHIP HORSE SHOW). Aug 19–29. Kentucky Fair and Expo Center, Louisville, KY. Midway, concerts by nationally known artists and the World's Championship Horse Show. Est attendance: 700,000. For info: Harold Workman, KY Fair and Expo Ctr, Box 37130, Louisville, KY 40233. Phone: (502) 367-5000.

★**NATIONAL AVIATION DAY.** Aug 19. Presidential Proclamation 2343, of July 25, 1939, covers all succeeding years. Always Aug 19 of each year since 1939. Observed annually on anniversary of birth of Orville Wright, who piloted "first self-powered flight in history," Dec 17, 1903. First proclaimed by President Franklin D. Roosevelt.

SPACE MILESTONE: *SPUTNIK 5* (USSR). Aug 19, 1960. Space menagerie satellite with dogs Belka and Strelka, mice, rats, houseflies and plants launched. These passengers became first living organisms recovered from orbit when the satellite returned safely to Earth the next day.

SWEDEN: SOUR HERRING PREMIERE. Aug 19. By ordinance, the year's supply of sour herring may begin to be sold on the third Thursday in August.

WRIGHT, ORVILLE: BIRTH ANNIVERSARY. Aug 19, 1871. Aviation pioneer (with his brother Wilbur) born at Dayton, OH, Aug 19, 1871, and died there Jan 30, 1948.

BIRTHDAYS TODAY

William Jefferson (Bill) Clinton, 53, 42nd president of the US, born Hope, AR, Aug 19, 1946.

John Stamos, 36, actor ("Full House"), born Cypress, CA, Aug 19, 1963.

Fred Thompson, 57, US Senator (R, Tennessee), actor (*In the Line of Fire*), born Sheffield, AL, Aug 19, 1942.

AUGUST 20 — FRIDAY
Day 232 — 133 Remaining

CALIFORNIA STATE FAIR. Aug 20–Sept 6. Sacramento, CA. Top-name entertainment, fireworks, California counties exhibits, livestock nursery, culinary delights, carnival rides, demolition derbies and award-winning wines and microbrews. For info: Cal Expo, PO Box 15649, Sacramento, CA 95852. Phone: (916) 263-3000. E-mail: SallyCSF@aol.com.

COLORADO STATE FAIR. Aug 20–Sept 6. State Fairgrounds, Pueblo, CO. One of the nation's oldest western fairs, it is also Colorado's largest single event, drawing more than a million visitors. Family fun, top-name entertainment, lots of food and festivities. For info: Colorado State Fair, Jerry Robbe, Pres/Genl Mgr, Pueblo, CO 81004. Phone: (719) 561-8484.

AUGUST 20
LAUNCH THE SCHOOL YEAR
WITH SPACE MILESTONES

Milestones of space exploration can launch the new school year. August has seen many successful "firsts," including the transmission of the first picture of Earth from space (Aug 7), the first flight of Earth organisms into space (Aug 19), the launch of *Voyager 2* (Aug 20), the first man-powered flight (Aug 23) and the launch of the space shuttle *Discovery* (Aug 30).

The space program launches rockets to explore and achieve scientific goals. A classroom can be viewed as a launching pad for academic goals. Brainstorming sessions about the new year's lessons can identify students' expectations about the topics they will be learning during the coming school days, weeks, months and year. Use their list of expectations to generate a "launching pad" list of classroom academic goals. Be sure to incorporate goals you as teacher must fulfill for district requirements. A launch pad bulletin board can serve as a constantly changing showcase for all student work that shows attainment of a goal, regardless of its size. Goals can include many kinds of "firsts": writing the letters of the alphabet, doing a math problem correctly, using scissors properly, producing a final draft of a composition, accomplishing reading goals, documenting science class observations and so on. Students can celebrate many "firsts," big and small, and recognize milestone achievements of classmates.

Art projects will get your student-generated bulletin board off to a quick start. Encourage kindergarten and primary students to draw a picture of something they would like to do in class this year. Time permitting, ask them to tell the class about their drawing— a good ice-breaker activity. Upper elementary and middle school students may write a paragraph, draw a picture or write a poem or a rap about what they want to accomplish during the school year. Small group discussions could explore ways some of the goals might be achieved.

GINZA HOLIDAY: JAPANESE CULTURAL FESTIVAL. Aug 20–22. Midwest Buddhist Temple, Chicago, IL. Experience the Waza (National Treasures tradition) by viewing 300 years of Edo craft tradition and seeing it come alive as master craftsmen from Tokyo demonstrate their arts. Japanese folk and classical dancing, martial arts, taiko (drums), flower arrangements and cultural displays. Chicken teriyaki, sushi, udon, shaved ice, corn on the cob and refreshments. Annually, the third weekend in August. Est attendance: 5,000. For info: Office Secretary, Midwest Buddhist Temple, 435 W Menomonee St, Chicago, IL 60614. Phone: (312) 943-7801. Fax: (312) 943-8069.

HARRISON, BENJAMIN: BIRTH ANNIVERSARY. Aug 20, 1833. The 23rd president of the US, born at North Bend, OH. He was the grandson of William Henry Harrison, 9th president of the US. His term of office, Mar 4, 1889–Mar 3, 1893, was preceded and followed by the presidential terms of Grover Cleveland (who thus became the 22nd and 24th president of the US). Harrison died at Indianapolis, IN, Mar 13, 1901.

August 1999	S	M	T	W	T	F	S
	1	2	3	4	5	6	7
	8	9	10	11	12	13	14
	15	16	17	18	19	20	21
	22	23	24	25	26	27	28
	29	30	31				

HUNGARY: NATIONAL DAY. Aug 20. National holiday. Commemorates the founding of Hungary by St. Stephen, ca. 1000. Celebrated as St. Stephen's Day.

O'HIGGINS, BERNARDO: BIRTH ANNIVERSARY. Aug 20, 1778. First ruler of Chile after its declaration of independence. Called the "Liberator of Chile." Born at Chillan, Chile. Died at Lima, Peru, Oct 24, 1842.

PERRY, OLIVER HAZARD: BIRTH ANNIVERSARY. Aug 20, 1785. American naval hero, born at South Kingston, RI. Died Aug 23, 1819, at sea. Best remembered is his announcement of victory at the Battle of Lake Erie, Sept 10, 1813 during the War of 1812: "We have met the enemy, and they are ours."

SPACE MILESTONE: *VOYAGER 2* (US). Aug 20, 1977. This unmanned spacecraft journeyed past Jupiter in 1979, Saturn in 1981, Uranus in 1986 and Neptune in 1989, sending photographs and data back to scientists on Earth.

BIRTHDAYS TODAY

Al Roker, 45, TV meteorologist ("Today Show"), born Brooklyn, NY, Aug 20, 1954.

AUGUST 21 — SATURDAY
Day 233 — 132 Remaining

HAWAII: ADMISSION DAY: 40th ANNIVERSARY. Aug 21, 1959. President Dwight Eisenhower signed a proclamation admitting Hawaii to the Union. The statehood bill had passed the previous March with a stipulation that statehood should be approved by a vote of Hawaiian residents. The referendum passed by a huge margin in June and Eisenhower proclaimed Hawaii the 50th state Aug 21. The third Friday in August is observed as a state holiday in Hawaii, commemorating statehood.

BIRTHDAYS TODAY

Steve Case, 41, president, America Online, born Honolulu, HI, Aug 21, 1958.
Arthur Yorinks, 46, author (*Hey, Al*), born Roslyn, NY, Aug 21, 1953.

AUGUST 22 — SUNDAY
Day 234 — 131 Remaining

BE AN ANGEL DAY. Aug 22. A day to do "one small act of service for someone. Be a blessing in someone's life." Annually, Aug 22. For info: Angel Heights Healing Center, Rev Jayne M. Howard, PO Box 95, Upperco, MD 21155. Phone: (410) 833-6912. Fax: (410) 429-4077. E-mail: blessing@erols.com. Web: drwnet.com/angel.

BELGIUM: WEDDING OF THE GIANTS. Aug 22. Traditional cultural observance. Annually, the fourth Sunday in August.

CAMEROON: VOLCANIC ERUPTION: ANNIVERSARY. Aug 22, 1986. Deadly fumes from a presumed volcanic eruption under Lake Nios at Cameroon killed more than 1,500 persons. A similar occurrence two years earlier had killed 37 persons.

DEBUSSY, CLAUDE: BIRTH ANNIVERSARY. Aug 22, 1862. (Achille) Claude Debussy, French musician and composer, especially remembered for his impressionistic "tone poems," was born at St. Germain-en-Laye, France. He died at Paris, France, Mar 25, 1918.

LITTLE LEAGUE BASEBALL WORLD SERIES. Aug 22–28 (tentative). Williamsport, PA. Eight teams from the US and foreign countries compete for the World Championship. Est attendance: 100,000. For info: Little League Baseball HQ, Box 3485,

Williamsport, PA 17701. Phone: (717) 326-1921. Fax: (717) 326-1074. Web: www.littleleague.org.

VIETNAM CONFLICT BEGINS: ANNIVERSARY. Aug 22, 1945. Less than a week after the Japanese surrender ended WWII, a team of Free French parachuted into southern Indochina in response to a successful coup by a Communist guerrilla named Ho Chi Minh in the French colony.

BIRTHDAYS TODAY

Ray Bradbury, 79, author (*The Toynbee Convector, Fahrenheit 451*), born Waukegan, IL, Aug 22, 1920.
Paul Molitor, 43, baseball player, born St. Paul, MN, Aug 22, 1956.

AUGUST 23 — MONDAY

Day 235 — 130 Remaining

FIRST MAN-POWERED FLIGHT: ANNIVERSARY. Aug 23, 1977. At Schafter, CA, Bryan Allen pedaled the 70-lb *Gossamer Condor* for a mile at a "minimal altitude of two pylons" in a flight certified by the Royal Aeronautical Society of Britain, winning a £50,000 prize offered by British industrialist Henry Kremer. See also: "First Man-Powered Flight Across English Channel: Anniversary" (June 12).

SWEDISH LANGUAGE AND CULTURE DAY CAMP. Aug 23–27. West Riverside Historic Site, Cambridge, MN. Children learn to speak Swedish and understand Swedish culture through songs, games, language classes and craft classes. Families see what their children have learned at a program at the end of the week. Annually, the last full week in August. For info: Valerie Arrowsmith, Isanti County Historical Society, PO Box 525, Cambridge, MN 55008. Phone: (612) 689-4229. Fax: (612) 689-5134.

VIRGO, THE VIRGIN. Aug 23–Sept 22. In the astronomical/astrological zodiac, which divides the sun's apparent orbit into 12 segments, the period Aug 23–Sept 22 is identified, traditionally, as the sun sign of Virgo, the Virgin. The ruling planet is Mercury.

BIRTHDAYS TODAY

Kobe Bryant, 21, basketball player, born Philadelphia, PA, Aug 23, 1978.
Rik Smits, 33, basketball player, born Eindhoven, The Netherlands, Aug 23, 1966.

AUGUST 24 — TUESDAY

Day 236 — 129 Remaining

ITALY: VESUVIUS DAY. Aug 24, AD 79. Anniversary of the eruption of Vesuvius, an active volcano in southern Italy, which destroyed the cities of Pompeii, Stabiae and Herculaneum.

MICHIGAN STATE FAIR. Aug 24–Sept 6. State Fairgrounds, Detroit, MI. Est attendance: 400,000. For info: State of Michigan, Dept of Agriculture, 1120 W State Fair Ave, Detroit, MI 48203. Phone: (313) 369-8250.

TAIWAN: CHENG CHENG KUNG BIRTH ANNIVERSARY. Aug 24. Joyous celebration of birth of Cheng Cheng Kung (Koxinga), born at Hirado, Japan, the Ming Dynasty loyalist who ousted the Dutch colonists from Taiwan in 1661. Dutch landing is commemorated annually Apr 29, but Cheng's birthday is honored on the 14th day of the seventh moon according to the Chinese lunar calendar. Cheng Cheng Kung died June 23, 1662, at Taiwan. See also: "Taiwan: Cheng Cheng Kung Landing Day" (Apr 29).

UKRAINE: INDEPENDENCE DAY. Aug 24. National day. Commemorates independence from the former Soviet Union in 1991.

WARNER WEATHER QUOTATION: ANNIVERSARY. Aug 24, 1897. Charles Dudley Warner, American newspaper editor for the *Hartford Courant*, published this now-famous and oft-quoted sentence, "Everybody talks about the weather, but nobody does anything about it." The quotation is often mistakenly attributed to his friend and colleague Mark Twain. Warner and Twain were part of the most notable American literary circle during the late 19th century. Warner was a journalist, essayist, novelist, biographer and author who collaborated with Mark Twain in writing *The Gilded Age* in 1873.

WASHINGTON, DC: INVASION ANNIVERSARY. Aug 24–25, 1814. During the War of 1812, British forces briefly invaded and raided Washington, DC, burning the Capitol, the president's house and most other public buildings. President James Madison and other high US government officials fled to safety until British troops (not knowing the strength of their position) departed the city two days later.

BIRTHDAYS TODAY

Max Cleland, 57, US Senator (D, Georgia), born Atlanta, GA, Aug 24, 1942.
Mike Huckabee, 44, Governor of Arkansas (R), born Hope, AR, Aug 24, 1955.
Reginald (Reggie) Miller, 34, basketball player, born Riverside, CA, Aug 24, 1965.
Kenny Quinn, 63, Governor of Nevada (R), born Garland, AR, Aug 24, 1936.
Calvin Edward (Cal) Ripken, Jr, 39, baseball player, born Havre de Grace, MD, Aug 24, 1960.
Merlin Tuttle, 58, scientist who works with bats, born Honolulu, HI, Aug 24, 1941.

AUGUST 25 — WEDNESDAY

Day 237 — 128 Remaining

BE KIND TO HUMANKIND WEEK. Aug 25–31. Life is too short to live it mean and grumpy. Change your attitude and make your life and those you share it with sweeter! It's nice to be nice. For info: Lorraine Jara, PO Box 586, Island Heights, NJ 08732-0586.

BERNSTEIN, LEONARD: BIRTH ANNIVERSARY. Aug 25, 1918. American conductor and composer Leonard Bernstein was born at Lawrence, MA. One of the greatest conductors in American music history, he first conducted the New York Philharmonic Orchestra at age 25 and was its director from 1959 to 1969. His musicals include *West Side Story* and *On the Town*, and his operas and operettas include *Candide*. He died five days after his retirement Oct 14, 1990, at New York, NY.

CHINA, PEOPLE'S REPUBLIC OF: FESTIVAL OF HUNGRY GHOSTS. Aug 25. Important Chinese festival, also known as Ghosts Month. According to Chinese legend, during the 7th lunar month the souls of the dead are released from purgatory to roam the Earth. Joss sticks are burnt in homes; prayers, food and "ghost money" are offered to appease the ghosts. Market stallholders combine to hold celebrations to ensure that their businesses will prosper in the coming year. Wayang (Chinese street opera) and puppet shows are performed, and fruit and Chinese delicacies are offered to the spirits of the dead. Chung Yuan (All Souls' Day) is observed on the 15th day of the 7th lunar month.

KELLY, WALT: BIRTH ANNIVERSARY. Aug 25, 1913. American cartoonist and creator of the comic strip "Pogo" was born at Philadelphia, PA. It was Kelly's character Pogo who paraphrased Oliver Hazard Perry to say, "We has met the enemy, and it is us." Kelly died at Hollywood, CA, Oct 18, 1973. See also: "Perry, Oliver Hazard: Birth Anniversary" (Aug 23).

NEVADA STATE FAIR. Aug 25–29. Reno Livestock Events Center, Reno, NV. State entertainment and carnival, with home arts, agriculture and commercial exhibits. Est attendance: 73,000. For info: Gary Lubra, CEO, Nevada State Fair, 1350-A N Wells Ave, Reno, NV 89512. Phone: (702) 688-5767. Fax: (702) 688-5763. E-mail: nvstatefair@inetworld.com. Web: www.nevadastatefair.org.

PARIS LIBERATED: 55th ANNIVERSARY. Aug 25, 1944. As dawn broke, the men of the 2nd French Armored Division entered Paris, ending the long German occupation of the City of Light. That afternoon General Charles de Gaulle led a parade down the Champs Elysées. Though Hitler had ordered the destruction of Paris, German occupying-officer General Dietrich von Choltitz refused that order and instead surrendered to French Major General Jacques Le Clerc.

SMITH, SAMANTHA: DEATH ANNIVERSARY. Aug 25. American schoolgirl whose interest in world peace drew praise and affection from people around the world. In 1982, the 10-year-old wrote a letter to Soviet leader Yuri Andropov asking him, "Why do you want to conquer the whole world, or at least our country?" The letter was widely publicized in the USSR and Andropov replied personally to her. Samantha Smith was invited to visit and tour the Soviet Union. On Aug 25, 1985, the airplane on which she was riding crashed at Maine, killing all aboard, including Samantha and her father. In 1986, minor planet No 3147, an asteroid between Mars and Jupiter, was named Samantha Smith in her memory.

URUGUAY: INDEPENDENCE DAY. Aug 25. National holiday. Gained independence from Brazil in 1828.

BIRTHDAYS TODAY

Albert Jojuan Belle, 33, baseball player, born Shreveport, LA, Aug 25, 1966.

	S	M	T	W	T	F	S
August		1	2	3	4	5	6	7
1999	8	9	10	11	12	13	14
	15	16	17	18	19	20	21
	22	23	24	25	26	27	28
	29	30	31				

Tim Burton, 41, producer (*The Nightmare Before Christmas*), born Burbank, CA, Aug 25, 1958.
Sean Connery, 69, actor (James Bond movies; *The Man Who Would Be King*), born Edinburgh, Scotland, Aug 25, 1930.
Kel Mitchell, 21, actor ("All That," "Kenan & Kel"), born Chicago, IL, Aug 25, 1978.

AUGUST 26 — THURSDAY
Day 238 — 127 Remaining

De FOREST, LEE: BIRTH ANNIVERSARY. Aug 26, 1873. American inventor of the electron tube, radio knife for surgery and the photoelectric cell and a pioneer in the creation of talking pictures and television. Born at Council Bluffs, IA, De Forest was holder of hundreds of patents but perhaps best remembered by the moniker he gave himself in the title of his autobiography, *Father of Radio*, published in 1950. So unbelievable was the idea of wireless radio broadcasting that De Forest was accused of fraud and arrested for selling stock to underwrite the invention that later was to become an essential part of daily life. De Forest died at Hollywood, CA, June 30, 1961.

FIRST BASEBALL GAMES TELEVISED: 60th ANNIVERSARY. Aug 26, 1939. WXBS television, at New York City, broadcast the first major league baseball games—a doubleheader between the Cincinnati Reds and the Brooklyn Dodgers at Ebbets Field. Announcer Red Barber interviewed Leo Durocher, manager of the Dodgers, and William McKechnie, manager of the Reds, between games.

KRAKATOA ERUPTION: ANNIVERSARY. Aug 26, 1883. Anniversary of the biggest explosion in historic times. The eruption of the Indonesian volcanic island, Krakatoa (Krakatau) was heard 3,000 miles away, created tidal waves 120 ft high (killing 36,000 persons), hurled five cubic miles of earth fragments into the air (some to a height of 50 miles) and affected the oceans and the atmosphere for years.

MINNESOTA STATE FAIR. Aug 26–Sept 6. St. Paul, MN. Major entertainers, agricultural displays, arts, crafts, food, carnival rides, animal judging and performances. Est attendance: 1,600,000. For info: Minnesota State Fair, 1265 Snelling Ave N, St. Paul, MN 55108-3099. Phone: (612) 642-2200. E-mail: fairinfo@statefair.gen.mn.us.

MONTGOLFIER, JOSEPH MICHEL: BIRTH ANNIVERSARY. Aug 26, 1740. French merchant and inventor, born at Vidalonlez-Annonay, France, who, with his brother Jacques Etienne in November 1782, conducted experiments with paper and fabric bags filled with smoke and hot air, which led to the invention of the hot-air balloon and man's first flight. Died at Balaruc-les-Bains, France, June 26, 1810. See also: "Montgolfier, Jacques Etienne: Birth Anniversary" (Jan 7), "First Balloon Flight: Anniversary" (June 5) and "Aviation History Month" (Nov 1).

MOON PHASE: FULL MOON. Aug 26. Moon enters Full Moon phase at 7:48 PM, EDT.

NEW YORK STATE FAIR. Aug 26–Sept 6. Empire Expo Center, Syracuse, NY. Agricultural and livestock competitions, top-name entertainment, the International Horse Show, business and industrial exhibits, the midway and ethnic presentations. Est attendance: 900,000. For info: Joseph LaGuardia, Dir of Mktg, NY State Fair, Empire Expo Ctr, Syracuse, NY 13209. Phone: (315) 487-7711. Fax: (315) 487-9260.

OREGON STATE FAIR. Aug 26–Sept 6. Salem, OR. Exhibits, products and displays illustrate Oregon's role as one of the nation's major agricultural and recreational states. Floral gardens, carnival, big-name entertainment, horse show and food. Annually, 12 days ending on Labor Day. Est attendance: 730,000. For info: Oregon State Fair, 2330 17th St NE, Salem, OR 97310-0140. Phone: (503) 378-3247.

SABIN, ALBERT BRUCE: BIRTH ANNIVERSARY. Aug 26, 1906. American medical researcher Albert Bruce Sabin was born at Bialystok, Poland. He is most noted for his oral vaccine for polio, which replaced Jonas Salk's injected vaccine because Sabin's provided lifetime protection. He was awarded the US National Medal of Science in 1971. Sabin died Mar 3, 1993, at Washington, DC.

★**WOMEN'S EQUALITY DAY.** Aug 26. Presidential Proclamation issued in 1973 and 1974 at request and since 1975 without request.

WOMEN'S EQUALITY DAY. Aug 26. Anniversary of certification as part of US Constitution, in 1920, of the 19th Amendment, prohibiting discrimination on the basis of sex with regard to voting. Congresswoman Bella Abzug's bill to designate Aug 26 of each year as "Women's Equality Day" in August 1974 became Public Law 93–382.

BIRTHDAYS TODAY

Macaulay Culkin, 19, actor (*Home Alone, My Girl*), born New York, NY, Aug 26, 1980.

Thomas J. Ridge, 54, Governor of Pennsylvania (R), born Munhall, PA, Aug 26, 1945.

Robert G. Torricelli, 48, US Senator (D, New Jersey), born Paterson, NJ, Aug 26, 1951.

AUGUST 27 — FRIDAY

Day 239 — 126 Remaining

ALASKA STATE FAIR/EXPO 99. Aug 27–Sept 6. Palmer, AK. Cows and critters, music and dancing, rides, excitement and family fun at the state's largest summer extravaganza. More than 500 events including demonstrations, high-caliber entertainment, rodeos, horse shows, homemaking and agricultural exhibits. Est attendance: 280,000. For info: Alaska State Fair, Inc, 2075 Glenn Hwy, Palmer, AK 99645. Phone: (907) 745-4827. Fax: (907) 745-7173.

DAWES, CHARLES GATES: BIRTH ANNIVERSARY. Aug 27, 1865. Thirtieth vice president of the US (1925–1929), born at Marietta, OH. Won the Nobel Peace Prize in 1925 for the "Dawes Plan" for German reparations. Died at Evanston, IL, Apr 23, 1951.

FIRST PLAY PRESENTED IN NORTH AMERICAN COLONIES: ANNIVERSARY. Aug 27, 1655. Acomac, VA, was the site of the first play presented in the North American colonies. The play was *Ye Bare and Ye Cubb*, by Phillip Alexander Bruce. Three local residents were arrested and fined for acting in the play. At the time, most colonies had laws prohibiting public performances; Virginia, however, had no such ordinance.

HAMLIN, HANNIBAL: BIRTH ANNIVERSARY. Aug 27, 1809. Fifteenth vice president of the US (1861–1865) born at Paris, ME. Died at Bangor, ME, July 4, 1891.

JOHNSON, LYNDON BAINES: BIRTH ANNIVERSARY. Aug 27, 1908. Thirty-sixth president of the US succeeded to the presidency following the assassination of John F. Kennedy. Johnson's term of office: Nov 22, 1963–Jan 20, 1969. In 1964, he said: "The challenge of the next half-century is whether we have the wisdom to use [our] wealth to enrich and elevate our national life—and to advance the quality of American civilization." Johnson was

born near Stonewall, TX, and died at San Antonio, TX, Jan 22, 1973. His birthday is observed as a holiday in Texas.

MOLDOVA: INDEPENDENCE DAY. Aug 27. Republic of Moldova declared its independence from the Soviet Union in 1991.

MOTHER TERESA: BIRTH ANNIVERSARY. Aug 27, 1910. Albanian Roman Catholic nun born Agnes Gonxha Bojaxhiu at Skopje, Macedonia. She founded the Order of the Missionaries of Charity, which cared for the destitute of Calcutta, India. She won the Nobel Peace Prize in 1979. She died at Calcutta, Sept 5, 1997.

NEBRASKA STATE FAIR. Aug 27–Sept 6. Lincoln, NE. Book fair, food booths, variety of entertainment, rodeos, amusement rides and tractor pulls. For info: Nebraska State Fair, PO Box 81223, Lincoln, NE 68501. Phone: (402) 473-4110. Fax: (402) 473-4114. E-mail: nestatefair@statefair.org.

BIRTHDAYS TODAY

Suzanne Fisher, 54, author (*Shabanu, Daughter of the Wind*), born Philadelphia, PA, Aug 27, 1945.

J. Robert Kerrey, 56, US Senator (D, Nebraska), born Lincoln, NE, Aug 27, 1943.

Paul Rubens (Pee-Wee Herman), 47, actor, writer ("Pee-Wee's Playhouse," *Pee-Wee's Big Adventure*), born Peekskill, NY, Aug 27, 1952.

AUGUST 28 — SATURDAY

Day 240 — 125 Remaining

CHILDREN'S DAY. Aug 28. Woodstock, VT. Traditional farm activities from corn shelling to sawing firewood—19th-century games, traditional spelling bee, ice cream and butter making, wagon rides. For info: Deborah Bulissa, Exec Asst, Billings Farm Museum, PO Box 489, Woodstock, VT 05091. Phone: (802) 457-2355. Fax: (802) 457-4663. E-mail: billings.farm@valley.net.

FEAST OF SAINT AUGUSTINE. Aug 28. Bishop of Hippo, author of *Confessions* and *The City of God*, born Nov 13, 354, at Tagaste, in what is now Algeria. Died Aug 28, 430, at Hippo, also in North Africa.

HAYES, LUCY WARE WEBB: BIRTH ANNIVERSARY. Aug 28, 1831. Wife of Rutherford Birchard Hayes, 19th president of the US, born at Chillicothe, OH. Died at Fremont, OH, June 25, 1889. She was nicknamed "Lemonade Lucy" because she and the president, both abstainers, served no alcoholic beverages at White House receptions.

MARCH ON WASHINGTON: ANNIVERSARY. Aug 28, 1963. More than 250,000 people attended this Civil Rights rally at Washington, DC, at which Reverend Dr. Martin Luther King, Jr made his famous "I have a dream" speech. See Curriculum Connection.

PETERSON, ROGER TORY: BIRTH ANNIVERSARY. Aug 28, 1908. Naturalist, author of *A Field Guide to Birds*, born at Jamestown, NY. Peterson died at Old Lyme, CT, July 28, 1996.

RADIO COMMERCIALS: ANNIVERSARY. Aug 28, 1922. Broadcasters realized radio could earn profits from the sale of advertising time. WEAF in New York ran a commercial "spot," which was sponsored by the Queensboro Realty Corporation of Jackson Heights to promote Hawthorne Court, a group of apartment buildings at Queens. The commercial rate was $100 for 10 minutes.

SETON, ELIZABETH ANN BAYLEY: 225th BIRTH ANNIVERSARY. Aug 28, 1774. First American-born saint was born at New York, NY. Seton died Jan 4, 1821, at Emmitsburg, MD.

AUGUST 28
"I HAVE A DREAM"

On Aug 28, 1963, Dr. Martin Luther King, Jr made his famous "I Have a Dream" speech during the March on Washington, a civil rights rally attended by more than 250,000 people. Although many people recognize the speech title, only some are familiar with its powerful, stirring text expressing hope for the future. *I Have a Dream*, by Dr. Martin Luther King Jr. (Scholastic, 0-590-20516-1, $16.95 All ages) presents the text of the speech, plus illustrations by 15 African American artists who have won a Coretta Scott King Award or honor book designation for their work. This excellent book provides a thought-provoking way for students to study the speech, and gives numerous starting points for classroom discussion on topics such as civil rights, the meaning of equality, race relations and how we can turn a social dream into a reality. Questions that arise from discussion groups can be used to generate student letters to government representatives.

Other books that explore the theme of civil rights include: *I Am Rosa Parks*, by Rosa Parks and Jim Haskins (Penguin, 0-8037-1206-5, $12.99 Gr. K–3); *Dear Dr. King: Letters from Today's Children to Dr. Martin Luther King, Jr.*, edited by Jan Colbert and Ann McMillan Harms (Hyperion, 0-7868-0417-3, $14.95 Gr. 4–7); and *Richard Wright and the Library Card*, William Miller (Publishers Group West, 1-8800-0057-1, $15.95 Gr. 3–8).

Schools with computer audio capabilities can access an audio version of Dr. King's speech at www.historychannel.com/gspeech/archive.html.

Students who want to turn a dream for a better society into reality can learn about Samantha Smith, the 10-year-old who wrote a letter to Soviet leader Yuri Andropov in the interest of peace. See Aug 25 entry for more details.

The founder of the American Sisters of Charity, the first American order of Roman Catholic nuns, she was canonized in 1975.

BIRTHDAYS TODAY

William S. Cohen, 59, US Secretary of Defense (Clinton administration), born Bangor, ME, Aug 28, 1940.
Michael Galeota, 15, actor (*Can't Be Heaven, Clubhouse Detectives*), born Long Island, NY, Aug 28, 1984.
Scott Hamilton, 41, Olympic gold medal figure skater, born Toledo, OH, Aug 28, 1958.
LeAnn Rimes, 17, singer, born Jackson, MS, Aug 28, 1982.
Allen Say, 62, illustrator and author (Caldecott for *Grandfather's Journey*), born Yokohama, Japan, Aug 28, 1937.

AUGUST 29 — SUNDAY
Day 241 — 124 Remaining

AMISTAD SEIZED: ANNIVERSARY. Aug 29, 1839. In January, 1839, 53 Africans were seized near modern-day Sierra Leone, taken to Cuba and sold as slaves. While being transferred to another part of the island on the ship *Amistad*, led by the African, Cinque, they seized control of the ship, telling the crew to take them back to Africa. However, the crew secretly changed course and the ship landed at Long Island, NY, where it and its "cargo" were seized as salvage. The *Amistad* was towed to New Haven, CT where the Africans were imprisoned and a lengthy legal battle began to determine if they were property to be returned to Cuba or free men. John Quincy Adams took their case all the way to the Supreme Court, where in 1841 it was determined that they were free and could return to Africa. A replica of the *Amistad* is being built at the Mystic Seaport Museum, Mystic, CT. For info: amistad.mysticseaport.org.

MARYLAND STATE FAIR. Aug 29–Sept 7. Timonium, MD. Home arts, agricultural and livestock presentations, midway rides, live entertainment and thoroughbred horse racing. Est attendance: 600,000. For info: Max Mosner, State Fairgrounds, PO Box 188, Timonium, MD 21094. Phone: (410) 252-0200.

SHAYS REBELLION: ANNIVERSARY. Aug 29, 1786. Daniel Shays, veteran of the battles of Lexington, Bunker Hill, Ticonderoga and Saratoga, was one of the leaders of more than 1,000 rebels who sought redress of grievances during the depression days of 1786–87. They prevented general court sessions and they prevented Supreme Court sessions at Springfield, MA, Sept 26. On Jan 25, 1787, they attacked the federal arsenal at Springfield; Feb 2, Shays's troops were routed and fled. Shays was sentenced to death but pardoned June 13, 1788. Later he received a small pension for services in the American Revolution.

SOVIET COMMUNIST PARTY SUSPENDED: ANNIVERSARY. Aug 29, 1991. The Supreme Soviet, the parliament of the USSR, suspended all activities of the Communist Party, seizing its property and bringing to an end the institution that ruled the Soviet Union for nearly 75 years. The action followed an unsuccessful coup Aug 19–21 that sought to overthrow the government of Soviet President Mikhail Gorbachev but instead prompted a sweeping wave of democratic change. Gorbachev quit as party leader Aug 24.

BIRTHDAYS TODAY

Karen Hesse, 47, author (Newbery for *Out of the Dust*), born Baltimore, MD, Aug 29, 1952.
Michael Jackson, 41, singer, songwriter ("We Are the World," *Bad, Thriller, Beat It*), born Gary, IN, Aug 29, 1958.
John Sidney McCain III, 63, US Senator (R, Arizona), born Panama Canal Zone, Aug 29, 1936.
Robert Rubin, 61, US Secretary of the Treasury (Clinton administration), born New York, NY, Aug 29, 1938.

AUGUST 30 — MONDAY
Day 242 — 123 Remaining

ARTHUR, ELLEN LEWIS HERNDON: BIRTH ANNIVERSARY. Aug 30, 1837. Wife of Chester Alan Arthur, 21st president of the US, born at Fredericksburg, VA. Died at New York, Jan 12, 1880.

BURTON, VIRGINIA LEE: BIRTH ANNIVERSARY. Aug 30, 1909. Author, illustrator, born at Newton Centre, MA. Her book *The Little House* won the Caldecott Medal in 1942. Other works include *Choo, Choo* and *Mike Mulligan and His Steam Shovel*. Burton died at Boston, MA, Oct 15, 1968.

FIRST WHITE HOUSE PRESIDENTIAL BABY: BIRTH ANNIVERSARY. Aug 30, 1893. Frances Folsom Cleveland (Mrs Grover Cleveland) was the first presidential wife to have a baby

August 1999

S	M	T	W	T	F	S
1	2	3	4	5	6	7
8	9	10	11	12	13	14
15	16	17	18	19	20	21
22	23	24	25	26	27	28
29	30	31				

at the White House when she gave birth to a baby girl (Esther). The first child ever born in the White House was a granddaughter to Thomas Jefferson in 1806.

HONG KONG: LIBERATION DAY. Aug 30. Public holiday to celebrate liberation from the Japanese in 1945. Annually, the last Monday in August.

MacMURRAY, FRED: BIRTH ANNIVERSARY. Aug 30, 1908. Born at Kankakee, IL, MacMurray's film and television career included a wide variety of roles, ranging from comedy (*The Absent-Minded Professor, Son of Flubber, The Shaggy Dog*) to serious drama (*The Caine Mutiny, Double Indemnity*). During 1960–72 he portrayed the father on "My Three Sons," which was second only to "Ozzie and Harriet" as network TV's longest running family sitcom. He died Nov 5, 1991, at Santa Monica, CA.

PERU: SAINT ROSE OF LIMA DAY. Aug 30. Saint Rose of Lima was the first saint of the western hemisphere. She lived at the time of the colonization by Spain in the 16th century. Patron saint of the Americas and the Philippines. Public holiday in Peru.

RUTHERFORD, ERNEST: BIRTH ANNIVERSARY. Aug 30, 1871. Physicist, born at Nelson, New Zealand. He established the nuclear nature of the atom, the electrical structure of matter and achieved the transmutation of elements, research which later resulted in the atomic bomb. Rutherford died at Cambridge, England, Oct 19, 1937.

SHELLEY, MARY WOLLSTONECRAFT: BIRTH ANNIVERSARY. Aug 30, 1797. English novelist Mary Shelley, daughter of the philosopher William Godwin and the feminist Mary Wollstonecraft and wife of the poet Percy Bysshe Shelley, was born at London and died there Feb 1, 1851. In addition to being the author of the famous novel *Frankenstein*, Shelley is important in literary history for her work in the editing and publishing of her husband's unpublished work after his early death.

SPACE MILESTONE: *DISCOVERY* (US). Aug 30, 1984. Space shuttle *Discovery* was launched from Kennedy Space Center, FL, for its maiden flight with six-member crew. During the flight the crew deployed three satellites and used a robot arm before landing at Edwards Air Force Base, CA, Sept 5.

TURKEY: VICTORY DAY. Aug 30. Commemorates victory in War of Independence in 1922. Military parades, performing of the Mehtar band (the world's oldest military band), fireworks.

WILKINS, ROY: BIRTH ANNIVERSARY. Aug 30, 1901. Roy Wilkins, grandson of a Mississippi slave, civil rights leader, active in the National Association for the Advancement of Colored People (NAACP), retired as its executive director in 1977. Born at St. Louis, MO, he died at New York, NY, Sept 8, 1981.

BIRTHDAYS TODAY

Ted Williams, 81, baseball Hall of Fame outfielder, born San Diego, CA, Aug 30, 1918.

AUGUST 31 — TUESDAY
Day 243 — 122 Remaining

CANADA; KLONDIKE ELDORADO GOLD DISCOVERY: ANNIVERSARY. Aug 31, 1896. Two weeks after the Rabbit/Bonanza Creek claim was filed, gold was discovered on Eldorado Creek, a tributary of Bonanza. More than $30 million worth of gold (worth some $600–$700 million in today's dollars) was mined from the Eldorado Claim in 1896.

KYRGYZSTAN: INDEPENDENCE DAY. Aug 31. National holiday. Commemorates independence from the former Soviet Union in 1991.

MALAYSIA: NATIONAL DAY. Aug 31. National holiday. Commemorates independence from Britain in 1957.

MONTESSORI, MARIA: BIRTH ANNIVERSARY. Aug 31, 1870. Italian physician and educator, born at Chiaraville, Italy. Founder of the Montessori method of teaching children. She believed that children need to work at tasks that interest them and if given the right materials and tasks, they learn best through individual attention. Montessori died at Noordwijk, Holland, May 6, 1952.

POLAND: SOLIDARITY FOUNDED: ANNIVERSARY. Aug 31, 1980. The Polish trade union Solidarity was formed at the Baltic Sea port of Gdansk, Poland. Outlawed by the government, many of its leaders were arrested. Led by Lech Walesa, Solidarity persisted in its opposition to the Communist-controlled government, and Aug 19, 1989, Polish president Wojcieck Jaruzelski astonished the world by nominating for the post of prime minister Tadeusz Mazowiecki, a deputy in the Polish Assembly, 1961–72, and editor-in-chief of Solidarity's weekly newspaper, bringing to an end 42 years of Communist Party domination.

TRINIDAD AND TOBAGO: INDEPENDENCE DAY. Aug 31. National holiday. Became Commonwealth nation in 1962.

BIRTHDAYS TODAY

Jennifer Azzi, 31, basketball player, born Oak Ridge, TN, Aug 31, 1968.

Edwin Corley Moses, 44, Olympic gold medal track athlete, born Dayton, OH, Aug 31, 1955.

Hideo Nomo, 31, baseball player, born Osaka, Japan, Aug 31, 1968.

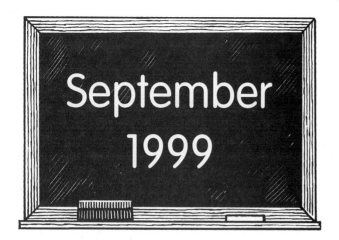

SEPTEMBER 1 — WEDNESDAY
Day 244 — 121 Remaining

BABY SAFETY MONTH. Sept 1–30. The Juvenile Products Manufacturers Association, Inc (JPMA), a national trade organization of juvenile product manufacturers devoted to helping parents keep baby safe, is disseminating information to parents, grandparents and other child caregivers about baby safety. The information from JPMA pertains to safe selection of juvenile products through the Association's Safety Certification Program and tips on correct use of products such as cribs, car seats, infant carriers and decorative accessories. For a free copy of JPMA's brochure "Safe and Sound for Baby," write to the address below and mark ATTN: JPMA Safety Brochure. Enclose a self-addressed stamped envelope and specify whether you want the brochure in English or Spanish. For info: JPMA, PR Dept, 236 Rte 38-W, Ste 100, Moorestown, NJ 08057.

BRAZIL: INDEPENDENCE WEEK. Sept 1–7. The independence of Brazil from Portugal in 1822 is commemorated with civic and cultural ceremonies promoted by federal, state and municipal authorities. On Sept 7, a grand military parade takes place and the National Defense League organizes the Running Race in Honor of the Symbolic Torch of the Brazilian Nation.

BURROUGHS, EDGAR RICE: BIRTH ANNIVERSARY. Sept 1, 1875. US novelist (*Tarzan of the Apes*), born at Chicago, IL. Correspondent for the *Los Angeles Times*, died at Encino, CA, Mar 19, 1950.

CARTIER, JACQUES: DEATH ANNIVERSARY. Sept 1, 1557. French navigator and explorer who sailed from St. Malo, France, Apr 20, 1534, in search of a northwest passage to the Orient. Instead, he discovered the St. Lawrence River, explored Canada's coastal regions and took possession of the country for France. Cartier was born at St. Malo, about 1491 (exact date unknown) and died there.

CHILDREN'S EYE HEALTH AND SAFETY MONTH. Sept 1–30. Prevent Blindness America® directs its educational efforts to common causes of eye injuries and common eye problems among children. Materials that can easily be posted or distributed to the community will be provided. For info: Prevent Blindness America®, 500 E Remington Rd, Schaumburg, IL 60173. Phone: (800) 331-2020. Fax: (847) 843-8458. Web: www.prevent blindness.org.

CHILDREN'S GOOD MANNERS MONTH. Sept 1–30. Starts the school year with a national program of teachers and parents encouraging good manners in children. The year-long program includes monthly objectives that work in conjunction with a reinforcing home program. For info: "Dr. Manners," Fleming Allaire, PhD, 35 Eastfield St, Manchester, CT 06040. Phone: (860) 643-0051.

CHILE: NATIONAL MONTH. Sept 1–30. A month of special significance in Chile: arrival of spring, Independence of Chile anniversary (proclaimed Sept 18, 1810), anniversary of the armed forces rising of Sept 11, 1973, to overthrow the government and celebration of the 1980 Constitution and Army Day, Sept 19.

D.A.R.E. LAUNCHED: ANNIVERSARY. Sept 1, 1983. D.A.R.E. (Drug Abuse Resistance Education) is a police officer-led series of classroom lessons that teaches students how to resist peer pressure and lead productive drug- and violence-free lives. The program, which was developed jointly by the Los Angeles Police Department and the Los Angeles Unified School District, initially focused on elementary school children but has now been expanded to include middle and high school students. D.A.R.E. has been implemented in 75 percent of US school districts and in 44 other countries. For info: D.A.R.E. America, PO Box 512090, Los Angeles, CA 90051-0090. Phone: (800) 223-DARE. Web: www.dare-america.com.

EMMA M. NUTT DAY. Sept 1. A day to honor the first woman telephone operator, Emma M. Nutt, who reportedly began her professional career at Boston, MA, Sept 1, 1878, and continued working as a telephone operator for some 33 years.

LIBRARY CARD SIGN-UP MONTH. Sept 1–30. National effort to sign up every child for a library card. Annually, the month of September. For info: Linda Wallace, American Library Assn, Public Information Office, 50 E Huron St, Chicago, IL 60611. Phone: (312) 280-5043 or (312) 280-5042. E-mail: pio@ala.org. Web: www.ala.org.

LIBYA: REVOLUTION DAY. Sept 1. Commemorates the revolution in 1969 when King Idris I was overthrown by Colonel Qaddafi. National holiday.

NATIONAL CHILDHOOD INJURY PREVENTION WEEK. Sept 1–7. To stress the importance of community involvement in protecting the nation's children from harm. Safety By Design® sponsors this week, providing a full week of opportunities to raise awareness of the problem of unintentional injury to children and highlight the roles members of the community play in reducing injury rates. Information and materials are available. For info: Safety By Design® Ltd, PO Box 4312, Great Neck, NY 11023. Phone and Fax: (516) 482-1475.

NATIONAL FOOD EDUCATION SAFETY MONTH. Sept 1–30. An initiative sponsored by the International Food Safety Council, a coalition of the restaurant and food service industry dedicated to food safety education. The goals are to encourage food safety training among all food service workers, to heighten awareness about the importance of food safety education and to build public understanding of the food service industry's expertise in food safety and its commitment to serving safe food. For info: Cindy Wilson, Intl Food Safety Council, 250 S Wacker Dr, Ste 1400, Chicago, IL 60606-5834. Phone: (312) 715-6770. Fax: (312) 715-0807. E-mail: cwilson@foodtrain.com.

September 1999

S	M	T	W	T	F	S
			1	2	3	4
5	6	7	8	9	10	11
12	13	14	15	16	17	18
19	20	21	22	23	24	25
26	27	28	29	30		

NATIONAL HISTORY DAY. Sept 1, 1999–June, 2000. This year-long project begins in September when curriculum and contest materials are distributed to coordinators and teachers around the country. District History Day contests are usually held in February or March and state contests in late April or early May. The national contest is held in June at the University of Maryland. There are two divisions of the competition: junior (Gr. 6–8) and senior (Gr. 9–12). Students can enter the contest with a paper, an individual or group exhibit, an individual or group performance or individual or group media, The theme for the 1999–2000 school year is "Science, Technology, Invention in History: Impact, Influence, Change." For info: National History Day, 0119 Cecil Hall, Univ of Maryland, College Park, MD 20742. Phone: (301) 314-9739. E-mail: hstryday@aol.com. Web: www.thehistorynet .com/NationalHistoryDay.

NATIONAL PEDICULOSIS PREVENTION MONTH. Sept 1–30. To promote awareness of how to prevent pediculosis (lice). For info: Natl Pediculosis Assn, PO Box 610189, Newton, MA 02161. Phone: (781) 449-NITS. Fax: (781) 449-8129. Web: www.headlice.org or www.licemeister.org.

NATIONAL PIANO MONTH. Sept 1–30. Recognizes America's most popular instrument and its more than 20 million players; also encourages piano study by people of all ages. For info: Donald W. Dillon, Exec Dir, Natl Piano Foundation, 4020 McEwen, Ste 105, Dallas, TX 75244-5019. Phone: (972) 233-9107. Fax: (972) 490-4219. E-mail: don@dondillon.com. Web: www.pianonet .com.

NATIONAL SCHOOL SUCCESS MONTH. Sept 1–30. Today's young people have many distractions from school and are sometimes overwhelmed when it comes to academics. Parents are often unskilled at effectively redirecting the attention of their children, especially their teenagers. This observance is to recognize parents who want to support and encourage their children to succeed in school and to explore ways to do that. Annually, the month of September. For info send SASE to: Teresa Langston, Dir, Parenting Without Pressure, 1330 Boyer St, Longwood, FL 32750-6311. Phone: (407) 767-2524.

PTA MEMBERSHIP ENROLLMENT MONTH IN TEXAS. Sept 1–30. Texas PTA is the largest child-advocacy organization in Texas with more than 750,000 members. National PTA is the largest child-advocacy organization in the nation with nearly 6.5 million members. For info: Joann Thurman, Texas PTA, 408 W 11th St, Austin, TX 78701-2199. Phone: (512) 476-6769 or (800) TALK-PTA. Fax: (512) 476-8152. E-mail: info@txpta.org. Web: www.txpta.org.

SAVE THE TIGER MONTH. Sept 1–30. Month devoted to preservation of endangered Siberian, Sumatran and Bengal tiger species.

Activities include fund-raising and promotional efforts for the San Diego Zoo and World Wildlife Foundation aimed at raising public awareness and activism. For info: Jacquie Malzat, Communications Mgr, 1280 Park Center Dr, Vista, CA 92083. Phone: (800) 999-4688. Fax: (619) 734-1372. Web: www.hotspring.com.

SEA CADET MONTH. Sept 1–30. Nationwide year-round youth program for boys and girls 11–17 teaches leadership and self-discipline with emphasis on nautically-oriented training without military obligation. Est attendance: 8,000. For info: US Naval Sea Cadet Corps, 2300 Wilson Blvd, Arlington, VA 22201. Phone: (703) 243-6910. Fax: (703) 243-3985. E-mail: mford@NAVY LEAGUE.org. Web: www.seacadets.org.

SLOVAKIA: NATIONAL DAY. Sept 1. Anniversary of the adoption of the Constitution of the Slovak Republic in 1992.

SOUTH DAKOTA STATE FAIR. Sept 1–7. Huron, SD. Grandstand entertainment nightly, 10 free stages with multiple shows daily, hundreds of commercial exhibits and thousands of livestock exhibits. One of the largest agricultural fairs in the US. Est attendance: 250,000. For info: Jewel Tschetter, Mgr, South Dakota State Fair, PO Box 1275, Huron, SD 57350-1275. Phone: (605) 353-7340. Fax: (605) 353-7348.

UZBEKISTAN: INDEPENDENCE DAY. Sept 1. National holiday. Commemorates independence from the Soviet Union in 1991.

BIRTHDAYS TODAY

Rosa Guy, 71, author (*Billy the Great*), born Trinidad, West Indies, Sept 1, 1928.
Tim Hardaway, 33, basketball player, born Chicago, IL, Sept 1, 1966.

SEPTEMBER 2 — THURSDAY

Day 245 — 120 Remaining

CALENDAR ADJUSTMENT DAY: ANNIVERSARY. Sept 2. Pursuant to the British Calendar Act of 1751, Britain (and the American colonies) made the "Gregorian Correction" in 1752. The Act proclaimed that the day following Wednesday, Sept 2, should become Thursday, Sept 14, 1752. There was rioting in the streets by those who felt cheated and who demanded the eleven days back. The Act also provided that New Year's Day (and the change of year number) should fall Jan 1 (instead of Mar 25) in 1752 and every year thereafter. See also: "Gregorian Calendar Adjustment: Anniversary" (Feb 24, Oct 4).

DAYS OF MARATHON: ANNIVERSARY. Sept 2–9, 490 BC. Anniversary of the event during the Persian Wars from which the marathon race is derived. Phidippides, "an Athenian and by profession and practice a trained runner," according to Herodotus, was dispatched from Marathon to Sparta (26 miles), Sept 2 to seek help in repelling the invading Persian army. Help being unavailable by religious law until after the next full moon, Phidippides ran the 26 miles back to Marathon Sept 4. Without Spartan aid, the Athenians defeated the Persians at the Battle of Marathon Sept 9. According to legend Phidippides carried the news of the battle to Athens and died as he spoke the words, "Rejoice, we are victorious." The marathon race was revived at the 1896 Olympic Games in Athens. Course distance, since 1924, is 26 miles, 385 yards.

ENGLAND: GREAT FIRE OF LONDON: ANNIVERSARY. Sept 2–5, 1666. The fire generally credited with bringing about our system of fire insurance started Sept 2, 1666, in the wooden house of a baker named Farryner, at London's Pudding Lane, near the Tower. During the ensuing three days more than 13,000 houses were destroyed, though it is believed that only six lives were lost in the fire.

FORTEN, JAMES: BIRTH ANNIVERSARY. Sept 2, 1766. James Forten was born of free black parents at Philadelphia, PA. As a powder boy on an American Revolutionary warship, he escaped being sold as a slave when his ship was captured due to the intervention of the son of the British commander. While in England he became involved with abolitionists. On his return to Philadelphia, he became an apprentice to a sailmaker and eventually purchased the company for which he worked. He was active in the abolition movement, and in 1816, his support was sought by the American Colonization Society for the plan to settle American blacks at Liberia. He rejected their ideas and their plans to make him the ruler of the colony. From the large profits of his successful sailmaking company, he contributed heavily to the abolitionist movement and was a supporter of William Lloyd Garrison's anti-slavery journal, *The Liberator*. Died at Philadelphia, PA, Mar 4, 1842.

McAULIFFE, CHRISTA: BIRTH ANNIVERSARY. Sept 2, 1948. Christa McAuliffe, a 37-year-old Concord, NH, high school teacher, was to have been the first "ordinary citizen" in space. Born Sharon Christa Corrigan at Boston, MA, she perished with six crew members in the Space Shuttle *Challenger* explosion Jan 28, 1986. See also: "Challenger Space Shuttle Explosion Anniversary" (Jan 28). For more info: www.cmp.state.nh.us.

MOON PHASE: LAST QUARTER. Sept 2. Moon enters Last Quarter phase at 6:17 PM, EDT.

SHERMAN ENTERS ATLANTA: ANNIVERSARY. Sept 2, 1864. After a four-week siege, Union General William Tecumseh Sherman entered Atlanta, GA. The city had been evacuated on the previous day by Confederate troops under General John B. Hood. Hood had mistakenly assumed Sherman was ending the siege Aug 27, when actually Sherman was beginning the final stages of his attack. Hood then sent troops to attack the Union forces at Jonesboro. Hood's troops were defeated, opening the way for the capture of Atlanta.

US TREASURY DEPARTMENT: ANNIVERSARY. Sept 2, 1789. The third presidential cabinet department, the Treasury Department, was established by Congress.

V-J DAY. Sept 2, 1945. Official ratification of Japanese surrender to the Allies occurred aboard the USS *Missouri* at Tokyo Bay Sept 2 (Far Eastern time) in 1945, thus prompting President Truman's declaration of this day as Victory-over-Japan Day. Japan's initial, informal agreement of surrender was announced by Truman and celebrated in the US Aug 14.

VIETNAM: INDEPENDENCE DAY. Sept 2. Ho Chi Minh formally proclaimed the independence of Vietnam from France and the establishment of the Democratic Republic of Vietnam in 1945. National holiday.

BIRTHDAYS TODAY

John Bierhorst, 63, author (*The Woman Who Fell from the Sky*), born Boston, MA, Sept 2, 1936.

Demi, 57, author (*One Grain of Rice*), born Charlotte Dumaresque Hunt, Cambridge, MA, Sept 2, 1942.

Bernard Most, 62, author and illustrator (*Where to Look for a Dinosaur*), born New York, NY, Sept 2, 1937.

Carlos Valderrama, 38, soccer player, born Santa Marta, Colombia, Sept 2, 1961.

SEPTEMBER 3 — FRIDAY
Day 246 — 119 Remaining

DOUGLASS ESCAPES TO FREEDOM: ANNIVERSARY. Sept 3, 1838. Dressed as a sailor and carrying identification papers borrowed from a retired merchant seaman, Frederick Douglass boarded a train at Baltimore, MD, a slave state, and rode to Wilmington, DE, where he caught a steamboat to the free city of Philadelphia. He then transferred to a train headed for New York City where he entered the protection of the Underground Railway network. Douglass later became a great orator and one of the leaders of the antislavery struggle.

ITALY SURRENDERS: ANNIVERSARY. Sept 3, 1943. General Giuseppe Castellano signed three copies of the "short armistice," effectively surrendering unconditionally for the Italian government. That same day the British Eighth Army, commanded by General Bernard Montgomery, invaded the Italian mainland.

QATAR: INDEPENDENCE DAY. Sept 3. National holiday. Commemorates the severing in 1971 of treaty with Britain which had handled Qatar's foreign relations.

SAN MARINO: NATIONAL DAY. Sept 3. Public holiday. Honors St. Marinus, the traditional founder of San Marino.

TREATY OF PARIS ENDS AMERICAN REVOLUTION: ANNIVERSARY. Sept 3, 1783. Treaty between Britain and the US, ending the Revolutionary War, signed at Paris, France. American signatories: John Adams, Benjamin Franklin and John Jay.

VERMONT STATE FAIR. Sept 3–12. Fairgrounds, Rutland, VT. Est attendance: 100,000. For info: Vermont State Fair, 175 S Main St, Rutland, VT 05701. Phone: (802) 775-5200.

BIRTHDAYS TODAY

Aliki, 70, Aliki Liacouras Brandenberg, author and illustrator (*Three Gold Pieces*), born Wildwood Crest, NJ, Sept 3, 1929.

Damon Stoudamire, 26, basketball player, born Portland, OR, Sept 3, 1973.

SEPTEMBER 4 — SATURDAY
Day 247 — 118 Remaining

LOS ANGELES, CALIFORNIA FOUNDED: ANNIVERSARY. Sept 4, 1781. Los Angeles founded by decree and called "El Pueblo de Nuestra Senora La Reina de Los Angeles de Porciuncula."

NATIONAL STORYTELLER OF THE YEAR CONTEST. Sept 4. Millersport, OH. Official Storyteller of the Year named at this event. Sponsored by the Creative Arts Institute, Inc, Adventures

September 1999	S	M	T	W	T	F	S
				1	2	3	4
	5	6	7	8	9	10	11
	12	13	14	15	16	17	18
	19	20	21	22	23	24	25
	26	27	28	29	30		

in *Storytelling Magazine* and the Ohio Arts Council. Annually, the Saturday before Labor Day. Est attendance: 500. For info: Donna Foster, Creative Arts, 8021 Kennedy Rd, Blacklick, OH 43004. Phone: (614) 759-9407. Fax: (614) 759-8480. E-mail: dfoster@freenet.columbus.oh.us.

NEWSPAPER CARRIER DAY. Sept 4. Anniversary of the hiring of the first "newsboy" in the US, 10-year-old Barney Flaherty, who is said to have answered the following classified advertisement which appeared in *The New York Sun*, in 1833: "To the Unemployed—a number of steady men can find employment by vending this paper. A liberal discount is allowed to those who buy to sell again."

POLK, SARAH CHILDRESS: BIRTH ANNIVERSARY. Sept 4, 1803. Wife of James Knox Polk, 11th president of the US. Born at Murfreesboro, TN, and died at Nashville, TN, Aug 14, 1891.

BIRTHDAYS TODAY

Joan Aiken, 75, author (the Mortimer series), born Rye, Sussex, England, Sept 4, 1924.

Jason David Frank, 26, actor (*Turbo: A Power Rangers Movie*, "Power Rangers Turbo"), born Covina, CA, Sept 4, 1973.

Mike Piazza, 31, baseball player, born Norristown, PA, Sept 4, 1968.

SEPTEMBER 5 — SUNDAY

Day 248 — 117 Remaining

BE LATE FOR SOMETHING DAY. Sept 5. To create a release from the stresses and strains resulting from a consistent need to be on time. For info: Les Waas, Pres, Procrastinators' Club of America, Inc, Box 712, Bryn Athyn, PA 19009. Phone: (215) 947-9020. Fax: (215) 947-7007.

FIRST CONTINENTAL CONGRESS ASSEMBLY: 225th ANNIVERSARY. Sept 5, 1774. The first assembly of this forerunner of the US Congress took place at Philadelphia, PA. All 13 colonies were represented except Georgia. Peyton Randolph, delegate from Virginia, was elected president. The second Continental Congress met beginning May 10, 1775, also at Philadelphia. For more information, visit the website of Carpenter's Hall, the building where the Continental Congress met, at www.liberty net.org/iha/carpen_html.

ITALY: HISTORICAL REGATTA. Sept 5. Venice. Traditional competition among two-oar racing gondolas, preceded by a procession of Venetian ceremonial boats of the epoch of the Venetian Republic. Annually, the first Sunday in September.

JAMES, JESSE: BIRTH ANNIVERSARY. Sept 5, 1847. Western legend and bandit Jesse Woodson James was born at Centerville (now Kearney), MO. His criminal exploits were glorified and romanticized by writers for Eastern readers looking for stories of Western adventure and heroism. After the Civil War, James and his brother, Frank, formed a group of eight outlaws who robbed banks, stagecoaches and stores. In 1873, the James gang began holding up trains. The original James gang was put out of business Sept 7, 1876, while attempting to rob a bank at Northfield, MN. Every member of the gang except for the James brothers was killed or captured. The brothers formed a new gang and resumed their criminal careers in 1879. Two years later, the governor of Missouri offered a $10,000 reward for their capture, dead or alive. On Apr 3, 1882 at St. Joseph, MO, Robert Ford, a member of the gang, shot 34-year-old Jesse in the back of the head and claimed the reward.

NIELSEN, ARTHUR CHARLES: BIRTH ANNIVERSARY. Sept 5, 1897. Marketing research engineer, founder of A.C. Nielsen Company, in 1923, known for radio and TV audience surveys and ratings, was born at Chicago, IL, and died there June 1, 1980.

SPACE MILESTONE: *VOYAGER 1* (US). Sept 5, 1977. Twin of *Voyager 2* which was launched Aug 20. On Feb 18, 1998, *Voyager 1* set a new distance record when after more than 20 years in space it reached 6.5 billion miles from Earth.

BIRTHDAYS TODAY

Paul Fleischman, 47, author, poet (Newbery for *Joyful Noise: Poems for Two Voices*), born Monterey, CA, Sept 5, 1952.

SEPTEMBER 6 — MONDAY

Day 249 — 116 Remaining

ADDAMS, JANE: BIRTH ANNIVERSARY. Sept 6, 1860. American worker for peace, social welfare and the rights of women. The founder of Chicago's Hull House settlement house, she was co-winner of Nobel Peace Prize in 1931. Born at Cedarville, IL, she died May 21, 1935, at Chicago, IL.

BALTIC STATES' INDEPENDENCE RECOGNIZED: ANNIVERSARY. Sept 6, 1991. The Soviet government recognized the independence of the Baltic states—Latvia, Estonia and Lithuania. The action came 51 years after the Baltic states were annexed by the Soviet Union. All three Baltic states had earlier declared their independence, and many nations had already recognized them diplomatically, including the US Sept 2, 1991.

CANADA: LABOR DAY. Sept 6. Annually, the first Monday in September.

LABOR DAY. Sept 6. Legal public holiday. Public Law 90–363 sets Labor Day on the first Monday in September. Observed in all states. First observance believed to have been a parade at 10 AM, Tuesday, Sept 5, 1882, at New York, NY, probably organized by Peter J. McGuire, a Carpenters and Joiners Union secretary. In 1883, a union resolution declared "the first Monday in September of each year a Labor Day." By 1893, more than half of the states were observing Labor Day on one or another day and a bill to establish Labor Day as a federal holiday was introduced in Congress. On June 28, 1894, President Grover Cleveland signed into law an act making the first Monday in September a legal holiday for federal employees and the District of Columbia. Canada also celebrates Labor Day on the first Monday in September. In most other countries, Labor Day is observed May 1. For links to Labor Day websites, go to: deil.lang.uiuc.edu/web.pages/holidays/labor.html.

LAFAYETTE, MARQUIS DE: BIRTH ANNIVERSARY. Sept 6, 1757. French general and aristocrat, Lafayette, whose full name was Marie-Joseph-Paul-Yves-Roch-Gilbert du Motier, came to America to assist in the revolutionary cause. He was awarded a major-generalship and began a lasting friendship with the American commander-in-chief, George Washington. After an alliance was signed with France, he returned to his native country and persuaded Louis XVI to send a 6,000-man force to assist the Americans. On his return, he was given command of an army at Virginia and was instrumental in forcing the surrender of Lord Cornwallis at Yorktown, leading to the end of the war and American independence. He was hailed as "The Hero of Two Worlds" and was appointed a brigadier general on his return to France in 1782. He became a leader of the liberal aristocrats during the early days of the French revolution, presenting to the National Assembly his draft of "A Declaration of the Rights of Man and of the Citizen." As the commander of the newly formed national guard of Paris, he rescued Louis XVI and Marie-Antoinette from a crowd that stormed Versailles Oct 6, 1789, returning them to Paris where they became hostages of the revolution. His popularity waned after his guards opened fire on angry demonstrators demanding abdication of the king in 1791. He fled to Austria with the overthrow of the monarchy in 1792, returning when Napoleon Bonaparte came to power. Born at Chavaniac, he died at Paris, May 20, 1834.

SAINT PETERSBURG NAME RESTORED: ANNIVERSARY. Sept 6, 1991. Russian legislators voted to restore the name Saint Petersburg to the nation's second largest city. The city had been known as Leningrad for 67 years in honor of the Soviet Union's founder, Vladimir I. Lenin. The city, founded in 1703 by Peter the Great, has had three names in the 20th century with Russian leaders changing its German-sounding name to Petrograd at the beginning of WWI in 1914 and Soviet Communist leaders changing its name to Leningrad in 1924 following their leader's death.

SWAZILAND: INDEPENDENCE DAY. Sept 6. Commemorates attainment of independence from Britain in 1968. National holiday.

BIRTHDAYS TODAY

Chad Scott, 25, football player, born Washington, DC, Sept 6, 1974.

SEPTEMBER 7 — TUESDAY
Day 250 — 115 Remaining

BRAZIL: INDEPENDENCE DAY. Sept 7. Declared independence from Portugal in 1822. National holiday.

NEITHER SNOW NOR RAIN DAY. Sept 7. Anniversary of the opening to the public, on Labor Day, 1914, of the New York Post Office Building at Eighth Avenue between 31st and 33rd Streets. On the front of this building was an inscription supplied by William M. Kendall of the architectural firm that planned the building. The inscription, a free translation from Herodotus, reads: "Neither snow nor rain nor heat nor gloom of night stays these couriers from the swift completion of their appointed

rounds." This has long been believed to be the motto of the US Post Office and Postal Service. They have, in fact, no motto . . . but the legend remains. [Info from: New York Post Office, Public Info Office and US Postal Service.]

QUEEN ELIZABETH I: BIRTH ANNIVERSARY. Sept 7, 1533. Queen of England, daughter of Henry VIII and Anne Boleyn, after whom the "Elizabethan Era" was named, was born at Greenwich Palace. She ascended the throne in 1558 at the age of 25. During her reign, the British defeated the Spanish Armada in July 1588, the Anglican Church was essentially established and England became a world power. She died at Richmond, England, Mar 24, 1603.

BIRTHDAYS TODAY

Daniel Ken Inouye, 75, US Senator (D, Hawaii), born Honolulu, HI, Sept 7, 1924.

SEPTEMBER 8 — WEDNESDAY
Day 251 — 114 Remaining

ANDORRA: NATIONAL HOLIDAY. Sept 8. Honors our Lady of Meritxell.

GALVESTON HURRICANE: ANNIVERSARY. Sept 8, 1900. The worst national disaster in US history in terms of lives lost. More than 6,000 people were killed when a hurricane struck Galveston, TX.

McGWIRE HITS 62nd HOME RUN: ANNIVERSARY. Sept 8, 1998. Mark McGwire of the St. Louis Cardinals hit his 62nd home run, breaking Roger Maris's 1961 record for the most home runs in a single season. McGwire hit his homer against pitcher Steve Trachsel of the Chicago Cubs at Busch Stadium at St. Louis as the Cardinals won, 6–3. A few days later, Sept 13, 1998, Sammy Sosa of the Chicago Cubs hit his 62nd homer. McGwire ended the season with a total of 70 home runs; Sosa with a total of 66.

NORTHERN PACIFIC RAILROAD COMPLETED: ANNIVERSARY. Sept 8, 1883. After 19 years of construction, the Northern Pacific Railroad became the second railroad to link the two coasts. The Union Pacific and Central Pacific lines met at Utah in 1869.

"STAR TREK" TV PREMIERE: ANNIVERSARY. Sept 8, 1966. The first of 79 episodes of the TV series "Star Trek" was aired on the NBC network. Although the science fiction show set in the future only lasted a few seasons, it has remained enormously popular through syndication reruns. It has been given new life through six motion pictures, a cartoon TV series and the very popular TV series "Star Trek: The Next Generation," "Star Trek: Deep Space Nine" and "Star Trek: Voyager." It has consistently ranked among the biggest titles in the motion picture, television, home video and licensing divisions of Paramount Pictures.

UNITED NATIONS: INTERNATIONAL LITERACY DAY. Sept 8. An international day observed by the organizations of the United Nations system. Info from: United Nations, Dept of Public Info, New York, NY 10017.

BIRTHDAYS TODAY

Jack Prelutsky, 59, poet (*The New Kid on the Block*), born Brooklyn, NY, Sept 8, 1940.

Jon Scieszka, 45, author (*The Stinky Cheese Man and Other Fairly Stupid Tales*), born Flint, MI, Sept 8, 1954.

Jonathan Taylor Thomas, 18, actor ("Home Improvement," voice of Simba in *The Lion King*), born Bethlehem, PA, Sept 8, 1981.

		S	M	T	W	T	F	S
September						1	2	3	4
1999		5	6	7	8	9	10	11
		12	13	14	15	16	17	18
		19	20	21	22	23	24	25
		26	27	28	29	30		

SEPTEMBER 9 — THURSDAY

Day 252 — 113 Remaining

AUNTS' DAY. Sept 9. A day of recognition for those special women in our lives who provide guidance and humor and that extra measure of caring that can make such an impact on our lives. For info: Susan Lupien, Pres, TLG, 1000 Ponce de Leon Blvd, #306, Miami, FL 33134. Phone: (305) 529-0473.

BONZA BOTTLER DAY™. Sept 9. To celebrate when the number of the day is the same as the number of the month. Bonza Bottler Day™ is an excuse to have a party at least once a month. For info: Gail M. Berger, 109 Matthew Ave, Poca, WV 25159. Phone: (304) 776-7746. E-mail: gberger5@aol.com.

CALIFORNIA: ADMISSION DAY: ANNIVERSARY. Sept 9. Became 31st state in 1850.

"FAT ALBERT AND THE COSBY KIDS" TV PREMIERE: ANNIVERSARY. Sept 9, 1972. This cartoon series was hosted by Bill Cosby, with characters based on his childhood friends at Philadelphia. Its central characters—Fat Albert, Weird Harold, Mush Mouth and Donald—were weird-looking but very human. The show sent messages of tolerance and harmony. In 1979 the show was renamed "The New Fat Albert Show."

KOREA, DEMOCRATIC PEOPLE'S REPUBLIC OF: NATIONAL DAY. Sept 9. National holiday in the Democratic People's Republic of [North] Korea.

LUXEMBOURG: ANNIVERSARY LIBERATION CEREMONY. Sept 9. Petange. Commemoration of liberation of Grand-Duchy by the Allied forces in 1944. Ceremony at monument of the American soldier.

MOON PHASE: NEW MOON. Sept 9. Moon enters New Moon phase at 6:02 PM, EDT.

TAJIKISTAN: INDEPENDENCE DAY. Sept 9. National holiday commemorating independence from the Soviet Union in 1991.

UTAH STATE FAIR. Sept 9–19. Salt Lake City, UT. Est attendance: 360,000. For info: Utah State Fair Park, 155 N 1000 W, Salt Lake City, UT 84116. Phone: (801) 538-8440. Fax: (801) 538-8455. E-mail: utstdonna@fiber.net.

WILLIAM, THE CONQUEROR: DEATH ANNIVERSARY. Sept 9, 1087. William I, The Conqueror, King of England and Duke of Normandy, whose image is portrayed in the Bayeux Tapestry, was born about 1028 at Falaise, Normandy. Victorious over Harold at the Battle of Hastings (the Norman Conquest) in 1066, William was crowned King of England at Westminster Abbey on Christmas Day of that year. Later, while waging war in France, William met his death at Rouen, Sept 9, 1087.

BIRTHDAYS TODAY

Benjamin Roy ("BJ") Armstrong, 32, basketball player, born Detroit, MI, Sept 9, 1967.
Adam Sandler, 33, actor (*The Waterboy, Billy Madison*), born Brooklyn, NY, Sept 9, 1966.
Mildred Pitts Walter, 77, author (*Justin and the Best Biscuits in the World*), born DeRidder, LA, Sept 9, 1922.

SEPTEMBER 10 — FRIDAY

Day 253 — 112 Remaining

BELIZE: SAINT GEORGE'S CAYE DAY. Sept 10. Public holiday celebrated in honor of the battle between the European Baymen Settlers and the Spaniards for the territory of Belize.

BRAXTON, CARTER: BIRTH ANNIVERSARY. Sept 10, 1736. American revolutionary statesman and signer of the Declaration of Independence. Born at Newington, VA, he died Oct 10, 1797, at Richmond, VA.

KANSAS STATE FAIR. Sept 10–19. Hutchinson, KS. Commercial and competitive exhibits, entertainment, carnival, car racing and other special attractions. Annually, beginning the first Friday after Labor Day. Est attendance: 335,000. For info: Bill Ogg, Gen Mgr, Kansas State Fair, 2000 N Poplar, Hutchinson, KS 67502. Phone: (316) 669-3600.

KEIKO RETURNS TO ICELAND: ANNIVERSARY. Sept 10, 1998. Keiko, the killer whale or orca who starred in the 1993 film *Free Willy*, was returned to his home in waters off Iceland after spending 19 years in captivity. Keiko was to be kept in a specially-built cage in the ocean until it was determined if he can return to the wild.

MARIS, ROGER: 65th BIRTH ANNIVERSARY. Sept 10, 1934. Roger Eugene Maris, baseball player born Roger Eugene Maras at Hibbing, MN. In 1961, Maris broke one of baseball's sacred records, hitting 61 home runs to surpass the mark set by Babe Ruth in 1927. This record wasn't broken until 1998. He won the American League MVP award in 1960 and 1961 and finished his career with the St. Louis Cardinals. Died at Houston, TX, Dec 14, 1985.

ROSH HASHANAH BEGINS AT SUNDOWN. Sept 10. Jewish New Year. See "Rosh Hashanah" (Sept 11).

TENNESSEE STATE FAIR. Sept 10–19. Nashville, TN. A huge variety of exhibits, carnival midway, animal and variety shows, live stage presentations, livestock, agricultural and craft competitions and food and game booths. Est attendance: 316,000. For info: Tennessee Fair Office, PO Box 40208, Melrose Station, Nashville, TN 37204. Phone: (615) 862-8980.

BIRTHDAYS TODAY

Matt Geiger, 30, baseball player, born Salem, MA, Sept 10, 1969.

SEPTEMBER 11 — SATURDAY

Day 254 — 111 Remaining

BATTLE OF BRANDYWINE: ANNIVERSARY. Sept 11, 1777. The largest engagement of the American Revolution, between the Continental Army led by General George Washington and British forces led by General William Howe. Howe was marching to take Philadelphia when Washington chose an area on the Brandywine Creek near Chadds Ford, PA to stop the advance. The American forces were defeated here and the British went on to take Philadelphia Sept 26. They spent the winter in the city while Washington's troops suffered in their encampment at Valley Forge, PA. For further info, visit the Independence Hall Association website at www.libertynet.org/iha/brandywine.html.

ETHIOPIA: NEW YEAR'S DAY. Sept 11. Public holiday. This day in 1999 begins the year 1993 on the Ethiopian calendar. This is also the beginning of the year 1716 on the Coptic calendar.

★**FEDERAL LANDS CLEANUP DAY.** Sept 11. Presidential Proclamation 5521, of Sept 5, 1986, covers all succeeding years. The first Saturday after Labor Day. (PL99–402 of Aug 27, 1986.)

KID'RIFIC. Sept 11–12. Hartford, CT. A two-day children's festival on Constitution Plaza in downtown Hartford, produced by the Hartford Downtown Council. Kid'rific will feature hands-on art and science activities, storytelling, master teaching artists' workshops, continuous stage entertainment, a petting zoo with a 13' tall giraffe and lots more. Annually, the first weekend after Labor Day. Est attendance: 50,000. For info: Steven A. Lazaroff, Dir for Events Programming, Hartford Downtown Council, 250 Constitution Plaza, Hartford, CT 06103. Phone: (860) 728-3089. Fax: (860) 527-9696. Web: www.hartford-hdc.com.

"LITTLE HOUSE ON THE PRAIRIE" TV PREMIERE: ANNIVERSARY. Sept 11, 1974. This hour-long family drama was based on the books by Laura Ingalls Wilder. It focused on the Ingalls family and their neighbors living at Walnut Grove, MN: Michael Landon as Charles (Pa), Karen Grassle as Caroline (Ma), Melissa Sue Anderson as daughter Mary, Melissa Gilbert as daughter Laura, from whose point of view the stories were told, Lindsay and Sidney Greenbush as daughter Carrie and Wendi and Brenda Turnbeugh as daughter Grace. The series spent one season at Winoka, Dakota. In its last season (1982), the show's name was changed to "Little House: A New Beginning," Landon appeared less often and the show centered around Laura and her husband.

NEW MEXICO STATE FAIR. Sept 11–27. Albuquerque, NM. Fireworks, blues, country, gospel, pop and rock entertainment. Rodeos, circus, auto thrill show, tractor pulls, horse racing and free grandstand shows. For info: New Mexico State Fair, Po Box 8546, Albuquerque, NM 87198. Phone: (505) 265-1791. Fax: (505) 266-7784.

911 DAY. Sept 11. To foster the implementation of a universal emergency telephone number system. For info: Natl Emergency Number Assn, 47849 Papermill Rd, Coshocton, OH 43812. Phone: (614) 622-8911. Fax: (614) 622-2090. Web: www.nena9-1-1.org.

PAKISTAN: FOUNDER'S DEATH ANNIVERSARY. Sept 11. Pakistan observes the death anniversary in 1948 of Quaid-i-Azam Mohammed Ali Jinnah (founder of Pakistan) as a national holiday.

PUBLIC LANDS DAY. Sept 11. To involve citizen volunteers in cleaning and maintaining public lands. Annually, the Saturday after Labor Day. Est attendance: 1,000,000. For info: Keep America Beautiful, Inc, Washington Square, 1010 Washington Blvd, Stamford, CT 06901. E-mail: keepamerbe@aol.com.

ROSH HASHANAH or JEWISH NEW YEAR. Sept 11–12. Jewish holy day; observed on following day also. Hebrew calendar date: Tishri 1, 5760. Rosh Hashanah (literally "Head of the Year") is the beginning of 10 days of repentance and spiritual renewal. (Began at sundown of previous day.)

SPACE MILESTONE: *MARS GLOBAL SURVEYOR* (US). Sept 11, 1997. Launched Nov 7, 1996, this unmanned vehicle was put in orbit around Mars on this date. It is designed to compile global

	S	**M**	**T**	**W**	**T**	**F**	**S**
September				1	2	3	4
1999	5	6	7	8	9	10	11
	12	13	14	15	16	17	18
	19	20	21	22	23	24	25
	26	27	28	29	30		

maps of Mars by taking high resolution photos. This mission inaugurated a new series of Mars expeditions in which NASA will launch pairs of orbiters and landers to Mars every 26 months into the next decade. *Mars Global Surveyor* was paired with the lander *Mars Pathfinder*. See also: "Space Milestone: *Mars Pathfinder*" (July 4).

BIRTHDAYS TODAY

Daniel Akaka, 75, US Senator (D, Hawaii), born Honolulu, HI, Sept 11, 1924.

SEPTEMBER 12 — SUNDAY
Day 255 — 110 Remaining

ENGLAND: BATTLE OF BRITAIN WEEK. Sept 12–18. Annually, the third week of September—the week containing Battle of Britain Day (Sept 15).

ETHIOPIA: NATIONAL REVOLUTION DAY. Sept 12. Observed as a national holiday. Commemorates the overthrow of Haile Selassie in 1974.

"FRAGGLE ROCK" TV PREMIERE: ANNIVERSARY. Sept 12, 1987. This children's show was a cartoon version of the live Jim Henson puppet production on HBO. It was set in the rock underneath a scientist's house and featured characters such as the Fraggles, the Doozers and the Gorgs.

"LASSIE" TV PREMIERE: ANNIVERSARY. Sept 12, 1954. This long-running series was originally about a boy and his courageous and intelligent dog, Lassie (played by more than six different dogs, all male). For the first few seasons, Lassie lived on the Miller farm and had lots of adventures. The family included Jeff (Tommy Rettig), his widowed mother Ellen (Jan Clayton) and George Cleveland as Gramps. Throughout the years there were many format and cast changes, as Lassie was exchanged from one family to another in order to have a variety of new perils and escapades. Other featured performers over the years include Cloris Leachman, June Lockhart and Larry Wilcox.

MARYLAND: DEFENDERS DAY. Sept 12. Maryland. Annual reenactment of bombardment of Fort McHenry in 1814 which inspired Francis Scott Key to write the "Star-Spangled Banner."

NATIONAL 5-A-DAY WEEK. Sept 12–18. To encourage all Americans to increase the amount of fruits and vegetables they eat to five or more servings per day, to better their health and reduce their risk of cancer and other chronic diseases. See Curriculum Connection. For info: Produce for Better Health Foundation, 5301 Limestone Rd, Ste 101, Wilmington, DE 19808. Phone: (302) 235-ADAY or (800) 4-CANCER. Fax: 302235555. Web: www.5aday.com.

★**NATIONAL GRANDPARENTS DAY.** Sept 12. Presidential Proclamation 4679, of Sept 6, 1979, covers all succeeding years. First Sunday in September following Labor Day (PL96–62 of Sept 6, 1979). First issued in 1978 (Proc 4580 of Aug 3, 1978), requested by Public Law 325 of July 28, 1978.

OWENS, JESSE: BIRTH ANNIVERSARY. Sept 12, 1913. James Cleveland (Jesse) Owens, American athlete, winner of four gold medals at the 1936 Olympic Games at Berlin, Germany, was born at Oakville, AL. Owens set 11 world records in track and field. During one track meet, at Ann Arbor, MI, May 23, 1935, Owens, representing Ohio State University, broke five world records and tied a sixth in the space of 45 minutes. Died at Tucson, AZ, Mar 31, 1980.

SPACE MILESTONE: *LUNA 2* (USSR). Sept 12, 1959. First spacecraft to land on moon was launched.

SEPTEMBER 12–18
A HEALTHIER YOU: NATIONAL 5-A-DAY WEEK

The order "Eat your vegetables!" makes many children hide peas under a napkin or smuggle food to the dog. However, research shows it's important for us to eat plenty of vegetables and fruits to stay healthy and reduce the risk of disease. National 5-A-Day Week helps you increase awareness of the role fruits and vegetables play in a balanced diet. They form part of the foundation of the US Department of Agriculture's food pyramid.

Before the start of 5-A-Day week ask your students to keep a daily chart of all the food they eat during the week. Don't let them know the theme of the approaching week. At week's end have students list the number of vegetables and fruits they've eaten, individually and as a class. The results can be charted and graphed as part of the math curriculum. Then, talk about 5-A-Day Week. Ask students to keep track of the new week's meals. Graph and compare 5-A-Day's results with the previous week's. Discuss vegetable likes and dislikes. A classroom book of recipes can make eating fruits and vegetables more fun. Young children can clean vegetables like broccoli, celery and carrots and serve them with a dip as a snack.

You may want to consider inviting a nutritionist to visit your class. A grocer or farmer, if available in your area, may offer an interesting perspective on the safe care and management of fresh fruits and vegetables.

Several books for young readers offer information on this and related topics: *The Edible Pyramid: Good Eating Every Day*, by Loreen Leedy (Holiday House, 0-8234-1126-5, $15.95 Gr. K–3); *The Food Pyramid*, by Joan Kalbacken (Children's Press, 0-516-20756-3, $21 Gr. 2–4); *Cool As a Cucumber, Hot as a Pepper: Fruit Vegetables*, by Meredith Hughes (Lerner, 0-8225-2832-0, $18.95 Gr. 5–7); *Stinky and Stringy: Stem and Bulb Vegetables*, by Meredith Hughes (Lerner, 0-8225-2833-9, $18.95 Gr. 5–7); *Where Food Comes From*, by Dorothy Hinshaw Patent (Holiday House, 0-8234-0877-9, $14.95 Gr. 1–5); and *Oliver's Fruit Salad*, by Vivian French (Orchard Books, 0-531-30087-0, $14.95 Gr. PreS–2).

For more information on the US Department of Agriculture's Food Pyramid and a printable pyramid, go to www.nal.usda.gov/fnic/Fpyr/pyramid.html on the web. A related event is Johnny Appleseed's birthday on Sept 26.

VIDEO GAMES DAY. Sept 12. A day for kids who love video games to celebrate the fun they have playing them and to thank their parents for all the cartridges and quarters they have provided to indulge this hobby.

BIRTHDAYS TODAY

Sam Brownback, 43, US Senator (R, Kansas), born Garnett, KS, Sept 12, 1956.
Peter Scolari, 45, actor ("Honey I Shrunk the Kids: The TV Show"), born Rochelle, IL, Sept 12, 1954.

SEPTEMBER 13 — MONDAY
Day 256 — 109 Remaining

BARRY, JOHN: DEATH ANNIVERSARY. Sept 13, 1803. Revolutionary War hero John Barry, first American to hold the rank of commodore, died at Philadelphia, PA. He was born at Tacumshane, County Wexford, Ireland, in 1745. He has been called the "Father of the American Navy."

DAHL, ROALD: BIRTH ANNIVERSARY. Sept 13, 1916. Author (*Charlie and the Chocolate Factory, James and the Giant Peach, Matilda*), born at Llandaff, South Wales, Great Britain. Died Nov 23, 1990, at Oxford, England.

FAST OF GEDALYA. Sept 13. Jewish holiday. Hebrew calendar date: Tishri 3, 5760. Tzom Gedalya begins at first light of day and commemorates the 6th-century BC assassination of Gedalya Ben Achikam.

"THE MUPPET SHOW" TV PREMIERE: ANNIVERSARY. Sept 13, 1976. This comedy variety show was hosted by Kermit the Frog from "Sesame Street." Other Jim Henson puppet characters included Miss Piggy, Fozzie the Bear and Gonzo the Great. Many celebrities made guest appearances on the show, which was broadcast in more than 100 countries. "Muppet Babies" was a Saturday morning cartoon spin-off that aired from 1984 to 1992. *The Muppet Movie* (1979) was the first of five films based on "The Muppet Show."

REED, WALTER: BIRTH ANNIVERSARY. Sept 13, 1851. American army physician especially known for his Yellow Fever research. Born at Gloucester County, VA, he served as an army surgeon for more than 20 years and as a professor at the Army Medical College. He died at Washington, DC, Nov 22, 1902. The US Army's general hospital at Washington, DC, is named in his honor.

"STAR-SPANGLED BANNER" INSPIRED: ANNIVERSARY. Sept 13–14, 1814. During the War of 1812, on the night of Sept 13, Francis Scott Key was aboard a ship that was delayed in Baltimore harbor by the British attack there on Fort Henry. Key had no choice but to anxiously watch the battle. That experience and seeing the American flag still flying over the fort the next morning inspired him to pen the verses that, coupled with the tune of a popular drinking song, became our official national anthem in 1931, 117 years after the words were written.

US CAPITAL ESTABLISHED AT NEW YORK CITY: ANNIVERSARY. Sept 13, 1789. Congress picked New York, NY, as the location of the new US government in place of Philadelphia, which had served as the capital up until this time. In 1790 the capital moved back to Philadelphia, and in 1800 moved permanently to Washington, DC.

BIRTHDAYS TODAY

William Janklow, 60, Governor of South Dakota (R), born Chicago, IL, Sept 13, 1939.
Ben Savage, 19, actor ("Boy Meets World"), born Chicago, IL, Sept 13, 1980.
Mildred D. Taylor, 56, author (Newbery for *Roll of Thunder, Hear My Cry*), born Jackson, MS, Sept 13, 1943.

SEPTEMBER 14 — TUESDAY
Day 257 — 108 Remaining

SOLO TRANSATLANTIC BALLOON CROSSING: 15th ANNIVERSARY. Sept 14–18, 1984. Joe W. Kittinger, 56-year-old balloonist, left Caribou, ME, in a 10-story-tall helium-filled balloon named *Rosie O'Grady's Balloon of Peace* Sept 14, 1984, crossed the Atlantic Ocean and reached the French coast, above the town of Capbreton, in bad weather Sept 17 at 4:29 PM, EDT. He crashlanded amid wind and rain near Savone, Italy, at 8:08 AM, EDT, Sept 18. His nearly 84-hour flight, covering about 3,535 miles, was the first solo balloon crossing of the Atlantic Ocean.

"THE WALTONS" TV PREMIERE: ANNIVERSARY. Sept 14, 1972. This epitome of the family drama spawned nearly a dozen knock-offs during its nine-year run on CBS. The drama was based on creator/writer Earl Hamner Jr's experiences growing up during the Depression in rural Virginia. It began as the TV movie "The Homecoming," which was so well-received that it was turned into a weekly series covering the years 1933–43. The cast went through numerous changes through the years; the principals were: Michael Learned as Olivia Walton, mother of the clan; Ralph Waite as John Walton, father; Richard Thomas as John-Boy, eldest son; Jon Walmsley as son Jason; Judy Norton as daughter Mary Ellen; Eric Scott as son Ben; Mary Elizabeth McDonough as daughter Erin; David W. Harper as son Jim-Bob and Kami Cotler as daughter Elizabeth. The Walton grandparents were played by Ellen Corby (Esther) and Will Geer (Zeb).

BIRTHDAYS TODAY

William Armstrong, 85, author (Newbery for *Sounder*), born Lexington, VA, Sept 14, 1914.

John Steptoe, 49, author and illustrator (*Mufaro's Beautiful Daughters: An African Tale*), born Brooklyn, NY, Sept 14, 1950.

SEPTEMBER 15 — WEDNESDAY

Day 258 — 107 Remaining

COOPER, JAMES FENIMORE: BIRTH ANNIVERSARY. Sept 15, 1789. American novelist, historian and social critic, born at Burlington, NJ, Cooper was one of the earliest American writers to develop a native American literary tradition. His most popular works are the five novels comprising *The Leatherstocking Tales*, featuring the exploits of one of the truly unique American fictional characters, Natty Bumppo. These novels, *The Deerslayer, The Last of the Mohicans, The Pathfinder, The Pioneers* and *The Prairie*, chronicle Natty Bumppo's continuing flight away from the rapid settlement of America. Cooper died Sept 14, 1851, at Cooperstown, NY, the town founded by his father.

COSTA RICA: INDEPENDENCE DAY. Sept 15. National holiday. Gained independence from Spain in 1821.

EL SALVADOR: INDEPENDENCE DAY. Sept 15. National holiday. Gained independence from Spain in 1821.

ENGLAND: BATTLE OF BRITAIN DAY. Sept 15. Commemorates end of biggest daylight bombing raid of Britain by German Luftwaffe, in 1940. Said to have been the turning point against Hitler's siege of Britain in WWII.

FIRST NATIONAL CONVENTION FOR BLACKS: ANNIVERSARY. Sept 15, 1830. The first national convention for blacks was held at Bethel Church, Philadelphia, PA. The convention was called to find ways to better the condition of black people and was attended by delegates from seven states. Bishop Richard Allen was elected as the first convention president.

GUATEMALA: INDEPENDENCE DAY. Sept 15. National holiday. Gained independence from Spain in 1821.

HONDURAS: INDEPENDENCE DAY. Sept 15. National holiday. Gained independence from Spain in 1821.

JAPAN: OLD PEOPLE'S DAY OR RESPECT FOR THE AGED DAY. Sept 15. National holiday.

	S	M	T	W	T	F	S
September 1999				1	2	3	4
	5	6	7	8	9	10	11
	12	13	14	15	16	17	18
	19	20	21	22	23	24	25
	26	27	28	29	30		

SEPTEMBER 15–OCTOBER 15 NATIONAL HISPANIC HERITAGE MONTH

Invite your class to a month-long fiesta celebrating the diverse Hispanic cultures whose heritage has enriched the US. The majority of Hispanic Americans came from Cuba, Puerto Rico, Mexico and Central and South America. Students can list and discuss where Hispanic influences can be found in the US. Place names are an obvious starting point. *The New York Public Library Amazing Hispanic American History: A Book of Answers for Kids*, by George Ochoa (Wiley, 0-471-19204-X, $12.95 Gr. 4 & up) is filled with trivia that will provoke discussion.

You and your students can also observe this month by learning some Spanish. Simple phrases like hola, adiós, cómo está?, and Spanish names for colors and common objects used in the classroom on a daily basis are good choices. Hispanic students in your class could lead the lessons. Check your local radio stations for a Spanish station you can turn on periodically.

A food fair is a tasty way to explore Hispanic heritage. Many cookbooks contain recipes from different regions and expose students to food other than fast-food tacos. Students can also make a piñata to top off the day's activities.

Recordings of Mexican mariachi and Afro-Cuban music are found in most library collections. Your students will enjoy these rhythms and might try learning a dance or two. The cha-cha, tango and rumba are Latin American dances.

Writers of children's literature with a Hispanic focus include Arthur Dorros, Gary Soto, Omar Castañeda, Nicholasa Mohr, Lulu Delacre, Vincent Martinez and Lori M. Carlson. Isabel Schon's *The Best of the Latino Heritage: A Guide to the Best Juvenile Books About Latino People and Cultures* (Scarecrow, 0-8108-3221-6, $37.50) lists books about Spanish-speakers in other countries and Latinos in the US. The teacher with Spanish-speaking students will want to consult Schon's *Recommended Books in Spanish for Children and Young Adults, 1991–1995* (Scarecrow, 0-8108-3235-6, $42.50). Finally, Schon's website at the Center for the Study of Books in Spanish for Children and Adolescents at California State University, San Marcos (www.csusm.edu/cwis/campus_centers/csbs) is a comprehensive guide.

There are many athletes of Hispanic heritage, such as baseball's Sammy Sosa, horse racing's Angel Cordero and golf's Nancy Lopez. Your students could search the sports pages and bring in articles about other Hispanic athletes.

For a classroom debate, the topic of bilingual education is currently in the news. Again, newspapers are a good source of information.

The Day of the Dead, which is celebrated from Oct 31 through Nov 2, is widely observed in Mexican American communities. For an excellent article that includes book and web sources and teaching approaches, see "Skeletons and Marigolds: Diás de los Muertos," by Jeanette Larson and Carolina Martìnez in the September 1998 issue of *Book Links* magazine.

KIRSTEN, SAMANTHA AND MOLLY DEBUT: ANNIVERSARY. Sept 15, 1986. The first three American Girl dolls representing different historical periods debuted. They were joined in later years by Addy, Felicity and Josefina. More than 4 million dolls and 48 million books about them have been sold. For more information: www.americangirl.com.

LIONS CLUBS INTERNATIONAL PEACE POSTER CONTEST. Sept 15. Contest for children ages 11–13. All entries must be sponsored by a local Lions Club. Today is the deadline for sponsorship requests by schools and youth groups. Posters due to sponsoring Lions Club by Nov 30, 1999. Finalist judging held at Chicago in February, 2000. For info: Public Relations Dept, Intl Assn of Lions Clubs, 300 22nd St, Oak Brook, IL 60523-8842. Phone: (630) 571-5466. Web: www.lionsclubs.org.

"THE LONE RANGER" TV PREMIERE: 50th ANNIVERSARY. Sept 15, 1949. This character was created for a radio serial in 1933 by George W. Trendle. The famous masked man was the alter ego of John Reid, a Texas Ranger who was the only survivor of an ambush. He was nursed back to health by his Native-American friend, Tonto. Both men traveled around the West on their trusty steeds, Silver and Scout, fighting injustice. On TV Clayton Moore played the Lone Ranger/John Reid and Jay Silverheels co-starred as Tonto. The theme music was Rossini's "William Tell Overture."

★ **NATIONAL HISPANIC HERITAGE MONTH.** Sept 15–Oct 15. Presidential Proclamation. Beginning in 1989, always issued for Sept 15–Oct 15 of each year (PL 100–402 of Aug 17, 1988). Previously issued each year for the week including Sept 15 and 16 since 1968 at request (PL90–498 of Sept 17, 1968). See Curriculum Connection.

NATIONAL SCHOOL PSYCHOLOGY DAY. Sept 15. A day of recognition for the field of school psychology and its contributions to education. Annually, Sept 15. For info: Alan W. Brue, 2006 NW 55th Ave, #H-5, Gainesville, FL 32653. E-mail: afn05660@afn.org.

NICARAGUA: INDEPENDENCE DAY. Sept 15. National holiday. Gained independence from Spain in 1821.

TAFT, WILLIAM HOWARD: BIRTH ANNIVERSARY. Sept 15, 1857. The 27th president of the US was born at Cincinnati, OH. His term of office was Mar 4, 1909–Mar 3, 1913. Following his presidency he became a law professor at Yale University until his appointment as Chief Justice of the US Supreme Court in 1921. Died at Washington, DC, Mar 8, 1930, and was buried at Arlington National Cemetery.

BIRTHDAYS TODAY

Tomie DePaola, 65, illustrator and author (*Strega Nona*), born Thomas DePaola, Meriden, CT, Sept 15, 1934.

Prince Harry, 15, Henry Charles Albert David, son of Prince Charles and Princess Diana, born London, England, Sept 15, 1984.

Robert McCloskey, 85, illustrator and author (Caldecott for *Time of Wonder, Make Way for Ducklings*), born John Robert McCloskey, Hamilton, OH, Sept 15, 1914.

SEPTEMBER 16 — THURSDAY

Day 259 — 106 Remaining

CHEROKEE STRIP DAY: ANNIVERSARY. Sept 16, 1893. Optional holiday, Oklahoma. Greatest "run" for Oklahoma land in 1893.

CORN ISLAND STORYTELLING FESTIVAL. Sept 16–18. Louisville, KY. 24th annual. More than 50 storytellers. Festival includes an "olio," mixture of tales, "Fest of Storytelling" and "ghost tales" told at Long Run Park. Est attendance: 16,000. For info: Joy Pennington, Intl Order of EARS, Inc, 12019 Donohue Ave, Louisville, KY 40243. Phone: (502) 245-0643. Fax: (502) 254-7542.

GENERAL MOTORS: FOUNDING ANNIVERSARY. Sept 16, 1908. The giant automobile manufacturing company was founded by William Crapo "Billy" Durant, a Flint, MI, entrepreneur.

MAYFLOWER DAY: ANNIVERSARY. Sept 16, 1620. Anniversary of the departure of the *Mayflower* from Plymouth, England with 102 passengers and a small crew. Vicious storms were encountered en route which caused serious doubt about the wisdom of continuing, but she reached Provincetown, MA, Nov 21, and discharged the Pilgrims at Plymouth, MA, Dec 26, 1620.

MEXICO: INDEPENDENCE DAY. Sept 16. National Day. The official celebration begins at 11 PM, Sept 15 and continues through Sept 16. On the night of the 15th, the President of Mexico steps onto the balcony of the National Palace at Mexico City and voices the same "El Grito" (Cry for Freedom) that Father Hidalgo gave on the night of Sept 15, 1810 which began Mexico's rebellion from Spain.

NATIONAL STUDENT DAY™. Sept 16. Created to recognize all students from preschool through postgraduate, this is the perfect day to show the students in our lives how proud we are of them, to recognize their hard work and to show support for their efforts. For info: Ralph E Williams, Exec Dir, National Assn of College Students, 8695 College Pkwy, Ste 300, Ft. Myers, FL 33919. Phone: (800) 500-4255 or (941) 489-1530. Fax: (941) 489-1142. E-mail: nacs@collegeknowledge.com. Web: www.collegeknowledge.com.

NATIONAL PLAY-DOH DAY. Sept 16. To commemorate the introduction of Play-Doh. Joe McVicker of Cincinnati sent some non-toxic wallpaper cleaner to his sister-in-law, a nursery school teacher. She found it to be an excellent replacement for modeling clay. In 1955, McVicker took the product to an educational convention and by 1956 Play-Doh was being sold commercially.

NORTHERN APPALACHIAN STORYTELLING FESTIVAL. Sept 16–19. Straughn Hall, Mansfield University, Mansfield, PA. Showcases the talent of the nation's top storytellers who share through their performances a sense of roots and cultural diversity. There are performances Saturday afternoon and Friday and Saturday evening, plus a ghost story session late Friday night. In addition, there are storytelling master classes Saturday morning and a workshop on Thursday and Friday. 19th annual. Annually, the third weekend in September. Est attendance: 1,700. For info: Dr. Priscilla M Travis, N Appalachian Storytelling Fest, PO Box 434, Mansfield, PA 16933. Phone: (717) 662-4785. Fax: (717) 662-4112. E-mail: ptravis@mnsfld.edu. Web: wso.net/storyfest/

PAPUA NEW GUINEA: INDEPENDENCE DAY. Sept 16. National holiday. Commemorates independence from Australian administration in 1975.

REY, H.A.: BIRTH ANNIVERSARY. Sept 16, 1898. Born Hans Augusto Rey at Hamburg, Germany. Rey illustrated the Curious George series, while his wife, Margaret Rey, wrote the stories. He died at Cambridge, MA, Aug 26, 1977.

UNITED NATIONS: INTERNATIONAL DAY FOR THE PRESERVATION OF THE OZONE LAYER. Sept 16. On Dec 19, 1994, the General Assembly proclaimed this day to commemorate the date in 1987 on which Montreal Protocol on Substances that Deplete the Ozone Layer was signed (Res 49/114). States are invited to devote the Day to promote, at the national level, activities in accordance with the objectives of the Protocol. The ozone layer filters sunlight and prevents the adverse effects of ultraviolet radiation from reaching the Earth's surface, thereby preserving life on the planet. For info: United Nations, Dept of Public Info, Public Inquiries Unit, Rm GA-57, New York, NY 10017. Phone: (212) 963-4475. Fax: (212) 963-0071. E-mail: inquiries@un.org.

BIRTHDAYS TODAY

David Copperfield, 43, magician, illusionist, born Metuchen, NJ, Sept 16, 1956.

Robin Yount, 44, Baseball Hall of Fame player, born Danville, IL, Sept 16, 1955.

SEPTEMBER 17 — FRIDAY

Day 260 — 105 Remaining

BATTLE OF ANTIETAM: ANNIVERSARY. Sept 17, 1862. This date has been called America's bloodiest day in recognition of the high casualties suffered in the Civil War battle between General Robert E. Lee's Confederate forces and General George McClellan's Union army. Estimates vary, but more than 25,000 Union and Confederate soldiers were killed or wounded in this battle on the banks of the Potomac River at Maryland.

THE BIG E. Sept 17–Oct 3. West Springfield, MA. New England's fall classic and one of the nation's largest fairs. Each September, The Big E features all free entertainment including top-name talent, a big-top circus and horse show. Also children's attractions, daily parade, historic village, Avenue of States, Better Living Center and much more. Annually, beginning the second Friday after Labor Day. Est attendance: 1,000,000. For info: Eastern States Exposition, 1305 Memorial Ave, West Springfield, MA 01089. Phone: (413) 737-2443. Ticket info: (800) 334-2443. Fax: (413) 787-0127. E-mail: sales@thebige.com. Web: www.thebige.com.

BURGER, WARREN E.: BIRTH ANNIVERSARY. Sept 17, 1907. Former Chief Justice of the US Warren E. Burger was born at St. Paul, MN. A conservative on criminal matters, but a progressive on social issues, he had the longest tenure (1969-86) of any chief justice in this century. Appointed by President Nixon, he voted in the majority on *Roe v Wade* (1973), which upheld a woman's right to an abortion, and on *US v Nixon* (1974), which forced Nixon to surrender audio tapes to the Watergate special prosecutor. He died June 25, 1995 at Washington, DC.

★**CITIZENSHIP DAY.** Sept 17. Presidential Proclamation always issued for Sept 17 at request (PL82–261 of Feb 29, 1952). Customarily issued as "Citizenship Day and Constitution Week." Replaces Constitution Day.

CONSTITUTION OF THE US: ANNIVERSARY. Sept 17, 1787. Delegations from 12 states at the Constitutional Convention at Philadelphia, PA, voted unanimously to approve the proposed

	S	M	T	W	T	F	S
September 1999				1	2	3	4
	5	6	7	8	9	10	11
	12	13	14	15	16	17	18
	19	20	21	22	23	24	25
	26	27	28	29	30		

document. Thirty-nine of the 42 delegates present signed it and the Convention adjourned, after drafting a letter of transmittal to the Congress. The proposed constitution stipulated that it would take effect when ratified by nine states. This day is a legal holiday in Arizona and Florida. For activities and lesson plans on the Constitution, visit the National Archives website at www.nara.gov/education/teaching/constitution/home.html.

★**CONSTITUTION WEEK.** Sept 17–23. Presidential Proclamation always issued for the period of Sept 17–23 each year since 1955 (PL 84–915 of Aug 2, 1956).

FOSTER, ANDREW (RUBE): BIRTH ANNIVERSARY. Sept 17, 1879. Rube Foster's efforts in baseball earned him the title of "The Father of Negro Baseball." He was a manager and star pitcher, pitching 51 victories in one year. In 1919, he called a meeting of black baseball owners and organized the first black baseball league, the Negro National League. He served as its president until his death in 1930. Foster was born at Calvert, TX, the son of a minister. He died Dec 9, 1930, at Kankakee, IL.

HENDRICKS, THOMAS ANDREWS: BIRTH ANNIVERSARY. Sept 17, 1819. Twenty-first vice president of the US (1885) born at Muskingum County, OH. Died at Indianapolis, IN, Nov 25, 1885.

MOON PHASE: FIRST QUARTER. Sept 17. Moon enters First Quarter phase at 4:06 PM, EDT.

NATIONAL CONSTITUTION CENTER CONSTITUTION WEEK. Sept 17–23. To celebrate and commemorate the signing of the US Constitution Sept 17, 1787. The National Constitution Center sponsors ceremonial signings of the Constitution nationwide. Everyone is invited to participate and receive educational materials about the world's oldest working Constitution. Est attendance: 1,000,000. For info: Natl Constitution Center, The Bourse, 111 S Independence Mall East, Ste 560, Philadelphia, PA 19106. Phone: (215) 923-0004. Fax: (215) 923-1749. Web: www.constitutioncenter.org.

NATIONAL FOOTBALL LEAGUE FORMED: ANNIVERSARY. Sept 17, 1920. The National Football League was formed at Canton, OH.

NATIVE AMERICAN DAY IN MASSACHUSETTS. Sept 17. Proclaimed annually by the governor for the third Friday in September.

SPACE MILESTONE: *PEGASUS 1* (US). Sept 17, 1978. This 23,000-pound research satellite broke up over Africa and fell to Earth. Major pieces are believed to have fallen into Atlantic Ocean off the coast of Angola. The satellite had been orbiting Earth for more than 13 years since being launched Feb 16, 1965.

STATE FAIR OF OKLAHOMA. Sept 17–Oct 3. Fairgrounds, Oklahoma City, Oklahoma. Third largest fair in North America includes seven buildings of commercial exhibits; Walt Disney's World on Ice, the State Fair Super Circus, PRCA championship rodeo, livestock competitions, top-name concerts and motorsports events. Annually, second Friday after Labor Day. Est attendance: 1,300,000. For info: Scott Munz, State Fair of Oklahoma, PO Box 74943, Oklahoma City, OK 73147. Phone: (405) 948-6700.

VON STEUBEN, BARON FRIEDRICH: BIRTH ANNIVERSARY. Sept 17, 1730. Prussian-born general, born at Magdeburg, Prussia, who served in the American Revolution. He died at Remsen, NY, Nov 28, 1794.

BIRTHDAYS TODAY

Paul Goble, 66, author and illustrator (Caldecott for *The Girl Who Loved Wild Horses*), born Surrey, England, Sept 17, 1933.

Charles Ernest Grassley, 66, US Senator (R, Iowa), born New Hartford, IA, Sept 17, 1933.

Philip D. (Phil) Jackson, 54, former basketball coach, former player, born Deer Lodge, MT, Sept 17, 1945.

Gail Carson Levine, 52, author (*Ella Enchanted*), born New York, NY, Sept 17, 1947.

David H. Souter, 60, Associate Justice of the US Supreme Court, born Melrose, MA, Sept 17, 1939.

SEPTEMBER 18 — SATURDAY

Day 261 — 104 Remaining

"THE ADDAMS FAMILY" TV PREMIERE: 35th ANNIVERSARY. Sept 18, 1964. Charles Addams' quirky *New Yorker* cartoon creations were brought to life in this ABC sitcom about a family full of oddballs. John Astin played lawyer Gomez Addams, with Carolyn Jones as his morbid wife Morticia, Ken Weatherwax as son Pugsley, Lisa Loring as daughter Wednesday, Jackie Coogan as Uncle Fester, Ted Cassidy as both Lurch, the butler, and Thing, a disembodied hand, Blossom Rock as Grandmama and Felix Silla as Cousin Itt. *The Addams Family* movie was released in 1991, starring Angelica Huston as Morticia, Raul Julia as Gomez, Christopher Lloyd as Uncle Fester and Christina Ricci as Wednesday.

CHILE: INDEPENDENCE DAY. Sept 18. National holiday. Gained independence from Spain in 1810.

DIEFENBAKER, JOHN: BIRTH ANNIVERSARY. Sept 18, 1895. Canadian lawyer, statesman and Conservative prime minister (1957–63). Born at Normandy Township, Ontario, Canada, he died at Ottawa, Ontario, Aug 16, 1979. Diefenbaker was a member of the Canadian Parliament from 1940 until his death.

IRON HORSE OUTRACED BY HORSE: ANNIVERSARY. Sept 18, 1830. In a widely celebrated race, the first locomotive built in America, the Tom Thumb, lost to a horse. Mechanical difficulties plagued the steam engine over the nine-mile course between Riley's Tavern and Baltimore, MD, and a boiler leak prevented the locomotive from finishing the race. In the early days of trains, engines were nicknamed "Iron Horses."

LAURA INGALLS WILDER FESTIVAL. Sept 18–19. Pepin, WI. 8th annual. Experience life in the mid-1800s with demonstrations of blacksmithing, woodworking, ironworking, weaving, quilting and wool-spinning by individuals dressed in period costumes. Stories and songs cited in Little House books are also performed and there's a Laura Ingalls look-alike contest. Additional attractions include a traveling exhibit of Wilder's written materials, sanctioned horse-pull, Civil War encampment, children's games from the period, parade, crafts and antiques at Laura Ingalls Wilder Memorial Park. For info: Wisconsin Dept of Tourism, Laura Ingalls Festival, PO Box 7976, Madison, WI 53707. Phone: (715) 442-2461 or (715) 442-2147. E-mail: tourism@laughlin.com. Web: tourism.state.wi.us.

NATIONAL KIDSDAY®. Sept 18. A national holiday to recognize the value, dignity and inherent worth of children everywhere (also known as National Children's Day™). Supervised and licensed by KidsPeace®, The National Center for Kids Overcoming Crisis, a private, not-for-profit organization that has been providing hope and healing to kids in crisis since 1882. KidsPeace offers the country's widest array of children's critical care services available under a "single roof" and crisis education to families across the US. Annually, the third Saturday in September. For info: Paula Knouse, KidsPeace, 5300 KidsPeace Dr, Orefield, PA 18069-9101. Phone: (610) 799-8325. Web: www.kidspeace.org.

READ, GEORGE: BIRTH ANNIVERSARY. Sept 18, 1733. Lawyer and signer of the Declaration of Independence, born at Cecil County, MD. Died Sept 21, 1798, at New Castle, DE.

STORY, JOSEPH: BIRTH ANNIVERSARY. Sept 18, 1779. Associate justice of the US Supreme Court (1811–45) was born at Marblehead, MA. "It is astonishing," he wrote a few months before his death, "how easily men satisfy themselves that the Constitution is exactly what they wish it to be." Story died Sept 10, 1845, at Cambridge, MA, having served 33 years on the Supreme Court bench.

US AIR FORCE ESTABLISHED: ANNIVERSARY. Sept 18, 1947. Although its heritage dates back to 1907 when the Army first established military aviation, the US Air Force became a separate military service on this date.

US CAPITOL CORNERSTONE LAID: ANNIVERSARY. Sept 18, 1793. President George Washington laid the Capitol cornerstone at Washington, DC, in a Masonic ceremony. That event was the first and last recorded occasion at which the stone with its engraved silver plate was seen. In 1958, during the extension of the east front of the Capitol, an unsuccessful effort was made to find it.

VIRGINIA CHILDREN'S FESTIVAL. Sept 18. Town Point Park, Norfolk, VA. An all-day family program hosted by nationally famous children's entertainers, costumed characters and five stages of entertainment. Also, magic, giant puppets, creative dance and many other activities for a day of fantasy and fun. Est attendance: 45,000. For info: Norfolk Festevents, Ltd, 120 W Main St, Norfolk, VA 23510. Phone: (757) 441-2345. Fax: (757) 441-5198.

BIRTHDAYS TODAY

Robert F. Bennett, 66, US Senator (R, Utah), born Salt Lake City, UT, Sept 18, 1933.

SEPTEMBER 19 — SUNDAY

Day 262 — 103 Remaining

CARROLL, CHARLES: BIRTH ANNIVERSARY. Sept 19, 1737. American Revolutionary leader and signer of the Declaration of Independence, born at Annapolis, MD. The last surviving signer of the Declaration, he died Nov 14, 1832, at Baltimore, MD.

DEAF AWARENESS WEEK. Sept 19–25. Nationwide celebration to promote deaf culture, American Sign Language and deaf heritage. Activities include library displays, interpreted story hours, Open Houses in residential schools and mainstream programs, exhibit booths in shopping malls with "Five Minute Sign Language Lessons," material distribution. For info: Natl Assn of the Deaf, 814 Thayer Ave, Silver Spring, MD 20910-4500. Fax: (301) 587-1791. E-mail: nadhq@juno.com. Web: www.nad.org.

MEXICO CITY EARTHQUAKE: ANNIVERSARY. Sept 19–20, 1985. Nearly 10,000 persons perished in the earthquakes (8.1 and 7.5 respectively, on the Richter Scale) that devastated Mexico City. Damage to buildings was estimated at more than $1 billion, and 100,000 homes were destroyed or severely damaged.

NATIONAL DOG WEEK. Sept 19–25. To promote the relationship of dogs to mankind and emphasize the need for the proper care and treatment of dogs. Annually, the last full week in September. For info: Morris Raskin, Secy, Dogs on Stamps Study Unit (DOSSU), 202 A Newport Rd, Cranbury, NJ 08512. Phone: (609) 655-7411.

NATIONAL FARM ANIMALS AWARENESS WEEK. Sept 19–25. A week to promote awareness of farm animals and their natural behaviors. Each day of the week is dedicated to learning about a specific group of farm animals and to appreciating their many interesting and unique qualities. Annually, the third full week in September. For info: David Kuemmerle, Project Coord, The Humane Soc of the US, Farm Animal Section, 2100 L St NW, Washington, DC 20037. Phone: (202) 452-1100. E-mail: hsusfarm @ix.netcom.com.

★**NATIONAL FARM SAFETY AND HEALTH WEEK.** Sept 19–25. Presidential Proclamation issued since 1982 for the third week in September. Previously, from 1944, for one of the last two weeks in July.

POWELL, LEWIS F., JR: BIRTH ANNIVERSARY. Sept 19, 1907. Former associate justice of the Supreme Court of the US, nominated by President Nixon Oct 21, 1971. (Took office Jan 7, 1972.) Justice Powell was born at Suffolk, VA. In 1987, he announced his retirement from the Court. He died Aug 25, 1998, at Richmond, VA.

SAINT CHRISTOPHER (SAINT KITTS) AND NEVIS: INDEPENDENCE DAY. Sept 19. National holiday. Commemorates the independence of these Caribbean islands from Britain in 1983.

SAINT JANUARIUS (GENNARO): FEAST DAY. Sept 19. Fourth-century bishop of Benevento, martyred near Naples, Italy, whose relics in the Naples Cathedral are particularly famous because on his feast days the blood in a glass vial is said to liquefy in response to prayers of the faithful. This phenomenon is said to occur also on the first Saturday in May.

YOM KIPPUR BEGINS AT SUNDOWN. Sept 19. Jewish Day of Atonement. See "Yom Kippur" (Sept 20).

BIRTHDAYS TODAY

James Haskins, 58, author (*Bayard Rustin: Behind the Scenes of the Civil Rights Movement*), born Montgomery, AL, Sept 19, 1941.

SEPTEMBER 20 — MONDAY
Day 263 — 102 Remaining

"THE COSBY SHOW" PREMIERE: ANNIVERSARY. Sept 20, 1984. Comedian Bill Cosby starred as Dr. Cliff Huxtable in this sitcom about an upper-middle class black family living at Brooklyn. Phylicia Rashad played his wife Claire, an attorney. Their five children were played by Sabrina Le Beauf, Lisa Bonet, Malcolm-Jamal Warner, Tempest Bledsoe and Keshia Knight Pulliam. "A Different World" was a spin-off, with daughter Denise (Lisa Bonet) attending her parents' alma mater, Hillman College.

YOM KIPPUR OR DAY OF ATONEMENT. Sept 20. Holiest Jewish observance. A day for fasting, repentance and seeking forgiveness. Hebrew calendar date: Tishri 10, 5760.

BIRTHDAYS TODAY

Arthur Geisert, 58, author and illustrator (*Roman Numerals I to M*), born Dallas, TX, Sept 20, 1941.

SEPTEMBER 21 — TUESDAY
Day 264 — 101 Remaining

ARMENIA: NATIONAL DAY. Sept 21. Public holiday. Commemorates independence from the Soviet Union in 1991.

BELIZE: INDEPENDENCE DAY. Sept 21. National holiday. Commemorates independence of the former British Honduras from Britain in 1981.

BIOSPHERE DAY. Sept 21. A day to remind all humanity of the fragility of our only life-support, with the consequent need to safeguard it our foremost human imperative. The Biosphere is that layer of our planet's periphery (solid, liquid and gaseous) in which any form of life exists naturally. Participants are resolved to spread fundamental information worldwide concerning the Biosphere and how to preserve it. It is the Biosphere that is gravely threatened by human overpopulation and profligacy, not the inert and more solid Planet Earth. A major Biosphere fund and substantial Biosphere Prizes are planned to support Biosphere Day and spread its vital message. For info: Dr. Nicholas Polunin, Pres, The Foundation for Environmental Conservation, 7 Chemin Taverney 1218, Grand-Saconnex, Geneva, Switzerland. Phone: (41) (22) 798-2383. Fax: (41) (22) 798-2344.

HURRICANE HUGO HITS AMERICAN COAST: 10th ANNIVERSARY. Sept 21, 1989. After ravaging the Virgin Islands, Hurricane Hugo hit the American coast at Charleston, SC. In its wake, Hugo left destruction totaling at least eight billion dollars.

JOSEPH, CHIEF: 95th DEATH ANNIVERSARY. Sept 21, 1904. Nez Percé chief, whose Indian name was In-Mut-Too-Yah-Lat-Lat, was born about 1840 at Wallowa Valley, Oregon Territory, and died on the Colville Reservation at Washington State.

	S	M	T	W	T	F	S
September				1	2	3	4
1999	5	6	7	8	9	10	11
	12	13	14	15	16	17	18
	19	20	21	22	23	24	25
	26	27	28	29	30		

Faced with war or resettlement to a reservation, Chief Joseph led a dramatic attempt to escape to Canada. After three months and more than 1,000 miles, he and his people were surrounded 40 miles from Canada and sent to a reservation at Oklahoma. Though the few survivors were later allowed to relocate to another reservation at Washington, they never regained their ancestral lands.

MALTA: INDEPENDENCE DAY: 35th ANNIVERSARY. Sept 21. National Day. Commemorates independence from Britain in 1964.

NETHERLANDS: PRINSJESDAG. Sept 21. Official opening of parliament at The Hague. The queen of the Netherlands, by tradition, rides in a golden coach to the hall of knights for the annual opening of parliament. Annually, on the third Tuesday in September.

TAYLOR, MARGARET SMITH: BIRTH ANNIVERSARY. Sept 21, 1788. Wife of Zachary Taylor, 12th president of the US, born at Calvert County, MD. Died Aug 18, 1852.

UNITED NATIONS: INTERNATIONAL DAY OF PEACE/OPENING DAY OF GENERAL ASSEMBLY. Sept 21. The United Nations General Assembly, Nov 30, 1981, declared "that the third Tuesday of September, the opening day of the regular sessions of the General Assembly, shall be officially proclaimed and observed as International Day of Peace and shall be devoted to commemorating and strengthening the ideals of peace both within and among all nations and peoples." An International Year of Peace was proclaimed for 1986. A Peace Month and a University for Peace also have been proposed. For more information, go the UN's website for children at www.un.org/Pubs/CyberSchool Bus/

BIRTHDAYS TODAY

Stephen King, 52, author (*Pet Sematary, The Shining, Misery*), born Portland, ME, Sept 21, 1947.

Bill Murray, 49, comedian ("Saturday Night Live"), actor (*Ghostbusters, Groundhog Day*), born Evanston, IL, Sept 21, 1950.

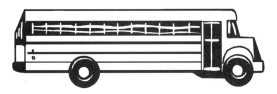

SEPTEMBER 22 — WEDNESDAY
Day 265 — 100 Remaining

ELEPHANT APPRECIATION DAY. Sept 22. Celebrate the earth's largest, most interesting and most noble endangered land animal. Free info kit from: Wayne Hepburn, Wild Heart Productions, PO Box 4710, Sarasota, FL 34230-4710. Phone: (941) 955-2950. Fax: (941) 955-5723. E-mail: mail@wildheart.com. Web: www.wildheart.com.

ICE CREAM CONE: BIRTHDAY. Sept 22, 1903. Italo Marchiony emigrated from Italy in the late 1800s and soon thereafter went into business at New York, NY, with a pushcart dispensing lemon ice. Success soon led to a small fleet of pushcarts, and the inventive Marchiony was inspired to develop a cone, first made of paper, later of pastry, to hold the tasty delicacy. On Sept 22, 1903, his application for a patent for his new mold was filed, and US Patent No 746971 was issued to him Dec 15, 1903.

MALI: INDEPENDENCE DAY. Sept 22. National holiday commemorating independence from France in 1960. Mali, in West Africa, was known as the French Sudan while a colony.

US POSTMASTER GENERAL ESTABLISHED: ANNIVERSARY. Sept 22, 1789. Congress established office of postmaster general, following the departments of state, war and treasury.

BIRTHDAYS TODAY

Bonnie Hunt, 35, actress (*Beethoven, Beethoven's 2*), born Chicago, IL, Sept 22, 1964.

Ronaldo, 23, Brazilian soccer star, born Ronaldo Luiz Nazario de Lima, Rio de Janeiro, Brazil, Sept 22, 1976.

SEPTEMBER 23 — THURSDAY
Day 266 — 99 Remaining

AUTUMN. Sept 23–Dec 22. In the Northern Hemisphere, autumn begins today with the autumnal equinox, at 7:31 AM, EDT. Note that in the Southern Hemisphere today is the beginning of spring. Everywhere on Earth (except near the poles) the sun rises due east and sets due west and daylight length is nearly identical—about 12 hours, 8 minutes.

"THE JETSONS" TV PREMIERE: ANNIVERSARY. Sept 23, 1962. "Meet George Jetson. His boy Elroy. Daughter Judy. Jane, his wife. . . . " These words introduced us to the Jetsons, a cartoon family living in the twenty-first century, the Flintstones of the Space Age. We followed the exploits of George and his family, as well as his unstable work relationship with his greedy, ruthless boss Cosmo Spacely. Voices were provided by George O'Hanlon as George, Penny Singleton as Jane, Janet Waldo as Judy, Daws Butler as Elroy, Don Messick as Astro, the family dog and Mel Blanc as Spacely. New episodes were created in 1985 which introduced a new pet, Orbity.

LIBRA, THE BALANCE. Sept 23–Oct 22. In the astronomical/astrological zodiac that divides the sun's apparent orbit into 12 segments, the period Sept 23–Oct 22 is identified traditionally as the sun sign of Libra, the Balance. The ruling planet is Venus.

McGUFFEY, WILLIAM HOLMES: BIRTH ANNIVERSARY. Sept 23, 1800. American educator and author of the famous *McGuffey Readers*, born at Washington County, PA. Probably no other textbooks have had a greater influence on American life. More than 120 million copies were sold. McGuffey died at Charlottesville, VA, May 4, 1873.

PLANET NEPTUNE DISCOVERY: ANNIVERSARY. Sept 23, 1846. Neptune is 2,796,700,000 miles from the sun (about 30 times as far from the sun as Earth). Eighth planet from the sun, Neptune takes 164.8 years to revolve around the sun. Diameter is about 31,000 miles compared to Earth at 7,927 miles. Discovered on this date by German astronomer Johann Galle.

SAUDI ARABIA: ANNIVERSARY KINGDOM UNIFICATION. Sept 23. National holiday. Commemorates unification in 1932.

STATE FAIR OF VIRGINIA ON STRAWBERRY HILL. Sept 23–Oct 3. Richmond, VA. The pride of Virginia's industry of agriculture can be seen in more than 3,000 exhibitions, competitions and shows. Virginia's greatest annual educational and entertainment event. Est attendance: 600,000. For info: Kieth T. Hessey, Genl Mgr, 600 E Laburnum Ave, Richmond, VA 23222. Phone: (804) 228-3200. Fax: (804) 228-3252. Web: www.statefair.com.

BIRTHDAYS TODAY

Bruce Brooks, 49, author (*What Hearts, The Moves Make the Man*), born Washington, DC, Sept 23, 1950.

Eric Scott Montross, 28, basketball player, born Indianapolis, IN, Sept 23, 1971.

SEPTEMBER 24 — FRIDAY
Day 267 — 98 Remaining

CHINA, PEOPLE'S REPUBLIC OF: MID-AUTUMN FESTIVAL. Sept 24. To worship the moon god. According to folk legend this day is also the birthday of the earth god T'u-ti Kung. The festival indicates the year's hard work in the fields will soon end with the harvest. People express gratitude to heaven as represented by the moon and earth as symbolized by the earth god for all good things from the preceding year. 15th day of eighth month of Chinese lunar calendar.

GUINEA-BISSAU: INDEPENDENCE DAY: 25th ANNIVERSARY. Sept 24. National holiday. Commemorates independence from Portugal in 1974.

HENSON, JIM: BIRTH ANNIVERSARY. Sept 24, 1936. Puppeteer, born at Greenville, MS. Jim Henson created a unique brand of puppetry known as the Muppets. Kermit the Frog, Big Bird, Rowlf, Bert and Ernie, Gonzo, Animal, Miss Piggy and Oscar the Grouch are a few of the puppets that captured the hearts of children and adults alike in television and film productions including "Sesame Street," "The Jimmy Dean Show," "The Muppet Show," *The Muppet Movie*, *The Muppets Take Manhattan*, *The Great Muppet Caper* and *The Dark Crystal*. Henson began his career in 1954 as producer of the TV show "Sam and Friends" at Washington, DC. He introduced the Muppets in 1956. His creativity was rewarded with 18 Emmy Awards, seven Grammy Awards, four Peabody Awards and five ACE Awards from the National Cable Television Association. Henson died unexpectedly May 16, 1990, at New York, NY.

KOREA: CHUSOK. Sept 24. Gala celebration by Koreans everywhere. Autumn harvest thanksgiving moon festival. Observed on 15th day of eighth lunar month (eighth full moon of lunar calendar) each year. Koreans pay homage to ancestors and express gratitude to guarding spirits for another year of rich crops. A time to visit tombs, leave food and prepare for coming winter season. Traditional food is "moon cake," made on eve of Chusok, with rice, chestnuts and jujube fruits. Games, dancing and gift exchanges. Observed since Silla Dynasty (beginning of First Millennium).

MARSHALL, JOHN: BIRTH ANNIVERSARY. Sept 24, 1755. Fourth Chief Justice of Supreme Court, born at Germantown, VA. Served in House of Representatives and as secretary of state under John Adams. Appointed by President Adams to the position of chief justice in January 1801, he became known as "The Great Chief Justice." Marshall's court was largely responsible for defining the role of the Supreme Court and basic organizing principles of government in the early years after adoption of the Constitution in such cases as *Marbury v Madison*, *McCulloch v Maryland*, *Cohens v Virginia* and *Gibbons v Ogden*. He died at Philadelphia, PA, July 6, 1835.

MOON FESTIVAL or MID-AUTUMN FESTIVAL. Sept 24. This festival, observed on the 15th day of the eighth moon of the lunar calendar year, is called by different names in different places, but is widely recognized throughout the Far East, including People's Republic of China, Taiwan, Korea, Singapore and Hong Kong. An important harvest festival at the time the moon is brightest, it is also a time for homage to ancestors. Special harvest foods are eaten, especially "moon cakes."

RAWLS, WILSON: BIRTH ANNIVERSARY. Sept 24, 1913. Author (*Where the Red Fern Grows*), born at Scraper, OK. Died Dec 16, 1984.

SOUTH AFRICA: HERITAGE DAY. Sept 24. A celebration of South African nationhood, commemorating the multicultural heritage of this rainbow nation.

STATE FAIR OF TEXAS. Sept 24–Oct 17. Fair Park, Dallas, TX. Features a Broadway musical, college football games, new car show, concerts, livestock shows and traditional events and entertainment including exhibits, creative arts and parades. Est attendance: 3,200,000. For info: Nancy Wiley, State Fair of Texas, PO Box 150009, Dallas, TX 75315. Phone: (214) 421-8716. Fax: (214) 421-8710. E-mail: pr@greatstatefair.com. Web: www.texfair.com/

SUKKOT BEGINS AT SUNDOWN. Sept 24. Jewish Feast of Tabernacles. See "Sukkot" (Sept 25).

BIRTHDAYS TODAY

Kevin Sorbo, 41, actor ("Hercules"), born Mound, MN, Sept 24, 1958.

SEPTEMBER 25 — SATURDAY
Day 268 — 97 Remaining

BANNED BOOKS WEEK—CELEBRATING THE FREEDOM TO READ. Sept 25–Oct 2. Brings to the attention of the general public the importance of the freedom to read and the harm censorship causes to our society. Sponsors: American Library Association, American Booksellers Association, American Booksellers Association for Free Expression, American Society of Journalists and Authors, Association of American Publishers, National Association of College Stores. For lists of frequently challenged books, visit the following websites: www.ala.org/bbooks/challenge.html and www.cs.cmu.edu/People/spok/most-banned.html. For info: Judith F. Krug, American Library Assn, Office for Intellectual Freedom, 50 E Huron St, Chicago, IL 60611. Phone: (312) 280-4223. Fax: (312) 280-4227. E-mail: oif@ala.org. Web: www.ala.org/bbooks.

FIRST AMERICAN NEWSPAPER PUBLISHED: ANNIVERSARY. Sept 25, 1690. The first (and only) edition of *Publick Occurrences Both Foreign and Domestick* was published by Benjamin Harris, at the London-Coffee-House, Boston, MA. Authorities considered this first newspaper published in the US offensive and ordered immediate suppression.

GREENWICH MEAN TIME BEGINS: ANNIVERSARY. Sept 25, 1676. On this day two very accurate clocks were set in motion at the Royal Observatory at Greenwich, England. Greenwich Mean Time (now called Universal Time) became standard for England; in 1884 it became standard for the world.

September 1999	S	M	T	W	T	F	S
				1	2	3	4
	5	6	7	8	9	10	11
	12	13	14	15	16	17	18
	19	20	21	22	23	24	25
	26	27	28	29	30		

HARVEST MOON. Sept 25. So called because the full moon nearest the autumnal equinox extends the hours of light into the evening and helps the harvester with his long day's work. Moon enters Full Moon phase at 6:51 AM, EDT.

KIWANIS KIDS' DAY. Sept 25. To honor and assist youth—our greatest resource. Annually, the fourth Saturday in September. For info: Kiwanis Intl, Program Dvmt Dept, 3636 Woodview Trace, Indianapolis, IN 46268. E-mail: kiwanismail@kiwanis.org. Web: www.kiwanis.org.

MAJOR LEAGUE BASEBALL'S FIRST DOUBLE HEADER: ANNIVERSARY. Sept 25, 1882. The first major league baseball double header was played between the Providence, RI and Worcester, MA teams.

MOON PHASE: FULL MOON. Sept 25. Moon enters Full Moon phase at 6:51 AM, EDT.

★**NATIONAL HUNTING AND FISHING DAY.** Sept 25. Presidential Proclamation 4682, of Sept 11, 1979, covers all succeeding years. Annually, the fourth Saturday of September.

PACIFIC OCEAN DISCOVERED: ANNIVERSARY. Sept 25, 1513. Vasco Núñez de Balboa, a Spanish conquistador, stood high atop a peak in the Darien, in present-day Panama, becoming the first European to look upon the Pacific Ocean, claiming it as the South Sea in the name of the King of Spain.

"THE PARTRIDGE FAMILY" PREMIERE: ANNIVERSARY. Sept 25, 1970. A fatherless family of five kids form a rock band with their mother Shirley (played by Shirley Jones), and go on the road. Son Keith was played by David Cassidy (who became a real-life rock star), daughter Laurie was played by Susan Dey, Danny Bonaduce played son Danny, youngest son Chris was played by Jeremy Gelbwaks and Brian Foster, and youngest daughter Tracy by Suzanne Crough. The TV family recorded several albums and songs such as "I Think I Love You" went on to be hits.

SEQUOIA NATIONAL PARK ESTABLISHED: ANNIVERSARY. Sept 25, 1890. Area in central California established as a national park. For further park info: Sequoia Natl Park, Three Rivers, CA 93271. Web: www.nps.gov/sequ.

SUKKOT, SUCCOTH or FEAST OF TABERNACLES, FIRST DAY. Sept 25. Hebrew calendar date: Tishri 15, 5760, begins nine-day festival in commemoration of Jewish people's 40 years of wandering in the desert and thanksgiving for the fall harvest. This high holiday season closes with Shemini Atzeret (see entry on Oct 2) and Simchat Torah (see entry on Oct 3).

BIRTHDAYS TODAY

Jim Murphy, 52, author of nonfiction (*The Great Fire*), born Newark, NJ, Sept 25, 1947.

Scottie Pippen, 34, basketball player, born Hamburg, AR, Sept 25, 1965.

Christopher Reeve, 47, actor (*Superman*), born New York, NY, Sept 25, 1952.

Will Smith, 31, actor ("The Fresh Prince of Bel Air"), born Philadelphia, PA, Sept 25, 1968.

Barbara Walters, 68, journalist, interviewer, TV host ("20/20"), born Boston, MA, Sept 25, 1931.

SEPTEMBER 26 — SUNDAY

Day 269 — 96 Remaining

APPLESEED, JOHNNY: 225th BIRTH ANNIVERSARY. Sept 26, 1774. John Chapman, better known as Johnny Appleseed, believed to have been born at Leominster, MA, Sept 26, 1774. Died at Allen County, IN, Mar 11, 1845. Planter of orchards and friend of wild animals, he was regarded as a great medicine man by the Indians.

"THE BRADY BUNCH" TV PREMIERE: ANNIVERSARY. Sept 26, 1969. This sitcom which spawned a whole industry starred Robert Reed as widower Mike Brady, who has three sons and is married to Carol (played by Florence Henderson), who has three daughters. Nutty housekeeper Alice was played by Ann B. Davis. Sons Peter (Christopher Knight), Greg (Barry Williams) and Bobby (Mike Lookinland) and daughters Marcia (Maureen McCormick), Jan (Eve Plumb) and Cindy (Susan Olsen) experienced the typical crises of youth. The show steered clear of social issues, portraying childhood as a time of innocence. This is probably why it has remained popular in reruns in the after-school time slot. "The Brady Kids" (1972–74) was a Sunday morning cartoon show. On "The Brady Bunch Hour" (1976–77) the family hosted a variety show. "The Brady Brides" (1981) was a sitcom about the two older girls adjusting to marriage. *A Very Brady Christmas* (1988) was CBS's highest-rated special for the season. *The Brady Bunch Movie* (1995) appealed to fans who had watched the show 25 years before.

FIRST TELEVISED PRESIDENTIAL DEBATE: ANNIVERSARY. Sept 26, 1960. The debate between presidential candidates John F. Kennedy and Richard Nixon was televised from a Chicago TV studio.

GERSHWIN, GEORGE: BIRTH ANNIVERSARY. Sept 26, 1898. American composer remembered for his many enduring songs and melodies, including: "The Man I Love," "Strike Up the Band," "Funny Face," "I Got Rhythm" and the opera *Porgy and Bess*. Many of his works were in collaboration with his brother, Ira. Born at Brooklyn, NY, he died of a brain tumor at Beverly Hills, CA, July 11, 1937. See also: "Gershwin, Ira: Birth Anniversary" (Dec 6). See Curriculum Connection.

★**GOLD STAR MOTHER'S DAY.** Sept 26. Presidential Proclamation always for last Sunday of each September since 1936. Proclamation 2424 of Sept 14, 1940, covers all succeeding years.

POPE PAUL VI: BIRTH ANNIVERSARY. Sept 26, 1897. Giovanni Battista Montini, 262nd pope of the Roman Catholic Church, born at Concesio, Italy. Elected pope June 21, 1963. Died at Castel Gandolfo, near Rome, Italy, Aug 6, 1978.

SHAMU'S BIRTHDAY. Sept 26. Shamu was born at Sea World at Orlando, FL, Sept 26, 1985, and is the first killer whale born in captivity to survive. Shamu is now living at Sea World's Texas park.

BIRTHDAYS TODAY

Christine T. Whitman, 53, Governor of New Jersey (R), born New York, NY, Sept 26, 1946.

SEPTEMBER 26
GEORGE GERSHWIN'S BIRTHDAY

George Gershwin is one of America's most famous composers. He wrote many songs and concert pieces that are still very popular today. The son of Russian immigrant parents, Gershwin began writing popular songs at age 15—the age when many of today's teens who play in local bands are first trying out their composing skills. His brother, Ira Gershwin, wrote the lyrics for many of George's show tunes. Biographies of Gershwin for children include *Introducing Gershwin*, by Roland Vernon (Silver Burdett, 0-382-39161-6, $22 Gr. 3–6) and *George Gershwin*, by Mike Venezia (Children's Press, 0-516-04536-9, $20 Gr. 3–6).

There are many ways Gershwin's music can be incorporated into the curriculum. From a language arts perspective, "I Got Rhythm" is a wonderful lead-in to poetry units, where students will be exploring rhythmic patterns. Gershwin's last symphonic piece was a piano and orchestral version of "I Got Rhythm" played with variations of the main musical theme. Comparisons can be drawn between how musicians play with notes and poets play with language. Rap is all about rhythm, and is a fun way for students to make a contemporary connection.

"Rhapsody in Blue" and "An American in Paris" are exciting musical pieces and introductions to quintessential American jazz and rhythmic compositions. Students can be encouraged to look for the movie *An American in Paris*, a musical with a plot constructed around Gershwin's piece. It's available on videocassette—free in public libraries. Also, don't miss *Porgy and Bess*, Gershwin's black "folk opera," and probably the best known of all American operas.

Recordings of Gershwin's music are widely available. If you don't have any in your personal music archives, public libraries offer cassettes, CDs and LPs.

Celebrating Gershwin's birthday rounds out September as National Piano Month. See entry under National Piano Month for more information.

SEPTEMBER 27 — MONDAY
Day 270 — 95 Remaining

ADAMS, SAMUEL: BIRTH ANNIVERSARY. Sept 27, 1722. Revolutionary leader and Massachusetts state politician Samuel Adams, cousin to President John Adams, was born at Boston. He died there Oct 2, 1803. As a delegate to the First and Second Continental Congresses Adams urged a vigorous stand against England. He signed the Declaration of Independence and the Articles of Confederation and supported the war for independence. Adams served as lieutenant governor of Massachusetts under John Hancock from 1789 to 1793 and then as governor until 1797.

ANCESTOR APPRECIATION DAY. Sept 27. A day to learn about and appreciate one's forebears. For info: W.D. Chase, A.A.D. Assn, PO Box 3, Montague, MI 49437-0003.

SAINT VINCENT DE PAUL: FEAST DAY. Sept 27. French priest, patron of charitable organizations, and founder of the Vincentian Order and co-founder of the Sisters of Charity. Canonized 1737 (lived 1581?–1660).

September *1999*	S	M	T	W	T	F	S
				1	2	3	4
	5	6	7	8	9	10	11
	12	13	14	15	16	17	18
	19	20	21	22	23	24	25
	26	27	28	29	30		

Martin Handford, 43, author and illustrator (*Where's Waldo?*), born London, England, Sept 27, 1956.

Stephen Douglas (Steve) Kerr, 34, basketball player, born Beirut, Lebanon, Sept 27, 1965.

Mike Schmidt, 50, Baseball Hall of Fame third baseman, born Dayton, OH, Sept 27, 1949.

Gerhard Schröder, 49, Chancellor of Germany, born Mossenberg, Germany, Sept 27, 1950.

SEPTEMBER 28 — TUESDAY
Day 271 — 94 Remaining

CABRILLO DAY: ANNIVERSARY OF DISCOVERY OF CALIFORNIA. Sept 28, 1542. California. Commemorates discovery of California by Portuguese navigator Juan Rodriguez Cabrillo who reached San Diego Bay. Cabrillo died at San Miguel Island, CA, Jan 3, 1543. His birth date is unknown. The Cabrillo National Monument marks his landfall and Cabrillo Day is still observed in California (in some areas on the Saturday nearest Sept 28).

TAIWAN: CONFUCIUS'S BIRTHDAY AND TEACHERS' DAY. Sept 28. National holiday, designated as Teachers' Day. Confucius is the Latinized name of Kung-futzu, born at Shantung province on the 27th day of the tenth moon (lunar calendar) in the 22nd year of Kuke Hsiang of Lu (551 BC). He died at age 72, having spent some 40 years as a teacher. Teachers' Day is observed annually on Sept 28.

WIGGIN, KATE DOUGLAS: BIRTH ANNIVERSARY. Sept 28, 1856. Kate Wiggin was born Kate Douglas Smith at Philadelphia, PA. She helped organize the first free kindergarten on the West Coast in 1878 at San Francisco and in 1880 she and her sister established the California Kindergarten Training School. After moving back to the East Coast she devoted herself to writing, producing a number of children's books including *The Birds' Christmas Carol*, *Polly Oliver's Problem* and *Rebecca of Sunnybrook Farm*. She died at Harrow, England, Aug 24, 1923.

WILLARD, FRANCES ELIZABETH CAROLINE: BIRTH ANNIVERSARY. Sept 28, 1839. American educator and reformer, president of the Women's Christian Temperance Union, 1879–98 and women's suffrage leader, born at Churchville, NY. Died at New York, NY, Feb 18, 1898.

Gwyneth Paltrow, 26, actress (*Hook, Emma*), born Los Angeles, CA, Sept 28, 1973.

SEPTEMBER 29 — WEDNESDAY
Day 272 — 93 Remaining

ENGLAND: SCOTLAND YARD: FIRST APPEARANCE ANNIVERSARY. Sept 29, 1829. The first public appearance of Greater London's Metropolitan Police occurred amid jeering and abuse from disapproving political opponents. Public sentiment turned to confidence and respect in the ensuing years. The Metropolitan Police had been established by an act of Parliament in June 1829, at the request of Home Secretary Sir Robert Peel, after whom the London police officers became more affectionately known as "bobbies." Scotland Yard, the site of their first headquarters near Charing Cross, soon became the official name of the force.

FERMI, ENRICO: BIRTH ANNIVERSARY. Sept 29, 1901. Nuclear physicist, born at Rome, Italy. Played a prominent role in the splitting of the atom and the construction of the first American nuclear reactor. Died at Chicago, IL, Nov 16, 1954.

MICHAELMAS. Sept 29. The feast of St. Michael and All Angels in the Greek and Roman Catholic Churches.

SPACE MILESTONE: *DISCOVERY* (US). Sept 29, 1988. Space Shuttle *Discovery*, after numerous reschedulings, launched from Kennedy Space Center, FL, with a five-member crew on board, and landed Oct 3 at Edwards Air Force Base, CA. It marked the first American manned flight since the Challenger tragedy in 1986. See also: "Challenger, Space Shuttle Explosion: Anniversary" (Jan 28).

BIRTHDAYS TODAY

Stan Berenstain, 76, author and illustrator, with his wife Jan (the Berenstain Bears series), born Philadelphia, PA, Sept 29, 1923.

Bryant Gumbel, 51, TV host ("Today," "The Public Eye"), sportscaster, born New Orleans, LA, Sept 29, 1948.

Lech Walesa, 56, Poland labor leader, Solidarity founder, born Popowo, Poland, Sept 29, 1943.

SEPTEMBER 30 — THURSDAY

Day 273 — 92 Remaining

BABE SETS HOME RUN RECORD: ANNIVERSARY. Sept 30, 1927. George Herman "Babe" Ruth hit his 60th home run of the season off Tom Zachary, of the Washington Senators. Ruth's record for the most homers in a single season stood for 34 years—until Roger Maris hit 61 in 1961. Maris's record was broken in 1998, first by Mark McGwire and then by Sammy Sosa.

BOTSWANA: INDEPENDENCE DAY. Sept 30. National holiday. The former Bechuanaland Protectorate (British Colony) became the independent Republic of Botswana in 1966.

FEAST OF SAINT JEROME. Sept 30. Patron saint of scholars and librarians.

"THE FLINTSTONES" TV PREMIERE: ANNIVERSARY. Sept 30, 1960. This Hanna Barbera cartoon comedy was set in prehistoric times. Characters included two Stone Age families, Fred and Wilma Flintstone and their neighbors Barney and Betty Rubble. In 1994 *The Flintstones* film was released, starring John Goodman, Rick Moranis, Elizabeth Perkins and Rosie O'Donnell.

MEREDITH ENROLLS AT OLE MISS: ANNIVERSARY. Sept 30, 1962. Rioting broke out when James Meredith became the first black to enroll in the all-white University of Mississippi. President Kennedy sent US troops to the area to force compliance with the law. Three people died in the fighting and 50 were injured. On June 6, 1966, Meredith was shot while participating in a civil rights march at Mississippi. On June 25 Meredith, barely recovered, rejoined the marchers near Jackson, MS.

BIRTHDAYS TODAY

Mike Damus, 20, actor ("Teen Angel"), born New York, NY, Sept 30, 1979.

Carol Fenner, 70, author (*Yolonda's Genius*), born New York, NY, Sept 30, 1929.

Martina Hingis, 19, tennis player, born Kosice, Slovakia, Sept 30, 1980.

Blanche Lambert Lincoln, 39, US Senator (D, Arkansas), born Helena, MT, Sept 30, 1960.

Dominique Moceanu, 18, gymnast, born Hollywood, CA, Sept 30, 1981.

October 1999

OCTOBER 1 — FRIDAY

Day 274 — 91 Remaining

ADOPT-A-SHELTER-ANIMAL MONTH. Oct 1–31. To promote the adoption of animals from local shelters, the ASPCA sponsors this important observance. For info: ASPCA Public Information Dept, 424 E 92nd St, New York, NY 10128. Phone: (212) 876-7700. E-mail: valeriea@aspca.org or press@aspca.org. Web: www.aspca .org.

BOOK IT! READING INCENTIVE PROGRAM. Oct 1, 1999–Feb 29, 2000. This is a five-month program for students in grades K-8 sponsored by Pizza Hut. Teachers set monthly reading goals for students. When a monthly reading goal is met, the child receives a certificate for a free pizza. If the whole class meets its goal, a pizza party is provided for the class. For info: Book It!, PO Box 2999, Wichita, KS 67201. Phone: (800) 4-BOOK IT. Fax: (316) 687-8937. Web: www.bookitprogram.com.

CHILD HEALTH MONTH. Oct 1–31. For info: American Academy of Pediatrics, 141 Northwest Point Blvd, Elk Grove Village, IL 60007. Phone: (847) 228-5005.

CHINA, PEOPLE'S REPUBLIC OF: NATIONAL DAY: 50th ANNIVERSARY. Oct 1. Commemorates the founding of the People's Republic of China in 1949.

COMPUTER LEARNING MONTH. Oct 1–31. A month-long focus of events and activities for learning new uses of computers and software, sharing ideas and helping others gain the benefits of computers and software. Numerous national contests are held to recognize students, educators and parents for their innovative ideas; computers and software are awarded to winning entries. Annually, the month of October. For info: Computer Learning Foundation, Dept CHS, PO Box 60007, Palo Alto, CA 94306-0007. Phone: (650) 327-3347. Fax: (650) 327-3349. E-mail: clf@ computerlearning.org. Web: www.computerlearning.org.

CYPRUS: INDEPENDENCE DAY. Oct 1. National holiday. Commemorates independence from Britain in 1960.

DISNEYWORLD OPENED: ANNIVERSARY. Oct 1, 1971. Disney's second theme park opened at Orlando, FL. See also "Disneyland Opened: Anniversary" (July 17).

	S	M	T	W	T	F	S
						1	2
October	3	4	5	6	7	8	9
1999	10	11	12	13	14	15	16
	17	18	19	20	21	22	23
	24	25	26	27	28	29	30
	31						

DIVERSITY AWARENESS MONTH. Oct 1–31. Celebrating, promoting and appreciating the diversity of our society. Also, a month to foster and further our understanding of the inherent value of all races, genders, nationalities, age groups, religions, sexual orientations, classes and disabilities. Annually, in October. See Curriculum Connection. For info: Carole Copeland Thomas, C. Thomas & Assoc, 400 W Cummings Park, Ste 1725-154, Woburn, MA 01801. Phone: (800) 801-6599. Fax: (617) 361-1355.

DOMESTIC VIOLENCE AWARENESS MONTH. Oct 1–31. Commemorated since 1987, this month attempts to raise awareness of efforts to end violence against women and their children. The Domestic Violence Awareness Month Project is a collaborative effort of the National Resource Center on Domestic Violence, Family Violence Prevention Fund, National Coalition Against Domestic Violence, National Domestic Violence Hotline and the National Network to End Domestic Violence. For info: Natl Resource Center on Domestic Violence, 6400 Flank Dr, Ste 1300, Harrisburg, PA 17112-2778. Phone: (800) 537-2238.

FAMILY HEALTH MONTH. Oct 1–31. For info: American Academy of Family Physicians, 8880 Ward Pkwy, Kansas City, MO 64114-2797. Phone: (800) 274-2237 or (816) 333-9700.

FAMILY HISTORY MONTH. Oct 1–31. To celebrate and publicize family history: the challenge of the research, the fascination of gathering family stories, customs and traditions, the fun of involving family members, its importance as an academic discipline and the value of passing it on to our children. Annually, the month of October. For info: Nancy O. Heydt, Monmouth County Genealogy Soc, PO Box 5, Lincroft, NJ 07738-0005. E-mail: jheydt@monmouth.com.

FIREPUP'S BIRTHDAY. Oct 1. Firepup spends his time teaching fire safety awareness to children in a fun-filled and nonthreatening manner. For info: Natl Fire Safety Council, Inc, PO Box 378, Michigan Center, MI 49254-0378. Phone: (517) 764-2811.

HARRISON, CAROLINE LAVINIA SCOTT: BIRTH ANNIVERSARY. Oct 1, 1832. First wife of Benjamin Harrison, 23rd president of the US, born at Oxford, OH. Died at Washington, DC, Oct 25, 1892. She was the second first lady to die in the White House.

MARIS HITS 61st HOME RUN: ANNIVERSARY. Oct 1, 1961. Roger Maris of the New York Yankees hit his 61st home run, breaking Babe Ruth's record for the most home runs in a season. Maris hit his homer against pitcher Tracy Stallard of the Boston Red Sox as the Yankees won, 1–0. Controversy over the record arose because the American League had adopted a 162-game schedule in 1961, and Maris played in 161 games. In 1927, when Ruth set his record, the schedule called for 154 games, and Ruth played in 151. On Sept 8, 1998, Mark McGwire of the St. Louis Cardinals hit his 62nd home run, breaking Maris's record, and a few days later, Sept 13, 1998, Sammy Sosa of the Chicago Cubs also hit his 62nd.

MONTH OF THE YOUNG ADOLESCENT. Oct 1–31. Youth between the ages of 10–15 undergo more extensive physical, mental, social and emotional changes than at any other time of life, with the exception of infancy. Initiated by the National Middle School Association and endorsed by 29 other national organizations focusing on youth, this month is designed to bring attention to the importance of this age in a person's development. For info: Natl Middle School Assn, 2600 Corporate Exchange Dr, Ste 370, Columbus, OH 43231. Phone: (800) 528-NMSA. Web: www.nmsa.org.

MONTH OF THE DINOSAUR. Oct 1–31. Promoting scientific awareness and educating everyone about our environment both present and past. Special on-line forums and activities as well as educational materials available to educators. For info: Ellen Sue Blakey, Big Horn Basin Foundation, PO Box 71, Thermopolis, WY 82443.

NATIONAL CAMPAIGN FOR HEALTHIER BABIES MONTH. Oct 1–31. For info: March of Dimes Birth Defects Foundation, 1275 Mamaroneck Ave, White Plains, NY 10605. Phone: (914) 997-4600.

NATIONAL CARAMEL MONTH. Oct 1–31. A month-long celebration of one of America's favorite treats, the caramel. First created in "sweet home" Chicago in 1875, Americans now consume more than 10 million pounds of the chewy, gooey sweets each year—as snacks as well as ingredients in favorite baked goods including brownies, bars, cookies, pies and cakes. Sponsored by Favorite Brands International, the makers of Farley's Original Chewy Caramels. From traditional caramel apples to haunting party recipes for Halloween gatherings, Caramel Month is a great excuse to go caramel crazy. For info send SASE: Favorite Brands Intl, Dept C, 25 Tri State International, Ste 400, Lincolnshire, IL 60069.

NATIONAL CRIME PREVENTION MONTH. Oct 1–31. During Crime Prevention Month, individuals can commit to working on at least one of three levels—family, neighborhood or community—to drive violence and drugs from our world. It is also a time to honor individuals who have accepted personal responsibility for their neighborhoods and groups who work for the community's common good. Annually, every October. For info: Natl Crime Prevention Council, 1700 K St, Second Floor, Washington, DC, 2006-1356. Phone: (202) 466-6272. Fax: (202) 296-1356. Web: www.weprevent.org or www.ncpc.org.

NATIONAL DENTAL HYGIENE MONTH. Oct 1–31. To increase public awareness of the importance of preventive oral health care and the dental hygienist's role as the preventive professional. Annually, during the month of October. For info: Public Relations, American Dental Hygienists' Assn, 444 N Michigan Ave, Ste 3400, Chicago, IL 60611. Phone: (312) 440-8900. Fax: (312) 440-6780. Web: www.adha.org.

★**NATIONAL DISABILITY EMPLOYMENT AWARENESS MONTH.** Oct 1–31. Presidential Proclamation issued for the month of October (PL100–630, Title III, Sec 301a of Nov 7, 1988). Previously issued as "National Employ the Handicapped Week" for a week beginning during the first week in October since 1945.

★**NATIONAL DOMESTIC VIOLENCE AWARENESS MONTH.** Oct 1–31.

NATIONAL FAMILY SEXUALITY EDUCATION MONTH. Oct 1–31. A national coalition effort to support parents as the first and primary sexuality educators of their children by providing information for parents and young people. For info: Planned Parenthood Federation of America, Education Dept, 810 Seventh Ave, New York, NY 10019. Phone: (800) 829-7732. Fax: (212) 247-6269. E-mail: education@ppfa.org. Web: www.planned parenthood.org.

NATIONAL ORTHODONTIC HEALTH MONTH. Oct 1–31. A beautiful healthy smile is only the most obvious benefit of orthodontic treatment. National Orthodontic Health Month spotlights the important role of orthodontic care in overall physical health and emotional well-being. The observance is sponsored by the American Association of Orthodontists (AAO), which supports research and education leading to quality patient care and promotes increased public awareness of the need for and benefits of orthodontic treatment. For info: Bill Beggs, Media Relations Mgr, The Hughes Group, 130 S Bemiston, St. Louis, MO 63105.

NATIONAL PASTA MONTH. Oct 1–31. To promote the nutritional value of pasta while educating the public about healthy, easy ways to prepare it. Annually, the month of October. For info: Emily A. Holt, Natl Pasta Assn, 2101 Wilson Blvd, Ste 920, Arlington, VA 22201. Phone: (703) 841-0818. Web: www.ilovepasta.org.

NATIONAL POPCORN POPPIN' MONTH. Oct 1–31. To celebrate the wholesome, economical, natural food value of popcorn, America's native snack. For info: The Popcorn Institute, 401 N Michigan Ave, Chicago, IL 60611-4267. Phone: (312) 644-6610. Fax: (312) 245-1083. Web: www.popcorn.org.

NATIONAL ROLLER SKATING MONTH. Oct 1–31. A month-long celebration recognizing the health benefits and recreational enjoyment of this long-loved pastime. Also includes in-line skating and an emphasis on Safe Skating. For info: Roller Skating Assn, 6905 Corporate Dr, Indianapolis, IN 46278. Phone: (317) 347-2626. Fax: (317) 347-2636. E-mail: RSA@oninternet.com. Web: www.rollerskating.com.

NATIONAL STAMP COLLECTING MONTH. Oct 1–31. Sponsored by the US Postal Service, which also sponsors STAMPERS, a program to introduce a new generation to the exciting world of stamp collecting. By calling the toll-free number 1-888-STAMP-FUN, children can receive free mailings which include magazines, posters and other educational items to help them start their own stamp collection. For info: Stamp Services, US Postal Service, 475 L'Enfant Plaza SW, Rm 4474-EB, Washington, DC 20260.

NATIONAL STORYTELLING FESTIVAL. Oct 1–3. Jonesborough, TN. Tennessee's oldest town plays host to the most dynamic storytelling event dedicated to the oral tradition. This three-day celebration showcases storytellers, stories and traditions from across America and around the world. Annually, the first full weekend in October. Est attendance: 10,000. For info: Natl Storytelling Assn (NSA), 116 W Main, Jonesborough, TN 37659. Phone: (800) 525-4514. Fax: (423) 753-9331. Web: www.story net.org.

NIGERIA: INDEPENDENCE DAY. Oct 1. National holiday. This West African nation became independent of Great Britain in 1960 and a republic in 1963.

PEDIATRIC CANCER AWARENESS MONTH. Oct 1–31. Cancer is the chief cause of death by disease in children. More than 1,000 children in the US die of cancer every year. For info: Bear Necessities Pediatric Cancer Foundation, 85 W Algonquin Rd, Ste 165, Arlington Heights, IL 60005. Phone: (847) 952-9164.

POLISH AMERICAN HERITAGE MONTH. Oct 1–31. A national celebration of Polish history, culture and pride, in cooperation with the Polish American Congress and Polonia Across America. For info: Michael Blichasz, Chair, Polish American Cultural Center, Natl HQ, 308 Walnut St, Philadelphia, PA 19106. Phone: (215) 922-1700. Fax: (215) 922-1518. Web: www.polish americancenter.org.

OCTOBER 1–31
DIVERSITY AWARENESS MONTH

The possibilities for celebrating this month in the classroom are endless. Here are a few that will get your creative thought processes flowing.

For the youngest primary students begin on a smaller scale, one that is concrete to very young children. Take a classroom poll on favorite colors. List students' names under each one. Make up other "favorite" categories—food, TV shows, books, animals. Talk about how some students share "favorites," others don't. Art projects focusing around the "likes" that students share provide a visual and concrete expression of similarities. Talk about our similarities: we are all people, everyone breathes, thinks and feels emotions. Other similarities include two eyes, ears, legs and arms. Then, discuss differences like hair, eye and skin color. Include discussion of differences caused by physical disabilities. Emphasize the way student "differences" make the classroom a more interesting and exciting place.

Older students may wish to explore differences by writing about family traditions that celebrate ethnic backgrounds. A bulletin board with pictures (student generated!) of the many cuisines we eat is a good idea.

Literature and music provide myriad opportunities for students of all ages to explore cultural differences. Ask students to share family favorites with their classmates. Teachers who need books that treat specific ethnic groups and/or promote discussion of diversity can consult the following: *Against Borders: Promoting Books for a Multicultural World*, by Hazel Rochman (American Library Association, 0-8389-0601-X, $25) which lists books for students in grades 6–12; *Our Family, Our Friends, Our World: An Annotated Guide to Significant Multicultural Books for Children and Teenagers*, by Lyn Miller-Lachmann (Bowker, 0-8352-3025-2, $49.95); and *This Land Is Our Land: A Guide to Multicultural Literature for Children and Young Adults*, by Althea K. Helbig and Agnes Regan Perkins (Greenwood, 0-313-28742-2, $49.95).

Older students can talk about stereotypes and misconceptions they hold about people who are a different gender, race or ethnic background. A teacher can provide prompts and moderate if the discussion gets too intense.

STOCKTON, RICHARD: BIRTH ANNIVERSARY. Oct 1, 1730. Lawyer and signer of the Declaration of Independence, born at Princeton, NJ. Died there, Feb 8, 1781.

SUPER MARIO BROTHERS RELEASED: ANNIVERSARY. Oct 1, 1985. In 1985 the Nintendo Entertainment System (NES) for home use was introduced and the popular game for the NES, Super Mario Brothers, was released on this date. In 1989 Nintendo introduced Game Boy, the first hand-held game system with interchangeable game paks. For further info: www.nintendo.com.

TUVALU: NATIONAL HOLIDAY. Oct 1. Commemorates independence from Great Britain in 1978.

UNITED NATIONS: INTERNATIONAL DAY OF OLDER PERSONS. Oct 1. On Dec 14, 1990, the General Assembly designated Oct 1 as the International Day for the Elderly. It appealed

for contributions to the Trust Fund for Aging (which supports projects in developing countries in implementation of the Vienna International Plan of Action on Aging adopted at the 1982 World Assembly on Aging) and endorsed an action program on aging for 1992 and beyond as outlined by the Secretary-General. (Res 45/106.) On Dec 21, 1995, the Assembly changed the name from "for the Elderly" to "of Older Persons" to conform with the 1991 UN Principles for Older Persons. 1999 has been declared the International Year of Older Persons by the UN. Info from: United Nations, Dept of Public Info, Public Inquiries Unit, Rm GA-57, New York, NY 10017. Phone: (212) 963-4475. Fax: (212) 963-0071. E-mail: inquiries@un.org.

US 2000 FEDERAL FISCAL YEAR BEGINS. Oct 1, 1999–Sept 30, 2000.

UNIVERSAL CHILDREN'S WEEK. Oct 1–7. To disseminate throughout the world info on the needs of children and to distribute copies of the Declaration of the Rights of the Child. For complete info, send $4 to cover expense of printing, handling and postage. Annually, the first seven days of October. For info: Dr. Stanley Drake, Pres, Intl Soc of Friendship and Good Will, 412 Cherry Hills Dr, Bakersfield, CA 93309-7902.

VEGETARIAN AWARENESS MONTH. Oct 1–31. This educational campaign advances awareness of the many surprising environmental, economic, health, humanitarian and other benefits of a vegetarian lifestyle. This event promotes personal and planetary healing with respect for all life. For info: Vegetarian Awareness Network/VEGANET, Communications Center, PO Box 321, Knoxville, TN 37901-0321. Phone: (800) USA-VEGE.

WORLD VEGETARIAN DAY. Oct 1. Celebration of vegetarianism's benefits to humans, animals and our planet. In addition to individuals, participants include libraries, schools, colleges, restaurants, food services, health-care centers, health food stores, workplaces and many more. For info: North American Vegetarian Soc, Box 72, Dolgeville, NY 13329. Phone: (518) 568-7970. Fax: (518) 568-7979. E-mail: navs@telenet.net. Web: www.cyberveg.org/navs.

YOSEMITE NATIONAL PARK ESTABLISHED: ANNIVERSARY. Oct 1, 1890. Yosemite Valley and Mariposa Big Tree Grove, granted to the State of California June 30, 1864, were combined and established as a national park. For further park info: Yosemite Natl Park, PO Box 577, Yosemite Natl Park, CA 95389 or www.nps.gov/yose/

BIRTHDAYS TODAY

Jimmy Carter (born James Earl Carter, Jr), 75, 39th US President, born Plains, GA, Oct 1, 1924.
Mark McGwire, 36, baseball player, born Pomona, CA, Oct 1, 1963.
William Hubbs Rehnquist, 75, Chief Justice of the US Supreme Court, born Milwaukee, WI, Oct 1, 1924.

	S	M	T	W	T	F	S
October						1	2
1999	3	4	5	6	7	8	9
	10	11	12	13	14	15	16
	17	18	19	20	21	22	23
	24	25	26	27	28	29	30
	31						

OCTOBER 2 — SATURDAY

Day 275 — 90 Remaining

BASKETBALL HALL OF FAME ENSHRINEMENT CEREMONIES. Oct 2. Springfield, MA. New electees are enshrined into the Basketball Hall of Fame. Est attendance: 1,500. For info: Robin Jonathan Deutsch, Public Relations & Publishing, Basketball Hall of Fame, 1150 W Columbus Ave, PO Box 179, Springfield, MA 01101-0179. Phone: (413) 781-6500.

CHARLIE BROWN AND SNOOPY: BIRTHDAY. Oct 2, 1950. Syndicated by United Feature Syndicate, Charles M. Schulz's "PEANUTS" comic strip now appears in 2,600 newspapers and is translated into 21 languages in 75 countries. For info: Lili Root, PR Mgr, United Media, 200 Madison Ave, New York, NY 10016. Phone: (212) 293-8520. Fax: (212) 293-8550. Web: www.snoopy.com.

GANDHI, MOHANDAS KARAMCHAND (MAHATMA): BIRTH ANNIVERSARY. Oct 2, 1869. Indian political and spiritual leader who achieved world honor and fame for his advocacy of nonviolent resistance as a weapon against tyranny was born at Porbandar, India. He was assassinated in the garden of his home at New Delhi, Jan 30, 1948. On the anniversary of Gandhi's birth (Gandhi Jayanti) thousands gather at the park on the Jumna River at Delhi where Gandhi's body was cremated. Hymns are sung, verses from the Gita, the Koran and the Bible are recited and cotton thread is spun on small spinning wheels (one of Gandhi's favorite activities). Other observances held at his birthplace and throughout India on this public holiday.

GUINEA: INDEPENDENCE DAY. Oct 2. National Day. Guinea gained independence from France in 1958.

MOON PHASE: LAST QUARTER. Oct 2. Moon enters Last Quarter phase at 12:02 AM, EDT.

NATIONAL CUSTODIAL WORKERS DAY. Oct 2. A day to honor custodial workers—those who clean up after us. For info: Bette Tadajewski, Saint John the Baptist Church, 2425 Frederick, Alpena, MI 49707. Phone: (517) 354-3019.

NATIONAL FRUGAL FUN DAY. Oct 2. A day to celebrate that having fun doesn't have to be costly. Do at least one fun thing for yourself and/or your family that is free of cost or under $5 a person: a concert or play, a hike, a meal out, a picnic, an art gallery or museum tour, a day trip, a boat ride. Annually, the first Saturday in October. For info: Shel Horowitz, PO Box 1164, Northampton, MA 01061-1164. Phone: (413) 586-2388. Fax: (617) 249-0153. E-mail: info@frugalfun.com. Web: www.frugalfun.com.

REDWOOD NATIONAL PARK ESTABLISHED: ANNIVERSARY. Oct 2, 1968. California's Redwood National Park was established. For further park info: Redwood Natl Park, 1111 Second St, Crescent City, CA 95531. Web: www.nps.gov/redw.

SHEMINI ATZERET. Oct 2. Hebrew calendar date: Tishri 22, 5760. The eighth day of Solemn Assembly, part of the Sukkot Festival (see entry on Sept 25), with memorial services and cycle of Biblical readings in the synagogue.

BIRTHDAYS TODAY

Thomas Muster, 32, tennis player, born Leibnitz, Austria, Oct 2, 1967.

OCTOBER 3 — SUNDAY

Day 276 — 89 Remaining

"THE ANDY GRIFFITH SHOW" TV PREMIERE: ANNIVERSARY. Oct 3, 1960. Marks the airing of the first episode of this popular show set at Mayberry, NC. Andy Griffith starred as Sheriff Andy Taylor, Ron Howard was his son Opie and Don Knotts played Deputy Barney Fife. The 12,000+ members of "The Andy Griffith Show" Rerun Watchers Club and others celebrate this day with festivities every year.

FIRE PREVENTION WEEK. Oct 3–9. To increase awareness of the dangers of fire and to educate the public on how to stay safe from fire. The theme this year is "Fire Drills: The Great Escape!" For info: Public Affairs Office, Natl Fire Protection Assn, One Batterymarch Park, Quincy, MA 02269. Phone: (617) 770-3000. Web: www.nfpa.org.

★**FIRE PREVENTION WEEK.** Oct 3–9 (approximate). Presidential Proclamation issued annually for the first or second week in October since 1925. For many years prior to 1925, National Fire Prevention Day was observed in October.

GERMAN REUNIFICATION: ANNIVERSARY. Oct 3, 1990. After 45 years of division, East and West Germany reunited, just four days short of East Germany's 41st founding anniversary (Oct 7, 1949). The new united Germany took the name the Federal Republic of Germany, the formal name of the former West Germany and adopted the constitution of the former West Germany. Today is a national holiday in Germany.

GET ORGANIZED WEEK. Oct 3–9. This is an opportunity to streamline your life, create more time, lower your stress and increase your profit. Simplify your situation and make it more manageable by taking advantage of this time to get organized. Annually, the first week in October. For info: Stephanie Denton, Natl Assn of Professional Organizers, 1033 LaPosada Dr, Ste 220, Austin, TX 78752-3880. Phone: (513) 871-8807. E-mail: 104340.14@compuserve.com.

HONDURAS: FRANCISCO MORAZAN HOLIDAY. Oct 3. Public holiday in honor of Francisco Morazan, national hero, who was born in 1799.

JAPAN: NEWSPAPER WEEK. Oct 3–9. During this week newspapers make an extensive effort to acquaint the public with their functions and the role of a newspaper in a free society. Annually, the first week in October.

KOREA: NATIONAL FOUNDATION DAY. Oct 3. National holiday also called Tangun Day, as it commemorates day when legendary founder of the Korean nation, Tangun, established his kingdom of Chosun in 2333 BC.

"MICKEY MOUSE CLUB" TV PREMIERE: ANNIVERSARY. Oct 3, 1955. This afternoon show for children was on ABC. Among its young cast members were Mouseketeers Annette Funicello and Shelley Fabares.

★**MINORITY ENTERPRISE DEVELOPMENT WEEK.** Oct 3–9. Presidential Proclamation issued without request since 1983 for the first full week in October except in 1991 when issued for

OCTOBER 3–9
NATIONAL METRIC WEEK

The United States is the only large industrialized country in the world that hasn't switched to the metric system. Though Congress passed the Metric Conversion Act in 1975, this system has been implemented only to a limited extent in the US. Don't leave your students clueless when it comes to the metric system; focus their attention during National Metric Week.

Converting height into centimeters always amuses children, whose size suddenly seems astronomical. Calculate and post classroom dimensions, measure desktops, have a recess 10-meter dash or meter high jump. Sports fans can figure the metric height of a basketball backboard, a football field or a baseball diamond.

Have fun with food measurements. Convert the ounces from soda cans and milk cartons into liters. Conversely, convert a liter soft drink bottle into ounces. Many food products today note both the customary and metric measure—have students look for examples at home and in the supermarket.

Car speeds zoom into high numbers when expressed as kilometers per hour.

Don't forget about Celsius degrees. What happens to the boiling and freezing points of water? What is a normal human body temperature?

Many Americans do use the metric system in their jobs on a daily basis. Discuss some occupations that use the metric system (engineers, chemists and some factory workers, for example) and why.

Get older students involved in a critical thinking debate on the pros and cons of switching to the metric system. After the debate, hold a classroom vote on "Should the US fully convert or not?"

You can also have fun with word play. Does an inchworm become a centiworm? What happens when you give someone an inch? Is this the end of the Quarter Pounder? For easy reference, post the conversion formulas in several easy-to-spot locations. Next to the classroom clock is a great place since eyes frequently turn in that direction.

The website of the US Metric Association provides a table of metric units and equivalents and other useful information at lamar.colostate.edu/~hillger.

Sept 22–28, in 1992 for Sept 27–Oct 3, to coincide with the National Conference and in 1997 for Sept 21-27.

NATIONAL METRIC WEEK. Oct 3–9. To maintain an awareness of the importance of the metric system as the primary system of measurement for the US. Annually, the first full week in October. See Curriculum Connection. For info: Natl Council of Teachers of Mathematics, 1906 Association Dr, Reston, VA 20191-1593. Phone: (703) 620-9840. Fax: (703) 476-2970. E-mail: info-central@nctm.org. Web: www.nctm.org.

ROBINSON NAMED BASEBALL'S FIRST BLACK MAJOR LEAGUE MANAGER: 25th ANNIVERSARY. Oct 3, 1974. The only major league player selected most valuable player in both the American and National Leagues, Frank Robinson was hired

		S	M	T	W	T	F	S
October							1	2
1999		3	4	5	6	7	8	9
		10	11	12	13	14	15	16
		17	18	19	20	21	22	23
		24	25	26	27	28	29	30
		31						

by the Cleveland Indians as baseball's first black major league manager. During his playing career Robinson represented the American League in four World Series playing for the Baltimore Orioles, led the Cincinnati Reds to a National League pennant and hit 586 home runs in 21 years of play.

SIMCHAT TORAH. Oct 3. Hebrew calendar date: Tishri 23, 5760. Rejoicing in the Torah concludes the nine-day Sukkot Festival (see entry on Sept 25). Public reading of the Pentateuch is completed and begun again, symbolizing the need for ever-continuing study.

WORLD COMMUNION SUNDAY. Oct 3. Communion is celebrated by Christians all over the world. Annually, the first Sunday in October.

BIRTHDAYS TODAY

Jeff Bingaman, 56, US Senator (D, New Mexico), born El Paso, TX, Oct 3, 1943.

OCTOBER 4 — MONDAY
Day 277 — 88 Remaining

"THE ALVIN SHOW" TV PREMIERE: ANNIVERSARY. Oct 4, 1961. This prime-time cartoon was based on Ross Bagdasarian's novelty group called The Chipmunks, which had begun as recordings with speeded-up vocals. In the series, the three chipmunks, Alvin, Simon and Theodore, sang and had adventures along with their songwriter-manager David Seville. Bagdasarian supplied the voices. Part of the show featured the adventures of inventor Clyde Crashcup. "Alvin" was more successful as a Saturday morning cartoon. It returned in reruns in 1979 and also prompted a sequel, called "Alvin and the Chipmunks," in 1983.

★**CHILD HEALTH DAY.** Oct 4. Presidential Proclamation always issued for the first Monday of October. Proclamation has been issued since 1928. In 1959 Congress changed celebration day from May 1 to the present observance (Pub Res No. 46 of May 18, 1928, and PL86–352 of Sept 22, 1959).

FESTIVAL IN THE SCHOOLS. Oct 4–8 (tentative). Nashville, TN, public and private schools. An artist-in-residence program brings area authors, storytellers, poets, songwriters, illustrators and cartoonists into classrooms to talk to children about their work. For info: Galyn Martin, Coordinator, Southern Festival of Books, Tennessee Humanities Council, 1003 18th Ave S, Nashville, TN 37212. Phone: (615) 320-7001 ext 15. Fax: (615) 321-4586. E-mail: gayln@tn-humanities.org.

GREGORIAN CALENDAR ADJUSTMENT: ANNIVERSARY. Oct 4, 1582. Pope Gregory XIII issued a bulletin that decreed that the day following Thursday, Oct 4, 1582, should be Friday, Oct 15, 1582, thus correcting the Julian Calendar, then 10 days out of date relative to the seasons. This reform was effective in most Catholic countries, though the Julian Calendar continued in use in Britain and the American colonies until 1752, in Japan until 1873, in China until 1912, in Russia until 1918, in Greece until 1923 and in Turkey until 1927. See also: "Gregorian Calendar Adjustment: Anniversary" (Feb 24) and "Calendar Adjustment Day: Anniversary" (Sept 2).

HAYES, RUTHERFORD BIRCHARD: BIRTH ANNIVERSARY. Oct 4, 1822. Nineteenth president of the US (Mar 4, 1877–Mar 3, 1881), born at Delaware, OH. In his inaugural address, Hayes said: "He serves his party best who serves the country best." He died at Fremont, OH, Jan 17, 1893.

JOHNSON, ELIZA McCARDLE: BIRTH ANNIVERSARY. Oct 4, 1810. Wife of Andrew Johnson, 17th president of the US, born at Leesburg, TN. Died at Greeneville, TN, Jan 15, 1876.

"LEAVE IT TO BEAVER" TV PREMIERE: ANNIVERSARY. Oct 4, 1957. This family sitcom was a stereotypical portrayal of American family life. It focused on Theodore "the Beaver" Cleaver (Jerry Mathers), his misadventures and his family: his patient, understanding, all-knowing and firm father, Ward (Hugh Beaumont), impeccably dressed housewife and mother June (Barbara Billingsley) and Wally (Tony Dow), Beaver's good-natured all-American brother. The "perfectness" of the Cleaver family was balanced by other, less than perfect characters. "Leave It to Beaver" remained popular in reruns and as a made-for-TV-movie in the '80s.

LESOTHO: NATIONAL DAY. Oct 4. National holiday. Commemorates independence from Britain in 1966.

NATIONAL WALK OUR CHILDREN TO SCHOOL WEEK. Oct 4–8. Parents are encouraged to walk their children to school to demonstrate the healthful effects of walking. For info: Walking Magazine, 45 Bromfield St, 8th Floor, Boston, MA 02108. Phone: (617) 574-0076. Fax: (617) 338-7433.

SAINT FRANCIS OF ASSISI: FEAST DAY. Oct 4. Giovanni Francesco Bernardone, religious leader, founder of the Friars Minor (Franciscan Order), born at Assisi, Umbria, Italy, in 1181. Died at Porziuncola, Oct 3, 1226. One of the best-loved saints of all time.

SPACE MILESTONE: *SPUTNIK* (USSR). Oct 4, 1957. Anniversary of launching of first successful man-made earth satellite. *Sputnik I* ("satellite") weighing 184 lbs was fired into orbit from the USSR's Tyuratam launch site. Transmitted radio signal for 21 days, decayed Jan 4, 1958. The beginning of the Space Age and man's exploration beyond Earth. This first-in-space triumph by the Soviets resulted in a stepped-up emphasis on the teaching of science in American classrooms.

STRATEMEYER, EDWARD L.: BIRTH ANNIVERSARY. Oct 4, 1862. American author of children's books, Stratemeyer was born at Elizabeth, NJ. He created numerous series of popular children's books including "The Bobbsey Twins," "The Hardy Boys," "Nancy Drew" and "Tom Swift." He and his Stratemeyer Syndicate, using 60 or more pen names, produced more than 800 books. More than four million copies were in print in 1987. Stratemeyer died at Newark, NJ, May 10, 1930.

SUPREME COURT 1999–2000 TERM BEGINS. Oct 4. Traditionally, the Supreme Court's annual term begins on the first Monday in October and continues with seven two-week sessions of oral arguments. Between the sessions are six recesses during which the opinions are written by the Justices. Ordinarily, all cases are decided by the following June or July. For a database of cases, biographies of the justices past and present and a virtual tour of the Supreme Court Building on the Web: oyez.nwu.edu.

UNITED NATIONS: WORLD HABITAT DAY. Oct 4. The United Nations General Assembly, by a resolution of Dec 17, 1985, has designated the first Monday of October each year as World Habitat Day. The first observance of this day, Oct 5, 1986, marked the 10th anniversary of the first international conference on the subject. (Habitat: United Nations Conference on Human Settlements, Vancouver, Canada, 1976.) Info from: United Nations, Dept of Public Info, Public Inquiries Unit, Rm GA-57, New York, NY 10017. Phone: (212) 963-4475. Fax: (212) 963-0071. E-mail: inquiries@un.org.

BIRTHDAYS TODAY

Karen Cushman, 58, author (*Catherine, Called Birdy*, Newbery for *The Midwife's Apprentice*), born Chicago, IL, Oct 4, 1941.

Chuck Hagel, 53, US Senator (R, Nebraska), born North Platte, NE, Oct 4, 1946.

Alicia Silverstone, 23, actress (*Batman & Robin*), born San Francisco, CA, Oct 4, 1976.

Donald Sobol, 75, author (the Encyclopedia Brown series), born New York, NY, Oct 4, 1924.

OCTOBER 5 — TUESDAY
Day 278 — 87 Remaining

ARTHUR, CHESTER ALAN: BIRTH ANNIVERSARY. Oct 5, 1829. The 21st president of the US, born at Fairfield, VT, succeeded to the presidency following the death of James A. Garfield. Term of office: Sept 20, 1881–Mar 3, 1885. Arthur was not successful in obtaining the Republican party's nomination for the following term. He died at New York, NY, Nov 18, 1886.

CHIEF JOSEPH SURRENDER: ANNIVERSARY. Oct 5, 1877. After a 1,700-mile retreat, Chief Joseph and the Nez Perce Indians surrendered to US Cavalry troops at Bear's Paw near Chinook, MT, Oct 5, 1877. Chief Joseph made his famous speech of surrender, "From where the sun now stands, I will fight no more forever."

FITZHUGH, LOUISE: BIRTH ANNIVERSARY. Oct 5, 1928. Author (*Harriet the Spy*), born at Memphis, TN. Died Nov 19, 1974.

GODDARD, ROBERT HUTCHINGS: BIRTH ANNIVERSARY. Oct 5, 1882. The "father of the Space Age," born at Worcester, MA. Largely ignored or ridiculed during his lifetime because of his dreams of rocket travel, including travel to other planets. Launched a liquid-fuel-powered rocket Mar 16, 1926, at Auburn, MA. Died Aug 10, 1945, at Baltimore, MD. See also: "Goddard Day" (Mar 16).

STONE, THOMAS: DEATH ANNIVERSARY. Oct 5, 1787. Signer of the Declaration of Independence, born 1743 (exact date unknown) at Charles County, MD. Died at Alexandria, VA.

TECUMSEH: DEATH ANNIVERSARY. Oct 5, 1813. Shawnee Indian chief and orator, born at Old Piqua near Springfield, OH, in March 1768. Tecumseh is regarded as one of the greatest of American Indians. He came to prominence between the years 1799 and 1804 as a powerful orator, defending his people against whites. He denounced as invalid all treaties by which Indians ceded their lands and condemned the chieftains who had entered into such agreements. With his brother Tenskwatawa, the Prophet, he established a town on the Tippecanoe River near Lafayette, IN, and then embarked on a mission to organize an Indian confederation to stop white encroachment. Although he advocated peaceful methods and negotiation, he did not rule out war as a last resort as he visited tribes throughout the country. While he was away, William Henry Harrison defeated the Prophet at the Battle of Tippecanoe Nov 7, 1811, and burned the town. Tecumseh organized a large force of Indian warriors and assisted the British in the War of 1812. Tecumseh was defeated and killed at the Battle of the Thames, Oct 5, 1813.

BIRTHDAYS TODAY

Grant Hill, 27, basketball player, born Dallas, TX, Oct 5, 1972.
Bil Keane, 77, cartoonist ("Family Circus"), born Philadelphia, PA, Oct 5, 1922.
Mario Lemieux, 34, Hall of Fame hockey player, born Montreal, Canada, Oct 5, 1965.
Patrick Roy, 34, hockey player, born Quebec City, Quebec, Canada, Oct 5, 1965.
Kate Winslet, 24, actress (*Titanic*), born Reading, England, Oct 5, 1975.

OCTOBER 6 — WEDNESDAY
Day 279 — 86 Remaining

EGYPT: ARMED FORCES DAY. Oct 6. The Egyptian Army celebrates crossing into Sinai in 1973. For info: Egyptian Tourist Authority, 645 N Michigan Ave, Ste 829, Chicago, IL 60611. Phone: (312) 280-4666. Fax: (312) 280-4788.

HONG KONG: BIRTHDAY OF CONFUCIUS. Oct 6. Religious observances are held by the Confucian Society at Confucius Temple at Causeway Bay. Observed on 27th day of 8th lunar month.

MISSISSIPPI STATE FAIR. Oct 6–12. Jackson, MS. Features nightly professional entertainment, livestock show, midway carnival, domestic art exhibits. Est attendance: 620,000. For info: Mississippi Fair Commission, PO Box 892, Jackson, MS 39205. Phone: (601) 961-4000. Fax: (601) 354-6545.

★**NATIONAL GERMAN-AMERICAN DAY.** Oct 6. Celebration of German heritage and contributions German Americans have made to the building of the nation. A Presidential Proclamation has been issued each year since 1987. Annually, Oct 6.

YOM KIPPUR WAR: ANNIVERSARY. Oct 6–25, 1973. A surprise attack by Egypt and Syria pushed Israeli forces several miles behind the 1967 cease-fire lines. Israel was caught off guard, partly because the attack came on the holiest Jewish religious day. After 18 days of fighting, hostilities were halted by the UN Oct 25. Israel

		S	M	T	W	T	F	S
October							1	2
1999		3	4	5	6	7	8	9
		10	11	12	13	14	15	16
		17	18	19	20	21	22	23
		24	25	26	27	28	29	30
		31						

partially recovered from the initial setback but failed to regain all the land lost in the fighting.

BIRTHDAYS TODAY

James Gilmore III, 50, Governor of Virginia (R), born Richmond, VA, Oct 6, 1949.
Betsy Hearne, 57, author (*Seven Brave Women*), born Wilsonville, AL, Oct 6, 1942.
Rebecca Lobo, 26, basketball player, born Southwick, MA, Oct 6, 1973.

OCTOBER 7 — THURSDAY
Day 280 — 85 Remaining

RODNEY, CAESAR: BIRTH ANNIVERSARY. Oct 7, 1728. Signer of the Declaration of Independence who cast a tie-breaking vote. Born near Dover, DE, he died at Dover, June 29, 1784.

SOUTH CAROLINA STATE FAIR. Oct 7–17 (tentative). Columbia, SC. Conklin Shows, musical entertainment, food booths and children's activities. Est attendance: 576,000. For info: South Carolina State Fair, PO Box 393, Columbia, SC 29202. Phone: (803) 799-3387. Fax: (803) 799-1760. E-mail: geninfo@scsn.net.

WALLACE, HENRY AGARD: BIRTH ANNIVERSARY. Oct 7, 1888. Thirty-third vice president of the US (1941–45) born at Adair County, IA. Died at Danbury, CT, Nov 18, 1965.

BIRTHDAYS TODAY

Desmond Tutu, 68, South African archbishop, Nobel Peace Prize winner, born Klerksdrop, South Africa, Oct 7, 1931.

OCTOBER 8 — FRIDAY
Day 281 — 84 Remaining

ALABAMA NATIONAL FAIR. Oct 8–16. Garrett Coliseum/Fairgrounds, Montgomery, AL. A midway filled with exciting rides and games, arts and crafts, exhibits, livestock shows, racing pigs, a circus, a petting zoo, food and entertainment. Est attendance: 227,000. For info: Hazel Ashmore, PO Box 3304, Montgomery, AL 36109-0304. Phone: (334) 272-6831. Fax: (334) 272-6835.

ARKANSAS STATE FAIR AND LIVESTOCK SHOW. Oct 8–17. Barton Coliseum and State Fairground, Little Rock, AR. Est attendance: 400,000. For info: Arkansas State Fair, PO Box 166660, Little Rock, AR 72216. Phone: (501) 372-8341. Fax: (501) 372-4197. Web: www.arkfairgrounds.com.

GEORGIA NATIONAL FAIR. Oct 8–17. Georgia National Fairgrounds, Perry, GA. Traditional state agricultural fair features thousands of entries in horse, livestock, horticultural, youth, home and fine arts categories. Family entertainment, education and fun. Sponsored by the State of Georgia. Annually, beginning the fifth Friday after Labor Day. Est attendance: 352,000. For info:

Georgia Natl Fair, PO Box 1367, 401 Larry Walker Pkwy, Perry, GA 31069. Phone: (912) 987-3247. Fax: (912) 987-7218. E-mail: mtreptow@alltell.net. Web: www.gnfa.com.

GREAT CHICAGO FIRE: ANNIVERSARY. Oct 8, 1871. Great fire of Chicago began, according to legend, when Mrs O'Leary's cow kicked over the lantern in her barn on DeKoven Street. The fire leveled 3½ sq miles, destroying 17,450 buildings and leaving 98,500 people homeless and about 250 people dead. Financially, the loss was $200 million. On the same day a fire destroyed the entire town of Peshtigo, WI, killing more than 1,100 people.

NATIONAL SCHOOL CELEBRATION. Oct 8. The National School Celebration will provide a high-profile celebration uniting our nation's youth during regular school hours for a patriotic observance. Every school in the nation is invited to participate. This event perpetuates the original spirit of the 1892 National School Celebration declared by President Benjamin Harrison, for which the first Pledge of Allegiance was written. Free resources available. Annually, the second Friday in October. For info: Paula Burton, Pres, Celebration USA, 17853 Santiago Blvd, Ste 107, Villa Park, CA 92667. Phone: (714) 283-1892. Web: www.american promise.com.

PERU: DAY OF THE NAVY. Oct 8. Public holiday in Peru, commemorating Combat of Angamos.

PESHTIGO FOREST FIRE: ANNIVERSARY. Oct 8, 1871. One of the most disastrous forest fires in history began at Peshtigo, WI, the same day the Great Chicago Fire began. The Wisconsin fire burned across six counties, killing more than 1,100 persons.

SOUTHERN FESTIVAL OF BOOKS: A CELEBRATION OF THE WRITTEN WORD. Oct 8–10 (tentative). War Memorial Plaza, Nashville, TN. To promote reading, writing, the literary arts and a broader understanding of the language and culture of the South, this annual festival will feature readings, talks and panel discussions by more than 200 authors, exhibit booths of publishing companies and bookstores, autographing sessions, a comprehensive children's program and the Cafe Stage, which is a performance corner for authors, storytellers and musicians. Est attendance: 30,000. For info: Galyn Martin, Coord, Southern Festival of Books, Tennessee Humanities Council, 1003 18th Ave S, Nashville, TN 37212. Phone: 6153207001 ext 15. Fax: (615) 321-4586. E-mail: galyn@tn-humanities.org.

BIRTHDAYS TODAY

Chevy Chase, 56, comedian, actor (*Christmas Vacation, Vegas Vacation*), born Cornelius Crane, New York, NY, Oct 8, 1943.

Matt Damon, 29, actor (*Saving Private Ryan*), born Cambridge, MA, Oct 8, 1970.

Jesse Jackson, 58, clergyman, civil rights leader ("I am somebody," "Keep hope alive"), born Greenville, NC, Oct 8, 1941.

Faith Ringgold, 69, artist, author (*Tar Beach, My Dream of Martin Luther King*), born New York, NY, Oct 8, 1930.

Rashaan Salaam, 25, football player, born San Diego, CA, Oct 8, 1974.

R.L. Stine, 56, author (the Goosebumps series), born Columbus, OH, Oct 8, 1943.

OCTOBER 9 — SATURDAY
Day 282 — 83 Remaining

ICELAND: LEIF ERIKSON DAY. Oct 9. Celebrates discovery of North America in the year 1000 by Norse explorer.

KOREA: ALPHABET DAY (HANGUL): ANNIVERSARY. Oct 9. Celebrates anniversary of promulgation of Hangul (24-letter phonetic alphabet) by King Sejong of the Yi Dynasty, in 1446.

★ **LEIF ERIKSON DAY.** Oct 9. Presidential Proclamation always issued for Oct 9 since 1964 (PL88–566 of Sept 2, 1964) at request. Honors the Norse explorer who is widely believed to have been the first European to visit the American continent. For information on the 1,000-year anniversary of this event to take place in 2000, visit the Leif Ericson Millennium Celebration website at www.leif.2000.

MOON PHASE: NEW MOON. Oct 9. Moon enters New Moon phase at 7:34 AM, EDT.

PLANET FRIENDS WEEK. Oct 9–15. Today's technology has moved children and teens out of their neighborhoods and on to a large multicultural playground called Planet Earth. Planet Friends Week encourages young people to think globally, experiencing new cultures and languages and to create their own network of Planet Friends all over the world. For info: Planet Friends, PO Box 10929, Pittsburgh, PA 15236.

UGANDA: INDEPENDENCE DAY. Oct 9. National holiday commemorating achievement of autonomy from Britain in 1962.

UNITED NATIONS: WORLD POST DAY. Oct 9. An annual special observance of Postal Administrations of the Universal Postal Union (UPU). For info: United Nations, Dept of Public Info, Public Inquiries Unit, Rm GA-57, New York, NY 10017. Phone: (212) 963-4475. Fax: (212) 963-0071. E-mail: inquiries@un.org.

BIRTHDAYS TODAY

Johanna Hurwitz, 62, author (*Busybody Nora*), born New York, NY, Oct 9, 1937.

Trent Lott, 58, US Senator (R, Mississippi), born Duck Hill, MS, Oct 9, 1941.

Mike Singletary, 41, Hall of Fame football player, born Houston, TX, Oct 9, 1958.

Annika Sorenstam, 29, golfer, born Stockholm, Sweden, Oct 9, 1970.

OCTOBER 10 — SUNDAY
Day 283 — 82 Remaining

AMERICAN SAMOA: WHITE SUNDAY. Oct 10. Second Sunday in October is "children's day" on the island. Children demonstrate skits, prayers, songs and special presentations for parents, friends and relatives. A feast is prepared by the parents and served to the children.

BONZA BOTTLER DAY™. Oct 10. To celebrate when the number of the day is the same as the number of the month. Bonza Bottler Day™ is an excuse to have a party at least once a month. For info: Gail M. Berger, 109 Matthew Ave, Poca, WV 25159. Phone: (304) 776-7746. E-mail: gberger5@aol.com.

DOUBLE TENTH DAY: ANNIVERSARY. Oct 10, 1911. Tenth day of 10th month, Double Tenth Day, is observed by many Chinese as the anniversary of the outbreak of the revolution against the imperial Manchu dynasty, Oct 10, 1911. Sun Yat-sen and Huan Hsing were among the revolutionary leaders.

FIJI: INDEPENDENCE DAY. Oct 10. National holiday. Commemorates independence from Britain in 1970.

GRANDMOTHER'S DAY IN FLORIDA AND KENTUCKY. Oct 10. A ceremonial day on the second Sunday in October.

JAPAN: HEALTH-SPORTS DAY ANNIVERSARY. Oct 10. National holiday to encourage physical activity for building sound

OCTOBER 10–16
NATIONAL WILDLIFE WEEK

This is a week to draw attention to the wide variety of wildlife (and their habitats) found throughout the US.

National Parks provide plenty of room for wildlife to roam. Student groups could present reports about National Parks from different areas of the US. Compare and contrast the kinds of habitats and wildlife found in national parks such as Acadia, the Everglades, Carlsbad Caverns, Death Valley, Canyonlands, Denali and Hawaii Volcanoes. These diverse climates and terrains support many different animals. Information can be found at the National Parks Service website: www.nps.gov.

Conservation issues are often highlighted in newspaper and magazine articles. Students can discuss and debate recent challenges to the Endangered Species Act. Coastal development and the destruction of wetlands are major threats to wildlife. Research and discuss construction practices that help and harm wildlife. The US Fish and Wildlife Service's Endangered Species website at www.fws.gov/r9endspp/endspp.htm has information for both teachers and students.

Students might find researching and reporting on unusual forms of wildlife interesting. Sea horses, armadillos, wolverines, manatees and gila monsters are a few examples. Facts about and artwork of the researched animals could be displayed on a bulletin board. Another board could focus on things we do that harm wildlife and what we can do to help.

Older students can debate the issue of wild animals being reintroduced into areas they formerly occupied. There are many sources for information on the reintroduction of wolves. *Wolf Wars*, by Hank Fischer (Falcon Press, 1-56044-352-9, $12.95) is a good teacher resource that explores the subject in depth. Students will enjoy *There's a Wolf in the Classroom*, by Bruce Weide and Patricia Tucker (Carolrhoda, 0-87614-958-1, $8.95 Gr. 3–7). Information is presented as a visiting wolf program. For additional sources and classroom activities see *Book Links* magazine article "Wolves: Fact and Fiction" in the September 1998 issue and National Geographic's website at www.nationalgeographic.com/resources/education/geoguide. Upper elementary and middle school classrooms may want to participate in the Journey North program which tracks spring's journey north via wildlife migration at www.learner.org/north.

body and mind. Created in 1966 to commemorate the day of the opening of the 18th Olympic Games at Tokyo, Oct 10, 1964.

NATIONAL SCHOOL LUNCH WEEK. Oct 10–16. To celebrate good nutrition and wholesome, low-cost school lunches. Annually, the second full week in October. For info: Communications Dept, American School Food Service Assn, 1600 Duke St, 7th Fl, Alexandria, VA 22314-3436. Phone: (703) 739-3900 x133.

★**NATIONAL SCHOOL LUNCH WEEK.** Oct 10–16. Presidential Proclamation issued for the week beginning with the second Sunday in October since 1962 (PL87–780 of Oct 9, 1962). Note: Not issued in 1981.

★**NATIONAL WILDLIFE WEEK.** Oct 10–16. A time for all Americans to learn about and celebrate the magnificent collec-

	S	M	T	W	T	F	S
October						1	2
1999	3	4	5	6	7	8	9
	10	11	12	13	14	15	16
	17	18	19	20	21	22	23
	24	25	26	27	28	29	30
	31						

tion of lands set aside for wildlife and for the American spirit. This is a time for renewed awareness and commitment to wildlife conservation. See Curriculum Connection.

SAMOA: WHITE SUNDAY. Oct 10. The second Sunday in October. For the children of Samoa, this is the biggest day of the year. Traditional roles are reversed, as children lead church services, are served special foods and receive gifts of new church clothes and other special items. All the children dress in white. The following Monday is an official holiday.

BIRTHDAYS TODAY

Brett Favre, 30, quarterback, born Gulfport, MS, Oct 10, 1969.
Robert San Souci, 53, author (*The Faithful Friend*), born San Francisco, CA, Oct 10, 1946.

OCTOBER 11 — MONDAY
Day 284 — 81 Remaining

CANADA: THANKSGIVING DAY. Oct 11. Observed on second Monday in October each year.

COLUMBUS DAY OBSERVANCE. Oct 11. Public Law 90–363 sets observance of Columbus Day on the second Monday in October. Applicable to federal employees and to the District of Columbia, but observed also in most states. Commemorates the landfall of Columbus in the New World, Oct 12, 1492. See also: "Columbus Day (Traditional)" (Oct 12). For links to Columbus Day websites, go to: deil.lang.uiuc.edu/web.pages/holidays/columbus.html.

★**COLUMBUS DAY.** Oct 11. Presidential Proclamation always the second Monday in October. Observed Oct 12 from 1934 to 1970 (Pub Res No 21 of Apr 30, 1934). PL90–363 of June 28, 1968, required that beginning in 1971 it would be observed on the second Monday in October.

★**GENERAL PULASKI MEMORIAL DAY.** Oct 11. Presidential Proclamation always issued for Oct 11 since 1929. Requested by Congressional Resolution each year from 1929–1946. (Since 1947 has been issued by custom.) Note: Proclamation 4869, of Oct 5, 1981, covers all succeeding years.

NATIONAL PET PEEVE WEEK. Oct 11–15. A chance for people to make others aware of all the little things in life they find so annoying, in the hope of changing some of them. Annually, the second full week of October. When requesting info, please send SASE. For info: Ad-America, Pine Tree Center Indust Park, 2215 29th St SE, Ste B-7, Grand Rapids, MI 49508. Phone: (616) 247-3797. Fax: (616) 247-3798. E-mail: adamerica@aol.com.

NATIVE AMERICANS' DAY IN SOUTH DAKOTA. Oct 11. Observed in the state of South Dakota as a legal holiday, dedicated to the remembrance of the great Native American leaders who contributed so much to the history of South Dakota. Annually, the second Monday in October.

ROBINSON, ROSCOE, JR: BIRTH ANNIVERSARY. Oct 11, 1928. The first black American to achieve the Army rank of four-star general. Born at St. Louis, MO, and died at Washington, DC, July 22, 1993.

ROOSEVELT, ANNA ELEANOR: BIRTH ANNIVERSARY. Oct 11, 1884. Wife of Franklin Delano Roosevelt, 32nd president of the US, was born at New York, NY. She led an active and independent life and was the first wife of a president to give her own news conference in the White House (1933). Widely known throughout the world, she was affectionately called "the first lady of the world." She served as US delegate to the United Nations

General Assembly for a number of years before her death at New York, NY, Nov 7, 1962. A prolific writer, she wrote in *This Is My Story*, "No one can make you feel inferior without your consent."

STONE, HARLAND FISKE: BIRTH ANNIVERSARY. Oct 11, 1872. Former associate justice and later chief justice of the US Supreme Court who wrote more than 600 opinions and dissents for that court, Stone was born at Chesterfield, NH. He served on the Supreme Court from 1925 until his death, at Washington, DC, Apr 22, 1946.

VATICAN COUNCIL II: ANNIVERSARY. Oct 11, 1962. The 21st ecumenical council of the Roman Catholic Church was convened by Pope John XXIII. It met in four annual sessions, concluding Dec 8, 1965. It dealt with the renewal of the Church and introduced sweeping changes, such as the use of the vernacular rather than Latin in the Mass.

VIRGIN ISLANDS–PUERTO RICO FRIENDSHIP DAY. Oct 11. Columbus Day (second Monday in October) also celebrates historical friendship between peoples of Virgin Islands and Puerto Rico.

YORKTOWN VICTORY DAY. Oct 11. Observed as a holiday in Virginia. Annually, the second Monday in October. See "Yorktown Day: Anniversary" (Oct 19).

BIRTHDAYS TODAY

Russell Freedman, 70, author (Newbery for *Lincoln: A Photobiography*), born San Francisco, CA, Oct 11, 1929.

Orlando Hernandez, 30, baseball player, known as "El Duque," born Villa Clara, Cuba, Oct 11, 1969.

Patty Murray, 49, US Senator (D, Washington), born Seattle, WA, Oct 11, 1950.

Michelle Trachtenberg, 14, actress (*Harriet the Spy*, "Pete & Pete"), born New York, NY, Oct 11, 1985.

Jon Steven "Steve" Young, 38, football player, born Salt Lake City, UT, Oct 11, 1961.

OCTOBER 12 — TUESDAY
Day 285 — 80 Remaining

BAHAMAS: DISCOVERY DAY. Oct 12. Commemorates the landing of Columbus in the Bahamas in 1492.

BOER WAR: 100th ANNIVERSARY. Oct 12, 1899. The Boers of the Transvaal and Orange Free State in southern Africa declared war on the British. The Boer states were annexed by Britain in 1900 but guerrilla warfare on the part of the Boers caused the war to drag on. It was finally ended May 31, 1902 by the Treaty of Vereeniging.

COLUMBUS DAY (TRADITIONAL). Oct 12. Public holiday in most countries in the Americas and in most Spanish-speaking countries. Observed under different names (Dia de la Raza or Day

of the Race) and on different dates (most often, as in US, on the second Monday in October). Anniversary of Christopher Columbus's arrival, Oct 12, 1492, after a dangerous voyage across "shoreless Seas," at the Bahamas (probably the island of Guanahani), which he renamed El Salvador and claimed in the name of the Spanish crown. In his *Journal*, he wrote: "As I saw that they (the natives) were friendly to us, and perceived that they could be much more easily converted to our holy faith by gentle means than by force, I presented them with some red caps, and strings of beads to wear upon the neck, and many other trifles of small value, wherewith they were much delighted, and became wonderfully attached to us." See also: "Columbus Day Observance" (Oct 11).

EQUATORIAL GUINEA: INDEPENDENCE DAY. Oct 12. National holiday. Gained independence from Spain in 1968.

MEXICO: DIA DE LA RAZA. Oct 12. Columbus Day is observed as the "Day of the Race," a fiesta time to commemorate the discovery of America as well as the common interests and cultural heritage of the Spanish and Indian peoples and the Hispanic nations.

SPAIN: NATIONAL HOLIDAY. Oct 12.

BIRTHDAYS TODAY

Kirk Cameron, 29, actor ("Growing Pains"), born Panorama City, CA, Oct 12, 1970.

John Engler, 51, Governor of Michigan (R), born Mt Pleasant, MI, Oct 12, 1948.

OCTOBER 13 — WEDNESDAY
Day 286 — 79 Remaining

BROWN, JESSE LEROY: BIRTH ANNIVERSARY. Oct 13, 1926. Jesse Leroy Brown was the first black American naval aviator and also the first black naval officer to lose his life in combat when he was shot down over Korea, Dec 4, 1950. On Mar 18, 1972, USS *Jesse L. Brown* was launched as the first ship to be named in honor of a black naval officer. Brown was born at Hattiesburg, MS.

PITCHER, MOLLY: BIRTH ANNIVERSARY. Oct 13, 1754. "Molly Pitcher," heroine of the American Revolution, was a water carrier at the Battle of Monmouth (Sunday, June 28, 1778) where she distinguished herself by loading and firing a cannon after her husband, John Hays, was wounded. Affectionately known as "Sergeant Molly" after General Washington issued her a warrant as a noncommissioned officer. Her real name was Mary Hays McCauley (née Ludwig). Born near Trenton, NJ, she died at Carlisle, PA, Jan 22, 1832.

PORTUGAL: PILGRIMAGE TO FATIMA. Oct 13. Crowds of pilgrims from Portugal and all over the world travel to Fatima to celebrate the last apparition of the Virgin to the little shepherds in 1917. For info: Portuguese Natl Tourist Office, 590 Fifth Ave, New York, NY 10036. Phone: (212) 354-4403.

RICHTER, CONRAD: BIRTH ANNIVERSARY. Oct 13, 1890. Author of books for children and adults, born at Pine Grove, PA. His book *The Light in the Forest* was made into a Disney film in 1958. *The Fields* won the Pulitzer Prize for fiction in 1951. Other works include *The Trees* and *The Town*. Richter died at Pottsville, PA, Oct 30, 1968.

UNITED NATIONS: INTERNATIONAL DAY FOR NATURAL DISASTER REDUCTION. Oct 13. The General Assembly made this designation for the second Wednesday of October each year as part of its efforts to foster international cooperation in reducing the loss of life, property damage and social and economic disruption caused by natural disasters. For info: United Nations, Dept of Public Info, New York, NY 10017.

US NAVY: AUTHORIZATION ANNIVERSARY. Oct 13, 1775. Commemorates legislation passed by Second Continental Congress authorizing the acquisition of ships and establishment of a navy.

WHITE HOUSE CORNERSTONE LAID: ANNIVERSARY. Oct 13, 1792. The cornerstone for the presidential residence at 1600 Pennsylvania Ave NW, Washington, DC, designed by James Hoban, was laid. The first presidential family to occupy it was that of John Adams, in November 1800. With three stories and more than 100 rooms, the White House is the oldest building at Washington. First described as the "presidential palace," it acquired the name "White House" about 10 years after construction was completed. Burned by British troops in 1814, it was reconstructed, refurbished and reoccupied by 1817. Take a virtual tour of the White House at www.whitehouse.gov. Young children can visit the White House for Kids site at www.whitehouse.gov/WH/kids/html/home.html.

BIRTHDAYS TODAY

Jerry Rice, 37, football player, born Starkville, MS, Oct 13, 1962.

Summer Sanders, 27, Olympic gold medal swimmer, host ("Figure It Out"), born Roseville, CA, Oct 13, 1972.

Paul Simon, 58, singer/songwriter, born Newark, NJ, Oct 13, 1941.

OCTOBER 14 — THURSDAY

Day 287 — 78 Remaining

ALASKA DAY CELEBRATION. Oct 14–18. Sitka, AK. Celebration of the transfer ceremony in which the Russian flag was lowered and the Stars and Stripes raised, formally transferring the ownership of Alaska to the US Oct 18, 1867. Annually, Oct 14–18. For info: Sitka Conv and Visitors Bureau, Box 1226, Sitka, AK 99835. Phone: (907) 747-5940.

BELIZE: COLUMBUS DAY. Oct 14. Public holiday.

CHICAGO INTERNATIONAL CHILDREN'S FILM FESTIVAL. Oct 14–24 (tentative). Cannes for Kids! Children's films from around the world plus workshops with directors, animators and movie makeup artists. For info: Chicago Intl Children's Film Festival, Facets Multimedia, 1517 W Fullerton Ave, Chicago, IL 606. Phone: (773) 281-9075. E-mail: kidsfest@facets.org. Web: www.cicff.org.

EISENHOWER, DWIGHT DAVID: BIRTH ANNIVERSARY. Oct 14, 1890. The 34th president of the US, born at Denison, TX. Served two terms as president, Jan 20, 1953–Jan 20, 1961. Nicknamed "Ike," he held the rank of five-star general of the army (resigned in 1952, and restored by act of Congress in 1961). He served as supreme commander of the Allied forces in western Europe during WWII. In his Farewell Address (Jan 17, 1961), speaking about the "conjunction of an immense military establishment and a large arms industry," he warned: "In the councils of government, we must guard against the acquisition of unwarranted influence, whether sought or unsought, by the military-industrial complex. The potential of the disastrous rise of

October 1999

S	M	T	W	T	F	S
					1	2
3	4	5	6	7	8	9
10	11	12	13	14	15	16
17	18	19	20	21	22	23
24	25	26	27	28	29	30
31						

misplaced power exists and will persist." An American hero, Eisenhower died at Washington, DC, Mar 28, 1969.

KING AWARDED NOBEL PEACE PRIZE: 35th ANNIVERSARY. Oct 14, 1964. Martin Luther King, Jr, became the youngest recipient of the Nobel Peace Prize when awarded the honor. Dr. King donated the entire $54,000 prize money to furthering the causes of the civil rights movement.

LENSKI, LOIS: BIRTH ANNIVERSARY. Oct 14, 1893. Children's author and illustrator, born at Springfield, OH. She wrote *Cotton In My Sack* and *Strawberry Girl*, which was awarded the Newbery Medal in 1946. Lenski died at Tarpon Springs, FL, Sept 11, 1974.

LITERATURE FESTIVAL. Oct 14. University of Kansas Union, Lawrence, KS. Festival of children's literature. For info: The Writing Conference, Inc, PO Box 664, Ottawa, KS 66067. Fax: (785) 242-0407. E-mail: jbushman@writingconference.com. Web: www.writingconference.com.

PENN, WILLIAM: BIRTH ANNIVERSARY. Oct 14, 1644. Founder of Pennsylvania, born at London, England. Penn died July 30, 1718, at Buckinghamshire, England. Presidential Proclamation 5284 of Nov 28, 1984, conferred honorary citizenship of the USA upon William Penn and his second wife, Hannah Callowhill Penn. They were the third and fourth persons to receive honorary US citizenship (following Winston Churchill and Raoul Wallenberg).

SOUND BARRIER BROKEN: ANNIVERSARY. Oct 14, 1947. Flying a Bell X-1 at Muroc Dry Lake Bed, CA, Air Force pilot Chuck Yeager flew faster than the speed of sound, ushering in the era of supersonic flight.

BIRTHDAYS TODAY

Jordan Brower, 18, actor ("Teen Angel"), born Vandenberg, CA, Oct 14, 1981.

OCTOBER 15 — FRIDAY

Day 288 — 77 Remaining

CROW RESERVATION OPENED FOR SETTLEMENT: ANNIVERSARY. Oct 15, 1892. By Presidential Proclamation 1.8 million acres of Crow Indian reservation were opened to settlers. The government had induced the Crow to give up a portion of their land in the mountainous western area in the state of Montana, for which they received 50 cents per acre.

"I LOVE LUCY" TV PREMIERE: ANNIVERSARY. Oct 15, 1951. This enormously popular sitcom, TV's first smash hit, starred the real-life husband and wife team of Cuban actor/bandleader Desi Arnaz and talented redheaded actress/comedienne Lucille Ball. They played Ricky and Lucy Ricardo, a New York bandleader and his aspiring actress/homemaker wife who was always scheming to get on stage. Costarring were William Frawley and Vivian Vance as Fred and Ethel Mertz, the Ricardos' landlords and good friends who participated in the escapades and dealt with the consequences of Lucy's well-intentioned plans. Other famous actors guest-starred on the show in later years, including Harpo Marx, Rock Hudson, William Holden and John Wayne. This was the first sitcom to be filmed live before a studio audience and it did extremely well in the ratings both the first time around and in reruns.

MY MOM IS A STUDENT DAY. Oct 15. Kids can show their support to their moms by treating them with new pens, paper clips and other little school supplies. They can also fix mom a school lunch with a supportive note inside. Annually, Oct 15. For info: Patti Veld, c/o Davenport College Library, 8200 Georgia St, Merrillville, IN 46410.

NATIONAL GROUCH DAY. Oct 15. Honor a grouch; all grouches deserve a day to be recognized. Annually, Oct 15. For info: Alan R. Miller, Carter Middle School, 300 Upland Dr, Room 207, Clio, MI 48420. Phone: (810) 591-0503.

NORTH CAROLINA STATE FAIR. Oct 15–24 (tentative). State Fairgrounds, Raleigh, NC. Agricultural fair with livestock, arts and crafts, home arts, entertainment and carnival. Est attendance: 750,000. For info: Sam Rand, Mgr, North Carolina State Fair, 1025 Blue Ridge Blvd, Raleigh, NC 27607. Phone: (919) 821-7400. Fax: (919) 733-5079. Web: www.agr.state.nc.us/fair/

SPACE MILESTONE: *CASSINI* (US). Oct 15, 1997. The plutonium-powered spacecraft is to arrive at Saturn in July 2004. It will orbit the planet, take pictures of its 18 known moons and dispatch a probe to Titan, the largest of these moons.

★**WHITE CANE SAFETY DAY.** Oct 15. Presidential Proclamation always issued for Oct 15 since 1964 (PL88–628 of Oct 6, 1964).

WILSON, EDITH BOLLING GALT: BIRTH ANNIVERSARY. Oct 15, 1872. Second wife of Woodrow Wilson, 28th president of the US, born at Wytheville, VA. She died at Washington, DC, Dec 28, 1961.

BIRTHDAYS TODAY

Barry Moser, 59, illustrator (*The Bird House*), born Chattanooga, TN, Oct 15, 1940.

OCTOBER 16 — SATURDAY

Day 289 — 76 Remaining

AMERICA'S FIRST DEPARTMENT STORE: ANNIVERSARY. Oct 16, 1868. Salt Lake City, UT. America's first department store, "ZCMI" (Zion's Co-Operative Mercantile Institution), is still operating at Salt Lake City. It was founded under the direction of Brigham Young. For info: Museum of Church History and Art, 45 North West Temple, Salt Lake City, UT 84150. Phone: (801) 240-4604.

BEN-GURION, DAVID: BIRTH ANNIVERSARY. Oct 16, 1886. First prime minister of the state of Israel. Born at Plonsk, Poland, died at Tel Aviv, Israel, Dec 1, 1973.

DICTIONARY DAY. Oct 16. The birthday of Noah Webster, American teacher and lexicographer, is occasion to encourage every person to acquire at least one dictionary—and to use it regularly. See Curriculum Connection.

OCTOBER 16
DICTIONARY DAY

On the birthday of Noah Webster, the compiler of the first dictionary of American English, start with a word jar or box and a designated dictionary (it can be an inexpensive paperback) in which words placed in the word jar will be highlighted with a yellow marker. Begin the collection with several words you think your students will find interesting. Your contributions might include onomatopoeia, really long words, silly words or useful words. Write each word on a slip of paper about the size of an index card. Include on the card the correct spelling of the word, its definition, an example of how it is used in a sentence and your name. Share your words with your students. Then hand out slips of paper to the class. Ask them to write down a word they like, along with the information suggested above. Emphasize that all words must have a student's name on them and that no profanity will be permitted. (If any finds its way in, throw it away without public acknowledgment.) Words deposited can be shared with the class as daily or weekly word study period, a blackboard list, a spelling test or prompt for a writing assignment.

On a weekly basis, students' slips are given to an official highlighter (rotate to a different student weekly), who highlights the words in the designated classroom dictionary. This dictionary is always available. Students checking out the page with their contribution will see what other words are on the page. Before they know it, they've read another word and definition—perhaps one to add to the jar.

If you add at least one word per week, it will continue stimulating student interest. By using words that occur during instructional periods or read aloud sessions, you can model the behavior you hope your students will use.

The index card slips can be stapled into weekly word booklets (with covers) that students can sign out, take home overnight or read at their desks. It's also fun to share them with other classes.

Children love to watch the yellow highlights increase in the dictionary, and it gives them a sense of accomplishment.

DOUGLAS, WILLIAM ORVILLE: BIRTH ANNIVERSARY. Oct 16, 1898. American jurist, world traveler, conservationist, outdoorsman and author. Born at Maine, MN, he served as justice of the US Supreme Court longer than any other (36 years). Died at Washington, DC, Jan 19, 1980.

GRANT PUT IN CHARGE OF THE MISSISSIPPI REGION: ANNIVERSARY. Oct 16, 1863. After his impressive success taking Vicksburg, MS, Ulysses S. Grant, a brigadier general of the militia, was appointed a general in the regular army and, with the subsequent reorganization of the departments of war at Ohio, Cumberland and Tennessee, was placed in charge of the newly formed Military Division of the Mississippi. Grant's first priority was to save the besieged and starving Union troops at Chattanooga, TN.

JOHN BROWN'S RAID: ANNIVERSARY. Oct 16, 1859. Abolitionist John Brown, with a band of about 20 men, seized the US Arsenal at Harpers Ferry, WV. Brown was captured and the insurrection put down by Oct 19. Brown was hanged at Charles Town, WV, Dec 2, 1859.

MILLION MAN MARCH: ANNIVERSARY. Oct 16, 1995. Hundreds of thousands of black men met at Washington, DC, for a "holy day of atonement and reconciliation" organized by Louis

Farrakhan, leader of the Nation of Islam. Marchers pledged to take responsibility for themselves, their families and their communities.

UNITED NATIONS: WORLD FOOD DAY. Oct 16. Annual observance to heighten public awareness of the world food problem and to strengthen solidarity in the struggle against hunger, malnutrition and poverty. Date of observance is anniversary of founding of Food and Agriculture Organization (FAO), Oct 16, 1945, at Quebec, Canada. For info: United Nations, Dept of Public Info, New York, NY 10017.

WEBSTER, NOAH: BIRTH ANNIVERSARY. Oct 16, 1758. American teacher and journalist whose name became synonymous with the word "dictionary" after his compilations of the earliest American dictionaries of the English language. Born at West Hartford, CT, he died at New Haven, CT, May 28, 1843. See Curriculum Connection.

WORLD FOOD DAY. Oct 16. To increase awareness, understanding and informed action on hunger. Annually, on the founding date of the UN Food and Agriculture Organization. For info: Patricia Young, US Natl Committee for World Food Day, 2175 K St NW, Washington DC, 20437. Phone: (202) 653-2404. Web: www.gsu.edu/~wwwwfd.

WORLD RAINFOREST WEEK. Oct 16–24. Rainforest activists from 140 worldwide action groups will sponsor events to increase public awareness of rainforest destruction and motivate people to protect the Earth's rainforest and support the rights of their inhabitants. The global rate of destruction of rainforests is 2.4 acres per second—equivalent to two US football fields. For info: M. Holmgren, Grassroots Coord, Rainforest Action Network, 221 Pine St, 5th Floor, San Francisco, CA 94104. Phone: (415) 398-4404. E-mail: rags@ran.org. Web: www.ran.org.

BIRTHDAYS TODAY

Joseph Bruchac, 57, author (*The Boy Who Lived with Bears and Other Iroquois Stories*), born Saratoga Springs, NY, Oct 16, 1942.

Paul Kariya, 25, hockey player, born Vancouver, British Columbia, Canada, Oct 16, 1974.

Kordell Stewart, 27, football player, born New Orleans, LA, Oct 16, 1972.

OCTOBER 17 — SUNDAY

Day 290 — 75 Remaining

AMERICA'S SAFE SCHOOLS WEEK. Oct 17–23. To motivate key education and law enforcement policymakers, as well as parents, students and community residents, to vigorously advocate schools that are safe and free of violence, weapons and drugs. Annually, the third week in October. For info: National School Safety Center, 4165 Thousand Oaks Blvd, Westlake Village, CA 91362. Phone: (805) 373-9977. Web: nssc1.org/safeweek.htm.

HAMMON, JUPITER: BIRTH ANNIVERSARY. Oct 17, 1711. America's first published black poet, whose birth anniversary is celebrated annually as Black Poetry Day (Oct 18 this year), was born into slavery, probably at Long Island, NY. He was taught to

	S	M	T	W	T	F	S
October						1	2
1999	3	4	5	6	7	8	9
	10	11	12	13	14	15	16
	17	18	19	20	21	22	23
	24	25	26	27	28	29	30
	31						

read, however, and as a trusted servant was allowed to use his master's library. "With the publication on Christmas Day, 1760, of the 88-line broadside poem 'An Evening Thought,' Jupiter Hammon, then 49, became the first black in America to publish poetry." Hammon died in 1790. The exact date and place of his death are unknown.

HONG KONG: CHUNG YEUNG FESTIVAL. Oct 17. This festival relates to the old story of the Han Dynasty, when a soothsayer advised a man to take his family to a high place on the ninth day of the ninth moon for 24 hours in order to avoid disaster. The man obeyed and found, on returning home, that all living things had died a sudden death in his absence. Part of the celebration is climbing to high places.

JOHNSON, RICHARD MENTOR: BIRTH ANNIVERSARY. Oct 17, 1780. Ninth vice president of the US (1837–41). Born at Floyd's Station, KY, he died at Frankfort, KY, Nov 19, 1850.

MOON PHASE: FIRST QUARTER. Oct 17. Moon enters First Quarter phase at 11 AM, EST.

★**NATIONAL FOREST PRODUCTS WEEK.** Oct 17–23. Presidential Proclamation always issued for the week beginning with the third Sunday in October since 1960 (PL86–753 of Sept 13, 1960).

NATIONAL SCHOOL BUS SAFETY WEEK. Oct 17–23. This week is set aside to focus attention on school bus safety—from the standpoint of the bus drivers, students and the motoring public. Annually, the third full week of October, starting on Sunday. For info: Natl School Bus Safety Week Committee, PO Box 2639, Springfield, VA 22152.

POPE JOHN PAUL I: BIRTH ANNIVERSARY. Oct 17, 1912. Albino Luciani, 263rd pope of the Roman Catholic Church. Born at Forno di Canale, Italy, he was elected pope Aug 26, 1978. Died at Rome, 34 days after his election, Sept 28, 1978. Shortest papacy since Pope Leo XI (Apr 1–27, 1605).

SAN FRANCISCO 1989 EARTHQUAKE: 10th ANNIVERSARY. Oct 17, 1989. The San Francisco Bay area was rocked by an earthquake registering 7.1 on the Richter scale at 5:04 PM, EDT, just as the nation's baseball fans settled in to watch the 1989 World Series. A large audience was tuned in to the pregame coverage when the quake hit and knocked the broadcast off the air. The quake caused damage estimated at $10 billion and killed 67 people, many of whom were caught in the collapse of the double-decked Interstate 80, at Oakland, CA.

TEEN READ WEEK. Oct 17–23. The teen years are a time when many kids reject reading as being just another dreary assignment. The goal of Teen Read Week is to encourage young adults to read for sheer pleasure as well as learning. Also to remind parents, teachers and others that reading for fun is important for teens as well as young children and to increase awareness of the resources available at libraries. For info: Young Adult Library Services Assn, American Library Assn, 50 E Huron St, Chicago, IL 60611. Phone: (800) 545-2433, ext 4390. E-mail: yalsa@ala.org. Web: www.ala.org/teenread.

UNITED NATIONS: INTERNATIONAL DAY FOR THE ERADICATION OF POVERTY. Oct 17. The General Assembly proclaimed this observance (Res 47/196) to promote public awareness of the need to eradicate poverty and destitution in all countries, particularly the developing nations. For further info, go to the UN's website for children at www.un.org/Pubs/Cyber SchoolBus/

BIRTHDAYS TODAY

Brandon Call, 23, actor ("Step By Step"), born Torrance, CA, Oct 17, 1976.

Judith Caseley, 48, author (*When Grandpa Came to Stay*), born Rahway, NJ, Oct 17, 1951.

Alan Garner, 65, author (*The Stone Book*), born Congleton, England, Oct 17, 1934.

Mae Jemison, 43, scientist, astronaut, host ("Susan B. Anthony Slept Here"), born Decatur, AL, Oct 17, 1956.

OCTOBER 18 — MONDAY

Day 291 — 74 Remaining

ALASKA DAY. Oct 18. Alaska. Anniversary of transfer of Alaska from Russia to the US which became official on Sitka's Castle Hill in 1867. This is a holiday in Alaska; when it falls on a weekend it is observed on the following Monday.

BLACK POETRY DAY. Oct 18 (tentative). To recognize the contribution of black poets to American life and culture and to honor Jupiter Hammon, first black in America to publish his own verse. Jupiter Hammon of Huntington, Long Island, NY, was born Oct 17, 1711. Est attendance: 200. For info: Alexis Levitin, Black Poetry Day Committee, Dept of English, SUNY-Plattsburgh, Plattsburgh, NY 12901-2681. Phone: (518) 564-2426. Fax: (518) 564-2140. E-mail: levitia@splava.cc.plattsburgh.edu.

JAMAICA: NATIONAL HEROES DAY. Oct 18. National holiday established in 1969. Always observed on third Monday of October.

NATIONAL HEALTH EDUCATION WEEK. Oct 18–24. Annually, the third week in October. For info: Lynne Whitt, Natl Center for Health Education, 72 Spring St, Ste 208, New York, NY 10012. Phone: (212) 334-9470.

SAINT LUKE: FEAST DAY. Oct 18. Patron saint of doctors and artists, himself a physician and painter, authorship of the third Gospel and Acts of the Apostles is attributed to him. Died about AD 68. Legend says that he painted portraits of Mary and Jesus.

VIRGIN ISLANDS: HURRICANE THANKSGIVING DAY. Oct 18. Third Monday of October is a legal holiday celebrating the end of hurricane season.

WATER POLLUTION CONTROL ACT: ANNIVERSARY. Oct 18, 1972. Overriding President Nixon's veto, Congress passed a $25 billion Water Pollution Control Act.

BIRTHDAYS TODAY

Joyce Hansen, 57, author (*I Thought My Soul Would Rise and Fly: The Diary of Patsy, a Freed Girl*), born New York, NY, Oct 18, 1942.

Jesse Helms, 78, US Senator (R, North Carolina), born Monroe, NC, Oct 18, 1921.

Shel Silverstein, 67, cartoonist, children's author (*A Light in the Attic, Where the Sidewalk Ends, The Giving Tree*), born Chicago, IL, Oct 18, 1932.

OCTOBER 19 — TUESDAY

Day 292 — 73 Remaining

JEFFERSON, MARTHA WAYLES SKELTON: BIRTH ANNIVERSARY. Oct 19, 1748. Wife of Thomas Jefferson, third president of the US. Born at Charles City County, VA, she died at Monticello, VA, Sept 6, 1782.

YORKTOWN DAY: "AMERICA'S REAL INDEPENDENCE DAY." Oct 19. Yorktown, VA. Representatives of the US, France and other nations involved in the American Revolution gather to celebrate the anniversary of the victory (Oct 19, 1781) that assured American independence. Parade and commemorative ceremonies. Annually, Oct 19. Est attendance: 2,000. For info: Activities Coord, Colonial National Historical Park, Box 210, Yorktown, VA 23690. Phone: (757) 898-3400. Web: www.nps.gov/colo.

YORKTOWN DAY: ANNIVERSARY. Oct 19, 1781. More than 7,000 English and Hessian troops, led by British General Lord Cornwallis, surrendered to General George Washington at Yorktown, VA, effectively ending the war between Britain and her American colonies. There were no more major battles, but the provisional treaty of peace was not signed until Nov 30, 1782, and the final Treaty of Paris, Sept 3, 1783.

BIRTHDAYS TODAY

Philip Pullman, 53, author of fantasy fiction (*The Subtle Knife*), born Norwich, England, Oct 19, 1946.

OCTOBER 20 — WEDNESDAY

Day 293 — 72 Remaining

DEWEY, JOHN: BIRTH ANNIVERSARY. Oct 20, 1859. Philosopher of education, born near Burlington, VT. A professor at the University of Chicago and Columbia University, Dewey was committed to child-centered education, learning by doing and integrating schools with the outside world. He died at New York, NY, June 2, 1952.

GUATEMALA: REVOLUTION DAY. Oct 20. Public holiday in Guatemala.

KENYA: KENYATTA DAY. Oct 20. Observed as a public holiday. Honors Jomo Kenyatta, first president of Kenya.

MacARTHUR RETURNS: US LANDINGS ON LEYTE, PHILIPPINES: 55TH ANNIVERSARY. Oct 20, 1944. In mid-September of 1944 American military leaders made the decision to begin the invasion of the Philippines on Leyte, a small island north of the Surigao Strait. With General Douglas MacArthur in overall command, US aircraft dropped hundreds of tons of bombs in the area of Dulag. Four divisions landed on the east coast, and after a few hours General MacArthur set foot on Philippine soil for the first time since he was ordered to Australia Mar 11, 1942, thus fulfilling his promise, "I shall return."

MANTLE, MICKEY: BIRTH ANNIVERSARY. Oct 20, 1931. Baseball Hall of Famer, born at Spavinaw, OK. Died Aug 13, 1995, at Dallas, TX.

MISSOURI DAY. Oct 20. Observed by teachers and pupils of schools with appropriate exercises throughout state of Missouri. Annually, the third Wednesday of October.

BIRTHDAYS TODAY

Peter Fitzgerald, 39, US Senator (R, Illinois), born Elgin, IL, Oct 20, 1960.
Nikki Grimes, 49, poet and author (*Meet Danitra Brown*), also writes as Naomi McMillen, born New York, NY, Oct 20, 1950.
Eddie Jones, 28, basketball player, born Pompano Beach, FL, Oct 20, 1971.

OCTOBER 21 — THURSDAY
Day 294 — 71 Remaining

ARIZONA STATE FAIR. Oct 21–Nov 7. Phoenix, AZ. Festival, concerts, flea markets, entertainment and food. For info: Marketing Dept, Arizona State Fair, PO Box 6728, Phoenix, AZ 85005. Phone: (602) 252-6771. Fax: (602) 495-1302.

THE DAY OF NATIONAL CONCERN ABOUT YOUNG PEOPLE AND GUN VIOLENCE. Oct 21. Students are encouraged on this day to sign a pledge that they will never carry a gun to school or resolve a dispute with a gun and they will urge their friends to do the same. More than 1,000,000 middle and high school students have signed the Pledge Against Gun Violence. For info: Student Pledge Against Gun Violence, 112 Nevada St, Northfield, MN 55057. Phone: (507) 645-5378. Web: www.pledge.org.

FILLMORE, CAROLINE CARMICHAEL McINTOSH: BIRTH ANNIVERSARY. Oct 21, 1813. Second wife of Millard Fillmore, 13th president of the US, born at Morristown, NJ. Died at New York, Aug 11, 1881.

INCANDESCENT LAMP DEMONSTRATED: ANNIVERSARY. Oct 21, 1879. Thomas A. Edison demonstrated the first incandescent lamp that could be used economically for domestic purposes. This prototype, developed at his Menlo Park, NJ, laboratory, could burn for 13- ½ hours.

NOBEL, ALFRED BERNHARD: BIRTH ANNIVERSARY. Oct 21, 1833. Swedish chemist and engineer who invented dynamite was born at Stockholm, Sweden, and died at San Remo, Italy, Dec 10, 1896. His will established the Nobel Prize.

SOMALIA DEMOCRATIC REPUBLIC: NATIONAL DAY. Oct 21. National holiday. Anniversary of the revolution.

TAIWAN: OVERSEAS CHINESE DAY. Oct 21. Thousands of overseas Chinese come to Taiwan for this and other occasions that make October a particularly memorable month.

	S	M	T	W	T	F	S
October						1	2
1999	3	4	5	6	7	8	9
	10	11	12	13	14	15	16
	17	18	19	20	21	22	23
	24	25	26	27	28	29	30
	31						

BIRTHDAYS TODAY

Janet Ahlberg, 55, illustrator (*The Jolly Postman*), born Croydon, England, Oct 21, 1944.
Nakia Burrise, 25, actress (*Turbo: A Power Rangers Movie*, "Power Rangers Turbo"), born San Diego, CA, Oct 21, 1974.
Ursula K. LeGuin, 70, author of science fiction (*The Tombs of Atuan*), born Berkeley, CA, Oct 21, 1929.
Jeremy Miller, 23, actor ("Growing Pains"), born West Covina, CA, Oct 21, 1976.
Benjamin Netanyahu, 50, Israeli prime minister, born Tel Aviv, Israel, Oct 21, 1949.

OCTOBER 22 — FRIDAY
Day 295 — 70 Remaining

FOXX, JIMMIE: BIRTH ANNIVERSARY. Oct 22, 1907. Baseball Hall of Fame first baseman born at Sudlersville, MD. Died at Miami, FL, July 21, 1967.

HOLY SEE: NATIONAL HOLIDAY. Oct 22. The state of Vatican City and the Holy See observe Oct 22 as a national holiday.

LISZT, FRANZ: BIRTH ANNIVERSARY. Oct 22, 1811. Hungarian pianist and composer (*Hungarian Rhapsodies*). Born at Raiding, Hungary, he died July 31, 1886, at Bayreuth, Germany.

RANDOLPH, PEYTON: DEATH ANNIVERSARY. Oct 22, 1775. First president of the Continental Congress, died at Philadelphia, PA. Born about 1721 (exact date unknown), at Williamsburg, VA.

STATE FAIR OF LOUISIANA. Oct 22–Nov 7. Fairgrounds, Shreveport, LA. Educational, agricultural, commercial exhibits, entertainment. Est attendance: 250,000. For info: Sam Giordano, Pres/Genl Mgr, Louisiana State Fairgrounds, PO Box 38327, Shreveport, LA 71133. Phone: (318) 635-1361. Fax: (318) 631-4909.

BIRTHDAYS TODAY

Brian Anthony Boitano, 36, Olympic gold medal figure skater, born Mountain View, CA, Oct 22, 1963.
John Hubbard Chafee, 77, US Senator (R, Rhode Island), born Providence, RI, Oct 22, 1922.
Jeff Goldblum, 47, actor (*The Lost World: Jurassic Park*), born Pittsburgh, PA, Oct 22, 1952.
Zachary Walker Hanson, 14, singer (Hanson), born Arlington, VA, Oct 22, 1985.
Bill Owens, 49, Governor of Colorado (R), born Fort Worth, TX, Oct 22, 1950.

OCTOBER 23 — SATURDAY
Day 296 — 69 Remaining

APPERT, NICOLAS: BIRTH ANNIVERSARY. Oct 23, 1752. Also known as "Canning Day," this is the anniversary of the birth of French chef, chemist, confectioner, inventor and author Nicolas Appert, at Chalons-Sur-Marne. Appert, who also invented the bouillon tablet, is best remembered for devising a system of heating foods and sealing them in airtight containers. Known as the "father of canning," Appert won a prize of 12,000 francs from the French government in 1809, and the title "Benefactor of Humanity" in 1812, for his inventions which revolutionized our previously seasonal diet. Appert died at Massy, France, June 3, 1841.

CHILDREN'S LITERATURE FESTIVAL. Oct 23. Keene State College, Keene, NH. To promote the reading, studying and use of children's literature. Speakers for the festival include Phyllis Reynolds Naylor, P.J. Lynch, Mark Teague, Janet Stevens and Denise Fleming. For info: Dr. David E. White, Festival Dir, Keene State College, 229 Main St, Keene, NH 03435. Phone: (603) 358-2302. E-mail: dwhite@keene.edu. Web: amazon.keene.edu.

HUNGARY: ANNIVERSARY OF 1956 REVOLUTION. Oct 23. National holiday.

HUNGARY DECLARED INDEPENDENT: 10th ANNIVERSARY. Oct 23, 1989. Hungary declared itself an independent republic, 33 years after Russian troops crushed a popular revolt against Soviet rule. The announcement followed a week-long purge by Parliament of the Stalinist elements from Hungary's 1949 constitution, which defined the country as a socialist people's republic. Acting head of state Matyas Szuros made the declaration in front of tens of thousands of Hungarians at Parliament Square, speaking from the same balcony from which Imre Nagy addressed rebels 33 years earlier. Nagy was hanged for treason after Soviet intervention. Free elections held in March 1990 removed the Communist party to the ranks of the opposition for the first time in four decades.

MAKE A DIFFERENCE DAY. Oct 23. This national day of community service is sponsored by *USA Weekend* (a Sunday supplement delivered in more than 500 newspapers). Volunteer projects completed are judged by well-known celebrities and 164 winning projects receive $2,000 each to donate to their charity of choice. Key projects are honored in April during National Volunteer Week at a special Make A Difference Day awards luncheon and at the White House. The Points of Light Foundation is a partner. More than one million people nationwide participate. For info: Make a Difference Day, USA Weekend, 1000 Wilson Blvd, Arlington, VA 22229-0012. Phone: (800) 416-3824 or (703) 276-4531. Web: www.usaweekend.com (keyword: diffday).

RHODE ISLAND FESTIVAL OF CHILDREN'S BOOKS AND AUTHORS. Oct 23–24. Lincoln School, Providence, RI. 11th annual. The festival provides an opportunity for readers of children's books to meet authors and illustrators. Kids can also enjoy performers, crafts, book-related videos and meeting popular book characters. For info: Development Office, Lincoln School, 301 Butler Ave, Providence, RI 02906-5545. Phone: (401) 331-9696.

SCORPIO, THE SCORPION. Oct 23–Nov 22. In the astronomical/astrological zodiac that divides the sun's apparent orbit into 12 segments, the period Oct 23–Nov 22 is identified, traditionally, as the sun sign of Scorpio, the Scorpion. The ruling planet is Pluto or Mars.

STEVENSON, ADLAI EWING: BIRTH ANNIVERSARY. Oct 23, 1835. Twenty-third vice president of the US (1893–97) born at Christian County, KY. Died at Chicago, IL, June 14, 1914. He was grandfather of Adlai E. Stevenson, the Democratic candidate for president in 1952 and 1956.

THAILAND: CHULALONGKORN DAY. Oct 23. Annual commemoration of the death of King Chulalongkorn the Great, who died Oct 23, 1910, after a 42-year reign. King Chulalongkorn abolished slavery in Thailand. Special ceremonies with floral tributes and incense at the foot of his equestrian statue in front of Bangkok's National Assembly Hall.

BIRTHDAYS TODAY

Jim Bunning, 68, US Senator (R, Kentucky), born Southgate, KY, Oct 23, 1931.
Pele, 59, former soccer player, born Edson Arantes do Nascimento, Tres Coracoes, Brazil, Oct 23, 1940.

Keith Van Horn, 24, basketball player, born Fullerton, CA, Oct 23, 1975.
"Weird Al" Yankovic, 40, singer, satirist ("The Weird Al Show"), born Lynwood, CA, Oct 23, 1959.

OCTOBER 24 — SUNDAY
Day 297 — 68 Remaining

HUNTER'S MOON. Oct 24. The full moon following Harvest Moon. So called because the moon's light in evening extends day's length for hunters. Moon enters Full Moon phase at 5:02 PM, EDT.

MOON PHASE: FULL MOON. Oct 24. Moon enters Full Moon phase at 5:02 PM, EDT.

SHERMAN, JAMES SCHOOLCRAFT: BIRTH ANNIVERSARY. Oct 24, 1855. Twenty-seventh vice president of the US (1909–12), born at Utica, NY. Died there Oct 30, 1912.

★ **UNITED NATIONS DAY.** Oct 24. Presidential Proclamation. Always issued for Oct 24 since 1948. (By unanimous request of the UN General Assembly.)

UNITED NATIONS DAY: ANNIVERSARY OF FOUNDING. Oct 24, 1945. Official United Nations holiday commemorates founding of the United Nations and effective date of the United Nations Charter. In 1971 the General Assembly recommended this day be observed as a public holiday by UN Member States (Res 2782/xxvi). For further info, visit the UN's website for children at www.un.org/Pubs/CyberSchoolBus/

UNITED NATIONS: DISARMAMENT WEEK. Oct 24–30. In 1978, the General Assembly called on member states to highlight the danger of the arms race, propagate the need for its cessation and increase public understanding of the urgent task of disarmament. Observed annually, beginning on the anniversary of the founding of the UN.

UNITED NATIONS: WORLD DEVELOPMENT INFORMATION DAY. Oct 24. Anniversary of adoption by United Nations General Assembly, in 1970, of the International Development Strategy for the Second United Nations Development Decade. Object is to "draw the attention of the world public opinion each year to development problems and the necessity of strengthening international cooperation to solve them." For info: United Nations, Dept of Public Info, New York, NY 10017.

ZAMBIA: INDEPENDENCE DAY: 35th ANNIVERSARY. Oct 24. Zambia. National holiday commemorates independence of what was then Northern Rhodesia from Britain in 1964. Celebrations in all cities, but main parades of military, labor and youth organizations are at capital, Lusaka.

Kweisi Mfume, 51, NAACP president, born Baltimore, MD, Oct 24, 1948.

Catherine Sutherland, 25, actress (*Turbo: A Power Rangers Movie*, "Power Rangers Turbo"), born Sydney, Australia, Oct 24, 1974.

OCTOBER 25 — MONDAY
Day 298 — 67 Remaining

PICASSO, PABLO RUIZ: BIRTH ANNIVERSARY. Oct 25, 1881. Called by many the greatest artist of the 20th century, Pablo Picasso excelled as a painter, sculptor and engraver. He is said to have commented once: "I am only a public entertainer who has understood his time." Born at Malaga, Spain, he died Apr 9, 1973, at Mougins, France.

STATE CONSTITUTION DAY IN MASSACHUSETTS. Oct 25. Proclaimed annually by the governor to commemorate the adoption of the state constitution in 1780.

TAIWAN: RETROCESSION DAY. Oct 25. Commemorates restoration of Taiwan to Chinese rule in 1945, after half a century of Japanese occupation.

BIRTHDAYS TODAY

Benjamin Gould, 19, actor ("Saved By the Bell: The New Class"), born Sacramento, CA, Oct 25, 1980.

Pedro Martinez, 28, baseball player, born Manoguyabo, Dominican Republic, Oct 25, 1971.

Midori, 28, violinist, born Qsaka, Japan, Oct 25, 1971.

OCTOBER 26 — TUESDAY
Day 299 — 66 Remaining

AUSTRIA: NATIONAL DAY. Oct 26. National holiday observed.

ERIE CANAL: ANNIVERSARY. Oct 26, 1825. The Erie Canal, first US major man-made waterway, was opened, providing a water route from Lake Erie to the Hudson River. Construction started July 4, 1817, and the canal cost $7,602,000. Cannons fired and celebrations were held all along the route for the opening. See Curriculum Connection.

MULE DAY. Oct 26. Anniversary of the first importation of Spanish jacks to the US, a gift from King Charles III of Spain. Mules are said to have been bred first in this country by George Washington from a pair delivered at Boston, Oct 26, 1785.

BIRTHDAYS TODAY

Hillary Rodham Clinton, 52, First Lady, wife of Bill Clinton, 42nd president of the US, born Park Ridge, IL, Oct 26, 1947.

Steven Kellogg, 58, author and illustrator (*Can I Keep Him?*), born Norwalk, CT, Oct 26, 1941.

	S	M	T	W	T	F	S
October						1	2
1999	3	4	5	6	7	8	9
	10	11	12	13	14	15	16
	17	18	19	20	21	22	23
	24	25	26	27	28	29	30
	31						

OCTOBER 26
ERIE CANAL OPENED

After eight long years of construction, the first barge, the *Seneca Chief*, floated the length of the Erie Canal on this day in 1825. For many years people dreamed of a waterway connecting the Great Lakes to the Atlantic Ocean. The first important waterway built in the US, the Erie Canal's length spanned 363 miles. Travel time from Troy and Albany, in eastern New York on the Hudson River, to Buffalo, on Lake Erie, was reduced from several weeks to less than ten days.

Learning about the Erie Canal is especially important for units on settling the American West. The opening of the Canal paved the way for a flood of settlers and manufactured goods into the country's interior. Also, agricultural products and timber from the western areas could be carried swiftly to the east coast.

Students can plot and trace the route of the canal on a map of New York. Discuss why that particular route was chosen and how difficulties were solved. The construction of locks was crucial. A group of students could draw diagrams or build a model of a lock.

Older students could enact DeWitt Clinton's petition to the New York state legislature for funds to build the canal. (The federal government had denied Clinton's request for building funds.) They could also compare and contrast the building of the Erie Canal with that of the Panama Canal, discussing the impact each had on its respective time period. Finally, they could research early railroads in America and the impact they had on canals.

Because Oct 26 is also Mule Day (see separate entry), students can learn the song "Erie Canal." Mules supplied the power needed to pull the barges along the canal. *The Amazing, Impossible Erie Canal*, by Cheryl Harness (Simon & Schuster, 0-02-742641-6, $16 Gr. 3–8) is an entertaining introduction to the building of the canal and also contains the lyrics and music to the song. Visit the New York State Canal System's website at www.canals.state.nys.us/canals/erie_canal.htm for additional information on the canal's history and recreational use today.

OCTOBER 27 — WEDNESDAY
Day 300 — 65 Remaining

BAGNOLD, ENID: BIRTH ANNIVERSARY. Oct 27, 1889. Novelist and playwright (*National Velvet*), born at Rochester, Kent, England. She died at London, England, Mar 31, 1981.

COOK, JAMES: BIRTH ANNIVERSARY. Oct 27, 1728. English sea captain and explorer who discovered the Hawaiian Islands and brought Australia and New Zealand into the British Empire. Born at Marton-in-Cleveland, Yorkshire, England and was killed Feb 14, 1779, at Hawaii.

HURRICANE MITCH: ANNIVERSARY. Oct 27, 1998. More than 6,000 people were killed in Honduras by flooding caused by Hurricane Mitch. Several thousand more were killed in other Central American countries, especially Nicaragua. On Sept 21, 1974, more than 8,000 people had been killed in Honduras by flooding caused by a hurricane.

NATIONAL FFA CONVENTION. Oct 27–30. Kentucky Fair & Exposition Center, Louisville, KY. This 72nd annual convention is an opportunity for recognition, business, elections and celebration. Delegates from each state discuss topics affecting the national agriculture education organization and elect a new team of national officers. Students compete in final rounds of leadership and career events and learn about education and career opportunities in a 300-exhibitor career show. Est attendance: 45,000. For info: Natl FFA Organization, 5632 Mt Vernon Memorial Hwy, Alexandria, VA 22309-0160. Phone: (703) 360-3600. Fax: (703) 360-5524. Web: www.ffa.org.

NAVY DAY. Oct 27. Observed since 1922.

NEW YORK CITY SUBWAY: 95th ANNIVERSARY. Oct 27, 1904. Running from City Hall to West 145th St, the New York City subway began operation. It was privately operated by the Interborough Rapid Transit Company and later became part of the system operated by the New York City Transit Authority.

ROOSEVELT, THEODORE: BIRTH ANNIVERSARY. Oct 27, 1858. Twenty-sixth president of the US, succeeded to the presidency on the assassination of William McKinley. His term of office: Sept 14, 1901–Mar 3, 1909. Roosevelt was the first president to ride in an automobile (1902), to submerge in a submarine (1905) and to fly in an airplane (1910). Although his best remembered quote is, "Speak softly and carry a big stick," he also said, "The first requisite of a good citizen in this Republic of ours is that he shall be able and willing to pull his weight." Born at New York, NY, Roosevelt died at Oyster Bay, NY, Jan 6, 1919. His last words: "Put out the light."

SAINT VINCENT AND THE GRENADINES: INDEPENDENCE DAY. Oct 27. National Day.

TURKMENISTAN: INDEPENDENCE DAY. Oct 27. National holiday. Commemorates independence from the Soviet Union in 1991.

"WALT DISNEY" TV PREMIERE: 45th ANNIVERSARY. Oct 27, 1954. This highly successful and long-running show appeared on different networks under different names but was essentially the same show. It was the first ABC series to break the Nielsen's Top Twenty and the first prime-time anthology series for kids. "Walt Disney" was originally titled "Disneyland" to promote the park and upcoming Disney releases. Later the title was changed to "Walt Disney Presents"; when it switched networks, it was called "Walt Disney's Wonderful World of Color" to highlight its being broadcast in color. Future titles included "The Wonderful World of Disney," "Disney's Wonderful World," "The Disney Sunday Movie" and "The Magical World of Disney." Presentations included edited versions of previously released Disney films and original productions (including natural history documentaries, behind-the-scenes at Disney shows and dramatic shows, including the popular Davy Crockett segments that were the first TV miniseries). The show went off the air in Dec 1980 after 25 years, making it the longest-running series in prime-time TV history.

BIRTHDAYS TODAY

Brad Radke, 27, baseball player, born Eau Claire, WI, Oct 27, 1972.

OCTOBER 28 — THURSDAY

Day 301 — 64 Remaining

CZECH REPUBLIC: FOUNDATION OF THE REPUBLIC: ANNIVERSARY. Oct 28, 1918. National Day, anniversary of the bloodless revolution in Prague, after which the Czechs and

Slovaks united to form Czechoslovakia (a union they dissolved without bloodshed in 1993).

GREECE: "OHI DAY." Oct 28. National holiday commemorating Greek resistance and refusal to open her borders when Mussolini's Italian troops attacked Greece in 1940. "Ohi" means no! Celebrated with military parades, especially at Athens and Thessaloniki.

NATIONAL MIDDLE SCHOOL ASSOCIATION ANNUAL CONFERENCE. Oct 28–Nov 1. Convention Center, Orlando, FL. For info: Natl Middle School Assn, 2600 Corporate Exchange Dr, Ste 370, Columbus, OH 43231. Phone: (614) 895-4730 or (800) 528-NMSA. Web: www.nmsa.org.

SAINT JUDE'S DAY. Oct 28. St. Jude, the saint of hopeless causes, was martyred along with St. Simon at Persia, and their feast is celebrated jointly. St. Jude was supposedly the brother of Jesus, and, like his brother, a carpenter by trade. He is most popular with those who attempt the impossible and with students, who often ask for his help on exams.

SALK, JONAS: 85th BIRTH ANNIVERSARY. Oct 28, 1914. Dr. Jonas Salk, developer of the Salk polio vaccine, was born at New York, NY. Salk announced his development of a successful vaccine in 1953, the year after a polio epidemic claimed some 3,300 lives in the US. Polio deaths were reduced by 95 percent after the introduction of the vaccine. Salk spent the last 10 years of his life doing AIDS research. He died June 23, 1995, at La Jolla, CA.

SPACE MILESTONE: INTERNATIONAL SPACE RESCUE AGREEMENT. Oct 28, 1970. US and USSR officials agreed upon space rescue cooperation.

STATUE OF LIBERTY: DEDICATION ANNIVERSARY. Oct 28, 1886. Frederic Auguste Bartholdi's famous sculpture, the statue of *Liberty Enlightening the World*, on Bedloe's Island at New York Harbor, was dedicated. Ground breaking for the structure was in April 1883. A sonnet by Emma Lazarus, inside the pedestal of the statue, contains the words: "Give me your tired, your poor, your huddled masses yearning to breathe free, the wretched refuse of your teeming shore. Send these, the homeless, tempest-tost to me, I lift my lamp beside the golden door!" For further info, visit the National Parks Service website at www.nps.gov/stli/main menu.htm.

BIRTHDAYS TODAY

Terrell Davis, 27, football player, born San Diego, CA, Oct 28, 1972.
Bill Gates, 44, computer software executive (Microsoft), born Seattle, WA, Oct 28, 1955.

OCTOBER 29 — FRIDAY

Day 302 — 63 Remaining

EMMETT, DANIEL DECATUR: BIRTH ANNIVERSARY. Oct 29, 1815. Creator of words and music for the song "Dixie," which became a fighting song for Confederate troops and unofficial "national anthem" of the South. Emmett was born at Mount Vernon, OH, and died there June 28, 1904.

SPACE MILESTONE: *DISCOVERY* (US): OLDEST MAN IN SPACE. Oct 29, 1998. Former astronaut and senator John Glenn became the oldest man in space when he traveled on the shuttle *Discovery* at the age of 77. In 1962 on *Friendship 7* he had been the first American to orbit Earth. See "Space Milestone: Friendship 7" (Feb 20).

STOCK MARKET CRASH: 70th ANNIVERSARY. Oct 29, 1929. Prices on the New York Stock Exchange plummeted and virtually collapsed four days after President Herbert Hoover had declared, "The fundamental business of the country . . . is on a sound and prosperous basis." More than 16 million shares were dumped and billions of dollars were lost. The boom was over and the nation faced nearly a decade of depression. Some analysts had warned that the buying spree, with prices 15 to 150 times above earnings, had to stop at some point. Frightened investors ordered their brokers to sell at whatever price. The resulting Great Depression, which lasted till about 1939, involved North America, Europe and other industrialized countries. In 1932 one out of four US workers was unemployed.

TURKEY: REPUBLIC DAY. Oct 29. Anniversary of the founding of the republic in 1923.

BIRTHDAYS TODAY

Dirk Kempthorne, 48, Governor of Idaho (R), born San Diego, CA, Oct 29, 1951.
Connie Mack III, 59, US Senator (R, Florida), born Philadelphia, PA, Oct 29, 1940.

OCTOBER 30 — SATURDAY

Day 303 — 62 Remaining

ADAMS, JOHN: BIRTH ANNIVERSARY. Oct 30, 1735. Second president of the US (term of office: Mar 4, 1797–Mar 3, 1801), born at Braintree, MA. Adams had been George Washington's vice president. He once wrote in a letter to Thomas Jefferson: "You and I ought not to die before we have explained ourselves to each other." John Adams and Thomas Jefferson died on the same day, July 4, 1826, the 50th anniversary of adoption of the Declaration of Independence. Adams's last words: "Thomas Jefferson still survives." Jefferson's last words: "Is it the fourth?" Adams was the father of John Quincy Adams (6th president of the US).

DEVIL'S NIGHT. Oct 30. Formerly a "Mischief Night" on the evening before Halloween and an occasion for harmless pranks, chiefly observed by children. However, in some areas of the US, the destruction of property and endangering of lives has led to the imposition of dusk-to-dawn curfews during the last two or three days of October. Not to be confused with "Trick or Treat"

or "Beggar's Night," usually observed on Halloween. See also: "Hallowe'en" (Oct 31).

FESTIVAL OF BOOKS FOR YOUNG PEOPLE. Oct 30. Iowa Memorial Union, Iowa City, IA. The 31st annual festival will feature talks by children's authors, booktalk sessions and exhibits of new books for young people. For info: School of Library and Information Science, Univ of Iowa, Iowa City, IA 52242-1420. Phone: (319) 335-5707. E-mail: ethel-bloesch@uiowa.edu.

POST, EMILY: BIRTH ANNIVERSARY. Oct 30, 1872. Emily Post was born at Baltimore, MD. Published in 1922, her book *Etiquette: The Blue Book of Social Usage* instantly became the American bible of manners and social behavior and established Post as the household name in matters of etiquette. It was in its 10th edition at the time of her death Sept 25, 1960, at New York, NY. *Etiquette* inspired a great many letters asking Post for advice on manners in specific situations. She used these letters as the basis for her radio show and for her syndicated newspaper column, which eventually appeared in more than 200 papers.

BIRTHDAYS TODAY

Diego Maradona, 39, former soccer player, born Lanus, Argentina, Oct 30, 1960.
Henry Winkler, 54, producer, actor ("The Fonz" on "Happy Days"), born New York, NY, Oct 30, 1945.

OCTOBER 31 — SUNDAY

Day 304 — 61 Remaining

FIRST BLACK PLAYS IN NBA GAME: ANNIVERSARY. Oct 31, 1950. Earl Lloyd became the first black ever to play in an NBA game when he took the floor for the Washington Capitols at Rochester, NY. Lloyd was actually one of three blacks to become NBA players in the 1950 season, the others being Nat "Sweetwater" Clifton, who was signed by the New York Knicks, and Chuck Cooper, who was drafted by the Boston Celtics (and debuted the night after Lloyd).

HALLOWE'EN or ALL HALLOW'S EVE. Oct 31. An ancient celebration combining Druid autumn festival and Christian customs. Hallowe'en (All Hallow's Eve) is the beginning of Hallowtide, a season that embraces the Feast of All Saints (Nov 1) and the Feast of All Souls (Nov 2). The observance, dating from the sixth or seventh centuries, has long been associated with thoughts of the dead, spirits, witches, ghosts and devils. In fact, the ancient Celtic Feast of Samhain, the festival that marked the beginning of winter and of the New Year, was observed Nov 1. See also: "Trick or Treat or Beggar's Night" (Oct 31). For links to sites about Halloween on the web go to: deil.lang.uiuc.edu/web.pages/holidays/halloween.html.

LOW, JULIET GORDON: BIRTH ANNIVERSARY. Oct 31, 1860. Founded Girl Scouts of the USA Mar 12, 1912, at Savannah, GA. Born at Savannah, she died there Jan 17, 1927.

	S	M	T	W	T	F	S
October						1	2
1999	3	4	5	6	7	8	9
	10	11	12	13	14	15	16
	17	18	19	20	21	22	23
	24	25	26	27	28	29	30
	31						

MOON PHASE: LAST QUARTER. Oct 31. Moon enters Last Quarter phase at 7:04 AM, EST.

MOUNT RUSHMORE COMPLETION: ANNIVERSARY. Oct 31, 1941. The Mount Rushmore National Memorial was completed after 14 years of work. First suggested by Jonah Robinson of the South Dakota State Historical Society, the memorial was dedicated in 1925, and work began in 1927. The memorial contains sculptures of the heads of Presidents George Washington, Thomas Jefferson, Abraham Lincoln and Theodore Roosevelt. The 60-foot-tall sculptures represent, respectively, the nation's founding, political philosophy, preservation, expansion and conservation. For more info: www.nps.gov/moru.

NATIONAL MAGIC DAY. Oct 31. Traditionally observed on the anniversary of the death of Harry Houdini in 1926.

★ **NATIONAL UNICEF DAY.** Oct 31. Presidential Proclamation 3817, of Oct 27, 1967, covers all succeeding years. Always Oct 31. For further info: www.unicef.org.

NEVADA: ADMISSION DAY: ANNIVERSARY. Oct 31. Became 36th state in 1864. Observed as a holiday in Nevada.

REFORMATION DAY: ANNIVERSARY. Oct 31, 1517. Anniversary on which Martin Luther nailed his 95 theses to the door of Wittenberg's Palace church, denouncing the selling of papal indulgences—the beginning of the Reformation in Germany. Observed by many Protestant churches as Reformation Sunday, on this day if it is a Sunday or on the Sunday before Oct 31.

TAIWAN: CHIANG KAI-SHEK DAY: ANNIVERSARY. Oct 31. National holiday to honor memory of Generalissimo Chiang Kai-Shek, the first constitutional president of the Republic of China, born in 1887.

TRICK OR TREAT or BEGGAR'S NIGHT. Oct 31. A popular custom on Hallowe'en, in which children wearing costumes visit neighbors' homes, calling out "Trick or Treat" and "begging" for candies or gifts to place in their beggars' bags. Some children Trick or Treat for UNICEF, collecting money for this organization. For more information, go to www.unicef.org. In recent years there has been increased participation by adults, often parading in elaborate or outrageous costumes and also requesting candy.

US: DAYLIGHT SAVING TIME ENDS; STANDARD TIME RESUMES. Oct 31–Apr 2, 2000. Standard Time resumes at 2 AM on the last Sunday in October in each time zone, as provided by the Uniform Time Act of 1966 (as amended in 1986 by Public Law 99–359). Many use the popular rule: "spring forward, fall back" to remember which way to turn their clocks.

BIRTHDAYS TODAY

Katherine Paterson, 67, author (Newbery for *The Bridge to Terabithia, Jacob Have I Loved*), born Qing Jiang, China, Oct 31, 1932.

Jane Pauley, 49, TV journalist ("Dateline"), born Indianapolis, IN, Oct 31, 1950.

Dan Rather, 68, journalist (co-anchor "CBS Evening News"), born Wharton, TX, Oct 31, 1931.

Adrienne Richard, 78, author (*Pistol*), born Evanston, IL, Oct 31, 1921.

November 1999

NOVEMBER 1 — MONDAY

Day 305 — 60 Remaining

ALGERIA: REVOLUTION ANNIVERSARY. Nov 1. National holiday commemorating revolution against France in 1954.

ALL HALLOWS or ALL SAINTS' DAY. Nov 1. Roman Catholic Holy Day of Obligation. Commemorates the blessed, especially those who have no special feast days. Observed Nov 1 since Pope Gregory IV set the date of recognition in 835. All Saints' Day is a legal holiday in Louisiana. Halloween is the evening before All Hallows Day.

ANTIGUA AND BARBUDA: NATIONAL HOLIDAY. Nov 1. Commemorates independence from Britain in 1981.

AUSTRALIA: RECREATION DAY. Nov 1. The first Monday in November is observed as Recreation Day at Northern Tasmania, Australia.

AVIATION HISTORY MONTH. Nov 1–30. Anniversary of aeronautical experiments in November 1782 (exact dates unknown), by Joseph Michel Montgolfier and Jacques Etienne Montgolfier, brothers living at Annonay, France. Inspired by Joseph Priestley's book *Experiments Relating to the Different Kinds of Air*, the brothers experimented with filling paper and fabric bags with smoke and hot air, leading to the invention of the hot-air balloon, man's first flight and the entire science of aviation and flight.

GUATEMALA: KITE FESTIVAL OF SANTIAGO SACATE-PEQUEZ. Nov 1. Long ago, when evil spirits disturbed the good spirits in the local cemetery, a magician told the townspeople a secret way to get rid of the evil spirits—by flying kites (because the evil spirits were frightened by the noise of wind against paper). Since then, the kite festival has been held at the cemetery each year Nov 1 or Nov 2, and it is said that "to this day no one knows of bad spirits roaming the streets or the cemetery of Santiago Sacatepequez," a village about 20 miles from Guatemala City. Nowadays, the youth of the village work for many weeks to make the elaborate and giant kites to fly on All Saints' Day (Nov 1) or All Souls' Day (Nov 2).

HOCKEY MASK INVENTED: 40th ANNIVERSARY. Nov 1, 1959. Tired of stopping hockey pucks with his face, Montreal

	S	M	T	W	T	F	S
November		1	2	3	4	5	6
1999	7	8	9	10	11	12	13
	14	15	16	17	18	19	20
	21	22	23	24	25	26	27
	28	29	30				

NOVEMBER 1–30
NATIONAL AMERICAN INDIAN HERITAGE MONTH

American Indian or Native American heritage encompasses diverse traditions that should be included in school curricula. All students will be enriched by learning about contributions the many tribes have made and are making to North American culture.

Native American tribes have a rich storytelling tradition. There are many myths and *porquoi* stories available for children; Joseph Bruchac and Gayle Ross are two author-storytellers who have published children's books that relate to these topics. Exposure to the Native American oral tradition is a way to encourage students to begin storytelling themselves. Michael Dorris wrote novels for young readers about first contacts between European explorers and Native Americans.

Because tribes are so diverse, small student study groups are more effective if they focus on one geographical region. Information can be presented to the class for comparing and contrasting with regional cultures studied by other groups.

Historical treatment of American Indians is integral to a well-balanced social studies curriculum. Chief Joseph's attempt to lead his people (Navajo) to freedom could be contrasted with the Cherokee peoples' forced march, called the Trail of Tears, from the southeastern states to Oklahoma.

For a literature connection about how Native American children were removed from their families in the early 1900s and required to attend faraway schools, see *Home to Medicine Mountain*, by Chiori Santiago (Children's Book Press, 0-892-39155-3, $15.95 Gr. 1–3). Russell Freedman's *Indian Chiefs* (Holiday House, 0-823-40625-3, $19.95 Gr. 3–8) is a fine collection of biographical sketches and photographs of famous chiefs.

Studying only historic Indian cultures may give children the impression American Indians no longer exist. It's important to include information about the lives of modern American Indians. The 13 volumes in Carolrhoda Books' series We Are Still Here: Native Americans Today contain a wealth of information on the lives of contemporary Native American children.

For a bibliography of additional materials, see *American Indian Reference and Resource Books for Children and Young Adults*, by Barbara J. Kuipers (2nd ed., Libraries Unlimited, 1-56308-258-6, $27.50).

Canadiens goalie Jacques Plante, having received another wound, reemerged from the locker room with seven new stitches—and a plastic face mask he had made from fiberglass and resin. Although Cliff Benedict had tried a leather mask back in the '20s, the idea didn't catch on but after Plante wore his, goalies throughout the NHL began wearing protective plastic face shields.

INTERNATIONAL DRUM MONTH. Nov 1–30. To celebrate the worldwide popularity of all types of drums. Annually, the month of November. For info: David Levine, Full Circle Management, Percussion Marketing Council, 12665 Kling St, Studio City, CA 91604. Phone: (818) 753-1310. Fax: (818) 753-1313. E-mail: DLEVINE360@aol.com.

MEDICAL SCHOOL FOR WOMEN OPENED AT BOSTON: ANNIVERSARY. Nov 1, 1848. Founded by Samuel Gregory, a pioneer in medical education for women, the Boston Female Medical School opened as the first medical school exclusively for women. The original enrollment was 12 students. In 1874, the school merged with the Boston University School of Medicine and formed one of the first co-ed medical schools in the world.

MERLIN'S SNUG HUGS FOR KIDS. Nov 1–Dec 15. Nationwide. Each community is encouraged to provide new winter outerwear for foster and needy children. Event runs for six weeks, and on the final day (Dec 15) Merlin's caravan collects the new winter clothes and delivers them to Children's Home & Aid Society. Sponsor: Merlin's Muffler & Brake. Annually, the first week of November through the third week of December. For info: Kathleen Quinn, ProQuest Communications, 626 Carriage Hill Dr, Glenview, IL 60025-5401. Phone: (847) 998-9950. Fax: (847) 998-9945. E-mail: proquest@aol.com. Web: www.merlins.com.

MEXICO: DAY OF THE DEAD. Nov 1–2. Observance begins during last days of October when "Dead Men's Bread" is sold in bakeries—round loaves, decorated with sugar skulls. Departed souls are remembered not with mourning but with a spirit of friendliness and good humor. Cemeteries are visited and graves are decorated.

★**NATIONAL ADOPTION MONTH.** Nov 1–30.

★**NATIONAL AMERICAN INDIAN HERITAGE MONTH.** Nov 1–30. See Curriculum Connection.

NATIONAL AUTHORS' DAY. Nov 1. This observance was adopted by the General Federation of Women's Clubs in 1929 and in 1949 was given a place on the list of special days, weeks and months prepared by the US Dept of Commerce. The resolution states: "by celebrating an Authors' Day as a nation, we would not only show patriotism, loyalty, and appreciation of the men and women who have made American literature possible, but would also encourage and inspire others to give of themselves in making a better America. . . ." It was also resolved "that we commemorate an Authors' Day to be observed on November First each year." See Curriculum Connection.

NATIONAL FAMILY LITERACY DAY®. Nov 1. Celebrated all over the country with special activities and events that showcase the importance of family literacy programs. Family literacy programs bring parents and children together in the classroom to learn and support each other in efforts to further their education and improve their life skills. Sponsored by the National Center for Family Literacy and Toyota. Annually, Nov 1. For info: Natl Center for Family Literacy, 325 W Main St, Ste 200, Louisville, KY 40202. Phone: (502) 584-1133. Fax: (502) 584-0172. E-mail: ncfl@famlit.org. Web: www.famlit.org.

NATIONAL HEALTHY SKIN MONTH. Nov 1–30. For info: American Academy of Dermatology, PO Box 681069, Schaumburg, IL 60168. Phone: (847) 330-0230.

PEANUT BUTTER LOVERS' MONTH. Nov 1–30. Celebration of America's favorite food and #1 sandwich. For info: Peanut Advisory Board, 500 Sugar Mill Rd, Ste 105A, Atlanta, GA 30350.

PRESIDENT FIRST OCCUPIES THE WHITE HOUSE: ANNIVERSARY. Nov 1, 1800. The federal government had been located at Philadelphia from 1790 until 1800. On Nov 1, 1800, President John Adams and his family moved into the newly-completed White House at Washington, DC, the nation's new capital. To take a virtual tour of the White House, go to: www.white house.gov.

PRIME MERIDIAN SET: ANNIVERSARY. Nov 1, 1884. Delegates from 25 nations met in October at Washington, DC at the International Meridian Conference to set up time zones for the world. On this day the treaty adopted by the Conference took effect, making Greenwich, England the Prime Meridian (i.e., zero longitude) and setting the International Date Line at 180° longi-

NOVEMBER 1
NATIONAL AUTHORS' DAY

Use this day to highlight favorite children's authors and to showcase your students' own work as authors.

In the classroom student authors can hold small group read aloud sessions of their work. Take care to give fiction, poetry and nonfiction equal attention. Use this day to draw special attention to the collection of classroom books that have been made by students.

Solicit family and peer input with a writing response form. The student should ask someone outside the classroom to read a piece of his or her work and respond to it. Response prompts could include: What did you like best about this piece? Did you feel any emotions while reading it? Were word choices varied and interesting?

Display books written by favorite authors and provide suggestions of read-alikes. *Booklist* magazine, published by the American Library Association, has regular columns that list read-alikes. Your public library should have a subscription to *Booklist* if your school library media center doesn't. Ask students to make bookmarks or posters celebrating their favorite authors or books.

Invite local authors to visit your classroom. Remember that people who write for local newspapers are authors, too. They are often willing to donate their time.

To give students a taste of the life of the professional writer, have them read an autobiography of one of their favorites. Some suggestions: *Author: A True Story*, by Helen Lester (Clarion, 0-395-82744-2, $10.95 Gr. K–2); *The Abracadabra Kid: A Writer's Life*, by Sid Fleischman (Greenwillow, 0-688014859-X, $16 Gr. 5 & up); *Blood on the Forehead: What I Know about Writing*, by M. E. Kerr (HarperCollins, 0-06-446207-2, $12.95 Gr. 6 & up); *Homesick: My Own Story*, by Jean Fritz (Putnam, 0-39-920933-6, $15.99 Gr. 4–6); *Knots In My Yo-Yo String: The Autobiography of a Kid*, by Jerry Spinelli (Knopf, 0-67-998791-6, $16.99 Gr. 4–6); *My Own Two Feet: A Memoir*, by Beverly Cleary (Morrow, 0-68-814267-2, $16 Gr. 6 & Up); *Bill Peet: An Autobiography*, by Bill Peet (Houghton Mifflin, 0-39-550932-7, $20 Gr. 4–6).

tude in the Pacific. Every 15° of longitude equals one hour and there are 24 meridians. While some countries do not strictly observe this system (for example, while China stretches over five time zones, it is the same time everywhere in China) it has brought predictability and logic to time throughout the world.

VIRGIN ISLANDS: LIBERTY DAY. Nov 1. Officially "D. Hamilton Jackson Memorial Day," commemorating establishment of the first press in the Virgin Islands in 1915.

WORLD COMMUNICATION WEEK. Nov 1–7. To stress the importance of communication among the more than five billion human beings in the world who speak more than 3,000 languages and to promote communication by means of the international language Esperanto. For complete info, send $4 to cover expense of printing, handling and postage. Annually, the first seven days of November. For info: Dr. Stanley Drake, Pres, Intl Soc of Friendship and Goodwill, 412 Cherry Hills Dr, Bakersfield, CA 93309-7902.

BIRTHDAYS TODAY

Fernando Anguamea Valenzuela, 39, baseball player, born Navojoa, Sonora, Mexico, Nov 1, 1960.

NOVEMBER 2 — TUESDAY
Day 306 — 59 Remaining

ALL SOULS' DAY. Nov 2. Commemorates the faithful departed. Catholic observance.

BOONE, DANIEL: BIRTH ANNIVERSARY. Nov 2, 1734. American frontiersman, explorer and militia officer, born at Berks County, near Reading, PA. In February 1778, he was captured at Blue Licks, KY, by Shawnee Indians, under Chief Blackfish, who adopted Boone when he was inducted into the tribe as "Big Turtle." Boone escaped after five months, and in 1781 was captured briefly by the British. He experienced a series of personal and financial disasters during his life, but continued a rugged existence, hunting until his 80s. Boone died at St. Charles County, MO, Sept 26, 1820. The bodies of Daniel Boone and his wife, Rebecca, were moved to Frankfort, KY, in 1845.

FIRST SCHEDULED RADIO BROADCAST: ANNIVERSARY. Nov 2, 1920. Station KDKA at Pittsburgh, PA broadcasted the results of the presidential election. By 1922 there were about 400 licensed radio stations in the US.

HARDING, WARREN GAMALIEL: BIRTH ANNIVERSARY. Nov 2, 1865. Twenty-ninth president of the US was born at Corsica, OH. His term of office: Mar 4, 1921–Aug 2, 1923 (died in office). His undistinguished administration was tainted by the Teapot Dome scandal, and his sudden death while on a western speaking tour (San Francisco, CA, Aug 2, 1923) prompted many rumors.

NORTH DAKOTA: ADMISSION DAY: ANNIVERSARY. Nov 2. Became 39th state in 1889.

POLK, JAMES KNOX: BIRTH ANNIVERSARY. Nov 2, 1795. The 11th president of the US was born at Mecklenburg County, NC. His term of office: Mar 4, 1845–Mar 3, 1849. A compromise candidate at the 1844 Democratic Party convention, Polk was awarded the nomination on the ninth ballot. He declined to be a candidate for a second term and declared himself to be "exceedingly relieved" at the completion of his presidency. He died shortly thereafter at Nashville, TN, June 15, 1849.

SOUTH DAKOTA: ADMISSION DAY: ANNIVERSARY. Nov 2. Became 40th state in 1889.

BIRTHDAYS TODAY

Danny Cooksey, 24, actor ("Pepper Ann," *The Little Mermaid*), born Moore, OK, Nov 2, 1975.

NOVEMBER 3 — WEDNESDAY
Day 307 — 58 Remaining

AUSTIN, STEPHEN FULLER: BIRTH ANNIVERSARY. Nov 3, 1793. A principal founder of Texas, for whom its capital city was named, Austin was born at Wythe County, VA. He first visited Texas in 1821 and established a settlement there the following year, continuing a colonization project started by his father, Moses Austin. Thrown in prison when he advocated formation of a separate state (Texas still belonged to Mexico), he was freed in 1835, lost a campaign for the presidency (of the Republic of Texas)

November 1999	S	M	T	W	T	F	S
		1	2	3	4	5	6
	7	8	9	10	11	12	13
	14	15	16	17	18	19	20
	21	22	23	24	25	26	27
	28	29	30				

to Sam Houston (q.v.) in 1836, and died (while serving as Texas secretary of state) at Austin, TX, Dec 27, 1836.

DOMINICA: NATIONAL DAY. Nov 3. National holiday. Commemorates the independence of this Caribbean island from Britain on this day in 1978.

JAPAN: CULTURE DAY. Nov 3. National holiday.

MICRONESIA, FEDERATED STATES OF: INDEPENDENCE DAY. Nov 3. National holiday commemorating independence from the US in 1986.

$$105 \times 3 = 315$$

NATIONAL ASSOCIATION FOR GIFTED CHILDREN CONVENTION. Nov 3–7. Albuquerque, NM. Educational sessions for administrators, counselors, coordinators, teachers and parents. Est attendance: 2,800. For info: Natl Assn for Gifted Children, 1707 L St NW, Ste 550, Washington, DC 20036. Phone: (202) 785-4268.

NATIONAL COUNCIL FOR GEOGRAPHIC EDUCATION MEETING. Nov 3–6. Boston, MA. For info: Natl Council for Geographic Education, 16A Leonard Hall, Indiana Univ of PA, Indiana, PA 15705. Phone: (412) 357-6290. Web: www.ncge.org.

PANAMA: INDEPENDENCE DAY. Nov 3. Panama declared itself independent of Colombia in 1903.

SANDWICH DAY: BIRTH ANNIVERSARY OF JOHN MONTAGUE. Nov 3, 1718. A day to recognize the inventor of the sandwich, John Montague, Fourth Earl of Sandwich, born at London, England. He was England's first lord of the admiralty, secretary of state for the northern department, postmaster general and the man after whom Captain Cook named the Sandwich Islands in 1778. A rake and a gambler, he is said to have invented the sandwich as a time-saving nourishment while engaged in a 24-hour-long gambling session in 1762. He died at London, England, Apr 30, 1792.

SPACE MILESTONE: *SPUTNIK 2* (USSR). Nov 3, 1957. A dog named Laika became the first animal sent into space. Total weight of craft and dog was 1,121 lbs. The satellite was not capable of returning the dog to Earth and she died when her air supply was gone. Nicknamed "Muttnik" by the American press.

WHITE, EDWARD DOUGLASS: BIRTH ANNIVERSARY. Nov 3, 1845. Ninth Chief Justice of the Supreme Court, born at La Fourche Parish, LA. During the Civil War, he served in the Confederate Army after which he returned to New Orleans to practice law. Elected to the US Senate in 1891, he was appointed to the Supreme Court by Grover Cleveland in 1894. He became Chief Justice under President William Taft in 1910 and served until 1921. He died at Washington, DC, May 19, 1921.

BIRTHDAYS TODAY

Brent Ashabranner, 78, author of nonfiction (*Our Beckoning Borders: Illegal Immigration to America*), born Shawnee, OK, Nov 3, 1921.
Roseanne, 46, comedienne, actress ("Roseanne," *She-Devil*), born Roseanne Barr, Salt Lake City, UT, Nov 3, 1953.

NOVEMBER 4 — THURSDAY
Day 308 — 57 Remaining

ITALY: VICTORY DAY. Nov 4. Commemorates the signing of a WWI treaty by Austria in 1918 which resulted in the transfer of Trentino and Trieste from Austria to Italy.

JEWISH BOOK MONTH. Nov 4–Dec 4. To promote interest in Jewish books. For info: Carolyn Starman Hessel, Jewish Book Council, 15 E 26th St, New York, NY 10010. Phone: (212) 532-4949. Fax: (212) 481-4174. Web: www.avotaynu.com/jbc.html.

KING TUT TOMB DISCOVERY: ANNIVERSARY. Nov 4, 1922. In 1922, one of the most important archaeological discoveries of modern times occurred at Luxor, Egypt. It was the tomb of Egypt's child-king, Tutankhamen, who became pharaoh at the age of nine and died, probably in the year 1352 BC, when he was 19. Perhaps the only ancient Egyptian royal tomb to have escaped plundering by grave robbers, it was discovered more than 3,000 years after Tutankhamen's death by English archaeologist Howard Carter, leader of an expedition financed by Lord Carnarvon. The priceless relics yielded by King Tut's tomb were placed in Egypt's National Museum at Cairo.

MISCHIEF NIGHT. Nov 4. Observed in England, Australia and New Zealand. Nov 4, the eve of Guy Fawkes Day, is occasion for bonfires and firecrackers to commemorate failure of the plot to blow up the Houses of Parliament Nov 5, 1605. See also: "England: Guy Fawkes Day" (Nov 5).

NATIONAL CHILDREN'S GOAL–SETTING DAY. Nov 4. Encourage parents to foster goal-setting habits in their children's lives so that their children can make their dreams come true. For info: Gary Ryan Blair, The GoalsGuy, 1201 E Fayette St, Syracuse, NY 13210. Phone: (800) 731-GOAL. Fax: (315) 474-6954. E-mail: kidsday@goalsguy.com. Web: www.goalsguy.com.

NORTH, STERLING: BIRTH ANNIVERSARY. Nov 4, 1906. Author (*Rascal*), born at Edgerton, WI. Died Dec 21, 1974.

PANAMA: FLAG DAY. Nov 4. Public holiday.

UNESCO: ANNIVERSARY. Nov 4, 1946. The United Nations Educational, Scientific and Cultural Organization was formed.

BIRTHDAYS TODAY

Gail E. Haley, 60, author and illustrator (Caldecott for *A Story, A Story*), born Charlotte, NC, Nov 4, 1939.
Ralph Macchio, 37, actor ("Eight Is Enough," *The Karate Kid*), born Huntington, NY, Nov 4, 1962.
Andrea McArdle, 36, singer, actress (Broadway's *Annie*), born Philadelphia, PA, Nov 4, 1963.

NOVEMBER 5 — FRIDAY
Day 309 — 56 Remaining

ENGLAND: GUY FAWKES DAY. Nov 5. United Kingdom. Anniversary of the "Gunpowder Plot." Conspirators planned to blow up the Houses of Parliament and King James I in 1605. Twenty barrels of gunpowder, which they had secreted in a cellar under Parliament, were discovered on the night of Nov 4, the very eve of the intended explosion, and the conspirators were arrested. They were tried and convicted, and Jan 31, 1606, eight (including Guy Fawkes) were beheaded and their heads displayed on pikes at London Bridge. Though there were at least 11 conspirators, Guy Fawkes is most remembered. In 1606, the Parliament, which was to have been annihilated, enacted a law establishing Nov 5 as a day of public thanksgiving. It is still observed, and on the night of Nov 5, the whole country lights up with bonfires and celebration. "Guys" are burned in effigy and the old verses repeated: "Remember, remember the fifth of November,/Gunpowder treason and plot;/I see no reason why Gunpowder Treason/Should ever be forgot."

ISRA AL MI'RAJ: ASCENT OF THE PROPHET MUHAMMAD. Nov 5. Islamic calendar date: Rajab 27, 1420. Commemorates the journey of the Prophet Muhammad from Mecca to Jerusalem, his ascension into the Seven Heavens and his return on the same night. Muslims believe that on that night Muhammad prayed together with Abraham, Moses and Jesus in the area of the Al-Aqsa Mosque at Jerusalem. The rock from which he is believed to have ascended to heaven to speak with God is the one inside The Dome of the Rock. Different methods for "anticipating" the visibility of the new moon crescent at Mecca are used by different Muslim groups. US date may vary.

ROGERS, ROY: BIRTH ANNIVERSARY. Nov 5, 1912. Known as the "King of the Cowboys," Rogers was born Leonard Slye at Cincinnati, OH. His many songs included "Don't Fence Me In" and "Happy Trails to You." He made his acting debut in *Under Western Stars* in 1935 and later hosted his own show, "The Roy Rogers Show," in 1951. Rogers died at Apple Valley, CA, July 6, 1998. See also: "The Roy Rogers Show" TV Premiere: Anniversary (Dec 30).

TEXAS BOOK FESTIVAL. Nov 5–7. Austin, TX. For info: Texas Book Festival, PO Box 13143, Austin, TX 78711. Phone: (512) 477-4055. Fax: (512) 322-0722. Web: link.tsl.state.tx.us/bookfest.

BIRTHDAYS TODAY

Tatum O'Neal, 36, actress (Oscar for *Paper Moon*; *Bad News Bears*), born Los Angeles, CA, Nov 5, 1963.
Jerry Stackhouse, 25, basketball player, born Kinston, NC, Nov 5, 1974.

NOVEMBER 6 — SATURDAY
Day 310 — 55 Remaining

"GOOD MORNING AMERICA" TV PREMIERE: ANNIVERSARY. Nov 6, 1975. This ABC morning program, set in a living room, is a mixture of news reports, features and interviews with newsmakers and people of interest. It was the first program to compete with NBC's "Today" show and initially aired as "A.M. America." Hosts have included David Hartman, Nancy Dussault, Sandy Hill, Charles Gibson, Joan Lunden, Lisa McRee and Kevin Newman.

NAISMITH, JAMES: BIRTH ANNIVERSARY. Nov 6, 1861. Inventor of the game of basketball was born at Almonte, Ontario, Canada. Died at Lawrence, KS, Nov 28, 1939. Basketball became an Olympic sport in 1936.

SADIE HAWKINS DAY. Nov 6. Widely observed in US, usually on the first Saturday in November. Tradition established in "Li'l Abner" comic strip in 1930s by cartoonist Al Capp. A popular occasion when women and girls are encouraged to take the initiative in inviting the man or boy of their choice for a date. A similar tradition is associated with Feb 29 in leap years.

SAXOPHONE DAY (ADOLPHE SAX BIRTH ANNIVERSARY). Nov 6. A day to recognize the birth anniversary of Adolphe Sax, Belgian musician and inventor of the saxophone and the saxotromba. Born at Dinant, Belgium in 1814, Antoine Joseph Sax, later known as Adolphe, was the eldest of 11 children of a musical instrument builder. Sax contributed an entire family of brass wind instruments for band and orchestra use. He was accorded fame and great wealth, but business misfortunes led to bankruptcy. Sax died in poverty at Paris, Feb 7, 1894.

SOUSA, JOHN PHILIP: BIRTH ANNIVERSARY. Nov 6, 1854. American composer and band conductor, remembered for stirring marches such as "The Stars and Stripes Forever," "Semper Fidelis," "El Capitan," born at Washington, DC. Died at Reading, PA, Mar 6, 1932. See also: "The Stars and Stripes Forever: Anniversary" (May 14).

SWEDEN: ALL SAINTS' DAY. Nov 6. Honors the memory of deceased friends and relatives. Annually, the Saturday following Oct 30.

SWEDEN: GUSTAVUS ADOLPHUS DAY. Nov 6. Honors Sweden's King and military leader killed in 1632.

BIRTHDAYS TODAY

Sally Field, 53, actress (Oscars for *Norma Rae*, *Places in the Heart*; *Mrs Doubtfire*), born Pasadena, CA, Nov 6, 1946.
Ethan Hawke, 29, actor (*Dead Poets Society*, *Reality Bites*), born Austin, TX, Nov 6, 1970.
Maria Owings Shriver, 44, broadcast journalist ("Today"), born Chicago, IL, Nov 6, 1955.

NOVEMBER 7 — SUNDAY

Day 311 — 54 Remaining

THE ART OF STORYTELLING CONFERENCE. Nov 7. Marietta, OH. Sharing the art of storytelling with a new generation. Est attendance: 150. For info: Donna Foster, Program Dir, Creative Arts Institute, Inc, 8021 Kennedy Rd, Blacklick, OH 43004. Phone: (614) 759-9407. Fax: (614) 759-8480.

CANADIAN PACIFIC RAILWAY: TRANSCONTINENTAL COMPLETION ANNIVERSARY. Nov 7, 1885. At 9:30 AM the last spike was driven at Craigellachie, British Columbia, completing the Canadian Pacific Railway's 2,980-mile transcontinental railroad track between Montreal, Quebec, in the east and Port Moody, British Columbia, in the west.

	S	M	T	W	T	F	S
November		1	2	3	4	5	6
1999	7	8	9	10	11	12	13
	14	15	16	17	18	19	20
	21	22	23	24	25	26	27
	28	29	30				

CURIE, MARIE SKLODOWSKA: BIRTH ANNIVERSARY. Nov 7, 1867. Polish chemist and physicist, born at Warsaw, Poland. In 1903 she was awarded, with her husband Pierre, the Nobel Prize for physics for their discovery of the element radium. Died near Sallanches, France, July 4, 1934. For further info: *Marie Curie*, by Leonard Everett Fisher (Macmillan, 0-02-735375-3, $14.95 Gr. 3–6).

FIRST BLACK GOVERNOR ELECTED: ANNIVERSARY. Nov 7, 1989. L. Douglas Wilder was elected governor of Virginia, becoming the first elected black governor in US history. Wilder had previously served as lieutenant governor of Virginia.

GREAT OCTOBER SOCIALIST REVOLUTION: ANNIVERSARY. Nov 7, 1917. This holiday in the old Soviet Union was observed for two days with parades, military displays and appearances by Soviet leaders. According to the old Russian calendar, the revolution took place Oct 25, 1917. Soviet calendar reform causes observance to fall Nov 7 (Gregorian). The Bolshevik Revolution began at Petrograd, Russia, on the evening of Nov 6 (Gregorian), 1917. A new government headed by Nikolai Lenin took office the following day under the name Council of People's Commissars. Leon Trotsky was commissar for foreign affairs and Josef Stalin became commissar of national minorities. In the mid-1990s, President Yeltsin issued a decree renaming this holiday the "Day of National Reconciliation and Agreement."

HALFWAY POINT OF AUTUMN. Nov 7. At 4:27 AM, EST, Nov 7, 1999, 44 days, 20 hours and 36 minutes of autumn will have elapsed and the equivalent will remain before 2:44 AM, EST, Dec 22 which is the winter solstice and the beginning of winter.

INDIA: DIWALI (DEEPAVALI). Nov 7. Diwali (or Divali), the five-day festival of lights, is the prettiest of all Indian festivals. It celebrates the return of Lord Rama to Ayodhya after a 14-year exile. Thousands of flickering lights illuminate houses and transform the drab urban landscape of cities and towns while fireworks add color and noise. The goddess of wealth, Lakshmi, is worshipped in Hindu homes on Diwali. Houses are white-washed and cleaned and elaborate designs drawn on thresholds with colored powder to welcome the fastidious goddess. Because there is no one universally accepted Hindu calendar, this holiday may be celebrated on a different date in some parts of India but it always falls in the months of October or November. For more info: *Divali*, by Dilip Kadodwala (Raintree, 0-8172-4616-9, $22.11 Gr. 4-6). For info: Govt of India Tourist Office, 30 Rockefeller Plaza, North Mezzanine, New York, NY 10112. Phone: (212) 586-4901.

MOON PHASE: NEW MOON. Nov 7. Moon enters New Moon phase at 10:53 PM, EST.

NATIONAL CHEMISTRY WEEK. Nov 7–13. To celebrate the contributions of chemistry to modern life and to help the public understand that chemistry affects every part of our lives. Activities include an array of outreach programs such as open houses, contests, workshops, exhibits and classroom visits. 10 million participants nationwide. For info: Natl Chemistry Week Office, American Chemical Society, 1155 16th St NW, Washington, DC 20036. Phone: (202) 872-6078. Fax: (202) 833-7722. E-mail: ncw@acs.org. Web: www.chemcenter.org.

NATIONAL SPLIT PEA SOUP WEEK. Nov 7–13. To promote the use of split peas in split pea soup. For info: Peter Mundt, USA Dry Pea and Lentil Council, 5071 Highway 8 W, Moscow, ID 83843-4023. Phone: (208) 882-3023. Fax: (208) 882-6406. E-mail: pulse@pea-lentil.com.

REPUBLICAN SYMBOL: 125th ANNIVERSARY. Nov 7, 1874. Thomas Nast used an elephant to represent the Republican Party in a satirical cartoon in *Harper's Weekly*. Today the elephant is still a well-recognized symbol for the Republican Party in political cartoons.

ROOSEVELT ELECTED TO FOURTH TERM: 55th ANNIVERSARY. Nov 7, 1944. Defeating Thomas Dewey, Franklin D. Roosevelt became the first, and only, person elected to four terms as President of the US. Roosevelt was inaugurated the following Jan 20 but died in office Apr 12, 1945, serving only 53 days of the fourth term.

RUSSIA: OCTOBER REVOLUTION. Nov 7. National holiday in Russia and Ukraine. Commemorates the Great Socialist Revolution which occurred in October, 1917 under the Old Style calendar. In the mid-1990s, President Yeltsin issued a decree renaming the holiday the "Day of National Reconciliation and Agreement."

YOUTH APPRECIATION WEEK. Nov 7–13. For info: Optimist Intl, 4494 Lindell Blvd, St. Louis, MO 63108. Phone: (314) 371-6000 or your local Optimist club.

BIRTHDAYS TODAY

Bill Nye, 64, host ("Bill Nye, the Science Guy"), born Washington, DC, Nov 7, 1935.

Mary Travers, 62, composer, singer (Peter, Paul and Mary, "Puff, the Magic Dragon"), born Louisville, KY, Nov 7, 1937.

NOVEMBER 8 — MONDAY
Day 312 — 53 Remaining

CORTÉS CONQUERS MEXICO: ANNIVERSARY. Nov 8, 1519. After landing on the Yucatan peninsula in April, Spaniard Hernan Cortés and his troops marched into the interior of Mexico to the Aztec capital and took the Aztec emperor Montezuma hostage.

HALLEY, EDMUND: BIRTH ANNIVERSARY. Nov 8, 1656. Astronomer and mathematician born at London, England. Astronomer Royal, 1721–42. Died at Greenwich, England, Jan 14, 1742. He observed the great comet of 1682 (now named for him), first conceived its periodicity and wrote in his *Synopsis of Comet Astronomy*: ". . . I may venture to foretell that this Comet will return again in the year 1758." It did, and Edmund Halley's memory is kept alive by the once-every-generation appearance of Halley's Comet. There have been 28 recorded appearances of this comet since 240 BC. Average time between appearances is 76 years. Halley's Comet is next expected to be visible in 2061.

MONTANA: ADMISSION DAY: ANNIVERSARY. Nov 8. Became 41st state in 1889.

X-RAY DISCOVERY DAY: ANNIVERSARY. Nov 8, 1895. Physicist Wilhelm Conrad Röntgen discovered X-rays, beginning a new era in physics and medicine. Although X-rays had been observed previously, it was Röntgen, a professor at the University of Wurzburg (Germany), who successfully repeated X-ray experimentation and who is credited with the discovery. For further info: *The Mysterious Rays of Dr. Röntgen*, by Beverly Gherman (Atheneum, 0-689-31839-1, $14.95 Gr. 2–5).

BIRTHDAYS TODAY

Mary Hart, 48, TV host, born Madison, SD, Nov 8, 1951.

Alfre Woodard, 46, actress (*Cross Creek*, *Miss Evers' Boys*), born Tulsa, OK, Nov 8, 1953.

NOVEMBER 9 — TUESDAY
Day 313 — 52 Remaining

AGNEW, SPIRO THEODORE: BIRTH ANNIVERSARY. Nov 9, 1918. Thirty-ninth vice president of the US, born at Baltimore, MD. Twice elected vice president (1968 and 1972), Agnew, Oct 10, 1973, became the second person to resign that office. Agnew entered a plea of no contest to a charge of income tax evasion (on contract kickbacks received while he was governor of Maryland and after he became vice president). He died Sept 17, 1996, at Berlin, MD. See also: "Calhoun, John Caldwell: Birth Anniversary" (Mar 18).

BANNEKER, BENJAMIN: BIRTH ANNIVERSARY. Nov 9, 1731. American astronomer, mathematician, clockmaker, surveyor and almanac author, called "first black man of science." Took part in original survey of city of Washington. Banneker's *Almanac* was published 1792–97. Born at Elliott's Mills, MD, he died at Baltimore, MD, Oct 9, 1806. A fire that started during his funeral destroyed his home, library, notebooks, almanac calculations, clocks and virtually all belongings and documents related to his life. For further info: *Dear Benjamin Banneker*, by Andrea Davis Pinkney (Harcourt, 0-15-200417-3, $14.95 Gr. 2–4).

BERLIN WALL OPENED: 10th ANNIVERSARY. Nov 9, 1989. After 28 years as a symbol of the Cold War, the Berlin Wall was opened. East Germany opened checkpoints along its border with West Germany after a troubled month that saw many citizens flee to the West through other countries. Coming amidst the celebration of East Germany's 40-year anniversary, the pro-democracy demonstrations led to the resignation of Erich Honecker, East Germany's head of state and party chief, who had supervised the construction of the Wall. He was replaced by Egon Krenz, who promised open political debate and a lessening of restrictions on travel in attempts to stem the flow of East Germans to the West. By opening the Berlin Wall, East Germany began a course that led to the de facto reunification of the two Germanys by summer 1990. The Berlin Wall was constructed Aug 13, 1961. Berlin was at the center of a superpower crisis as US President Kennedy increased troop strength in response to the blockade of West Berlin by the Soviets. Honecker started construction, with Soviet leader Krushchev's blessing, of the 27.9-mile wall across the city. Many attempts to scale or breech the wall ensued throughout the years. But on the evening of Nov 9, 1989, citizens of both sides walked freely through the barrier as others danced atop the structure to celebrate the end of an era.

CAMBODIA: INDEPENDENCE DAY. Nov 9. National Day. Commemorates independence from France in 1949.

EAST COAST BLACKOUT: ANNIVERSARY. Nov 9, 1965. Massive electric power failure starting in western New York state at 5:16 PM, cut electric power to much of northeastern US and Ontario and Quebec in Canada. More than 30 million persons in an area of 80,000 square miles were affected. The experience provoked studies of the vulnerability of 20th-century technology.

KRISTALLNACHT (CRYSTAL NIGHT): ANNIVERSARY. Nov 9–10, 1938. During the evening of Nov 9 and into the morning of Nov 10, 1938, mobs in Germany destroyed thousands of shops and homes carrying out a pogrom against Jews. Synagogues were burned down or demolished. There were bonfires in every Jewish neighborhood, fueled by Jewish prayer books, Torah scrolls and volumes of philosophy, history and poetry. More than 30,000 Jews were arrested and 91 killed. The night got its name from the smashing of glass store windows.

NATIONAL CHILD SAFETY COUNCIL: FOUNDING ANNIVERSARY. Nov 9, 1955. National Child Safety Council (NCSC) at Jackson, MI. NCSC is the oldest and largest nonprofit organization in the US dedicated solely to the personal safety and well-being of young children. For info: Barbara Handley Huggett, Dir Research and Development, NCSC, Box 1368, Jackson, MI 49204-1368. Phone: (517) 764-6070.

BIRTHDAYS TODAY

Lois Ehlert, 65, author and illustrator (*Hands, Nuts to You*), born Beaver Dam, WI, Nov 9, 1934.
Lou Ferrigno, 48, actor (*Pumping Iron*, "The Incredible Hulk"), former bodybuilder, born Brooklyn, NY, Nov 9, 1951.
Robert Graham, 63, US Senator (D, Florida), born Dade County, FL, Nov 9, 1936.
Lynn Hall, 62, author (the Dragon series), born Lombard, IL, Nov 9, 1937.

NOVEMBER 10 — WEDNESDAY
Day 314 — 51 Remaining

AMERICAN ASSOCIATION OF SCHOOL LIBRARIANS CONFERENCE. Nov 10–14. Birmingham, AL. A joint conference with the International Association of School Librarianship. For info: American Assn of School Librarians, 50 E. Huron St, Chicago, IL 60611. Phone: (800) 545-2433. Web: www.ala.org.

EDMUND FITZGERALD SINKING: ANNIVERSARY. Nov 10, 1975. The ore carrier *Edmund Fitzgerald* broke in two during a heavy storm in Lake Superior (near Whitefish Point). There were no survivors of this, the worst Great Lakes ship disaster of the decade, which took the lives of 29 crew members.

MARINE CORPS BIRTHDAY. Nov 10. Commemorates the Marine Corps' establishment in 1775. Originally part of the navy, it became a separate unit July 11, 1789.

MICROSOFT RELEASES WINDOWS: ANNIVERSARY. Nov 10, 1983. In 1980, Microsoft signed a contract with IBM to design an operating system, MS-DOS, for a personal computer that IBM was developing. On this date Microsoft released Windows, an extension of MS-DOS with a graphical user interface.

NATIONAL YOUNG READER'S DAY. Nov 10. Pizza Hut and the Center for the Book in the Library of Congress established National Young Reader's Day to remind Americans of the joys and importance of reading for young people. Schools, libraries, families and communities nationwide use this day to celebrate youth reading in a variety of creative and educational ways. Ideas on ways you can celebrate this special day available. For info: Shelley Morehead, The BOOK IT! Program, PO Box 2999, Wichita, KS 67201. Phone: (800) 426-6548. Fax: (316) 636-9500. E-mail: read@bookitprogram.com. Web: www.bookitprogram.com.

NATIONAL ASSOCIATION FOR THE EDUCATION OF YOUNG CHILDREN CONFERENCE. Nov 10–13. New Orleans, LA. For info: Natl Assn for the Education of Young Children, 1509 16th St NW, Washington, DC 20036. Phone: (202) 232-8777. Fax: (202) 328-1846. E-mail: naeyc@naeyc.org. Web: www.naeyc.org.

"SESAME STREET" TV PREMIERE: 30th ANNIVERSARY. Nov 10, 1969. An important, successful long-running children's show, "Sesame Street" educates children while they have fun. It takes place along a city street, featuring a diverse cast of humans and puppets. Through singing, puppetry, film clips and skits, kids are taught letters, numbers, concepts and other lessons. Shows are "sponsored" by letters and numbers. Human cast members have included: Loretta Long, Matt Robinson, Roscoe Orman, Bob McGrath, Linda Bove, Buffy St. Marie, Ruth Buzzi, Will Lee, Northern J. Calloway, Emilio Delgado and Sonia Manzano. Favorite Jim Henson muppets include Ernie, Bert, Grover, Oscar the Grouch, Kermit the Frog, the Cookie Monster, life-sized Big Bird and Mr Snuffleupagus.

SPACE MILESTONE: *LUNA 17* (USSR). Nov 10, 1970. This unmanned spacecraft landed and released *Lunakhod 1* (8-wheel, radio-controlled vehicle) on Moon's Sea of Rains Nov 17, which explored lunar surface, sending data back to Earth.

BIRTHDAYS TODAY

Sinbad, 43, actor (*Unnecessary Roughness*, "A Different World"), born Benton Harbor, MI, Nov 10, 1956.

NOVEMBER 11 — THURSDAY
Day 315 — 50 Remaining

ANGOLA: INDEPENDENCE DAY. Nov 11. National holiday. The West African state of Angola gained its independence from Portugal in 1975.

	S	M	T	W	T	F	S
November		1	2	3	4	5	6
1999	7	8	9	10	11	12	13
	14	15	16	17	18	19	20
	21	22	23	24	25	26	27
	28	29	30				

BONZA BOTTLER DAY™. Nov 11. To celebrate when the number of the day is the same as the number of the month. Bonza Bottler Day™ is an excuse to have a party at least once a month. For info: Gail M. Berger, 109 Matthew Ave, Poca, WV 25159. Phone: (304) 776-7746. E-mail: gberger5@aol.com.

CANADA: REMEMBRANCE DAY. Nov 11. Public holiday.

FRENCH WEST INDIES: CONCORDIA DAY. Nov 11. St. Martin. Public holiday. Parades and joint ceremony by French and Dutch officials at the obelisk Border Monument commemorating the long-standing peaceful coexistence of both countries. For info: Ms Michel Coutosiev, Mktg Challenges Int'l, 10 E 21st St, New York, NY 10010. Phone: (212) 529-9069.

"GOD BLESS AMERICA" FIRST PERFORMED: ANNIVERSARY. Nov 11, 1938. Irving Berlin wrote this song especially for Kate Smith. She first sang it during her regular radio broadcast. It quickly became a great patriotic favorite of the nation and one of Smith's most requested songs.

MARTINMAS. Nov 11. The Feast Day of St. Martin of Tours, who lived about AD 316–397. A bishop, he became one of the most popular saints of the Middle Ages. The period of warm weather often occurring about the time of his feast day is sometimes called St. Martin's Summer (especially in England).

POLAND: INDEPENDENCE DAY. Nov 11. Poland regained independence in 1918, after having been partitioned among Austria, Prussia and Russia for more than 120 years.

SPACE MILESTONE: *GEMINI 12* (US). Nov 11, 1966. Last Project Gemini manned Earth orbit launched. Buzz Aldrin spent five hours on a space walk, setting a new record.

SWEDEN: SAINT MARTIN'S DAY. Nov 11. Originally in memory of St. Martin of Tours; also associated with Martin Luther, who is celebrated the day before. Marks the end of the autumn's work and the beginning of winter activities.

VETERANS DAY. Nov 11. Veterans Day was observed Nov 11 from 1919 through 1970. Public Law 90–363, the "Monday Holiday Law," provided that, beginning in 1971, Veterans Day would be observed on "the fourth Monday in October." This movable observance date, which separated Veterans Day from the Nov 11 anniversary of WWI Armistice, proved unpopular. State after state moved its observance back to the traditional Nov 11 date, and finally Public Law 94–97 of Sept 18, 1975, required that, effective Jan 1, 1978, the observance of Veterans Day revert to Nov 11. See also: "Armistice Day" (Nov 11). For more information about Veterans Day, go to the website of the Veterans of Foreign Wars at www.vfw.com/amesm/origins.shtml.

★ **VETERANS DAY.** Nov 11. Presidential Proclamation. Formerly called "Armistice Day" and proclaimed each year since 1926 for Nov 11. PL83–380 of June 1, 1954, changed the name to "Veterans Day." PL90–363 of June 28, 1968, required that beginning in 1971 it would be observed the fourth Monday in October. PL 94–97 of Sept 18, 1975, required that effective Jan 1, 1978, the observance would revert to Nov 11. See Curriculum Connection.

WASHINGTON: ADMISSION DAY: ANNIVERSARY. Nov 11. Became 42nd state in 1889.

WORLD WAR I ARMISTICE: ANNIVERSARY. Nov 11, 1918. Anniversary of armistice between Allied and Central Powers ending WWI, signed at 5 AM, Nov 11, 1918, in Marshal Foch's railway car in the Forest of Compiegne, France. Hostilities ceased at 11 AM. Recognized in many countries as Armistice Day, Remembrance Day, Veterans Day, Victory Day or World War I Memorial Day. Many places observe silent memorial at the 11th hour of the 11th day of the 11th month each year. See also: "Veterans Day" (Nov 11).

NOVEMBER 11
WORLD WAR I ARMISTICE DAY/VETERANS DAY

Veterans Day, or Armistice Day, as it is called in many countries outside the US, has been a legal federal holiday since 1938. However, many children today do not know its significance or why people wear red poppies. This day commemorates the end of World War I in 1918. In 1919, President Woodrow Wilson proclaimed it as Armistice Day, to remind all Americans of the tragedies of war. In 1954, Congress changed the name to Veterans Day, to honor and recognize veterans of all wars.

This is a day for reflection on the sacrifices made during wars. Compromise and nonviolent conflict resolution are alternative topics. There are many books available on war and its effects. *In Flanders Fields: the Story of the Poem by John McCrae*, by Linda Granfield (Doubleday, 0-385-32228-3, $15.95 Gr. 3 & up) intersperses double-page spreads of the poem with information about World War I, including the significance of red poppies. *Casey Over There*, by Staton Rabin (Harcourt Brace, 0-15-253186-6, $14.95 Gr. K–3) is a picture book about one family's experience during WWI. *After the Dancing Days*, by Margaret Rostkowski (HarperCollins, 0-06-440248-7, $4.95 Gr. 6 & up) is about a young girl's relationship with a WWI veteran who is recovering in a veteran's hospital. *War and the Pity of War*, edited by Neil Philip (Clarion, 0-395-84982-9, $20 Gr. 6 & up) is an anthology of poems inspired by war. The poems reflect a range of experiences, including heroism, sardonic humor and horror.

BIRTHDAYS TODAY

Barbara Boxer, 59, US Senator (D, California), born Brooklyn, NY, Nov 11, 1940.

Leonardo DiCaprio, 24, actor (*Parenthood*, *Titanic*), born Ridgewood, NJ, Nov 11, 1975.

Peg Kehret, 63, author (*Horror at the Haunted House*), born LaCrosse, WI, Nov 11, 1936.

Kurt Vonnegut, Jr, 77, novelist (*Slaughterhouse Five*, *Cat's Cradle*), born Indianapolis, IN, Nov 11, 1922.

NOVEMBER 12 — FRIDAY
Day 316 — 49 Remaining

BLACKMUN, HARRY A.: BIRTH ANNIVERSARY. Nov 12, 1908. Retired associate justice of the Supreme Court of the US, nominated by President Nixon Apr 14, 1970. Justice Blackmun was born at Nashville, IL. He retired from the Court Aug 3, 1994, and died Mar 4, 1999, at Arlington, VA.

STANTON, ELIZABETH CADY: BIRTH ANNIVERSARY. Nov 12, 1815. American woman suffragist and reformer, Elizabeth Cady Stanton was born at Johnstown, NY. "We hold these truths to be self-evident," she said at the first Women's Rights Convention, in 1848, "that all men and women are created equal." She died at New York, NY, Oct 26, 1902.

SUN YAT-SEN: BIRTH ANNIVERSARY (TRADITIONAL). Nov 12. Although his actual birth date in 1866 is not known, Dr. Sun Yat-Sen's traditional birthday commemoration is held Nov 12. Heroic leader of China's 1911 revolution, he died at Peking, Mar 12, 1925. The death anniversary is also widely observed. See also: "Sun Yat-Sen: Death Anniversary" (Mar 12).

TYLER, LETITIA CHRISTIAN: BIRTH ANNIVERSARY. Nov 12, 1790. First wife of John Tyler, 10th president of the US, born at New Kent County, VA. Died at Washington, DC, Sept 10, 1842.

BIRTHDAYS TODAY

Jack Reed, 50, US Senator (D, Rhode Island), born Providence, RI, Nov 12, 1949.

Sammy Sosa, 31, baseball player, born San Pedro de Macoris, Dominican Republic, Nov 12, 1968.

NOVEMBER 13 — SATURDAY

Day 317 — 48 Remaining

BRANDEIS, LOUIS DEMBITZ: BIRTH ANNIVERSARY. Nov 13, 1856. American jurist, associate justice of US Supreme Court (1916–39), born at Louisville, KY. Died at Washington, DC, Oct 5, 1941.

CIRCLE K INTERNATIONAL SERVICE DAY. Nov 13. This day is set aside for all Circle K clubs worldwide to perform a campus and community service project to benefit children ages 6-13. Circle K is a college student service organization sponsored by Kiwanis. For info: Circle K Intl, 3636 Woodview Trace, Indianapolis, IN 46268-3196. Phone: (317) 875-8755 or (317) 875-8755. Fax: (317) 879-0204. E-mail: cki@kiwanis.org.

STEVENSON, ROBERT LOUIS: BIRTH ANNIVERSARY. Nov 13, 1850. Scottish author, born at Edinburgh, Scotland, known for his *Child's Garden of Verses* and novels such as *Treasure Island* and *Kidnapped*. Died at Samoa, Dec 3, 1894.

STOKES BECOMES FIRST BLACK MAYOR IN US: ANNIVERSARY. Nov 13, 1967. Carl Burton Stokes became the first black in the US elected mayor when he won the Cleveland, OH, mayoral election. Died Apr 3, 1996.

BIRTHDAYS TODAY

Whoopi Goldberg, 50, comedienne, actress (*Ghost, Sister Act, The Color Purple*), born New York, NY, Nov 13, 1949.

Garry Marshall, 65, producer, director (*Beaches, Pretty Woman*), actor ("Murphy Brown"), born New York, NY, Nov 13, 1934.

Vincent (Vinny) Testaverde, 36, football player, born New York, NY, Nov 13, 1963.

NOVEMBER 14 — SUNDAY

Day 318 — 47 Remaining

★**AMERICAN EDUCATION WEEK.** Nov 14–20. Presidential Proclamation 5403, of Oct 30, 1985, covers all succeeding years. Always the first full week preceding the fourth Thursday in November. Issued from 1921–25 and in 1936, sometimes for a week in December and sometimes as National Education Week. After an absence of a number of years, this proclamation was issued each year from 1955–82 (issued in 1955 as a prelude to the White House Conference on Education). Previously, Proclamation 4967, of Sept 13, 1982, covered all succeeding years as the second week in November.

AMERICAN EDUCATION WEEK. Nov 14–20. Focuses attention on the importance of education and all that it stands for.

		S	M	T	W	T	F	S
November			1	2	3	4	5	6
1999		7	8	9	10	11	12	13
		14	15	16	17	18	19	20
		21	22	23	24	25	26	27
		28	29	30				

NOVEMBER 14–20
NATIONAL GEOGRAPHY AWARENESS WEEK

Research results reveal that large numbers of American students are unable to locate the US on a map or a globe. National Geography Awareness Week gives you the perfect opportunity to put students on the right road to geography literacy.

Map skills are crucial. Children begin to grasp the concept that maps "stand for" something by kindergarten age. Help the youngest students understand what maps are and how they are used by asking them to draw maps relevant to their lives. A map of the student (head, arms and legs labeled), the classroom, the student's bedroom and house or apartment are good places to start. Successfully following directions and reading a treasure map of the school could lead to a classroom treat.

Older students can have fun with geography in many ways. Sports fans can locate the cities, states and countries where their favorite teams play. The same exercise can be used for clothing manufacturers, food products or celebrity birthplaces. Students of all ages can "pin" the place where they (or siblings) were born on a classroom map.

Those who enjoy competition might want to participate in a Geography Bee. Similar to a Spelling Bee, students would locate places. Several age divisions would allow more student participation. For kindergartners questions could include places found around the school building and in the community. The National Geographic Society sponsors a national geography bee. See Oct 15 for information on registering your school.

Me On The Map, Joan Sweeney (Random House, 0-517-88557-3, $6.99 Gr. K–2) introduces the basic concept of mapmaking. Sorting states and their capital cities can be a daunting task. *The Scrambled States of America*, by Laurie Keller (Henry Holt, 0-8050-5802-8, $15.95 Gr. K–4) is a humorous story about states switching places, filled with facts and geographical fun.

The US Geological Survey, which maps the US, has lesson plans on its website at www.usgs.gov/education/learnweb/index.html.

Annually, the week preceding the week of Thanksgiving. For info: Connie Morris, Natl Education Assn (NEA), 1201 16th St NW, Washington, DC 20036. Phone: (202) 822-7262. Fax: (202) 822-7292. Web: www.nea.org.

AROUND THE WORLD IN 72 DAYS: ANNIVERSARY. Nov 14, 1889. Newspaper reporter Nellie Bly (pen name used by Elizabeth Cochrane Seaman) set off in 1889, to attempt to break Jules Verne's imaginary hero Phileas Fogg's record of voyaging around the world in 80 days. She did beat Fogg's record, taking 72 days, 6 hours, 11 minutes and 14 seconds to make the trip.

BLOOD TRANSFUSION: ANNIVERSARY. Nov 14, 1666. Samuel Pepys, diarist and Fellow of the Royal Society, wrote in his diary for Nov 14, 1666: "Dr. Croone told me. . .there was a pretty experiment of the blood of one dog let out, till he died, into the body of another on one side, while all his own run out on the other side. The first died upon the place, and the other very well and likely to do well. This did give occasion to many pretty wishes, as of the blood of a Quaker to be let into an Archbishop, and such like; but, as Dr. Croone says, may, if it takes, be of mighty use to man's health, for the amending of bad blood by borrowing from a better body."

EISENHOWER, MAMIE DOUD: BIRTH ANNIVERSARY.
Nov 14, 1896. Wife of Dwight David Eisenhower, 34th president of the US, born at Boone, IA. Died Nov 1, 1979, at Gettysburg, PA.

GERMANY: VOLKSTRAUERTAG. Nov 14. Memorial Day and national day of mourning in all German states. Observed on the Sunday before Totensonntag. See also: "Germany: Totensonntag" (Nov 21).

GUINEA-BISSAU: RE-ADJUSTMENT MOVEMENT'S DAY.
Nov 14. National holiday.

INDIA: CHILDREN'S DAY. Nov 14. Holiday observed throughout India.

JORDAN: KING HUSSEIN'S BIRTHDAY. Nov 14. H.M. King Hussein is honored each year on the anniversary of his birth in 1935. He died Feb 6, 1999, at Jordan.

MILES, MISKA: BIRTH ANNIVERSARY. Nov 14, 1899. Author (*Annie and the Old One*), whose real name was Patricia Miles Martin, born at Cherokee, KS. Died Jan 1, 1986.

MONET, CLAUDE: BIRTH ANNIVERSARY. Nov 14, 1840. French Impressionist painter (*Water Lillies*), born at Paris. Died at Giverny, France, Dec 5, 1926.

NATIONAL GEOGRAPHY AWARENESS WEEK. Nov 14–20. Focus public awareness on the importance of the knowledge of geography. To be on the mailing list for information on obtaining a Geography Awareness Week packet of teaching materials, send your name and mailing address to Geography Education Program, Natl Geographic Soc, PO Box 98190, Washington, DC 20090-8190. More than 225,000 packets mailed out last year. For additional information, visit the Society's website at www.nationalgeographic.com. See Curriculum Connection.

NEHRU, JAWAHARLAL: BIRTH ANNIVERSARY. Nov 14, 1889. Indian leader and first prime minister after independence. Born at Allahabad, India, he died May 27, 1964, at New Delhi.

BIRTHDAYS TODAY

Ben Cayetano, 60, Governor of Hawaii (D), born Honolulu, HI, Nov 14, 1939.
Prince Charles, 51, Prince of Wales, heir to the British throne, born London, England, Nov 14, 1948.
Astrid Lindgren, 92, children's author (*Pippi Longstocking, The Brothers Lionheart*), born Vimmerby, Sweden, Nov 14, 1907.
Curt Schilling, 33, baseball player, born Anchorage, AK, Nov 14, 1966.
William Steig, 92, cartoonist, illustrator and author (*Dr. DeSoto*, Caldecott for *Sylvester and the Magic Pebble*), born New York, NY, Nov 14, 1907.

NOVEMBER 15 — MONDAY

Day 319 — 46 Remaining

BRAZIL: REPUBLIC DAY. Nov 15. Commemorates the Proclamation of the Republic in 1889.

JAPAN: SHICHI-GO-SAN. Nov 15. Annual children's festival. The *Shichi-Go-San* (Seven-Five-Three) rite, observed Nov 15, is "the most picturesque event in the autumn season." Parents take their three-year-old children of either sex, five-year-old boys and seven-year-old girls to the parish shrines dressed in their best clothes. There the guardian spirits are thanked for the healthy growth of the children and prayers are offered for their further development.

NOVEMBER 15
GEORGIA O'KEEFFE'S BIRTHDAY

Georgia O'Keeffe is one of America's best-known artists. Her paintings of flowers and desert landscapes, particularly those including skulls, command instant recognition. Students will enjoy looking at her artwork, which can be found reprinted in books, calendars and postcards. Discuss the way O'Keeffe explored shape and varying light conditions. Talk about her use of bright, vibrant colors.

O'Keeffe's work was closely tied to nature. This provides a tie-in to the science curriculum. Units on plants, animals and rocks and minerals are full of materials well-suited to an O'Keeffe celebration and exhibit. Ask students to find a rock, leaf or twig with an interesting shape. If outside observation is possible, students can look at cloud shapes and tree bark patterns, the shapes found on an animal's paw or the texture of its fur. An assignment would be to draw or paint the object they have seen, paying special attention to shape, texture and color. Encourage students to highlight the part of their object which intrigues them most by drawing it larger than life-size. An additional activity could include a list of descriptive and sensory words for the object the student has drawn or painted. The list will provide a starting point for the student to write a poem or short essay. Artwork and written pieces should be displayed in the classroom or hall.

There are a number of juvenile and adult biographies about O'Keeffe; for example, *My Name Is Georgia: A Portrait*, by Jeanette Winter (Harcourt Brace, 0-15-201649-X, $16 Gr. 2–4). Check your library for video interviews and documentaries available about her life and work. An excellent website with reproductions of paintings is at www.ionet.net/~jellenc/okeeffe5.html.

NATIONAL CHILDREN'S BOOK WEEK. Nov 15–21. To encourage the enjoyment of reading for young people. Each year, the week has a theme. For the 80th annual celebration, the theme is "Plant a Seed: Read." Posters and a suggested activity brochure are available from the sponsor. For info: The Children's Book Council, Inc, 568 Broadway, Ste 404, New York, NY 10012. Phone: (212) 966-1990. Fax: (212) 966-2073. E-mail: staff@cbcbooks.org. Web: www.cbcbooks.org.

O'KEEFFE, GEORGIA: BIRTH ANNIVERSARY. Nov 15, 1887. Described as one of the greatest American artists of the 20th century, O'Keeffe painted desert landscapes and flower studies. Born at Sun Prairie, WI, she was married to the famous photographer Alfred Stieglitz. She died at Santa Fe, NM, Mar 6, 1986. See Curriculum Connection.

BIRTHDAYS TODAY

Daniel Pinkwater, 58, author (*Smarkout Boys and the Avocado of Death*), born Memphis, TN, Nov 15, 1941.

NOVEMBER 16 — TUESDAY

Day 320 — 45 Remaining

MOON PHASE: FIRST QUARTER. Nov 16. Moon enters First Quarter phase at 4:03 AM, EST.

NATIONAL COMMUNITY EDUCATION DAY. Nov 16. To recognize and promote strong relationships between public schools and the communities they serve and to help schools develop new relationships with parents, community members, local organizations and agencies. Annually, the Tuesday of American Education Week. For info: Natl Community Education Assn, 3929 Old Lee Hwy, Ste 91-A, Fairfax, VA 22030-2401. Phone: (703) 359-8973. Fax: (703) 359-0972. E-mail: ncea@ncea.com.

OKLAHOMA: ADMISSION DAY: ANNIVERSARY. Nov 16. Became 46th state in 1907.

RIEL, LOUIS: HANGING ANNIVERSARY. Nov 16, 1885. Born at St. Boniface, Manitoba, Canada, Oct 23, 1844, Louis Riel, leader of the Metis (French/Indian mixed ancestry), was elected to Canada's House of Commons in 1873 and 1874, but never seated. Confined to asylums for madness (feigned or falsely charged, some said), Riel became a US citizen in 1883. In 1885 he returned to western Canada to lead the North West Rebellion. Defeated, he surrendered and was tried for treason, convicted and hanged, at Regina, Northwest Territory, Canada. Seen as a patriot and protector of French culture in Canada, Riel's life and death became a legend and a symbol of the problems between French and English Canadians.

ROMAN CATHOLICS ISSUE NEW CATECHISM: ANNIVERSARY. Nov 16, 1992. For the first time since 1563, the Roman Catholic Church issued a new universal catechism, which addressed modern-day issues.

SAINT EUSTATIUS, WEST INDIES: STATIA AND AMERICA DAY: ANNIVERSARY. Nov 16. St. Eustatius, Leeward Islands. To commemorate the first salute to an American flag by a foreign government, from Fort Oranje in 1776. Festivities include sports events and dancing. During the American Revolution St. Eustatius was an important trading center and a supply base for the colonies.

SPACE MILESTONE: *VENERA 3* (USSR). Nov 16, 1965. This unmanned space probe crashed into Venus, Mar 1, 1966. First manmade object on another planet.

UNITED NATIONS: INTERNATIONAL DAY FOR TOLERANCE. Nov 16. On Dec 12, 1996, the General Assembly established the International Day for Tolerance, to commemorate the adoption by UNESCO member states of the Declaration of Principles on Tolerance Nov 16, 1995. For info: United Nations, Dept of Public Info, New York, NY 10017.

BIRTHDAYS TODAY

Oksana Baiul, 22, Olympic figure skater, born Dniepropetrovsk, Ukraine, Nov 16, 1977.

	S	M	T	W	T	F	S
November		1	2	3	4	5	6
1999	7	8	9	10	11	12	13
	14	15	16	17	18	19	20
	21	22	23	24	25	26	27
	28	29	30				

Lisa Bonet, 32, actress ("The Cosby Show," "A Different World"), born San Francisco, CA, Nov 16, 1967.
Jean Fritz, 84, author (Laura Ingalls Wilder Medal for *The Cabin Faced West*), born Hankow, China, Nov 16, 1915.
Dwight Eugene Gooden, 35, baseball player, born Tampa, FL, Nov 16, 1964.
Robin McKinley, 47, author (Newbery for *The Hero and the Crown*), born Jennifer Carolyn Robin McKinley, Warren, OH, Nov 16, 1952.

NOVEMBER 17 — WEDNESDAY
Day 321 — 44 Remaining

GERMANY: BUSS UND BETTAG. Nov 17. Buss und Bettag (Repentance Day) is observed on the Wednesday before the last Sunday of the church year. A legal public holiday in all German states except Bavaria (where it is observed only in communities with predominantly Protestant populations).

NATIONAL EDUCATIONAL SUPPORT PERSONNEL DAY. Nov 17. A mandate of the delegates to the 1987 National Education Association Representative Assembly called for a special day during American Education Week to honor the contributions of school support employees. Local associations and school districts salute support staff on this 13th annual observance, the Wednesday of American Education Week. For info: Connie Morris, Natl Education Assn (NEA), 1201 16th St NW, Washington, DC 20036. Phone: (202) 822-7262. Fax: (202) 822-7292. Web: www.nea.org.

WORLD PEACE DAY. Nov 17. World Peace Day was created to give the common person a way to demonstrate their desire for peace. To do this, people pray for peace all day, drive with their headlights on, wear a white ribbon for peace (everyday) and sign our petition for peace (available on our web page) or print our petition for peace and have 20 people sign it. Annually, Nov 17. For info: Don Morris, PO Box 565245, Miami, FL 33256-5245. Phone: (305) 270-8890. E-mail: peaceguy@peaceday.org. Web: www.peaceday.org.

BIRTHDAYS TODAY

Justin Cooper, 11, actor (*Liar, Liar,* "Brother's Keeper"), born Los Angeles, CA, Nov 17, 1988.
Howard Dean, 51, Governor of Vermont (D), born East Hampton, NY, Nov 17, 1948.
Danny DeVito, 55, actor (*Twins, Matilda*), born Neptune, NJ, Nov 17, 1944.
(Clarke) Isaac Hanson, 19, singer (Hanson), born Tulsa, OK, Nov 17, 1980.
James M. Inhofe, 65, US Senator (R, Oklahoma), born Des Moines, IA, Nov 17, 1934.

NOVEMBER 18 — THURSDAY
Day 322 — 43 Remaining

AMERICAN SPEECH–LANGUAGE–HEARING ASSOCIATION CONVENTION. Nov 18–21. San Francisco, CA. Scientific sessions held on language, speech disorders, hearing science and hearing disorders and matters of professional interest to speech-language pathologists and audiologists. Est attendance: 10,000. For info: Cheryl Russell, Conv Dir, American Speech–Language–Hearing Assn, 10801 Rockville Pike, Rockville, MD 20852-3279. Phone: (301) 897-5700.

DAGUERRE, LOUIS JACQUES MANDE: BIRTH ANNIVERSARY. Nov 18, 1789. French tax collector, theatre scene-painter, physicist and inventor, was born at Cormeilles-en-Parisis,

France. He is remembered for his invention of the daguerreotype photographic process—one of the earliest to permit a photographic image to be chemically fixed to provide a permanent picture. The process was presented to the French Academy of Science Jan 7, 1839. Daguerre died near Paris, France, July 10, 1851.

GREAT AMERICAN SMOKEOUT. Nov 18. A day observed annually to celebrate smoke-free environments. Annually, the third Thursday in November. For info: PR Dept, American Cancer Soc, 1599 Clifton Rd NE, Atlanta, GA 30329. Phone: (404) 329-5735. Web: www.cancer.org.

LATVIA: INDEPENDENCE DAY. Nov 18. National holiday. Commemorates the declaration of an independent Latvia in 1918.

MICKEY MOUSE'S BIRTHDAY. Nov 18. The comical activities of squeaky-voiced Mickey Mouse first appeared in 1928, on the screen of the Colony Theatre at New York City. The film, Walt Disney's "Steamboat Willie," was the first animated cartoon talking picture.

NATIONAL COUNCIL OF TEACHERS OF ENGLISH ANNUAL CONVENTION. Nov 18–23. Denver, CO. For info: Natl Council of Teachers of English, 1111 W Kenyon Rd, Urbana, IL 61801-1096. Phone: (800) 369-6283 or (217) 328-3870. Web: www.ncte.org.

NATIONAL COUNCIL FOR THE SOCIAL STUDIES ANNUAL MEETING. Nov 18–21. Orange County Convention Center, Orlando, FL. For info: Natl Council for the Social Studies, 3501 Newark St NW, Washington, DC 20016. Phone: (202) 966-7840. Web: www.ncss.org.

OMAN: NATIONAL HOLIDAY. Nov 18. Sultanate of Oman celebrates its national day.

SHEPARD, ALAN: BIRTH ANNIVERSARY. Nov 18, 1923. Astronaut, born East Derry, NH. Shepard was the first American in space when he flew *Freedom 7* in 1961, just 23 days after Russian Yuri Gargarin was the first man in space. Shepard died July 21, 1998, near Monterey, CA.

SOUTH AFRICA ADOPTS NEW CONSTITUTION: ANNIVERSARY. Nov 18, 1993. After more than 300 years of white majority rule, basic civil rights were finally granted to blacks in South Africa. The constitution providing such rights was approved by representatives of the ruling party, as well as members of 20 other political parties.

US UNIFORM TIME ZONE PLAN: ANNIVERSARY. Nov 18, 1883. Charles Ferdinand Dowd, a Connecticut school teacher and one of the early advocates of uniform time, proposed a time zone plan of the US (four zones of 15 degrees), which he and others persuaded the railroads to adopt and place in operation. Info from National Bureau of Standards Monograph 155. See also: "US Standard Time Act: Anniversary" (Mar 19).

BIRTHDAYS TODAY

Dante Bichette, 36, baseball player, born West Palm Beach, FL, Nov 18, 1963.
Wilma Mankiller, 54, Chief of the Cherokee Nation 1985–95, born Tahlequah, OK, Nov 18, 1945.
Ted Stevens, 76, US Senator (R, Alaska), born Indianapolis, IN, Nov 18, 1923.

NOVEMBER 19 — FRIDAY

Day 323 — 42 Remaining

BELIZE: GARIFUNA DAY. Nov 19. Public holiday celebrating the first arrival of Black Caribs from St. Vincent and Rotan to Southern Belize.

CAMPANELLA, ROY: BIRTH ANNIVERSARY. Nov 19, 1921. Baseball Hall of Fame catcher born at Philadelphia, PA. Died at Woodland Hills, CA, June 26, 1993.

COLD WAR FORMALLY ENDED: ANNIVERSARY. Nov 19–21, 1990. A summit was held at Paris with the leaders of the Conference on Security and Cooperation in Europe (CSCE) Nov 19–21, 1990. The highlight of the summit was the signing of a treaty to dramatically reduce conventional weapons in Europe, thereby ending the Cold War.

GARFIELD, JAMES ABRAM: BIRTH ANNIVERSARY. Nov 19, 1831. The 20th president of the US (and the first left-handed president) was born at Orange, OH. Term of office: Mar 4–Sept 19, 1881. While walking into the Washington, DC, railway station on the morning of July 2, 1881, Garfield was shot by disappointed office seeker Charles J. Guiteau. He survived, in very weak condition, until Sept 19, 1881, when he succumbed to blood poisoning at Elberon, NJ (where he had been taken for recuperation). Guiteau was tried, convicted and hanged at the jail at Washington, June 30, 1882.

HAVE A BAD DAY DAY. Nov 19. For those who are filled with revulsion at being told endlessly to "have a nice day," this day is a brief respite. Store and business owners are to ask workers to tell customers to "have a bad day." Annually, Nov 19. [© 1998 by WPL] For info: Thomas or Ruth Roy, Wellness Permission League, PO Box 662, Mt. Gretna, PA 17064-0662. Phone: (717) 964-1308. Fax: (717) 964-1335. E-mail: wellcat@desupernet.net.

LINCOLN'S GETTYSBURG ADDRESS: ANNIVERSARY. Nov 19, 1863. Seventeen acres of the Civil War battlefield at Gettysburg, PA, were dedicated as a national cemetery. Noted orator Edward Everett spoke for two hours; the address that Lincoln delivered in less than two minutes was later recognized as one of the most eloquent of the English language. Five manuscript copies in Lincoln's hand survive, including the rough draft begun in ink at the executive mansion at Washington and concluded in pencil at Gettysburg on the morning of the dedication (kept at the Library of Congress). For more info: *The Gettysburg Address* (Houghton Mifflin, 0-395-69824-3, $14.95 Gr. 3-5).

MONACO: NATIONAL HOLIDAY. Nov 19.

PUERTO RICO: DISCOVERY DAY. Nov 19. Public holiday. Columbus discovered Puerto Rico in 1493 on his second voyage to the New World.

RETIRED TEACHER'S DAY IN FLORIDA. Nov 19. A ceremonial day to honor the retired teachers of the state.

"ROCKY AND HIS FRIENDS" TV PREMIERE: 40th ANNIVERSARY. Nov 19, 1959. This popular cartoon featured the adventures of a talking squirrel, Rocky (Rocket J. Squirrel), and his friend Bullwinkle, a flaky moose. The tongue-in-cheek dialogue contrasted with the simple plots in which Rocky and Bullwinkle tangled with Russian bad guys Boris Badenov and Natasha (who worked for Mr Big). Other popular segments on the show included the adventures of Sherman and Mr Peabody (an intelligent talking dog). In 1961 the show was renamed "The Bullwinkle Show," but the cast of characters remained the same.

SCHAEFER, JACK: BIRTH ANNIVERSARY. Nov 19, 1907. Author of the bestseller *Shane*, which was later made into an award-winning film. Born at Cleveland, OH, Schaefer died Jan 24, 1991, at Santa Fe, NM.

TEXAS PTA CONVENTION. Nov 19–22. Rivercenter Marriott, San Antonio, TX. The 90th annual business meeting of the Texas PTA. General business meeting includes adoption of legislative positions and resolutions. More than 40 workshops are presented on parenting and parent involvement issues. Est attendance: 2,000. For info: Joan Thurman, Texas PTA, 408 W 11th St, Austin, TX 78701-2199. Phone: (512) 476-6769 or (800) TALK-PTA. Fax: (512) 476-8152. E-mail: info@txpta.org. Web: www.txpta.org.

BIRTHDAYS TODAY

Gail Devers, 33, Olympic gold medal sprinter, born Seattle, WA, Nov 19, 1966.

Jodie Foster, 37, actress (*Little Man Tate, Nell*), director (*Home for the Holidays*), born Los Angeles, CA, Nov 19, 1962.

Thomas R. Harkin, 60, US Senator (D, Iowa), born Cumming, IA, Nov 19, 1939.

Jim Hodges, 43, Governor of South Carolina (D), born Lancaster, SC, Nov 19, 1956.

Ahmad Rashad (born Bobby Moore), 50, sportscaster, former football player, born Portland, OR, Nov 19, 1949.

Meg Ryan, 38, actress (*Sleepless in Seattle*), born Fairfield, CT, Nov 19, 1961.

Kerri Strug, 22, Olympic gymnast, born Tucson, AZ, Nov 19, 1977.

Tommy G. Thompson, 58, Governor of Wisconsin (R), born Elroy, WI, Nov 19, 1941.

Ted Turner, 61, baseball, basketball and cable TV executive, born Cincinnati, OH, Nov 19, 1938.

NOVEMBER 20 — SATURDAY
Day 324 — 41 Remaining

BILL OF RIGHTS: ANNIVERSARY OF FIRST STATE RATIFICATION. Nov 20, 1789. New Jersey became the first state to ratify 10 of the 12 amendments to the US Constitution proposed by Congress Sept 25. These 10 amendments came to be known as the Bill of Rights. See also: "First Proposed Amendments to the US Constitution: Anniversary" (Sept 25).

KENNEDY, ROBERT FRANCIS: BIRTH ANNIVERSARY. Nov 20, 1925. US Senator and younger brother of John F. Kennedy (35th president) was born at Brookline, MA. An assassin shot him at Los Angeles, CA, June 5, 1968, while he was campaigning for the presidential nomination. He died the next day. Sirhan Sirhan was convicted of his murder.

LAURIER, SIR WILFRED: BIRTH ANNIVERSARY. Nov 20, 1841. Canadian statesman (premier, 1896–1911), born at St. Lin, Quebec. Died Feb 17, 1919, at Ottawa, Ontario.

MEXICO: REVOLUTION ANNIVERSARY. Nov 20. Anniversary of the social revolution launched by Francisco I. Madero in 1910. National holiday.

November 1999	S	M	T	W	T	F	S
		1	2	3	4	5	6
	7	8	9	10	11	12	13
	14	15	16	17	18	19	20
	21	22	23	24	25	26	27
	28	29	30				

THAILAND: ELEPHANT ROUND-UP AT SURIN. Nov 20. Elephant demonstrations in morning, elephant races and tug-of-war between 100 men and one elephant. Observed since 1961 on third Saturday in November. Special trains from Bangkok on previous day.

UNITED NATIONS: UNIVERSAL CHILDREN'S DAY. Nov 20. Designated by the United Nations General Assembly as Universal Children's Day. First observance was in 1953. A time to honor children with special ceremonies and festivals and to make children's needs known to governments. Observed on different days in more than 120 nations; Nov 20 marks the day in 1959 when the General Assembly adopted the Declaration of the Rights of the Child.

WOLCOTT, OLIVER: BIRTH ANNIVERSARY. Nov 20, 1726. Signer of the Declaration of Independence, Governor of Connecticut, born at Windsor, CT. Died Dec 1, 1797, at Litchfield, CT.

BIRTHDAYS TODAY

Marion Dane Bauer, 61, author (*On My Honor*), born Oglesby, IL, Nov 20, 1938.

Joseph Robinette Biden, Jr, 57, US Senator (D, Delaware), born Scranton, PA, Nov 20, 1942.

Robert C. Byrd, 82, US Senator (D, West Virginia), born North Wilkesboro, NC, Nov 20, 1917.

NOVEMBER 21 — SUNDAY
Day 325 — 40 Remaining

CONGRESS FIRST MEETS IN WASHINGTON: ANNIVERSARY. Nov 21, 1800. Congress met at Philadelphia from 1790 to 1800, when the north wing of the new Capitol at Washington, DC was completed. The House and Senate were scheduled to meet in the new building Nov 17, 1800 but a quorum wasn't achieved until Nov 21. To take a virtual tour of the Capitol, go to: www.senate.gov/vtour.

MAN'S FIRST FREE FLIGHT (BALLOON): ANNIVERSARY. Nov 21, 1783. Jean Francois Pilatre de Rozier and the Marquis Francois Laurent d'Arlandes became the first men to fly when they ascended in a Montgolfier hot-air balloon at Paris, France, less than six months after the first public balloon flight demonstration (June 5, 1783), and only a year after the first experiments with small paper and fabric balloons by the Montgolfier brothers, Joseph and Jacques, at Annonay, France, in November 1782. The first manned free flight lasted about 25 minutes and carried the passengers nearly six miles at a height of about 300 feet, over the city of Paris. Benjamin Franklin was one of the spectators at the flight.

NATIONAL ADOPTION WEEK. Nov 21–27. To commemorate the success of three kinds of adoption—infant, special needs and intercountry—through a variety of special events. Annually, the week of Thanksgiving. Est attendance: 15,000. For info: Natl Council for Adoption, 1930 17th St NW, Washington, DC 20009-6207. Phone: (202) 328-1200. Fax: (202) 332-0935.

NATIONAL BIBLE WEEK. Nov 21–28. An interfaith campaign to promote reading and study of the Bible. Resource packets available. Governors and mayors across the country proclaim National Bible Week observance in their constituencies. Annually, from the Sunday preceding Thanksgiving to the following Sunday. For info: Thomas R. May, Exec Dir, Natl Bible Assn, 1865 Broadway, 7th Fl, New York, NY 10023. Phone: (212) 408-1390.

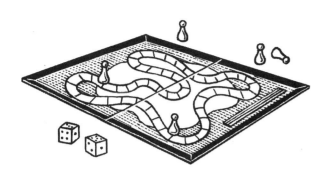

NATIONAL GAME AND PUZZLE WEEK. Nov 21–27. To increase appreciation of games and puzzles while conserving the tradition of investing time with family and friends. Annually, the last week in November. For info: Dana Heideman, Patch Products, PO Box 268, Beloit, WI 53512-0268. Phone: (608) 362-6896. Fax: (608) 362-8178. E-mail: patch@patchproducts.com. Web: www.patchproducts.com.

NORTH CAROLINA: RATIFICATION DAY. Nov 21. Became 12th state to ratify Constitution in 1789.

SPEARE, ELIZABETH GEORGE: BIRTH ANNIVERSARY. Nov 21, 1908. Author (Newbery for *The Bronze Bow, The Witch of Blackbird Pond*), born at Melrose, MA. Died 1994.

UNITED NATIONS: WORLD TELEVISION DAY. Nov 21. On Dec 17, 1996, the General Assembly proclaimed this day as World Television Day, commemorating the date in 1996 on which the first World Television Forum was held at the UN. Info from: United Nations, Dept of Public Info, New York, NY 10017.

WORLD HELLO DAY. Nov 21. Everyone who participates greets 10 people. People in 179 countries have participated in this annual activity for advancing peace through personal communication. Heads of state of 114 countries have expressed approval of the event. 27th annual observance. For info: Michael McCormack, The McCormack Brothers, Box 993, Omaha, NE 68101.

BIRTHDAYS TODAY,1981

Troy Aikman, 33, quarterback, born West Covina, CA, Nov 21, 1966.

Richard J. Durbin, 55, US Senator (D, Illinois), born East St. Louis, IL, Nov 21, 1944.

George Kenneth (Ken) Griffey, Jr, 30, baseball player, born Donora, PA, Nov 21, 1969.

Stanley ("Stan the Man") Musial, 79, Baseball Hall of fame outfielder and first baseman, born Donora, PA, Nov 21, 1920.

Marlo Thomas, 61, actress ("That Girl"), author (*Free to Be . . . You and Me*), born Detroit, MI, Nov 21, 1938.

Megan Whalen Turner, 34, author (*The Thief*), born Fort Sill, OK, Nov 21, 1965.

NOVEMBER 22 — MONDAY

Day 326 — 39 Remaining

ADAMS, ABIGAIL SMITH: BIRTH ANNIVERSARY. Nov 22, 1744. Wife of John Adams, second president of the US, born at Weymouth, MA. Died Oct 28, 1818, at Quincy, MA.

FINLAND: INTERNATIONAL CHILDREN'S FILM FESTIVAL. Nov 22–28. Oulu. This one-week event gives festival visitors an opportunity to view several dozen feature-length films. Est attendance: 10,000. For info: Finnish Tourist Board, 655 Third Ave, New York, NY 10017. Phone: (212) 885-9700 or (358) (8) 881-1293. Fax: (358) (8) 8811290. Web: www.ouka.fi/oek/

GARNER, JOHN NANCE: BIRTH ANNIVERSARY. Nov 22, 1868. Thirty-second vice president of US (1933–41) born at Red River County, TX. Died at Uvalde, TX, Nov 7, 1967.

LEBANON: INDEPENDENCE DAY. Nov 22. National Day. Gained independence from France in 1943.

NATIONAL STOP THE VIOLENCE DAY. Nov 22. Radio and television stations across the nation are encouraged to promote "Peace on the Streets" and help put an end to gang (and other) violence through Stop the Violence Day. Participating stations unite to call for a one-day cease fire, the idea being, "If we can stop the violence for one day, we can stop the violence everyday, one day at a time." Stations also encourage listeners/viewers to wear and display white ribbons that day and drive with their headlights on as show of peace. Many stations hold peace rallies with local community leaders and also conduct a moment of silence on the air in honor of the year's victims of violence. Begun in 1990. Annually, on the anniversary of President John F. Kennedy's assassination. For info: Cliff Berkowitz, Pres, Lost Coast Communications, Inc, PO Box 25, Ferndale, CA 95536. Phone: (707) 786-5104. Fax: (707) 786-5100.

BIRTHDAYS TODAY

Boris Franz Becker, 32, tennis player, born Leimen, Germany, Nov 22, 1967.

Guion S. Bluford, Jr, 57, first black astronaut in space, born West Philadelphia, PA, Nov 22, 1942.

NOVEMBER 23 — TUESDAY

Day 327 — 38 Remaining

JAPAN: LABOR THANKSGIVING DAY. Nov 23. National holiday.

MOON PHASE: FULL MOON. Nov 23. Moon enters Full Moon phase at 2:04 AM, EST.

PERIGEAN SPRING TIDES. Nov 23. Spring tides, the highest possible tides, occur when New Moon or Full Moon takes place within 24 hours of the moment the Moon is nearest Earth (perigee) in its monthly orbit, at 5 PM, EST. The word spring refers not to the season but comes from the German word *springen*, "to rise up."

PIERCE, FRANKLIN: BIRTH ANNIVERSARY. Nov 23, 1804. The 14th president of the US was born at Hillsboro, NH. Term of office: Mar 4, 1853–Mar 3, 1857. Not nominated until the 49th ballot at the Democratic party convention in 1852, he was refused his party's nomination in 1856 for a second term. Pierce died at Concord, NH, Oct 8, 1869.

RUTLEDGE, EDWARD: 250th BIRTH ANNIVERSARY. Nov 23, 1749. Signer of the Declaration of Independence, governor of South Carolina, born at Charleston, SC. Died there Jan 23, 1800.

SAGITTARIUS, THE ARCHER. Nov 23–Dec 21. In the astronomical/astrological zodiac that divides the sun's apparent orbit into 12 segments, the period Nov 22–Dec 21 is identified, traditionally, as the sun-sign of Sagittarius, the Archer. The ruling planet is Jupiter.

BIRTHDAYS TODAY

Vin Baker, 28, basketball player, born Lake Wales, FL, Nov 23, 1971.

Mary L. Landrieu, 44, US Senator (D, Louisiana), born Arlington, VA, Nov 23, 1955.

Charles E. Schumer, 49, US Senator (D, New York), born Brooklyn, NY, Nov 23, 1950.

NOVEMBER 24 — WEDNESDAY

Day 328 — 37 Remaining

BARKLEY, ALBEN WILLIAM: BIRTH ANNIVERSARY. Nov 24, 1877. Thirty-fifth vice president of the US (1949–53), born at Graves County, KY. Died at Lexington, VA, Apr 30, 1956.

BURNETT, FRANCES HODGSON: BIRTH ANNIVERSARY. Nov 24, 1849. Children's author, noted for her classics, *Little Lord Fauntleroy, The Secret Garden* and *A Little Princess.* Born at Manchester, England, she died at Long Island, NY, Oct 29, 1924.

TAYLOR, ZACHARY: BIRTH ANNIVERSARY. Nov 24, 1784. The soldier who became 12th president of the US was born at Orange County, VA. Term of office: Mar 4, 1849–July 9, 1850. He was nominated at the Whig party convention in 1848, but, the story goes, he did not accept the letter notifying him of his nomination because it had postage due. He cast his first vote in 1846, when he was 62 years old. Becoming ill July 4, 1850, he died at the White House, July 9.

"WHAT DO YOU LOVE ABOUT AMERICA" DAY. Nov 24. One day to talk about what's great about our country and its people. In the midst of cynicism, let's talk to each other about what we love. For info: Chuck Sutherland, 6236 Del Norte Ln, Dallas, TX 75225. Phone: (214) 696-9214. Fax: (214) 696-6742. E-mail: sutherla@swbell.net.

BIRTHDAYS TODAY

Sylvia Louise Engdahl, 66, author (*Enchantress from the Stars*), born Los Angeles, CA, Nov 24, 1933.

Dan Glickman, 55, US Secretary of Agriculture, born Wichita, KS, Nov 24, 1944.

Meredith Henderson, 16, actress ("The Adventures of Shirley Holmes: Detective"), born Ottawa, Canada, Nov 24, 1983.

Yoshiko Uchida, 78, author (*Journey to Topaz: A Story of Japanese-American Evacuation*), born Alameda, CA, Nov 24, 1921.

NOVEMBER 25 — THURSDAY

Day 329 — 36 Remaining

AMERICA'S THANKSGIVING PARADE. Nov 25. Woodward Ave, Detroit, MI. The 72nd annual parade kicks off the holiday season with nearly 100 units marching. Annually, on Thanksgiving morning. Est attendance: 1,300,000. For info: Dennis Carnovale, The Parade Co, 9600 Mt Elliott, Detroit, MI 48211. Phone: (313) 923-7400. Fax: (313) 923-2920.

AUTOMOBILE SPEED REDUCTION: ANNIVERSARY. Nov 25, 1973. Anniversary of the presidential order requiring a cutback from the 70 mile-per-hour speed limit due to the energy crisis. The 55 mile-per-hour National Maximum Speed Limit (NMSL) was established by Congress in January 1974. The National Highway Traffic Administration reported that "the 55 mph NMSL forestalled 48,310 fatalities through 1980. There were also reductions in crash-related injuries and property damage." Motor fuel savings were estimated at 2.4 billion gallons per year. Notwithstanding, in 1987 Congress permitted states to increase speed limits on rural interstate highways to 65 miles per hour.

CARNEGIE, ANDREW: BIRTH ANNIVERSARY. Nov 25, 1835. American financier, philanthropist and benefactor of more than 2,500 libraries, was born at Dunfermline, Scotland. Carnegie Hall, Carnegie Foundation and the Carnegie Endowment for International Peace are among his gifts. Carnegie wrote in 1889, "Surplus wealth is a sacred trust which its possessor is bound to administer in his lifetime for the good of the community.... The man who dies . . . rich dies disgraced." Carnegie died at his summer estate, "Shadowbrook," MA, Aug 11, 1919.

EASTMAN, P.D.: BIRTH ANNIVERSARY. Nov 25, 1909. Philip Dey Eastman was born at Amherst, MA. His *Are You My Mother?* and *Go, Dog, Go!* rank among the bestselling children's books of all time. He died Jan 7, 1986.

MACY'S THANKSGIVING DAY PARADE. Nov 25. New York, NY. Starts at 9 AM, EST, in Central Park West. A part of everyone's Thanksgiving, the parade grows bigger and better each year. Featuring floats, giant balloons, marching bands and famous stars, the parade is televised for the whole country. 71st annual parade. For info: New York Conv/Visitors Bureau, 810 Seventh Ave, New York, NY 10019. Phone: (212) 484-1222. Web: www.nycvisit.com.

POPE JOHN XXIII: BIRTH ANNIVERSARY. Nov 25, 1881. Angelo Roncalli, 261st pope of the Roman Catholic Church, born at Sotte il Monte, Italy. Elected pope, Oct 28, 1958. Died June 3, 1963, at Rome, Italy.

SHOPPING REMINDER DAY. Nov 25. One month before Christmas, a reminder to shoppers that there are only 24 more shopping days (excluding Sundays, Thanksgiving and Christmas Eve) after today until Christmas, and that one month from today a new countdown will begin for Christmas 2000.

6ABC/BOSCOV'S THANKSGIVING DAY PARADE. Nov 25. Philadelphia, PA. Est attendance: 300,000. For info: Valerie Lagauskas, Parade Dir, WPVI-TV, 4100 City Line Ave, Philadelphia, PA 19131. Phone: (215) 581-4529.

SURINAME: INDEPENDENCE DAY. Nov 25. Holiday. Gained independence from the Netherlands in 1975.

★**THANKSGIVING DAY.** Nov 25. Presidential Proclamation. Always issued for the fourth Thursday in November. See also: "First US Holiday by Presidential Proclamation: Anniversary" (Nov 26).

THANKSGIVING DAY. Nov 25. Legal public holiday. (Public Law 90–363 sets Thanksgiving Day on the fourth Thursday in November). Observed in all states. In most states, the Friday after Thanksgiving is also a holiday; in Nevada it is called Family Day. For links to sites about Thanksgiving on the web, go to: deil.lang.uiuc.edu/web.pages/holidays/thanksgiving.html.

November 1999	S	M	T	W	T	F	S
		1	2	3	4	5	6
	7	8	9	10	11	12	13
	14	15	16	17	18	19	20
	21	22	23	24	25	26	27
	28	29	30				

Marc Brown, 53, illustrator and author (the Arthur series), born Erie, PA, Nov 25, 1946.

Joe DiMaggio, 85, Baseball Hall of Fame outfielder, born Martinez, CA, Nov 25, 1914.

Crescent Dragonwagon, 47, author (*Half a Moon and One Whole Star*), born New York, NY, Nov 25, 1952.

John F. Kennedy, Jr, 39, lawyer, editor (*George*), born Washington, DC, Nov 25, 1960.

NOVEMBER 26 — FRIDAY

Day 330 — 35 Remaining

BLACK FRIDAY. Nov 26. The traditional beginning of the Christmas shopping season on the Friday after Thanksgiving.

BUY NOTHING DAY. Nov 26. A 24-hour moratorium on consumer spending, a celebration of simplicity, about getting our runaway consumer culture back onto a sustainable path. Annually, on the first shopping day after Thanksgiving. For info: The Media Foundation, 1243 W. 7th Ave, Vancouver, BC, Canada V6H 1B7. Phone: (800) 663-1243. Fax: (604) 737-6021. E-mail: buy nothingday@adbusters.org.

CUSTER BATTLEFIELD BECOMES LITTLE BIGHORN BATTLEFIELD: ANNIVERSARY. Nov 26, 1991. The US Congress approved a bill renaming Custer Battlefield National Monument as Little Bighorn Battlefield National Monument. The bill also authorized the construction of a memorial to the Native Americans who fought and died at the battle known as Custer's Last Stand. Introduced by then Representative Ben Nighthorse Campbell, the only Native American in Congress, the bill was signed into law by President George Bush.

FAMILY DAY IN NEVADA. Nov 26. Observed annually on the Friday following the fourth Thursday in November.

FIRST US HOLIDAY BY PRESIDENTIAL PROCLAMATION: ANNIVERSARY. Nov 26, 1789. President George Washington proclaimed Nov 26, 1789, to be Thanksgiving Day. Both Houses of Congress, by their joint committee, had requested him to recommend a day of public thanksgiving and prayer, to be observed by acknowledging with grateful hearts the many and signal favors of Almighty God, especially by affording them an opportunity to peaceably establish a form of government for their safety and happiness. Proclamation issued Oct 3, 1789.

SLINKY INTRODUCED: ANNIVERSARY. Nov 26, 1945. In 1943 engineer Richard James was working in a Philadelphia shipyard trying to find a way to stabilize a piece of equipment on a ship in heavy seas. One idea was to suspend it on springs. One day a spring tumbled off his desk, giving him the idea for a toy. The accidental plaything was introduced by James and his wife in a Philadelphia department store during the 1945 Christmas season. Today more than 250,000,000 Slinkys have been sold. For further info: www.poof-toys.com.

TRUTH, SOJOURNER: DEATH ANNIVERSARY. Nov 26, 1883. A former slave who had been sold four different times, Sojourner Truth became an evangelist who argued for abolition and women's rights. After a troubled early life, she began her evangelical career in 1843, traveling through New England until she discovered the utopian colony called the Northampton Association of Education and Industry. It was there she was exposed to, and became an advocate for, the cause of abolition, working with Frederick Douglass, Wendall Phillips, William Lloyd Garrison and others. In 1850 she befriended Lucretia Mott, Elizabeth Cady Stanton and other feminist leaders and actively began supporting calls for women's rights. In 1870 she attempted to petition Congress to create a "Negro State" on public lands in the West. Born at Ulster County, NY, about 1790, she died Nov 26, 1883, at Battle Creek, MI.

BIRTHDAYS TODAY

Shannon Dunn, 27, Olympic snowboarder, born Arlington Heights, IL, Nov 26, 1972.

Shawn Kemp, 30, NBA forward, member of Dream Team II, born Elkhart, IN, Nov 26, 1969.

Laurence Pringle, 64, science writer (*An Extraordinary Life: The Story of a Monarch Butterfly*), born Rochester, NY, Nov 26, 1935.

Charles Monroe Schulz, 77, cartoonist ("Peanuts"), born Minneapolis, MN, Nov 26, 1922.

NOVEMBER 27 — SATURDAY

Day 331 — 34 Remaining

LIVINGSTON, ROBERT R.: BIRTH ANNIVERSARY. Nov 27, 1746. Member of the Continental Congress, farmer, diplomat and jurist, born at New York, NY. It was Livingston who administered the oath of office to President George Washington in 1789. He died at Clermont, NY, Feb 26, 1813.

THIRD PARLIAMENT OF THE WORLD'S RELIGIONS. Nov 27–Dec 4. Cape Town, South Africa. The first meeting of the interfaith Parliament was held at the World's Columbian Exposition at Chicago in 1893; the second was held at Chicago in 1993. For info: Dr. Jim Kenney, Council for a Parliament of the World's Religions, 105 W Adams, Ste 800, Chicago, IL 60690-1630. Phone: (312) 629-2990. Fax: (312) 629-2991. E-mail: spiritcpwr@aol.com. Web: www.cpwr.org.

WEIZMANN, CHAIM: 125th BIRTH ANNIVERSARY. Nov 27, 1874. Israeli statesman born near Pinsk, Byelorussia. He played an important role in bringing about the British government's Balfour Declaration, calling for the establishment of a national home for Jews at Palestine. He died at Tel Aviv, Israel, Nov 9, 1952.

BIRTHDAYS TODAY

Kevin Henkes, 39, author and illustrator (*Owen, Lily's Purple Plastic Purse*), born Racine, WI, Nov 27, 1960.

Nick Van Exel, 28, basketball player, born Kenosha, WI, Nov 27, 1971.

Jaleel White, 23, actor ("Family Matters"), born Los Angeles, CA, Nov 27, 1976.

NOVEMBER 28 — SUNDAY

Day 332 — 33 Remaining

ADVENT, FIRST SUNDAY. Nov 28. Advent includes the four Sundays before Christmas: Nov 28, Dec 5, Dec 12 and Dec 19 in 1999.

ALBANIA: INDEPENDENCE DAY. Nov 28. National holiday. Commemorates independence from the Ottoman Empire in 1912.

MAURITANIA: INDEPENDENCE DAY. Nov 28. National holiday. This country in the northwest part of Africa attained sovereignty from France on this day in 1960.

MEXICO: GUADALAJARA INTERNATIONAL BOOK FAIR.
Nov 28–Dec 6. Mexico's largest book fair with exhibitors from all over the Spanish-speaking world. Est attendance: 275,000. For info: David Unger, Guadalajara Book Fair–US Office, Div of Hum, NAC 6293, City College, New York, NY 10031. Phone: (212) 650-7925. Fax: (212) 650-7912. E-mail: daucc@cunyvm.cuny.edu.

PANAMA: INDEPENDENCE FROM SPAIN. Nov 28. Public holiday. Commemorates the independence of Panama (which at the time was part of Colombia) from Spain in 1821.

PASADENA DOO DAH PARADE. Nov 28. Pasadena, CA. No theme, no judging, no prizes, no order of march, no motorized vehicles and no animals. Annually, the Sunday following Thanksgiving Day.

BIRTHDAYS TODAY

Ed Harris, 49, actor (*The Right Stuff*), born Englewood, NJ, Nov 28, 1950.

Mary Lyons, 52, author of biographies (*Catching the Fire: Philip Simmons, Blacksmith*), born Macon, GA, Nov 28, 1947.

Ed Young, 68, author and illustrator (Caldecott for *Lon Po Po: A Red-Riding Hood Story from China*), born Tientsin, China, Nov 28, 1931.

NOVEMBER 29 — MONDAY
Day 333 — 32 Remaining

ALCOTT, LOUISA MAY: BIRTH ANNIVERSARY. Nov 29, 1832. American author, born at Philadelphia, PA. Died at Boston, MA, Mar 6, 1888. Her most famous novel was *Little Women*, the classic story of Meg, Jo, Beth and Amy.

CZECHOSLOVAKIA ENDS COMMUNIST RULE: 10th ANNIVERSARY. Nov 29, 1989. Czechoslovakia ended 41 years of one-party communist rule when the Czechoslovak parliament voted unanimously to repeal the constitutional clauses giving the Communist Party a guaranteed leading role in the country and promoting Marxism-Leninism as the state ideology. The vote came at the end of a 12-day revolution sparked by the beating of protestors Nov 17. Although the Communist party remained in power, the tide of reform led to its ouster by the Civic Forum,

November 1999	S	M	T	W	T	F	S
		1	2	3	4	5	6
	7	8	9	10	11	12	13
	14	15	16	17	18	19	20
	21	22	23	24	25	26	27
	28	29	30				

headed by playwright Vaclav Havel. The Civic Forum demanded free elections with equal rights for all parties, a mixed economy and support for foreign investment. In the first free elections in Czechoslovakia since WWII, Vaclav Havel was elected president.

"KUKLA, FRAN AND OLLIE" TV PREMIERE: ANNIVERSARY. Nov 29, 1948. This popular children's show featured puppets created and handled by Burr Tillstrom and was equally popular with adults. Fran Allison was the only human on the show. Tillstrom's lively and eclectic cast of characters, called the "Kuklapolitans," included the bald, high-voiced Kukla, the big-toothed Oliver J. Dragon (Ollie), Fletcher Rabbit, Cecil Bill, Beulah the Witch, Colonel Crackie, Madame Ooglepuss and Dolores Dragon. Most shows were performed without scripts.

LEWIS, C.S. (CLIVE STAPLES): BIRTH ANNIVERSARY. Nov 29, 1898. British scholar, novelist and author (*The Screwtape Letters, Chronicles of Narnia*), born at Belfast, Ireland. *The Lion, the Witch and the Wardrobe*, the first volume in the seven-volume Chronicles of Narnia series, was published in 1950. Died at Oxford, England, Nov 22, 1963.

MOON PHASE: LAST QUARTER. Nov 29. Moon enters Last Quarter phase at 6:18 PM, EST.

WAITE, MORRISON R.: BIRTH ANNIVERSARY. Nov 29, 1816. Seventh Chief Justice of the Supreme Court, born at Lyme, CT. Appointed Chief Justice by President Ulysses S. Grant Jan 19, 1874. The Waite Court is remembered for its controversial rulings that did much to rehabilitate the idea of states' rights after the Civil War and early Reconstruction years. Waite died at Washington, DC, Mar 23, 1888.

BIRTHDAYS TODAY

Jacques Rene Chirac, 67, French President, born Paris, France, Nov 29, 1932.

Madeleine L'Engle, 81, author (Newbery for *A Wrinkle in Time*), born New York, NY, Nov 29, 1918.

Howie Mandel, 44, actor, producer ("Bobby's World"), born Toronto, Canada, Nov 29, 1955.

Andrew McCarthy, 37, actor (*Pretty in Pink, Weekend at Bernie's*), born Westfield, NJ, Nov 29, 1962.

NOVEMBER 30 — TUESDAY
Day 334 — 31 Remaining

BARBADOS: INDEPENDENCE DAY. Nov 30. National holiday. Gained independence from Great Britain in 1966.

CLEMENS, SAMUEL LANGHORNE (MARK TWAIN): BIRTH ANNIVERSARY. Nov 30, 1835. Celebrated American author, whose books include: *The Adventures of Tom Sawyer, The Adventures of Huckleberry Finn* and *The Prince and the Pauper*. Born at Florida, MO, Twain is quoted as saying, "I came in with Halley's Comet in 1835. It is coming again next year, and I expect to go out with it." He did. Twain died at Redding, CT, Apr 21, 1910 (just one day after Halley's Comet perihelion).

NATIONAL GEOGRAPHY BEE, SCHOOL LEVEL. Nov 29, 1999–Jan 14, 2000. Principals must register their schools by Oct 15, 1999. Nationwide contest involving millions of students at the school level. The Bee is designed to encourage the teaching and study of geography. There are three levels of competition. A student must win school-level Bee in order to win the right to take a written exam. The written test determines the top 100 students in each state who are eligible to go on to the state level. National

Geographic brings the state winner and his/her teacher to Washington for the national level in May. Alex Trebek moderates the national level. For info: Natl Geography Bee, Natl Geographic Soc, 1145 17th St NW, Washington, DC 20036. Phone: (202) 857-7001.

PHILIPPINES: BONIFACIO DAY. Nov 30. Also known as National Heroes' Day. Commemorates birth in 1863 of Andres Bonifacio, leader of the 1896 revolt against Spain.

SAINT ANDREW'S DAY. Nov 30. Feast day of the apostle and martyr, Andrew, who died about AD 60. Patron saint of Scotland.

ZEMACH, MARGOT: BIRTH ANNIVERSARY. Nov 30, 1931. Illustrator (Caldecott for *Duffy and the Devil*), born at Los Angeles, CA. Died May 21, 1989.

BIRTHDAYS TODAY

Joan Ganz Cooney, 70, founder of the Children's Television Workshop and developer of "Sesame Street," born Nov 30, 1929.

Des'ree, 29, singer (*I Ain't Movin'*), born London, England, Nov 30, 1970.

Mandy Patinkin, 47, actor (Tony for *Evita; Sunday in the Park with George*, "Chicago Hope"), born Chicago, IL, Nov 30, 1952.

Ivan Rodriguez, 28, baseball player, born Vega Baja, Puerto Rico, Nov 30, 1971.

Paul Stookey, 62, singer, songwriter (Peter, Paul and Mary), born Baltimore, MD, Nov 30, 1937.

Natalie Williams, 29, basketball player, born Long Beach, CA, Nov 30, 1970.

DECEMBER 1 — WEDNESDAY
Day 335 — 30 Remaining

BASKETBALL CREATED: ANNIVERSARY. Dec 1, 1891. James Naismith was a teacher of physical education at the International YMCA Training College at Springfield, MA. In order to create an indoor sport that could be played during the winter months, he nailed up peach baskets at opposite ends of the gym and gave students soccer balls to toss into them. Thus was born the game of basketball.

CHRISTMAS TREE AT ROCKEFELLER CENTER. Dec 1. (Date approximate.) New York, NY. Lighting of the huge Christmas tree in Rockefeller Plaza signals the opening of the holiday season at New York City. Date is usually a weekday during the first week of December.

HUG-A-WEEK FOR THE HEARING IMPAIRED. Dec 1–31. Give a hug to someone who doesn't hear so well, each week until the end of the year. As we approach the holiday season, start with a weekly hug and find out how you might proactively include people with hearing loss in the season's festivities. A little extra time and a few special moments may help someone who can't hear so well be included and more able to share throughout the season. Annually, the month of December. For info: Carol MacKenzie, Communicate with Care, 12 Kayla Cir, Plymouth, MA 02362. Phone: (508) 224-3640. E-mail: commwcare@aol.com.

NATIONAL COMMUNITY EDUCATION ASSOCIATION CONFERENCE. Dec 1–4. Orlando Hyatt, Orlando, FL. 34th annual. Largest national gathering for community educators and others interested in promoting parent-community involvement in education, forming community partnerships to address community needs and expanding lifelong learning opportunities for all community residents. Est attendance: 700. For info: Ursula Ellis, Dir of Communications, Natl Community Education Assn, 3929 Old Lee Hwy, Ste 91-A, Fairfax, VA 22030-2401. Phone: (703) 359-8973. Fax: (703) 359-0972. E-mail: ncea@ncea.com.

PORTUGAL: INDEPENDENCE DAY. Dec 1. Public holiday. Became independent of Spain in 1640.

	S	M	T	W	T	F	S
December				1	2	3	4
1999	5	6	7	8	9	10	11
	12	13	14	15	16	17	18
	19	20	21	22	23	24	25
	26	27	28	29	30	31	

ROMANIA: NATIONAL DAY. Dec 1. National holiday. Commemorates unification of Romania and Transylvania in 1918.

ROSA PARKS DAY: ANNIVERSARY OF ARREST. Dec 1, 1955. Anniversary of the arrest of Rosa Parks, at Montgomery, AL, for refusing to give up her seat and move to the back of a municipal bus. Her arrest triggered a yearlong boycott of the city bus system and led to legal actions which ended racial segregation on municipal buses throughout the southern US. The event has been called the birth of the modern civil rights movement. Rosa McCauley Parks was born at Tuskegee, AL, on Feb 4, 1913.

SAFE TOYS AND GIFTS MONTH. Dec 1–31. What are the top 10 dangerous toys to children's eyesight? Prevent Blindness America® issues a list of toys hazardous to eyesight. Tips on how to choose age-appropriate toys will be distributed. For info: Prevent Blindness America®, 500 E Remington Rd, Schaumburg, IL 60173. Phone: (800) 331-2020. Fax: (847) 843-8458. Web: www.prevent blindness.org.

UNITED NATIONS: WORLD AIDS DAY. Dec 1. In 1988 the World Health Organization of the United Nations declared Dec 1 as World AIDS Day, an international day of awareness and education about AIDS. The WHO is the leader in global direction and coordination of AIDS prevention, control, research and education. A program called UN-AIDS was created to bring together the skills and expertise of the World Bank, UNDP, UNESCO, UNICEF, UNFPA and the WHO to strengthen and expand national capacities to respond to the pandemic. Also see the World AIDS Day entry (Dec 1) for information address in US.

UNIVERSAL HUMAN RIGHTS MONTH. Dec 1–31. To disseminate throughout the world information about human rights and distribute copies of the Universal Declaration of Human Rights in English and other languages. Please send $4 to cover expense of printing, handling and postage. Annually, the month of December. For info: Dr. Stanley Drake, Pres, Intl Soc of Friendship & Good Will, 412 Cherry Hills Dr, Bakersfield, CA 93309-7902.

WORLD AIDS DAY. Dec 1. US observance of UN day to focus world attention on the fight against HIV/AIDS. For info: American Assn for World Health, World AIDS Day, 1825 K St NW, Ste 1208, Washington, DC 20006. Phone: (202) 466-5883. Fax: (202) 466-5896. E-mail: aawhstaff@aol.com. Web: www.aawhworld health.org.

BIRTHDAYS TODAY

Jan Brett, 50, author and illustrator (*Trouble with Trolls*), born Hingham, MA, Dec 1, 1949.

Larry Walker, 33, baseball player, born Maple Ridge, British Columbia, Dec 1, 1966.

DECEMBER 2 — THURSDAY
Day 336 — 29 Remaining

ARTIFICIAL HEART TRANSPLANT: ANNIVERSARY. Dec 2, 1982. Barney C. Clark, 61, became the first recipient of a permanent artificial heart. The operation was performed at the University of Utah Medical Center at Salt Lake City. Near death at the time of the operation, Clark survived almost 112 days after the implantation. He died Mar 23, 1983.

FIRST SELF-SUSTAINING NUCLEAR CHAIN REACTION: ANNIVERSARY. Dec 2, 1942. Physicist Enrico Fermi led a team of scientists at the University of Chicago in producing the first

DECEMBER 2
GEORGES SEURAT'S BIRTHDAY

Celebrate the birth of Georges Seurat (pronounced zhawrzh suh-RAH) and familiarize students with an interesting style of painting. Born at Paris, France, in 1859, Seurat was one of the inventors of pointillism, a painting style that experiments with pure color and dots rather than brush strokes. In pointillist paintings, facial expression and detailed textures are not as important as capturing the intensity of color and the play of light. Seurat's most famous pointillist painting is *Sunday Afternoon on the Island of La Grande Jatte*, painted in 1886, which depicts a crowd of people enjoying a Sunday afternoon on an island in the Seine River. Shown strolling, fishing or relaxing on blankets, the people and the surrounding landscape are an exploration and celebration of color.

Pointillists did not mix colors. Instead, they used dots of pure color positioned side by side. Different shades were obtained by varying the intensity, or number, of dots of a particular color in certain areas. When seen from a distance, the viewer's eyes blend the colors.

Bring in examples of Seurat and pointillist-influenced paintings done by Paul Gauguin, Vincent Van Gogh, Claude Monet and Jan Vermeer. Many art books contain color reproductions of their work. Encourage students to draw or paint their own pointillist art. In addition to pen and paint, markers work well for pointillist pictures. Before beginning the actual art piece, have students experiment with dot intensity. For example, investigate how adding yellow dots in varying numbers changes a blue or a red dotted area. How much yellow must be added before the viewer's eye blends the blue and yellow into green? Display student work in a classroom exhibit.

A research project could include an investigation of pointillism in modern technology. The pictures on color television are made with dots of color. The number of pixels, or dots, on a computer's monitor screen control the clarity and intensity of the images we see.

controlled, self-sustaining nuclear chain reaction. As part of the "Manhattan Project," their first simple nuclear reactor was built under the stands of the University's football stadium. This work led to the development of the atomic bomb, first tested on July 16, 1945, at Alamogordo, NM.

LAOS: NATIONAL DAY: ANNIVERSARY. Dec 2. National holiday commemorating proclamation of Lao People's Democratic Republic in 1975.

MONROE DOCTRINE: ANNIVERSARY. Dec 2, 1823. President James Monroe, in his annual message to Congress, enunciated the doctrine that bears his name and that was long hailed as a statement of US policy. ". . . In the wars of the European powers in matters relating to themselves we have never taken any part . . . we should consider any attempt on their part to extend their system to any portion of this hemi-sphere as dangerous to our peace and safety. . . ."

★ **PAN AMERICAN HEALTH DAY.** Dec 2. Presidential Proclamation 2447, of Nov 23, 1940, covers all succeeding years. Always Dec 2. The 1940 Pan American Conference of National Directors of Health adopted a resolution recommending that a "Health Day" be held annually in the countries of the Pan American Union.

SEURAT, GEORGES: BIRTH ANNIVERSARY. Dec 2, 1859. French Neo-Impressionist painter, born at Paris, France. Died there Mar 29, 1891. Seurat is known for his style of painting with small dots of color called "pointillism." See Curriculum Connection.

UNITED ARAB EMIRATES: NATIONAL DAY: ANNIVERSARY OF INDEPENDENCE. Dec 2. Anniversary of the day in 1971 when a federation of seven sheikdoms declared independence and became known as the United Arab Emirates.

BIRTHDAYS TODAY

Wayne Allard, 56, US Senator (R, Colorado), born Fort Collins, CO, Dec 2, 1943.

Randy Gardner, 41, figure skater, born Marina del Rey, CA, Dec 2, 1958.

David Macaulay, 53, illustrator and author (*Cathedral*, Caldecott for *Black and White*), born Burton-on-Trent, England, Dec 2, 1946.

Stone Phillips, 45, anchor ("Dateline," "20/20"), born Texas City, TX, Dec 2, 1954.

Harry Reid, 60, US Senator (D, Nevada), born Searchlight, NV, Dec 2, 1939.

Monica Seles, 26, tennis player, born Novi Sad, Yugoslavia, Dec 2, 1973.

William Wegman, 56, artist/photographer (of dogs), born Holyoke, MA, Dec 2, 1943.

DECEMBER 3 — FRIDAY
Day 337 — 28 Remaining

ILLINOIS: ADMISSION DAY: ANNIVERSARY. Dec 3. Became 21st state in 1818.

UNITED NATIONS: INTERNATIONAL DAY OF DISABLED PERSONS. Dec 3. On Oct 14, 1992 (Res 47/3), at the end of the Decade of Disabled Persons, the General Assembly proclaimed Dec 3 to be an annual observance to promote the continuation of integrating the disabled into general society.

BIRTHDAYS TODAY

Brian Bonsall, 18, actor (*Blank Check*, "Family Ties"), born Torrance, CA, Dec 3, 1981.

Anna Chlumsky, 19, actress (*My Girl*, *My Girl 2*), born Chicago, IL, Dec 3, 1980.

Brendan Fraser, 31, actor (*George of the Jungle*), born Indianapolis, IN, Dec 3, 1968.

Katarina Witt, 34, Olympic figure skater, born Karl-Marx-Stadt, East Germany, Dec 3, 1965.

DECEMBER 4 — SATURDAY
Day 338 — 27 Remaining

CHANUKAH. Dec 4–11. Feast of Lights or Feast of Dedication. This festival lasting eight days commemorates victory of Maccabees over Syrians (165 BC) and rededication of Temple of Jerusalem. Begins on Hebrew calendar date Kislev 25, 5760. For more info: *A Hanukkah Treasury*, edited by Eric A. Kimmel (Holt, 0-8050-5293-3, $19.95 All ages).

LEAF, MUNRO: BIRTH ANNIVERSARY. Dec 4, 1905. Born at Hamilton, MD. Leaf authored and illustrated the children's book *The Story of Ferdinand*. He died at Garrett Park, MD, Dec 21, 1976.

SPACE MILESTONE: *ENDEAVOUR* SPACE STATION LAUNCH (US). Dec 4, 1998. The shuttle *Endeavour* took a US component of the space station named Unity into orbit 220 miles from Earth where spacewalking astronauts fastened it to a component launched by the Russians on Nov 20, 1998. It will take a total of 45 US and Russian launches over the next five years before the space station is complete.

BIRTHDAYS TODAY

George Ancona, 70, author (*Pablo Remembers: The Fiesta of the Day of the Dead*), born New York, NY, Dec 4, 1929.

Jeff Blake, 29, football player, born Sanford, FL, Dec 4, 1970.

DECEMBER 5 — SUNDAY

Day 339 — 26 Remaining

"THE ABBOTT AND COSTELLO SHOW" TV PREMIERE: ANNIVERSARY. Dec 5, 1952. Bud Abbott and Lou Costello made 52 half-hour films for television incorporating many of their best burlesque routines. The show ran for two seasons, until 1954. Costello died in 1959. In 1966 Hanna-Barbera Productions produced an animated cartoon based on the characters of Abbott and Costello. Abbott supplied his own voice while Stan Irwin imitated Costello. Bud Abbott died in 1974.

AFL-CIO FOUNDED: ANNIVERSARY. Dec 5. The American Federation of Labor and the Congress of Industrial Organizations joined together in 1955, following 20 years of rivalry, to become the nation's leading advocate for trade unions.

CLERC-GALLAUDET WEEK. Dec 5–11. Week in which to celebrate the birth anniversaries of Laurent Clerc (Dec 26, 1785) and Thomas Hopkins Gallaudet (Dec 10, 1787). Clerc and Gallaudet pioneered education for the deaf in the US while serving as role models to both deaf and hearing people and together they helped to promote literacy and lifelong learning for all people. Activities will include a lecture on Clerc and Gallaudet, storytelling for all ages and a library display of books, videotapes, magazines, newspapers and posters. Library Kit available for $3.95. For info: FOLDA, Inc, 2930 Craiglawn Rd, Silver Spring, MD 20904-1816. Phone: (301) 572-5168. Fax: (301) 572-4134. E-mail: alhagemeyer@juno.com.

DISNEY, WALT: BIRTH ANNIVERSARY. Dec 5, 1901. Animator, filmmaker, born at Chicago, IL. Disney died at Los Angeles, CA, Dec 15, 1966.

HAITI: DISCOVERY DAY: ANNIVERSARY. Dec 5. Commemorates the discovery of Haiti by Christopher Columbus in 1492. Public holiday.

MONTGOMERY BUS BOYCOTT BEGINS: ANNIVERSARY. Dec 5, 1955. Rosa Parks was arrested at Montgomery, AL, on Dec 1, 1955, for refusing to give up her seat on a bus to a white man. In support of Parks, and to protest the arrest, the black community of Montgomery organized a boycott of the bus system. The boycott lasted from Dec 5, 1955, to Dec 20, 1956, when a US Supreme Court ruling was implemented at Montgomery, integrating the public transportation system.

December	S	M	T	W	T	F	S
December				1	2	3	4
1999	5	6	7	8	9	10	11
	12	13	14	15	16	17	18
	19	20	21	22	23	24	25
	26	27	28	29	30	31	

DECEMBER 5
UNITED NATIONS INTERNATIONAL VOLUNTEER DAY

In our busy lives we often forget the importance of volunteering our time to organizations and people who need a helping hand. Out of a growing concern that some children do not understand the value of being a volunteer, some school districts are making community service hours a graduation requirement. Familiarizing primary and middle school children with volunteer service helps them discover the rewards—on personal and community levels—of helping others.

Parent/teacher groups within the school system are an example of how volunteers make a difference in students' lives. Many towns have service organizations, such as Kiwanis, Knights of Columbus, food pantries and homeless shelters. Community-based groups may be willing to provide a school speaker.

Students can volunteer in school: sorting the Lost and Found items, reading aloud to younger students, setting up a tutoring program and helping with playground trash pick-up are a few volunteer projects that don't involve transportation. With access to transportation, usually with parent volunteers, students can donate time at local nursing homes or soup kitchens with age-appropriate activities and supervision.

Encourage students to find stories of people engaging in volunteer work. Collecting newspaper stories and photographs showing people involved in disaster relief after floods, tornadoes, earthquakes or hurricanes is one way to illustrate volunteerism. A "We Make a Difference" bulletin board of volunteers school wide keeps students aware of areas that can use help.

The key to success is making students aware of needs in the community.

THAILAND: KING'S BIRTHDAY AND NATIONAL DAY. Dec 5. Celebrated throughout the kingdom with colorful pageantry. Stores and houses decorated with spectacular illuminations at night. Public holiday.

TWENTY-FIRST AMENDMENT TO THE US CONSTITUTION RATIFIED: ANNIVERSARY. Dec 5, 1933. Prohibition ended with the repeal of the Eighteenth Amendment by the Twenty-First Amendment.

UNITED NATIONS: INTERNATIONAL VOLUNTEER DAY FOR ECONOMIC AND SOCIAL DEVELOPMENT. Dec 5. In a resolution of Dec 17, 1985, the United Nations General Assembly recognized the desirability of encouraging the work of all volunteers. It invited governments to observe, annually Dec 5, the "International Volunteer Day for Economic and Social Development," urging them to take measures to heighten awareness of the important contribution of volunteer service." A day commemorating the establishment in December 1970 of the UN Volunteers program and inviting world recognition of volunteerism in the international development movement. For info: United Nations, Dept of Public Info, Public Inquiries Unit, Rm GA-57, New York, NY 10017. Phone: (212) 963-4475. Fax: (212) 963-0071. E-mail: inquiries@un.org. See Curriculum Connection.

VAN BUREN, MARTIN: BIRTH ANNIVERSARY. Dec 5, 1782. Eighth president of the US (term of office: Mar 4, 1837–Mar 3, 1841), was the first to have been born a citizen of the US. He had served as vice-president under Andrew Jackson. He was a widower for nearly two decades before he entered the White House. His daughter-in-law, Angelica, served as White House hostess during an administration troubled by bank and business failures, depression and unemployment. Van Buren was born at Kinderhook, NY, and died there July 24, 1862.

WHEATLEY, PHILLIS: DEATH ANNIVERSARY. Dec 5, 1784. Born at Senegal, West Africa about 1753, Phillis Wheatley was brought to the US in 1761 and purchased as a slave by a Boston tailor named John Wheatley. She was allotted unusual privileges for a slave, including being allowed to learn to read and write. She wrote her first poetry at age 14, and her first work was published in 1770. Wheatley's fame as a poet spread throughout Europe as well as the US after her *Poems on Various Subjects, Religious and Moral* was published at England in 1773. She was invited to visit George Washington's army headquarters after he read a poem she had written about him in 1776. Phillis Wheatley died at about age 30 at Boston, MA.

BIRTHDAYS TODAY

Strom Thurmond, 97, US Senator (R, South Carolina), born Edgefield, SC, Dec 5, 1902.

DECEMBER 6 — MONDAY
Day 340 — 25 Remaining

CENTRAL AFRICAN REPUBLIC: NATIONAL DAY OBSERVED. Dec 6. Commemorates Proclamation of the Republic Dec 1, 1958. Usually observed on the first Monday in December.

ECUADOR: DAY OF QUITO. Dec 6. Commemorates founding of city of Quito by Spaniards in 1534.

FINLAND: INDEPENDENCE DAY. Dec 6. National holiday. Declaration of independence from Russia in 1917.

GERALD FORD SWEARING-IN AS VICE PRESIDENT: ANNIVERSARY. Dec 6, 1973. Gerald Ford was sworn in as vice president under Richard Nixon, following the resignation of Spiro Agnew who pled no contest to a charge of income tax evasion. See also: "Agnew, Spiro Theodore: Birth Anniversary" (Nov 9).

GERSHWIN, IRA: BIRTH ANNIVERSARY. Dec 6, 1896. Pulitzer Prize–winning American lyricist and author who collaborated with his brother, George, and with many other composers. Among his Broadway successes: *Lady Be Good, Funny Face, Strike Up the Band* and such songs as "The Man I Love," "Someone to Watch Over Me," "I Got Rhythm" and hundreds of others. Born at New York, NY, he died at Beverly Hills, CA, Aug 17, 1983. See also: "Gershwin, George: Birth Anniversary" (Sept 26).

HALIFAX, NOVA SCOTIA, DESTROYED: ANNIVERSARY. Dec 6, 1917. More than 1,650 people were killed at Halifax when the Norwegian ship *Imo* plowed into the French munitions ship *Mont Blanc. Mont Blanc* was loaded with 4,000 tons of TNT, 2,300 tons of picric acid, 61 tons of other explosives and a deck of highly flammable benzene, which ignited and touched off an explosion. In addition to those killed, 1,028 were injured. A tidal wave, caused by the explosion, washed much of the city out to sea.

MISSOURI EARTHQUAKES: ANNIVERSARY. Dec 6, 1811. The most violent and prolonged series of earthquakes in US history occurred not in California, but in the Midwest at New Madrid, MO. They lasted until Feb 12, 1812. There were few deaths because of the sparse population.

SAINT NICHOLAS DAY. Dec 6. One of the most venerated saints of both eastern and western Christian churches, of whose life little is known, except that he was Bishop of Myra in what is now Turkey in the fourth century, and that from early times he has been one of the most often pictured saints, especially noted for his charity. Santa Claus and the presentation of gifts is said to derive from Saint Nicholas.

THIRTEENTH AMENDMENT TO THE US CONSTITUTION RATIFIED: ANNIVERSARY. Dec 6, 1865. The Thirteenth Amendment to the Constitution was ratified, abolishing slavery in the US. "Neither slavery nor involuntary servitude, save as a punishment for crime whereof the party shall have been duly convicted, shall exist within the United States, or any place subject to their jurisdiction." This amendment was proclaimed Dec 18, 1865. The Thirteenth, Fourteenth and Fifteenth amendments are considered the Civil War Amendments. See also: "Emancipation Proclamation: Anniversary" (Jan 1) for Lincoln's proclamation freeing slaves in the rebelling states.

BIRTHDAYS TODAY

Andrew Cuomo, 42, US Secretary of Housing and Urban Development (Clinton administration), born Queens, NY, Dec 6, 1957.
John Reynolds Gardiner, 55, author (*Stone Fox, Top Secret*), born Los Angeles, CA, Dec 6, 1944.
Don Nickles, 51, US Senator (R, Oklahoma), born Ponca City, OK, Dec 6, 1948.

DECEMBER 7 — TUESDAY
Day 341 — 24 Remaining

DELAWARE RATIFIES CONSTITUTION: ANNIVERSARY. Dec 7, 1787. Delaware became the first state to ratify the proposed Constitution. It did so by unanimous vote.

MOON PHASE: NEW MOON. Dec 7. Moon enters New Moon phase at 5:32 PM, EST.

PEARL HARBOR DAY: ANNIVERSARY. Dec 7, 1941. At 7:55 AM (local time), "a date that will live in infamy," nearly 200 Japanese aircraft attacked Pearl Harbor, Hawaii, long considered the US "Gibraltar of the Pacific." The raid, which lasted little more than one hour, left nearly 3,000 dead. Nearly the entire US Pacific Fleet was at anchor there, and few ships escaped damage. Several were sunk or disabled, while 200 US aircraft on the ground were destroyed. The attack on Pearl Harbor brought about immediate US entry into WWII, a Declaration of War being requested by President Franklin D. Roosevelt and approved by the Congress Dec 8, 1941.

SPACE MILESTONE: *GALILEO* (US). Dec 7, 1995. Launched Oct 18, 1989 by the space shuttle *Atlantis*, the spacecraft *Galileo* entered the orbit of Jupiter on this date after a six-year journey. It orbited Jupiter for two years, sending out probes to study three of its moons. Organic compounds, the ingredients of life, were found on them.

TUNIS, JOHN: BIRTH ANNIVERSARY. Dec 7, 1889. Author of sports books (*The Kid Comes Back, Iron Duke*), born at Boston, MA. Died Feb 4, 1975.

UNITED NATIONS: INTERNATIONAL CIVIL AVIATION DAY. Dec 7. On Dec 6, 1996, the General Assembly proclaimed Dec 7 as International Civil Aviation Day. On Dec 7, 1944, the convention on International Civil Aviation, which established the International Civil Aviation Organization, was signed. Info from: United Nations, Dept of Public Info, New York, NY 10017.

BIRTHDAYS TODAY

Larry Bird, 43, basketball coach, former player, born West Baden, IN, Dec 7, 1956.

Thad Cochran, 62, US Senator (R, Mississippi), born Pontotoc, MS, Dec 7, 1937.

Susan M. Collins, 47, US Senator (R, Maine), born Caribou, ME, Dec 7, 1952.

Anne Fine, 52, author (*The Tulip Touch, Alias Madame Doubtfire*), born County Durham, England, Dec 7, 1947.

DECEMBER 8 — WEDNESDAY

Day 342 — 23 Remaining

AMERICAN FEDERATION OF LABOR (AFL) FOUNDED: ANNIVERSARY. Dec 8, 1886. Originally founded at Pittsburgh, PA, as the Federation of Organized Trades and Labor Unions of the United States and Canada in 1881, the union was reorganized in 1886 under the name American Federation of Labor (AFL). The AFL was dissolved as a separate entity in 1955 when it merged with the Congress of Industrial Organizations to form the AFL-CIO. See also: "AFL-CIO Founding: Anniversary (Dec 5)."

CHINESE NATIONALISTS MOVE TO FORMOSA: 50th ANNIVERSARY. Dec 8, 1949. The government of Chiang Kai–Shek moved to Formosa (Taiwan) after being driven out of mainland China by the Communists led by Mao Tse– Tung.

CIVIL RIGHTS WEEK IN MASSACHUSETTS. Dec 8–14. Proclaimed annually by the governor.

December 1999

S	M	T	W	T	F	S
			1	2	3	4
5	6	7	8	9	10	11
12	13	14	15	16	17	18
19	20	21	22	23	24	25
26	27	28	29	30	31	

FEAST OF THE IMMACULATE CONCEPTION. Dec 8. Roman Catholic Holy Day of Obligation.

FIRST STEP TOWARD A NUCLEAR-FREE WORLD: ANNIVERSARY. Dec 8, 1987. The former Soviet Union and the US signed a treaty at Washington eliminating medium-range and shorter-range missiles. This was the first treaty completely doing away with two entire classes of nuclear arms. These missiles, with a range of 500 to 5,500 kilometers, were to be scrapped under strict supervision within three years of the signing.

GUAM: LADY OF CAMARIN DAY HOLIDAY: ANNIVERSARY. Dec 8. Declared a legal holiday by Guam legislature, Mar 2, 1971.

NAFTA SIGNED: ANNIVERSARY. Dec 8, 1993. President Clinton signed the North American Free Trade Agreement which cut tariffs and eliminated other trade barriers between the US, Canada and Mexico. The Agreement went into effect Jan 1, 1994.

SEGAR, ELZIE CRISLER: BIRTH ANNIVERSARY. Dec 8, 1894. Creator of *Thimble Theater*, the comic strip that came to be known as *Popeye*. Centered on the Oyl family, especially daughter Olive, the strip introduced a new central character in 1929. A one-eyed sailor with bulging muscles, Popeye became the strip's star attraction almost immediately. Popeye made it to the silver screen in animated form and in 1980 became a movie with Robin Williams playing the lead. Segar was born at Chester, IL. He died Oct 13, 1938, at Santa Monica, CA.

SOVIET UNION DISSOLVED: ANNIVERSARY. Dec 8, 1991. The Union of Soviet Socialist Republics ceased to exist, as the republics of Russia, Byelorussia and Ukraine signed an agreement at Minsk, Byelorussia, creating the Commonwealth of Independent States. The remaining republics, with the exception of Georgia, joined in the new Commonwealth as it began the slow and arduous process of removing the yoke of Communism and dealing with strong separatist and nationalistic movements within the various republics.

THURBER, JAMES: BIRTH ANNIVERSARY. Dec 8, 1894. Author for adults and children (*The Thirteen Clocks*), born at Columbus, OH. Died at New York, NY, Nov 2, 1961.

BIRTHDAYS TODAY

Kim Basinger, 46, actress (*The Natural, My Stepmother Is an Alien*), born Athens, GA, Dec 8, 1953.

Teri Hatcher, 35, actress ("Lois & Clark"), born Sunnyvale, CA, Dec 8, 1964.

DECEMBER 9 — THURSDAY

Day 343 — 22 Remaining

BIRDSEYE, CLARENCE: BIRTH ANNIVERSARY. Dec 9, 1886. American industrialist who developed a way of deep-freezing foods. He was marketing frozen fish by 1925 and was one of the founders of General Foods Corporation. Born at Brooklyn, NY, he died at New York City, Oct 7, 1956.

BRUNHOFF, JEAN DE: 100th BIRTH ANNIVERSARY. Dec 9, 1899. Author and illustrator of *The Story of Babar* and *The Little Elephant*. Born at Paris, France, Brunhoff died at Switzerland, Oct 16, 1937. In later years, the Babar series was continued by his son Laurent.

COMPUTER MOUSE DEVELOPED: ANNIVERSARY. Dec 9, 1968. Designed as a pointing device to help users interact with their computers, the mouse was first developed in 1968 but its use didn't become widespread until 1984 when Apple attached it to its Macintosh computer.

HARRIS, JOEL CHANDLER: BIRTH ANNIVERSARY. Dec 9, 1848. American author, creator of the Uncle Remus stories, born at Eatonton, GA. Died July 3, 1908, at Atlanta, GA.

RAMADAN: THE ISLAMIC MONTH OF FASTING. Dec 9, 1999–Jan 7, 2000. Begins on Islamic lunar calendar date Ramadan 1, 1420. Ramadan, the ninth month of the Islamic calendar, is holy because it was during this month that the Holy Qur'an [Koran] was revealed. All adults of sound body and mind fast from dawn (before sunrise) until sunset to achieve spiritual and physical purification and self-discipline, abstaining from food, drink and intimate relations. It is a time for feeling a common bond with the poor and needy, a time of piety and prayer. Different methods for "anticipating" the visibility of the new moon crescent at Mecca are used by different Muslim groups. US date may vary. For links to Ramadan sites on the web, go to: deil.lang.uiuc.edu/web.pages/holidays/ramadan.html.

TANZANIA: INDEPENDENCE AND REPUBLIC DAY. Dec 9. Tanganyika became independent of Britain in 1961. The republics of Tanganyika and Zanzibar joined to become one state (Apr 27, 1964) renamed (Oct 29, 1964) the United Republic of Tanzania.

BIRTHDAYS TODAY

Joan W. Blos, 71, author (Newbery for *A Gathering of Days: A New England Girl's Journal, 1830–1832*), born New York, NY, Dec 9, 1928.

Thomas Andrew Daschle, 52, US Senator (D, South Dakota), born Aberdeen, SD, Dec 9, 1947.

Mary Downing Hahn, 62, author (*The Doll in the Garden: A Ghost Story*), born Washington, DC, Dec 9, 1937.

Eloise McGraw, 84, author (*Moorchild*), born Houston, TX, Dec 9, 1915.

Donny Osmond, 42, actor, singer ("Donny and Marie;" stage: *Joseph and the Amazing Technicolor Dreamcoat*), born Ogden, UT, Dec 9, 1957.

DECEMBER 10 — FRIDAY

Day 344 — 21 Remaining

DEWEY, MELVIL: BIRTH ANNIVERSARY. Dec 10, 1851. American librarian and inventor of the Dewey decimal book classification system was born at Adams Center, NY. Born Melville Louis Kossuth Dewey, he was an advocate of spelling reform, urged use of the metric system and was interested in many other education reforms. Dewey died at Highlands County, FL, Dec 26, 1931.

DICKINSON, EMILY: BIRTH ANNIVERSARY. Dec 10, 1830. One of America's greatest poets, Emily Dickinson was born at Amherst, MA. She was reclusive and frail in health. She died May 15, 1886, at Amherst. Seven of her poems were published during her life, but after her death her sister, Lavinia, discovered almost 2,000 more poems locked in her bureau. They were published gradually, over 50 years, beginning in 1890. The little-known Emily Dickinson who was born, lived and died at Amherst now is recognized as one of the most original poets of the English-speaking world.

FIRST US SCIENTIST RECEIVES NOBEL PRIZE: ANNIVERSARY. Dec 10, 1907. University of Chicago professor Albert Michelson, eminent physicist known for his research on the speed of light and optics, became the first US scientist to receive the Nobel Prize, Dec 10, 1907.

DECEMBER 10–16
HUMAN RIGHTS WEEK

In the United States we stress the importance of individual rights. During this week you can call your students' attention to this in many ways.

What constitutes a "right"? Today many people are confused about the difference between "rights" and "privileges." A list of rights might include: respect, housing, education, fair representation in the eyes of the law, gender and racial equality. Privileges might include: a driver's license or owning a VCR and TV. A list of classroom rights and privileges will help clarify the issue.

For a historical perspective, examine why early settlers came to North America; for example, for the right of religious freedom. Bill of Rights Day falls within this week on Dec 15, the date in 1791 when the first ten amendments to the Constitution took effect. Does our Bill of Rights address all possible human rights? The topic "What happens when the rights of one group infringe upon the rights of others?" can lead to thought-provoking debate. Pushing Native Americans off their traditional lands or the hotly debated "right to bear arms" are examples. The Franklin Watts series What Do We Mean by Human Rights? for grades 4–6 has volumes that address specific rights, such as freedom of speech and workers' rights.

Older students can explore US policies regarding countries that violate human rights. A good resource is your local or regional chapter of Amnesty International.

An end-of-the-week discussion of the responsibilities we share and the things we can do to ensure all people are accorded basic rights will help motivate and direct students.

United Nations Human Rights Day occurs on Dec 10th to commemorate the adoption of the Universal Declaration of Human Rights in 1948. The UN has a website especially for students with information on this topic at www.un.org/Pubs/CyberSchoolBus/.

GALLAUDET, THOMAS HOPKINS: BIRTH ANNIVERSARY. Dec 10, 1787. A hearing educator who, with Laurent Clerc, founded the first public school for deaf people, Connecticut Asylum for the Education and Instruction of Deaf and Dumb Persons (now the American School for the Deaf), at Hartford, CT, Apr 15, 1817. Gallaudet was born at Philadelphia, PA, and died Sept 9, 1851, at Hartford, CT.

GODDEN, RUMER: BIRTH ANNIVERSARY. Dec 10, 1907. Author of the popular children's tales *The Mousewife* and *The Story of Holly & Ivy*. Born at Sussex, England, Godden died at Thornhill, Scotland, Nov 8, 1998.

★**HUMAN RIGHTS DAY.** Dec 10. Presidential Proclamation 2866, of Dec 6, 1949, covers all succeeding years. Customarily issued as "Bill of Rights Day, Human Rights Day and Week."

★**HUMAN RIGHTS WEEK.** Dec 10–16. Presidential Proclamation issued since 1958 for the week of Dec 10–16, except in 1986. See also: "Human Rights Day" (Dec 10) and "Bill of Rights Day" (Dec 15). See Curriculum Connection.

MISSISSIPPI: ADMISSION DAY: ANNIVERSARY. Dec 10. Became 20th state in 1817.

NOBEL PRIZE AWARDS CEREMONIES. Dec 10. Oslo, Norway and Stockholm, Sweden. Alfred Nobel, Swedish chemist and inventor of dynamite who died in 1896, provided in his will that income from his $9 million estate should be used for annual prizes to be awarded to people who are judged to have made the most valuable contributions to the good of humanity. The Nobel Peace Prize is awarded by a committee of the Norwegian parliament and the presentation is made at the Oslo City Hall. Five other prizes, for physics, chemistry, medicine, literature and economics, are presented in a ceremony at Stockholm, Sweden. Both ceremonies traditionally are held on the anniversary of the death of Alfred Nobel. The current value of each prize is about $1,000,000. See also: "Nobel, Alfred Bernhard: Death Anniversary" (Dec 10).

NORTON, MARY: BIRTH ANNIVERSARY. Dec 10, 1903. British children's writer known for The Borrowers series, for which she received the Carnegie Medal. Her book *Bed-Knob and Broomstick* was made into a movie by Disney in 1971. Born at London, England, she died at Hartland, Devon, England, Aug 29, 1992.

RALPH BUNCHE AWARDED NOBEL PEACE PRIZE: ANNIVERSARY. Dec 10, 1950. Dr. Ralph Johnson Bunche became the first black man awarded the Nobel Peace Prize. Bunche was awarded the prize for his efforts in mediation between Israel and neighboring Arab states in 1949.

RED CLOUD: 90th DEATH ANNIVERSARY. Dec 10, 1909. Sioux Indian chief Red Cloud was born in 1822 (exact date unknown), near North Platte, NE. A courageous leader and defender of Indian rights, Red Cloud was the son of Lone Man and Walks as She Thinks. His unrelenting determination caused US abandonment of the Bozeman trail and of three forts that interfered with Indian hunting grounds. Red Cloud died at Pine Ridge, SD.

THAILAND: CONSTITUTION DAY. Dec 10. A public holiday throughout Thailand.

TREATY OF PARIS ENDS SPANISH-AMERICAN WAR: ANNIVERSARY. Dec 10, 1898. Following the conclusion of the Spanish-American War in 1898, American and Spanish ambassadors met at Paris, France, to negotiate a treaty. Under the terms of this treaty, Spain granted the US the Philippine Islands and the islands of Guam and Puerto Rico, and agreed to withdraw from Cuba. Senatorial debate over the treaty centered on the US's move toward imperialism by acquiring the Philippines. A vote was taken Feb 6, 1899 and the treaty passed by a one-vote margin. President William McKinley signed the treaty Feb 10, 1899.

UNITED NATIONS: HUMAN RIGHTS DAY: ANNIVERSARY. Dec 10. Official United Nations observance day. Date is the anniversary of adoption of the "Universal Declaration of Human Rights" in 1948. The Declaration sets forth basic rights and fundamental freedoms to which all men and women everywhere in the world are entitled. For further info, go to the UN's website for children at www.un.org/Pubs/CyberSchoolBus/

UNITED NATIONS: THIRD DECADE TO COMBAT RACISM AND RACIAL DISCRIMINATION: YEAR SIX. Dec 10. In 1973 the United Nations General Assembly proclaimed the years 1973–83, beginning Dec 10, UN Human Rights Day, as the Decade to Combat Racism and Racial Discrimination. Renewing its efforts, the UN designated the years 1983–93 as the Second Decade to Combat Racism and Racial Discrimination. The adopted Program of Action states the decade's goals and outlines

the measures to be taken at the regional, national and international levels to achieve them. In Res 47/77 of Dec 16, 1992, the Assembly called upon the international community to provide resources for the program to be carried out during a third decade (1993–2003), particularly for the monitoring of the transition from apartheid in South Africa. Info from: United Nations, Dept of Public Info, New York, NY 10017.

BIRTHDAYS TODAY

Raven Symone, 14, actress ("The Cosby Show," *Doctor Dolittle*), born Atlanta, GA, Dec 10, 1985.

DECEMBER 11 — SATURDAY
Day 345 — 20 Remaining

BURKINA FASO: NATIONAL DAY. Dec 11.

INDIANA: ADMISSION DAY: ANNIVERSARY. Dec 11. Became 19th state in 1816.

SPACE MILESTONE: *MARS CLIMATE ORBITER* (US). Dec 11, 1998. This unmanned rocket will track the movement of water vapor over Mars which it is scheduled to reach in Sept 1999. On Jan 3, 1999 *Mars Polar Lander* was launched. It will burrow into the ground and analyze the soil.

UNITED NATIONS: UNICEF ANNIVERSARY. Dec 11, 1946. Anniversary of the establishment by the United Nations General Assembly of the United Nations International Children's Emergency Fund (UNICEF). For info: United Nations, Dept of Public Info, New York, NY 10017. Web: www.unicef.org.

BIRTHDAYS TODAY

Max Baucus, 58, US Senator (D, Montana), born Helena, MT, Dec 11, 1941.

Jermaine Jackson, 45, singer, musician (Jackson 5, "Daddy's Home," "Let's Get Serious"), born Gary, IN, Dec 11, 1954.

John F. Kerry, 56, US Senator (D, Massachusetts), born Denver, CO, Dec 11, 1943.

Rider Strong, 20, actor ("Boy Meets World"), born San Francisco, CA, Dec 11, 1979.

DECEMBER 12 — SUNDAY
Day 346 — 19 Remaining

BONZA BOTTLER DAY™. Dec 12. To celebrate when the number of the day is the same as the number of the month. Bonza Bottler Day™ is an excuse to have a party at least once a month. For info: Gail M. Berger, 109 Matthew Ave, Poca, WV 25159. Phone: (304) 776-7746. E-mail: gberger5@aol.com.

December 1999	S	M	T	W	T	F	S
				1	2	3	4
	5	6	7	8	9	10	11
	12	13	14	15	16	17	18
	19	20	21	22	23	24	25
	26	27	28	29	30	31	

DAY OF OUR LADY OF GUADALUPE. Dec 12. The legend of Guadalupe tells how in December 1533, an Indian, Juan Diego, saw the Virgin Mother on a hill near Mexico City, who instructed him to go to the bishop and have him build a shrine to her on the site of the vision. After his request was initially rebuffed, the Virgin Mother appeared to Juan Diego three days later. She instructed him to pick roses growing on a stony and barren hillside nearby and take them to the bishop as proof. Although flowers do not normally bloom in December, Juan Diego found the roses and took them to the bishop. As he opened his mantle to drop the roses on the floor, an image of the Virgin Mary appeared among them. The bishop built the sanctuary as instructed. Our Lady of Guadalupe became the patroness of Mexico City and by 1746 was the patron saint of all New Spain and by 1910 of all Latin America.

FIRST BLACK SERVES IN US HOUSE OF REPRESENTATIVES: ANNIVERSARY. Dec 12, 1870. Joseph Hayne Rainey of Georgetown, SC, was sworn in as the first black to serve in the US House of Representatives. Rainey filled the seat of Benjamin Franklin Whittemore, which had been declared vacant by the House. He served until Mar 3, 1879.

INTERNATIONAL SHAREWARE DAY. Dec 12. A day to take the time to reward the efforts of thousands of computer programmers who trust that if we try their programs and like them, we will pay for them. Unfortunately, very few payments are received, thus stifling the programmers' efforts. This observance is meant to prompt each of us to inventory our PCs and Macs, see if we are using any shareware, and then take the time in the holiday spirit to write payment checks to the authors. Hopefully this will keep shareware coming. Annually, the second Sunday in December. For info: David Lawrence, Host, Online Today, c/o Noblestar, 3141 Fairview Park Dr, Ste 400, Falls Church, VA 22042. E-mail: david@online-today.com. Web: online-today.com.

JAY, JOHN: BIRTH ANNIVERSARY. Dec 12, 1745. American statesman, diplomat and first chief justice of the US Supreme Court (1789–95), coauthor (with Alexander Hamilton and James Madison) of the influential *Federalist* papers, was born at New York, NY. Jay died at Bedford, NY, May 17, 1829.

KENYA: JAMHURI DAY. Dec 12. Jamhuri Day (Independence Day) is Kenya's official National Day, commemorating proclamation of the republic and independence from the UK in 1963.

MEXICO: GUADALUPE DAY. Dec 12. One of Mexico's major celebrations. Honors the "Dark Virgin of Guadalupe," the republic's patron saint. Parties and pilgrimages, with special ceremonies at the Shrine of Our Lady of Guadalupe, at Mexico City.

NATIONAL CHILDREN'S MEMORIAL DAY. Dec 12. A day to remember the more than 79,000 young people who die in the US every year. Annually, the second Sunday in December. For info: The Compassionate Friends, Inc, PO Box 3696, Oak Brook, IL 60522-3696. Phone: (630) 990-0010. E-mail: tcf_national@prodigy.com. Web: www.compassionatefriends.com.

PENNSYLVANIA RATIFIES CONSTITUTION: ANNIVERSARY. Dec 12, 1787. Pennsylvania became the second state to ratify the US Constitution, by a vote of 46 to 23.

POINSETTIA DAY (JOEL ROBERTS POINSETT: DEATH ANNIVERSARY). Dec 12. A day to enjoy poinsettias and to honor Dr. Joel Roberts Poinsett, the American diplomat who introduced the Central American plant which is named for him into the US. Poinsett was born at Charleston, SC, Mar 2, 1799. He also served as a member of Congress and as secretary of war. He died near Statesburg, SC, Dec 12, 1851. The poinsettia has become a favorite Christmas season plant.

RUSSIA: CONSTITUTION DAY. Dec 12. National holiday commemorating adoption of new constitution in 1993.

TELL SOMEONE THEY'RE DOING A GOOD JOB WEEK. Dec 12–18. Every day this week tell someone "you're doing a good job." For info: Joe Hoppel, Radio Station WCMS, 900 Commonwealth Place, Virginia Beach, VA 23464. Phone: (757) 424-1050. Fax: (804) 424-3479. E-mail: wcms@norfolk.infi.net. Web: www.wcms.com.

BIRTHDAYS TODAY

Tracy Ann Austin, 37, former tennis player, born Rolling Hills Estates, CA, Dec 12, 1962.

Mayim Bialik, 24, actress ("Blossom"), born San Diego, CA, Dec 12, 1975.

DECEMBER 13 — MONDAY
Day 347 — 18 Remaining

LINCOLN, MARY TODD: BIRTH ANNIVERSARY. Dec 13, 1818. Wife of Abraham Lincoln, 16th president of the US, born at Lexington, KY. Died at Springfield, IL, July 16, 1882.

MALTA: REPUBLIC DAY. Dec 13. National holiday. Malta became a republic in 1974.

NEW ZEALAND FIRST SIGHTED BY EUROPEANS: ANNIVERSARY. Dec 13, 1642. Captain Abel Tasman of the Dutch East India Company first sighted New Zealand but was kept from landing by Maori warriors. In 1769 Captain James Cook landed and claimed formal possession for Great Britain.

NORTH AND SOUTH KOREA END WAR: ANNIVERSARY. Dec 13, 1991. North and South Korea signed a treaty of reconciliation and nonaggression, formally ending the Korean War— 38 years after fighting ceased in 1953. This agreement was not hailed as a peace treaty, and the armistice that was signed July 27, 1953, between the UN and North Korea, was to remain in effect until it could be transformed into a formal peace.

SWEDEN: SANTA LUCIA DAY. Dec 13. Nationwide celebration of festival of light, honoring St. Lucia. Many hotels have their own Lucia, a young girl attired in a long, flowing white gown with a wreath of candles in her hair, who serves guests coffee and lussekatter (saffron buns) in the early morning.

BIRTHDAYS TODAY

Sergei Federov, 30, hockey player, born Pskov, Russia, Dec 13, 1969.

Dick Van Dyke, 74, actor, comedian (*Mary Poppins*, "The Dick Van Dyke Show"), born West Plains, MO, Dec 13, 1925.

Tom Vilsack, 49, Governor of Iowa (D), born Pittsburgh, PA, Dec 13, 1950.

DECEMBER 14 — TUESDAY
Day 348 — 17 Remaining

ALABAMA: ADMISSION DAY: ANNIVERSARY. Dec 14. Became the 22nd state in 1819.

SOUTH POLE DISCOVERY: ANNIVERSARY. Dec 14, 1911. The elusive object of many expeditions dating from the 7th century, the South Pole was located and visited by Roald Amundsen with four companions and 52 sled dogs. All five men and 12 of the dogs returned to base camp safely. Next to visit the South Pole, Jan 17, 1912, was a party of five led by Captain Robert F. Scott, all of whom perished during the return trip. A search party found their frozen bodies 11 months later. See also: "Amundsen, Roald: Birth Anniversary" (July 16).

SUTCLIFFE, ROSEMARY: BIRTH ANNIVERSARY. Dec 14, 1920. Author of historical novels for children (*The Mark of the Horse Lord*), born at East Clanden, England. Died July 23, 1992.

WASHINGTON, GEORGE: 200th DEATH ANNIVERSARY. Dec 14, 1799. First president of the US. Born at Westmoreland County, VA, Feb 22, 1732, he died at Mount Vernon, VA.

BIRTHDAYS TODAY

Craig Biggio, 34, baseball player, born Smithtown, NY, Dec 14, 1965.

Rhoda Blumberg, 82, author (*Commodore Perry in the Land of the Shogun*), born New York, NY, Dec 14, 1917.

Patty Duke, 53, actress (Oscar for *The Miracle Worker*; Emmy for *My Sweet Charlie*), born New York, NY, Dec 14, 1946.

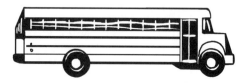

DECEMBER 15 — WEDNESDAY

Day 349 — 16 Remaining

★**BILL OF RIGHTS DAY.** Dec 15. Presidential Proclamation. Has been proclaimed each year since 1962, but was omitted in 1967 and 1968. (Issued in 1941 and 1946 at Congressional request and in 1947 without request.) Since 1968 has been included in Human Rights Day and Week Proclamation.

BILL OF RIGHTS: ANNIVERSARY. Dec 15, 1791. The first 10 amendments to the US Constitution, known as the Bill of Rights, became effective following ratification by Virginia. The anniversary of ratification and of effect is observed as Bill of Rights Day.

CURACAO: KINGDOM DAY AND ANTILLEAN FLAG DAY. Dec 15. This day commemorates the Charter of Kingdom, signed at the Knight's Hall at The Hague in 1954, granting the Netherlands Antilles complete autonomy. The Antillean Flag was hoisted for the first time Dec 15, 1959.

"DAVY CROCKETT" TV PREMIERE: ANNIVERSARY. Dec 15, 1954. This show, a series of five segments, can be considered TV's first miniseries. Shown on Walt Disney's "Disneyland" show, it starred Fess Parker as American western hero Davy Crockett and was immensely popular. The show spawned Crockett paraphernalia, including the famous coonskin cap (even after we found out that Boone never wore a coonskin hat).

EIFFEL, ALEXANDRE GUSTAVE: BIRTH ANNIVERSARY. Dec 15, 1832. Eiffel, the French engineer who designed the 1,000 ft-high, million-dollar, open-lattice wrought iron Eiffel Tower, and who participated in designing the Statue of Liberty, was born at Dijon, France. The Eiffel Tower, weighing more than 7,000 tons, was built for the Paris International Exposition of 1889. Eiffel died at Paris, France, Dec 23, 1923.

December 1999

S	M	T	W	T	F	S
			1	2	3	4
5	6	7	8	9	10	11
12	13	14	15	16	17	18
19	20	21	22	23	24	25
26	27	28	29	30	31	

HALCYON DAYS. Dec 15–29. Traditionally, the seven days before and the seven days after the winter solstice. To the ancients a time when fabled bird (called the halcyon–pronounced hal-cee-on) calmed the wind and waves—a time of calm and tranquility.

MOON PHASE: FIRST QUARTER. Dec 15. Moon enters First Quarter phase at 7:50 PM, EST.

PUERTO RICO: NAVIDADES. Dec 15–Jan 6. Traditional Christmas season begins mid-December and ends on Three Kings Day. Elaborate nativity scenes, carolers, special Christmas foods and trees from Canada and US. Gifts on Christmas Day and on Three Kings Day.

SITTING BULL: DEATH ANNIVERSARY. Dec 15, 1890. Famous Sioux Indian leader, medicine man and warrior of the Hunkpapa Teton band. Known also by his native name, Tatankayatanka, Sitting Bull was born on the Grand River, SD. He first accompanied his father on the warpath at the age of 14 against the Crow and thereafter rapidly gained influence within his tribe. In 1886 he led a raid on Fort Buford. His steadfast refusal to go to a reservation led General Phillip Sheridan to initiate a campaign against him which led to the massacre of Lieutenant Colonel George Custer's men at Little Bighorn, after which Sitting Bull fled to Canada, remaining there until 1881. Although many in his tribe surrendered on their return, Sitting Bull remained hostile until his death in a skirmish with the US soldiers along the Grand River.

SMITH, BETTY: BIRTH ANNIVERSARY. Dec 15, 1904. Author born at New York, NY. Her books include *A Tree Grows in Brooklyn*, *Tomorrow Will be Better* and *Joy In the Morning*. Smith died at Shelton, CT, Jan 17, 1972.

BIRTHDAYS TODAY

Garrett Wang, 31, actor ("Star Trek: Voyager"), born Riverside, CA, Dec 15, 1968.

DECEMBER 16 — THURSDAY

Day 350 — 15 Remaining

BAHRAIN: INDEPENDENCE DAY. Dec 16. National holiday. Commemorates independence from British protection in 1971.

BANGLADESH: VICTORY DAY. Dec 16. National holiday. Commemorates victory over Pakistan in 1971. The former East Pakistan became Bangladesh.

BATTLE OF THE BULGE: 55th ANNIVERSARY. Dec 16, 1944. By late 1944 the German Army was in retreat and Allied forces were on German soil. But a surprise German offensive was launched in the Belgian Ardennes Forest on this date. The Nazi commanders, hoping to minimize any aerial counterattack by the Allies, chose a time when foggy, rainy weather prevailed and the initial attack by eight armored divisions along a 75-mile front took the Allies by surprise, the 5th Panzer Army penetrating to within 20 miles of crossings on the Meuse River. US troops were able to hold fast at bottlenecks in the Ardennes, but by the end of December the German push had penetrated 65 miles into the Allied lines (though their line had narrowed from the initial 75 miles to 20 miles). By that time the Allies began to respond and the Germans were stopped by Montgomery on the Meuse and by Patton at Bastogne. The weather cleared and Allied aircraft began to bomb the German forces and supply lines by Dec 26. The German Army withdrew from the Ardennes, Jan 21, 1945, having lost 120,000 men.

BEETHOVEN, LUDWIG VAN: BIRTH ANNIVERSARY. Dec 16, 1770. Regarded by many as the greatest orchestral composer of all time, Ludwig van Beethoven was born at Bonn, Germany. Impairment of his hearing began before he was 30, but even total deafness did not halt his composing and conducting. His last appearance on the concert stage was to conduct the premiere of his *Ninth Symphony*, at Vienna, May 7, 1824. He was unable to hear either the orchestra or the applause. Of a stormy temperament, he is said to have died during a violent thunderstorm Mar 26, 1827, at Vienna.

BOSTON TEA PARTY: ANNIVERSARY. Dec 16, 1773. Anniversary of Boston patriots' boarding of British vessel at anchor at Boston Harbor. Contents of nearly 350 chests of tea were dumped into the harbor to protest the British monopoly on tea imports. This was one of several events leading to the American Revolution.

KAZAKHSTAN, REPUBLIC OF: REPUBLIC DAY. Dec 16. National Day. Commemorates independence from the Soviet Union in 1991.

MEXICO: POSADAS. Dec 16–24. A nine-day annual celebration throughout Mexico. Processions of "pilgrims" knock at doors asking for posada (shelter), commemorating the search by Joseph and Mary for a shelter in which the infant Jesus might be born. Pilgrims are invited inside, and fun and merrymaking ensue with blindfolded guests trying to break a "piñata" (papier mache decorated earthenware utensil filled with gifts and goodies) suspended from the ceiling. Once the piñata is broken, the gifts are distributed and celebration continues.

PHILIPPINES: SIMBANG GABI. Dec 16–25. Nationwide. A nine-day novena of predawn masses, also called "Misa de Gallo." One of the traditional Filipino celebrations of the holiday season.

SOUTH AFRICA: RECONCILIATION DAY. Dec 16. National holiday. Celebrates the spirit of reconciliation, national unity and peace amongst all citizens.

BIRTHDAYS TODAY

Bill Brittain, 69, author (*The Wish Giver: Three Tales of Coven Tree*), born Rochester, NY, Dec 16, 1930.

DECEMBER 17 — FRIDAY

Day 351 — 14 Remaining

AZTEC CALENDAR STONE DISCOVERY: ANNIVERSARY. Dec 17, 1790. One of the wonders of the western hemisphere—the Aztec Calendar or Solar Stone—was found beneath the ground by workmen repairing Mexico City's Central Plaza. The intricately carved stone, 11 ft, 8 inches in diameter and weighing nearly 25 tons, proved to be a highly developed calendar monument to the sun. Believed to have been carved in the year 1479, this extraordinary time-counting basalt tablet originally stood in the Great Temple of the Aztecs. Buried along with other Aztec idols, soon after the Spanish conquest in 1521, it remained hidden until 1790. Its 52-year cycle had regulated many Aztec ceremonies, including human sacrifices to save the world from destruction by the gods.

FLOYD, WILLIAM: BIRTH ANNIVERSARY. Dec 17, 1734. Signer of the Declaration of Independence, member of Congress, born at Brookhaven, Long Island. Died at Westernville, NY, Aug 4, 1821.

KING, W.L. MACKENZIE: BIRTH ANNIVERSARY. Dec 17, 1874. Former Canadian prime minister, born at Berlin, Ontario. Served 21 years, the longest term of any prime minister in the English-speaking world. Died at Kingsmere, Canada, July 22, 1950.

★**PAN AMERICAN AVIATION DAY.** Dec 17. Presidential Proclamation 2446, of Nov 18, 1940, covers all succeeding years (Pub Res No. 105 of Oct 10, 1940).

UNDERDOG DAY. Dec 17. To salute, before the year's end, all of the underdogs and unsung heroes—the Number Two people who contribute so much to the Number One people we read about. (Sherlock Holmes's Dr. Watson and Robinson Crusoe's Friday are examples.) Annually, the third Friday in December. For info: P. Moeller, Chief Underdog, Box 71, Clio, MI 48420-1042.

★**WRIGHT BROTHERS DAY.** Dec 17. Presidential Proclamation always issued for Dec 17 since 1963 (PL88–209 of Dec 17, 1963). Issued twice earlier at Congressional request in 1959 and 1961.

WRIGHT BROTHERS FIRST POWERED FLIGHT: ANNIVERSARY. Dec 17, 1903. Orville and Wilbur Wright, brothers, bicycle shop operators, inventors and aviation pioneers, after three years of experimentation with kites and gliders, achieved the first documented successful powered and controlled flights of an airplane. The flights, near Kitty Hawk, NC, piloted first by Orville then by Wilbur Wright, were sustained for less than one minute but represented man's first powered airplane flight and the beginning of a new form of transportation. Orville Wright was born at Dayton, OH, Aug 19, 1871, and died there Jan 30, 1948. Wilbur Wright was born at Millville, IN, Apr 16, 1867, and died at Dayton, OH, May 30, 1912. For further info: *The Wright Brothers: How They Invented the Airplane*, by Russell Freedman (Holiday, 0-8234-0875-2, $18.95 Gr. 4–6).

BIRTHDAYS TODAY

David Kherdian, 68, author (*The Road from Home: The Story of an Armenian Girl*), born Racine, WI, Dec 17, 1931.

DECEMBER 18 — SATURDAY

Day 352 — 13 Remaining

NEW JERSEY RATIFICATION DAY: ANNIVERSARY. Dec 18, 1787. New Jersey became the third state to ratify the Constitution (following Delaware and Pennsylvania). It did so unanimously.

NIGER: REPUBLIC DAY. Dec 18. National holiday. This West African nation gained autonomy within the French community on this day in 1958.

BIRTHDAYS TODAY

Brad Pitt, 35, actor (*Interview with a Vampire, A River Runs Through It*), born Shawnee, OK, Dec 18, 1964.

Marilyn Sachs, 72, author (the Veronica Ganz series), born Bronx, NY, Dec 18, 1927.

Steven Spielberg, 52, producer, director (*E.T.: The Extra-Terrestrial, Indiana Jones, Close Encounters of the Third Kind, Jurassic Park*), born Cincinnati, OH, Dec 18, 1947.

Kiefer Sutherland, 33, actor (*Flatliners, A Few Good Men*), born Los Angeles, CA, Dec 18, 1966.

DECEMBER 19 — SUNDAY

Day 353 — 12 Remaining

ASARAH B'TEVET. Dec 19. Hebrew calendar date: Tevet 10, 5760. The Fast of the 10th of Tevet begins at first morning light and commemorates the beginning of the Babylonian siege of Jerusalem in the 6th century BC.

CHRISTMAS GREETINGS FROM SPACE: ANNIVERSARY. Dec 19, 1958. At 3:15 PM, EST, the US Earth satellite *Atlas* transmitted the first radio voice broadcast from space, a 58-word recorded Christmas greeting from President Dwight D. Eisenhower: "to all mankind America's wish for peace on earth and good will toward men everywhere." The satellite had been launched from Cape Canaveral Dec 18.

LA FARGE, OLIVER: BIRTH ANNIVERSARY. Dec 19, 1901. American author and anthropologist, born at New York, NY. La Farge wrote the children's book *Laughing Boy*. He died at Albuquerque, NM, Aug 2, 1963.

REENACTMENT OF THE BOSTON TEA PARTY. Dec 19. Congress Street Bridge, Boston, MA. Reenactment of "Boston's most notorious protest, the single most important event leading to the American Revolution." Annually, the Sunday closest to Dec 16. Starts at Old South Meeting House 5:30 PM. Est attendance: 1,000. For info: Boston Tea Party Ship, Congress St Bridge, Boston, MA 02210. Phone: (617) 338-1773. Fax: (617) 338-1974.

WOODSON, CARTER GODWIN: BIRTH ANNIVERSARY. Dec 19, 1875. Historian who introduced black studies to colleges and universities, born at New Canton, VA. His scholarly works included *The Negro in Our History, The Education of the Negro Prior to 1861*. Known as the father of Black history, he inaugurated Negro History Week. Woodson was working on a six-volume *Encyclopaedia Africana* when he died at Washington, DC, Apr 3, 1950.

BIRTHDAYS TODAY

Eve Bunting, 71, author (*Sixth-Grade Sleepover, Smoky Night*), born Anne Evelyn Bolton, Maghera, Ireland, Dec 19, 1928.

Alyssa Milano, 27, actress ("Who's the Boss," "Melrose Place"), born Brooklyn, NY, Dec 19, 1972.

Warren Sapp, 27, football player, born Plymouth, FL, Dec 19, 1972.

Reggie White, 38, football player, born Chattanooga, TN, Dec 19, 1961.

	S	M	T	W	T	F	S
December				1	2	3	4
1999	5	6	7	8	9	10	11
	12	13	14	15	16	17	18
	19	20	21	22	23	24	25
	26	27	28	29	30	31	

DECEMBER 20 — MONDAY

Day 354 — 11 Remaining

AMERICAN POET LAUREATE ESTABLISHMENT: ANNIVERSARY. Dec 20, 1985. A bill empowering the Librarian of Congress to name, annually, a Poet Laureate/Consultant in Poetry was signed into law by President Ronald Reagan. In return for a $10,000 stipend as Poet Laureate and a salary (about $35,000) as the Consultant in Poetry, the person named will present at least one major work of poetry and will appear at selected national ceremonies. The first Poet Laureate of the US was Robert Penn Warren, appointed to that position by the Librarian of Congress Feb 26, 1986.

LOUISIANA PURCHASE DAY. Dec 20, 1803. One of the greatest real estate deals in history, when more than a million square miles of the Louisiana Territory were turned over to the US by France, for a price of about $20 per square mile. It nearly doubled the size of the US, extending the western border to the Rocky Mountains.

MACAU: REVERTS TO CHINESE CONTROL: ANNIVERSARY. Dec 20, 1999. Macau, a tiny province on the southeast coast of China, reverts to Chinese rule today. It has been a Portuguese colony since 1557. With the return of Hong Kong in 1997 and the return of Macau, no part of mainland China is occupied by a foreign power.

PRESIDENT CLINTON IMPEACHED: ANNIVERSARY. Dec 20, 1998. President Bill Clinton was impeached by a House of Representatives that was divided along party lines. He was charged with perjury and obstruction of justice stemming from a sexual relationship with a White House intern. He was tried by the Senate in January 1999. On Feb 12, 1999, he was acquitted on both charges. Clinton was only the second US president to undergo impeachment proceedings. Andrew Johnson was impeached by the House in 1868 but the Senate voted against impeachment.

SACAGAWEA: DEATH ANNIVERSARY. Dec 20, 1812. As a young Shoshone Indian woman, Sacagawea in 1805 (with her two-month-old boy strapped to her back) traveled with the Lewis and Clark Expedition, serving as an interpreter. It is said that the expedition could not have succeeded without her aid. She was born about 1787 and died at Fort Manuel on the Missouri River. Few other women have been so often honored. There are statues, fountains and memorials of her, and her name has been given to a mountain peak. In 2000 the US Mint is issuing a $1 coin with Sacagawea's picture on it.

SAMUEL SLATER DAY IN MASSACHUSETTS. Dec 20. Proclaimed annually by the governor, this day commemorates Samuel Slater, the founder of the American factory system. He came to America from England and built a cotton mill at Rhode Island in 1790. He directed many New England mills until his death in 1835.

SOUTH CAROLINA: SECESSION ANNIVERSARY. Dec 20, 1860. South Carolina's legislature voted to secede from the US, the first state to do so. By Feb 1, 1861, 10 more states had seceded and formed the Confederate States of America (Alabama, Arkansas, Florida, Georgia, Louisiana, Mississippi, North Carolina, South Carolina, Tennessee, Texas and Virginia).

VIRGINIA COMPANY EXPEDITION TO AMERICA: ANNIVERSARY. Dec 20, 1606. Three small ships, the *Susan Constant*, the *Godspeed* and the *Discovery*, commanded by Captain Christopher Newport, departed London, England, bound for America, where the royally chartered Virginia Company's approximately 120 persons established the first permanent English settlement in what is now the US at Jamestown, VA, May 14, 1607.

BIRTHDAYS TODAY

Uri Geller, 53, psychic, clairvoyant, born Tel Aviv, Israel, Dec 20, 1946.

DECEMBER 21 — TUESDAY

Day 355 — 10 Remaining

FIRST CROSSWORD PUZZLE: ANNIVERSARY. Dec 21, 1913. The first crossword puzzle was compiled by Arthur Wynne and published in a supplement to the *New York World*.

HUMBUG DAY. Dec 21. Allows all those preparing for Christmas to vent their frustrations. Twelve "humbugs" allowed. [© 1998 by WPL] For info: Tom or Ruth Roy, Wellness Permission League, PO Box 662, Mt. Gretna, PA 17064-0662. Phone: (717) 964-1308. Fax: (717) 964-1335. E-mail: wellcat@desupernet.net.

PILGRIM LANDING: ANNIVERSARY. Dec 21, 1620. According to Governor William Bradford's *History of Plymouth Plantation*, "On Munday," [Dec 21, 1620, New Style] the Pilgrims, aboard the *Mayflower*, reached Plymouth, MA, "sounded ye harbor, and founde it fitt for shipping; and marched into ye land, & founde diverse cornfields, and ye best they could find, and ye season & their presente necessitie made them glad to accepte of it. . . . And after wards tooke better view of ye place, and resolved wher to pitch their dwelling; and them and their goods." Plymouth Rock, the legendary place of landing since it first was "identified" in 1769, nearly 150 years after the landing, has been a historic shrine since. The landing anniversary is observed in much of New England as Forefathers' Day.

SPACE MILESTONE: *APOLLO 8* **(US).** Dec 21, 1968. First moon voyage launched, manned by Colonel Frank Borman, Captain James A. Lovell, Jr and Major William A. Anders. Orbited moon Dec 24, returned to Earth Dec 27. First men to orbit the moon and see the side of the moon away from Earth.

YALDA. Dec 21. Yalda, the longest night of the year, is celebrated by Iranians. The ceremony has an Indo-Iranian origin, where Light and Good were considered to struggle against Darkness and Evil. With fires burning and lights lit, family and friends gather to stay up through the night helping the sun in its battle against darkness. They recite poetry, tell stories and eat special fruits and nuts until the sun, triumphant, reappears in the morning. For info: Yassaman Djalali, Librarian, West Valley Branch Library, 1243 San Tomas Aquino Rd, San Jose, CA 95117. Phone: (408) 244-4766.

BIRTHDAYS TODAY

Chris Evert Lloyd, 45, broadcaster and former tennis player, born Ft Lauderdale, FL, Dec 21, 1954.

DECEMBER 22 — WEDNESDAY

Day 356 — 9 Remaining

CAPRICORN, THE GOAT. Dec 22–Jan 19. In the astronomical and astrological zodiac that divides the sun's apparent orbit into 12 segments, the period Dec 22–Jan 19 is identified, traditionally, as the sun-sign of Capricorn, the Goat. The ruling planet is Saturn.

"DING DONG SCHOOL" TV PREMIERE: ANNIVERSARY. Dec 22, 1952. Named by a three-year-old after watching a test broadcast of the opening sequence (a hand ringing a bell), "Ding Dong School" was one of the first children's educational series. Miss Frances (Dr. Frances Horwich, head of Roosevelt College's education department at Chicago) was the host of this weekday show.

FIRST GORILLA BORN IN CAPTIVITY: BIRTH ANNIVERSARY. Dec 22, 1956. "Colo" was born at the Columbus, OH, zoo, weighing in at 3¼ pounds, the first gorilla born in captivity.

MOON PHASE: FULL MOON. Dec 22. Moon enters Full Moon phase at 12:31 PM, EST.

OGLETHORPE, JAMES EDWARD: BIRTH ANNIVERSARY. Dec 22, 1696. English general, author and colonizer of Georgia. Founder of the city of Savannah. Oglethorpe was born at London. He died June 30, 1785, at Cranham Hall, Essex, England.

PERIGEAN SPRING TIDES. Dec 22. Spring tides, the highest possible tides, which occur when New Moon or Full Moon takes place within 24 hours of the moment the Moon is nearest Earth (perigee) in its monthly orbit at 6 AM, EST. The word spring refers not to the season but comes from the German word *springen*, "to rise up."

WINTER. Dec 22–Mar 20. In the Northern Hemisphere winter begins today with the winter solstice, at 2:44 AM, EST. Note that in the Southern Hemisphere today is the beginning of summer. Between Equator and Arctic Circle the sunrise and sunset points on the horizon are farthest south for the year and daylight length is minimum (ranging from 12 hours, 8 minutes, at the equator to zero at the Arctic Circle).

BIRTHDAYS TODAY

Hector Elizondo, 63, actor (*Pretty Woman*, "Chicago Hope"), born New York, NY, Dec 22, 1936.

Claudia Alta "Lady Bird" Johnson, 87, former First Lady, widow of Lyndon Johnson, the 36th president of the US, born Karnack, TX, Dec 22, 1912.

Jerry Pinkney, 60, illustrator (*John Henry*), born Philadelphia, PA, Dec 22, 1939.

Diane K. Sawyer, 53, journalist ("60 Minutes," "Prime Time Live"), born Glasgow, KY, Dec 22, 1946.

☆ *The Teacher's Calendar, 1999–2000* ☆

DECEMBER 23 — THURSDAY
Day 357 — 8 Remaining

FIRST NONSTOP FLIGHT AROUND THE WORLD WITHOUT REFUELING: ANNIVERSARY. Dec 23, 1987. Dick Rutan and Jeana Yeager set a new world record of 216 hours of continuous flight, breaking their own record of 111 hours set July 15, 1986. The aircraft *Voyager* departed from Edwards Air Force Base at California Dec 14, 1987, and landed Dec 23, 1987. The journey covered 24,986 miles at an official speed of 115 miles per hour.

JAPAN: BIRTHDAY OF THE EMPEROR. Dec 23. National Day. Holiday honoring Emperor Akihito, born in 1933.

METRIC CONVERSION ACT: ANNIVERSARY. Dec 23, 1975. The Congress of the US passed Public Law 94–168, known as the Metric Conversion Act of 1975. This act declares that the SI (International System of Units) will be this country's basic system of measurement and establishes the United States Metric Board which is responsible for the planning, coordination and implementation of the nation's voluntary conversion to SI. (Congress had authorized the metric system as a legal system of measurement in the US by an act passed July 28, 1866. In 1875, the US became one of the original signers of the Treaty of the Metre, which established an international metric system.)

MEXICO: FEAST OF THE RADISHES. Dec 23. Oaxaca. Figurines of people and animals cleverly carved out of radishes are sold during festivities.

TRANSISTOR INVENTED: ANNIVERSARY. Dec 23, 1947. John Bardeen, Walter Brattain and William Shockley of Bell Laboratories shared the Nobel Prize for their invention of the transistor, which led to a revolution in communications and electronics.

BIRTHDAYS TODAY

Akihito, 66, Emperor of Japan, born Tokyo, Japan, Dec 23, 1933.
Avi, 62, author (*The True Confessions of Charlotte Doyle*), born Avi Wortis, New York, NY, Dec 23, 1937.
Corey Haim, 27, actor (*Murphy's Romance, The Lost Boys*), born Toronto, Ontario, Canada, Dec 23, 1972.
Martin Kratt, 34, zoologist, co-host with his brother Chris of "Kratts' Creatures," born Summit, NJ, Dec 23, 1965.

DECEMBER 24 — FRIDAY
Day 358 — 7 Remaining

AUSTRIA: "SILENT NIGHT, HOLY NIGHT" CELEBRATIONS. Dec 24. Oberndorf, Hallein and Wagrain, Salzburg, Austria. Commemorating the creation of the Christmas carol here in 1818.

CARSON, CHRISTOPHER "KIT": BIRTH ANNIVERSARY. Dec 24, 1809. American frontiersman, soldier, trapper, guide and Indian agent best known as Kit Carson. Born at Madison County, KY, he died at Fort Lyon, CO, May 23, 1868.

		S	M	T	W	T	F	S
December					1	2	3	4
1999		5	6	7	8	9	10	11
		12	13	14	15	16	17	18
		19	20	21	22	23	24	25
		26	27	28	29	30	31	

CHRISTMAS EVE. Dec 24. Family gift-giving occasion in many Christian countries.

HOLY YEAR 2000. Dec 24, 1999–Jan 6, 2001. An estimated 13 million people will travel to Rome to celebrate the Great Jubilee of the Incarnation of Christ. Among the events will be a Jubilee of the Children on Jan 2, 2000, a World Eucharistic Congress, June 19–25 and World Youth Day, Aug 19–20. For info: Great Jubilee 2000, Vatican City, 00120. Web: www.vatican.va/

LIBYA: INDEPENDENCE DAY. Dec 24. Libya gained its independence from Italy in 1951.

BIRTHDAYS TODAY

Eddie Pope, 26, soccer player, born Greensboro, NC, Dec 24, 1973.
Jeff Sessions, 53, US Senator (R, Alabama), born Hybart, AL, Dec 24, 1946.

DECEMBER 25 — SATURDAY
Day 359 — 6 Remaining

BARTON, CLARA: BIRTH ANNIVERSARY. Dec 25, 1821. Clarissa Harlowe Barton, American nurse and philanthropist, founder of the American Red Cross, was born at Oxford, MA. In 1881, she became first president of the American Red Cross (founded May 21, 1881). She died at Glen Echo, MD, Apr 12, 1912.

CHRISTMAS. Dec 25. Christian festival commemorating the birth of Jesus of Nazareth. Most popular of Christian observances, Christmas as a Feast of the Nativity dates from the 4th century. Although Jesus's birth date is not known, the Western church selected Dec 25 for the feast, possibly to counteract the non-Christian festivals of that approximate date. Many customs from non-Christian festivals (Roman Saturnalia, Mithraic sun's birthday, Teutonic yule, Druidic and other winter solstice rites) have been adopted as part of the Christmas celebration (lights, mistletoe, holly and ivy, holiday tree, wassailing and gift giving, for example). Some Orthodox Churches celebrate Christmas Jan 7 based on the "old calendar" (Julian). Theophany (recognition of the divinity of Jesus) is observed Dec 25 and also Jan 6, especially by the Eastern Orthodox Church. For links to sites about Christmas on the web, go to: deil.lang.uiuc.edu/web.pages/holidays/christmas.edu.

BIRTHDAYS TODAY

Rickey Henderson, 41, baseball player, born Chicago, IL, Dec 25, 1958.
Sissy Spacek (Mary Elizabeth), 50, actress (Oscar for *Coal Miner's Daughter; Missing*), born Quitman, TX, Dec 25, 1949.

DECEMBER 26 — SUNDAY

Day 360 — 5 Remaining

BAHAMAS: JUNKANOO. Dec 26. Kaleidoscope of sound and spectacle combining a bit of Mardi Gras, mummer's parade and ancient African tribal rituals. Revelers in colorful costumes parade through the streets to sounds of cowbells, goat skin drums and many other homemade instruments. Always on Boxing Day.

BOXING DAY. Dec 26. Ordinarily observed on the first day after Christmas. A legal holiday in Canada, the United Kingdom and many other countries. Formerly a day when Christmas gift boxes were expected by a postman, the lamplighter, the trash man and others who render services to the public at large. When Boxing Day falls on a Saturday or Sunday, the Monday or Tuesday immediately following may be proclaimed or observed as a bank or public holiday.

CHRISTMAS AT THE TOP MUSEUM. Dec 26–27. Spinning Top Museum, Burlington, WI. Enjoy the traditional, universal toys of tops and top games, well-loved Christmas gifts around the world in the 2-hour museum program: 35 hands-on games and experiments, two videos, view the exhibit of 2,000 items, plus a live show by top collector. Reservations required. For info: Spinning Top Museum, 533 Milwaukee Ave (Hwy 36), Burlington, WI 53105. Phone: (414) 763-3946.

CLERC, LAURENT: BIRTH ANNIVERSARY. Dec 26, 1785. The first deaf teacher in America, Laurent Clerc assisted Thomas Hopkins Gallaudet in establishing the first public school for the deaf, Connecticut Asylum for the Education and Instruction of Deaf and Dumb Persons (now the American School for the Deaf), at Hartford, CT, in 1817. For 41 years Clerc trained new teachers in the use of sign language and in methods of teaching the deaf. Clerc was born at LaBalme, France, and died July 18, 1869.

KIDS AFTER CHRISTMAS. Dec 26–Jan 2. Mystic, CT. Everyone pays the youth admission and enjoys a full day of crafts, entertainment and the lore of the sea. Est attendance: 3,000. For info: Mystic Seaport, 75 Greenmanville Ave, Box 6000, Mystic, CT 06355. Phone: (860) 572-5315 or (888) 9SEAPORT. Web: www.mysticseaport.org.

KWANZAA. Dec 26–Jan 1, 1999. American black family observance created in 1966 by Dr. Maulana Karenga in recognition of traditional African harvest festivals. This seven-day festival stresses self-reliance and unity of the black family, with a harvest feast (karamu) on the next to the last day and a day of meditation on the final one. Each day is dedicated to a principle that African Americans should live by— Day 1: Unity; Day 2: Self-determination; Day 3: Collective work and responsibility; Day 4: Cooperative economics; Day 5: Purpose; Day 6: Creativity; Day 7: Faith. Kwanzaa means "first fruit" in Swahili. For further info: *The Children's Book of Kwanzaa: A Guide to Celebrating the Holiday*, by Dolores Johnson (Atheneum, 0-68-980864-X, $16 Gr. 4-6).

MAO TSE-TUNG: BIRTH ANNIVERSARY. Dec 26, 1893. Chinese librarian, teacher, communist revolutionist and "founding father" of the People's Republic of China, born at Hunan Province, China. Died at Beijing, Sept 9, 1976.

NATIONAL WHINER'S DAY™. Dec 26. A day dedicated to whiners, especially those who return Christmas gifts and need lots of attention. People are encouraged to be happy about what they do have, rather than unhappy about what they don't have. The most famous whiner(s) of the year will be announced. Nominations accepted through Dec 15. For more info, please send SASE to: Rev. Kevin C. Zaborney, 4900 Campau Dr, Midland, MI 48640. Phone: (517) 631-5740. E-mail: kzaborney@aol.com.

NELSON, THOMAS: BIRTH ANNIVERSARY. Dec 26, 1738. Merchant and signer of the Declaration of Independence, born at Yorktown, VA. Died at Hanover County, VA, Jan 4, 1789.

RADIUM DISCOVERED: ANNIVERSARY. Dec 26, 1898. French scientists Pierre and Marie Curie discovered the element radium, for which they later won the Nobel Prize for Physics.

SAINT STEPHEN'S DAY. Dec 26. One of the seven deacons named by the apostles to distribute alms. Died during 1st century. Feast Day is observed as a public holiday in Austria.

SECOND DAY OF CHRISTMAS. Dec 26. Observed as holiday in many countries.

SOUTH AFRICA: DAY OF GOODWILL. Dec 26. National holiday. Replaces Boxing Day.

BIRTHDAYS TODAY

Evan Bayh, 44, US Senator (D, Indiana), born Shirkieville, IN, Dec 26, 1955.

Susan Butcher, 45, sled dog racer, born Cambridge, MA, Dec 26, 1954.

Gray Davis, 57, Governor of California (D), born Bronx, NY, Dec 26, 1942.

DECEMBER 27 — MONDAY

Day 361 — 4 Remaining

"HOWDY DOODY" TV PREMIERE: ANNIVERSARY. Dec 27, 1947. The first popular children's show was brought to TV by Bob Smith and was one of the first regular NBC shows to be shown in color. The show was set in the circus town of Doodyville, populated by people and puppets. Children sat in the bleachers' "Peanut Gallery" and participated in activities such as songs and stories. Human characters were Buffalo Bob (Bob Smith), the silent clown Clarabell (Bob Keeshan, Bobby Nicholson and Lew Anderson), storekeeper Cornelius Cobb (Nicholson), Chief Thunderthud (Bill LeCornec), Princess Summerfall Winterspring (Judy Tyler and Linda Marsh), Bison Bill (Ted Brown) and wrestler Ugly Sam (Dayton Allen). Puppet costars included Howdy Doody, Phineas T. Bluster, Dilly Dally, Flub-a-Dub, Captain Scuttlebutt, Double Doody and Heidi Doody. The filmed adventures of Gumby were also featured. In the final episode, Clarabell broke his long silence to say, "Goodbye, kids."

PASTEUR, LOUIS: BIRTH ANNIVERSARY. Dec 27, 1822. French chemist-bacteriologist born at Dole, Jura, France. Died at

Villeneuve l'Etang, France, Sept 28, 1895. Among his contributions to the germ theory of disease, he was the discoverer of prophylactic inoculation against rabies. He also proved that the spoilage of perishable food products could be prevented by the technique of heat treatment. This process, pasteurization, was named for him.

SAINT JOHN, APOSTLE-EVANGELIST: FEAST DAY. Dec 27. Son of Zebedee, Galilean fisherman, and Salome. Died about AD 100. Roman Rite Feast Day is Dec 27. (Observed May 8 by Byzantine Rite.)

BIRTHDAYS TODAY

Lisa Jakub, 19, actress (*Mrs Doubtfire, A Pig's Tale*), born Toronto, Canada, Dec 27, 1980.
Diane Stanley, 56, author and illustrator (*Rumpelstiltskin's Daughter*), born Abilene, TX, Dec 27, 1943.
Ernesto Zedillo Ponce de Leon, 48, president of Mexico, born Mexico City, Mexico, Dec 27, 1951.

DECEMBER 28 — TUESDAY
Day 362 — 3 Remaining

AUSTRALIA: PROCLAMATION DAY. Dec 28. Observed in South Australia.

HOLY INNOCENTS DAY (CHILDERMAS). Dec 28. Commemoration of the massacre of children at Bethlehem, ordered by King Herod who wanted to destroy, among them, the infant Savior. Early and medieval accounts claimed as many as 144,000 victims, but more recent writers, noting that Bethlehem was a very small town, have revised the estimates of the number of children killed to between six and 20.

IOWA: ADMISSION DAY: ANNIVERSARY. Dec 28. Became 29th state in 1846.

***POOR RICHARD'S ALMANACK* : ANNIVERSARY.** Dec 28, 1732. The *Pennsylvania Gazette* carried the first known advertisement for the first issue of *Poor Richard's Almanack* by Richard Saunders (Benjamin Franklin) for the year 1733. The advertisement promised "many pleasant and witty verses, jests and sayings . . ." America's most famous almanac, *Poor Richard's* was published through the year 1758 and has been imitated many times since. From *The Autobiography of Benjamin Franklin*: "In 1732 I first publish'd my Almanack, under the name of *Richard Saunders*; it was continu'd by me about twenty-five years, commonly call'd *Poor Richard's Almanack*. I endeavor'd to make it both entertaining and useful, and it accordingly came to be in such demand, that I reap'd considerable profit from it, vending annually near ten thousand. And observing that it was generally read, scarce any neighborhood in the province being without it, I consider'd it as a proper vehicle for conveying instruction among the common people, who bought scarcely any other books; I therefore filled all the little spaces that occurr'd between the remarkable days in the calendar with proverbial sentences, chiefly such as inculcated industry and frugality, as the means of procuring wealth, and

December 1999	S	M	T	W	T	F	S
				1	2	3	4
	5	6	7	8	9	10	11
	12	13	14	15	16	17	18
	19	20	21	22	23	24	25
	26	27	28	29	30	31	

thereby securing virtue; it being more difficult for a man in want, to act always honestly, as, to use here one of those proverbs, *it is hard for an empty sack to stand upright*."

WILSON, WOODROW: BIRTH ANNIVERSARY. Dec 28, 1856. The 28th president of the US was born Thomas Woodrow Wilson at Staunton, VA. Twice elected president (1912 and 1916), it was Wilson who said, "The world must be made safe for democracy," as he asked the Congress to declare war on Germany, Apr 2, 1917. His first wife, Ellen, died Aug 6, 1914, and he married Edith Bolling Galt, Dec 18, 1915. He suffered a paralytic stroke Sept 16, 1919, never regaining his health. There were many speculations about who (possibly Mrs Wilson?) was running the government during his illness. His second term of office ended Mar 3, 1921, and he died at Washington, DC, Feb 3, 1924.

BIRTHDAYS TODAY

Cynthia DeFelice, 48, author (*The Apprenticeship of Lucas Whitaker*), born Philadelphia, PA, Dec 28, 1951.
Tim Johnson, 53, US Senator (D, South Dakota), born Canton, SD, Dec 28, 1946.
Patrick Rafter, 27, tennis player, born Mount Isa, Queensland, Australia, Dec 28, 1972.
Todd Richards, 30, Olympic snowboarder, born Worcester, MA, Dec 28, 1969.
Denzel Washington, 45, actor ("St. Elsewhere," *Glory, Malcolm X*), born Mt Vernon, NY, Dec 28, 1954.

DECEMBER 29 — WEDNESDAY
Day 363 — 2 Remaining

ATWATER, RICHARD: BIRTH ANNIVERSARY. Dec 29, 1892. Author, with his wife Florence, of the Newbery Award winner *Mr Popper's Penguins*. Born at Chicago, IL, he died Aug 21, 1948.

JOHNSON, ANDREW: BIRTH ANNIVERSARY. Dec 29, 1808. Seventeenth president of the US, Andrew Johnson was born at Raleigh, NC. Upon Abraham Lincoln's assassination Johnson became president. He was the only US president to be impeached, and he was acquitted Mar 26, 1868. After his term of office as president (Apr 15, 1865–Mar 3, 1869) he made several unsuccessful attempts to win public office. Finally he was elected to the US Senate from Tennessee and served in the Senate from Mar 4, 1875, until his death, at Carter's Station, TN, July 31, 1875.

LAILAT UL QADR: THE NIGHT OF POWER. Dec 29 (also Dec 31, 1999, Jan 2, 4 or 6, 2000). "The Night of Power" falls on one of the last 10 days of Ramadan on an odd-numbered day (Islamic calendar dates: Ramadan 21, 23, 25, 27 or 29, 1420). The Holy Qur'an states that praying on this night is better than praying 1,000 months. Since it is not known which day it is, Muslims feel it is best to pray on each of the possible nights. Different methods for "anticipating" the visibility of the new moon crescent at Mecca are used by different Muslim sects or groups. US date may vary.

MOON PHASE: LAST QUARTER. Dec 29. Moon enters Last Quarter phase at 9:04 AM, EST.

NEPAL: BIRTHDAY OF HIS MAJESTY THE KING. Dec 29. National holiday of Nepal commemorating birth of King in 1945. Three-day celebration with huge public rally at Tundikkel, gay pageantry, musical bands and illumination in the towns at night.

TEXAS: ADMISSION DAY: ANNIVERSARY. Dec 29. Became 28th state in 1845.

UNITED NATIONS: INTERNATIONAL DAY FOR BIOLOGICAL DIVERSITY. Dec 29. On Dec 19, 1994, the General Assembly proclaimed this observance for Dec 29, the date of entry into force of the Convention on Biological Diversity (Res 49/119). Designation of the Day had been recommended by the Conference of the Parties to the Convention, held at Nassau Nov 28–Dec 9, 1994. For info: United Nations, Dept of Public Info, New York, NY 10017.

WOUNDED KNEE MASSACRE: ANNIVERSARY. Dec 29, 1890. Anniversary of the massacre of more than 200 Native American men, women and children by the US 7th Cavalry at Wounded Knee Creek, SD. Government efforts to suppress a ceremonial religious practice, the Ghost Dance (which called for a messiah who would restore the bison to the plains, make the white men disappear and bring back the old Native American way of life), had resulted in the death of Sitting Bull Dec 15, 1890, which further inflamed the disgruntled Native Americans and culminated in the slaughter at Wounded Knee Dec 29. For more info: *Wounded Knee, 1890: The End of the Plains Indian Wars*, by Tom Streissguth (Facts on File, 0-8160-3600-4, $19.95 Gr. 7-12).

YMCA ORGANIZED: ANNIVERSARY. Dec 29, 1851. The first US branch of the Young Men's Christian Association was organized at Boston. It was modeled on an organization begun at London in 1844.

BIRTHDAYS TODAY

Molly Bang, 56, author and illustrator (*The Paper Crane*), born Princeton, NJ, Dec 29, 1943.

Irene Brady, 56, science author and illustrator (*Wild Mouse*), born Ontario, OR, Dec 29, 1943.

Ted Danson, 52, actor ("Cheers," *Three Men and a Baby*), born San Diego, CA, Dec 29, 1947.

DECEMBER 30 — THURSDAY

Day 364 — 1 Remaining

KIPLING, RUDYARD: BIRTH ANNIVERSARY. Dec 30, 1865. English poet, novelist and short story writer, Nobel prize laureate, Kipling was born at Bombay, India. After working as a journalist at India, he traveled around the world. He married an American and lived at Vermont for several years. Kipling is best known for his children's stories, such as the *Jungle Book* and *Just So Stories* and poems such as "The Ballad of East and West" and "If." He died at London, England, Jan 18, 1936.

MADAGASCAR: NATIONAL HOLIDAY. Dec 30. Anniversary of the change of the name Malagasy Republic to the Democratic Republic of Madagascar in 1975.

PHILIPPINES: RIZAL DAY: ANNIVERSARY. Dec 30. Commemorates martyrdom of Dr. Jose Rizal in 1896.

"THE ROY ROGERS SHOW" TV PREMIERE: ANNIVERSARY. Dec 30, 1951. This very popular TV western starred Roy Rogers and his wife, Dale Evans, as themselves. It also featured Pat Brady as Rogers's sidekick who rode a jeep named Nellybelle, the singing group Sons of the Pioneers, Rogers's horse Trigger, Evans's horse Buttermilk and a German shepherd named Bullet. This half-hour show was especially popular with young viewers.

BIRTHDAYS TODAY

Jane Langton, 77, author (*The Fledgling*), born Boston, MA, Dec 30, 1922.

Matt Lauer, 42, news anchor ("Today"), born New York, NY, Dec 30, 1957.

Mercer Mayer, 56, author and illustrator (*East of the Sun, West of the Moon*), born Little Rock, AR, Dec 30, 1943.

Julianne Moore, 39, actress (*The Lost World: Jurassic Park*), born Fayetteville, NC, Dec 30, 1960.

Tracey Ullman, 40, actress, singer ("The Tracey Ullman Show," *I Love You to Death*), born Buckinghamshire, England, Dec 30, 1959.

Tiger (Eldrick) Woods, 24, golfer, born Cypress, CA, Dec 30, 1975.

DECEMBER 31 — FRIDAY

Day 365 — 0 Remaining

FIRST BANK OPENS IN US: ANNIVERSARY. Dec 31, 1781. The first modern bank in the US, the Bank of North America, was organized by Robert Morris and received its charter from the Confederation Congress in 1781. It began operations Jan 7, 1782, at Philadelphia.

LEAP SECOND ADJUSTMENT TIME. Dec 31. One of the times that have been favored for the addition or subtraction of a second from clock time (to coordinate atomic and astronomical time). The determination to adjust is made by the Central Bureau of the International Earth Rotation Service at Paris.

DECEMBER 31
THE END OF A MILLENNIUM?

With the excitement of the digits rolling from 1999 to 2000 this New Year's Eve, it probably won't matter much to global partygoers that the beginning of the next millennium is still a year away.

There is a lot of confusion about when the present millennium ends and a new one begins. A millennium is a period of 1,000 years. Our era is divided into two periods, BC (before Christ) and AD (anno Domini, which means "in the year of our Lord"), based on the birth of Jesus Christ. However, in the eighth century when this system started to be widely used, Arabic numerals were not yet known in Europe. The Roman numerals then in use did not have a symbol for zero so the first year of the first millennium was AD 1 and the year 1000 was the 1,000th year. This means that Jan 1, 1001 was the first day of the second millennium and Jan 1, 2001 will be the first day of the third millennium.

Leaflets from the Old Royal Observatory at Greenwich, England explain this in greater detail. These are available on the Web at www.ast.cam.ac.uk/pubinfo/leaflets/new_mill.html. For activities related to the millennium, see *The Kids Guide to the Millennium*, by Ann Love and Jane Drake (Kids Can Press, 1-5507-4436-4, $7.95 Gr. 4-6).

MAKE UP YOUR MIND DAY. Dec 31. A day for all those people who have a hard time making up their minds. Make a decision today and follow through with it! Annually, Dec 31. For info: A.C. Moeller and M.A. Dufour, Box 71, Clio, MI 48420-1042.

MATISSE, HENRI: BIRTH ANNIVERSARY. Dec 31, 1869. Painter born at Le Cateau, France. Matisse also designed textiles and stained glass windows. Died at Nice, France, Nov 3, 1954.

NEW YEAR'S EVE. Dec 31. The last evening of the Gregorian calendar year, traditionally a night for merrymaking to welcome in the new year. Although technically the second millennium doesn't end until New Year's Eve, 2000, most of the world will be welcoming the third millennium tonight. See Curriculum Connection.

ORANGE BOWL PARADE. Dec 31. Miami, FL. Annual New Year's Eve parade for the past 62 years. Nationally televised, parade moves 2.2 miles along downtown Miami's Biscayne Boulevard by the bay. Est attendance: 500,000. For info: John Shaffer, Orange Bowl Committee, 601 Brickell Key Dr, Ste 206, Miami, FL 33131. Phone: (305) 371-4600.

PANAMA: ASSUMES CONTROL OF CANAL: ANNIVERSARY. Dec 31, 1999. With the expiration of the Panama Canal Treaty of 1979 at noon, the Republic of Panama will assume full responsibility for the canal and the US Panama Canal Commission will cease to exist.

BIRTHDAYS TODAY

Anthony Hopkins, 62, actor (*Amistad*), born Port Talbot, Wales, Great Britain, Dec 31, 1937.

Val Kilmer, 40, actor (*Batman Forever*), born Los Angeles, CA, Dec 31, 1959.

JANUARY 1 — SATURDAY

Day 1 — 365 Remaining

SATURDAY, JANUARY ONE, 2000. Jan 1. First day of the first month of the Gregorian calendar year, Anno Domini 2000, being a Leap Year, and (until July 4th) the 224th year of American independence. The New Year begins just west of the International Date Line in the Pacific and travels with the day around the world in an westerly direction, so the year 2000 will arrive first in Asia, then in Europe and Africa, and finally in the Americas. New Year's Day is a public holiday in the US and in many other countries. Traditionally, it is a time for personal stocktaking, for making resolutions for the coming year and sometimes for recovering from the festivities of New Year's Eve. Financial accounting begins anew for businesses and individuals whose fiscal year is the calendar year. Jan 1 has been observed as the beginning of the year in most English-speaking countries since the British Calendar Act of 1751, prior to which the New Year began Mar 25 (approximating the vernal equinox). Earth begins another orbit of the sun, during which it, and we, will travel some 583,416,000 miles in 365.24219 days. New Year's Day has been called "Everyman's Birthday," and in some countries a year is added to everyone's age Jan 1 rather than on the anniversary of each person's birth.

AUSTRALIA: COMMONWEALTH FORMED: ANNIVERSARY. Jan 1, 1901. The six colonies of Victoria, New South Wales, Queensland, South Australia, Western Australia and Northern Territory were united into one nation. The British Parliament had passed the Commonwealth Constitution Bill in the spring of 1900 and Queen Victoria signed the document Sept 17, 1900. Australia will celebrate its centennial as a nation in 2001.

AUTISM AWARENESS MONTH. Jan 1–31. A month filled with events such as poster contests, a state proclamation by the governor and family activities on autism. This is a national celebration. Annually, the month of January. For info: Linda Ryan, Coord of Mktg and PR, COSAC, 1450 Parkside Ave, Ste 22, Ewing, NJ 08638. Phone: (609) 883-8100. Fax: (609) 883-5509. E-mail: njautism@aol.com. Web: members.aol.com/njautism.

BEANIE BABIES INTRODUCED: ANNIVERSARY. Jan 1, 1994. During this month the first nine Beanie Babies were introduced. Since then, more than 135 models of the plush animals have been released. For more info: www.ty.com.

BONZA BOTTLER DAY™. Jan 1. (Also Feb 2, Mar 3, Apr 4, May 5, June 6, July 7, Aug 8, Sept 9, Oct 10, Nov 11 and Dec 12.) To celebrate when the number of the day is the same as the number of the month. Bonza Bottler Day™ is an excuse to have a party at least once a month. For info: Gail M. Berger, Bonza Bottler Day, 109 Matthew Ave, Poca, WV 25159. Phone: (304) 776-7746. E-mail: gberger5@aol.com.

CUBA: ANNIVERSARY OF THE REVOLUTION. Jan 1. National holiday celebrating the overthrow of the government of Fulgencio Batista in 1959 by the revolutionary forces of Fidel Castro, which had begun a civil war in 1956.

CUBA: LIBERATION DAY: ANNIVERSARY. Jan 1. A national holiday that celebrates the end of Spanish rule in 1899. Cuba, the largest island of the West Indies, was a Spanish possession from its discovery by Columbus (Oct 27, 1492) until 1899. Under US military control 1899–1902 and 1906–09, a republican government took over Jan 28, 1909 and controlled the island until overthrown Jan 1, 1959, by Fidel Castro's revolutionary movement.

CZECH-SLOVAK DIVORCE: ANNIVERSARY. Jan 1, 1993. As Dec 31, 1992, gave way to Jan 1, 1993, the 74-year-old state of Czechoslovakia separated into two nations—the Czech and Slovak Republics. The Slovaks held a celebration through the night in the streets of Bratislava amid fireworks, bell ringing, singing of the new country's national anthem and the raising of the Slovak flag. In the new Czech Republic no official festivities took place, but later in the day the Czechs celebrated with a solemn oath by their parliament. The nation of Czechoslovakia ended peacefully though polls showed that most Slovaks and Czechs would have preferred that Czechoslovakia survive. Before the split Czech Prime Minister Vaclav Klaus and Slovak Prime Minister Vladimir Meciar reached agreement on dividing everything from army troops and gold reserves to the art on government building walls.

ELLIS ISLAND OPENED: ANNIVERSARY. Jan 1, 1892. Ellis Island was opened on New Year's Day in 1892. Over the years more than 20 million individuals were processed through the immigration station. The island was used as a point of deportation as well; in 1932 alone, 20,000 people were deported from Ellis Island. When the US entered WWII in 1941, Ellis Island became a Coast Guard Station. It closed Nov 12, 1954, and was declared a national park in 1956. After years of disuse it was restored and was reopened as a museum in 1990. For more info: www.nps.gov/stli/serv02.htm.

EMANCIPATION PROCLAMATION: ANNIVERSARY. Jan 1, 1863. Two of the most important presidential proclamations of American history are those of Sept 22, 1862, and Jan 1, 1863, in which Abraham Lincoln, by executive proclamation, freed the slaves in the rebelling states. "That on . . . [Jan 1, 1863] . . . all persons held as slaves within any state or designated part of a state, the people whereof shall then be in rebellion against the United States, shall be then, thenceforward, and forever, free. . . ." See also: "13th Amendment: Anniversary" (Dec 18) for abolition of slavery in all states.

EURO INTRODUCED: ANNIVERSARY. Jan 1, 1999. The euro, the common currency of 11 members of the European Union, was introduced for use by banks. The value of the currencies of Austria, Belgium, Finland, France, Germany, Ireland, Italy, Luxembourg, the Netherlands, Portugal and Spain are locked in at a permanent conversion rate to the euro. On Jan 1, 2002, euro bills and coins will begin circulating and other currencies will be phased out.

HAITI: INDEPENDENCE DAY. Jan 1. A national holiday commemorating the proclamation of independence in 1804. Haiti, occupying the western third of the island Hispaniola (second largest of the West Indies), was a Spanish colony from the time of its discovery by Columbus in 1492 until 1697, then a French colony until the proclamation of independence in 1804.

JAPANESE ERA NEW YEAR. Jan 1–3. Celebration of the beginning of the year Heisei Twelve, the 12th year of Emperor Akihito's reign.

KLIBAN, B(ERNARD): 65th BIRTH ANNIVERSARY. Jan 1, 1935. Cartoonist B. Kliban was born at Norwalk, CT. He was known for his satirical drawings of cats engaged in human pursuits, which appeared in the books *Cat* (1975), *Never Eat Anything Bigger than Your Head & Other Drawings* (1976) and *Whack Your Porcupine* (1977). His drawings appeared on T-shirts, greeting cards, calendars, bedsheets and other merchandise, creating a $50 million industry before his death at San Francisco, CA, Aug 12, 1990.

MARCH OF DIMES BIRTH DEFECTS PREVENTION MONTH. Jan 1–31. To heighten awareness of birth defects and how they may be prevented, to inform the public about the work of the March of Dimes and to offer opportunities to new volunteers for service in the prevention of birth defects. For info: March of Dimes Birth Defects Foundation, 1275 Mamaroneck Ave, White Plains, NY 10605. Phone: (914) 997-4600.

MEXICO: ZAPATISTA REBELLION: ANNIVERSARY. Jan 1, 1994. Declaring war against the government of President Carlos Salinas de Gortari, the Zapatista National Liberation Army seized four towns in the state of Chiapas in southern Mexico. The rebel group, which took its name from the early 20th-century Mexican revolutionary Emiliano Zapata, issued a declaration stating that they were protesting discrimination against the Indian population of the region and against their severe poverty.

MUMMERS PARADE. Jan 1. Philadelphia, PA. World famous New Year's Day parade of 20,000 spectacularly costumed Mummers in a colorful parade that goes on all day. Est attendance: 100,000. For info: Mummers Parade, 1100 S 2nd St, Philadelphia, PA 19147. Phone: (215) 636-1666. E-mail: mummersmus@aol.com.

NATIONAL BATH SAFETY MONTH. Jan 1–31. To raise awareness of the potential of hazards that exist and encourage people to conduct a bathroom safety audit. For info: Linda Maiorana, Homecare America, 5 Wellwood Ave, Farmingdale, NY 11735. Phone: (516) 454-6664. Fax: (516) 454-8572. E-mail: lmaiorana@homecareamerica.com. Web: www.homecareamerica.com.

NATIONAL BOOK MONTH. Jan 1–31. When the world demands more and more of our time, National Book Month invites everyone in America to take time out to treat themselves to a unique pleasure: reading a good book. Readers participate in National Book Month annually through literary events held at schools, bookstores, libraries, community centers and arts organizations. The organization also sponsors the annual National Book Awards, which include an award for a children's book. For info: Natl Book Foundation, 260 Fifth Ave, Rm 904, New York, NY 10001. Phone: (212) 685-0261. Fax: (212) 235-6570. E-mail: NatBkFdn@mindspring.com.

NATIONAL ENVIRONMENTAL POLICY ACT: 30th ANNIVERSARY. Jan 1, 1970. The National Environmental Policy Act of 1969, establishing the Council on Environmental Quality and making it federal government policy to protect the environment.

NATIONAL EYE CARE MONTH. Jan 1–31. Sponsored by the American Academy of Ophthalmology, this month promotes awareness of eye health, importance of medical eye care and prevention to avoid eye injuries and disease. A free kit of materials is available to businesses and organizations to increase awareness at local and community levels. Fax a copy of your mailing label with your request. For info: American Academy of Ophthalmology–NECM, PO Box 7424, San Francisco, CA 94140-7424. Fax: (415) 561-8567. E-mail: PIMR@aao.org. Web: www.eyenet.org.

NATIONAL HOT TEA MONTH. Jan 1–31. To celebrate one of nature's most popular, soothing and relaxing beverages; the only beverage in America commonly served hot or iced, anytime, anywhere, for any occasion. For info: Joseph P. Simrany, Pres, The Tea Council of the USA, 420 Lexington Ave, Ste 825, New York, NY 10170. Phone: (212) 986-6998. Fax: (212) 697-8658.

NATIONAL PERSONAL SELF-DEFENSE AWARENESS MONTH. Jan 1–31. To educate Americans about realistic self-defense options, tactics and techniques in an increasingly aggressive world. Seminars and related events nationally focus on issues of awareness, prevention, risk reduction, confrontation avoidance and physical self-defense techniques to encourage individuals to take a pro-active role in their self-defense and in building self-confidence. For info: Natl Self-Defense Inst Inc, 1521 Alton Rd, Box 131, Miami Beach, FL 33139. Phone: (305) 868-NSDI or (305) 577-8811. Fax: (305) 577-8312.

NATIONAL SOUP MONTH. Jan 1–31. To celebrate one of the world's favorite foods and its relevance to today's lifestyles. For info: Kevin Lowery, Public Affairs, Campbell Soup Co, Campbell Place, Camden, NJ 08103-1799. Phone: (800) 257-8443. Web: www.campbellsoups.com.

NEW YEAR'S DAY. Jan 1. Legal holiday in all states and territories of the US and in most other countries. The world's most widely celebrated holiday.

NEW YEAR'S DISHONOR LIST. Jan 1. Since 1976, America's dishonor list of words banished from the Queen's English. Overworked words and phrases (e.g., *uniquely unique, first time ever, safe sex*). Send nominations to the following address: PR Office, Lake Superior State Univ, Sault Ste. Marie, MI 49783. Phone: (906) 635-2315. Fax: (906) 635-2111. Web: www.lssu.edu.

OATMEAL MONTH. Jan 1–31. "Celebrate oatmeal, a low-fat, sodium-free, whole grain that when eaten daily as a part of a diet that's low in saturated fat and cholesterol may help reduce the risk of heart disease. Delicious recipes, helpful hints and tips from Quaker® Oats, The Oat Expert, will make enjoying the heart health benefits oatmeal has to offer easy, convenient and, above all, delicious." For info: The Oat Expert, 225 W Washington, Ste 1440, Chicago, IL 60606. Phone: (312) 629-1234.

PHILIPPINES: BLACK NAZARENE FIESTA. Jan 1–9. Manila. A traditional nine-day fiesta honors Quiapo district's patron saint. Cultural events, fireworks and parades culminate in a procession

	S	M	T	W	T	F	S
January 2000							1
	2	3	4	5	6	7	8
	9	10	11	12	13	14	15
	16	17	18	19	20	21	22
	23	24	25	26	27	28	29
	30	31					

with the life-size statue of the Black Nazarene. Procession begins at the historic Quiapo Church.

REVERE, PAUL: BIRTH ANNIVERSARY. Jan 1, 1735. American patriot, silversmith and engraver, maker of false teeth, eyeglasses, picture frames and surgical instruments. Best remembered for his famous ride Apr 18, 1775, to warn patriots that the British were coming, celebrated in Longfellow's poem, "The Midnight Ride of Paul Revere." Born at Boston, MA, died there May 10, 1818. See also: "Paul Revere's Ride: Anniversary" (Apr 18).

ROSE BOWL GAME. Jan 1. Pasadena, CA. Football conference champions from Big Ten and Pac-10 meet in the Rose Bowl game. Tournament of Roses has been an annual New Year's Day event since 1890; Rose Bowl football game since 1902. Michigan defeated Stanford 49-0 in what was the first postseason football game. Called the Rose Bowl since 1923, it is preceded each year by the Tournament of Roses Parade. Est attendance: 100,000. For info: Bridget Schinnerer, Program Coord, Rose Bowl Stadium, 1001 Rose Bowl Drive, Pasadena, CA 91103. Phone: (626) 449-4100. Fax: (626) 449-9066. Web: www.tournamentofroses .com.

ROSS, BETSY: BIRTH ANNIVERSARY. Jan 1, 1752. According to legend based largely on her grandson's revelations in 1870, needleworker Betsy Ross created the first stars-and-stripes flag in 1775, under instructions from George Washington. Her sewing and her making of flags were well known, but there is little corroborative evidence of her role in making the first stars-and-stripes. The account is generally accepted, however, in the absence of any documented claims to the contrary. She was born Elizabeth Griscom at Philadelphia, PA, and died there Jan 30, 1836.

RUSSIA: NEW YEAR'S DAY OBSERVANCE. Jan 1–2. National holiday. Modern tradition calls for setting up New Year's trees in homes, halls, clubs, palaces of culture and the hall of the Kremlin Palace. Children's parties with Granddad Frost and his granddaughter, Snow Girl. Games, songs, dancing, special foods, family gatherings and exchanges of gifts and New Year's cards.

SAINT BASIL'S DAY. Jan 1. St. Basil's or St. Vasily's feast day observed by Eastern Orthodox churches. Special traditions for the day include serving St. Basil cakes, each of which contains a coin. Feast day observed Jan 14 by those churches using the Julian calendar.

SOLEMNITY OF MARY, MOTHER OF GOD. Jan 1. Holy Day of Obligation in Roman Catholic Church since calendar reorganization of 1969, replacing the Feast of the Circumcision, which had been recognized for more than 14 centuries.

SUDAN: INDEPENDENCE DAY. Jan 1. National holiday. Sudan was proclaimed a sovereign independent republic Jan 1, 1956, ending its status as an Anglo-Egyptian condominium (since 1899).

TOURNAMENT OF ROSES PARADE. Jan 1. Pasadena, CA. 111th annual parade. Rose Parade starting at 8 AM, PST, includes floats, bands and equestrians. Est attendance: 1,000,000. For info: Pasadena Tournament of Roses Assn, 391 S Orange Grove Blvd, Pasadena, CA 91184. Phone: (626) 449-4100. Fax: (626) 449-9066. Web: www.tournamentofroses.com.

UNITED NATIONS: DECADE AGAINST DRUG ABUSE: YEAR TEN. Jan 1–Dec 31. United Nations program for the decade 1991–2000 to strengthen international, regional and national efforts in the fight against drug abuse. Proclaimed by the General Assembly Feb 23, 1990 (Res S-17/2). Info from: United Nations, Dept of Public Info, New York, NY 10017.

UNITED NATIONS: DECADE FOR HUMAN RIGHTS EDUCATION: YEAR SIX. Jan 1–Dec 31. On Dec 23, 1994, the General Assembly proclaimed this decade to begin in 1995, and welcomed the Plan of Action for the Decade submitted by the Secretary-General (Res 49/184). The Assembly expressed its conviction that human rights education should constitute a lifelong process, by which people learn respect for the dignity of others. Info from: United Nations, Dept of Public Info, New York, NY 10017.

UNITED NATIONS: DECADE FOR THE ERADICATION OF POVERTY: YEAR FOUR. Jan 1–Dec 31. General Assembly, Dec 20, 1995 (Res 50/107 II), proclaimed 1997–2006 (the decade following the International Year for the Eradication of Poverty—1996) to be a time for governments and organizations to pursue implementation of the recommendations of the major UN conferences on this issue, particularly the World Summit for Social Development held in Copenhagen in March 1995. Info from: United Nations, Dept of Public Info, New York, NY 10017.

UNITED NATIONS: INTERNATIONAL DECADE OF THE WORLD'S INDIGENOUS PEOPLE: YEAR SEVEN. Jan 1–Dec 9. Proclaimed by the General Assembly, Dec 21, 1993 (Res 48/163), this decade (1994–2003) focuses international attention and cooperation on the problems of indigenous people in a range of areas, such as human rights, health, education, development and environment. Governments are encouraged to include representatives of these people in planning and executing goals and activities for the decade. Info from: United Nations, Dept of Public Info, New York, NY 10017.

WAYNE, "MAD ANTHONY": BIRTH ANNIVERSARY. Jan 1, 1745. American Revolutionary War general whose daring, sometimes reckless, conduct earned him the nickname "Mad Anthony" Wayne. His courage and shrewdness as a soldier made him a key figure in the capture of Stony Point, NY (1779), preventing Benedict Arnold's delivery of West Point to the British, and in subduing hostile Indians of the Northwest Territory (1794). He was born at Waynesboro, PA and died at Presque Isle, PA, Dec 15, 1796.

Z DAY. Jan 1. To give recognition on the first day of the year to all persons and places whose names begin with the letter "Z" and who are always listed or thought of last in any alphabetized list. For info: Tom Zager, 4545 Kirkwood Dr, Sterling Heights, MI 48310.

BIRTHDAYS TODAY

Ernest F. Hollings, 78, US Senator (D, South Carolina), born Charleston, SC, Jan 1, 1922.

Gary Johnson, 47, Governor of New Mexico (R), born Minot, ND, Jan 1, 1953.

Tony Knowles, 57, Governor of Alaska (D), born Tulsa, OK, Jan 1, 1943.

JANUARY 2 — SUNDAY

Day 2 — 364 Remaining

ASIMOV, ISAAC: 80th BIRTH ANNIVERSARY. Jan 2, 1920. Although Isaac Asimov was one of the world's best-known writers of science fiction, his almost 500 books dealt with subjects as diverse as the Bible, works for preschoolers, college textbooks, mysteries, chemistry, biology, limericks, Shakespeare, Gilbert and Sullivan and modern history. During his prolific career he helped to elevate science fiction from pulp magazines to a more intellectual level. Some of his works include the *Foundation Trilogy, The Robots of Dawn, Robots and Empire, Nemesis, Murder at the A.B.A.* (in which he himself was a character), *The Gods Themselves* and *I, Robot,* in which he posited the famous Three Laws of Robotics. *The Clock We Live On* is an accessible explanation of the origins of calendars. Asimov was born near Smolensk, Russia, and died at New York, NY, Apr 6, 1992.

55-MPH SPEED LIMIT: ANNIVERSARY. Jan 2, 1974. President Richard Nixon signed a bill requiring states to limit highway speeds to a maximum of 55 mph. This measure was meant to conserve energy during the crisis precipitated by the embargo imposed by the Arab oil-producing countries. A plan, used by some states, limited sale of gasoline on odd-numbered days for cars whose plates ended in odd numbers and even-numbered days for even-numbered plates. Some states limited purchases to $2–$3 per auto and lines as long as six miles resulted in some locations. See also: "Arab Oil Embargo Lifted: Anniversary" (Mar 13).

GEORGIA: RATIFICATION DAY. Jan 2, 1788. By unanimous vote, Georgia became the fourth state to ratify the Constitution.

HAITI: ANCESTORS' DAY. Jan 2. Commemoration of the ancestors. Also known as Hero's Day. Public holiday.

JAPAN: KAKIZOME. Jan 2. Traditional Japanese festival gets under way when the first strokes of the year are made on paper with the traditional brushes.

SPACE MILESTONE: *LUNA 1* (USSR). Jan 2, 1959. Launch of robotic moon probe that missed the moon and became the first spacecraft from Earth to orbit the sun.

SPAIN CAPTURES GRANADA: ANNIVERSARY. Jan 2, 1492. Spaniards took the city of Granada from the Moors, ending seven centuries of Muslim rule in Spain.

TAFT, HELEN HERRON: BIRTH ANNIVERSARY. Jan 2, 1861. Wife of William Howard Taft, 27th President of the US, born at Cincinnati, OH. Died at Washington, DC, May 22, 1943.

WOLFE, JAMES: BIRTH ANNIVERSARY. Jan 2, 1727. English general who commanded the British army's victory over Montcalm's French forces on the Plains of Abraham at Quebec City in 1759. As a result, France surrendered Canada to England. Wolfe was born at Westerham, Kent, England. He died at the Plains of Abraham of battle wounds, Sept 13, 1759.

January 2000	S	M	T	W	T	F	S
							1
	2	3	4	5	6	7	8
	9	10	11	12	13	14	15
	16	17	18	19	20	21	22
	23	24	25	26	27	28	29
	30	31					

David Cone, 37, baseball player, born Kansas City, MO, Jan 2, 1963.

Dennis Hastert, 58, Speaker of the House of Representatives, born Aurora, IL, Jan 2, 1942.

Richard Riley, 67, US Secretary of Education, born Greenville, SC, Jan 2, 1933.

JANUARY 3 — MONDAY

Day 3 — 363 Remaining

ALASKA: ADMISSION DAY: ANNIVERSARY. Jan 3. Alaska, which had been purchased from Russia in 1867, became the 49th state in 1959. The area of Alaska is nearly one-fifth the size of the rest of the US.

CONGRESS ASSEMBLES. Jan 3. The Constitution provides that "the Congress shall assemble at least once in every year...." and the 20th Amendment specifies "and such meeting shall begin at noon on the 3rd day of January, unless they shall by law appoint a different day."

COOLIDGE, GRACE ANNA GOODHUE: BIRTH ANNIVERSARY. Jan 3, 1879. Wife of Calvin Coolidge, 30th president of the US, born at Burlington, VT. Died at Northampton, MA, July 8, 1957.

DRINKING STRAW PATENTED: ANNIVERSARY. Jan 3, 1888. A drinking straw made out of paraffin-covered paper was patented by Marvin Stone of Washington, DC. It replaced natural rye straws.

EARTH AT PERIHELION. Jan 3. At approximately midnight, EST, planet Earth will reach Perihelion, that point in its orbit when it is closest to the sun (about 91,400,000 miles). The Earth's mean distance from the sun (mean radius of its orbit) is reached early in the months of April and October. Note that Earth is closest to the sun during Northern Hemisphere winter. See also: "Earth at Aphelion" (July 3).

FRISBEE INTRODUCED: ANNIVERSARY. Jan 3, 1957. Legend has it that in the 1920s New England college students tossed pie tins from the Frisbie Baking Company of Bridgeport, CT. The first plastic flying disc was released as the Pluto Platter, for its resemblance to a UFO. In 1958 it was re-named the Frisbee. More than 100 million Frisbees have been sold and there are numerous Frisbee tournaments across America every year.

MOTT, LUCRETIA (COFFIN): BIRTH ANNIVERSARY. Jan 3, 1793. American teacher, minister, antislavery leader and (with Elizabeth Cady Stanton) one of the founders of the women's rights movement in the US. Born at Nantucket, MA, she died near Philadelphia, PA, Nov 11, 1880.

RUSSIA: PASSPORT PRESENTATION. Jan 3. A ceremony for 16-year-olds, who are recognized as citizens of the country. Always on the first working day of the New Year.

TOLKIEN, J[OHN] R[ONALD] R[EUEL]: BIRTH ANNIVERSARY. Jan 3, 1892. Author of *The Hobbit* (1937) and the trilogy *The Lord of the Rings.* Though best known for his fantasies,

Tolkien was also a serious philologist. Born at Bloemfontein, South Africa, he died at Bournemouth, England, Sept 2, 1973.

BIRTHDAYS TODAY

Alma Flor Ada, 62, author (*Yours Truly, Goldilocks*), born Camaguey, Cuba, Jan 3, 1938.

Joan Walsh Anglund, 74, author, illustrator of children's books (*Crocus in the Snow, Bedtime Book*), born Hinsdale, IL, Jan 3, 1926.

Mel Gibson, 44, actor (*Lethal Weapon*, voice of John Smith in *Pocahontas*), born New York, NY, Jan 3, 1956.

Robert (Bobby) Hull, 61, Hockey Hall of Fame left wing, born Point Anne, Ontario, Canada, Jan 3, 1939.

Jason Marsden, 25, actor ("Step By Step"), born Providence, RI, Jan 3, 1975.

JANUARY 4 — TUESDAY

Day 4 — 362 Remaining

BRAILLE, LOUIS: BIRTH ANNIVERSARY. Jan 4, 1809. The inventor of a widely used touch system of reading and writing for the blind was born at Coupvray, France. Permanently blinded at the age of three by a leatherworking awl in his father's saddle-making shop, Braille developed a system of writing that used, ironically, an awl-like stylus to punch marks in paper that could be felt and interpreted by the blind. The system was largely ignored until after Braille died in poverty, suffering from tuberculosis, at Paris, Jan 6, 1852.

GENERAL TOM THUMB: BIRTH ANNIVERSARY. Jan 4, 1838. Charles Sherwood Stratton, perhaps the most famous midget in history, was born at Bridgeport, CT. His growth almost stopped during his first year, but he eventually reached a height of three feet, four inches and a weight of 70 pounds. "Discovered" by P.T. Barnum in 1842, Stratton, as "General Tom Thumb," became an internationally known entertainer and on tour performed before Queen Victoria and other heads of state. On Feb 10, 1863, he married another midget, Lavinia Warren. Stratton died at Middleborough, MA, July 15, 1883.

GRIMM, JACOB: BIRTH ANNIVERSARY. Jan 4, 1785. Librarian, mythologist and philologist, born at Hanau, Germany. Most remembered for *Grimms' Fairy Tales* (in collaboration with his brother Wilhelm). Died at Berlin, Germany, Sept 20, 1863. See Curriculum Connection.

MYANMAR: INDEPENDENCE DAY. Jan 4. National Day. The British controlled the country from 1826 until 1948 when it was granted independence. Formerly Burma, the country's name was changed to the Union of Myanmar in 1989 to reflect that the population is made up not just of the Burmese but of many other ethnic groups as well.

NEWTON, ISAAC: BIRTH ANNIVERSARY. Jan 4, 1643. Sir Isaac Newton was the chief figure of the scientific revolution of the 17th century, a physicist and mathematician who laid the foundations of calculus, studied the mechanics of planetary motion and discovered the law of gravitation. Born at Woolsthorpe, England, he died at London, England, Mar 20, 1727. Newton was born before Great Britain adopted the Gregorian calendar. His Julian (Old Style) birth date is Dec 25, 1642.

POLISH-AMERICAN IN THE HOUSE: ANNIVERSARY. Jan 4, 1977. Maryland Democrat Barbara Mikulski took her seat in the US House of Representatives, the first Polish-American ever to do so. An able voice for female as well as working class Baltimore constituents of the 3rd District, Mikulski went on to be elected to the US Senate.

JANUARY 4
JAKOB LUDWIG GRIMM — BIRTHDAY

Jakob Grimm and his brother Wilhelm collected and published many of our most beloved fairy tales, including Sleeping Beauty, Rumpelstiltskin, Hansel and Gretel, Rapunzel and Cinderella. Traditional literature (fairy tales) introduces children to a wide variety of cultural groups and has universal appeal. Familiarity with traditional literature characters and situations is part of being culturally literate. The rich, descriptive language found in original versions of Grimms' tales exposes children to an enriching experience. Moral issues are very clear in Grimms' fairy tales. Good and evil are very distinct. Good triumphs in the end, often with harsh consequences for the wrongdoers.

Grimms' fairy tales are wonderful readalouds for students in grades K–8. Many picture book versions are suitable for adapting into plays or as Reader's Theater scripts.

A scholarly, but fun, treatment is to compare and contrast one of the Grimms' tales with its variants found in other cultures. Make a literary criticism chart with the headings: Title, Hero or Heroine, Setting, Magic, Wrongdoers, Punishment, Story's End. As a group, read the original Grimm version of the tale. Then choose two or more cultural variants of the same tale. Divide the class into groups and assign one tale to each group. After reading and discussing them, regroup as a class. Each group reports to the class and fills in their information on the classroom literary criticism chart. Discuss ways the different cultures have adapted the tale.

Cinderella is a good first choice. Its many variants include: *The Golden Sandal: A Middle Eastern Cinderella Story*, by Rebecca Hickox (Holiday House, 0-8234-1331-4, $15.95 Gr. K–3); *Mufaro's Beautiful Daughters*, by John Steptoe (Morrow, 0-688-04045-4, $16 Gr. K–3); *The Way Meat Loves Salt: A Cinderella Tale from the Jewish Tradition*, by Nina Jaffe (Holt, 0-8050-4384-5, $15.95 Gr. K–3); *Kongi and Potgi: A Cinderella Story from Korea*, by Oki Han (Dial, 0-8037-1571-4, $14.99 Gr. K–3); *Sootface: An Ojibwa Cinderella Story*, by Robert San Souci (Doubleday, 0-385-31202-4, $16.95 Gr. 1–4); *Cendrillon: A Caribbean Cinderella*, by Robert San Souci (Simon & Schuster, 0-689-80668-X, $16 Gr. K–3); and *Yeh-Shen: A Cinderella Story from China*, by Ai-Ling Louie (Paperstar, 0-698-11388-8, $5.95 Gr. 1–4). Primary and middle school students enjoy doing literary comparisons using these books and the many other fairy tale variants available.

POP MUSIC CHART INTRODUCED: ANNIVERSARY. Jan 4, 1936. *Billboard* magazine published the first list of best-selling pop records, covering the week that ended Dec 30, 1935. On the list were recordings by the Tommy Dorsey and the Ozzie Nelson orchestras.

TRIVIA DAY. Jan 4. In celebration of those who know all sorts of facts and/or have doctorates in uselessology. For info: Robert L. Birch, Puns Corps, Box 2364, Falls Church, VA 22042-0364. Phone: (703) 533-3668.

UTAH: ADMISSION DAY: ANNIVERSARY. Jan 4. Became the 45th state in 1896.

BIRTHDAYS TODAY

Robert Burleigh, 64, poet (*Hoops*), born Chicago, IL, Jan 4, 1936.

Phyllis Reynolds Naylor, 67, author (Newbery for *Shiloh*), born Anderson, IN, Jan 4, 1933.

JANUARY 5 — WEDNESDAY
Day 5 — 361 Remaining

AILEY, ALVIN: BIRTH ANNIVERSARY. Jan 5, 1931. Born at Rogers, TX, Alvin Ailey began his career as a choreographer in the late 1950s after a successful career as a dancer. He founded the Alvin Ailey American Dance Theater, drawing from classical ballet, jazz, Afro-Caribbean and modern dance idioms to create the 79 ballets of the company's repertoire. He and his work played a central part in establishing a role for blacks in the world of modern dance. Ailey died Dec 1, 1989, at New York, NY.

CARVER, GEORGE WASHINGTON: DEATH ANNIVERSARY. Jan 5, 1943. Black American agricultural scientist, author, inventor and teacher. Born into slavery at Diamond Grove, MO, probably in 1864. His research led to the creation of synthetic products made from peanuts, potatoes and wood. Carver died at Tuskegee, AL. His birthplace became a national monument in 1953. For further info: *George Washington Carver: Nature's Trailblazer*, by Theresa Rogers (Twenty-First Century, 0-8050-2115-9, $14.95 Gr. 5–7).

DECATUR, STEPHEN: BIRTH ANNIVERSARY. Jan 5, 1779. American naval officer (whose father and grandfather, both also named Stephen Decatur, were also seafaring men) born at Sinepuxent, MD. In a toast at a dinner in Norfolk in 1815, Decatur spoke his most famous words: "Our country! In her intercourse with foreign nations may she always be in the right; but our country, right or wrong." Mortally wounded in a duel with Commodore James Barron, at Bladensburg, MD, on the morning of Mar 22, 1820, Decatur was carried to his home at Washington where he died a few hours later.

ITALY: EPIPHANY FAIR. Jan 5. Piazza Navona, Rome, Italy. On the eve of Epiphany a fair of toys, sweets and presents takes place among the beautiful Bernini Fountains.

PICCARD, JEANNETTE RIDLON: BIRTH ANNIVERSARY. Jan 5, 1895. First American woman to qualify as a free balloon pilot (1934). One of the first women to be ordained an Episcopal priest (1976). Pilot for record-setting balloon ascent into stratosphere (57,579 ft) from Dearborn, MI, Oct 23, 1934, with her husband, Jean Felix Piccard. She was an identical twin married to an identical twin. Born at Chicago, IL, she died at Minneapolis, MN, May 17, 1981. See also: "Piccard, Jean Felix: Birth Anniversary" (Jan 28).

TWELFTH NIGHT. Jan 5. Evening before Epiphany. Twelfth Night marks the end of medieval Christmas festivities and the end of Twelfthtide (the 12-day season after Christmas ending with Epiphany). Also called Twelfth Day Eve.

WYOMING INAUGURATES FIRST WOMAN GOVERNOR IN US: 75th ANNIVERSARY. Jan 5, 1925. Nellie Tayloe (Mrs William B.) Ross became the first woman to serve as governor upon her inauguration as governor of Wyoming. She had previously finished out the term of her husband, who had died in office. In 1974 Ella Grasso of Connecticut became the first woman to be elected governor in her own right.

January 2000	S	M	T	W	T	F	S
							1
	2	3	4	5	6	7	8
	9	10	11	12	13	14	15
	16	17	18	19	20	21	22
	23	24	25	26	27	28	29
	30	31					

BIRTHDAYS TODAY

Mike DeWine, 53, US Senator (R, Ohio), born Springfield, OH, Jan 5, 1947.
Warrick Dunn, 25, football player, born Baton Rouge, LA, Jan 5, 1975.
Walter Frederick "Fritz" Mondale, 72, 42nd vice-president of the US and candidate for president in 1984, born Ceylon, MN, Jan 5, 1928.

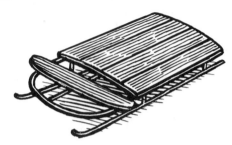

JANUARY 6 — THURSDAY
Day 6 — 360 Remaining

ARMENIAN CHRISTMAS. Jan 6. Christmas is observed in the Armenian Church, the oldest national Christian church.

CARNIVAL SEASON. Jan 6–Mar 7. A secular festival preceding Lent. A time of merrymaking and feasting before the austere days of Lenten fasting and penitence (40 weekdays between Ash Wednesday and Easter Sunday). The word *carnival* probably is derived from the Latin *carnem levare*, meaning "to remove meat." Depending on local custom, the carnival season may start any time between Nov 11 and Shrove Tuesday. Conclusion of the season is much less variable, being the close of Shrove Tuesday in most places. Celebrations vary considerably, but the festival often includes many theatrical aspects (masks, costumes and songs) and has given its name (in the US) to traveling amusement shows that may be seen throughout the year. Observed traditionally in Roman Catholic countries from Epiphany through Shrove Tuesday.

EPIPHANY or TWELFTH DAY. Jan 6. Known also as Old Christmas Day and Twelfthtide. On the twelfth day after Christmas, Christians celebrate the visit of the Magi or Wise Men to the baby Jesus. In many countries, this is the day children receive gifts, rather than Christmas day. Epiphany of Our Lord, one of the oldest Christian feasts, is observed in Roman Catholic churches in the US on a Sunday between Jan 2 and 8. Theophany of the Eastern Orthodox Church is observed on this day in churches using the Gregorian calendar and Jan 19 in those churches using the Julian calendar and celebrates the manifestation of the divinity of Jesus at the time of his baptism in the Jordan River by John the Baptist.

ITALY: LA BEFANA. Jan 6. Epiphany festival in which the "Befana," a kindly witch, bestows gifts on children—toys and candy for those who have been good, but a lump of coal or a pebble for those who have been naughty. The festival begins on the night of Jan 5 with much noise and merrymaking (when the Befana is supposed to come down the chimney on her broom, leaving gifts in children's stockings) and continues with fairs, parades and other activities.

MOON PHASE: NEW MOON. Jan 6. Moon enters New Moon phase at 1:14 PM, EST.

NATIONAL SMITH DAY. Jan 6. The commonest surname in the English-speaking world is Smith. There are an estimated

2,382,500 Smiths in the US. This special day honors the birthday in 1580 of Captain John Smith, the leader of the English colonists who settled at Jamestown, VA, in 1607, thus making him one of the first American Smiths. On this special day, all derivatives, such as Goldsmith, are invited to participate. For info: Adrienne Sioux Koopersmith, 1437 W Rosemont, 1W, Chicago, IL 60660-1319. Phone: (773) 743-5341. Fax: (773) 743-5395. E-mail: kooper@interaccess.com.

NEW MEXICO: ADMISSION DAY: ANNIVERSARY. Jan 6. Became 47th state in 1912.

PAN AM CIRCLES EARTH: ANNIVERSARY. Jan 6, 1942. A Pan American Airways plane arrived in New York to complete the first around-the-world trip by a commercial aircraft.

SANDBURG, CARL: BIRTH ANNIVERSARY. Jan 6, 1878. American poet ("Fog," "Chicago"), biographer of Lincoln, historian and folklorist, born at Galesburg, IL. Died at Flat Rock, NC, July 22, 1967.

SMITH, JEDEDIAH STRONG: BIRTH ANNIVERSARY. Jan 6, 1799. Mountain man, fur trader and one of the first explorers of the American West, Smith helped develop the Oregon Trail. He was the first American to reach California by land and first to travel by land from San Diego, up the West Coast to the Canadian border. Smith was born at Jericho (now Bainbridge), NY, and was killed by Comanche Indians along the Santa Fe Trail in what is now Kansas, May 27, 1831.

SPACE MILESTONE: *LUNAR EXPLORER* **(US).** Jan 6, 1998. NASA headed back to the moon for the first time since the Apollo 17 flight 25 years before. This unmanned probe searches for evidence of frozen water on the moon.

THREE KINGS DAY. Jan 6. Major festival of Christian Church observed in many parts of the world with gifts, feasting, last lighting of Christmas lights and burning of Christmas greens. In many European countries children get their Christmas presents on Three Kings Day. Twelfth and last day of the Feast of the Nativity. Commemorates visit of the Three Wise Men (Kings or Magi) to Bethlehem.

BIRTHDAYS TODAY

Johnny Yong Bosch, 24, actor (*Turbo: A Power Rangers Movie*, "Power Rangers Turbo"), born Topeka, KS, Jan 6, 1976.

Gabrielle Reece, 30, pro volleyball player, born La Jolla, CA, Jan 6, 1970.

JANUARY 7 — FRIDAY
Day 7 — 359 Remaining

FILLMORE, MILLARD: 200th BIRTH ANNIVERSARY. Jan 7, 1800. Thirteenth president of the US (July 10, 1850–Mar 3, 1853). Fillmore succeeded to the presidency upon the death of Zachary Taylor, but he did not get the hoped-for nomination from his party in 1852. He ran for president unsuccessfully in 1856 as candidate of the "Know-Nothing Party," whose platform demanded, among other things, that every government employee (federal, state and local) should be a native-born citizen. Fillmore was born at Locke, NY, and died at Buffalo, NY, Mar 8, 1874.

FIRST BALLOON FLIGHT ACROSS ENGLISH CHANNEL: ANNIVERSARY. Jan 7, 1785. Dr. John Jeffries, a Boston physician, and Jean-Pierre Blanchard, French aeronaut, crossed the English Channel from Dover, England, to Calais, France, landing in a forest after being forced to throw overboard all ballast, equipment and even most of their clothing to avoid a forced landing

JANUARY 7–14
UNIVERSAL LETTER WRITING WEEK

Receiving letters is so much nicer than getting junk mail. But the key to receiving letters is writing them.

"A Letter a Day" makes a nice theme for this week and fits in well with the language arts curriculum. Make Monday the kick-off with letter writing on a classroom level. Put all students' names in a box. Add yours if the total is an odd number. Have each student pick a name. Each student writes a letter to the student whose name she or he picked. Set a minimum number of sentences to be included in each letter. Suggest: an initial comment about the weather; one thing they think the other student does well; their favorite subject in school; an activity he or she did over the holidays; or a hobby interest. Ask one question in the letter. Distribute letters and have students write a reply to the letter they received as homework.

Tuesday, have students write a letter to a city official in your town (prepare a list of names in advance)—the mayor, a council representative, a firefighter, the person in charge of parks. Ask them to comment on things they like and dislike in the town. Wednesday, let them write a letter to a real friend, family member or other person who lives in a different city. Avoid the famous, to increase the likelihood of a response. Thursday, start a campaign for a pen pal. World Pen Friends provides pen pals for young people ages 10–20 in 175 countries and charges $3 per pen pal, with group rates for classes of ten or more. Write to World Pen Friends, PO Box 337, Saugerties, NY 12477-0337 for information. Friday could be e-mail day, if you have access to computers. Explain how e-mail works and discuss its good and bad aspects.

Monday and Tuesday's letters can be "mailed" without stamps. Drop the letters to city officials off at your town hall. Or see if the school district interbuilding mail run could include swinging by the town hall. For letters on Wednesday and Thursday, using the US Postal Service, either ask students to bring in two stamps or the money to buy two stamps from you. Request funds to purchase stamps for students who may be unable to afford them from your school's parent organization.

in the icy waters of the English Channel. Blanchard's trousers are said to have been the last article thrown overboard.

GERMANY: MUNICH FASCHING CARNIVAL. Jan 7–Mar 7. Munich. From Jan 7 through Shrove Tuesday is Munich's famous carnival season. Costume balls are popular throughout carnival. High points on Fasching Sunday (Mar 5) and Shrove Tuesday (Mar 7) with great carnival outside at the Viktualienmarkt and on Pedestrian Mall.

JAPAN: NANAKUSA. Jan 7. Festival dates back to the 7th century and recalls the seven plants served to the emperor that are believed to have great medicinal value—shepherd's purse, chickweed, parsley, cottonweed, radish, hotoke-no-za and aona.

JAPAN: USOKAE (BULLFINCH EXCHANGE FESTIVAL). Jan 7. Dazaifu, Fukuoka Prefecture. "Good Luck" gilded wood bullfinches, mixed among many plain ones, are sought after by the throngs as priests of the Dazaifu Shrine pass them out in the dim light of a small bonfire.

MONTGOLFIER, JACQUES ETIENNE: BIRTH ANNIVERSARY. Jan 7, 1745. Merchant and inventor born at Vidalon-lez Annonay, Ardèche, France. With his older brother, Joseph Michel, in November 1782, conducted experiments with paper and fabric bags filled with smoke and hot air, which led to invention of the hot-air balloon and human's first flight. Died at Serrieres, France, Aug 2, 1799. See also: "First Balloon Flight: Anniversary" (June 5); "Aviation History Month" (Nov 1).

OLD CALENDAR ORTHODOX CHRISTMAS. Jan 7. Some Orthodox Churches celebrate Christmas which is the "Old" (Julian) calendar date.

RUSSIA: CHRISTMAS OBSERVANCE. Jan 7. National holiday.

TRANSATLANTIC PHONING: ANNIVERSARY. Jan 7, 1927. Commercial transatlantic telephone service between New York and London was inaugurated. There were 31 calls made the first day.

UNIVERSAL LETTER-WRITING WEEK. Jan 7–14. The purpose of this week is for people all over the world to get the new year off to a good start by sending letters and cards to friends and acquaintances not only in their own country but to people throughout the world. For complete information and suggestions about writing good letters, send $4 to cover expense of printing, handling and postage. For info: Dr. Stanley Drake, Pres, Intl Soc of Friendship and Goodwill, 412 Cherry Hills Dr, Bakersfield, CA 93309-7902. See Curriculum Connection.

BIRTHDAYS TODAY

Katie Couric, 43, cohost, "Today Show," born Arlington, VA, Jan 7, 1957.

Minfong Ho, 49, author (*Hush! A Thai Lullaby*), born Rangoon, Burma, Jan 7, 1951.

JANUARY 8 — SATURDAY
Day 8 — 358 Remaining

AT&T DIVESTITURE: ANNIVERSARY. Jan 8, 1982. In the most significant antitrust suit since the breakup of Standard Oil in 1911, American Telephone and Telegraph agreed to give up its 22 local Bell System companies ("Baby Bells"). These companies represented 80 percent of AT&T's assets. This ended the corporation's virtual monopoly on US telephone service.

BATTLE OF NEW ORLEANS: ANNIVERSARY. Jan 8, 1815. British forces suffered crushing losses (more than 2,000 casualties) in an attack on New Orleans, LA. Defending US troops were led by General Andrew Jackson, who became a popular hero as a result of the victory. Neither side knew that the War of 1812 had ended two weeks previously with the signing of the Treaty of Ghent, Dec 24, 1814. Battle of New Orleans Day is observed in Louisiana.

CHOU EN-LAI: DEATH ANNIVERSARY. Jan 8, 1976. Anniversary of the death of Chou En-Lai, premier of the State Council of the People's Republic of China. He was born in 1898 (exact date unknown).

EARTH'S ROTATION PROVED: ANNIVERSARY. Jan 8, 1851. Using a device now known as Foucault's pendulum in his Paris home, physicist Jean Foucault demonstrated that the Earth rotates on its axis.

January *2000*	S	M	T	W	T	F	S
							1
	2	3	4	5	6	7	8
	9	10	11	12	13	14	15
	16	17	18	19	20	21	22
	23	24	25	26	27	28	29
	30	31					

EID-AL-FITR: CELEBRATING THE FAST. Jan 8. Islamic calendar date: Shawwal 1, 1420. This feast/festival celebrates having completed the Ramadan fasting (which began Dec 9, 1999) and usually lasts for several days. Everyone wears new clothes; children receive gifts from parents and relatives; games, folktales, plays, puppet shows, trips to amusement parks; children allowed to stay up late. Different methods for "anticipating" the visibility of the new moon crescent at Mecca are used by different Muslim groups. US date may vary.

GREECE: MIDWIFE'S DAY or WOMEN'S DAY. Jan 8. Midwife's Day or Women's Day is celebrated Jan 8 each year to honor midwives and all women. "On this day women stop their housework and spend their time in cafés, while the men do all the housework chores and look after the children." In some villages, men caught outside "will be stripped . . . and drenched with cold water."

NATIONAL JOYGERM DAY. Jan 8. Joygerm junkies invade and pervade the earth with merriment and mirth, joy and cheer, kindness and courtesy, silliness and sacredness and happiness and humor. Festivities include smile check-up clinics, chuckling, chortling and grinning and winning over gruff and grumpy grouches to the Joygerm Generation. For info: Joygerm Joan E. White, Founder, Joygerms Unlimited, PO Box 219, Eastwood Station, Syracuse, NY 13206-0219. Phone: (315) 472-2779.

PRESLEY, ELVIS AARON: 65th BIRTH ANNIVERSARY. Jan 8, 1935. Popular American rock singer, born at Tupelo, MS. Although his middle name was spelled incorrectly as "Aron" on his birth certificate, Elvis had it legally changed to "Aaron," which is how it is spelled on his gravestone. Died at Memphis, TN, Aug 16, 1977.

WAR ON POVERTY: ANNIVERSARY. Jan 8, 1964. President Lyndon Johnson declared a War on Poverty in his State of the Union address. He stressed improved education as one of the cornerstones of the program. The following Aug 20, he signed a $947.5 million anti-poverty bill designed to assist more than 30 million citizens.

BIRTHDAYS TODAY

Nancy Bond, 55, author (*A String in the Harp*), born Bethesda, MD, Jan 8, 1945.

Slade Gorton, 72, US Senator (R, Washington), born Chicago, IL, Jan 8, 1928.

Lauren Hewett, 19, actress ("Spellbinder: Land of the Dragon Lord"), born Sydney, Australia, Jan 8, 1981.

Bob Taft, 58, Governor of Ohio (R), born Boston, MA, Jan 8, 1942.

JANUARY 9 — SUNDAY
Day 9 — 357 Remaining

AVIATION IN AMERICA: ANNIVERSARY. Jan 9, 1793. A Frenchman, Jean-Pierre Blanchard, made the first manned free-balloon flight in America's history at Philadelphia, PA. The event was watched by President George Washington and many other high government officials. The hydrogen-filled balloon rose to a height of about 5,800 feet, traveled some 15 miles and landed 46 minutes later. Reportedly Blanchard had one passenger on the flight—a little black dog.

CATT, CARRIE LANE CHAPMAN: BIRTH ANNIVERSARY. Jan 9, 1859. American women's rights leader, founder (in 1919) of National League of Women Voters. Born at Ripon, WI, she died at New Rochelle, NY, Mar 9, 1947.

CONNECTICUT RATIFIES CONSTITUTION: ANNIVERSARY. Jan 9, 1788. By a vote of 128 to 40, Connecticut became the fifth state to ratify the Constitution.

NIXON, RICHARD MILHOUS: BIRTH ANNIVERSARY. Jan 9, 1913. Richard Nixon served as the 36th vice president of the US (under President Dwight D. Eisenhower) Jan 20, 1953 to Jan 20, 1961. He was the 37th president of the US, serving Jan 20, 1969, to Aug 9, 1974, when he resigned the presidency while under threat of impeachment. First US president to resign that office. He was born at Yorba Linda, CA, and died at New York, NY, Apr 22, 1994.

PANAMA: MARTYRS' DAY. Jan 9. Public holiday.

PHILIPPINES: FEAST OF THE BLACK NAZARENE. Jan 9. Culmination of a nine-day fiesta. Manila's largest procession takes place in the afternoon of Jan 9, in honor of the Black Nazarene, whose shrine is at the Quiapo Church.

SECRET PAL DAY. Jan 9. A day for secret pals to remember and do something special for each other. Annually, the second Sunday in January. For info: Eagles Lodge #4080, PO Box 1319, Hayden Lake, ID 83835. Phone: (208) 772-4901 or (208) 772-0687.

SWITZERLAND: MEITLISUNNTIG. Jan 9. On Meitlisunntig, the second Sunday in January, the girls of Meisterschwanden and Fahrwangen, in the Seetal district of Aargau, Switzerland, stage a procession in historical uniforms and a military parade before a female General Staff. According to tradition, the custom dates from the Villmergen War of 1712, when the women of both communes gave vital help that led to victory. Popular festival follows the procession.

BIRTHDAYS TODAY

Clyde Robert Bulla, 86, author (*The Chalk Box Kid*), born King City, MO, Jan 9, 1914.
Bill Graves, 47, Governor of Kansas (R), born Salina, KS, Jan 9, 1953.
Joely Richardson, 35, actress (*101 Dalmatians*), born London, England, Jan 9, 1965.

JANUARY 10 — MONDAY
Day 10 — 356 Remaining

ENGLAND: PLOUGH MONDAY. Jan 10. Always the Monday after Twelfth Day. Work on the farm is resumed after the festivities of the 12 days of Christmas. On preceding Sunday ploughs may be blessed in churches. Celebrated with dances and plays.

LEAGUE OF NATIONS: 80th ANNIVERSARY. Jan 10, 1920. Through the Treaty of Versailles, the League of Nations came into existence. Fifty nations entered into a covenant designed to avoid war. The US never joined the League of Nations, which was dissolved Apr 18, 1946.

NATIONAL CLEAN-OFF-YOUR-DESK DAY. Jan 10. To provide one day early each year for every desk worker to see the top of the desk and prepare for the following year's paperwork. Annually, the second Monday in January. For info: A.C. Moeller, Box 71, Clio, MI 48420-1042.

NATIONAL THANK GOD IT'S MONDAY! DAY. Jan 10. Besides holidays, such as President's Day, being celebrated on Mondays, people everywhere start new jobs, have birthdays, celebrate promotions and begin vacations on Mondays. A day in recognition of this first day of the week. Annually, the second Monday in January. For info: Dorothy Zjawin, 61 W Colfax Ave, Roselle Park, NJ 07204. Phone: (908) 241-6241. Fax: (908) 241-6241.

UNITED NATIONS GENERAL ASSEMBLY: ANNIVERSARY. Jan 10, 1946. On the 26th anniversary of the establishment of the unsuccessful League of Nations, delegates from 51 nations met at London, England, for the first meeting of the UN General Assembly.

WOMEN'S SUFFRAGE AMENDMENT INTRODUCED IN CONGRESS: ANNIVERSARY. Jan 10, 1878. Senator A. A. Sargent of California, a close friend of Susan B. Anthony, introduced into the US Senate a women's suffrage amendment known as the Susan B. Anthony Amendment. It wasn't until Aug 26, 1920, 42 years later, that the amendment was signed into law.

BIRTHDAYS TODAY

Glenn Robinson, 27, basketball player, member of 1996 Dream Team, born Gary, IN, Jan 10, 1973.

JANUARY 11 — TUESDAY
Day 11 — 355 Remaining

CUCKOO DANCING WEEK. Jan 11–17. To honor the memory of Laurel and Hardy, whose theme, "The Dancing Cuckoos," shall be heard throughout the land as their movies are seen and their antics greeted by laughter by old and new fans of these unique masters of comedy. [Originated by the late William T. Rabe of Sault Ste. Marie, MI.]

"DESIGNATED HITTER" RULE ADOPTED: ANNIVERSARY. Jan 11, 1973. American League adopted the "designated hitter" rule, whereby an additional player is used to bat for the pitcher.

FIRST BLACK SOUTHERN LIEUTENANT GOVERNOR: ANNIVERSARY. Jan 11, 1986. L. Douglas Wilder was sworn in as lieutenant governor of Virginia. He was the first black elected to statewide office in the South since Reconstruction. He later served as governor of Virginia.

HOSTOS, EUGENIO MARIA: BIRTH ANNIVERSARY. Jan 11, 1839. Puerto Rican patriot, scholar and author of more than 50 books. Born at Rio Canas, Puerto Rico, he died at Santo Domingo, Dominican Republic, Aug 11, 1903. The anniversary of his birth is observed as a public holiday in Puerto Rico.

MacDONALD, JOHN A.: BIRTH ANNIVERSARY. Jan 11, 1815. Canadian statesman, first prime minister of Canada. Born at Glasgow, Scotland, he died June 6, 1891, at Ottawa, Canada.

NEPAL: NATIONAL UNITY DAY. Jan 11. Celebration paying homage to King Prithvinarayan Shah (1723–75), founder of the present house of rulers of Nepal and creator of the unified Nepal of today.

O'BRIEN, ROBERT C.: BIRTH ANNIVERSARY. Jan 11, 1918. Author (Newbery for *Mrs Frisby and the Rats of NIMH*), born Robert Conly at Brooklyn, NY. Died at Washington, DC, Mar 5, 1973.

US SURGEON GENERAL DECLARES CIGARETTES HAZARDOUS: ANNIVERSARY. Jan 11, 1964. US Surgeon General Luther Terry issued the first government report saying that smoking may be hazardous to one's health.

BIRTHDAYS TODAY

Jean Chretien, 66, 20th prime minister of Canada, born Shawinigan, Quebec, Jan 11, 1934.

JANUARY 12 — WEDNESDAY
Day 12 — 354 Remaining

"BATMAN" TV PREMIERE: ANNIVERSARY. Jan 12, 1966. ABC's crime-fighting show gained a place in Nielsen's top 10 ratings in its first season. The series was based on the DC Comic characters created by Bob Kane in 1939. Adam West starred as millionaire Bruce Wayne and superhero alter ego, Batman. Burt Ward co-starred as Dick Grayson/Robin, the Boy Wonder. A colorful assortment of villains guest-starring each week included: Cesar Romero as the Joker, Eartha Kitt and Julie Newmar as Catwoman, Burgess Meredith as the Penguin and Frank Gorshin as the Riddler. Some other stars making memorable appearances included Liberace, Vincent Price, Milton Berle, Tallulah Bankhead and Ethel Merman. The series played up its comic-strip roots with innovative and sharply skewed camera angles, bright bold colors and wild graphics. "Batman's" memorable theme song, composed by Neal Hefti, can be heard today with some 120 episodes in syndication. Many Batman movies have been made, the first in 1943. The most recent is *Batman & Robin*, starring George Clooney and Chris O'Donnell.

HANCOCK, JOHN: BIRTH ANNIVERSARY. Jan 12, 1737. American patriot and statesman, first signer of the Declaration of Independence. Born at Braintree, MA, he died at Quincy, MA, Oct 8, 1793. Because his signature was the most conspicuous one on the Declaration, Hancock's name has become part of the American language, referring to any handwritten signature, as in "Put your John Hancock on that!"

HAYES, IRA HAMILTON: BIRTH ANNIVERSARY. Jan 12, 1922. Ira Hayes was one of six US Marines who raised the American flag on Iwo Jima's Mount Suribachi, Feb 23, 1945, following a US assault on the Japanese stronghold. The event was immortalized by AP photographer Joe Rosenthal's famous photo and later by a Marine War Memorial monument at Arlington, VA. Hayes was born on a Pima Indian Reservation at Arizona. He

	S	M	T	W	T	F	S
January							1
2000	2	3	4	5	6	7	8
	9	10	11	12	13	14	15
	16	17	18	19	20	21	22
	23	24	25	26	27	28	29
	30	31					

returned home after WWII a much celebrated hero. A hero to everyone except himself, Hayes was unable to cope with fame. He was found dead of "exposure to freezing weather and over-consumption of alcohol" on the Sacaton Indian Reservation at Arizona, Jan 24, 1955.

LONDON, JACK: BIRTH ANNIVERSARY. Jan 12, 1876. American author of more than 50 books: short stories, novels and travel stories of the sea and of the far north, many marked by brutal realism. His most widely known work is *The Call of the Wild*, the great dog story published in 1903. London was born at San Francisco, CA. He died by suicide Nov 22, 1916, near Santa Rosa, CA.

NATIONAL HANDWRITING DAY. Jan 12. Popularly observed on the birthday of John Hancock to encourage more legible handwriting.

PESTALOZZI, JOHANN HEINRICH: BIRTH ANNIVERSARY. Jan 12, 1746. Swiss educational reformer, born at Zurich. His theories laid the groundwork for modern elementary education. He died Feb 17, 1827, at Brugg, Switzerland.

TANZANIA: ZANZIBAR REVOLUTION DAY. Jan 12. National day. Zanzibar became independent in December 1963, under a sultan.

BIRTHDAYS TODAY

Kirstie Alley, 45, actress (*Look Who's Talking*), born Wichita, KS, Jan 12, 1955.

Andrew Lawrence, 12, actor ("Brotherly Love," *Prince for a Day*), born Philadelphia, PA, Jan 12, 1988.

JANUARY 13 — THURSDAY
Day 13 — 353 Remaining

ALGER, HORATIO, JR: BIRTH ANNIVERSARY. Jan 13, 1834. American clergyman and author of more than 100 popular books for boys (some 20 million copies sold). Honesty, frugality and hard work assured that the heroes of his books would find success, wealth and fame. Born at Revere, MA, he died at Natick, MA, July 18, 1899.

POETRY BREAK. Jan 13. Celebrate poetry by announcing a "poetry break and reading a poem aloud—at home, at school, in the office, in the market . . . anywhere!" See Curriculum Connection. For info: Dr. Caroline Feller Bauer, 10155 Collins Ave, #402, Miami Beach, FL 33154-1636. Phone: (305) 868-9991. Fax: (305) 868-9992. E-mail: caroline@spctnet.com.

RADIO BROADCASTING: 90th ANNIVERSARY. Jan 13, 1910. Radio pioneer and electron tube inventor Lee De Forest arranged the world's first radio broadcast to the public at New

JANUARY 13
POETRY BREAK

Take time out for a daily poetry break. If you don't already have a collection of short poems to read aloud, you might want to start one. Look for poems that you can write on an index card, one per card. Keep them in a file box in the classroom and take one or two for reading during standing-in-line times like going into the gym or lunchroom.

Start the day with a poem. Read another one after lunch. You can ask students to share a favorite poem too. Write a class poem. Doing this together helps students understand creative and writing processes. After deciding on a subject, if the class if going to write a rhyming poem have students list rhyming words about the subject before you begin.

For quick poetry, explain couplets and have students write a couplet that tells something about themselves. Example: My name is Lou/My eyes are blue. If they wish, students could continue on to four, six or eight lines.

Another poetry exercise is to play with similes. Ask students to think of a favorite color, word, food or book. Have them describe the item in terms of a simile. Example: Blue is like a huge iceberg, *Goosebumps* books by R. L. Stine are like fingernails scratching a chalkboard.

Jack Prelutsky and Shel Silverstein have published popular collections of poetry for young readers. Also look for books by Myra Cohn Livingston, Paul B. Janeczko, Eloise Greenfield and Paul Fleischman. Recent collections containing poems that will enrich your poetry break include: *Old Elm Speaks: Tree Poems*, by Kristine O'Connell George (Clarion, 0-395-87611-7, $15 Gr. K–5); *Doodle Dandies: Poems That Take Shape*, by J. Patrick Lewis (Atheneum, 0-689-81075-X, $16 All ages) and *The Beauty of the Beast: Animal Poems*, selected by Jack Prelutsky (Random House, 0-679-87058-X, $25 All ages).

York, NY. He succeeded in broadcasting the voice of Enrico Caruso along with other stars of the Metropolitan Opera to several receiving locations in the city where listeners with earphones marveled at wireless music from the air. Though only a few were equipped to listen, it was the first broadcast to reach the public and the beginning of a new era in which wireless radio communication became almost universal. See also: "First Scheduled Radio Broadcast: Anniversary" (Nov 2).

★ **STEPHEN FOSTER MEMORIAL DAY.** Jan 13. Presidential Proclamation 2957 of Dec 13, 1951 (designating Jan 13, 1952), covers all succeeding years. (PL82–225 of Oct 27, 1951.) Observed on the anniversary of Foster's death, Jan 13, 1864, at New York, NY. See also: "Foster, Stephen: Birth Anniversary" (July 4).

TOGO: LIBERATION DAY. Jan 13. National holiday. Commemorates 1963 uprising.

BIRTHDAYS TODAY

Michael Bond, 74, author (*A Bear Called Paddington, Paddington At Work*), born Newbury, Berkshire, England, Jan 13, 1926.

JANUARY 14 — FRIDAY
Day 14 — 352 Remaining

ARNOLD, BENEDICT: BIRTH ANNIVERSARY. Jan 14, 1741. American officer who deserted to the British during the Revolutionary War and whose name has since become synonymous with treachery. Born at Norwich, CT, he died June 14, 1801, at London, England.

LOFTING, HUGH: BIRTH ANNIVERSARY. Jan 14, 1886. Author and illustrator, known for the Doctor Dolittle series of children's books. In his books the famous Dr. Dolittle has the ability to talk with animals. *The Voyages of Dr. Dolittle* won the Newbery Medal in 1923. Born at Maidenhead, England, Lofting died at Santa Monica, CA, Sept 26, 1947.

MOON PHASE: FIRST QUARTER. Jan 14. Moon enters First Quarter phase at 8:34 AM, EST.

RATIFICATION DAY. Jan 14, 1784. Anniversary of the act that officially ended the American Revolution and established the US as a sovereign power. On Jan 14, 1784, the Continental Congress, meeting at Annapolis, MD, ratified the Treaty of Paris, thus fulfilling the Declaration of Independence of July 4, 1776.

"THE SIMPSONS" TV PREMIERE: 10th ANNIVERSARY. Jan 14, 1990. TV's hottest animated family, "The Simpsons," premiered as a half-hour weekly sitcom. The originator of Homer, Marge, Bart, Lisa and Maggie is cartoonist Matt Groening.

SPACE MILESTONE: *SOYUZ 4 (USSR).* Jan 14, 1969. First docking of two manned spacecraft (with *Soyuz 5*) and first interchange of spaceship personnel in orbit by means of space walks.

WHIPPLE, WILLIAM: BIRTH ANNIVERSARY. Jan 14, 1730. American patriot and signer of the Declaration of Independence. Born at Kittery, ME, he died at Portsmouth, NH, Nov 10, 1785.

BIRTHDAYS TODAY

Shannon Lucid, 57, astronaut, holds the record for longest stay in space by an American, born Shanghai, China, Jan 14, 1943.

JANUARY 15 — SATURDAY
Day 15 — 351 Remaining

"HAPPY DAYS" PREMIERE: ANNIVERSARY. Jan 15, 1974. This nostalgic comedy was set in Milwaukee in the 1950s. Teenager Richie Cunningham was played by Ron Howard and his best friends "Potsie" Weber and Ralph Malph by Anson Williams and Don Most. Richie's parents were played by Tom Bosley and Marion Ross and his sister, Joanie, was played by Erin Moran. "The Fonz"—Arthur "Fonzie" Fonzarelli—was played by Henry Winkler. "Happy Days" aired until 1984 and has been in syndication ever since. "Laverne and Shirley" was a spin-off of this popular program.

JAPAN: COMING-OF-AGE DAY. Jan 15. National holiday for youth of the country who have reached adulthood during the preceding year.

KING, MARTIN LUTHER, JR: BIRTH ANNIVERSARY. Jan 15, 1929. Black civil rights leader, minister, advocate of non-violence and recipient of the Nobel Peace Prize (1964). Born at Atlanta, GA, he was assassinated at Memphis, TN, Apr 4, 1968. After his death many states and territories observed his birthday as a holiday. In 1983 the Congress approved HR 3706, "A bill to amend Title 5, United States Code, to make the birthday of Martin Luther King, Jr, a legal public holiday." Signed by the president on Nov 2, 1983, it became Public Law 98–144. The law sets the third Monday in January for observance of King's birthday. First observance was Jan 20, 1986. See also: "King, Martin Luther, Jr: Birthday Observed" (Jan 17).

LIVINGSTON, PHILIP: BIRTH ANNIVERSARY. Jan 15, 1716. Merchant and signer of the Declaration of Independence, born at Albany, NY. Died at York, PA, June 12, 1778.

MINORITY SCIENTISTS SHOWCASE. Jan 15–17. St. Louis, MO. Open new doors to future science careers and interests during Martin Luther King Jr weekend with hands-on activities and information available as part of a free program. Meet and talk with African Americans working in science-related fields throughout the St. Louis area. Annually, Martin Luther King Jr weekend. Est attendance: 2,000. For info: Bev Pfeifer-Harms, St. Louis Science Center, 5050 Oakland Ave, St. Louis, MO 63110. Phone: (314) 289-4419. Fax: (314) 533-8687. E-mail: bpharms@slsc.org. Web: www.slsc.org.

PHILIPPINES: ATI-ATIHAN FESTIVAL. Jan 15–16. Kalibo, Aklan. One of the most colorful celebrations in the Philippines, the Ati-Atihan Festival commemorates the peace pact between the Ati of Panay (pygmies) and the Malays, who were early migrants in the islands. The townspeople blacken their bodies with soot, don colorful and bizarre costumes and sing and dance in the streets. The festival also celebrates the Feast Day of Santo Niño (the infant Jesus). Annually, the third weekend in January.

BIRTHDAYS TODAY

Andrea Martin, 53, actress (*Bogus, Anastasia*), born Portland, ME, Jan 15, 1947.

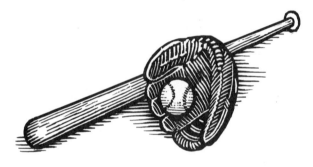

JANUARY 16 — SUNDAY
Day 16 — 350 Remaining

DEAN, DIZZY: BIRTH ANNIVERSARY. Jan 16, 1911. Jay Hanna "Dizzy" Dean, major league pitcher (St. Louis Cardinals) and Baseball Hall of Fame member was born at Lucas, AR. Following his baseball career, Dean established himself as a radio and TV sports announcer and commentator, becoming famous for his innovative delivery. "He slud into third," reported Dizzy, who on another occasion explained that "Me and Paul [baseball player brother Paul "Daffy" Dean] . . . didn't get much education." Died at Reno, NV, July 17, 1974.

INTERNATIONAL PRINTING WEEK. Jan 16–22. To develop public awareness of the printing/graphic arts industry. Annually, the week including Ben Franklin's birthday, Jan 17. For info: Kevin P. Keane, Exec Dir, Intl Assn of Printing House Craftsmen, 7042 Brooklyn Blvd, Minneapolis, MN 55429-1370. Phone: (612) 560-1620. Web: www.iaphc.org.

	S	M	T	W	T	F	S
January							1
2000	2	3	4	5	6	7	8
	9	10	11	12	13	14	15
	16	17	18	19	20	21	22
	23	24	25	26	27	28	29
	30	31					

JAPAN: HARU-NO-YABUIRI. Jan 16. Employees and servants who have been working over the holidays are given a day off.

NATIONAL NOTHING DAY: ANNIVERSARY. Jan 16. Anniversary of National Nothing Day, an event created by newspaperman Harold Pullman Coffin and first observed in 1973 "to provide Americans with one national day when they can just sit without celebrating, observing or honoring anything." Since 1975, though many other events have been listed on this day, lighthearted traditional observance of Coffin's idea has continued. Coffin, a native of Reno, NV, died at Capitola, CA, Sept 12, 1981.

PERSIAN GULF WAR BEGINS: ANNIVERSARY. Jan 16, 1991. Allied forces launched a major air offensive against Iraq to begin the Gulf War. The strike was designed to destroy Iraqi air defenses, command, control and communication centers. As Desert Shield became Desert Storm, the world was able to see and hear for the first time an initial engagement of war as CNN broadcasters, stationed at Baghdad, broadcast the attack live.

PROHIBITION (EIGHTEENTH) AMENDMENT: ANNIVERSARY. Jan 16, 1919. Nebraska became the 36th state to ratify the prohibition amendment on this date, and the 18th Amendment became part of the US Constitution. One year later, Jan 16, 1920, the 18th Amendment took effect and the sale of alcoholic beverages became illegal in the US with the Volstead Act providing for enforcement. This was the first time that an amendment to the Constitution dealt with a social issue. The 21st Amendment, repealing the 18th, went into effect Dec 6, 1933.

RELIGIOUS FREEDOM DAY. Jan 16, 1786. The legislature of Virginia adopted a religious freedom statute that protected Virginians against any requirement to attend or support any church and against discrimination. This statute, which had been drafted by Thomas Jefferson and introduced by James Madison, later was the model for the First Amendment to the US Constitution.

BIRTHDAYS TODAY

Kate McMullan, 53, author (the Dragon Slayers' Academy Series), born St. Louis, MO, Jan 16, 1947.
Martha Weston, 53, author and illustrator (*Bad Baby Brother*), born Asheville, NC, Jan 16, 1947.

JANUARY 17 — MONDAY
Day 17 — 349 Remaining

FIRST NUCLEAR-POWERED SUBMARINE VOYAGE: 45th ANNIVERSARY. Jan 17, 1955. The world's first nuclear-powered submarine, the *Nautilus*, now forms part of the *Nautilus* Memorial Submarine Force Library and Museum at the Naval Submarine Base New London at Groton, CT. At 11 AM, EST, her commanding officer, Commander Eugene P. Wilkerson, ordered all lines cast off and sent the historic message: "Under way on nuclear power." Highlights of the *Nautilus*: keel laid by President Harry S Truman June 14, 1952; christened and launched by Mrs Dwight D. Eisenhower Jan 21, 1954; commissioned to the US Navy Sept 30, 1954.

FRANKLIN, BENJAMIN: BIRTH ANNIVERSARY. Jan 17, 1706. "Elder statesman of the American Revolution," oldest signer of both the Declaration of Independence and the Constitution, scientist, diplomat, author, printer, publisher, philosopher, philanthropist and self-made, self-educated man. Author, printer and publisher of *Poor Richard's Almanack* (1733–58). Born at Boston, MA, Franklin died at Philadelphia, PA, Apr 17, 1790. In 1728

Franklin wrote a premature epitaph for himself. It first appeared in print in Ames's 1771 almanac: "The Body of BENJAMIN FRANKLIN/Printer/Like a Covering of an old Book/Its contents torn out/And stript of its Lettering and Gilding,/Lies here, Food for Worms;/But the work shall not be lost,/It will (as he believ'd) appear once more/In a New and more beautiful Edition/Corrected and amended/By the Author."

JAPAN SUFFERS MAJOR EARTHQUAKE: 5th ANNIVERSARY.
Jan 17, 1995. Japan suffered its second most deadly earthquake in the 20th century when a 20-second temblor left 5,500 dead and more than 21,600 people injured. The epicenter was six miles beneath Awaji Island at Osaka Bay. This was just 20 miles west of Kobe, Japan's sixth-largest city and a major port that accounted for 12 percent of the country's exports. Measuring 7.2 on the Richter scale, the quake collapsed or badly damaged more than 30,400 buildings and left 275,000 people homeless.

KING, MARTIN LUTHER, JR: BIRTHDAY OBSERVED.
Jan 17. Public Law 98–144 designates the third Monday in January as an annual legal public holiday observing the birth of Martin Luther King, Jr. First observed in 1986. In New Hampshire, this day is designated Civil Rights Day. See also: "King, Martin Luther, Jr: Birth Anniversary" (Jan 15). For links to sites on the Web about Dr. King, go to: deil.lang.uiuc.edu/web.pages/holidays/king.html.

LEE-JACKSON-KING DAY IN VIRGINIA.
Jan 17. Annually, the third Monday in January.

LEWIS, SHARI: BIRTH ANNIVERSARY.
Jan 17, 1934. Puppeteer Shari Lewis, creator of Lamb Chop and Charlie Horse, was born Shari Hurwitz at New York, NY. She died Aug 3, 1998, at Los Angeles, CA.

★ MARTIN LUTHER KING, JR FEDERAL HOLIDAY.
Jan 17. Presidential Proclamation has been issued without request each year for the third Monday in January since 1986.

MEXICO: BLESSING OF THE ANIMALS AT THE CATHEDRAL.
Jan 17. Church of San Antonio at Mexico City or Xochimilco provide best sights of chickens, cows and household pets gaily decorated with flowers. (Saint's day for San Antonio Abad, patron saint of domestic animals.)

SOUTHERN CALIFORNIA EARTHQUAKE: ANNIVERSARY.
Jan 17, 1994. An earthquake measuring 6.6 on the Richter scale struck the Los Angeles area about 4:20 AM. The epicenter was at Northridge in the San Fernando Valley, about 20 miles northwest of downtown Los Angeles. A death toll of 51 was announced Jan 20. Sixteen of the dead were killed in the collapse of one apartment building. More than 25,000 people were made homeless by the quake and 680,000 lost electric power. Many buildings were destroyed and others made uninhabitable due to structural damage. A section of the Santa Monica Freeway, part of the Simi Valley Freeway and three major overpasses collapsed. Hundreds of aftershocks occurred in the following several weeks. Costs to repair the damages were estimated at 15–30 billion dollars.

BIRTHDAYS TODAY

Muhammad Ali (Cassius Marcellus Clay, Jr), 58, former heavyweight champion boxer who changed his name after converting to Islam, born Louisville, KY, Jan 17, 1942.

Jim Carrey, 38, actor (*Dumb and Dumber, Mask, Ace Ventura*), comedian, born Ontario, Canada, Jan 17, 1962.

Robert Cormier, 73, author (*I Am the Cheese*), born Leominster, MA, Jan 17, 1927.

JANUARY 18 — TUESDAY
Day 18 — 348 Remaining

FIRST BLACK US CABINET MEMBER: ANNIVERSARY.
Jan 18, 1966. Robert Clifton Weaver was sworn in as Secretary of Housing and Urban Development, becoming the first black cabinet member in US history. He was nominated by President Lyndon Johnson. Born Dec 29, 1907 at Washington, DC, Weaver died at New York, NY, July 17, 1997.

POOH DAY: A.A. MILNE: BIRTH ANNIVERSARY.
Jan 18, 1882. Anniversary of the birth of A(lan) A(lexander) Milne, English author, especially remembered for his children's stories: *Winnie the Pooh* and *The House at Pooh Corner*. Also the author of *Mr Pim Passes By, When We Were Very Young* and *Now We Are Six*. Born at London, England, he died at Hartfield, England, Jan 31, 1956.

ROGET, PETER MARK: BIRTH ANNIVERSARY.
Jan 18, 1779. English physician, best known as author of Roget's *Thesaurus of English Words and Phrases*, first published in 1852. Roget was also the inventor of the "log-log" slide rule. Born at London, England, Roget died at West Malvern, Worcestershire, England, Sept 12, 1869. See Curriculum Connection.

BIRTHDAYS TODAY

Mark Messier, 39, hockey player, born Edmonton, Alberta, Canada, Jan 18, 1961.

Alan Schroeder, 39, author of biographies (*Ragtime Tumpie*), born Alameda, CA, Jan 18, 1961.

JANUARY 18
PETER MARK ROGET'S BIRTHDAY

It was a good party. No, it was a *very* good party. No, it was a…a…a… If you've ever grasped for an elusive word or synonym, it's likely you've also reached for a thesaurus. Today is the day to celebrate, honor and observe the author of the first thesaurus.

Roget's Thesaurus is a valuable tool for older writers. The classified arrangement with its cross-referenced numbering system may be confusing, but explanation and practice will clarify its usage. Today there are thesauruses that list words alphabetically, which makes them easier for young students to use. Among them are *The American Heritage Children's Thesaurus*, by Paul Hellwig (Houghton Mifflin, 0-395-84977-2, $17 Gr. 3–7) and *Scholastic Children's Thesaurus*, by John K. Bollard (Scholastic, 0-590-96785-1, $15.95 Gr. 3–7).

Here's a Roget's Day exercise suitable for all students. Write a sentence on the board, such as, "After school, the girl walked into her house." Now, ask students to substitute another word for walked or any weak verb or adjective you've deliberately chosen in your sentence. Offer prompts if necessary. When you run out of classroom suggestions, use the thesaurus to show even more possible words.

A thesaurus written by the students can also be a fun, year-long activity. List words that crop up frequently in student writings (*said, then, run*). Students can suggest and illustrate alternative words on sheets of paper that can be collated into a classroom book. The prompt sentence could be, "Instead of (walk), use (skip) if you are (happy)."

You'll all have a good, wonderful, marvelous time.

JANUARY 19 — WEDNESDAY

Day 19 — 347 Remaining

CÉZANNE, PAUL: BIRTH ANNIVERSARY. Jan 19, 1839. French post-Impressionist painter known for his landscapes, born at Aix-en-Provence, France. He died at Aix, Oct 22, 1906.

CONFEDERATE HEROES DAY. Jan 19. Observed on anniversary of Robert E. Lee's birthday. Official holiday in Texas.

LEE, ROBERT E.: BIRTH ANNIVERSARY. Jan 19, 1807. Greatest military leader of the Confederacy, son of Revolutionary War General Henry (Light Horse Harry) Lee. His surrender Apr 9, 1865, to Union General Ulysses S. Grant brought an end to the Civil War. Born at Westmoreland County, VA, he died at Lexington, VA, Oct 12, 1870. His birthday is observed in Florida, Kentucky, Louisiana, South Carolina and Tennessee. Observed on third Monday in January in Alabama, Arkansas and Mississippi.

POE, EDGAR ALLAN: BIRTH ANNIVERSARY. Jan 19, 1809. American poet and story writer, called "America's most famous man of letters." Born at Boston, MA, he was orphaned in dire poverty in 1811 and was raised by Virginia merchant John Allan. In 1836 he married his 13-year-old cousin, Virginia Clemm. A magazine editor of note, he is best remembered for his poetry (especially "The Raven") and for his tales of suspense. Died at Baltimore, MD, Oct 7, 1849.

TIN CAN PATENT: 175th ANNIVERSARY. Jan 19, 1825. Ezra Daggett and Thomas Kensett obtained a patent for a process for storing food in tin cans.

BIRTHDAYS TODAY

Nina Bawden, 75, author (*Carrie's War*), born London, England, Jan 19, 1925.

Jodie Sweetin, 18, actress ("Full House"), born Los Angeles, CA, Jan 19, 1982.

JANUARY 20 — THURSDAY

Day 20 — 346 Remaining

AQUARIUS, THE WATER CARRIER. Jan 20–Feb 19. In the astronomical/astrological zodiac, which divides the sun's apparent orbit into 12 segments, the period Jan 20–Feb 19 is identified, traditionally, as the sun-sign of Aquarius, the Water Carrier. The ruling planet is Uranus or Saturn.

January 2000	S	M	T	W	T	F	S
							1
	2	3	4	5	6	7	8
	9	10	11	12	13	14	15
	16	17	18	19	20	21	22
	23	24	25	26	27	28	29
	30	31					

BRAZIL: NOSSO SENHOR DO BONFIM FESTIVAL. Jan 20–30. Salvador, Bahia, Brazil. Our Lord of the Happy Ending Festival is one of Salvador's most colorful religious feasts. Climax comes with people carrying water to pour over church stairs and sidewalks to cleanse them of impurities.

CAMCORDER DEVELOPED: ANNIVERSARY. Jan 20, 1982. Five companies (Hitachi, JVC, Philips, Matsushita and Sony) agreed to cooperate on the construction of a camera with a built-in videocassette recorder.

GUINEA-BISSAU: NATIONAL HEROES DAY. Jan 20. National holiday.

LUNAR ECLIPSE. Jan 20–21. Total eclipse of the moon. Moon enters penumbra at approximately 9:02 PM, EST, Jan 20, reaches middle of eclipse at 11:43 PM and leaves penumbra at 2:24 AM, Jan 21. Visible in North America, except the Aleutian Islands, Central America, South America, most of Africa, Europe, western Asia, Greenland, the arctic region, the Palmer Peninsula of Antartica, the Atlantic Ocean and the eastern Pacific Ocean; the end visible in North America, Hawaii, Central America, South America, extreme western Africa, Europe except the southeastern portion, Greenland, the arctic region, the Palmer Peninsula of Antarctica, the North Pacific Ocean except the southwestern portion, the eastern South Pacific Ocean, the North Atlantic Ocean and the South Atlantic Ocean except the southeastern portion.

MOON PHASE: FULL MOON. Jan 20. Moon enters Full Moon phase at 11:40 PM, EST.

US REVOLUTIONARY WAR: CESSATION OF HOSTILITIES: ANNIVERSARY. Jan 20, 1783. The British and US Commissioners signed a preliminary "Cessation of Hostilities," which was ratified by England's King George III Feb 14 and led to the Treaties of Paris and Versailles, Sept 3, 1783, ending the war.

BIRTHDAYS TODAY

Edwin "Buzz" Aldrin, 70, former astronaut, one of first three men on moon, born Montclair, NJ, Jan 20, 1930.

Paul D. Coverdell, 61, US Senator (R, Georgia), born Des Moines, IA, Jan 20, 1939.

JANUARY 21 — FRIDAY

Day 21 — 345 Remaining

ALLEN, ETHAN: BIRTH ANNIVERSARY. Jan 21, 1738. Revolutionary War hero and leader of the Vermont "Green Mountain Boys." Born at Litchfield, CT, he died at Burlington, VT, Feb 12, 1789.

ARBOR DAY IN FLORIDA. Jan 21. A ceremonial day on the third Friday in January.

BRECKINRIDGE, JOHN CABELL: BIRTH ANNIVERSARY. Jan 21, 1821. Fourteenth vice president of the US (1857–61), serving under President James Buchanan. Born at Lexington, KY, he died there May 17, 1875.

FIRST CONCORDE FLIGHT: ANNIVERSARY. Jan 21, 1976. The supersonic Concorde airplane was put into service by Britain and France.

JACKSON, THOMAS JONATHAN "STONEWALL": BIRTH ANNIVERSARY. Jan 21, 1824. Confederate general and one of the most famous soldiers of the American Civil War, best known as "Stonewall" Jackson. Born at Clarksburg, VA (now WV), Jackson died of wounds received in battle near Chancellorsville, VA, May 10, 1863.

Hakeem Abdul Olajuwon, 37, basketball player, born Lagos, Nigeria, Jan 21, 1963.

JANUARY 22 — SATURDAY
Day 22 — 344 Remaining

ANSWER YOUR CAT'S QUESTION DAY. Jan 22. If you will stop what you are doing and take a look at your cat, you will observe that the cat is looking at you with a serious question. Meditate upon it, then answer the question! Annually, Jan 22. [© 1998 by WPL] For info: Tom or Ruth Roy, Wellness Permission League, PO Box 662, Mount Gretna, PA 17064-0662. Phone: (717) 964-1308. Fax: (717) 964-1335. E-mail: wellcat@desupernet.net.

TU B'SHVAT. Jan 22. Hebrew calendar date: Shebat 15, 5760. The 15th day of the month of Shebat in the Hebrew calendar year is set aside as Hamishah Asar (New Year of the Trees or Jewish Arbor Day), a time to show respect and appreciation for trees and plants.

VINSON, FRED M.: BIRTH ANNIVERSARY. Jan 22, 1890. The 13th Chief Justice of the US Supreme Court, born at Louisa, KY. Served in the House of Representatives, appointed Director of War Mobilization during WWII and Secretary of the Treasury under Harry Truman. Nominated by Truman to succeed Harlan F. Stone as Chief Justice. Died at Washington, DC, Sept 8, 1953.

BIRTHDAYS TODAY

Blair Lent, 70, author and illustrator (*Tikki Tikki Tembo*), born Boston, MA, Jan 22, 1930.

Rafe Martin, 54, author (*The Boy Who Lived with the Seals*), born Rochester, NY, Jan 22, 1946.

Beverly Mitchell, 19, actress (*Mother of the Bride*, "7th Heaven"), born Arcadia, CA, Jan 22, 1981.

JANUARY 23 — SUNDAY
Day 23 — 343 Remaining

BLACKWELL, ELIZABETH, AWARDED MD: ANNIVERSARY. Jan 23, 1849. Dr. Elizabeth Blackwell became the first woman to receive an MD degree. The native of Bristol, England, was awarded her degree by the Medical Institution of Geneva, NY.

HEWES, JOSEPH: BIRTH ANNIVERSARY. Jan 23, 1730. Signer of the Declaration of Independence. Born at Princeton, NJ, he died Nov 10, 1779 at Philadelphia, PA.

MANET, ÉDOUARD: BIRTH ANNIVERSARY. Jan 23, 1832. French artist (*Déjeuner dur l'herbe*, *Olympia*), born at Paris, France. He died at Paris, Apr 30, 1883.

NATIONAL PIE DAY. Jan 23. To focus attention on pie as an American art form, culinary inheritance and taste delight through pie tastings, pie-making classes for adults and kids, pie recipe collections and competitions. For info: John Lehndorff, 512 Concord Ave, Boulder, CO 80304. Phone: (303) 499-0165. E-mail: nibble man@aol.com.

STEWART, POTTER: 85th BIRTH ANNIVERSARY. Jan 23, 1915. Associate Justice of the Supreme Court of the US, nominated by President Eisenhower, Jan 17, 1959. (Oath of office, May 15, 1959.) Born at Jackson, MI, he retired in July 1981 and died Dec 7, 1985, at Putney, VT. Buried at Arlington National Cemetery.

TWENTIETH AMENDMENT TO US CONSTITUTION RATIFIED: ANNIVERSARY. Jan 23, 1933. The 20th Amendment was ratified, fixing the date of the presidential inauguration at the current Jan 20 instead of the previous Mar 4. It also specified that were the president-elect to die before taking office, the vice president-elect would succeed to the presidency. In addition, it set Jan 3 as the official opening date of Congress each year.

TWENTY-FOURTH AMENDMENT TO US CONSTITUTION RATIFIED: ANNIVERSARY. Jan 23, 1964. Poll taxes and other taxes were eliminated as a prerequisite for voting in all federal elections by the 24th Amendment.

BIRTHDAYS TODAY

Frank R. Lautenberg, 76, US Senator (D, New Jersey), born Paterson, NJ, Jan 23, 1924.

JANUARY 24 — MONDAY
Day 24 — 342 Remaining

BOLIVIA: ALACITIS FAIR. Jan 24–26. La Paz. Traditional annual celebration by Aymara Indians with prayers and offerings to god of prosperity.

CALIFORNIA GOLD DISCOVERY: ANNIVERSARY. Jan 24, 1848. James W. Marshal, an employee of John Sutter, accidentally discovered gold while building a sawmill near Coloma, CA. Efforts to keep the discovery secret failed, and the gold rush got under way in 1849. Had the Gold Rush not occurred, it might have taken California years to reach the population of 60,000 necessary for statehood, but the 49ers increased the population beyond that figure in one year and in 1850 California became a state. For more information, visit the California Sesquicentennial website at www.tgifdirectory.com/cal150.

BIRTHDAYS TODAY

Tatyana M. Ali, 21, actress ("Sesame Street," "The Fresh Prince of Bel Air"), born Long Island, NY, Jan 24, 1979.

Mary Lou Retton, 32, Olympic gold medal gymnast, born Fairmont, WV, Jan 24, 1968.

JANUARY 25 — TUESDAY
Day 25 — 341 Remaining

CURTIS, CHARLES: BIRTH ANNIVERSARY. Jan 25, 1860. Thirty-first vice president of the US (1929–33). Born at Topeka, KS, he died at Washington, DC, Feb 8, 1936.

FIRST SCHEDULED TRANSCONTINENTAL FLIGHT: ANNIVERSARY. Jan 25, 1959. American Airlines opened the jet age in the US with the first scheduled transcontinental flight on a Boeing 707 nonstop from California to New York.

SCOTLAND: UP HELLY AA. Jan 25. Lerwick, Shetland Islands. Norse galley burned in impressive ceremony symbolizing sacrifice to the sun. Old Viking custom. Annually, the last Tuesday in January. Tourist Information Centre, Market Cross, Lerwick, Shetland, Scotland ZE1 0LU. Phone: (44) (1595) 693434. Fax: (44) (1595) 695807.

BIRTHDAYS TODAY

Conrad Burns, 65, US Senator (R, Montana), born Gallatin, MO, Jan 25, 1935.

Chris Chelios, 38, hockey player, born Chicago, IL, Jan 25, 1962.

Christine Lakin, 21, actress ("Step By Step"), born Dallas, TX, Jan 25, 1979.

JANUARY 26 — WEDNESDAY

Day 26 — 340 Remaining

AUSTRALIA: AUSTRALIA DAY—FIRST BRITISH SETTLEMENT: ANNIVERSARY. Jan 26, 1788. A shipload of convicts arrived briefly at Botany Bay (which proved to be unsuitable) and then at Port Jackson (later the site of the city of Sydney). Establishment of an Australian prison colony was to relieve crowding of British prisons. Australia Day, formerly known as Foundation Day or Anniversary Day, has been observed since about 1817 and has been a public holiday since 1838. Observed Jan 26 if a Monday, otherwise on the first Monday thereafter (Jan 31 in 2000).

COLEMAN, BESSIE: BIRTH ANNIVERSARY. Jan 26, 1893. The first African American to receive a pilot's license, Coleman had to go to France to study flying, since she was denied admission to aviation schools in the US because of her race and sex. She took part in acrobatic air exhibitions where her stunt-flying and figure eights won her many admirers. Born at Atlanta, TX, she died in a plane crash at Jacksonville, FL, Apr 30, 1926.

DENTAL DRILL PATENT: 125th ANNIVERSARY. Jan 26, 1875. George F. Green, of Kalamazoo, MI, patented the electric dental drill.

DODGE, MARY MAPES: BIRTH ANNIVERSARY. Jan 26, 1831. Children's author, known for her book *Hans Brinker or, The Silver Skates*. Born at New York, NY, she died at Ontenora Park, NY, Aug 21, 1905.

DOMINICAN REPUBLIC: NATIONAL HOLIDAY. Jan 26. An official public holiday celebrates the birth anniversary of Juan Pablo Duarte, one of the fathers of the republic.

FRANKLIN PREFERS TURKEY: ANNIVERSARY. Jan 26, 1784. In a letter to his daughter, Benjamin Franklin expressed his unhappiness over the choice of the eagle as the symbol of America. He preferred the turkey. See Curriculum Connection.

GRANT, JULIA DENT: BIRTH ANNIVERSARY. Jan 26, 1826. Wife of Ulysses Simpson Grant, 18th president of the US. Born at St. Louis, MO, died at Washington, DC, Dec 14, 1902.

INDIA: REPUBLIC DAY. Jan 26. National holiday. Anniversary of Proclamation of the Republic, Basant Panchmi. In 1929, Indian National Congress resolved to work for establishment of a sovereign republic, a goal that was realized Jan 26, 1950, when India became a democratic republic.

MICHIGAN: ADMISSION DAY: ANNIVERSARY. Jan 26. Became 26th state in 1837.

NATIONAL COMPLIMENT DAY. Jan 26. This day is set aside to compliment at least five people. Not only are compliments appreciated by the receiver, they lift the spirit of the giver. Compliments provide a quick and easy way to connect positively with those you come in contact with. Giving compliments forges bonds, dispels loneliness and just plain feels good. Annually, the fourth Wednesday in January. For info: Deborah Hoffman, Positive Results Seminars, 12 Campion Circle, Concord, NH 03303-3410. Phone: (603) 225-0991. E-mail: prseminars@compuserve.com. or

January 2000	S	M	T	W	T	F	S
							1
	2	3	4	5	6	7	8
	9	10	11	12	13	14	15
	16	17	18	19	20	21	22
	23	24	25	26	27	28	29
	30	31					

JANUARY 26
FRANKLIN PREFERS TURKEY DAY

History (and Ben Franklin) come alive when you investigate this unfamiliar historical fact.

Ask your students to share what they know about turkeys, making a list on the board. Next, tell them that Ben Franklin thought the choice of an eagle as our national symbol was a poor one; he preferred the turkey. When your students finish laughing, ask why they think he liked this bird and list their reasons. Have students gather information from the learning center about turkeys and eagles. First, they should discover that there are domesticated turkeys, like those raised as a food crop, and wild turkeys, which were what Franklin had in mind. They should find enough similarities and differences to compare and contrast both kinds of turkeys and eagles. Jim Arnosky's book *All About Turkeys* (Scholastic, 0-590-48147-9, $15.95 Gr. 1–5) contains a wealth of information about turkeys. *Soaring With the Wind: The Bald Eagle*, by Gail Gibbons (Morrow, 0-688-13730-X, $16 Gr. 2–4) gives a good overview of bald eagles.

After the students have done some research, read aloud the section of the letter Franklin wrote to his daughter Sarah Bache on the subject. "I wish the bald eagle had not been chosen as the representative of our country; he is a bird of bad moral character; like those among men who live by sharping and robbing; he is generally poor, and often very lousy. The turkey is a much more respectable bird, and withal a true original native of America."

As a persuasive writing extension, ask students to write letters to the country's founding fathers in support of Franklin's candidate. Another extension would be to ask students to choose another animal they feel best represents this country and write a statement telling why the animal should be chosen.

Katherine Chamberlain, Heart to Heart Seminars, 724 Park Ave, Contoocook, NH 03229-3089. Phone: (603) 746-6227. E-mail: Kathiecham@aol.com.

NATIONAL SCHOOL NURSE DAY. Jan 26. A day to honor and recognize the school nurse, School Nurse Day has been established to foster a better understanding of the role of school nurses in the educational setting. Annually, the fourth Wednesday in January. Brochures available for purchase. For info: Judy Barker, Adm Asst, Natl Assn of School Nurses, Inc, PO Box 1300, Scarborough, ME 04070-1300. Phone: (207) 883-2117. Fax: (207) 883-2683. E-mail: nasn@aol.com.

BIRTHDAYS TODAY

Wayne Gretzky, 39, hockey player, born Brantford, Ontario, Canada, Jan 26, 1961.

JANUARY 27 — THURSDAY

Day 27 — 339 Remaining

APOLLO I: SPACECRAFT FIRE: ANNIVERSARY. Jan 27, 1967. Three American astronauts, Virgil I. Grissom, Edward H. White and Roger B. Chaffee, died when fire suddenly broke out at 6:31 PM in *Apollo I* during a launching simulation test, as it stood on the ground at Cape Kennedy, FL, Jan 27, 1967. First launching in the Apollo program had been scheduled for Feb 27, 1967.

DODGSON, CHARLES LUTWIDGE (LEWIS CARROLL): BIRTH ANNIVERSARY. Jan 27, 1832. English mathematician and author, better known by his pseudonym, Lewis Carroll, creator of *Alice's Adventures in Wonderland*, was born at Cheshire, England. *Alice* was written for Alice Liddell, daughter of a friend, and first published in 1886. *Through the Looking-Glass*, a sequel, and *The Hunting of the Snark* followed. Dodgson's books for children proved equally enjoyable to adults, and they overshadowed his serious works on mathematics. Dodgson died at Guildford, Surrey, England, Jan 14, 1898.

MOZART, WOLFGANG AMADEUS: BIRTH ANNIVERSARY. Jan 27, 1756. One of the world's greatest music makers. Born at Salzburg, Austria, into a gifted musical family, Mozart began performing at age three and composing at age five. Some of the best known of his more than 600 compositions include the operas *Marriage of Figaro, Don Giovanni, Cosi fan tutte* and *The Magic Flute*, his unfinished Requiem Mass, his C major symphony known as the "Jupiter" and many quartets and piano concertos. He died at Vienna, Dec 5, 1791.

VIETNAM WAR ENDS: ANNIVERSARY. Jan 27, 1973. US and North Vietnam, along with South Vietnam and the Viet Cong, signed an "Agreement on ending the war and restoring peace in Vietnam." Signed at Paris, France, to take effect Jan 28 at 8 AM Saigon time, thus ending US combat role in a war that had involved American personnel stationed in Vietnam since defeated French forces had departed under terms of the Geneva Accords in 1954. Longest war in US history. More than one million combat deaths (US deaths: 46,079).

BIRTHDAYS TODAY

Julie Foudy, 29, soccer player, born San Diego, CA, Jan 27, 1971.
Julius B. Lester, 61, author (*To Be a Slave, Black Folktales*), born St. Louis, MO, Jan 27, 1939.

JANUARY 28 — FRIDAY
Day 28 — 338 Remaining

CHALLENGER SPACE SHUTTLE EXPLOSION: ANNIVERSARY. Jan 28, 1986. At 11:39 AM, EST, the Space Shuttle *Challenger STS-51L* exploded, 74 seconds into its flight and about 10 miles above the earth. Hundreds of millions around the world watched television replays of the horrifying event that killed seven people, destroyed the billion-dollar craft, suspended all shuttle flights and halted, at least temporarily, much of the US manned space flight program. Killed were teacher Christa McAuliffe (who was to have been the first ordinary citizen in space) and six crew members: Francis R. Scobee, Michael J. Smith, Judith A. Resnik, Ellison S. Onizuka, Ronald E. McNair and Gregory B. Jarvis.

MacKENZIE, ALEXANDER: BIRTH ANNIVERSARY. Jan 28, 1822. The man who became the first Liberal prime minister of Canada (1873–78) was born at Logierait, Perth, Scotland. He died at Toronto, Apr 17, 1892.

MARTÍ, JOSÉ JULIAN: BIRTH ANNIVERSARY. Jan 28, 1853. Cuban author and political activist born at Havana, Cuba, Martí was exiled to Spain, where he studied law before coming to the US in 1890. He was killed in battle at Dos Rios, Cuba, May 19, 1895.

MOON PHASE: LAST QUARTER. Jan 28. Moon enters Last Quarter phase at 2:57 AM, EST.

PICCARD, AUGUSTE: BIRTH ANNIVERSARY. Jan 28, 1884. Scientist and explorer, born at Basel, Switzerland. Record-setting balloon ascents into stratosphere and ocean depth descents and explorations. Twin brother of Jean Felix Piccard. Died at Lausanne, Switzerland, Mar 24, 1962. See also: "Piccard, Jean Felix: Birth Anniversary" (Jan 28).

PICCARD, JEAN FELIX: BIRTH ANNIVERSARY. Jan 28, 1884. Scientist, engineer, explorer, born at Basel, Switzerland. Noted for cosmic-ray research and record-setting balloon ascensions into stratosphere. Reached 57,579 ft in sealed gondola piloted by his wife, Jeannette, in 1934. Twin brother of Auguste Piccard. Died at Minneapolis, MN, Jan 28, 1963. See also: "Piccard, Jeannette Ridlon: Birth Anniversary" (Jan 5) and "Piccard, Auguste: Birth Anniversary" (Jan 28).

BIRTHDAYS TODAY

Jeanne Shaheen, 53, Governor of New Hampshire (D), born St. Charles, MO, Jan 28, 1947.
Elijah Wood, 19, actor (*Flipper, Deep Impact*), born Cedar Rapids, IA, Jan 28, 1981.

JANUARY 29 — SATURDAY
Day 29 — 337 Remaining

KANSAS: ADMISSION DAY: ANNIVERSARY. Jan 29. Became the 34th state in 1861.

McKINLEY, WILLIAM: BIRTH ANNIVERSARY. Jan 29, 1843. Twenty-fifth president of the US, born at Niles, OH. Died in office, at Buffalo, NY, Sept 14, 1901, as the result of a gunshot wound by an anarchist assassin Sept 6, 1901, while he was attending the Pan-American Exposition.

BIRTHDAYS TODAY

Christopher Collier, 70, author of historical fiction, with his brother James Lincoln Collier (*My Brother Sam Is Dead*), born New York, NY, Jan 29, 1930.
Dominik Hasek, 35, hockey player, born Pardubice, Czech Republic, Jan 29, 1965.
Ronald Stacey King, 33, basketball player, born Lawton, OK, Jan 29, 1967.
Bill Peet, 85, author and illustrator (*Whingdingdilly, The Wump World*), born Grandview, IN, Jan 29, 1915.
Jason James Richter, 20, actor (*Free Willy*), born Medford, OR, Jan 29, 1980.
Rosemary Wells, 57, author and illustrator (*Noisy Nora, Benjamin and Tulip*, The Max series), born New York, NY, Jan 29, 1943.
Oprah Winfrey, 46, TV talk show hostess (Emmys for "The Oprah Winfrey Show"), actress (*Beloved*), born Kosciusko, MS, Jan 29, 1954.

JANUARY 30 — SUNDAY
Day 30 — 336 Remaining

NATIONAL INANE ANSWERING MESSAGE DAY. Jan 30. Annually, the day set aside to change, shorten, replace or delete those ridiculous and/or annoying answering machine messages that waste the time of anyone who must listen to them. [© 1998 by WPL]. For info: Thomas and Ruth Roy, Wellness Permission League, PO Box 662, Mount Gretna, PA 17064-0662. Phone: (717) 964-1308. Fax: (717) 964-1335. E-mail: wellcat@desupernet.net.

NATIONAL POPCORN DAY. Jan 30. A salute to popcorn. "What's more American than a super bowl of popcorn while watching the Super Bowl?" Annually, Superbowl Sunday. For info: Polly Peterson, WROE-FM, PO Box 1035, Neenah, WI 54957-1035. Phone: (414) 725-4447. Fax: (414) 725-0463.

ROOSEVELT, FRANKLIN DELANO: BIRTH ANNIVERSARY. Jan 30, 1882. Thirty-second president of the US (Mar 4, 1933–Apr 12, 1945). The only president to serve more than two terms, FDR was elected four times. He supported the Allies in WWII before the US entered the struggle by supplying them with war materials through the Lend-Lease Act; he became deeply involved in broad decision making after the Japanese attack on Pearl Harbor Dec 7, 1941. Born at Hyde Park, NY, he died a few months into his fourth term at Warm Springs, GA, Apr 12, 1945.

SUPER BOWL XXXIV. Jan 30. Atlanta, GA. The battle between the NFC and AFC champions. Annually, the last Sunday in January. For info: PR Dept, The Natl Football League, 410 Park Ave, New York, NY 10022. Phone: (212) 758-1500. Web: www.nfl.com.

BIRTHDAYS TODAY

Lloyd Alexander, 76, author (*The Black Cauldron*, Newbery for *The High King*), born Philadelphia, PA, Jan 30, 1924.

Allan W. Eckert, 69, author (*Incident at Hawk's Hill*), born Buffalo, NY, Jan 30, 1931.

Frank O'Bannon, 70, Governor of Indiana (D), born Louisville, KY, Jan 30, 1930.

JANUARY 31 — MONDAY
Day 31 — 335 Remaining

McDONALD'S INVADES THE SOVIET UNION: 10th ANNIVERSARY. Jan 31, 1990. McDonald's Corporation opened its first fast-food restaurant in the Soviet Union.

NAURU: NATIONAL HOLIDAY. Jan 31. Republic of Nauru. Commemorates independence in 1968 from a UN trusteeship administered by Australia, New Zealand and the UK.

ROBINSON, JACKIE: BIRTH ANNIVERSARY. Jan 31, 1919. Jack Roosevelt Robinson, athlete and business executive, first black to enter professional major league baseball (Brooklyn Dodgers, 1947–56). Voted National League's Most Valuable Player in 1949 and elected to the Baseball Hall of Fame in 1962. Born at Cairo, GA, Robinson died at Stamford, CT, Oct 24, 1972.

SPACE MILESTONE: *EXPLORER 1* (US). Jan 31, 1958. The first successful US satellite. Although launched four months later than the Soviet Union's *Sputnik*, *Explorer* reached a higher altitude and detected a zone of intense radiation inside Earth's magnetic field. This was later named the Van Allen radiation belts. More than 65 subsequent *Explorer* satellites were launched through 1984.

SPACE MILESTONE: PROJECT MERCURY TEST (US). Jan 31, 1961. A test of Project Mercury spacecraft accomplished the first US recovery of a large animal from space. Ham, the chimpanzee, successfully performed simple tasks in space.

BIRTHDAYS TODAY

Queen Beatrix, 62, Queen of the Netherlands, born Sostdijk, Netherlands, Jan 31, 1938.

Gerald McDermott, 59, illustrator and author (Caldecott for *Arrow to the Sun*), born Detroit, MI, Jan 31, 1941.

(Lynn) Nolan Ryan, 53, Baseball Hall of Fame player, born Refugio, TX, Jan 31, 1947.

FEBRUARY 1 — TUESDAY

Day 32 — 334 Remaining

★**AMERICAN HEART MONTH.** Feb 1–29. Presidential Proclamation issued each year for February since 1964. (PL88–254 of Dec 30, 1963.)

AMERICAN HEART MONTH. Feb 1–29. Volunteers across the country spend one to four weeks canvassing neighborhoods and providing educational information about heart disease and stroke. For info: Cathy Yarbrough, News Media Relations, American Heart Association, 7272 Greenville Ave, Dallas, TX 75231. Phone: (800) AHA-USA1. Fax: (214) 369-3685. Web: www.american heart.org.

BLACK HISTORY MONTH. Feb 1–29. Traditionally the month containing Abraham Lincoln's birthday (Feb 12) and Frederick Douglass's presumed birthday (Feb 14). Observance of a special period to recognize achievements and contributions by African Americans dates from February 1926, when it was launched by Dr. Carter G. Woodson and others. Variously designated Negro History, Black History, Afro-American History, African-American History, Black Heritage and Black Expressions, the observance period was initially one week, but since 1976 has been the entire month of February. Each year Black History Month has a theme. Visit the website of the Association for African-American Life and History for the theme for the current year and information on a theme-related kit you can purchase from the Association. The price for the 1999 kit was $49.95. *Black History Month Resource Book* (2nd ed., Gale, 0-7876-1755-X, $47) includes both programmatic ideas and lists of resources in all media for all ages. See Curriculum Connection. For info: Assn for Afro-American Life and History, 1407 14th St NW, Washington, DC 20005-3704. Phone: (202) 667-2822. Fax: (202) 387-9802. Web: www.art noir.com/asalh/.

BLACK MARIA STUDIO: ANNIVERSARY. Feb 1, 1893. The first moving picture studio was completed, built on Thomas Edison's laboratory compound at West Orange, NJ, at a cost of less than $700. The wooden structure of irregular oblong shape was covered with black tar paper. It had a sharply sloping roof hinged at one edge so that half of it could be raised to admit sunlight. Fifty feet in length, it was mounted on a pivot enabling it to be swung around to follow the changing position of the sun. There was a stage draped in black at one end of the single room. Though the structure was officially called a Kinetographic Theater, it was nicknamed the "Black Maria" because it resembled an old-fash-

FEBRUARY 1–29
BLACK HISTORY MONTH

Celebrate the many contributions African Americans have made to the arts throughout the history of the United States. Here are some suggestions that will familiarize your students with African American artists.

In language arts you might feature poets Phillis Wheatley, Langston Hughes and Countee Cullen. *I, Too, Sing America: Three Centuries of African American Poetry*, selected by Catherine Clinton (Houghton Mifflin, 0-395-89599-5, $20 All ages) contains these poets and many more. To give the words impact, let students present poems orally as choral readings, scripted in different ways. Mildred Taylor's novel *Roll of Thunder, Hear My Cry* (Dial, 0-803-77473-7, $15.99 Gr. 3–7) has a number of short, powerful scenes appropriate for middle school students to script for Reader's Theater.

African Americans have contributed to theater as playwrights and actors. Lorraine Hansberry, the author of *A Raisin in the Sun*, is the subject of a biography: *Young, Black, and Determined*, by Fredrick L. McKissack and Patricia C. McKissack (Holiday House, 0-8234-1300-4, $18.95 Gr. 6–12). Also discuss Pulitzer Prize-winning playwrights August Wilson and Charles Gordone.

Clementine Hunter was an African American folk artist. Children will relate to her paintings of everyday life. For more information see *Talking With Tebé: Clementine Hunter, Memory Artist*, edited by Mary Lyons (Houghton Mifflin, 0-395-72031-1, $16 Gr. 3–8). Lyons has also written books on African American artists Horace Pippin and Harriet Powers. Jacob Lawrence is another African American painter whose work will appeal to children. *The Great Migration: An American Story*, by Jacob Lawrence (HarperCollins, 0-06-023037-1, $23.50 Gr. 4–6) reproduces his series of paintings that tells the story of the movement of African Americans out of the South. For information about Lawrence's life, see *Story Painter: The Life of Jacob Lawrence*, by John Duggleby (Chronicle, 0-8118-2082-3, $16.95 Gr. 5–8).

African Americans have contributed to classical music and are responsible for the uniquely American art form, jazz. Jessye Norman, Leontyne Price and Kathleen Battle are internationally recognized opera singers. Show video selections from operas that feature these singers. No child should grow up without hearing the rags composed by Scott Joplin, the singing of Paul Robeson or the music of jazz artists Dizzy Gillespie, Duke Ellington and Ella Fitzgerald. Find recordings in the library and play them for your students.

Dance, by noted African American dancer/choreographer Bill T. Jones and Susan Kuklin (Hyperion, 0-7868-0362-2, $14.95 Gr. 1–4) brings the delights of modern dance to young children. Also discuss such black dancers/choreographers as Alvin Ailey and Arthur Mitchell.

There are countless possibilities for bringing African American artists to life for your students. Contact your Learning Center director and local public library for additional suggestions.

ioned police wagon. It was described as "hot and cramped" by "Gentleman" Jim Corbett, the pugilistic idol who was the subject of an early movie made in the studio.

CAR INSURANCE FIRST ISSUED: ANNIVERSARY. Feb 1, 1898. Travelers Insurance Company issued the first car insurance against accidents with horses.

FREEDOM DAY: ANNIVERSARY. Feb 1. Anniversary of President Abraham Lincoln's approval, Feb 1, 1865, of the 13th Amendment to the US Constitution (abolishing slavery): "1. Neither slavery nor involuntary servitude, except as a punishment for crime whereof the party shall have been duly convicted, shall exist within the United States or any place subject to their jurisdiction. 2. Congress shall have power to enforce this article by appropriate legislation." The amendment had been proposed by the Congress Jan 31, 1865; ratification was completed Dec 18, 1865.

GREENSBORO SIT-IN: 40th ANNIVERSARY. Feb 1, 1960. Commercial discrimination against blacks and other minorities provoked a nonviolent protest. At Greensboro, NC, four students from the Agricultural and Technical College at Greensboro (Ezell Blair, Jr, Franklin McCain, Joseph McNeill and David Richmond) sat down at a Woolworths store lunch counter and ordered coffee. Refused service, they remained all day. The following days similar sit-ins took place at the Woolworths lunch counter. Before the week was over they were joined by a few white students. The protest spread rapidly, especially in southern states. More than 1,600 persons were arrested before the year was over for participating in sit-ins. Civil rights for all became a cause for thousands of students and activists. In response, equal accommodation regardless of race became the rule at lunch counters, hotels and business establishments in thousands of places.

LIBRARY LOVERS' MONTH. Feb 1–29. A month-long celebration of school, public and private libraries of all types. This is a time for everyone, especially library support groups, to recognize the value of libraries and to work to assure that the nation's libraries will continue to serve. For info: Stephanie Stokes, 1980 Washington, No 107, San Francisco, CA 94109-2930. Phone: (415) 749-0130. Fax: (415) 749-0735. E-mail: librarylovers@calibraries .org. Web: www.calibraries.org/librarylovers.

★**NATIONAL AFRICAN AMERICAN HISTORY MONTH.** Feb 1–29.

NATIONAL CHERRY MONTH. Feb 1–29. To publicize the colorful red tart cherry. Recipes, posters and table tents available. For info: Jane Baker, Mktg Dir, Cherry Marketing Institute, PO Box 30285, Lansing, MI 48909-7785. Phone: (517) 669-4264. Fax: (517) 669-3354. E-mail: jbaker@cherrymkt.org. Web: www.cherrymkt .org.

NATIONAL CHILDREN'S DENTAL HEALTH MONTH. Feb 1–29. To increase dental awareness and stress the importance of

regular dental care. For info: American Dental Assn, 211 E Chicago Ave, Chicago, IL 60611. To purchase materials, phone in US: (800) 947-4746. Web: www.ada.org.

★**NATIONAL FREEDOM DAY.** Feb 1. Presidential Proclamation 2824, Jan 25, 1949, covers all succeeding years (PL80–842 of June 30, 1948).

NATIONAL SIGN UP FOR SUMMER CAMP MONTH. Feb 1–29. Every year more than eight million children continue a national tradition by attending day or resident camps. Building self-confidence, learning new skills and making memories that last a lifetime are just a few examples of what makes camp special and why camp does children a world of good. To find the right program, parents begin looking at summer camps during this month—and sign their children up while there are still vacancies. For info: Public Relations, American Camping Assn, 5000 State Rd 67N, Martinsville, IN 46151. Phone: (765) 342-8456. E-mail: bschultz@aca-camps.org. Web: www.aca-camps.org. For a guide to accredited camps, call (800) 428-CAMPS.

FEBRUARY 1
ROBINSON CRUSOE DAY

In 1704, following an argument with his ship's captain, Alexander Selkirk requested to be put ashore on an uninhabited island in the southeast Pacific. He remained on the island for almost four years. He was rescued on Feb 1, 1709. When Daniel Defoe wrote *Robinson Crusoe* in 1719, the main character's story of island survival was based on Selkirk's adventures.

Upper middle school and junior high students who are interested may want to read *Robinson Crusoe*. Some prior discussion and explanation of period writing style and language usage would be helpful. Although the day receives its name from the book, it isn't necessary to read *Robinson Crusoe* to enjoy the day. Survival, adventure and self-reliance are themes all students can relate to.

Incorporate these themes into the language arts curriculum in several ways. One could be as a message in a bottle. Ask students to pretend they are on a deserted island. A corked bottle washes ashore. What will they use as paper and ink and what would they write in a rescue note? Ask students who like computer or virtual reality games to write a proposal that outlines and summarizes a plot and setting for a new computer survival game. On a lighter note, students could write a survival guide for the school day, week or year. Perhaps these could be shared with younger students as a read aloud session.

Science tie-ins could include methods of survival in differing ecosystems. For example: what would people do in a rainforest, a desert or Alaska? Also, while studying ocean units, students could chart a floating bottle's likely path on an ocean current— the Gulf Stream would be one possibility.

Many excellent survival stories have been written for young readers. Offer *The Transall Saga*, by Gary Paulsen (Delacorte, 0-385-32196-1, $15.95 Gr. 6–8); *Climb or Die*, by Edward Myers (Hyperion, 0-786-81129-3, $4.95 Gr. 3–6); *Toughboy and Sister*, by Kirkpatrick Hill (Puffin, 0-14-034866-2, $3.99 Gr. 4–7); *Earthquake Terror*, by Peg Kehret (Puffin, 0-14-038343-3, $3.99 Gr. 3–7); and *Invitation to the Game*, by Monica Hughes (Simon & Schuster, 0-671-86692-3, $3.95 Gr. 6 & up) to students who are looking for great adventure. *Survival Themes in Fiction for Children and Young People*, 2nd edition, by Binnie Tate Wilkin (Scarecrow, 0-8108-2676-3, $27.50) is an annotated bibliography arranged by theme, "survival" being used in the very broadest sense of the word.

	S	M	T	W	T	F	S
February			1	2	3	4	5
2000	6	7	8	9	10	11	12
	13	14	15	16	17	18	19
	20	21	22	23	24	25	26
	27	28	29				

NATIONAL WILD BIRD FEEDING MONTH. Feb 1–29. To recognize that February is one of the most difficult winter months in much of the US for birds to survive in the wild and to encourage people to provide food, water and shelter to supplement the wild birds' natural diet of weed seeds and harmful insects. For info: Sue Wells, Exec Dir, Natl Bird-Feeding Soc, PO Box 23, Northbrook, IL 60065-0023. Phone: (847) 272-0135.

NORTH CAROLINA SWEETPOTATO MONTH. Feb 1–29. To educate the public about the nutritional benefits and versatility of sweet potatoes. North Carolina farmers want America to know that sweet potatoes aren't just for turkeys anymore. Available year-round, sweet potatoes are loaded with beta carotene and vitamin C. They can be boiled, baked, microwaved, grilled, broiled, fried, mashed, sauteed, candied or served raw. North Carolina produces more sweet potatoes than any other state. For info: Sue Johnson-Langdon, North Carolina SweetPotato Commission, 1327 N Brightleaf Blvd, Ste H, Smithfield, NC 27577. Phone: (919) 989-7323. Fax: (919) 989-3015. E-mail: ncsweetsue@aol.com.

RETURN SHOPPING CARTS TO THE SUPERMARKET MONTH. Feb 1–29. A month-long opportunity to return stolen shopping carts, milk crates, bread trays and ice cream baskets to supermarkets and to avoid the increased food prices that these thefts cause. Annually, the month of February. Sponsor: Illinois Food Retailers Association. For info: Anthony A. Dinolfo, Grocer, Retired, 8148 S Homan Ave, Chicago, IL 60652. Phone: (773) 737-6540.

ROBINSON CRUSOE DAY. Feb 1. Anniversary of the rescue, Feb 1, 1709, of Alexander Selkirk, Scottish sailor who had been put ashore (in September 1704) on the uninhabited island, Juan Fernandez, at his own request after a quarrel with his captain. His adventures formed the basis for Daniel Defoe's book *Robinson Crusoe*. A day to be adventurous and self-reliant. See Curriculum Connection.

ST. LAURENT, LOUIS STEPHEN: BIRTH ANNIVERSARY. Feb 1, 1882. Canadian lawyer and prime minister, born at Compton, Quebec. Died at Quebec City, July 25, 1973.

BIRTHDAYS TODAY

Michael B. Enzi, 56, US Senator (R, Wyoming), born Bremerton, WA, Feb 1, 1944.

Jerry Spinelli, 59, author (*Wringer*, Newbery for *Maniac Magee*), born Norristown, PA, Feb 1, 1941.

Boris Yeltsin, 69, Russian president, born Sverdlovsk, Russia, Feb 1, 1931.

FEBRUARY 2 — WEDNESDAY

Day 33 — 333 Remaining

BABE VOTED INTO BASEBALL HALL OF FAME: ANNIVERSARY. Feb 2, 1936. The five charter members of the brand-new Baseball Hall of Fame at Cooperstown, NY, were announced. Of 226 ballots cast, Ty Cobb was named on 222, Babe Ruth on 215, Honus Wagner on 215, Christy Mathewson on 205 and Walter Johnson on 189. A total of 170 votes were necessary to be elected to the Hall of Fame.

BAN ON AFRICAN NATIONAL CONGRESS LIFTED: 10th ANNIVERSARY. Feb 2, 1990. The 30-year ban on the African National Congress was lifted by South African President F. W. de Klerk. De Klerk also vowed to free Nelson Mandela and lift restrictions on 33 other opposition groups.

BONZA BOTTLER DAY™. Feb 2. To celebrate when the number of the day is the same as the number of the month. Bonza Bottler Day™ is an excuse to have a party at least once a month. For info: Gail M. Berger, 109 Matthew Ave, Poca, WV 25159. Phone: (304) 776-7746. E-mail: gberger5@aol.com.

CALIFORNIA KIWIFRUIT DAY. Feb 2. National campaign to educate Americans about the nutritional benefits of kiwifruit, the most nutrient-dense fruit (they provide twice the vitamin C of oranges); ways to enjoy kiwifruit and kiwifruit's colorful history. Annually, Feb 2. For info: Laura Bachmann, Porter Novelli, 444 Market St, Ste 3000, San Francisco, CA 94111. Fax: (415) 733-1770.

CANDLEMAS DAY or PRESENTATION OF THE LORD. Feb 2. Observed in Roman Catholic and Eastern Orthodox Churches. Commemorates presentation of Jesus in the Temple and the purification of Mary 40 days after his birth. Candles have been blessed since the 11th century. Formerly called the Feast of Purification of the Blessed Virgin Mary. Old Scottish couplet proclaims: "If Candlemas is fair and clear/There'll be two winters in the year."

GROUNDHOG DAY. Feb 2. Old belief that if the sun shines on Candlemas Day, or if the groundhog sees his shadow when he emerges on this day, six weeks of winter will ensue. For links to websites about Groundhog Day, go to deil.lang.uiuc.edu/web.pages/holidays/groundhog.html.

GROUNDHOG DAY IN PUNXSUTAWNEY, PENNSYLVANIA. Feb 2. Widely observed traditional annual Candlemas Day event at which "Punxsutawney Phil, king of the weather prophets," is the object of a search. Tradition is said to have been established by early German settlers. The official trek (which began in 1887) is followed by a weather prediction for the next six weeks. [Phil made his dramatic film debut with Bill Murray in *Groundhog Day*.]

MEXICO: DIA DE LA CANDELARIA. Feb 2. All Mexico celebrates Candlemas Day with dances, processions, bullfights.

THE RECORD OF A SNEEZE : ANNIVERSARY. Feb 2, 1893. One day after Thomas Edison's "Black Maria" studio was completed at West Orange, NJ, a studio cameraman took the first "close-up" in film history. *The Record of a Sneeze*, starring Edison's assistant Fred P. Ott, was also the first motion picture to receive a copyright (1894). See also: "Black Maria Studio: Anniversary" (Feb 1).

TREATY OF GUADALUPE HIDALGO: ANNIVERSARY. Feb 2, 1848. The war between Mexico and the US formally ended with the signing of the Treaty of Guadalupe Hidalgo, signed in the village for which it was named. The treaty provided for Mexico's cession to the US of the territory that became the states of California, Nevada, Utah, most of Arizona and parts of New Mexico, Colorado and Wyoming, in exchange for $15 million from the US. In addition, Mexico relinquished all rights to Texas north of the Rio Grande. The Senate ratified the treaty Mar 10, 1848.

WALTON, GEORGE: DEATH ANNIVERSARY. Feb 2, 1804. Signer of the Declaration of Independence. Born at Prince Edward County, VA, 1749 (exact date unknown). Died at Augusta, GA.

BIRTHDAYS TODAY

Judith Viorst, 69, author (*The Tenth Good Thing About Barney*), born Newark, NJ, Feb 2, 1931.

FEBRUARY 3 — THURSDAY

Day 34 — 332 Remaining

FIFTEENTH AMENDMENT TO US CONSTITUTION RATIFIED: ANNIVERSARY. Feb 3, 1870. The 15th Amendment granted that the right of citizens to vote shall not be denied on account of race, color or previous condition of servitude.

FLORIDA STATE FAIR. Feb 3–13 (tentative). Florida State Fair Grounds, Tampa, FL. The fair features the best arts, crafts, competitive exhibits, equestrian shows, livestock, entertainment and food found in Florida. Also not to be missed is "Cracker Country," where cultural and architectural history has been preserved. Est attendance: 500,000. For info: Sherry Powell, Mktg & Advertising Mgr, Florida State Fair, PO Box 11766, Tampa, FL 33680. Phone: (813) 621-7821 or (813) 622-PARK. Web: www.fl-ag.com/statefair.

INCOME TAX BIRTHDAY: SIXTEENTH AMENDMENT TO US CONSTITUTION: RATIFICATION ANNIVERSARY. Feb 3, 1913. The 16th Amendment granted Congress the authority to levy taxes on income. (Church bells did not ring throughout the land and no dancing in the streets was reported.)

JAPAN: BEAN-THROWING FESTIVAL (SETSUBUN). Feb 3. Setsubun marks the last day of winter according to the lunar calendar. Throngs at temple grounds throw beans to drive away imaginary devils.

NORTH AMERICA'S COLDEST RECORDED TEMPERATURE: ANNIVERSARY. Feb 3, 1947. At Snag, in Canada's Yukon Territory, a temperature of 81 degrees below zero (Fahrenheit) was recorded on this date, a record low for all of North America.

SPACE MILESTONE: *CHALLENGER STS-10* (US). Feb 3, 1984. Shuttle *Challenger* launched from Kennedy Space Center, FL, with a crew of five (Vance Brand, Robert Gibson, Ronald McNair, Bruce McCandless and Robert Stewart). On Feb 7 two astronauts became the first to fly freely in space (propelled by their backpack jets), untethered to any craft. Landed at Cape Canaveral, FL, Feb 11.

BIRTHDAYS TODAY

Joan Lowery Nixon, 73, author (the Orphan Train series), born Los Angeles, CA, Feb 3, 1927.

Paul S. Sarbanes, 67, US Senator (D, Maryland), born Salisbury, MD, Feb 3, 1933.

Maura Tierney, 35, actress (*Liar, Liar*), born Boston, MA, Feb 3, 1965.

FEBRUARY 4 — FRIDAY
Day 35 — 331 Remaining

APACHE WARS BEGAN: ANNIVERSARY. Feb 4, 1861. The period of conflict known as the Apache Wars began at Apache Pass, AZ, when Army Lieutenant George Bascom arrested Apache Chief Cochise for raiding a ranch. Cochise escaped and declared war. The wars lasted 25 years under the leadership of Cochise and, later, Geronimo.

HALFWAY POINT OF WINTER. Feb 4. At 2:35 AM, EST, Feb 4, 44 days, 23 hours and 51 minutes of winter will have elapsed and the equivalent remain before 2:35 AM, EST, Mar 20, 2000, which is the spring equinox and the beginning of spring.

LINDBERGH, CHARLES AUGUSTUS: BIRTH ANNIVERSARY. Feb 4, 1902. American aviator Charles "Lucky Lindy" Lindbergh was the first to fly solo and nonstop over the Atlantic Ocean, New York to Paris, May 20–21, 1927. Born at Detroit, MI, he died

February 2000	S	M	T	W	T	F	S
			1	2	3	4	5
	6	7	8	9	10	11	12
	13	14	15	16	17	18	19
	20	21	22	23	24	25	26
	27	28	29				

at Kipahula, Maui, HI, Aug 27, 1974. See also: "Lindbergh Flight: Anniversary" (May 20).

SRI LANKA: INDEPENDENCE DAY. Feb 4. Democratic Socialist Republic of Sri Lanka observes National Day. On Feb 4, 1948, Ceylon (as it was then known) obtained independence from Great Britain. The name Sri Lanka was adopted in 1972.

BIRTHDAYS TODAY

Rod Grams, 52, US Senator (R, Minnesota), born Princeton, MN, Feb 4, 1948.

Russel Hoban, 75, author of books illustrated by his wife Lillian (*Bedtime for Frances*), born Lansdale, PA, Feb 4, 1925.

Rosa Lee Parks, 87, civil rights leader who refused to give up her seat on the bus, born Tuskegee, AL, Feb 4, 1913.

FEBRUARY 5 — SATURDAY
Day 36 — 330 Remaining

CHINESE NEW YEAR. Feb 5. Traditional Chinese lunar year begins at sunset on the day of second New Moon following the winter solstice. The New Year can begin any time from Jan 10 through Feb 19. Begins year 4698 of the ancient Chinese calendar, designated as the Year of the Dragon. Generally celebrated until the Lantern Festival 15 days later, but merchants usually reopen their stores and places of business on the fifth day of the first lunar month (Feb 9, 2000). See also: "China: Lantern Festival" (Feb 19). This holiday is celebrated as Tet in Vietnam. For more info: *Celebrating Chinese New Year*, by Diane Hoyt-Goldsmith (Holiday House, 0-8234-1393-4, $16.95 Gr. 3-5).

FAMILY-LEAVE BILL: ANNIVERSARY. Feb 5, 1993. President William Clinton signed legislation requiring companies with 50 or more employees (and all government agencies) to allow employees to take up to 12 weeks unpaid leave in a 12-month period to deal with the birth or adoption of a child or to care for a relative with a serious health problem. The bill became effective Aug 5, 1993.

LAURA INGALLS WILDER GINGERBREAD SOCIABLE. Feb 5. Pomona, CA. The 32nd annual event commemorates the birthday (Feb 7, 1867) of the renowned author of the Little House books. The library has on permanent display the handwritten manuscript of *Little Town on the Prairie* and other Wilder memorabilia. Entertainment by fiddlers, craft displays, apple cider and gingerbread. Annually, the first Saturday in February. Est attendance: 300. For info: Marguerite F. Raybould, Friends of the Pomona Public Library, 625 S Garey Ave, Pomona, CA 91766. Phone: (909) 620-2017. Fax: (909) 620-3713.

MEXICO: ANNIVERSARY OF THE CONSTITUTION. Feb 5. The present constitution, embracing major social reforms, was adopted in 1917.

MOON PHASE: NEW MOON. Feb 5. Moon enters New Moon phase at 8:03 AM, EST.

SOLAR ECLIPSE. Feb 5. Partial eclipse of the sun. Eclipse begins at 5:55 AM, EST, reaches greatest eclipse at 7:49 AM and ends at 9:43 AM. Visible in Antarctica, central southern Indian Ocean.

WEATHERMAN'S [WEATHERPERSON'S] DAY. Feb 5. Commemorates the birth of one of America's first weathermen, John Jeffries, a Boston physician who kept detailed records of weather conditions, 1774–1816. Born at Boston, Feb 5, 1744, and died there Sept 16, 1819. See also: "First Balloon Flight Across English Channel: Anniversary" (Jan 7).

WITHERSPOON, JOHN: BIRTH ANNIVERSARY. Feb 5, 1723. Clergyman, signer of the Declaration of Independence and reputed coiner of the word *Americanism* (in 1781). Born near Edinburgh, Scotland. Died at Princeton, NJ, Nov 15, 1794.

BIRTHDAYS TODAY

Henry Louis (Hank) Aaron, 66, baseball executive, Baseball Hall of Fame outfielder, all-time home-run leader, born Mobile, AL, Feb 5, 1934.

Patricia Lauber, 76, author (the Let's Read and Find Out science series, *Volcano: The Eruption and Healing of Mount St. Helens*), born New York, NY, Feb 5, 1924.

David Wiesner, 43, author and illustrator (Caldecott for *Tuesday*), born Bridgewater, NJ, Feb 5, 1957.

FEBRUARY 6 — SUNDAY

Day 37 — 329 Remaining

ACCESSION OF QUEEN ELIZABETH II: ANNIVERSARY. Feb 6, 1952. Princess Elizabeth Alexandra Mary succeeded to the British throne (becoming Elizabeth II, Queen of the United Kingdom of Great Britain and Northern Ireland and Head of the Commonwealth) upon the death of her father, King George VI, Feb 6, 1952. Her coronation took place June 2, 1953, at Westminster Abbey at London.

AFRICAN AMERICAN READ-IN. Feb 6–7. Schools, libraries and community organizations are urged to make literacy a significant part of Black History Month by hosting Read-Ins in their communities. Report your results by submitting the 2000 African American Read-In Chain Report Card. This 11th national Read-In is sponsored by the Black Caucus of the National Council of Teachers of English. For a Read-In Chain Packet: Dr. Sandra E. Gibbs, NCTE Special Programs, 1111 W Kenyon Rd, Urbana, IL 61801-1096. Phone: (217) 328-3870. E-mail: sgibbs@ncte.org. Web: www.ncte.org/spot/aa-read-in.html.

BOY SCOUTS OF AMERICA ANNIVERSARY WEEK. Feb 6–12. Commemorating the founding of the organization Feb 8, 1910. For info: Boy Scouts of America, 1325 W Walnut Hill Ln, Irving, TX 75015-2079. Phone: (214) 580-2263. Web: www.bsa.scouting.org.

BURR, AARON: BIRTH ANNIVERSARY. Feb 6, 1756. Third vice president of the US (Mar 4, 1801–Mar 3, 1805). While vice president, Burr challenged political enemy Alexander Hamilton to a duel and mortally wounded him July 11, 1804, at Weehawken, NJ. Indicted for the challenge and for murder, he returned to Washington to complete his term of office (during which he presided over the impeachment trial of Supreme Court Justice Samuel Chase). In 1807 Burr was arrested, tried for treason (in an alleged scheme to invade Mexico and set up a new nation in the West) and acquitted. Born at Newark, NJ, he died at Staten Island, NY, Sept 14, 1836.

MASSACHUSETTS RATIFIES CONSTITUTION: ANNIVERSARY. Feb 6, 1788. By a vote of 187 to 168, Massachusetts became the sixth state to ratify the Constitution.

★**NATIONAL CHILD PASSENGER SAFETY AWARENESS WEEK.** Feb 6–12. For info: Office of Occupant Protection, Natl Highway Safety Administration, 400 Seventh St SW, Washington, DC 20590. Phone: (202) 366-9550.

NEW ZEALAND: WAITANGI DAY. Feb 6. National Day. Commemorates signing of the Treaty of Waitangi in 1840 (at Waitangi, Chatham Islands, New Zealand). The treaty, between the native Maori and the European peoples, provided for development of New Zealand under the British Crown.

RUTH, "BABE": BIRTH ANNIVERSARY. Feb 6, 1895. One of baseball's greatest heroes, George Herman "Babe" Ruth was born at Baltimore, MD. The left-handed pitcher—"the Sultan of Swat,"—hit 714 home runs in 22 major league seasons of play and played in 10 World Series. Died at New York, NY, Aug 16, 1948.

SWITZERLAND: HOMSTROM. Feb 6. Scuol. Burning of straw men on poles as a symbol of winter's imminent departure. Annually, the first Sunday in February.

BIRTHDAYS TODAY

Ronald Reagan, 89, 40th president of the US, born Tampico, IL, Feb 6, 1911.

FEBRUARY 7 — MONDAY

Day 38 — 328 Remaining

BALLET INTRODUCED TO THE US: ANNIVERSARY. Feb 7, 1827. Renowned French danseuse Mme Francisquy Hutin introduced ballet to the US with a performance of *The Deserter*, staged at the Bowery Theater, New York, NY. A minor scandal erupted when the ladies in the lower boxes left the theater upon viewing the light and scanty attire of Mme Hutin and her troupe.

DICKENS, CHARLES: BIRTH ANNIVERSARY. Feb 7, 1812. English social critic and novelist, born at Portsmouth, England. Among his most successful books: *Oliver Twist*, *The Posthumous Papers of the Pickwick Club*, *David Copperfield* and *A Christmas Carol*. Died at Gad's Hill, England, June 9, 1870, and was buried at Westminster Abbey.

ELEVENTH AMENDMENT TO US CONSTITUTION (SOVEREIGNTY OF THE STATES): RATIFICATION ANNIVERSARY. Feb 7, 1795. The 11th Amendment to the Constitution was ratified, curbing the powers of the federal judiciary in relation to the states. The amendment reaffirmed the sovereignty of the states by prohibiting suits against them.

GIPSON, FRED: BIRTH ANNIVERSARY. Feb 7, 1908. Born near Mason, TX. Gipson is known for such works as *Old Yeller*, *Savage Sam* and *Little Arliss*. In 1959, he won the William Allen White Children's Book Award and the First Sequoyah Award. Gipson died at Mason County, TX, Aug 17, 1973.

GRENADA: INDEPENDENCE DAY. Feb 7. National Day. Commemorates independence from Great Britain in 1974.

NATIONAL SCHOOL COUNSELING WEEK. Feb 7–11. Promotes counseling in the school and community. For info: American School Counselor Assn, 801 N Fairfax St, Ste 310, Alexandria, VA 22314. Phone: (800) 306-4722. Fax: (703) 683-1619. E-mail: asca@erols.com. Web: www.schoolcounselor.org.

WILDER, LAURA INGALLS: BIRTH ANNIVERSARY. Feb 7, 1867. Author of *The Little House on the Prairie* and its sequels. Born at Pepin, WI, Wilder died Feb 10, 1957, at Mansfield, MO. For further info, go to the Little House on the Prairie Home Page at www.vvv.com/~jenslegg/index.htm.

BIRTHDAYS TODAY

Garth Brooks, 38, singer, born Tulsa, OK, Feb 7, 1962.

Juwan Howard, 27, basketball player, born Chicago, IL, Feb 7, 1973.

Herb Kohl, 65, US Senator (D, Wisconsin), born Milwaukee, WI, Feb 7, 1935.

Pete Postlethwaite, 55, actor (*The Lost World: Jurassic Park*), born London, England, Feb 7, 1945.

FEBRUARY 8 — TUESDAY
Day 39 — 327 Remaining

BOY SCOUTS OF AMERICA FOUNDED: 90th ANNIVERSARY. Feb 8, 1910. The Boy Scouts of America was founded at Washington, DC, by William Boyce, based on the work of Sir Robert Baden-Powell with the British Boy Scout Association. For more info: www.bsa.scouting.org.

JAPAN: HA-RI-KU-YO (NEEDLE MASS). Feb 8. Ha-Ri-Ku-Yo, a Needle Mass, may be observed on either Feb 8 or Dec 8. Girls do no needlework; instead they gather old and broken needles, which they dedicate to the Awashima Shrine at Wakayama. Girls pray to Awashima Myozin (their protecting deity) that their needlework, symbolic of love and marriage, will be good. Participation in the Needle Mass hopefully leads to a happy marriage.

JAPAN: SNOW FESTIVAL. Feb 8–12. Sapporo, Hokkaido. Huge, elaborate snow and ice sculptures are erected on the Odori-Koen Promenade.

OPERA DEBUT IN THE COLONIES: ANNIVERSARY. Feb 8, 1735. The first opera produced in the colonies was performed at the Courtroom, at Charleston, SC. The opera was *Flora; or the Hob in the Well*, written by Colley Cibber.

SHERMAN, WILLIAM TECUMSEH: BIRTH ANNIVERSARY. Feb 8, 1820. Born at Lancaster, OH, General Sherman is especially remembered for his devastating march through Georgia during the Civil War and his statement "War is hell." Died at New York, NY, Feb 14, 1891.

SPACE MILESTONE: *ARABSAT-1*: 15th ANNIVERSARY. Feb 8, 1985. League of Arab States communications satellite launched into geosynchronous orbit from Kourou, French Guiana, by European Space Agency.

VERNE, JULES: BIRTH ANNIVERSARY. Feb 8, 1828. French writer, sometimes called "the father of science fiction," born at Nantes, France. Author of *Around the World in Eighty Days, Twenty Thousand Leagues Under the Sea* and many other novels. Died at Amiens, France, Mar 24, 1905.

BIRTHDAYS TODAY

Alonzo Mourning, 30, basketball player, born Chesapeake, VA, Feb 8, 1970.

FEBRUARY 9 — WEDNESDAY
Day 40 — 326 Remaining

HARRISON, WILLIAM HENRY: BIRTH ANNIVERSARY. Feb 9, 1773. Ninth president of the US (Mar 4–Apr 4, 1841). His term of office was the shortest in our nation's history—32 days. He was the first president to die in office (of pneumonia contracted during inaugural ceremonies). Born at Berkeley, VA, he died at Washington, DC, Apr 4, 1841.

February *2000*	S	M	T	W	T	F	S
			1	2	3	4	5
	6	7	8	9	10	11	12
	13	14	15	16	17	18	19
	20	21	22	23	24	25	26
	27	28	29				

BIRTHDAYS TODAY

David Gallagher, 15, actor ("7th Heaven"), born College Point, NY, Feb 9, 1985.

Joe Pesci, 57, actor (*Home Alone, Home Alone 2*), born Newark, NJ, Feb 9, 1943.

FEBRUARY 10 — THURSDAY
Day 41 — 325 Remaining

CHILDREN'S LITERATURE 2000. Feb 10–12. Ohio State University, Columbus, OH. For info: Roy Wilson, Ohio State Univ. Phone: (614) 292-7902. E-mail: wilson.418@osu.edu.

MALTA: FEAST OF ST. PAUL'S SHIPWRECK. Feb 10. Valletta. Holy day of obligation. Commemorates shipwreck of St. Paul on the north coast of Malta in AD 60.

TWENTY-FIFTH AMENDMENT TO US CONSTITUTION RATIFIED (PRESIDENTIAL SUCCESSION, DISABILITY): ANNIVERSARY. Feb 10, 1967. Procedures for presidential succession were further clarified by the 25th Amendment, along with provisions for continuity of power in the event of a disability or illness of the president. The 25th Amendment was ratified Feb 10, 1967.

BIRTHDAYS TODAY

Kirk Fordice, 66, Governor of Mississippi (R), born Memphis, TN, Feb 10, 1934.

Frank Keating, 56, Governor of Oklahoma (R), born St. Louis, MO, Feb 10, 1944.

E.L. Konigsburg, 70, author (Newbery for *The View From Saturday, From the Mixed-up Files of Mrs Basil E. Frankweiler*), born Elaine Lobl, New York, NY, Feb 10, 1930.

FEBRUARY 11 — FRIDAY
Day 42 — 324 Remaining

CAMEROON: YOUTH DAY. Feb 11. Public holiday.

EDISON, THOMAS ALVA: BIRTH ANNIVERSARY. Feb 11, 1847. American inventive genius and holder of more than 1,200 patents (including the incandescent electric lamp, phonograph, electric dynamo and key parts of many now-familiar devices such as the movie camera, telephone transmitter, etc). Edison said, "Genius is 1 percent inspiration and 99 percent perspiration." His birthday is now widely observed as Inventor's Day. Born at Milan, OH, and died at Menlo Park, NJ, Oct 18, 1931.

FULLER, MELVILLE WESTON: BIRTH ANNIVERSARY. Feb 11, 1833. Eighth chief justice of the US Supreme Court. Born at Augusta, ME, he died at Sorrento, ME, July 4, 1910.

IRAN, ISLAMIC REPUBLIC OF: NATIONAL DAY. Feb 11. National holiday. Commemorates the founding of the republic in 1979.

JAPAN: NATIONAL FOUNDATION DAY: ANNIVERSARY. Feb 11. Marks the founding of the Japanese nation. In 1872 the government officially set Feb 11, 660 BC, as the date of accession to the throne of the Emperor Jimmu (said to be Japan's first emperor) and designated the day a national holiday by the name of Empire Day. The holiday was abolished after WWII, but was revived as National Foundation Day in 1966. Ceremonies are held with Their Imperial Majesties the Emperor and Empress, the Prime Minister and other dignitaries attending. National holiday.

MANDELA, NELSON: PRISON RELEASE: 10th ANNIVERSARY. Feb 11, 1990. After serving more than 27½ years of a life sentence (convicted, with eight others, of sabotage and conspiracy to overthrow the government), South Africa's Nelson Mandela, 71 years old, walked away from the Victor Verster prison farm at Paarl, South Africa, a free man. He had survived the governmental system of apartheid. Mandela greeted a cheering throng of well-wishers, along with hundreds of millions of television viewers worldwide, with demands for an intensification of the struggle for equality for blacks, who make up nearly 75 percent of South Africa's population.

SPACE MILESTONE: *OSUMI* (JAPAN): 30th ANNIVERSARY. Feb 11, 1970. First Japanese satellite launched. Japan became fourth nation to send a satellite into space.

VATICAN CITY: INDEPENDENCE ANNIVERSARY. Feb 11, 1929. The Lateran Treaty, signed by Pietro Cardinal Gasparri and Benito Mussolini, guaranteed the independence of the State of Vatican City and recognized the sovereignty of the Holy See over it. Area is about 109 acres.

BIRTHDAYS TODAY

Brandy (Norwood), 21, singer, actress ("Cinderella," "Moesha"), born Macomb, MS, Feb 11, 1979.

Jeb Bush, 47, Governor of Florida (R), born Midland, TX, Feb 11, 1953.

Mel Carnahan, 66, Governor of Missouri (D), born Birch Tree, MO, Feb 11, 1934.

Matthew Lawrence, 20, actor ("Brotherly Love," "Boy Meets World"), born Abington, PA, Feb 11, 1980.

Mike Leavitt, 49, Governor of Utah (R), born Cedar City, UT, Feb 11, 1951.

Jane Yolen, 61, author (*Owl Moon*), born New York, NY, Feb 11, 1939.

FEBRUARY 12 — SATURDAY

Day 43 — 323 Remaining

ADAMS, LOUISA CATHERINE JOHNSON: 225th BIRTH ANNIVERSARY. Feb 12, 1775. Wife of John Quincy Adams, 6th president of the US. Born at London, England, she died at Washington, DC, May 14, 1852.

DARWIN, CHARLES ROBERT: BIRTH ANNIVERSARY. Feb 12, 1809. Author and naturalist born at Shrewsbury, England. Best remembered for his books *On the Origin of Species by Means of Natural Selection, or the Preservation of Favoured Races in the Struggle for Life* and *The Descent of Man and Selection in Relation to Sex*. Died at Down, Kent, England, Apr 19, 1882. For further info: *Charles Darwin: Revolutionary Biologist*, by J. Edward Evans (Lerner, 0-8225-4914-X, $21.50 Gr. 6–9).

KOSCIUSKO, THADDEUS: BIRTH ANNIVERSARY. Feb 12, 1746. Polish patriot and American Revolutionary War figure. Born at Lithuania, he died at Solothurn, Switzerland, Oct 15, 1817. The governor of Massachusetts proclaims the first Sunday in February as Kosciusko Day (Feb 6 in 2000).

LINCOLN, ABRAHAM: BIRTH ANNIVERSARY. Feb 12, 1809. Sixteenth president of the US (Mar 4, 1861–Apr 15, 1865) and the first to be assassinated (on Good Friday, Apr 14, 1865, at Ford's Theatre at Washington, DC). His presidency encompassed the tragic Civil War. Especially remembered are his Emancipation Proclamation (Jan 1, 1863) and his Gettysburg Address (Nov 19, 1863). Born at Hardin County, KY, he died at Washington, DC, Apr 15, 1865. Lincoln's birthday is observed as part of President's Day in most states, but is a legal holiday in Florida, Illinois and Kentucky and an optional bank holiday in Iowa, Maryland, Michigan, Pennsylvania, Washington and West Virginia. See also: "Presidents' Day," (Feb 21). For more info: *Lincoln: A Photobiography*, by Russell Freedman (Houghton Mifflin, 0-89-919380-3, $17 Gr. 4-6) and *Lincoln: In His Own Words*, edited by Milton Meltzer (Harcourt Brace, 0-15-245437-3, $22.95 Gr. 6-8). For links to Lincoln sites on the web, go to: deil.lang.uiuc.edu/web.pages/holidays/lincoln.html.

LOST PENNY DAY©. Feb 12. Today is set aside to put all of those pennies stashed in candy dishes, bowls and jars back in circulation. Take those pennies and give them to a shelter or agency that assists the homeless or your local Humane Society. Annually, on President Abraham Lincoln's birthday, the man depicted on the copper penny. For info: Adrienne Sioux Koopersmith, 1437 W Rosemont, #1W, Chicago, IL 60660-1319. Phone: (773) 743-5341. Fax: (773) 743-5395. E-mail: kooper@interaccess.com.

LUXEMBOURG: BURGSONNDEG. Feb 12. Young people build a huge bonfire on a hill to celebrate the victorious sun, marking the end of winter. A tradition dating to pre-Christian times.

MOON PHASE: FIRST QUARTER. Feb 12. Moon enters First Quarter phase at 6:21 PM, EST.

NAACP FOUNDED: ANNIVERSARY. Feb 12, 1909. The National Association for the Advancement of Colored People was founded by W.E.B. Dubois and Ida Wells-Barnett, among others, to wage a militant campaign against lynching and other forms of racial oppression. Its legal wing brought many lawsuits that successfully challenged segregation in the 1950s and 60s.

SAFETYPUP'S® BIRTHDAY. Feb 12. This year Safetypup®, created by the National Child Safety Council, joyously celebrates his birthday by bringing safety awareness/education messages to children in a positive, nonthreatening manner. Safetypup® has achieved a wonderful balance of safety sense, caution and childlike enthusiasm about life and helping kids "Stay Safe and Sound." For info: Barbara Handley Huggett, Dir, NCSC, Research and Development, Box 1368, Jackson, MI 49204-1368. Phone: (517) 764-6070.

BIRTHDAYS TODAY

Judy Blume, 62, author (*Blubber, Superfudge*), born Elizabeth, NJ, Feb 12, 1938.

Joanna Kerns, 47, actress ("Growing Pains"), born San Francisco, CA, Feb 12, 1953.

Christina Ricci, 20, actress (*Casper, Addams Family Values*), born Santa Monica, CA, Feb 12, 1980.

Arlen Specter, 70, US Senator (R, Pennsylvania), born Wichita, KS, Feb 12, 1930.

Jacqueline Woodson, 36, author (*I Hadn't Meant to Tell You This*), born Columbus, OH, Feb 12, 1964.

FEBRUARY 13 — SUNDAY

Day 44 — 322 Remaining

FIRST MAGAZINE PUBLISHED IN AMERICA: ANNIVERSARY. Feb 13, 1741. Andrew Bradford published *The American Magazine* just three days ahead of Benjamin Franklin's *General Magazine*.

GET A DIFFERENT NAME DAY. Feb 13. If you dislike your name, or merely find it boring, today is the day to adopt the moniker of your choice. [© 1998 by WPL] For info: Thomas or Ruth Roy, Wellness Permission League, PO Box 662, Mt Gretna, PA 17064-0662. Phone: (717) 964-1308. Fax: (717) 964-1335. E-mail: wellcat@desupernet.net.

HOMES FOR BIRDS WEEK. Feb 13–19. A week to encourage people to clean out, fix up and put up homes for wild birds. Annually, the third week in February. For info: John F. Gardner, Pres, Wild Bird Marketplace, 1891 Santa Barbara Dr, Ste 106, Lancaster, PA 17601. Phone: (717) 581-5310. Fax: (717) 581-5312. E-mail: jfg@wildbird.com. Web: www.wildbird.com.

TRUMAN, BESS (ELIZABETH) VIRGINIA WALLACE: BIRTH ANNIVERSARY. Feb 13, 1885. Wife of Harry S Truman, 33rd president of the US. Born at Independence, MO and died there Oct 18, 1982.

WOOD, GRANT: BIRTH ANNIVERSARY. Feb 13, 1892. American artist, especially noted for his powerful realism and satirical paintings of the American scene, was born near Anamosa, IA. He was a printer, sculptor, woodworker and high school and college teacher. Among his best-remembered works are *American Gothic, Fall Plowing* and *Stone City*. Died at Iowa City, IA, Feb 12, 1942.

BIRTHDAYS TODAY

Janet Taylor Lisle, 53, author (*Afternoon of the Elves*), born Englewood, NJ, Feb 13, 1947.

Ouida Sebestyen, 76, author (*Words by Heart*), born Vernon, TX, Feb 13, 1924.

Simms Taback, 68, author and illustrator (*There Was an Old Lady Who Swallowed a Fly*), born New York, NY, Feb 13, 1932.

Chuck Yeager, 77, pilot who broke sound barrier, born Myra, WV, Feb 13, 1923.

FEBRUARY 14 — MONDAY

Day 45 — 321 Remaining

ARIZONA: ADMISSION DAY: ANNIVERSARY. Feb 14. Became the 48th state in 1912.

FERRIS WHEEL DAY. Feb 14, 1859. Anniversary of the birth of George Washington Gale Ferris, American engineer and inventor, at Galesburg, IL. Among his many accomplishments as a civil engineer, Ferris is best remembered as the inventor of the Ferris wheel, which he developed for the World's Columbian Exposition

February *2000*	S	M	T	W	T	F	S
			1	2	3	4	5
	6	7	8	9	10	11	12
	13	14	15	16	17	18	19
	20	21	22	23	24	25	26
	27	28	29				

at Chicago, IL, in 1893. Built on the Midway Plaisance, the 250-feet-in-diameter Ferris wheel (with 36 coaches, each capable of carrying 40 passengers), proved one of the greatest attractions of the fair. It was America's answer to the Eiffel Tower of the Paris International Exposition of 1889. Ferris died at Pittsburgh, PA, Nov 22, 1896.

FIRST PRESIDENTIAL PHOTOGRAPH: ANNIVERSARY. Feb 14, 1849. President James Polk became the first US president to be photographed while in office. The photographer was Mathew B. Brady, who would become famous for his photography during the American Civil War.

OREGON: ADMISSION DAY: ANNIVERSARY. Feb 14. Became 33rd state in 1859.

RACE RELATIONS DAY. Feb 14. A day designated by some churches to recognize the importance of interracial relations. Formerly was observed on Abraham Lincoln's birthday or on the Sunday preceding it. Since 1970 observance has generally been Feb 14.

RANDOM ACTS OF KINDNESS WEEK. Feb 14–20. A global grass roots awareness campaign and celebration of the power of Random Acts of Kindness as a counterbalance to random acts of violence. Our goal is to reverse the tide of anger and violence in our society by deepening our connection with others through the practice of simple, day-to-day kindness to our fellow humankind. Annually, Monday–Sunday including Feb 14. For info: Melissa Fumia, Dir, Random Acts of Kindness Foundation, 2322 6th St, Ste 106, Berkeley, CA 94710. Phone: (510) 845-2471. Fax: (510) 845-2142. E-mail: rakday@aol.com. Web: www.ReadersNdex.com/randomacts/

READ TO YOUR CHILD DAY. Feb 14. Motto: "Show your kids you love them: Read to them." To encourage parents, teachers and other caregivers to engage in the wonderfully beneficial and delightfully fun practice of reading to children. A packet of materials is available, including ideas for campaigns to promote literacy, plus reproducible flyers on classroom reading, family reading at home and sharing books with babies. Flyers describe the benefits of read-aloud sessions, give tips for oral reading and list books people can read for more information. Annually, on Valentine's Day. For packet send business-sized, stamped, self-addressed envelope plus two first class stamps tucked inside (to cover photocopy expenses) to Dee Anderson, 1023 25 St, #1, Moline, IL 61265.

VALENTINE'S DAY. Feb 14. St. Valentine's Day celebrates the feasts of two Christian martyrs of this name. One, a priest and physician, was beheaded at Rome, Italy, Feb 14, AD 269, during the reign of Emperor Claudius II. Another Valentine, the Bishop of Terni, is said to have been beheaded, also at Rome, Feb 14 (possibly in a later year). Both history and legend are vague and contradictory about details of the Valentines and some say that Feb 14 was selected for the celebration of Christian martyrs as a diversion from the ancient pagan observance of Lupercalia. An old legend has it that birds choose their mates on Valentine's Day. Now it is one of the most widely observed unofficial holidays. It is an occasion for the exchange of gifts (usually books, flowers or sweets) and greeting cards with affectionate or humorous messages. For links to Valentine's Day sites on the web go to: deil.lang.uiuc.edu/web.pages/holidays/valentine.html.

BIRTHDAYS TODAY

Drew Bledsoe, 28, football player, born Ellensburg, WA, Feb 14, 1972.

Judd Gregg, 53, US Senator (R, New Hampshire), born Nashua, NH, Feb 14, 1947.

Jamake Highwater, 58, author (*Anpao: An American Indian Odyssey*), born Glacier County, MT, Feb 14, 1942.

Donna Shalala, 59, US Secretary of Health and Human Services (Clinton administration), born Cleveland, OH, Feb 14, 1941.

Paul O. Zelinsky, 47, illustrator (Caldecott for *Rapunzel*), born Evanston, IL, Feb 14, 1953.

FEBRUARY 15 — TUESDAY
Day 46 — 320 Remaining

CLARK, ABRAHAM: BIRTH ANNIVERSARY. Feb 15, 1726. Signer of the Declaration of Independence, farmer and lawyer. Born at Elizabethtown, NJ and died there Sept 15, 1794.

GALILEI, GALILEO: BIRTH ANNIVERSARY. Feb 15, 1564. Physicist and astronomer who helped overthrow medieval concepts of the world, born at Pisa, Italy. He proved the theory that

---

FEBRUARY 15
GALILEO

Give the science curriculum a February boost by celebrating Galileo's birthday. Although Galileo didn't invent the telescope, he improved the lens and began stargazing. His observations of planetary motions converted him to Copernicus' theory of a sun-centered solar system, a personal "discovery" that led to heresy charges by the Roman Catholic Church. In 1610, he discovered four moons that circle Jupiter.

If possible, borrow a telescope. Ask students to write how it changes their perceptions of distant objects. With parental coordination, organize an evening in the classroom when students can look at the stars through the telescope. Ahead of time, choose one or two constellations (the Big Dipper is an easily spotted one) that students can search for. Many cultures have myths about the formation of constellations. Students can write their own explanations.

Planetary mobiles really brighten up a classroom, as do dioramas. Making constellations with cellophane and construction paper is another colorful classroom decoration. Scratch board-style crayon artwork (with black crayon covering an underlayer of colors) is also fun.

Pisa, Galileo's birthplace, is a quick geography and science link. The Leaning Tower is a landmark with world recognition. Students can research what has caused the tower to lean.

Older students (junior high) could read Bertolt Brecht's play *Galileo* and enact scenes as Reader's Theater. Involve the class in a discussion of Galileo's imprisonment in later life for adhering to beliefs he held. *Starry Messenger*, by Peter Sís (Farrar, Straus, 0-374-37191-1, $16 Gr. 2–6) is another literature connection.

NASA has chosen to honor Galileo by naming a spacecraft after him. In 1995 the spacecraft *Galileo* entered the orbit of Jupiter after taking six years to journey there. (See the entry for Dec 7.) It continues to orbit, studying several of Jupiter's moons. Older students will want to visit NASA's *Galileo* website at www.jpl.nasa.gov/galileo/index.html. The site also has a Galileo Education Resources page for K-12 teachers at www.jpl.nasa.gov/galileo/education.html.

---

all bodies, large and small, descend at equal speed and gathered evidence to support Copernicus's theory that the Earth and other planets revolve around the sun. Galileo died at Florence, Italy, Jan 8, 1642. See Curriculum Connection.

SUTTER, JOHN AUGUSTUS: BIRTH ANNIVERSARY. Feb 15, 1803. Born at Kandern, Germany, Sutter established the first white settlement on the site of Sacramento, CA, in 1839, and owned a large tract of land there, which he named New Helvetia. The first great gold strike in the US was on his property, at Sutter's Mill, Jan 24, 1848. His land was soon overrun by gold seekers who, he claimed, slaughtered his cattle and stole or destroyed his property. Sutter was bankrupt by 1852. Died at Washington, DC, June 18, 1880.

BIRTHDAYS TODAY

Norman R. Bridwell, 72, author and illustrator (*Clifford, the Big Red Dog*), born Kokomo, IN, Feb 15, 1928.

Matt Groening, 46, cartoonist ("The Simpsons"), born Portland, OR, Feb 15, 1954.

Doris Orgel, 71, author (*The Devil in Vienna*), born Vienna, Austria, Feb 15, 1929.

FEBRUARY 16 — WEDNESDAY
Day 47 — 319 Remaining

ASSOCIATION FOR EDUCATIONAL COMMUNICATION AND TECHNOLOGY CONFERENCE. Feb 16–20. Long Beach, CA. For info: Assn for Educational Communication and Technology, 1025 Vermont Ave NW, Ste 820, Washington, DC 20005-3516. Phone: (202) 347-7834. Fax: (202) 347-7839. Web: www.aect.org.

HEART 2 HEART DAY. Feb 16. Confide something to your diary—start young and you'll write a whole book before you know it! Annually, two days after Valentine's Day. For info: Fine Print Publishing Co, PO Box 916401, Longwood, FL 32791-6401. Phone: (407) 814-7777. Fax: (407) 814-7677.

LITHUANIA: INDEPENDENCE DAY. Feb 16. National Day. The anniversary of Lithuania's declaration of independence in 1918 is observed as the Baltic state's Independence Day. In 1940, Lithuania became a part of the Soviet Union under an agreement between Joseph Stalin and Adolf Hitler. On Mar 11, 1990, Lithuania declared its independence from the Soviet Union, the first of the Soviet republics to do so. After demanding independence, Lithuania set up a border police force and aided young men in efforts to avoid the Soviet military draft, prompting then Soviet leader Mikhail Gorbachev to send tanks into the capital of Vilnius and impose oil and gas embargoes. In the wake of the failed coup attempt in Moscow Aug 19, 1991, Lithuanian independence finally was recognized.

WILSON, HENRY: BIRTH ANNIVERSARY. Feb 16, 1812. Eighteenth vice president of the US (1873–75). Born at Farmington, NH, died at Washington, DC, Nov 22, 1875.

BIRTHDAYS TODAY

Jerome Bettis, 28, football player, born Detroit, MI, Feb 16, 1972.

FEBRUARY 17 — THURSDAY
Day 48 — 318 Remaining

GERONIMO: DEATH ANNIVERSARY. Feb 17, 1909. American Indian of the Chiricahua (Apache) tribe was born about 1829 in Arizona. He was the leader of a small band of warriors whose devastating raids in Arizona, New Mexico and Mexico caused the

US Army to send 5,000 men to recapture him after his first escape. He was confined at Fort Sill, OK, where he died Feb 17, 1909, after dictating, for publication, the story of his life.

NATIONAL PTA FOUNDERS' DAY: ANNIVERSARY. Feb 17, 1897. Celebrates the PTA's founding by Phoebe Apperson Hearst and Alice McLellan Birney. For info: Natl PTA, 330 N Wabash, Ste 2100, Chicago, IL 60611. Phone: (312) 670-6782. Fax: (312) 670-6783. E-mail: info@pta.org. Web: www.pta.org.

BIRTHDAYS TODAY

Joseph Gordon-Levitt, 19, actor ("3rd Rock from the Sun," *Halloween H20*), born Los Angeles, CA, Feb 17, 1981.

Michael Jeffrey Jordan, 37, former basketball player, former minor league baseball player, born Brooklyn, NY, Feb 17, 1963.

Robert Newton Peck, 72, author (the Soup series, *A Day No Pigs Would Die*), born Vermont, Feb 17, 1928.

Craig Thomas, 67, US Senator (R, Wyoming), born Cody, WY, Feb 17, 1933.

FEBRUARY 18 — FRIDAY
Day 49 — 317 Remaining

COW MILKED WHILE FLYING IN AN AIRPLANE: 70th ANNIVERSARY. Feb 18, 1930. Elm Farm Ollie became the first cow to fly in an airplane. During the flight, which was attended by reporters, she was milked and the milk was sealed in paper containers and parachuted over St. Louis, MO.

DAVIS, JEFFERSON: INAUGURATION ANNIVERSARY. Feb 18, 1861. In the years before the Civil War, Jefferson Davis was the acknowledged leader of the Southern bloc in the US Senate and a champion of states' rights, but he had little to do with the secessionist movement until after his home state of Mississippi joined the Confederacy Jan 9, 1861. Davis withdrew from the Senate that same day. He was unanimously chosen as president of the Confederacy's provisional government and inaugurated at Montgomery, AL, Feb 18. Within the next year he was elected to a six-year term by popular vote and was inaugurated a second time Feb 22, 1862, at Richmond, VA.

GAMBIA: INDEPENDENCE DAY: 35th ANNIVERSARY. Feb 18, 1965. National holiday. Independence from Britain granted. Referendum in April 1970 established Gambia as a republic within the Commonwealth.

BIRTHDAYS TODAY

John William Warner, 73, US Senator (R, Virginia), born Washington, DC, Feb 18, 1927.

FEBRUARY 19 — SATURDAY
Day 50 — 316 Remaining

CHINA: LANTERN FESTIVAL. Feb 19. Traditional Chinese festival falls on 15th day of first month of Chinese lunar calendar year. Lantern processions mark end of the Chinese New Year holiday season. See also: "Chinese New Year" (Feb 5).

COPERNICUS, NICOLAUS: BIRTH ANNIVERSARY. Feb 19, 1473. Polish astronomer and priest who revolutionized scientific

thought with what came to be called the Copernican theory, that placed the sun instead of the Earth at the center of our planetary system. Born at Torun, Poland, died at East Prussia, May 24, 1543.

JAPANESE INTERNMENT: ANNIVERSARY. Feb 19, 1942. As a result of President Franklin Roosevelt's Executive Order 9066, some 110,000 Japanese-Americans living in coastal Pacific areas were placed in concentration camps in remote areas of Arizona, Arkansas, inland California, Colorado, Idaho, Utah and Wyoming. The interned Japanese-Americans (two-thirds were US citizens) lost an estimated $400 million in property. For more info: *Life in a Japanese American Internment Camp*, by Diane Yancey (Lucent, 1-56006-345-9, $17.96 Gr. 6-12).

MOON PHASE: FULL MOON. Feb 19. Moon enters Full Moon phase at 11:27 AM, EST.

TAIWAN: LANTERN FESTIVAL AND TOURISM DAY. Feb 19. Fifteenth day of the First Moon of the lunar calendar marks end of New Year holiday season. Lantern processions and contests.

BIRTHDAYS TODAY

Jeff Daniels, 45, actor (*101 Dalmatians, Fly Away Home*), born Chelsea, MI, Feb 19, 1955.

Jill Krementz, 60, author and photographer (*A Very Young Dancer*, the How It Feels series), born New York, NY, Feb 19, 1940.

FEBRUARY 20 — SUNDAY
Day 51 — 315 Remaining

ADAMS, ANSEL: BIRTH ANNIVERSARY. Feb 20, 1902. American photographer, known for his photographs of Yosemite National Park, born at San Francisco, CA. Adams died at Monterey, CA, Apr 22, 1984.

BROTHERHOOD/SISTERHOOD WEEK. Feb 20–26. A kickoff period for programs emphasizing a commitment to brotherhood/sisterhood. The National Program Office develops educational materials for use during this period that can be used year round. Annually, the third full week in February. Sponsor: The National Conference (founded as the National Conference of Christians and Jews). For info: The Natl Conference, 71 Fifth Ave, New York, NY 10003. Phone: (212) 206-0006.

DOUGLASS, FREDERICK: DEATH ANNIVERSARY. Feb 20, 1895. American journalist, orator and antislavery leader. Born at Tuckahoe, MD, probably in February 1817. Died at Anacostia Heights, Washington, DC. His original name before his escape from slavery was Frederick Augustus Washington Bailey.

NATIONAL ENGINEERS WEEK. Feb 20–26. The 50th annual observance, cosponsored by 21 national engineering societies and 15 major national corporations, will feature classroom programs in elementary and secondary schools throughout the US, shopping mall exhibits, engineering workplace tours and other events. Also, the Future Cities Competition national finals held at Washington, DC. For more info: Natl Engineers Week Headquarters, 1420 King St, Alexandria, VA 22314. Phone: (703) 684-2852. E-mail: eweek@nspe.org. Web: www.eweek.org.

NORTHERN HEMISPHERE HOODIE-HOO DAY. Feb 20. At high noon (local time) citizens are asked to go outdoors and yell "Hoodie-Hoo" to chase away winter and make ready for spring, one month away. [© 1998 by WPL] For info: Tom or Ruth Roy, Wellness Permission League, PO Box 662, Mt Gretna, PA 17064-0662. Phone: (717) 964-1308. Fax: (717) 964-1335. E-mail: wellcat @desupernet.net.

February 2000	S	M	T	W	T	F	S
			1	2	3	4	5
	6	7	8	9	10	11	12
	13	14	15	16	17	18	19
	20	21	22	23	24	25	26
	27	28	29				

PISCES, THE FISH. Feb 20–Mar 20. In the astronomical/astrological zodiac, which divides the sun's apparent orbit into 12 segments, the period Feb 20–Mar 20 is identified, traditionally, as the sun sign of Pisces, the Fish. The ruling planet is Neptune.

SPACE MILESTONE: *FRIENDSHIP 7* (US): FIRST AMERICAN TO ORBIT EARTH. Feb 20, 1962. John Herschel Glenn, Jr, became the first American, and the third man, to orbit Earth. Aboard the capsule *Friendship 7*, he made three orbits of Earth. Spacecraft was *Mercury-Atlas 6*. In 1998 the 77-year-old Glenn went into space once again on the space shuttle *Discovery* to study the effects of aging.

SPACE MILESTONE: *MIR* SPACE STATION (USSR). Feb 20, 1986. A "third-generation" orbiting space station, *Mir* (Peace), was launched without crew from the Baikonur space center at Leninsk, Kazakhstan. Believed to be 40 feet long, weigh 47 tons and have six docking ports. Russian and American crews have used the station for more than 10 years. After many equipment failures in 1998, the Russians decided to take Mir out of service in 1999.

STUDENT VOLUNTEER DAY. Feb 20. To honor students who give of themselves and of their personal time to improve the lives of others and their communities. Annually, Feb 20. Est attendance: 250. For info: Susquehanna Univ, Center for Service Learning and Volunteer Programs, 514 University Avenue, Selinsgrove, PA 17870-1001. Phone: (717) 372-4139. Fax: (717) 372-2745. E-mail: woodsd@susqu.edu.

BIRTHDAYS TODAY

Charles Wade Barkley, 37, basketball player, born Leeds, AL, Feb 20, 1963.

Mitch McConnell, 58, US Senator (R, Kentucky), born Colbert County, AL, Feb 20, 1942.

FEBRUARY 21 — MONDAY

Day 52 — 314 Remaining

BANGLADESH: MARTYRS DAY. Feb 21. National mourning day or Shaheed Day in memory of martyrs of the Bengali Language Movement in 1952.

BATTLE OF VERDUN: ANNIVERSARY. Feb 21–Dec 18, 1916. The German High Command launched an offensive on the Western Front at Verdun, France which became WWI's single longest battle. An estimated one million men were killed, decimating both the German and French armies.

FIRST WOMAN TO GRADUATE FROM DENTAL SCHOOL: ANNIVERSARY. Feb 21, 1866. Lucy Hobbs became the first woman to graduate from a dental school at Cincinnati, OH.

PRESIDENTS' DAY. Feb 21. Presidents' Day observes the birthdays of George Washington (Feb 22) and Abraham Lincoln (Feb 12). With the adoption of the Monday Holiday Law (which moved the observance of George Washington's birthday from Feb 22 each year to the third Monday in February), some of the specific significance of the event was lost and added impetus was given to the popular description of that holiday as Presidents' Day. Present usage often regards Presidents' Day as a day to honor all former presidents of the US. Annually, the third Monday in February. See Curriculum Connection.

WASHINGTON, GEORGE: BIRTHDAY OBSERVANCE (LEGAL HOLIDAY). Feb 21. Legal public holiday (Public Law 90–363 sets Washington's birthday observance on the third Monday in February each year—applicable to federal employees and

FEBRUARY 21
WASHINGTON MONUMENT DEDICATED
AND PRESIDENTS' DAY

The area in Washington, DC known as the Mall contains familiar US architectural monuments, especially those dedicated to presidents. Unfortunately, many children do not have the opportunity to visit our capital city. This year Presidents' Day falls on the dedication day (in 1885) of the Washington Monument. The year 2000 is also the 200th anniversary of the federal government's move from Philadelphia to the new city of Washington. In 1800, President John Adams and his family moved into the White House, Congress met for the first time in the new Capitol building and the Library of Congress was founded. There will be bicentennial celebrations in Washington this year commemorating these events. Start your class on a geography and history field trip to DC without actually leaving the room.

Divide your students into four groups, each representing a compass direction. Designate each wall as a direction of a compass. Through research, artwork and photographs, let your students bring the Mall in Washington DC, to your room. Students on the west wall would focus on the Lincoln Memorial, the Vietnam Veterans Memorial and the large reflecting pool. The south group works on the Franklin Delano Roosevelt and Thomas Jefferson Memorials. Those in the north group do the Washington Monument (which is actually in the center of the Mall) and the White House. There is also a new sculpture in the center of the Mall honoring nurses who served during war times. Members of the east group research the United States Capitol and the Library of Congress.

Small groups can give presentations to the class on the history of these buildings and biographies of the people they commemorate. Students can look for depictions of these memorials. For example, the Lincoln Memorial is on the penny and the $5 bill. The White House is on the $20 bill. Presentations might feature important events that took place during the years the presidents governed or events that have occurred in each building.

Learning center directors can steer you toward the many books available for young readers. Congressional representatives are usually glad to send a map and other information about the city (particularly tourist attractions) to a class that writes and requests them. If you have Internet access, the Library of Congress is online at www.loc.gov, the White House at www.whitehouse.gov and you can tour the capitol at www.senate.gov.

to the District of Columbia). Observed on this day in all states. See also: "Washington, George: Birth Anniversary" (Feb 22). For links to web sites about this holiday and George Washington, go to: deil.lang.uiuc.edu/web.pages/holidays/washington.html.

WASHINGTON MONUMENT DEDICATED: ANNIVERSARY. Feb 21, 1885. Monument to the first president was dedicated at Washington, DC. See Curriculum Connection.

BIRTHDAYS TODAY

Jennifer Love Hewitt, 21, actress (*I Know What You Did Last Summer*, "Party of Five"), born Waco, TX, Feb 21, 1979.

Victor Martinez, 46, author (National Book Award for *Parrot in the Oven: Mi Vida*), born Fresno, CA, Feb 21, 1954.

Olympia J. Snowe, 53, US Senator (R, Maine), born Augusta, ME, Feb 21, 1947.

FEBRUARY 22 — TUESDAY
Day 53 — 313 Remaining

BADEN-POWELL, ROBERT: BIRTH ANNIVERSARY. Feb 22, 1857. British army officer who founded the Boy Scouts and Girl Guides. Born at London, England, he died at Kenya, Africa, Jan 8, 1941.

MONTGOMERY BOYCOTT ARRESTS: ANNIVERSARY. Feb 22, 1956. On Feb 20 white city leaders of Montgomery, AL, issued an ultimatum to black organizers of the three-month-old Montgomery bus boycott. They said if the boycott ended immediately there would be "no retaliation whatsoever." If it did not end, it was made clear they would begin arresting black leaders. Two days later, 80 well-known boycotters, including Rosa Parks, Martin Luther King, Jr and E.D. Nixon, marched to the sheriff's office in the county courthouse, where they gave themselves up for arrest. They were booked, fingerprinted and photographed. The next day the story was carried by newspapers all over the world.

SAINT LUCIA: INDEPENDENCE DAY: ANNIVERSARY. Feb 22. National holiday. Commemorates independence from Britain in 1979.

WADLOW, ROBERT PERSHING: BIRTH ANNIVERSARY. Feb 22, 1918. Tallest man in recorded history, born at Alton, IL. Though only 9 lbs at birth, by age 10 Wadlow already stood more than 6 feet tall and weighed 210 lbs. When Wadlow died at age 22, he was a remarkable 8 feet 11.1 inches tall, 490 lbs. His gentle, friendly manner in the face of constant public attention earned him the name "Gentle Giant." Wadlow died July 15, 1940, at Manistee, MI, of complications resulting from a foot infection.

WASHINGTON, GEORGE: BIRTH ANNIVERSARY. Feb 22, 1732. First president of the US ("First in war, first in peace and first in the hearts of his countrymen" in the words of Henry "Light-Horse Harry" Lee). Born at Westmoreland County, VA, Feb 22 (New Style), Feb 11 (Old Style), 1732, he died at Mount Vernon, VA, Dec 14, 1799. See also: "Washington, George: Birthday Observance (Legal Holiday)" (Feb 21 in 2000).

WOOLWORTHS FIRST OPENED: ANNIVERSARY. Feb 22, 1879. First chain store, Woolworths, opened at Utica, NY. In 1997, the closing of the chain was announced.

BIRTHDAYS TODAY

Drew Barrymore, 25, actress (*Ever After*), born Los Angeles, CA, Feb 22, 1975.

Michael Te Pei Chang, 28, tennis player, born Hoboken, NJ, Feb 22, 1972.

	S	M	T	W	T	F	S
February			1	2	3	4	5
2000	6	7	8	9	10	11	12
	13	14	15	16	17	18	19
	20	21	22	23	24	25	26
	27	28	29				

Lisa Fernandez, 29, softball player, born Long Beach, CA, Feb 22, 1971.

William Frist, 48, US Senator (R, Tennessee), born Nashville, TN, Feb 22, 1952.

Edward Moore (Ted) Kennedy, 68, US Senator (D, Massachusetts), born Boston, MA, Feb 22, 1932.

Jayson Williams, 32, basketball player, born Ritter, SC, Feb 22, 1968.

FEBRUARY 23 — WEDNESDAY
Day 54 — 312 Remaining

BRUNEI DARUSSALAM: NATIONAL DAY. Feb 23. National holiday.

DUBOIS, W.E.B.: BIRTH ANNIVERSARY. Feb 23, 1868. William Edward Burghardt Dubois, American educator and leader of the movement for black equality. Born at Great Barrington, MA, he died at Accra, Ghana, Aug 27, 1963. "The cost of liberty," he wrote in 1909, "is less than the price of repression."

FIRST CLONING OF AN ADULT ANIMAL: ANNIVERSARY. Feb 23, 1997. Researchers in Scotland announced the first cloning of an adult animal, a lamb they named Dolly with a genetic makeup identical to that of her mother. This led to worldwide speculation about the possibility of human cloning. On Mar 4, President Clinton imposed a ban on the federal funding of human cloning research.

GUYANA: 30th ANNIVERSARY OF REPUBLIC. Feb 23, 1970. National holiday.

HANDEL, GEORGE FREDERICK: BIRTH ANNIVERSARY. Feb 23, 1685. Born at Halle, Saxony, Germany, Handel and Bach (See also: "Bach, Johann Sebastian: Birth Anniversary" [Mar 21]), born the same year, were perhaps the greatest masters of Baroque music. Handel's most frequently performed work is the oratorio *Messiah*, which was first heard in 1742. He died at London, England, Apr 14, 1759.

TAYLOR, GEORGE: DEATH ANNIVERSARY. Feb 23, 1781. Signer of the Declaration of Independence. Born 1716 at British Isles (exact date unknown). Died at Easton, PA.

BIRTHDAYS TODAY

Laura Geringer, 52, author (the Myth Men series), born New York, NY, Feb 23, 1948.

Patricia Richardson, 48, actress ("Home Improvement"), born Bethesda, MD, Feb 23, 1952.

Rodney Slater, 45, US Secretary of Transportation, born Tutwyler, MS, Feb 23, 1955.

FEBRUARY 24 — THURSDAY
Day 55 — 311 Remaining

ESTONIA: INDEPENDENCE DAY. Feb 24. National holiday. Commemorates declaration of independence from the Soviet Union in 1918. However, independence was brief; Estonia was to be part of the Soviet Union until 1991.

GREGORIAN CALENDAR DAY: ANNIVERSARY. Feb 24, 1582. Pope Gregory XIII, enlisting the expertise of distinguished astronomers and mathematicians, issued a bill correcting the Julian calendar that was then 10 days in error. The new calendar named for him, the Gregorian calendar, became effective Oct 4, 1582, in most Catholic countries, in 1752 in Britain and the American colonies, in 1918 in Russia and in 1923 in Greece. It is the most widely used calendar in the world today. See also: "Calendar Adjustment Day: Anniversary" (Sept 2) and "Gregorian Calendar Adjustment: Anniversary" (Oct 4).

GRIMM, WILHELM CARL: BIRTH ANNIVERSARY. Feb 24, 1786. Mythologist and author, born at Hanau, Germany. Best remembered for *Grimms' Fairy Tales*, in collaboration with his brother, Jacob. Died at Berlin, Germany, Dec 16, 1859. See also: "Grimm, Jacob: Birth Anniversary" (Jan 4).

VOTE TO IMPEACH PRESIDENT ANDREW JOHNSON: ANNIVERSARY. Feb 24, 1867. In a showdown over reconstruction policy following the Civil War, the House of Representatives voted to impeach President Andrew Johnson. During the two years following the end of the war, the Republican-controlled Congress had sought to severely punish the South by undoing the policies of President Johnson. Congress passed the Reconstruction Act that divided the South into five military districts headed by officers who were to take their orders from General Grant, the head of the army, instead of from President Johnson. In addition, Congress passed the Tenure of Office Act, which required Senate approval before Johnson could remove any official whose appointment was originally approved by the Senate. Johnson vetoed this act but the veto was overridden by Congress. To test the constitutionality of the act, Johnson dismissed Secretary of War Edwin Stanton, triggering the impeachment vote.

WAGNER, HONUS: BIRTH ANNIVERSARY. Feb 24, 1874. American baseball great, born John Peter Wagner at Carnegie, PA. Nicknamed the "Flying Dutchman," Wagner was among the first five players elected to the Baseball Hall of Fame in 1936. Died at Carnegie, Dec 6, 1955.

BIRTHDAYS TODAY

Beth Broderick, 41, actress ("Sabrina, the Teenage Witch"), born Long Beach, CA, Feb 24, 1959.

Steven Jobs, 45, founder of Apple computer company, born Los Altos, CA, Feb 24, 1955.

Joseph I. Lieberman, 58, US Senator (D, Connecticut), born Stamford, CT, Feb 24, 1942.

George Ryan, 66, Governor of Illinois (R), born Maquoketa, IA, Feb 24, 1934.

Don Siegelman, 54, Governor of Alabama (D), born Mobile, AL, Feb 24, 1946.

FEBRUARY 25 — FRIDAY

Day 56 — 310 Remaining

CLAY BECOMES HEAVYWEIGHT CHAMP: ANNIVERSARY. Feb 25, 1964. Twenty-two-year-old Cassius Clay (later Muhammad Ali) became world heavyweight boxing champion by defeating Sonny Liston. At the height of his athletic career Ali was well known for both his fighting ability and personal style. His most famous saying was, "I am the greatest!" In 1967 he was convicted of violating the Selective Service Act and was stripped of his title for refusing to be inducted into the armed services during the Vietnam War. Ali cited religious convictions as his reason for refusal. In 1971 the Supreme Court reversed the conviction. Ali is the only fighter to win the heavyweight title three separate times. He defended that title nine times.

KUWAIT: NATIONAL DAY. Feb 25. National holiday.

NATIONAL BANK CHARTERED BY CONGRESS: ANNIVERSARY. Feb 25, 1791. The First Bank of the US at Philadelphia, PA, was chartered. Proposed as a national (or central) bank by Alexander Hamilton, it lost its charter in 1811. The Second Bank of the US received a charter in 1816 which expired in 1836. Since that time, the US has had no central bank. Central banking functions are carried out by the Federal Reserve System, established in 1913.

RENOIR, PIERRE AUGUSTE: BIRTH ANNIVERSARY. Feb 25, 1841. Impressionist painter, born at Limoges, France, Renoir's paintings are known for their joy and sensuousness as well as his use of light. In his later years he was crippled by arthritis and would paint with the brush strapped to his hand. He died at Cagnes-sur-Mer, Provence, France, Dec 17, 1919.

BIRTHDAYS TODAY

Cynthia Voigt, 58, author (Newbery for *Dicey's Song*), born Boston, MA, Feb 25, 1942.

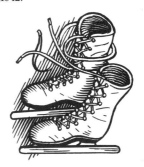

FEBRUARY 26 — SATURDAY

Day 57 — 309 Remaining

CODY, WILLIAM FREDERIC "BUFFALO BILL": BIRTH ANNIVERSARY. Feb 26, 1846. American frontiersman who claimed to have killed more than 4,000 buffaloes, born at Scott County, IA. Subject of many heroic yarns, Cody became successful as a showman, taking his Wild West Show across the US and to Europe. Died Jan 10, 1917, at Denver, CO.

FEDERAL COMMUNICATIONS COMMISSION CREATED: ANNIVERSARY. Feb 26, 1934. President Franklin D. Roosevelt ordered the creation of a Communications Commission, which became the FCC. It was created by Congress June 19, 1934 to oversee communication by radio, wire or cable. TV and satellite communication later became part of its charge.

GRAND CANYON NATIONAL PARK ESTABLISHED: ANNIVERSARY. Feb 26, 1919. By an act of Congress, Grand Canyon National Park was established. An immense gorge cut through the high plateaus of northwest Arizona by the raging Colorado River and covering 1,218,375 acres, Grand Canyon National Park is considered one of the most spectacular natural phenomena in the world. For further info: www.nps.gov/grca.

MOON PHASE: LAST QUARTER. Feb 26. Moon enters Last Quarter phase at 10:53 PM, EST.

STRAUSS, LEVI: BIRTH ANNIVERSARY. Feb 26, 1829. Bavarian immigrant Levi Strauss created the world's first pair of jeans—Levi's 501 jeans—for California's gold miners in 1850. Born at Buttenheim, Bavaria, Germany, he died in 1902.

BIRTHDAYS TODAY

Sarah Ezer, 19, actress ("The Adventures of Shirley Holmes: Detective"), born Vancouver, British Columbia, Feb 26, 1981.

Marshall Faulk, 27, football player, born New Orleans, LA, Feb 26, 1973.

Sharon Bell Mathis, 63, author (*The Hundred Penny Box*), born Atlantic City, NJ, Feb 26, 1937.

Jenny Thompson, 27, Olympic swimmer, born Dover, NH, Feb 26, 1973.

Bernard Wolf, 70, author of nonfiction (*HIV Positive*), born New York, NY, Feb 26, 1930.

FEBRUARY 27 — SUNDAY

Day 58 — 308 Remaining

DOMINICAN REPUBLIC: INDEPENDENCE DAY. Feb 27. National Day. Independence gained in 1844 with the withdrawal of Haitians, who had controlled the area for 22 years.

KUWAIT LIBERATED AND 100-HOUR WAR ENDS: ANNIVERSARY. Feb 27, 1991. Allied troops entered Kuwait City, Kuwait, four days after launching a ground offensive. President George Bush declared Kuwait to be liberated and ceased all offensive military operations in the Gulf War. The end of military operations at midnight EST came 100 hours after the beginning of the land attack.

LONGFELLOW, HENRY WADSWORTH: BIRTH ANNIVERSARY. Feb 27, 1807. American poet and writer born at Portland, ME. He is best remembered for his classic narrative poems, such as *The Song of Hiawatha, Paul Revere's Ride* and *The Wreck of the Hesperus*. Died at Cambridge, MA, Mar 24, 1882. For more info: *Henry Wadsworth Longfellow: America's Beloved Poet*, by Bonnie Lukes (Morgan Reynolds, 1-883846-31-5, $19.95 Gr. 6-12).

NO BRAINER DAY. Feb 27. This is a day where you can slack off, play hookey or find the easy way out. If you are going to do anything at all, make it a no brainer, something you can do without any serious thought. A drop in heart attacks is found on days like this-just what the doctor ordered. You have the rest of the year for a hectic schedule. For info: Adrienne Sioux Koopersmith, 1437 W Rosemont, 1W, Chicago, IL 60660-1319. Phone: (773) 743-5341. Fax: (773) 743-5395. E-mail: kooper@interaccess.com.

TWENTY-SECOND AMENDMENT TO US CONSTITUTION (TWO-TERM LIMIT): 50th RATIFICATION ANNIVERSARY. Feb 27, 1950. After the four successive presidential terms of Franklin Roosevelt, the 22nd Amendment limited the tenure of presidential office to two terms.

BIRTHDAYS TODAY

Uri Shulevitz, 65, author and illustrator (*The Treasure*), born Warsaw, Poland, Feb 27, 1935.

FEBRUARY 28 — MONDAY

Day 59 — 307 Remaining

TENNIEL, JOHN: BIRTH ANNIVERSARY. Feb 28, 1820. Illustrator and cartoonist, born at London, England. Best remembered for his illustrations for Lewis Carroll's *Alice's Adventures in Wonderland*. Died at London, Feb 25, 1914.

BIRTHDAYS TODAY

Eric Lindros, 27, hockey player, born London, Ontario, Feb 28, 1973.
Dean Smith, 69, basketball coach, born Emporia, KS, Feb 28, 1931.

FEBRUARY 29 — TUESDAY

Day 60 — 306 Remaining

LEAP YEAR DAY. Feb 29. A day added to the calendar to bring our calendar more nearly into accord with the Earth's orbital period (365.24219 days). This adjustment is made every four years except for century years that are not exactly divisible by 400. Since 2000 is exactly divisible by 400, it is a leap year, but 1900 was not. A "common year" (any year that is not a leap year) has an exact number of weeks (52) plus one day. That extra day means that if a given date falls on a Monday one year, it will fall on a Tuesday the next year. However, the rule changes for leap years, which have 52 weeks plus two days. After Feb 29, a date that fell on a Monday the previous year will fall on Wednesday during the leap year—it has leaped over a day. This "leap" will occur from Mar 1, 2000 through Feb 28, 2001.

LEE, ANN: BIRTH ANNIVERSARY. Feb 29, 1736. The founder of Shakerism in America, born at Manchester, England. In 1758, Ann Lee joined a society called the Shaking Quakers, or Shakers, which had been formed by Jane and James Wardley. Public confessing of sin, meditating, trembling, shaking, shouting, marching and singing characterized the society's form of worship. After serious health problems and the deaths of her four children in infancy, she became obsessed with the idea that sexual relations were sinful and began preaching celibacy. She was hailed as the Wardleys' successor and her positions on sex and marriage were incorporated in Shaker beliefs. At 38 Lee sailed for the American colonies, arriving at New York, NY, Aug 6, 1774. Lee joined a Shaker group near Albany. She became celebrated for the gift of tongues and an ability to work miracles and to cure diseases. Pacifists, the Shakers refused to bear arms in the American Revolution. Accused of British sympathies, Lee was charged with high treason July 17, 1780, and was jailed for 4½ months. She was regarded by many of her followers as a second coming of Christ. Known as "Ann the Word" or "Mother Ann." She died at Watervliet, NY, Sept 8, 1784.

BIRTHDAYS TODAY

David R. Collins, 60, author of biographies for children (*Arthur Ashe: Against the Wind*), born Marshalltown, IA, Feb 29, 1940.

March 2000

MARCH 1 — WEDNESDAY

Day 61 — 305 Remaining

★**AMERICAN RED CROSS MONTH.** Mar 1–31. Presidential Proclamation for Red Cross Month issued each year for March since 1943. Issued as American Red Cross Month since 1987.

THE ARRIVAL OF MARTIN PINZON: ANNIVERSARY.

Mar 1, 1493. Martin Alonzo Pinzon (1440–1493), Spanish shipbuilder and navigator (and co-owner of the *Niña* and the *Pinta*), accompanied Christopher Columbus on his first voyage, as commander of the *Pinta*. Storms separated the ships on their return voyage, and the *Pinta* first touched land at Bayona, Spain, where Pinzon gave Europe its first news of the discovery of the New World before Columbus's landing at Palos. Pinzon's brother, Vicente Yanez Pinzon, was commander of the third caravel of the expedition, the *Niña*.

ARTICLES OF CONFEDERATION RATIFIED: ANNIVERSARY.

Mar 1, 1781. This compact made among the original 13 states had been adopted by the Continental Congress Nov 15, 1777, and submitted to the states for ratification Nov 17, 1777. Maryland was the last state to approve, Feb 27, 1781, but Congress named Mar 1, 1781, as the day of formal ratification. The Articles of Confederation remained the supreme law of the nation until Mar 4, 1789, when Congress first met under the Constitution.

BIBLE WOMEN AWARENESS MONTH.

Mar 1–31. To help raise awareness of the women in the Bible and the stories of their lives which are role models for women today and the heritage of all who live in our Judeo-Christian society. For info send SASE: Christian Women's Ministries, PO Box 8716, Portland, OR 97207. E-mail: christine@christianwomen.com. Web: www.christian women.com/ministries.

BOSNIA AND HERZEGOVINA: INDEPENDENCE DAY.

Mar 1. Commemorates independence in 1991.

HEMOPHILIA MONTH.

Mar 1–31. For info: Natl Hemophilia Foundation, 116 W 32nd St, 11th Floor, New York, NY 10001. Phone: (800) 42-HANDI.

★**IRISH-AMERICAN HERITAGE MONTH.** Mar 1–31. Presidential Proclamation called for by House Joint Resolution 401 (PL 103–379).

JAPAN: OMIZUTORI (WATER-DRAWING FESTIVAL).

Mar 1–14. Todaiji, Nara. At midnight, a solemn rite is performed in the flickering light of pine torches. People rush for sparks from

MARCH 1–31
MUSIC IN OUR SCHOOLS MONTH

There are many ways to bring music into your classroom, even if you don't sing or play an instrument! Link recorded songs with literature: "Wild Thing," recorded by the Trogs, with *Where the Wild Things Are*, by Maurice Sendak (HarperCollins, 0-06-025492-0, $16.95 Gr. K–3); "Tar Beach," recorded by John Sebastian with *Tar Beach*, by Faith Ringgold (Crown, 0-5175-8031-4, $18.99 Gr. K–3); "What a Wonderful World," recorded by Louis Armstrong with *What a Wonderful World*, by G. D. Weiss and Bob Thiele (Atheneum, 0-68-980097-8, $16 All ages). On a folksy sing-a-long note link "Take Me Out to the Ballgame" with *Teammates*, by Peter Golenbock (Harcourt Brace, 0-15-200603-6, $16 Gr. K–3); "Frog Went A Courting" with *Frog Went A-Courtin'*, by John Langstaff (Harcourt Brace, 0-15-230214-X, $16 Gr. K–3) and "I Know an Old Lady Who Swallowed a Fly" with any of the several children's book versions. Even hearing impaired students can relate to music. See *Moses Goes to a Concert*, by Isaac Millman (Farrar Straus, 0-374-35067-1, $16 Gr. K–4) for a story about deaf children going to a concert.

To expose students to the classics, recordings are available of Sergei Prokofiev's symphonic fairy tale *Peter and the Wolf* (read aloud one of the many versions of this fairy tale), Saint-Saens' *Danse Macabre* (read aloud Cynthia de Felice's *The Dancing Skeleton* (Aladdin, 0-68-980453-9, $5.99 Gr. K–3) before playing this) and Maurice Ravel's orchestration of Mussorgsky's *Pictures at an Exhibition* (perfect for students to draw their ideas of what the pictures might look like).

Jazz is an authentically American art form. Explore it with recordings of Ella Fitzgerald (the Queen of Scat singing), Benny Goodman's big band sound, bebop by Charlie Parker and Thelonius Monk and Dixieland jazz. For noninstrumental fun check out Bobby McFerrin. It's hard to believe the musical sounds he makes—without any instruments!

The traditional music of Asia ranges from stringed instruments to Japan's Kodo Drummers. Try one of their recordings and your students will be hopping. South American traditional music tugs at your heart and your feet. Sukay is one of the many groups who record South American music. African pop music has become very popular in this country. Explore your library's music collection.

Invite students and parents who play instruments to talk about their instruments and play a tune or two. Perhaps some musically-inclined students would like to compose a song or a rap.

The way you bring music into your students' lives doesn't matter as much as the fact that you do it. Everyone relates to music—you just have to find the right kind. It will enrich students' lives in ways you could never imagine.

the torches, which are believed to have magic power against evil. Most spectacular on the night of Mar 12. The ceremony of drawing water is observed at 2 AM Mar 13, to the accompaniment of ancient Japanese music.

KOREA: SAMILJOL or INDEPENDENCE MOVEMENT DAY.

Mar 1. Koreans observe the anniversary of the independence movement against Japanese colonial rule in 1919.

MENTAL RETARDATION AWARENESS MONTH.

Mar 1–31. To educate the public about the needs of this nation's more than seven million citizens with mental retardation and about ways to prevent retardation. The Arc is a national organization on mental retardation, formerly the Association for Retarded Citizens. For info: Liz Moore, The Arc, 500 E Border St, Ste 300, Arlington, TX 76010. Phone: (817) 261-6003. Fax: (817) 277-3491. Web: thearc.org/welcome.html.

MUSIC IN OUR SCHOOLS MONTH. Mar 1–31. To draw public awareness to the importance of music education as part of a balanced curriculum. Additional information and awareness items are available from MENC. See Curriculum Connection. For info: Mark Trevino, Mgr Special Programs, Music Educators Natl Conference (MENC), 1806 Robert Fulton Dr, Reston, VA 20191. Phone: (800) 336-3768 or (703) 860-4000. Fax: (703) 860-1531.

NATIONAL CRAFT MONTH. Mar 1–31. Promoting the fun and creativity of hobbies and crafts. For info: Hobby Industry Assn, Natl Craft Month, Richartz and Fliss, 400 Morris Ave, Denville, NJ 07834. Phone: (973) 627-8180. Fax: (973) 672-8410. Web: www.i-craft.com. Info also available from: Assn of Crafts and Creative Industries, 1100-H Brandywine Blvd, PO Box 2188, Zanesville, OH 43702-2188. Phone: (614) 452-4541.

NATIONAL FROZEN FOOD MONTH. Mar 1–31. Promotes a national awareness of the economical and nutritional benefits of frozen foods. Annually, the month of March. For info: Lori B. Pohlman, VP Communications & New Media, Natl Frozen Food Assn, 4755 Linglestown Rd, Ste 300, Harrisburg, PA 17112. Phone: (717) 657-8601. Fax: (717) 657-9862. E-mail: nffm@nffa.org. Web: www.nffa.org.

NATIONAL MIDDLE LEVEL EDUCATION MONTH. Mar 1–31. To encourage middle level schools to schedule local events focusing on the educational needs of early adolescents. For info: Dir of Middle Level Services, Natl Assn of Secondary School Principals, 1904 Association Dr, Reston, VA 20190. Phone: (703) 860-7263.

NATIONAL NUTRITION MONTH. Mar 1–31. To educate consumers about the importance of good nutrition by providing the latest practical information on how simple it can be to eat healthfully. For info: The American Dietetic Assn, Natl Center for Nutrition and Dietetics, 216 W Jackson Blvd, Chicago, IL 60606-6995. Phone: (312) 899-0040. Fax: (312) 899-1739. E-mail: nnm@eat right.org. Web: www.eatright.org.

NATIONAL PIG DAY. Mar 1. To accord to the pig its rightful, though generally unrecognized, place as one of man's most intelligent and useful domesticated animals. Annually, Mar 1. For further information send SASE to: Ellen Stanley, 7006 Miami, Lubbock, TX 79413.

NATIONAL PROCRASTINATION WEEK. Mar 1–7. To promote the benefits of relaxing through putting off until tomorrow everything that needn't be done today. For info: Les Waas, Pres, Procrastinators' Club of America Inc, PO Box 712, Bryn Athyn, PA 19009. Phone: (215) 947-9020. Fax: (215) 947-7007.

NATIONAL TALK WITH YOUR TEEN ABOUT SEX MONTH. Mar 1–31. The importance of frank talk with teenagers about sex is emphasized. Parents are encouraged to provide their teenage children with current, accurate information and open lines for communication, as well as support their self-esteem, reduce misinformation and guide teenagers toward making responsible decisions regarding sex. Annually, the month of March. For info send SASE to: Teresa Langston, Dir, Parenting

	S	M	T	W	T	F	S
March				1	2	3	4
2000	5	6	7	8	9	10	11
	12	13	14	15	16	17	18
	19	20	21	22	23	24	25
	26	27	28	29	30	31	

MARCH 1–31
WOMEN'S HISTORY MONTH

There have been two movements for women's rights in this country. Elizabeth Cady Stanton and Susan B. Anthony were among the early crusaders for women's rights in the nineteenth century. Like many in the women's suffrage movement, they were both abolitionists. Their ideas that women should have voting rights, equal educational opportunities and the right to own property were radical and hotly contested. It was not until 1920 that women finally won the right to vote with the passage of the Nineteenth Amendment to the Constitution.

The first Woman's Rights Convention was held July 19, 1848, at Seneca Falls, NY. After learning about the convention, middle grade students can make posters and banners that they might have carried if they were representatives attending the first Convention. Ask your students to draw political cartoons about women's suffrage.

Stanton and Anthony pioneered many women's rights issues. Junior high students can research, then compare and contrast them with issues raised during the equal rights movements of the 1960s and 1970s, the second wave of the women's movement. Betty Friedan and Gloria Steinem figured prominently in that movement. Now that women had the vote, what were the issues raised by the equal rights movement? What does the word feminism mean? Did the equal rights movement only benefit women or were there benefits for men as well? Students might want to read back issues of *MS* magazine. They can also survey women in their families and find out how the movement has affected their lives. In what way, if any, did they participate or benefit?

Women's fashions have changed in many ways throughout history. Discuss how wearing trousers changed women's lives. Compare and contrast historical conceptions of beauty with modern ideas. The tradition of Chinese foot binding, the European custom of removing a rib or two to achieve a tiny waist and today's craze for body piercing, tattooing and henna decoration are topics that will interest students.

There is a wealth of children's literature about famous women and their contributions to the sciences, the arts and politics but *Seven Brave Women*, by Betsy Hearne (Morrow, 0-688-14502-7, $15 All ages) is an outstanding book that celebrates the importance of contributions that fall outside the category of fame. This picture book describes seven generations of women in one family who demonstrated bravery by conquering the challenges of everyday living.

Young Oxford History of Women in the United States, edited by Nancy Cott (11 vols, Oxford University Press, 0-19-508830-1, $242 Gr. 6 & up) is an excellent survey of American women's history.

Without Pressure (PWOP), 1330 Boyer St, Longwood, FL 32750-6311. Phone: (407) 767-2524.

NATIONAL UMBRELLA MONTH. Mar 1–31. In honor of one of the most versatile and underrated inventions of the human race, this month is dedicated to the purchase, use of and conversation about umbrellas. Annually, the month of March. For info: Thomas Edward Knibb, 8819 Adventure Ave, Walkersville, MD 21793-7828. Phone: (301) 898-3009. E-mail: tomknibb@hotmail .com.

NATIONAL WOMEN'S HISTORY MONTH. Mar 1–31. A time for reexamining and celebrating the wide range of women's contributions and achievements that are too often overlooked in the telling of US history. A theme kit on Women's History Month for

Simplify your life
with The Teacher's Calendar . . .

We offer you a complete day-by-day calendar that lets you find out quickly what's going on—today . . . tomorrow . . . every day of the year—and to plan ahead. It's easy to make sure you receive the newest edition of *The Teacher's Calendar* as soon as it is available.

Simply return one of the Pre-Publication Order Forms below. Your copy of *The Teacher's Calendar, 2000–2001* will be reserved immediately and shipped just as soon as it is off the press.

This convenient order option carries our unconditional guarantee—you may return *The Teacher's Calendar* for any reason within 10 days of receipt for a full refund. Why not order today and be sure of starting the 2000–2001 school year with *The Teacher's Calendar* at your fingertips!

The Teacher's Calendar, 2000–2001

Mail to: NTC/Contemporary Publishing Group

4255 W. Touhy Ave., Lincolnwood, IL 60646-1975

YES! Send me _____ copies of

The Teacher's Calendar, 2000–2001 at $19.95 each*

   Quantity Discounts:

   Deduct 10% per copy for 3–9 copies

   Deduct 20% per copy for 10 or more copies $ _____

Sales Tax:

   Add applicable tax in AL, CA, FL, IL, NC, NJ,

   NY, OH, PA, TX, WA $ _____

Shipping and Handling:

   Add $5.00 for first copy, $3.50 for each

   additional copy $ _____

☐ Check ☐ Money Order

   (payable to NTC/Contemporary Publishing Group)   TOTAL $ _____

☐ VISA ☐ MasterCard ☐ AmEx ☐ Discover

Acct. _____ Exp. ___/___

X_____

Signature if charging to bank card

_____

Name (please print)

SHIP TO:

_____

Name

_____

Address

_____

Address

_____

City   State   Zip

*Prices subject to change without notice.

Mail to: NTC/Contemporary Publishing Group

4255 W. Touhy Ave., Lincolnwood, IL 60646-1975

YES! Send me _____ copies of

The Teacher's Calendar, 2000–2001 at $19.95 each*

   Quantity Discounts:

   Deduct 10% per copy for 3–9 copies

   Deduct 20% per copy for 10 or more copies $ _____

Sales Tax:

   Add applicable tax in AL, CA, FL, IL, NC, NJ,

   NY, OH, PA, TX, WA $ _____

Shipping and Handling:

   Add $5.00 for first copy, $3.50 for each

   additional copy $ _____

☐ Check ☐ Money Order

   (payable to NTC/Contemporary Publishing Group)   TOTAL $ _____

☐ VISA ☐ MasterCard ☐ AmEx ☐ Discover

Acct. _____ Exp. ___/___

X_____

Signature if charging to bank card

_____

Name (please print)

SHIP TO:

_____

Name

_____

Address

_____

Address

_____

City   State   Zip

*Prices subject to change without notice.

grades 5-12 is available each year from the National Women's History Project. See Curriculum Connection. For info: Natl Women's History Project, 7738 Bell Rd, Dept P, Windsor, CA 95492. Phone: (707) 838-6000. Fax: (707) 838-0478. E-mail: nwhp@aol.com. Web: www.nwhp.org.

NATIONAL ASSOCIATION OF INDEPENDENT SCHOOLS ANNUAL CONFERENCE. Mar 1–4. Baltimore, MD. For info: Natl Assn of Independent Schools, 1620 L St NW, Ste 1100, Washington, DC 20036. Phone: (202) 973-9700. E-mail: confpreview@ nais-schools.org. Web: www.nais.org.

NEBRASKA: ADMISSION DAY: ANNIVERSARY. Mar 1. Became 37th state in 1867.

NEWSCURRENTS STUDENT EDITORIAL CARTOON CONTEST DEADLINE. Mar 1. Students in grades K-12 can win US Savings Bonds and get their work published in a national book by entering the annual Newscurrents Student Editorial Cartoon Contest. Participants must submit original cartoons on any subject of nationwide interest. Complete rules available. For info: Jeff Robbins, Knowledge Unlimited, PO Box 52, Madison, WI 53701. Phone: (800) 356-2303. Fax: (800) 618-1570. E-mail: jrobbins@ku.com. Web: www.knowledgeunlimited.com.

OHIO: ADMISSION DAY: ANNIVERSARY. Mar 1. Became 17th state in 1803.

OPTIMISM MONTH. Mar 1–31. To encourage people to boost their optimism. Research proves optimists achieve more health, prosperity and happiness than pessimists. Use this month-long celebration to practice optimism and turn optimism into a delightful, permanent habit. Free "Tip Sheets" available. For info: Dr. Michael Mercer & Dr. Maryann Troiani, The Mercer Group, Inc, 25597 Drake Rd, Barrington, IL 60010. Phone: (847) 382-0690. For media interviews, Victoria Sterling. Phone: (847) 382-6420.

PEACE CORPS FOUNDED: ANNIVERSARY. Mar 1, 1961. Official establishment of the Peace Corps by President John F. Kennedy's signing of executive order. The Peace Corps has sent more than 150,000 volunteers to 132 developing countries to help people help themselves. The volunteers assist in projects such as health, education, water sanitation, agriculture, nutrition and forestry. For info: Peace Corps, 1990 K St, Washington, DC 20526. Phone: (800) 424-8580 or (202) 606-3010. Fax: (202) 606-3110. Web: www.peacecorps.gov.

PLAY-THE-RECORDER MONTH. Mar 1–31. American Recorder Society members all over the continent will celebrate the organization's annual Play-the-Recorder Month by performing in public places such as libraries, bookstores, museums and shopping malls. Some will offer workshops on playing the recorder or demonstrations in schools. Founded in 1939, the ARS is the membership organization for all recorder players, including amateurs to leading professionals. Annually, the month of March. For info: American Recorder Soc, PO Box 631, Littleton, CO 80160-0631. Phone: (303) 347-1120. E-mail: recorder@compuserve.com.

RED CROSS MONTH. Mar 1–31. To make the public aware of American Red Cross service in the community. There are some 1,300 Red Cross offices nationwide; each local office plans its own activities. For info on activities in your area, contact your local Red Cross office. For info: American Red Cross Natl HQ, Public Inquiry Center, 8111 Gatehouse Rd, Falls Church, VA 22042. Phone: (703) 206-7090. Fax: (703) 206-7507. E-mail: info@usa.redcross.org. Web: www.redcross.org.

RETURN THE BORROWED BOOKS WEEK. Mar 1–7. To remind you to make room for those precious old volumes that will be returned to you, by cleaning out all that worthless trash that your friends are waiting for. Annually, the first seven days of March. For info: Inter-Global Society for Prevention of Cruelty to Cartoonists, Al Kaelin, Secy, 3119 Chadwick Dr, Los Angeles, CA 90032. Phone: (213) 221-7909.

SLAYTON, DONALD "DEKE" K.: BIRTH ANNIVERSARY. Mar 1, 1924. "Deke" Slayton, longtime chief of flight operations at the Johnson Space Center, was born at Sparta, WI. Slayton was a member of Mercury Seven, the original group of young military aviators chosen to inaugurate America's sojourn into space. Unfortunately, a heart problem prevented him from participating in any of the Mercury flights. When in 1971 the heart condition mysteriously went away, Slayton flew on the last Apollo Mission. The July 1975 flight, involving a docking with a Soviet Soyuz spacecraft, symbolized a momentary thaw in relations between the two nations. During his years as chief of flight operations, Slayton directed astronaut training and selected the crews for nearly all missions. He died June 13, 1993, at League City, TX.

SWITZERLAND: CHALANDRA MARZ. Mar 1. Engadine. Springtime traditional event when costumed young people, ringing bells and cracking whips, drive away the demons of winter.

WALES: SAINT DAVID'S DAY. Mar 1. Celebrates patron saint of Wales. Welsh tradition calls for the wearing of a leek on this day.

★ **WOMEN'S HISTORY MONTH.** Mar 1–31.

YELLOWSTONE NATIONAL PARK: ANNIVERSARY. Mar 1, 1872. The first area in the world to be designated a national park, most of Yellowstone is in Wyoming, with small sections in Montana and Idaho. It was established by an act of Congress. For further info: www.nps.gov/yell.

YOUTH ART MONTH. Mar 1–31. To emphasize the value and importance of participation in art in the development of all children and youth. For info: Council for Art Education, Inc, 100 Boylston St, Ste 1050, Boston, MA 02116. Phone: (617) 426-6400.

BIRTHDAYS TODAY

John B. Breaux, 56, US Senator (D, Louisiana), born Crowley, LA, Mar 1, 1944.

Yolanda Griffith, 30, basketball player, born Chicago, IL, Mar 1, 1970.

Ron Howard, 46, actor ("Happy Days," "Andy Griffith Show"), producer (*Parenthood*, *Far and Away*), born Duncan, OK, Mar 1, 1954.

Alan Thicke, 53, actor ("Growing Pains"), born Ontario, Canada, Mar 1, 1947.

MARCH 2 — THURSDAY
Day 62 — 304 Remaining

ETHIOPIA: ADWA DAY. Mar 2, 1896. Ethiopian forces under Menelik II inflicted a crushing defeat on the invading Italians at Adwa.

GEISEL, THEODOR "DR. SEUSS": BIRTH ANNIVERSARY. Mar 2, 1904. Theodor Seuss Geisel, the creator of *The Cat in the Hat* and *How the Grinch Stole Christmas*, was born at Springfield, MA. Known to children and parents as Dr. Seuss, his books have sold more than 200 million copies and have been translated into 20 languages. His career began with *And to Think That I Saw It on Mulberry Street*, which was turned down by 27 publishing houses before being published by Vanguard Press. His books included many messages, from environmental consciousness in *The Lorax* to the dangers of pacifism in *Horton Hatches the Egg* and *Yertel the Turtle*'s thinly veiled references to Hitler as the title character. He was awarded a Pulitzer Prize in 1984 "for his contribution over nearly half a century to the education and enjoyment of America's children and their parents." He died Sept 24, 1991, at La Jolla, CA.

HOUSTON, SAM: BIRTH ANNIVERSARY. Mar 2, 1793. American soldier and politician, born at Rockbridge County, VA, is remembered for his role in Texas history. Houston was a congressman (1823–27) and governor (1827–29) of Tennessee. He resigned his office as governor in 1829 and rejoined the Cherokee Indians (with whom he had lived for several years as a teenage runaway), who accepted him as a member of their tribe. Houston went to Texas in 1832 and became commander of the Texan army in the War for Texan Independence, which was secured when Houston routed the much larger Mexican forces led by Santa Ana, Apr 21, 1836, at the Battle of San Jacinto. After Texas's admission to the Union, Houston served as US senator and later as governor of the state. He was deposed in 1861 when he refused to swear allegiance to the Confederacy. Houston, the only person to have been elected governor of two different states, failed to serve his full term of office in either. The city of Houston, TX, was named for him. He died July 26, 1863, at Huntsville, TX.

MOUNT RAINIER NATIONAL PARK ESTABLISHED: ANNIVERSARY. Mar 2, 1899. Located in the Cascade Range in north-central Washington state, this is the fourth oldest park in the national park system. For further info: www.nps.gov/mora.

READ ACROSS AMERICA DAY. Mar 2. A national reading campaign that advocates that all children read a book the evening of Mar 2. Celebrated on Dr. Seuss's birthday. For info: Natl Education Assn, 1201 16th St, NW, Washington, DC, 20036. Phone: (202) 822-7830. Fax: (888) 747-READ. Web: www.nea.org/read across.

SPACE MILESTONE: *PIONEER 10* (US). Mar 2, 1972. This unmanned probe began a journey on which it passed and photographed Jupiter and its moons, 620 million miles from Earth, in December 1973. It crossed the orbit of Pluto, and then in 1983 become the first known Earth object to leave our solar system. On Sept 22, 1987 *Pioneer 10* reached another space milestone at 4:19 PM, when it reached a distance 50 times farther from the sun than the sun is from Earth.

SPACE MILESTONE: *SOYUZ 28* (USSR). Mar 2, 1978. Cosmonauts Alexi Gubarev and Vladimir Remek linked with *Salyut 6* space station Mar 3, visiting crew of *Soyuz 26*. Returned to Earth Mar 10. Remek, from Czechoslovakia, was the first person in space from a country other than the US or USSR. Launched Mar 2, 1978.

TEXAS INDEPENDENCE DAY. Mar 2, 1836. Texas adopted Declaration of Independence from Mexico.

BIRTHDAYS TODAY

Leo Dillon, 67, illustrator, with his wife Diane Dillon (Caldecotts for *Why Mosquitoes Buzz in People's Ears*, *Ashanti to Zulu: African Traditions*), born Brooklyn, NY, Mar 2, 1933.

Russell D. Feingold, 47, US Senator (D, Wisconsin), born Janesville, WI, Mar 2, 1953.

MARCH 3 — FRIDAY
Day 63 — 303 Remaining

BONZA BOTTLER DAY™. Mar 3. To celebrate when the number of the day is the same as the number of the month. Bonza Bottler Day™ is an excuse to have a party at least once a month. For info: Gail M. Berger, 109 Matthew Ave, Poca, WV 25159. Phone: (304) 776-7746. E-mail: gberger5@aol.com.

BULGARIA: LIBERATION DAY. Mar 3. Grateful tribute to the Russian, Romanian and Finnish soldiers and Bulgarian volunteers who, in the Russo-Turkish War, 1877–78, liberated Bulgaria from five centuries of Ottoman rule.

FLORIDA: ADMISSION DAY: ANNIVERSARY. Mar 3. Became 27th state in 1845.

I WANT YOU TO BE HAPPY DAY. Mar 3. A day dedicated to reminding people to be thoughtful of others by showing love and care and concern, even if things are not going well for them. For info: Harriette W. Grimes, Grandmother, PO Box 545, Winter Garden, FL 34777-0545. Phone: (407) 656-3830. Fax: (407) 656-2790.

JAPAN: HINAMATSURI (DOLL FESTIVAL). Mar 3. This special festival for girls is observed throughout Japan. Annually, Mar 3.

MALAWI: MARTYR'S DAY. Mar 3. Public holiday in Malawi.

MOROCCO: ANNIVERSARY OF THE THRONE. Mar 3. National holiday commemorating King Hassan II's accession to the throne in 1961.

NATIONAL ANTHEM DAY. Mar 3, 1931. The bill designating "The Star-Spangled Banner" as our national anthem was adopted by the US Senate and went to President Herbert Hoover for signature. The president signed it the same day.

***TIME* MAGAZINE FIRST PUBLISHED: ANNIVERSARY.** Mar 3, 1923. The first issue of *Time* bore this date. The magazine was founded by Henry Luce and Briton Hadden.

WORLD DAY OF PRAYER. Mar 3. An ecumenical event that reinforces bonds between peoples of the world as they join in a global circle of prayer. Annually, the first Friday in March. Sponsor: International Committee for World Day of Prayer. Church Women United is the National World Day of Prayer Committee for the US. For info: Mary Cline Detrick, Dir for Ecumenical Celebrations, Church Women United, 475 Riverside Dr, 5th Fl, New York, NY 10115. Phone: (212) 870-2347 or (800) 298-5551. Fax: (212) 870-2338.

	S	M	T	W	T	F	S
March				1	2	3	4
2000	5	6	7	8	9	10	11
	12	13	14	15	16	17	18
	19	20	21	22	23	24	25
	26	27	28	29	30	31	

Jacqueline (Jackie) Joyner-Kersee, 38, Olympic gold medal heptathlete, born East St. Louis, IL, Mar 3, 1962.

Patricia MacLachlan, 62, author (Newbery for *Sarah, Plain and Tall*), born Cheyenne, WY, Mar 3, 1938.

MARCH 4 — SATURDAY

Day 64 — 302 Remaining

ADAMS, JOHN QUINCY: RETURN TO CONGRESS ANNIVERSARY. Mar 4, 1830. On this day, John Quincy Adams returned to the House of Representatives to represent the district of Plymouth, MA. He was the first former president to do so and served for eight consecutive terms.

BRAZIL: CARNIVAL. Mar 4–7. Especially in Rio de Janeiro, this carnival is one of the great folk festivals, and the big annual event in the life of Brazilians. Begins on Saturday night before Ash Wednesday and continues through Shrove Tuesday.

CONGRESS: ANNIVERSARY OF FIRST MEETING UNDER CONSTITUTION. Mar 4, 1789. The first Congress met at New York, NY. A quorum was obtained in the House on Apr 1, in the Senate Apr 5 and the first Congress was formally organized Apr 6. Electoral votes were counted, and George Washington was declared president (69 votes) and John Adams vice president (34 votes).

FRENCH WEST INDIES: CARNIVAL. Mar 4–8. Martinique. For five days, business comes to a halt. Streets spill over with parties and parades. Carnival Queen is elected. For info: Ms Muriel Wiltord, Martinique Promo Bureau, 444 Madison Ave, 16th Floor, New York, NY 10022. Phone: (800) 391-4909. Fax: (212) 838-7855. E-mail: martinique@nyo.com. Web: www.martinique.org.

GROVER CLEVELAND'S SECOND PRESIDENTIAL INAUGURATION: ANNIVERSARY. Mar 4, 1893. Grover Cleveland was inaugurated for a second but nonconsecutive term as president. In 1885 he had become 22nd President of the US and in 1893 the 24th. Originally a source of some controversy, the Congressional Directory for some time listed him only as the 22nd president. The Directory now lists him as both the 22nd and 24th presidents though some historians continue to argue that one person cannot be both. Benjamin Harrison served during the intervening term, defeating Cleveland in electoral votes, though not in the popular vote.

OLD INAUGURATION DAY. Mar 4. Anniversary of the date set for beginning the US presidential term of office, 1789–1933. Although the Continental Congress had set the first Wednesday of March 1789 as the date for the new government to convene, a quorum was not present to count the electoral votes until Apr 6. Though George Washington's term of office began Mar 4, he did not take the oath of office until Apr 30, 1789. All subsequent presidential terms (except successions following the death of an incumbent), until Franklin D. Roosevelt's second term, began Mar 4. The 20th Amendment (ratified Jan 23, 1933) provided that "the terms of the President and Vice President shall end at noon on the 20th day of January . . . and the terms of their successors shall then begin."

PENNSYLVANIA DEEDED TO WILLIAM PENN: ANNIVERSARY. Mar 4, 1681. To satisfy a debt of £16,000, King Charles II of England granted a royal charter, deed and governorship of Pennsylvania to William Penn.

***PEOPLE* MAGAZINE: ANNIVERSARY.** Mar 4, 1974. The popular gossip magazine was officially launched with the Mar 4, 1974, issue featuring a cover photo of Mia Farrow.

PULASKI, CASIMIR: BIRTH ANNIVERSARY. Mar 4, 1747. American Revolutionary hero, General Kazimierz (Casimir) Pulaski, born at Winiary, Mazovia, Poland, the son of a count. He was a patriot and military leader in Poland's fight against Russia of 1770–71 and went into exile at the partition of Poland in 1772. He went to America in 1777 to join the Revolution, fighting with General Washington at Brandywine and also serving at Germantown and Valley Forge. He organized the Pulaski Legion to wage guerrilla warfare against the British. Mortally wounded in a heroic charge at the siege of Savannah, GA, he died aboard the warship *Wasp* Oct 11, 1779. Pulaski Day is celebrated Oct 11 in Massachusetts and on the first Monday of March in Illinois.

ROCKNE, KNUTE: BIRTH ANNIVERSARY. Mar 4, 1888. Legendary Notre Dame football coach born at Voss, Norway. Known for such sayings as "Win one for the Gipper," he died at Cottonwood Falls, KS, Mar 31, 1931.

SPACE MILESTONE: *OGO 5* (US). Mar 4, 1968. Orbiting Geophysical Observatory (OGO) collected data on sun's influence on Earth. Launched Mar 4, 1968. Six OGOs were launched in all.

TELEVISION ACADEMY HALL OF FAME: FIRST INDUCTEES ANNOUNCED: ANNIVERSARY. Mar 4, 1984. The Television Academy of Arts and Sciences announced the formation of the Television Academy Hall of Fame at Burbank, CA. The first inductees were Lucille Ball, Milton Berle, Paddy Chayefsky, Norman Lear, Edward R. Murrow, William S. Paley and David Sarnoff.

VERMONT: ADMISSION DAY: ANNIVERSARY. Mar 4. Became 14th state in 1791.

Peyton Manning, 24, football player, born New Orleans, LA, Mar 4, 1976.

Dav Pilkey, 34, author and illustrator (The Dumb Bunnies series, *The Paperboy*), born Cleveland, OH, Mar 4, 1966.

Peggy Rathmann, 47, author and illustrator (Caldecott for *Officer Buckle and Gloria*), born St. Paul, MN, Mar 4, 1953.

MARCH 5 — SUNDAY

Day 65 — 301 Remaining

BOSTON MASSACRE: ANNIVERSARY. Mar 5, 1770. A skirmish between British troops and a crowd at Boston, MA, became widely publicized and contributed to the unpopularity of the British regime in America before the American Revolution. Five men were killed and six more were injured by British troops commanded by Captain Thomas Preston.

CRISPUS ATTUCKS DAY: DEATH ANNIVERSARY. Mar 5, 1770. Honors Crispus Attucks, possibly a runaway slave, who was the first to die in the Boston Massacre.

FASCHING SUNDAY. Mar 5. Germany and Austria. The last Sunday before Lent.

ITALY: CARNIVAL WEEK. Mar 5–11. Milan. Carnival week is held according to local tradition, with shows and festive events for children on Tuesday and Thursday. Parades of floats, figures in the costume of local folk characters Meneghin and Cecca, parties and more traditional events are held on Saturday. Annually, the Sunday–Saturday of Ash Wednesday week.

MERCATOR, GERHARDUS: BIRTH ANNIVERSARY. Mar 5, 1512. Cartographer-geographer Mercator was born at Rupelmonde, Belgium. His Mercator projection for maps provided an accurate ratio of latitude to longitude and is still used today. He also introduced the term "atlas" for a collection of maps. He died at Duisberg, Germany, Dec 2, 1594.

SAINT PIRAN'S DAY. Mar 5. Celebrates the birthday of St. Piran, the patron saint of Cornish tinners. Cornish worldwide celebrate this day. For info: The Cornish American Heritage Soc, 2405 N Brookfield Rd, Brookfield, WI 53045. Phone: (414) 786-9358. E-mail: jjolliff@post.its.mcw.edu.

SAVE YOUR VISION WEEK. Mar 5–11. To remind Americans that vision is one of the most vital of all human needs and its protection is of great significance to the health and welfare of every individual. Annually, the first full week in March. For info: American Optometric Assn, 243 N Lindbergh Blvd, St. Louis, MO 63141. Phone: (314) 991-4100. Fax: (314) 991-4101. E-mail: opt-info@aol.com. Web: www.aoanet.org/

★ **SAVE YOUR VISION WEEK.** Mar 5–11. Presidential Proclamation issued for the first week of March since 1964, except 1971 and 1982 when issued for the second week of March. (PL88–1942, of Dec 30, 1963.)

SHROVETIDE. Mar 5–7. The three days before Ash Wednesday: Shrove Sunday, Monday and Tuesday—a time for confession and for festivity before the beginning of Lent.

BIRTHDAYS TODAY

Merrion Frances (Mem) Fox, 54, author (*Possum Magic, Koala Lou*), born Australia, Mar 5, 1946.

John Kitzhaber, 53, Governor of Oregon (D), born Colfax, WA, Mar 5, 1947.

MARCH 6 — MONDAY
Day 66 — 300 Remaining

BROWNING, ELIZABETH BARRETT: BIRTH ANNIVERSARY. Mar 6, 1806. English poet, author of *Sonnets from the Portuguese*, wife of poet Robert Browning and subject of the play *The Barretts of Wimpole Street*, was born near Durham, England. She died at Florence, Italy, June 29, 1861.

CARNIVAL. Mar 6–7. Period of festivities, feasts, foolishness and gaiety immediately before Lent begins on Ash Wednesday. Ordinarily Carnival includes only Fasching (the Feast of Fools), being the Monday and Tuesday immediately preceding Ash Wednesday. The period of Carnival may also be extended to include longer periods in some areas.

DENMARK: STREET URCHINS' CARNIVAL. Mar 6. Observed on Shrove Monday.

FALL OF THE ALAMO: ANNIVERSARY. Mar 6, 1836. Anniversary of the fall of the Texan fort, the Alamo. The siege, led by Mexican general Santa Ana, began Feb 23 and reached its climax Mar 6, when the last of the defenders was slain. Texans, under General Sam Houston, rallied with the war cry "Remember the Alamo" and, at the Battle of San Jacinto, Apr 21, defeated and captured Santa Ana, who signed a treaty recognizing Texas's independence.

FASCHING. Mar 6–7. In Germany and Austria, Fasching, also called Fasnacht, Fasnet or Feast of Fools, is a Shrovetide festival with processions of masked figures, both beautiful and grotesque.

	S	M	T	W	T	F	S
March				1	2	3	4
2000	5	6	7	8	9	10	11
	12	13	14	15	16	17	18
	19	20	21	22	23	24	25
	26	27	28	29	30	31	

MARCH 6
THE ARTIST INSIDE YOU— MICHELANGELO'S BIRTHDAY

Michelangelo Buonarroti, born Mar 6, 1475, is an artist whose first name is recognized by almost everyone. While Michelangelo had a particular love of sculpting, he also painted spectacular pictures and was interested in architecture. One of his most famous works is the painting on the ceiling of the Sistine Chapel in Rome.

Art in the classroom lets creative students showcase and develop talents beyond academic abilities, which helps them gain self-confidence and earn peer respect. Celebrating Michelangelo's birthday offers many art possibilities for the classroom. (March is also Youth Art Month. See that entry for more information.) Pictures of Michelangelo's paintings and sculpture can be used to set up a mini art gallery. Students of all ages can experiment with clay, paint, ink, charcoal, chalk and crayons and produce their own work. Older students may want to explore sculpture with soap (flakes and bar carving), wire and papier-mâché.

Freedom to choose among various media gives each student a greater chance of personal satisfaction. The truly adventurous may want to experiment by painting while lying on their backs, the way Michelangelo did while working on the Sistine Chapel. Completed student artwork can be displayed in the classroom or in display cases throughout the building, simultaneously celebrating Michelangelo's birthday and Youth Art Month.

Michelangelo is especially noted for his portrayal of the human body. His human figures are restrained, yet show considerable animation because Michelangelo made a practice of studying anatomy. This dovetails nicely with science curriculum units on the human body. Make the connection between muscle structure and how Michelangelo uses it to give life to their figures. Encourage students to draw a picture of their own hand, showing how their bones and muscles stand out.

There are many books available about Michelangelo. For a look at his playful side try *Michelangelo's Surprise*, by Tony Parillo (Farrar Straus, 0-374-34961-4, $16 Gr. PreS–3). Mike Venezia's *Michelangelo* (Children's Press, 0-5164-2293-6, $6.95 Gr. K–2) is a biography and contains illustrations of Michelangelo's paintings and sculptures. This is one book in the Getting to Know the World's Great Artists series. *Muscles*, by Seymour Simon (Morrow, 0-688-14642-2, $16 Gr. 3 & up) nicely complements the science connection.

Always the two days (Rose Monday and Shrove Tuesday) between Fasching Sunday and Ash Wednesday.

GHANA: INDEPENDENCE DAY. Mar 6. National holiday. Received independence from Great Britain in 1957.

GUAM: DISCOVERY DAY or MAGELLAN DAY. Mar 6. Commemorates discovery of Guam in 1521. Annually, the first Monday in March.

ICELAND: BUN DAY. Mar 6. Children invade homes in the morning with colorful sticks and receive gifts of whipped cream buns (on the Monday before Shrove Tuesday).

MICHELANGELO: 525th BIRTH ANNIVERSARY. Mar 6, 1475. Anniversary of the birth, at Caprese, Italy, of Michelangelo di Lodovico Buonarroti Simoni, a prolific Renaissance painter, sculptor, architect and poet who had a profound impact on Western art. Michelangelo's fresco painting on the ceiling of the Sistine Chapel at the Vatican at Rome, Italy, is often considered the

MARCH 6–10
NEWSPAPER IN EDUCATION WEEK

This week-long focus on newspapers is just what you need to get your students into a life-long habit of reading. You can start in a number of ways. Many local papers are glad to donate free copies for educational use. (More than 700 newspapers around the country sponsor Newspaper in Education Week.) A classroom subscription assures regular reading. Sometimes parent-teacher organizations will provide a school year's subscription to the Learning Center. Add the newspaper to the "reader's corner" of your classroom so students can browse the paper when they have finished in-class assignments.

Each day of the week focuses on a different section of the paper. Categories might include: international news items, editorial pages, sports, health and fashion, entertainment, travel and classified ads. Collect items that pertain to curriculum content areas—science, particularly medicine, environmental concerns and space exploration—to supplement textbook information with up-to-the-minute discoveries. Have students clip articles and start subject files they can refer to during the balance of the school year. Discuss what makes an attention-grabbing headline. Start a collection of new words and their definitions. Look for grammatical and spelling errors. Make opportunities for students to share the news they've read about with each other.

See if your local paper has a web address. For a directory of newspapers on the web, go to www.newspapers.com. Fast-breaking news stories can be followed up by consulting newspaper sites on the Internet.

For older children, try to find several different newspapers and encourage students to analyze the manner in which the news is presented; for example, sensationalism versus a well-researched story supported with facts. Ask students to compare the coverage of an important event in the newspaper with the coverage given the event by television news. What are the advantages and disadvantages of the news in printed form and on TV?

Students may be interested in starting a classroom newspaper. The National Elementary Schools Press Association website at www.nespa.org has suggestions. Many areas of the curriculum, especially history and social studies, provide great opportunities for newspaper-style rewrites. At the end of the week, your students may be surprised to find how much they look forward to reading the daily news.

For additional resources, contact your local newspaper or the website of the Newspaper Association of America at www.naa.org/foundation/resources.html.

pinnacle of his achievement in painting, as well as the highest achievement of the Renaissance. Also among his works were the sculptures *David* and *The Pieta*. Appointed architect of St. Peter's in 1542, a post he held until his death Feb 18, 1564, at Rome. See Curriculum Connection.

MOON PHASE: NEW MOON. Mar 6. Moon enters New Moon phase at 12:17 AM, EST.

NATIONAL SCHOOL BREAKFAST WEEK. Mar 6–10. To focus on the importance of a nutritious breakfast served in the schools, giving children a good start to their day. Annually, the first full week in March (weekdays). For info: American School Food Service Assn, 1600 Duke St, 7th Fl, Alexandria, VA 22314-3436. Phone: (703) 739-3900. Web: www.asfsa.org.

NEWSPAPER IN EDUCATION WEEK. Mar 6–10. A week-long celebration using newspapers in the classroom as living textbooks.

More than 700 newspapers in the US and Canada participate in this event annually. Annually, the first full week in March (weekdays). See Curriculum Connection. For info: Mgr Education Programs, Newspaper Assn of America Foundation, 1921 Gallows Rd, Ste 600, Vienna, VA 22182-3900. Phone: (703) 902-1730. E-mail: guntr@naa.org. Web: www.naa.org.

SHROVE MONDAY. Mar 6. The Monday before Ash Wednesday. In Germany and Austria, this is called Rose Monday.

TRINIDAD: CARNIVAL. Mar 6–7. Port of Spain. Called by islanders "the mother of all carnivals," a special tradition that brings together people from all over the world in an incredible colorful setting that includes the world's most celebrated calypsonians, steel band players, costume designers and masqueraders. Annually, the two days before Ash Wednesday. For info: Natl Carnival Commission, Tourism and Industrial Development Co, Administration Bldg, Queen Park Savannah, Port of Spain, Trinidad and Tobago, West Indies. Phone: (809) 623-1932. Fax: (809) 623-3848.

BIRTHDAYS TODAY

Christopher Samuel Bond, 61, US Senator (R, Missouri), born St. Louis, MO, Mar 6, 1939.
Alan Greenspan, 74, economist, Chairman of the Federal Reserve Board, born New York, NY, Mar 6, 1926.
Shaquille Rashan O'Neal, 28, basketball player, born Newark, NJ, Mar 6, 1972.

MARCH 7 — TUESDAY
Day 67 — 299 Remaining

BURBANK, LUTHER: BIRTH ANNIVERSARY. Mar 7, 1849. Anniversary of birth of American naturalist and author, creator and developer of many new varieties of flowers, fruits, vegetables and trees. Luther Burbank's birthday is observed by some as Bird and Arbor Day. Born at Lancaster, MA, he died at Santa Rosa, CA, Apr 11, 1926.

HOPKINS, STEPHEN: BIRTH ANNIVERSARY. Mar 7, 1707. Colonial governor (Rhode Island) and signer of the Declaration of Independence. Born at Providence, RI and died there July 13, 1785.

ICELAND: BURSTING DAY. Mar 7. Feasts with salted mutton and thick pea soup. (Shrove Tuesday.)

MARDI GRAS. Mar 7. Celebrated especially at New Orleans, LA, Mobile, AL, and certain Mississippi and Florida cities. Last feast before Lent. Although Mardi Gras (Fat Tuesday, literally) is properly limited to Shrove Tuesday, it has come to be popularly applied to the preceding two weeks of celebration.

MONOPOLY INVENTED: ANNIVERSARY. Mar 7, 1933. Monopoly was mass marketed by Parker Brothers beginning in 1935.

SHROVE TUESDAY. Mar 7. Always the day before Ash Wednesday. Sometimes called Pancake Tuesday. A legal holiday in certain counties in Florida.

TOWN MEETING DAY IN VERMONT. Mar 7. The first Tuesday in March is an official state holiday in Vermont. Nearly every town elects officers, approves budget items and deals with a multitude of other items in a day-long public meeting of the voters.

BIRTHDAYS TODAY

Michael Eisner, 58, Disney executive, born Mount Kisco, NY, Mar 7, 1942.

MARCH 8 — WEDNESDAY
Day 68 — 298 Remaining

ASH WEDNESDAY. Mar 8. Marks the beginning of Lent. Forty weekdays and six Sundays (Saturday considered a weekday) remain until Easter Sunday. Named for use of ashes in ceremonial penance.

FIRST US INCOME TAX: ANNIVERSARY. Mar 8, 1913. The Internal Revenue Service began to levy and collect income taxes.

GRAHAME, KENNETH: BIRTH ANNIVERSARY. Mar 8, 1859. Scottish author, born at Edinburgh. His children's book, *The Wind in the Willows*, has as its main characters a mole, a rat, a badger and a toad. He died July 6, 1932, at Pangbourne, Berkshire.

INTERNATIONAL (WORKING) WOMEN'S DAY. Mar 8. A day to honor women, especially working women. Said to commemorate an 1857 march and demonstration at New York, NY, by female garment and textile workers. Believed to have been first proclaimed for this date at an international conference of women held at Helsinki, Finland, in 1910, "that henceforth Mar 8 should be declared International Women's Day." The 50th anniversary observance, at Peking, China, in 1960, cited Clara Zetkin (1857–1933) as "initiator of Women's Day on Mar 8." This is perhaps the most widely observed holiday of recent origin and is unusual among holidays originating in the US in having been widely adopted and observed in other nations, including socialist countries. In Russia it is a national holiday, and flowers or gifts are presented to women workers.

LENT BEGINS. Mar 8–Apr 22. Most Christian churches observe period of fasting and penitence (40 weekdays and six Sundays—Saturday considered a weekday) beginning on Ash Wednesday and ending on the Saturday before Easter.

NATIONAL MUSIC EDUCATION CONVENTION. Mar 8–11. Washington, DC. For info: Music Educators Natl Conference, 1806 Robert Fulton Dr, Reston, VA 22091. Phone: (703) 860-4000. Web: www.menc.org.

RUSSIA: INTERNATIONAL WOMEN'S DAY. Mar 8. National holiday.

SYRIAN ARAB REPUBLIC REVOLUTION DAY: ANNIVERSARY. Mar 8, 1963. Official public holiday commemorating assumption of power by Revolutionary National Council.

		S	M	T	W	T	F	S
March						1	2	3	4
2000		5	6	7	8	9	10	11
		12	13	14	15	16	17	18
		19	20	21	22	23	24	25
		26	27	28	29	30	31	

UNITED NATIONS: INTERNATIONAL WOMEN'S DAY. Mar 8. An international day observed by the organizations of the United Nations system. For more information, visit the UN's website for children at www.un.org/Pubs/CyberSchoolBus/

VAN BUREN, HANNAH HOES: BIRTH ANNIVERSARY. Mar 8, 1783. Wife of Martin Van Buren, 8th president of the US. Born at Kinderhook, NY, she died at Albany, NY, Feb 5, 1819.

BIRTHDAYS TODAY

James Van Der Beek, 23, actor ("Dawson's Creek"), born Cheshire, CT, Mar 8, 1977.

MARCH 9 — THURSDAY
Day 69 — 297 Remaining

BARBIE DEBUTS: ANNIVERSARY. Mar 9, 1959. The popular doll debuted in stores. More than 800 million dolls have been sold. For more info: www.barbie.com.

BELGIUM: CAT FESTIVAL. Mar 9. Traditional cultural observance. Annually, on the second day of Lent.

BELIZE: BARON BLISS DAY. Mar 9. Official public holiday. Celebrated in honor of Sir Henry Edward Ernest Victor Bliss, a great benefactor of Belize.

CHILDREN AND HEALTHCARE WEEK™. Mar 9–17. The goal of this observance is to increase awareness among families, schools, local communities and all health care professionals of the special needs of children and their families in health care settings. A comprehensive guide of planning materials is available for $10. For info: Assn for the Care of Children's Health, 19 Mantua Rd, Mt Royal, NJ 08061. Phone: (609) 224-1742. Fax: (609) 423-3420. E-mail: amk@smarthub.com. Web: www.look.net/acch.

GRANT COMMISSIONED COMMANDER OF ALL UNION ARMIES: ANNIVERSARY. Mar 9, 1864. In Washington, DC, Ulysses S. Grant accepted his commission as Lieutenant General, becoming the commander of all the Union armies.

PANIC DAY. Mar 9. Run around all day in a panic, telling others you can't handle it anymore. [© 1998 by WPL] For info: Tom or Ruth Roy, Wellness Permission League, PO Box 662, Mt Gretna, PA 17064-0662. Phone: (717) 964-1308. Fax: (717) 964-1335. E-mail: wellcat@desupernet.net.

VESPUCCI, AMERIGO: BIRTH ANNIVERSARY. Mar 9, 1451. Italian navigator, merchant and explorer for whom the Americas were named. Born at Florence, Italy. He participated in at least two expeditions between 1499 and 1502 which took him to the coast of South America, where he discovered the Amazon and Plata rivers. Vespucci's expeditions were of great importance because he believed that he had discovered a new continent, not just a new route to the Orient. Neither Vespucci nor his exploits achieved the fame of Columbus, but the New World was to be named for Amerigo Vespucci, by an obscure German geographer and mapmaker, Martin Waldseemuller. Ironically, in his work as an outfitter of ships, Vespucci had been personally acquainted with Christopher Columbus. Vespucci died at Seville, Spain, Feb 22, 1512. See also: "Waldseemuller, Martin: Remembrance Day" (Apr 25).

BIRTHDAYS TODAY

Emmanuel Lewis, 29, actor ("Webster"), born Brooklyn, NY, Mar 9, 1971.

MARCH 10 — FRIDAY
Day 70 — 296 Remaining

SALVATION ARMY IN THE US: ANNIVERSARY. Mar 10, 1880. Commissioner George Scott Railton and seven women officers landed at New York to officially begin the work of the Salvation Army in the US.

SHABBAT ACROSS AMERICA. Mar 10. More than 600 participating synagogues (Conservative, Orthodox, Reform and Reconstructionist) encourage Jews to observe the Sabbath on this Friday night. For info: Natl Jewish Outreach Program, 485 5th Ave, New York, NY 10017-6104. Phone: (888) SHA-BBAT or (212) 986-7450. Web: www.njop.org/saapage/saa2.htm.

TELEPHONE INVENTION: ANNIVERSARY. Mar 10, 1876. Alexander Graham Bell transmitted the first telephone message to his assistant in the next room: "Mr Watson, come here, I want you," at Cambridge, MA. See also: "Bell, Alexander Graham: Birth Anniversary" (Mar 3).

TUBMAN, HARRIET: DEATH ANNIVERSARY. Mar 10, 1913. American abolitionist, Underground Railroad leader, born a slave at Bucktown, Dorchester County, MD, about 1820 or 1821. She escaped from a Maryland plantation in 1849 and later helped more than 300 slaves reach freedom. Died at Auburn, NY. For further info: *Minty: A Story of Young Harriet Tubman*, by Alan Schroeder (Dial, 0-8037-1889-6, $16.99 Gr. K-3). For more info on the Underground Railroad, visit www.undergroundrailroad.com.

US PAPER MONEY ISSUED: ANNIVERSARY. Mar 10, 1862. The first paper money was issued in the US on this date. The denominations were $5 (Hamilton), $10 (Lincoln) and $20 (Liberty). They were not legal tender when first issued but became so by Act of Mar 17, 1862.

BIRTHDAYS TODAY

Kim Campbell, 53, first woman prime minister of Canada, born Vancouver Island, British Columbia, Canada, Mar 10, 1947.

MARCH 11 — SATURDAY
Day 71 — 295 Remaining

BUREAU OF INDIAN AFFAIRS ESTABLISHED: ANNIVERSARY. Mar 11, 1824. The US War Department created the Bureau of Indian Affairs.

FLU PANDEMIC OF 1918 HITS US: ANNIVERSARY. Mar 11, 1918. The first cases of the "Spanish" influenza were reported in the US when 107 soldiers became sick at Fort Riley, KS. By the end of 1920 nearly 25 percent of the US population had had it. As many as 500,000 civilians died from the virus, exceeding the number of US troops killed abroad in WWI. Worldwide, more than 1 percent of the global population, or 22 million people, had died by 1920. The origin of the virus was never determined absolutely, though it was probably somewhere in Asia. The name "Spanish" influenza came from the relatively high number of cases in that country early in the epidemic. Due to the panic, cancellation of public events was common and many public service workers wore masks on the job. Emergency tent hospitals were set up in some locations due to overcrowding.

GAG, WANDA: BIRTH ANNIVERSARY. Mar 11, 1893. Author and illustrator (*Millions of Cats*), born at New Ulm, MN. Died at Milford, NJ, June 27, 1946.

JOHNNY APPLESEED DAY (JOHN CHAPMAN DEATH ANNIVERSARY). Mar 11, 1845. Anniversary of the death of John Chapman, better known as Johnny Appleseed, believed to have been born at Leominster, MA, Sept 26, 1774. The planter of orchards and friend of wild animals was regarded by the Indians as a great medicine man. He died at Allen County, IN. See also: "Johnny Appleseed: Birth Anniversary" (Sept 26).

KEATS, EZRA JACK: BIRTH ANNIVERSARY. Mar 11, 1916. Author and illustrator (Caldecott for *The Snowy Day*), born at Brooklyn, NY. Died May 6, 1983, at New York, NY.

PAINE, ROBERT TREAT: BIRTH ANNIVERSARY. Mar 11, 1731. Jurist and signer of the Declaration of Independence. Born at Boston, MA, died there May 11, 1814.

BIRTHDAYS TODAY

Roy Barnes, 52, Governor of Georgia (D), born Mableton, GA, Mar 11, 1948.
Curtis Brown, Jr, 44, astronaut, commander of the 1998 shuttle *Discovery*, born Elizabethtown, NC, Mar 11, 1956.
Jonathan London, 53, author (the Froggy series), born Brooklyn, NY, Mar 11, 1947.
Antonin Scalia, 64, Associate Justice of the US Supreme Court, born Trenton, NJ, Mar 11, 1936.

MARCH 12 — SUNDAY
Day 72 — 294 Remaining

BOYCOTT, CHARLES CUNNINGHAM: BIRTH ANNIVERSARY. Mar 12, 1832. Charles Cunningham Boycott, born at Norfolk, England, has been immortalized by having his name become part of the English language. In County Mayo, Ireland, the Tenants' "Land League" in 1880 asked Boycott, an estate agent, to reduce rents (because of poor harvest and dire economic conditions). Boycott responded by serving eviction notices on the tenants, who retaliated by refusing to have any dealings with him. Charles Stewart Parnell, then President of the National Land League and agrarian agitator, retaliated against Boycott by formulating and implementing the method of economic and social ostracism that came to be called a "boycott." Boycott died at Suffolk, England, June 19, 1897.

GIRL SCOUT WEEK. Mar 12–18. To observe the anniversary of the founding of the Girl Scouts of the USA, the largest voluntary organization for girls and women in the world, which began Mar 12, 1912. Special observances include: Girl Scout Sabbath, Mar 17, Girl Scout Sunday, Mar 12, when Girl Scouts gather to attend religious services together, and Girl Scout Birthday, Mar 12. For info: Media Services, Girl Scouts of the USA, 420 Fifth Ave, New York, NY 10018. Phone: (212) 852-8000. Fax: (212) 852-6514. Web: www.gsusa.org.

GIRL SCOUTS OF THE USA FOUNDING: ANNIVERSARY. Mar 12, 1912. Juliet Low founded the Girl Scouts of the USA at Savannah, GA.

LESOTHO: MOSHOESHOE'S DAY. Mar 12. National holiday. Commemorates the great leader, Chief Moshoeshoe I, who unified the Basotho people, beginning in 1820.

MAURITIUS: INDEPENDENCE DAY. Mar 12. National holiday commemorates attainment of independent nationhood (within the British Commonwealth) by this island state in the western Indian Ocean on this day in 1968.

★ **NATIONAL POISON PREVENTION WEEK.** Mar 12–18. Presidential Proclamation issued each year for the third week of March since 1962. (PL87–319 of Sept 26, 1961.)

PIERCE, JANE MEANS APPLETON: BIRTH ANNIVERSARY. Mar 12, 1806. Wife of Franklin Pierce, 14th president of the US. Born at Hampton, NH, she died at Concord, NH, Dec 2, 1863.

SUN YAT-SEN: DEATH ANNIVERSARY. Mar 12, 1925. The heroic leader of China's 1911 revolution is remembered on the anniversary of his death at Peking, China. Observed as Arbor Day in Taiwan.

BIRTHDAYS TODAY

Kent Conrad, 52, US Senator (D, North Dakota), born Bismarck, ND, Mar 12, 1948.

Virginia Hamilton, 64, author (*The People Could Fly, M.C. Higgins the Great*), born Yellow Springs, OH, Mar 12, 1936 (some sources say 1933).

Darryl Eugene Strawberry, 38, baseball player, born Los Angeles, CA, Mar 12, 1962.

MARCH 13 — MONDAY

Day 73 — 293 Remaining

ARAB OIL EMBARGO LIFTED: ANNIVERSARY. Mar 13, 1974. The oil-producing Arab countries agreed to lift their five-month embargo on petroleum sales to the US. During the embargo prices went up 300 percent and a ban was imposed on Sunday gasoline sales. The embargo was in retaliation for US support of Israel during the October 1973 Middle-East War.

CAMP FIRE BOYS AND GIRLS BIRTHDAY WEEK. Mar 13–19. To celebrate the 90th anniversary of Camp Fire Boys and Girls (founded in 1910 as Camp Fire Girls). For info: Camp Fire Boys and Girls, 4601 Madison Ave, Kansas City, MO 64112. Phone: (816) 756-1950. Fax: (816) 756-0258. E-mail: info@campfire.org. Web: www.campfire.org.

CYPRUS: GREEN MONDAY. Mar 13. Green, or Clean, Monday is the first Monday of Lent on the Orthodox calendar. Lunch in the fields, with bread, olives and uncooked vegetables and no meat or dairy products.

DEAF HISTORY MONTH. Mar 13–Apr 15. Observance of three of the most important anniversaries for deaf Americans: Apr 15, 1817, establishment of the first public school for the deaf in America, later known as The American School for the Deaf; Apr 8, 1864, charter signed by President Lincoln authorizing the Board of Directors of the Columbia Institution (now Gallaudet University) to grant college degrees to deaf students; Mar 13, 1988, the victory of the Deaf President Now movement at Gallaudet. To help

set up a program at libraries, schools and other organizations, the Friends of Libraries for Deaf Action, Inc (FOLDA, Inc) has developed resources promoting public awareness about the deaf community and its rich history. For info: FOLDA, Inc, 2930 Craiglawn Rd, Silver Spring, MD 20904-1816. Phone: (301) 572-5168. Fax: (301) 572-4134. E-mail: alhagemeyer@juno.com.

EARMUFFS PATENTED: ANNIVERSARY. Mar 13, 1887. Chester Greenwood of Maine received a patent for earmuffs.

FILLMORE, ABIGAIL POWERS: BIRTH ANNIVERSARY. Mar 13, 1798. First wife of Millard Fillmore, 13th president of the US. Born at Stillwater, NY. It is said that the White House was without any books until Abigail Fillmore, formerly a teacher, made a room on the second floor into a library. Within a year, Congress appropriated $250 for the president to spend on books for the White House. Died at Washington, DC, Mar 30, 1853.

MOON PHASE: FIRST QUARTER. Mar 13. Moon enters First Quarter phase at 1:59 AM, EST.

NATIONAL OPEN AN UMBRELLA INDOORS DAY. Mar 13. The purpose of this day is for people to open umbrellas indoors and note whether they have any bad luck. Annually, Mar 13. For info: Thomas Edward Knibb, 8819 Adventure Ave, Walkersville, MD 21793-7828. Phone: (301) 898-3009. E-mail: tomknibb@hotmail.com.

ORTHODOX LENT. Mar 13–Apr 22. Great Lent or Easter Lent, observed by Eastern Orthodox Churches, lasts until Holy Week begins on Orthodox Palm Sunday (Apr 23).

PLANET URANUS DISCOVERY: ANNIVERSARY. Mar 13, 1781. German-born English astronomer Sir William Herschel discovered the seventh planet from the sun, Uranus.

PRIESTLY, JOSEPH: BIRTH ANNIVERSARY. Mar 13, 1733. English clergyman and scientist, discoverer of oxygen, born at Fieldhead, England. He and his family narrowly escaped an angry mob attacking their home because of his religious and political views. They moved to the US in 1794. Died at Northumberland, PA, Feb 6, 1804.

SAINT AUBIN, HELEN "CALLAGHAN" CANDAELE: BIRTH ANNIVERSARY. Mar 13, 1929. Helen Candaele St. Aubin, known as Helen Callaghan during her baseball days, was born at Vancouver, British Columbia, Canada. Saint Aubin and her sister, Margaret Maxwell, were recruited for the All-American Girls Professional Baseball League, which flourished in the 1940s when many major league players were off fighting WWII. She first played at age 15 for the Minneapolis Millerettes, an expansion team that moved to Indiana and became the Fort Wayne Daisies. For the 1945 season the left-handed outfielder led the league with a .299 average and 24 extra base hits. In 1946 she stole 114 bases in 111 games. Her son Kelly Candaele's documentary on the women's baseball league inspired the film *A League of Their Own*. Saint Aubin, who was known as the "Ted Williams of women's baseball," died Dec 8, 1992, at Santa Barbara, CA.

UNITED KINGDOM: COMMONWEALTH DAY. Mar 13. Replaces Empire Day observance recognized until 1958. Observed on second Monday in March. Also observed in the British Virgin Islands, Gibraltar and Newfoundland, Canada.

BIRTHDAYS TODAY

Diane Dillon, 67, illustrator, with her husband Leo Dillon (Caldecotts for *Why Mosquitoes Buzz in People's Ears, Ashanti to Zulu: African Traditions*), born Glendale, CA, Mar 13, 1933.

Ellen Raskin, 72, author (Newbery for *The Westing Game*), born Milwaukee, WI, Mar 13, 1928 (some sources say 1925).

		S	M	T	W	T	F	S
March					1	2	3	4
2000		5	6	7	8	9	10	11
		12	13	14	15	16	17	18
		19	20	21	22	23	24	25
		26	27	28	29	30	31	

MARCH 14 — TUESDAY

Day 74 — 292 Remaining

DE ANGELI, MARGUERITE: BIRTH ANNIVERSARY. Mar 14, 1889. Author and illustrator, born at Lampeer, MI. She won the Newbery Medal in 1950 for her classic *The Door in the Wall*. Her first book was *Ted & Nina Go to the Grocery Store* in 1935. She died at Detroit, MI, June 16, 1987.

EINSTEIN, ALBERT: BIRTH ANNIVERSARY. Mar 14, 1879. Theoretical physicist best known for his theory of relativity. Born at Ulm, Germany, he won the Nobel Prize in 1921. Died at Princeton, NJ, Apr 18, 1955.

JONES, CASEY: BIRTH ANNIVERSARY. Mar 14, 1864. Railroad engineer and hero of ballad, whose real name was John Luther Jones. Born near Cayce, KY, he died in a railroad wreck near Vaughn, MS, Apr 30, 1900.

MARSHALL, THOMAS RILEY: BIRTH ANNIVERSARY. Mar 14, 1854. Twenty-eighth vice president of the US (1913–21). Born at North Manchester, IN, he died at Washington, DC, June 1, 1925.

MOTH-ER DAY. Mar 14. A day set aside to honor moth collectors and specialists. Celebrated in museums or libraries with moth collections. For info: Bob Birch, Puns Corps Grand Punscorpion, Box 2364, Falls Church, VA 22042-0364. Phone: (703) 533-3668.

TAYLOR, LUCY HOBBS: BIRTH ANNIVERSARY. Mar 14, 1833. Lucy Beaman Hobbs, first woman in America to receive a degree in dentistry (Ohio College of Dental Surgery, 1866) and to be admitted to membership in a state dental association. Born at Franklin County, NY. In 1867 she married James M. Taylor, who also became a dentist (after she instructed him in the essentials). Active women's rights advocate. Died at Lawrence, KS, Oct 3, 1910.

BIRTHDAYS TODAY

Jordan Taylor Hanson, 17, singer (Hanson), born Jenks, OK, Mar 14, 1983.

MARCH 15 — WEDNESDAY

Day 75 — 291 Remaining

CHILDREN'S BOOK FESTIVAL. Mar 15–17 (tentative). Hattiesburg, MS. This three-day spring festival brings together children's authors and illustrators for workshops, question and answer sessions and storytelling. For info: Kalicia Henderson, Children's Book Festival, USM Continuing Education, Box 5055B, Hattiesburg, MS 39406. Phone: (601) 266-4186. E-mail: Kalicia.Henderson@usm.edu. Web: ocean.st.usm.edu/~mhamilto/

IDES OF MARCH. Mar 15. On the Roman calendar, each month had three division days: Kalends, Nones and Ides. The Ides occurred on the 15th of the month (or on the 13th in months with less than 31 days). Julius Caesar was assassinated on this day in 44 BC.

JACKSON, ANDREW: BIRTH ANNIVERSARY. Mar 15, 1767. Seventh president of the US (Mar 4, 1829–Mar 3, 1837) was born in a log cabin at Waxhaw, SC. Jackson was the first president since George Washington who had not attended college. He was a military hero in the War of 1812. His presidency reflected his democratic and egalitarian values. Died at Nashville, TN, June 8, 1845. His birthday is observed as a holiday in Tennessee.

MAINE: ADMISSION DAY: ANNIVERSARY. Mar 15. Became 23rd state in 1820. Prior to this date, Maine had been part of Massachusetts.

WASHINGTON'S ADDRESS TO CONTINENTAL ARMY OFFICERS: ANNIVERSARY. Mar 15, 1783. George Washington addressed a meeting at Newburgh, NY of Continental Army officers who were dissatisfied and rebellious for want of back pay, food, clothing and pensions. General Washington called for patience, opening his speech with the words: "I have grown grey in your service. . . ." Congress later acted to satisfy most of the demands.

YAWM ARAFAT: THE STANDING AT ARAFAT. Mar 15. Islamic calendar date: Dhu-Hijjah 9, 1420. The day when people on the Hajj (pilgrimage to Mecca) assemble for "the Standing" at the plain of Arafat at Mina, Saudi Arabia, near Mecca. This gathering is a foreshadowing of the Day of Judgment. Different methods for "anticipating" the visibility of the new moon crescent at Mecca are used by different Muslim groups. US date may vary.

BIRTHDAYS TODAY

Ruth Bader Ginsburg, 67, Associate Justice of the US Supreme Court, born Brooklyn, NY, Mar 15, 1933.

Don Sundquist, 64, Governor of Tennessee (R), born Moline, IL, Mar 15, 1936.

Ruth White, 58, author (*Belle Prater's Boy*), born Whitewood, VA, Mar 15, 1942.

MARCH 16 — THURSDAY

Day 76 — 290 Remaining

ABSOLUTELY INCREDIBLE KID DAY. Mar 16. Camp Fire Boys and Girls, one of the nation's oldest and largest youth development organizations, holds its fourth annual event to encourage adults to write a letter to a child in their life to tell children how special they are and how much they mean to them. Annually, the third Thursday in March. For info: Camp Fire Boys and Girls, 4601 Madison Ave, Kansas City, MO 64112. Phone: (816) 756-1950. Fax: (816) 756-0258. E-mail: info@campfire.org. Web: www.campfire.org.

BLACK PRESS DAY: ANNIVERSARY OF THE FIRST BLACK NEWSPAPER. Mar 16, 1827. Anniversary of the founding of the first black newspaper in the US, *Freedom's Journal*, on Varick Street at New York, NY.

CLYMER, GEORGE: BIRTH ANNIVERSARY. Mar 16, 1739. Signer of the Declaration of Independence and of the US Constitution. Born at Philadelphia, PA and died there Jan 24, 1813.

EID-AL-ADHA: FEAST OF THE SACRIFICE. Mar 16. Islamic calendar date: Dhu-Hijja 10, 1420. Commemorates Abraham's willingness to sacrifice his son Ishmael in obedience to God. It is part of the Hajj (pilgrimage to Mecca). The day begins with the sacrifice of an animal in remembrance of the Angel Gabriel's substitution of a lamb as Abraham's offering. One-third of the meat is given to the poor and the rest is shared with friends and family. Celebrated with gifts and general merrymaking, the festival usually continues for several days. It is celebrated as Tabaski in

Benin, Burkina Faso, Guinea, Guinea-Bissau, Ivory Coast, Mali, Niger and Senegal and as Kurban Bayram in Turkey and Bosnia. Different methods for "anticipating" the visibility of the moon crescent at Mecca are used by different Muslim groups. US date may vary.

GODDARD DAY. Mar 16, 1926. Commemorates first liquid-fuel-powered rocket flight, devised by Robert Hutchings Goddard (1882–1945) at Auburn, MA.

"THE GUMBY SHOW" TV PREMIERE: ANNIVERSARY. Mar 16, 1957. This kids' show was a spin-off from "Howdy Doody," where the character of Gumby was first introduced in 1956. Gumby and his horse Pokey were clay figures whose adventures were filmed using the process of "Claymation." "The Gumby Show," created by Art Clokey, was first hosted by Bobby Nicholson and later by Pinky Lee. It was syndicated in 1966 and again in 1988.

MADISON, JAMES: BIRTH ANNIVERSARY. Mar 16, 1751. Fourth president of the US (Mar 4, 1809–Mar 3, 1817), born at Port Conway, VA. He was president when British forces invaded Washington, DC, requiring Madison and other high officials to flee while the British burned the Capitol, the president's residence and most other public buildings (Aug 24–25, 1814). Died at Montpelier, VA, June 28, 1836.

NIXON, THELMA CATHERINE PATRICIA RYAN: BIRTH ANNIVERSARY. Mar 16, 1912. Wife of Richard Milhous Nixon, 37th president of the US. Born at Ely, NV, she died at Park Ridge, NJ, June 22, 1993.

BIRTHDAYS TODAY

Sid Fleischman, 80, author (Newbery for *The Whipping Boy*), born Albert Sidney Fleischman, Brooklyn, NY, Mar 16, 1920.

William Mayne, 72, author (*Lady Muck*), born Kingston-upon-Hull, England, Mar 16, 1928.

Daniel Patrick Moynihan, 73, US Senator (D, New York), born Tulsa, OK, Mar 16, 1927.

MARCH 17 — FRIDAY
Day 77 — 289 Remaining

CAMP FIRE BOYS AND GIRLS: 90th ANNIVERSARY. Mar 17. To commemorate the 90th anniversary of the founding of Camp Fire Boys and Girls and the service given to children and youth across the nation. Founded in 1910 as Camp Fire Girls. For info: Camp Fire Boys and Girls, 4601 Madison Ave, Kansas City, MO 64112. Phone: (816) 756-1950. Fax: (816) 756-0258. E-mail: info@campfire.org. Web: www.campfire.org.

March 2000	S	M	T	W	T	F	S
				1	2	3	4
	5	6	7	8	9	10	11
	12	13	14	15	16	17	18
	19	20	21	22	23	24	25
	26	27	28	29	30	31	

EVACUATION DAY IN MASSACHUSETTS. Mar 17, 1776. Proclaimed annually by the governor, Evacuation Day commemorates the anniversary of the evacuation from Boston of British troops.

IRELAND: NATIONAL DAY. Mar 17. St. Patrick's Day is observed in the Republic of Ireland as a legal national holiday.

NORTHERN IRELAND: SAINT PATRICK'S DAY HOLIDAY. Mar 17. National Holiday.

RUSTIN, BAYARD: 90th BIRTH ANNIVERSARY. Mar 17, 1910. Black pacifist and civil rights leader, Bayard Rustin was an organizer and participant in many of the great social protest marches—for jobs, freedom and nuclear disarmament. He was arrested and imprisoned more than 20 times for his civil rights and pacifist activities. Born at West Chester, PA, Rustin died at New York, NY, Aug 24, 1987.

SAINT PATRICK'S DAY. Mar 17. Commemorates the patron saint of Ireland, Bishop Patrick (389–461 AD) who, about 432 AD, left his home in the Severn Valley, England, and introduced Christianity into Ireland. Feast Day in the Roman Catholic Church. A national holiday in Ireland and Northern Ireland. For links to websites about St. Patrick's Day, go to: deil.lang.uiuc.edu/web.pages/holidays/stpatrick.html.

SAINT PATRICK'S DAY PARADE. Mar 17. Fifth Avenue, New York, NY. Held since 1762, the parade of 125,000 begins the two-mile march at 11:30 AM and lasts about six hours. Starts on 42nd Street and 5th Avenue and ends at 86th Street and First Avenue. Est attendance: 1,000,000. For info: NY Conv and Visitors Bureau, 810 Seventh Ave, New York, NY 10019. Phone: 800NYC-VISIT or (212) 484-1222.

SOUTH AFRICAN WHITES VOTE TO END MINORITY RULE: ANNIVERSARY. Mar 17, 1992. A referendum proposing ending white minority rule through negotiations was supported by a whites-only ballot. The vote of 1,924,186 (68.6 percent) whites in support of President F.W. de Klerk's reform policies was greater than expected.

TANEY, ROGER B.: BIRTH ANNIVERSARY. Mar 17, 1777. Fifth Chief Justice of the Supreme Court, born at Calvert County, MD. Served as Attorney General under President Andrew Jackson. Nominated as Secretary of the Treasury, he became the first presidential nominee to be rejected by the Senate because of his strong stance against the Bank of the United States as a central bank. A year later, he was nominated to the Supreme Court as an associate justice by Jackson, but his nomination was stalled until the death of Chief Justice John Marshall July 6, 1835. Taney was nominated to fill Marshall's place on the bench and after much resistance he was sworn in as Chief Justice in March 1836. His tenure on the Supreme Court is most remembered for the Dred Scott decision. He died at Washington, DC, Oct 12, 1864.

BIRTHDAYS TODAY

Patrick Duffy, 51, actor ("Step By Step"), born Townsend, MT, Mar 17, 1949.

MARCH 18 — SATURDAY
Day 78 — 288 Remaining

ARUBA: FLAG DAY. Mar 18. Aruba national holiday. Display of flags, national music and folkloric events.

CALHOUN, JOHN CALDWELL: BIRTH ANNIVERSARY. Mar 18, 1782. American statesman and first vice president of the US to resign that office (Dec 28, 1832). Born at Abbeville District, SC, he died at Washington, DC, Mar 31, 1850.

CLEVELAND, GROVER: BIRTH ANNIVERSARY. Mar 18, 1837. The 22nd and 24th president of the US was born Stephen Grover Cleveland at Caldwell, NJ. Terms of office as president: Mar 4, 1885–Mar 3, 1889, and Mar 4, 1893–Mar 3, 1897. He ran for president for the intervening term and received a plurality of votes cast but failed to win electoral college victory for that term. Only president to serve two nonconsecutive terms. Also the only president to be married in the White House. He married 21-year-old Frances Folsom, his ward. Their daughter, Esther, was the first child of a president to be born in the White House. Died at Princeton, NJ, June 24, 1908.

JORDAN'S BACK!: 5th ANNIVERSARY. Mar 18, 1995. Michael Jordan, considered one of the National Basketball Association's greatest all-time players, made history again when he announced that he was returning to professional play after a 17-month break. The 32-year-old star had retired just before the start of the 1993–94 season, following the murder of his father, James Jordan. Jordan, who averaged 32.3 points a game during regular season play, had led the Chicago Bulls to three successive NBA titles. While retired, he tried a baseball career, playing for the Chicago White Sox minor league team. After returning to the Bulls, he led them to three more NBA titles. He announced his retirement again Jan 13, 1999 after the six-month NBA lockout was resolved.

NATIONAL ASSOCIATION OF ELEMENTARY SCHOOL PRINCIPALS ANNUAL CONFERENCE. Mar 18–21. Convention Center, New Orleans, LA. For info: Natl Assn of Elementary School Principals, 1615 Duke St, Alexandria, VA 22314. Phone: 703684-3345 or (800) 38-NAESP. Fax: (800) 39N-AESP. E-mail: naesp@naesp.org. Web: www.naesp.org.

SAVE THE FLORIDA PANTHER DAY. Mar 18. A ceremonial day on the third Saturday in March.

SPACE MILESTONE: *VOSKHOD 2* (USSR): 35th ANNIVERSARY. Mar 18, 1965. Colonel Leonov stepped out of the capsule for 20 minutes in a special space suit, the first man to leave a spaceship. It was two months prior to the first US space walk. See also: "Space Milestone: *Gemini 4* US" (June 3).

BIRTHDAYS TODAY

Bonnie Blair, 36, former Olympic gold medal speed skater, born Cornwall, NY, Mar 18, 1964.

Queen Latifah, 30, singer, actress ("Living Single"), born East Orange, NJ, Mar 18, 1970.

MARCH 19 — SUNDAY

Day 79 — 287 Remaining

BRADFORD, WILLIAM: BIRTH ANNIVERSARY. Mar 19, 1589. Pilgrim father, governor of Plymouth Colony. Born at Yorkshire, England, and baptized Mar 19, 1589. Sailed from Southampton, England, on the *Mayflower* in 1620. Died at Plymouth, MA, May 9, 1657.

CAMP FIRE BOYS AND GIRLS BIRTHDAY SUNDAY. Mar 19. A day when Camp Fire Boys and Girls commemorate the organization's founding and worship together and participate in the services of their churches or temples. For info: Camp Fire Boys and Girls, 4601 Madison Ave, Kansas City, MO 64112. Phone: (816) 756-1950. Fax: (816) 756-0258. E-mail: info@campfire.org. Web: www.campfire.org.

EARP, WYATT: BIRTH ANNIVERSARY. Mar 19, 1848. Born at Monmouth, IL, and died Jan 13, 1929, at Los Angeles, CA. A legendary figure of the Old West, Earp worked as a railroad hand, saloonkeeper, gambler, lawman, gunslinger, miner and real estate

MARCH 19–25
NATIONAL AGRICULTURE WEEK

National Agriculture Week can be observed in the science curriculum with an experiment. Have students plant three bean seeds early in the week before Agriculture Week. The first will be placed on top of several layers of damp paper towels placed in the bottom of a paper cup. The towels must be kept moist, so water them daily. The second seed should be planted in soil and watered as necessary. The third seed should be planted in soil, but be watered and fed with a plant fertilizer. Students can hypothesize about the results. During Agriculture Week the seeds will sprout. Students can measure, draw and note changes they observe over the next few weeks. Have them answer the question: Do fertilizers make a difference? For ideas about other plant-related activities, see *Garden Wizardry for Kids*, by L. Patricia Kite (Barron's, 0-8120-1317-4, $21.95 Gr. 4–6) which describes more than 300 projects.

A geographical focus could include mapping the areas of the country that supply your region with meat and produce your students eat. *Harvest Year*, by Cris Peterson (Boyds Mills Press, 1-56397-571-8, $15.95 Gr. K–3) uses maps and photographs to show that every month something is being harvested somewhere in the United States. What is the most important agricultural product grown in your state? Other topics to explore this week include: Getting food to the marketplace; Family farms vs. large corporate farms; and Organic farming vs. use of herbicides and pesticides. Books like *The American Family Farm: A Photo Essay*, by George Ancona and Joan Anderson (Harcourt Brace, 0-15-203025-5, $18.94 Gr. 4–6) will help introduce farming to urban children. *Farms Feed the World*, by Lee S. Hill (Carolrhoda, 1-57505-075-7, $14.95 Gr. K–3) describes different types of farms. *Becoming Felix*, by Nancy Hope Wilson (Farrar Straus, 0-374-30664-8, $16 Gr. 4–7) is a novel about a family's struggle to maintain their farm.

A related holiday in March is the birthday of Cesar Chavez (Mar 31), a Mexican American who founded the first union for farm workers in the US. *Cesar Chavez: a Photo-Illustrated Biography*, by Lucile Davis (Bridgestone, 1-56065-569-0, $14 Gr. 2–4) and *Farmer's Friend: The Story of Cesar Chavez*, David R. Collins (Carolrhoda, 1-57505-031-5, $6.95 Gr. 4–7) are two biographies with information for young readers.

investor at various times. Best known for his involvement in the gunfight at the OK Corral Oct 26, 1881, at Tombstone, AZ.

MOON PHASE: FULL MOON. Mar 19. Moon enters Full Moon phase at 11:44 PM, EST.

NATIONAL AGRICULTURE WEEK. Mar 19–25. To honor America's providers of food and fiber and to educate the general public about the US agricultural system. Annually, the week that includes the first day of spring. See Curriculum Connection. For info: Agriculture Council of America, 11020 King St, Ste 205, Overland Park, KS 66210. Phone: (913) 491-1895. Fax: (913) 491-6502. E-mail: info@agday.org. Web: www.agday.org.

NATIONAL POISON PREVENTION WEEK. Mar 19–25. To aid in encouraging the American people to learn of the dangers of accidental poisoning and to take preventive measures against it. Annually, the third full week in March. For info: Ken Giles, Secy, Poison Prevention Week Council, Box 1543, Washington, DC 20013. E-mail: kgiles@cpsc.gov. Web: www.cpsc.gov.

SWALLOWS RETURN TO SAN JUAN CAPISTRANO. Mar 19. Traditional date (St. Joseph's Day), since 1776, for swallows to return to old mission of San Juan Capistrano, CA.

US STANDARD TIME ACT: ANNIVERSARY. Mar 19, 1918. Anniversary of passage by the Congress of the Standard Time Act, which authorized the Interstate Commerce Commission to establish standard time zones for the US. The Act also established "Daylight Saving Time," to save fuel and to promote other economies in a country at war. Daylight-saving time first went into operation on Easter Sunday, Mar 31, 1918. The Uniform Time Act of 1966, as amended in 1986, by Public Law 99–359, now governs standard time in the US. See also: "US: Daylight Saving Time Begins" (Apr 2).

WARREN, EARL: BIRTH ANNIVERSARY. Mar 19, 1891. American jurist, 14th Chief Justice of the US Supreme Court. Born at Los Angeles, CA, died at Washington, DC, July 9, 1974.

BIRTHDAYS TODAY

Glenn Close, 53, actress (*101 Dalmatians*), born Greenwich, CT, Mar 19, 1947.

Bruce Willis, 45, actor (*Die Hard*, voice in *Look Who's Talking 2*), born Penn's Grove, NJ, Mar 19, 1955.

MARCH 20 — MONDAY
Day 80 — 286 Remaining

ANONYMOUS GIVING WEEK. Mar 20–26. A time to celebrate the true spirit of giving. Experience the joy in random acts of kindness. Leave a legacy of anonymous contribution. Perfect for a one-time or all-week adventure designed to share time, talent and treasure. For info: Janna Krammer, Legacy Institute, 42805 Blackhawk Rd, Harris, MN 55032. Phone: (612) 674-0227. Fax: (612) 674-0228. E-mail: legacyinst@aol.com.

AUSTRALIA: CANBERRA DAY. Mar 20. Australian Capital Territory. Public holiday the third Monday in March.

LEGOLAND OPENS: ANNIVERSARY. Mar 20, 1999. The Legoland theme park for children ages 2–12 opened on this day at Carlsbad, CA. Since its beginnings in the 1950s, the Danish maker has manufactured more than 189 billion Lego blocks. Legos were introduced in the US in 1962. For info: Legoland, One Lego Dr, Carlsbad, CA 92008. Phone: (760) 918-LEGO. Web: www.legoland.dk.

NATIONAL AGRICULTURE DAY. Mar 20. A day to honor America's providers of food and fiber and to educate the general public about the US agricultural system. Week of celebration: Mar 19–25. Annually, the first day of spring. See Curriculum Connection. For info: Agriculture Council of America, 11020 King St, Ste 205, Overland Park, KS 66210. Phone: (913) 491-1895. Fax: (913) 491-6502. E-mail: aca@nama.org. Web: www.agday.org.

NATIONAL ENERGY EDUCATION WEEK. Mar 20–24. To make energy education part of the school curriculum. The week ending in the second to last Friday in March. For info: Natl Energy Education Development Project, PO Box 2518, Reston, VA 20195. Phone: (800) 875-5029.

SPRING. Mar 20–June 20. In the Northern Hemisphere spring begins today with the vernal equinox, at 2:35 AM, EST. Note that in the Southern Hemisphere today is the beginning of autumn. Sun rises due east and sets due west everywhere on Earth (except near poles) and the daylight length (interval between sunrise and

March 2000	S	M	T	W	T	F	S
				1	2	3	4
	5	6	7	8	9	10	11
	12	13	14	15	16	17	18
	19	20	21	22	23	24	25
	26	27	28	29	30	31	

sunset) is virtually the same everywhere today: 12 hours, 8 minutes.

TA'ANIT ESTHER (FAST OF ESTHER). Mar 20. Hebrew calendar date: Adar 13, 5760. Commemorates Queen Esther's fast, in the 6th century BC, to save the Jews of ancient Persia. Ordinarily observed Adar 13, the Fast of Esther is observed on the previous Thursday (Adar 11) when Adar 13 is a Sabbath.

TUNISIA: INDEPENDENCE DAY. Mar 20. Commemorates treaty in 1956 by which France recognized Tunisian autonomy.

BIRTHDAYS TODAY

Mitsumasa Anno, 74, illustrator (*Topsy-Turvies, Anno's Alphabet*), born Tsuwano, Japan, Mar 20, 1926.

Lois Lowry, 63, author (Newbery for *Number the Stars, The Giver*), born Honolulu, HI, Mar 20, 1937.

Patrick James (Pat) Riley, 55, basketball coach and former player, born Schenectady, NY, Mar 20, 1945.

Fred Rogers, 72, producer, TV personality ("Mr Rogers' Neighborhood"), born Latrobe, PA, Mar 20, 1928.

Louis Sachar, 46, author (National Book Award for *Holes*), born East Meadow, NY, Mar 20, 1954.

MARCH 21 — TUESDAY
Day 81 — 285 Remaining

AMERICAN ALLIANCE FOR HEALTH, PHYSICAL EDUCATION, RECREATION AND DANCE ANNUAL MEETING. Mar 21–25. Orlando, FL. For info: American Alliance for Health, Physical Education, Recreation & Dance, 1900 Association Dr, Reston, VA 20191-1599. Phone: (800) 213-7193 or (703) 476-3400. Web: www.aahperd.org.

ARIES, THE RAM. Mar 21–Apr 19. In the astronomical/astrological zodiac, which divides the sun's apparent orbit into 12 segments, the period Mar 21–Apr 19 is identified, traditionally, as the sun sign of Aries, the Ram. The ruling planet is Mars.

BACH, JOHANN SEBASTIAN: BIRTH ANNIVERSARY. Mar 21, 1685. Organist and composer, one of the most influential composers in musical history. Born at Eisenach, Germany, he died at Leipzig, Germany, July 28, 1750.

IRANIAN NEW YEAR: NORUZ. Mar 21. National celebration for all Iranians, this is the traditional Persian New Year. (In Iran spring comes Mar 21.) It is a celebration of nature's rebirth. Every household spreads a special cover with symbols for the seven good angels on it. These symbols are sprouts, wheat germ, apples, hyacinth, fruit of the jujube, garlic and sumac heralding life, rebirth, health, happiness, prosperity, joy and beauty. A fish bowl is also customary, representing the end of the astrological year, and wild rue is burnt to drive away evil and bring about a happy New Year. This pre-Islamic holiday, a legacy of Zoroastrianism, is also celebrated as Navruz, Nau-Roz or Noo Roz in Afghanistan, Albania, Azerbaijan, Kazakhstan, Kyrgyzstan, Tajikistan and Turkmenistan. For info: Mahvash Tafreshi, Librarian, Farmingdale Public Library, 116 Merritts Rd, Farmingdale, NY 11735. Phone: (516) 249-9090. Fax: (516) 694-9697 or Yassaman Djalali, Librarian, West Valley Branch Library, 1243 San Tomas Aquino Rd, San Jose, CA 95117. Phone: (408) 244-4766.

JUAREZ, BENITO: BIRTH ANNIVERSARY. Mar 21, 1806. A full-blooded Zapotec Indian, Benito Pablo Juarez was born at Oaxaca, Mexico and grew up to become the president of Mexico. He learned Spanish at age 12. Juarez became judge of the civil court in Oaxaca in 1842, a member of congress in 1846 and governor in 1847. In 1858, following a rebellion against the constitution, the presidency was passed to Juarez. He died at Mexico City, July 18, 1872. A symbol of liberation and of Mexican resistance to foreign intervention, his birthday is a public holiday in Mexico.

LEWIS, FRANCIS: BIRTH ANNIVERSARY. Mar 21, 1713. Signer of the Declaration of Independence, born at Wales. Died Dec 31, 1802, at Long Island, NY.

NAMIBIA: INDEPENDENCE DAY. Mar 21. National Day. Commemorates independence from South Africa in 1990.

NAW-RUZ. Mar 21. Baha'i New Year's Day. Astronomically fixed to commence the year. One of the nine days of the year when Baha'is suspend work. For info: Pamela Zivari, Baha'is of the US, Office of Public Info, 866 UN Plaza, Ste 120, New York, NY 10017-1822. Phone: (212) 803-2500. Fax: (212) 803-2573. E-mail: usopi-ny@bic.org.

POCAHONTAS (REBECCA ROLFE): DEATH ANNIVERSARY. Mar 21, 1617. Pocahontas, daughter of Powhatan, born about 1595, near Jamestown, VA, leader of the Indian union of Algonkin nations, helped to foster good will between the colonists of the Jamestown settlement and her people. Pocahontas converted to Christianity, was baptized with the name Rebecca and married John Rolfe Apr 5, 1614. In 1616, she accompanied Rolfe on a trip to his native England, where she was regarded as an overseas "ambassador." Pocahontas's stay in England drew so much attention to the Virginia Company's Jamestown settlement that lotteries were held to help support the colony. Shortly before she was scheduled to return to Jamestown, Pocahontas died at Gravesend, Kent, England, of either smallpox or pneumonia.

PURIM. Mar 21. Hebrew calendar date: Adar 14, 5760. Feasts, gifts, charity and the reading of the Book of Esther mark this joyous commemoration of Queen Esther's intervention, in the 6th century BC, to save the Jews of ancient Persia. Haman's plot to exterminate the Jews was thwarted, and he was hanged on the very day he had set for execution of the Jews.

SINGLE PARENTS DAY. Mar 21. Dedicated to recognizing and heightening awareness of Americans to the issues related to single-parent households. In 1984, Congress established Mar 21 as Single Parents Day. Each year the Coalition for Single Parents gives out the Single Parent of the Year Award. 1998 recipient: Rosie O'Donnell. For info: Janice S. Moglen, PO Box 61014, Denver, CO 80206. Phone: (303) 899-4971. Fax: (303) 832-1667. E-mail: daymar21@privatei.com. Web: www2.privatei.com/~daymar21.

SOUTH AFRICA: HUMAN RIGHTS DAY. Mar 21. National holiday. Commemorates the massacre in 1960 at Sharpeville and all those who lost their lives in the struggle for equal rights as citizens of South Africa.

UNITED NATIONS: INTERNATIONAL DAY FOR THE ELIMINATION OF RACIAL DISCRIMINATION. Mar 21. Initiated by the United Nations General Assembly in 1966 to be observed annually Mar 21, the anniversary of the killing of 69 African demonstrators at Sharpeville, South Africa in 1960, as a day to remember "the victims of Sharpeville and those countless others in different parts of the world who have fallen victim to racial injustice" and to promote efforts to eradicate racial discrimination worldwide. Info from: United Nations, Dept of Public Info, New York, NY 10017.

BIRTHDAYS TODAY

Margaret Mahy, 64, author (*The Rattlebang Picnic*), born Whakatane, New Zealand, Mar 21, 1936.

Rosie O'Donnell, 38, talk show host, actress (*A League of Their Own, The Flintstones*), born Commack, NY, Mar 21, 1962.

David Wisniewski, 47, illustrator and author (Caldecott for *Golem*), born Middlesex, England, Mar 21, 1953.

MARCH 22 — WEDNESDAY
Day 82 — 284 Remaining

CALDECOTT, RANDOLPH: BIRTH ANNIVERSARY. Mar 22, 1846. Illustrator who brought greater beauty to children's books, born at Chester, England. He died at St. Augustine, FL, Feb 12, 1886. The Caldecott Medal given annually by the American Library Association for the most distinguished American picture book for children is named in his honor.

EQUAL RIGHTS AMENDMENT SENT TO STATES FOR RATIFICATION: ANNIVERSARY. Mar 22, 1972. The Senate passed the 27th Amendment, prohibiting discrimination on the basis of sex, sending it to the states for ratification. Hawaii led the way as the first state to ratify and by the end of the year 22 of the required states had ratified it. On Oct 6, 1978, the deadline for ratification was extended to June 30, 1982, by Congress. The amendment still lacked three of the required 38 states for ratification. This was the first extension granted since Congress set seven years as the limit for ratification. The amendment failed to achieve ratification as the deadline came and passed and no additional states ratified the measure.

FIRST WOMEN'S COLLEGIATE BASKETBALL GAME: ANNIVERSARY. Mar 22, 1893. The first women's collegiate basketball game was played at Smith College at Northampton, MA. Senda Berenson, then Smith's director of physical education and "mother of women's basketball," supervised the game, in which Smith's sophomore team beat the freshman team 5–4. For info: Dir of Media Relations, Smith College, Office of College Relations, Northampton, MA 01063. Phone: (413) 585-2190. Fax: (413) 585-2174. E-mail: lfenlason@colrel.smith.edu.

INTERNATIONAL GOOF-OFF DAY. Mar 22. A day of relaxation and a time to be oneself; a day for some good-humored fun and some good-natured silliness. Everyone needs one special day each year to goof off. For info: Monica A. Dufour, 471 S Vanburen Circle, Davison, MI 48423-8535. Phone: (810) 658-3147.

LASER PATENTED: 40th ANNIVERSARY. Mar 22, 1960. The first patent for a laser (Light Amplification by Stimulated Emission of Radiation) was granted to Arthur Schawlow and Charles Townes.

SPACE MILESTONE: RECORD TIME IN SPACE: 5th ANNIVERSARY. Mar 22, 1995. A Russian cosmonaut returned to Earth after setting a record of 439 days in space aboard *Mir*. Previous records include three Soviet cosmonauts who spent 237 days in space at *Salyut 7* space station in 1984, a Soviet cosmonaut who spent 326 days aboard *Mir* in 1987 and two Soviets who spent 366 days aboard *Mir* in 1988. The longest stay in space by any US astronaut was Shannon Lucid's 188-day stay on *Mir* in 1996. This also set a record for women in space.

UNITED NATIONS: WORLD DAY FOR WATER. Mar 22. The General Assembly declared this observance (Res 47/193) to promote public awareness of how water resource development contributes to economic productivity and social well-being.

BIRTHDAYS TODAY

Shawn Bradley, 28, basketball player, born Landstuhl, West Germany, Mar 22, 1972.

Robert Quinlan (Bob) Costas, 48, sportscaster, born New York, NY, Mar 22, 1952.

Orrin Grant Hatch, 66, US Senator (R, Utah), born Pittsburgh, PA, Mar 22, 1934.

Cristen Powell, 21, race car driver, born Portland, OR, Mar 22, 1979.

William Shatner, 69, actor (Captain Kirk of "Star Trek"; "TJ Hooker"), author (*Tek* novels), born Montreal, Quebec, Canada, Mar 22, 1931.

Elvis Stojko, 28, skater, born Newmarket, Ontario, Canada, Mar 22, 1972.

MARCH 23 — THURSDAY
Day 83 — 283 Remaining

CHILDREN'S LITERATURE FESTIVAL. Mar 23–25. Central Missouri State University, Warrensburg, MO. Designed for teachers to introduce them to authors of children's and young adult literature. Est attendance: 7,000. For info: Pal V. Rao, Children's Literature Festival, Central Missouri State Univ, Warrensburg, MO 64093. Phone: (660) 543-4140. Fax: (660) 543-8001. E-mail: Pal@libserv.csmu.edu. Web: library.csmu.edu/deanpage.htm.

COLFAX, SCHUYLER: BIRTH ANNIVERSARY. Mar 23, 1823. Seventeenth vice president of the US (1869–73). Born at New York, NY. Died Jan 13, 1885, at Mankato, MN.

LIBERTY DAY: 225th ANNIVERSARY. Mar 23, 1775. Anniversary of Patrick Henry's speech for arming the Virginia militia at St. Johns Church, Richmond, VA. "I know not what course others may take, but as for me, give me liberty or give me death."

NEAR MISS DAY. Mar 23, 1989. A mountain-sized asteroid passed within 500,000 miles of Earth, a very close call according to NASA. Impact would have equaled the strength of 40,000 hydrogen bombs, created a crater the size of the District of Columbia and devastated everything for 100 miles in all directions.

NEW ZEALAND: OTAGO AND SOUTHLAND PROVINCIAL ANNIVERSARY. Mar 23. In addition to the statutory public holidays of New Zealand, there is in each provincial district a holiday for the provincial anniversary. This is observed in Otago and Southland.

PAKISTAN: REPUBLIC DAY: 60th ANNIVERSARY. Mar 23. National holiday. The All-India-Muslim League adopted a resolution calling for a Muslim homeland in 1940. On the same day in 1956 Pakistan declared itself a republic.

UNITED NATIONS: WORLD METEOROLOGICAL DAY. Mar 23. An international day observed by meteorological services throughout the world and by the organizations of the UN system. For info: United Nations, Dept of Public Info, New York, NY 10017.

		S	M	T	W	T	F	S
March					1	2	3	4
2000		5	6	7	8	9	10	11
		12	13	14	15	16	17	18
		19	20	21	22	23	24	25
		26	27	28	29	30	31	

BIRTHDAYS TODAY

Eleanor Cameron, 88, author (*The Court of the Stone Children*), born Winnipeg, Manitoba, Canada, Mar 23, 1912.

Jason Kidd, 27, basketball player, born San Francisco, CA, Mar 23, 1973.

Moses Eugene Malone, 46, former basketball player, born Petersburg, VA, Mar 23, 1954.

MARCH 24 — FRIDAY
Day 84 — 282 Remaining

EXXON VALDEZ OIL SPILL: ANNIVERSARY. Mar 24, 1989. The tanker *Exxon Valdez* ran aground at Prince William Sound, leaking 11 million gallons of oil into one of nature's richest habitats.

HOUDINI, HARRY: BIRTH ANNIVERSARY. Mar 24, 1874. Magician and escape artist. Born at Budapest, Hungary, died at Detroit, MI, Oct 31, 1926. Lecturer, athlete, author, expert on history of magic, exposer of fraudulent mediums and motion picture actor. Was best known for his ability to escape from locked restraints (handcuffs, straitjackets, coffins, boxes and milk cans). Anniversary of his death (Halloween) has been the occasion for meetings of magicians and attempts at communication by mediums.

PHILIPPINE INDEPENDENCE: ANNIVERSARY. Mar 24, 1934. President Franklin Roosevelt signed a bill granting independence to the Philippines. The bill, which took effect July 4, 1946, brought to a close almost half a century of US control of the islands.

RHODE ISLAND VOTERS REJECT CONSTITUTION: ANNIVERSARY. Mar 24, 1788. In a popular referendum, Rhode Island rejected the new Constitution by a vote of 2,708 to 237. The state later (May 29, 1790) ratified the Constitution and ratified the Bill of Rights, June 7, 1790.

TAIWAN: BIRTHDAY OF KUAN YIN, GODDESS OF MERCY. Mar 24. Nineteenth day of Second Moon of the lunar calendar, celebrated at Taipei's Lungshan (Dragon Mountain) and other temples.

TB BACILLUS DISCOVERED: ANNIVERSARY. Mar 24, 1882. The tuberculosis bacillus was discovered by German scientist Robert Koch.

BIRTHDAYS TODAY

Dr. Roger Bannister, 71, distance runner, broke the 4-minute-mile record in 1954, born Harrow, Middlesex, England, Mar 24, 1929.

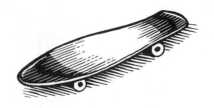

MARCH 25 — SATURDAY
Day 85 — 281 Remaining

ASSOCIATION FOR SUPERVISION AND CURRICULUM DEVELOPMENT CONFERENCE. Mar 25–27. New Orleans, LA. For info: Assn for Supervision and Curriculum Development, 1703 N Beauregard St, Alexandria, VA 22311-1714. Phone: (703) 578-9600. Fax: (703) 575-5400. Web: www.ascd.org.

BORGLUM, GUTZON: BIRTH ANNIVERSARY. Mar 25, 1871. American sculptor who created the huge sculpture of four American presidents (Washington, Jefferson, Lincoln and Theodore Roosevelt) at Mount Rushmore National Memorial in the Black Hills of South Dakota. Born John Gutzon de la Mothe Borglum at Bear Lake, ID, the son of Mormon pioneers, he worked the last 14 years of his life on the Mount Rushmore sculpture. He died at Chicago, IL, Mar 6, 1941.

FEAST OF ANNUNCIATION. Mar 25. Celebrated in the Roman Catholic Church in commemoration of the message of the Angel Gabriel to Mary that she was to be the Mother of Christ.

GREECE: INDEPENDENCE DAY. Mar 25. National holiday. Celebrates the beginning of the Greek revolt for independence from the Ottoman Empire in 1821. Greece attained independence in 1829.

MARYLAND DAY. Mar 25. Commemorates arrival of Lord Baltimore's first settlers in Maryland in 1634.

PECAN DAY: 225th ANNIVERSARY. Mar 25, 1775. Anniversary of the planting by George Washington, of pecan trees (some of which still survive) at Mount Vernon. The trees were a gift to Washington from Thomas Jefferson, who had planted a few pecan trees from the southern US at Monticello, VA. The pecan, native to southern North America, is sometimes called "America's own nut." First cultivated by American Indians, it has been transplanted to other continents but has failed to achieve wide use or popularity outside the US.

TRIANGLE SHIRTWAIST FIRE: ANNIVERSARY. Mar 25, 1911. At about 4:30 PM, fire broke out at the Triangle Shirtwaist Company at New York, NY, minutes before the seamstresses were to go home. Some workers were fatally burned while others leaped to their deaths from the windows of the 10-story building. The fire lasted only 18 minutes but left 146 workers dead, most of them young immigrant women. It was found that some of the deaths were a direct result of workers being trapped on the ninth floor by a locked door. Labor law forbade locking factory doors while employees were at work, and owners of the company were indicted on charges of first- and second-degree manslaughter. The tragic fire became a turning point in labor history, bringing about reforms in health and safety laws.

BIRTHDAYS TODAY

Cammi Granato, 29, Olympic ice hockey player, born Maywood, IL, Mar 25, 1971.
Elton John, 53, singer, songwriter, born Reginald Kenneth Dwight, Pinner, England, Mar 25, 1947.

MARCH 26 — SUNDAY

Day 86 — 280 Remaining

BANGLADESH: INDEPENDENCE DAY. Mar 26. Commemorates East Pakistan's independence in 1971 as the state of Bangladesh. Celebrated with parades, youth festivals and symposia.

CAMP DAVID ACCORD SIGNED: ANNIVERSARY. Mar 26, 1979. Israeli Prime Minister Menachem Begin and Egyptian President Anwar Sadat signed the Camp David peace treaty, ending 30 years of war between their two countries. The agreement was fostered by President Jimmy Carter.

EUROPE: SUMMER DAYLIGHT SAVING TIME. Mar 26–Oct 29. Many European countries observe daylight-saving (summer) time from 2 AM on the last Sunday in March until 3 AM on the last Sunday in October.

FROST, ROBERT LEE: BIRTH ANNIVERSARY. Mar 26, 1874. American poet who tried his hand at farming, teaching, shoemaking and editing before winning acclaim as a poet. Pulitzer Prize winner. Born at San Francisco, CA, he died at Boston, MA, Jan 29, 1963.

MAKE UP YOUR OWN HOLIDAY DAY. Mar 26. This day is a day you may name for whatever you wish. Reach for the stars! Make up a holiday! Annually, Mar 26. [© 1998 by WPL] For info: Thomas and Ruth Roy, Wellness Permission League, PO Box 662, Mt Gretna, PA 17064-0662. Phone: (717) 964-1308. Fax: (717) 964-1335. E-mail: wellcat@desupernet.net.

PRINCE JONAH KUHIO KALANIANOLE DAY. Mar 26. Hawaii. Commemorates the man, who as Hawaii's delegate to the US Congress, introduced the first bill for statehood in 1919. Not until 1959 did Hawaii become a state.

SOVIET COSMONAUT RETURNS TO NEW COUNTRY: ANNIVERSARY. Mar 26, 1992. After spending 313 days in space in the Soviet *Mir* space station, cosmonaut Serge Krikalev returned to Earth and to what was for him a new country. He left Earth May 18, 1991, a citizen of the Soviet Union, but during his stay aboard the space station, the Soviet Union crumbled and became the Commonwealth of Independent States. Originally scheduled to return in October 1991, Krikalev's return was delayed by five months due to his country's disintegration and the ensuing monetary problems.

UNITED KINGDOM: SUMMER TIME. Mar 26–Oct 29. "Summer Time" (one hour in advance of Standard Time), similar to daylight-saving time, is observed from 0100 hours on the day after the fourth Saturday in March until 0100 hours on the day after the fourth Saturday in October.

BIRTHDAYS TODAY

Marcus Allen, 40, football player, born San Diego, CA, Mar 26, 1960.
Sandra Day O'Connor, 70, Associate Justice of the US Supreme Court, born El Paso, TX, Mar 26, 1930.
John Houston Stockton, 38, basketball player, born Spokane, WA, Mar 26, 1962.

MARCH 27 — MONDAY

Day 87 — 279 Remaining

EARTHQUAKE STRIKES ALASKA: ANNIVERSARY. Mar 27, 1964. The strongest earthquake in North American history (8.4 on the Richter scale) struck Alaska, east of Anchorage. 117 people were killed.

FUNKY WINKERBEAN: ANNIVERSARY. Mar 27, 1972. Anniversary of the nationally syndicated comic strip. For info: Tom Batiuk, Creator, 2750 Substation Rd, Medina, OH 44256. Phone: (330) 722-8755.

MOON PHASE: LAST QUARTER. Mar 27. Moon enters Last Quarter phase at 7:21 PM, EST.

NATIONAL SLEEP AWARENESS WEEK. Mar 27–Apr 4. All Americans are urged to recognize the dangers of untreated sleep disorders and the importance of proper sleep to their health, safety and productivity. "8ZZZs, please!" For info: Natl Sleep Foundation, 729 15th St NW, 4th Floor, Washington, DC 20005. Phone: (888) NSF-SLEEP.

RÖNTGEN, WILHELM KONRAD: BIRTH ANNIVERSARY. Mar 27, 1845. German scientist who discovered x-rays (1895) and won a Nobel Prize in 1901. Born at Lennep, Prussia, he died at Munich, Germany, Feb 10, 1923. See also: "X-Ray Discovery Day: Anniversary" (Nov 8).

SEWARD'S DAY: ANNIVERSARY OF THE ACQUISITION OF ALASKA. Mar 27. Observed in Alaska near anniversary of its acquisition from Russia in 1867. The treaty of purchase was signed between the Russians and the Americans Mar 30, 1867, and ratified by the Senate May 28, 1867. The territory was formally transferred Oct 18, 1867. Annually, the last Monday in March.

BIRTHDAYS TODAY

Mariah Carey, 30, singer, born New York, NY, Mar 27, 1970.

MARCH 28 — TUESDAY
Day 88 — 278 Remaining

AMERICAN DIABETES ALERT. Mar 28. A one-day "wake-up call" for those eight million Americans who have diabetes and don't even know it. During the Alert, local ADA affiliates use the diabetes risk test—a simple paper-and-pencil quiz—to communicate the risk factors and symptoms of the disease. For more information, call 1-800-DIABETES (342-2383). Annually, the fourth Tuesday in March. For info: (800) 232-3472.

CZECH REPUBLIC: TEACHERS' DAY. Mar 28. Celebrates birth on this day of Jan Amos Komensky (Comenius), Moravian educational reformer (1592–1671).

"GREATEST SHOW ON EARTH" FORMED: ANNIVERSARY. Mar 28, 1881. P.T. Barnum and James A. Bailey merged their circuses to form the "Greatest Show on Earth."

SPACE MILESTONE: *NOAA 8* (US). Mar 28, 1983. Search and Rescue Satellite (SARSAT) launched from Vandenburg Air Force Base, CA, to aid in locating ships and aircraft in distress. *Kosmos 1383*, launched July 1, 1982, by the USSR, in a cooperative rescue effort, is credited with saving more than 20 lives.

THREE MILE ISLAND NUCLEAR POWER PLANT ACCIDENT: ANNIVERSARY. Mar 28, 1979. A series of accidents beginning at 4 AM, EST, at Three Mile Island on the Susquehanna River about 10 miles southeast of Harrisburg, PA, was responsible for extensive reevaluation of the safety of existing nuclear power generating operations. Equipment and other failures reportedly brought Three Mile Island close to a meltdown of the uranium core, threatening extensive radiation contamination.

BIRTHDAYS TODAY

Byrd Baylor, 76, author (*I'm in Charge of Celebrations*), born San Antonio, TX, Mar 28, 1924.
Frank Hughes Murkowski, 67, US Senator (R, Alaska), born Seattle, WA, Mar 28, 1933.

MARCH 29 — WEDNESDAY
Day 89 — 277 Remaining

"AMERICA'S SUBWAY" DAY: ANNIVERSARY. Mar 29, 1976. The Washington (DC) Metropolitan Area Transit Authority ran its first Metrorail passenger train 24 years ago. The Metro system consisted of only five stations and 4.6 miles on the Red Line Route. In 1999 two more stations and three miles of track were added to the system. Metro now consists of 78 stations and 98 miles of service. Passengers make more than 500,000 trips each weekday in the nation's capital and the greater Washington area. Many of these are made by tourists from across the country and around the world — hence the moniker "America's Subway." For info: Cheryl Johnson, Washington Metropolitan Area Transit Authority, 600 Fifth St NW, Washington, DC 20001. Phone: (202) 962-1051. Fax: (202) 962-2897.

CANADA: BRITISH NORTH AMERICA ACT: ANNIVERSARY. Mar 29, 1867. This act of the British Parliament established the Dominion of Canada, uniting Ontario, Quebec, Nova Scotia and New Brunswick. Union was proclaimed July 1, 1867. The remaining colonies in Canada were still ruled directly by Great Britain until Manitoba joined the Dominion in 1870, British Columbia in 1871, Prince Edward Island in 1873, Alberta and Saskatchewan in 1905 and Newfoundland in 1949. See also: "Canada: Canada Day" (July 1).

HOOVER, LOU HENRY: 125th BIRTH ANNIVERSARY. Mar 29, 1875. Wife of Herbert Clark Hoover, 31st president of the US. Born at Waterloo, IA, she died at Palo Alto, CA, Jan 7, 1944.

MADAGASCAR: COMMEMORATION DAY. Mar 29. Commemoration Day for the victims of the rebellion in 1947 against French colonization.

TAIWAN: YOUTH DAY. Mar 29.

TEXAS LOVE THE CHILDREN DAY. Mar 29. A day recognizing every child's right and need to be loved. Promoting the hope that one day all children will live in loving, safe environments and will be given proper health care and equal learning opportunities. Precedes the start of National Child Abuse Prevention Month (April). For info: Patty Murphy, 7713 Chasewood Dr, North Richland Hills, TX 76180. Phone: (817) 498-5840. E-mail: MURPH0@flash.net.

TWENTY-THIRD AMENDMENT TO US CONSTITUTION RATIFIED: ANNIVERSARY. Mar 29, 1961. District of Columbia residents were given the right to vote in presidential elections under the 23rd Amendment.

TYLER, JOHN: BIRTH ANNIVERSARY. Mar 29, 1790. Tenth president of the US (Apr 6, 1841–Mar 3, 1845). Born at Greenway, VA, Tyler succeeded to the presidency upon the death of William Henry Harrison. Tyler's first wife died while he was president, and he remarried before the end of his term of office, becoming the first president to marry while in office. Fifteen children were born of the two marriages. In 1861 he was elected to the Congress of the Confederate States but died at Richmond, VA, Jan 18, 1862, before being seated. His death received no official tribute from the US government.

YOUNG, DENTON TRUE (CY): BIRTH ANNIVERSARY. Mar 29, 1867. Baseball Hall of Fame pitcher born at Gilmore, OH. Young is baseball's all-time winningest pitcher, having accumulated 511 victories in his 22-year career. The Cy Young Award is

	S	M	T	W	T	F	S
March 2000				1	2	3	4
	5	6	7	8	9	10	11
	12	13	14	15	16	17	18
	19	20	21	22	23	24	25
	26	27	28	29	30	31	

given each year in his honor to major league's best pitcher. Inducted into the Hall of Fame in 1937. Died at Peoli, OH, Nov 4, 1955.

BIRTHDAYS TODAY

Lucy Lawless, 32, actress ("Xena"), born Mount Albert, Auckland, New Zealand, Mar 29, 1968.

MARCH 30 — THURSDAY
Day 90 — 276 Remaining

ANESTHETIC FIRST USED IN SURGERY: ANNIVERSARY. Mar 30, 1842. Dr. Crawford W. Long, having seen the use of nitrous oxide and sulfuric ether at "laughing gas" parties, observed that individuals under their influences felt no pain. On this date, he removed a tumor from the neck of a man who was under the influence of ether.

DOCTORS' DAY. Mar 30. Traditional annual observance since 1933 to honor America's physicians on anniversary of occasion when Dr. Crawford W. Long became the first acclaimed physician to use ether as an anesthetic agent in a surgical technique, Mar 30, 1842. The red carnation has been designated the official flower of Doctors' Day.

ITALY: BOLOGNA INTERNATIONAL CHILDREN'S BOOK FAIR. Mar 30–Apr 2 (tentative). Bologna, Italy. Publishers from 79 countries exhibit their books to the trade. Est attendance: 25,000. For info: Bologna Children's Book Fair, Piazza Costituzione, Italy. Phone: 51-282-361. Fax: 51-282-333. E-mail: dir.com@bolognafiere.it. Web: www.bolognafiere.it/BookFair.

PENCIL PATENTED: ANNIVERSARY. Mar 30, 1858. First pencil with the eraser top was patented by Hyman Lipman.

SEWELL, ANNA: BIRTH ANNIVERSARY. Mar 30, 1820. Born at Yarmouth, England, Anna Sewell is best known for her book *Black Beauty*. Published in 1877, her tale centers around the abuses and injustices to horses she saw while growing up. She died at Old Catton, Norfolk, England, Apr 25, 1878.

TRINIDAD AND TOBAGO: SPIRITUAL BAPTIST LIBERATION SHOUTER DAY. Mar 30. Public Holiday. For info: Information Dept, Tourism Div, Tourism and Industrial Development Co, 10-14 Phillips St, Port of Spain, Trinidad, West Indies.

VAN GOGH, VINCENT: BIRTH ANNIVERSARY. Mar 30, 1853. Dutch post-Impressionist painter, especially known for his bold and powerful use of color (*Sunflowers, The Starry Night*). Born at Groot Zundert, Netherlands, he died at Auvers-sur-Oise, France, July 29, 1890.

BIRTHDAYS TODAY

Robert C. Smith, 59, US Senator (R, New Hampshire), born Tuftonboro, NH, Mar 30, 1941.

MARCH 31 — FRIDAY
Day 91 — 275 Remaining

CHAVEZ, CESAR ESTRADA: BIRTH ANNIVERSARY. Mar 31, 1927. Labor leader who organized migrant farm workers in support of better working conditions. Chavez initiated the National Farm Workers Association in 1962, attracting attention to the migrant farm workers' plight by organizing boycotts of products including grapes and lettuce. He was born at Yuma, AZ, and died Apr 23, 1993, at San Luis, AZ. His birthday is a holiday in California.

CHESNUT, MARY BOYKIN MILLER: BIRTH ANNIVERSARY. Mar 31, 1823. Born at Pleasant Hill, SC, and died Nov 22, 1886, at Camden, SC. During the Civil War Chesnut accompanied her husband, a Confederate staff officer, on military missions. She kept a journal of her experiences and observations, which was published posthumously as *A Diary from Dixie*, a perceptive portrait of Confederate military and political leaders and insightful view of Southern life during the Civil War.

EIFFEL TOWER: ANNIVERSARY. Mar 31, 1889. Built for the Paris Exhibition of 1889, the tower was named for its architect, Alexandre Gustave Eiffel, and is one of the world's best known landmarks.

JOHNSON, JOHN (JACK) ARTHUR: BIRTH ANNIVERSARY. Mar 31, 1878. In 1908 Jack Johnson became the first black to win the heavyweight boxing championship when he defeated Tommy Burns at Sydney, Australia. Unable to accept a black's triumph, the boxing world tried to find a white challenger. Jim Jeffries, former heavyweight title holder, was badgered out of retirement. On July 4, 1919, at Reno, NV, the "battle of the century" proved to be a farce when Johnson handily defeated Jeffries. Race riots swept the US and plans to exhibit the film of the fight were canceled. Johnson was born at Galveston, TX, and died in an automobile accident June 10, 1946, at Raleigh, NC. He was inducted into the Boxing Hall of Fame in 1990. The film *The Great White Hope* is based on his life.

US AIR FORCE ACADEMY ESTABLISHED: ANNIVERSARY. Mar 31, 1954. The US Air Force Academy was established at Colorado Springs, CO, to train officers for the Air Force.

VIRGIN ISLANDS: TRANSFER DAY. Mar 31. Commemorates transfer resulting from purchase of the Virgin Islands by the US from Denmark, Mar 31, 1917, for $25 million.

BIRTHDAYS TODAY

William Daniels, 73, actor ("Boy Meets World"), born Brooklyn, NY, Mar 31, 1927.

Al Gore, 52, 45th vice-president of the US, born Albert Gore, Jr, Washington, DC, Mar 31, 1948.

Angus King, Jr, 56, Governor of Maine (I), born Alexandria, VA, Mar 31, 1944.

Patrick J. Leahy, 60, US Senator (D, Vermont), born Montpelier, VT, Mar 31, 1940.

Steve Smith, 31, basketball player, born Highland Park, MI, Mar 31, 1969.

APRIL 1 — SATURDAY
Day 92 — 274 Remaining

ALCOHOL AWARENESS MONTH. Apr 1–30. To help raise awareness among community prevention leaders and citizens about the problem of underage drinking. Concentrates on community grassroots activities. For info: Public Info Dept, Natl Council on Alcoholism and Drug Dependence, Inc, 12 W 21st St, New York, NY 10010. Phone: (212) 206-6770. Fax: (212) 645-1690. Web: www.ncadd.org.

APRIL FOOLS' or ALL FOOLS' DAY. Apr 1. "The joke of the day is to deceive persons by sending them upon frivolous and nonsensical errands; to pretend they are wanted when they are not, or, in fact, any way to betray them into some supposed ludicrous situation, so as to enable you to call them 'An April Fool.'"–Brady's *Clavis Calendaria*, 1812. For links to April Fools' Day sites on the web, go to: deil.lang.uiuc.edu/web.pages/holidays/aprilfool.html.

BE KIND TO ANIMALS KIDS CONTEST DEADLINE. Apr 1. Application deadline for this contest. The national winner will receive a $5,000 scholarship. For info: American Humane Assn, 63 Inverness Dr East, Englewood, CO 80112. Phone: (303) 792-9900. Web: www.americanhumane.org.

BULGARIA: SAINT LASARUS'S DAY. Apr 1. Ancient Slavic holiday of young girls, in honor of the goddess of spring and love.

CANADA: NUNAVUT INDEPENDENCE: ANNIVERSARY. Apr 1, 1999. Nunavut became Canada's third independent territory. This self-governing territory with an Inuit majority was created from the eastern half of the Northwest Territories. In 1992 Canada's Inuit people accepted a federal land-claim package granting them control over the new territory.

★**CANCER CONTROL MONTH.** Apr 1–30.

EXCHANGE CLUB CHILD ABUSE PREVENTION MONTH. Apr 1–30. Nationwide effort to raise awareness of child abuse and how to prevent it. For info: The Natl Exchange Club, Foundation for Prevention of Child Abuse, 3050 Central Ave, Toledo, OH 43606-1700. Phone: (419) 535-3232 or (800) 760-3413. Fax: (419) 535-1989. E-mail: info@preventchildabuse.com. Web: www.preventchildabuse.com.

	S	M	T	W	T	F	S
April							1
2000	2	3	4	5	6	7	8
	9	10	11	12	13	14	15
	16	17	18	19	20	21	22
	23	24	25	26	27	28	29
	30						

GOLDEN RULE WEEK. Apr 1–7. The purpose of this week is to remind everyone of the importance of the Golden Rule in making this a better world in which we all may live. For a copy of the Golden Rule of 10 religions, send $4 to cover printing and postage. For info: Dr. Stanley J. Drake, Pres, Intl Soc of Friendship and Goodwill, 412 Cherry Hills Dr, Bakersfield, CA 93309-7902.

HARVEY, WILLIAM: BIRTH ANNIVERSARY. Apr 1, 1578. Physician, born at Folkestone, England. The first to discover the mechanics of the circulation of the blood. Died at Roehampton, England, June 3, 1657.

INTERNATIONAL AMATEUR RADIO MONTH. Apr 1–30. To disseminate information about the important part amateur radio operators or "hams" throughout the world are playing in promoting friendship, peace and good will. To obtain complete information about becoming an International Good Will Ambassador as well as a list of amateur radio operators in many countries, send $4 to cover expense of printing, handling and postage. Annually, the month of April. For info: Dr. Stanley Drake, Pres, Intl Soc of Friendship and Good Will, 412 Cherry Hills Dr, Bakersfield, CA 93309-7902.

KEEP AMERICA BEAUTIFUL MONTH. Apr 1–30. To educate Americans about their personal responsibility for litter prevention, proper waste disposal and environmental improvement through various community projects. Annually, the month of April. For info: Evan Jones, Dir of Communications, Keep America Beautiful, Inc, Washington Square, 1010 Washington Blvd, Stamford, CT 06901. Phone: (203) 323-8987. Fax: (203) 325-9199. E-mail: keepamerbe@aol.com.

MATHEMATICS EDUCATION MONTH. Apr 1–30. An opportunity for students, teachers, parents and the community as a whole to focus on the importance of mathematics and the changes taking place in the mathematics curriculum. See Curriculum Connection. For info: Communications Manager, Natl Council of Teachers of Mathematics, 1906 Association Dr, Reston, VA 20191-1593. Phone: (703) 620-9840. Fax: (703) 476-2970. E-mail: info central@nctm.org. Web: www.nctm.org.

MONTH OF THE YOUNG CHILD®. Apr 1–30. Michigan. To promote awareness of the importance of young children and their specific needs in today's society. Many communities celebrate with special events for children and families. For info: Michigan Assn for Education of Young Children, Beacon Pl, Ste 1-D, 4572 S Hagadorn Road, East Lansing, MI 48823-5385. Phone: (800) 336-6424 or (517) 336-9700. Fax: (517) 336-9790. E-mail: moyc@miaeyc.com. Web: www.miaeyc.com.

NATIONAL BLUE RIBBON WEEK. Apr 1–7. Wear a blue ribbon to show your concern about and objection to child abuse. Nationwide public awareness effort. For info: The Natl Exchange Club, 3050 Central Ave, Toledo, OH 43606-1700. Phone: (419) 535-3232 or (800) 924-2643. Fax: (419) 535-1989. E-mail: nechq@aol.com. Web: www.nationalexchangeclub.com.

NATIONAL HUMOR MONTH. Apr 1–30. Focuses on the joy and therapeutic value of laughter and how it can reduce stress, improve job performance and enrich the quality of life. For info: send SASE (55¢) to: Larry Wilde, Dir, The Carmel Institute of Humor, 25470 Canada Dr, Carmel, CA 93923-8926. E-mail: larry wilde@aol.com. Web: www.larrywilde.com.

NATIONAL KNUCKLES DOWN MONTH. Apr 1–30. To recognize and revive the American tradition of playing and collecting marbles and keep it rolling along. Please send self-addressed, stamped envelope with inquiries. For info: Cathy C. Runyan-Svacina, The Marble Lady, 7812 NW Hampton Rd, Kansas City, MO 64152. Phone: (816) 587-8687. Fax: Same as Phone.

APRIL 1–30
MATH EDUCATION MONTH

Make enjoyable math activities the focus this month. Primary students can work as partners and take turns acting as storekeepers and customers. Give students play money to "purchase" items they would regularly use for the day in class: paper, books from the classroom library, scissors or paste. Prices should reflect amounts that will lead to most student success, depending on the purpose of the lesson. In first grade, prices might be the face value of coins. For higher levels of interaction, set amounts at prices that will require making change.

Use data from attendance records and cafeteria lunch choices to work with bar graphs and percentages. The same can be done with class polls on favorite foods, singers, stories or school subjects.

Calculators provide hours of entertainment. *Calculator Riddles*, by David Adler (Holiday House, 0-8234-1186-9, $14.95 Gr. 3–7) is informative and fun. Encourage students to invent their own riddles.

Language arts blends into the math curriculum when you incorporate books like *Hickory Dickory Math: Teaching Math with Nursery Rhymes and Fairy Tales*, by Cecilia Dinio-Durkin (Scholastic, 0-590-06541-6, $9.95 Gr. K–2), *Marvelous Math: A Book of Poems*, selected by Lee B. Hopkins (Simon & Schuster, 0-68-980658-2, $17 All ages), and *Mother Goose Math*, by Emily Bolam (Viking, 0-67-087569-4, $14.99 PreS–2). Have students write and publish a classroom book of math poetry. *Counting Caterpillars and Other Math Poems*, by Betsy Franco (Scholastic, 0-590-64210-3, $9.95 Gr. K–2) is a teacher resource with instant activities. For additional book suggestions, consult *Read Any Good Math Lately? Children's Books for Mathematical Learning*, by David J. Whitin and Sandra Wilde (Heinemann, 0-435-08334-1, $22) and *Math Through Children's Literature: Making the NCTM Standards Come Alive*, by Kathryn L. Braddon, Nancy J. Hall and Dale Taylor (Teacher Ideas Press, 0-87287-932-1, $23.50).

Divide students into groups and ask them to brainstorm about the places they use math without realizing it. Examples could include the room's clock, a pizza and shoe sizes.

The Math Forum is a website with links to math education materials for teachers at all levels at forum.swarthmore.edu. One feature of this site is MathMagic, a project that uses e-mail to help students engage in a problem-solving dialog with children at another school. MathMagic posts challenges in each of four categories (Gr. K–3, 4–6, 7–9 and 10–12). A team of students works via e-mail with a team at another school to solve the problem. Go to forum.swarthmore.edu/mathmagic to learn more.

NATIONAL POETRY MONTH. Apr 1–30. Annual observance to pay tribute to the great legacy and ongoing achievement of American poets and the vital place of poetry in American culture. In a proclamation issued in honor of the first observance, President Bill Clinton called it "a welcome opportunity to celebrate not only the unsurpassed body of literature produced by our poets in the past, but also the vitality and diversity of voices reflected in the works of today's American poets . . . Their creativity and wealth of language enrich our culture and inspire a new generation of Americans to learn the power of reading and writing at its best." Spearheaded by the Academy of American Poets, this is the largest and most extensive celebration of poetry in American history. For info: Academy of American Poets, 584 Broadway, Ste 1208, New York, NY 10012-3250. Phone: (212) 274-0343. Web: www.poets.org.

NATIONAL SLEEP DAY. Apr 1. Sleep-deprived Americans are urged "8ZZZs, please!" For info: Natl Sleep Foundation, 729 15th St NW, 4th Floor, Washington, DC 20005. Phone: (888) NSF-SLEEP. Web: www.sleepfoundation.org.

NATIONAL YOUTH SPORTS SAFETY MONTH. Apr 1–30. Bringing public attention to the prevalent problem of injuries in youth sports. This event promotes safety in sports activities and is supported by more than 60 national sports and medical organizations. For info: Michelle Glassman, Exec Dir, Natl Youth Sports Safety Fdtn, 333 Longwood Ave, Ste 202, Boston, MA 02115. Phone: (617) 277-1171. Fax: (617) 277-2278. E-mail: NYSSF@aol.com. Web: www.nyssf.org.

PREVENTION OF CRUELTY TO ANIMALS MONTH. Apr 1–30. The ASPCA sponsors this crucial month which is designed to prevent cruelty to animals by focusing on public awareness and public education campaigns. For info: ASPCA Public Information Dept, 424 E 92nd St, New York, NY 10128. Phone: (212) 876-7700. E-mail: valeriea@aspca.org or press@aspca.org. Web: www.aspca.org.

SCHOOL LIBRARY MEDIA MONTH. Apr 1–30. Celebrates the work of school library media specialists in our nation's elementary and secondary schools. For info: American Assn of School Librarians, American Library Assn, 50 E Huron St, Chicago, IL 60611. Phone: (800) 545-2433. E-mail: AASL@ala.org. Web: www.ala.org/aasl.

SPORTS EYE SAFETY MONTH. Apr 1–30. During this month's observance, Prevent Blindness America will encourage young athletes to wear eye/face protection when participating in sports. Materials that can easily be posted or distributed to the community will be provided. For info: Prevent Blindness America®, 500 E Remington Rd, Schaumburg, IL 60173. Phone: (800) 331-2020. Fax: (847) 843-8458. Web: www.preventblindness.org.

US HOUSE OF REPRESENTATIVES ACHIEVES A QUORUM: ANNIVERSARY. Apr 1, 1789. First session of Congress was held Mar 4, 1789, but not enough representatives arrived to achieve a quorum until Apr 1.

ZAM! ZOO AND AQUARIUM MONTH. Apr 1–30. A national celebration to focus public attention on the role of zoos and aquariums in wildlife education and conservation. Held at 184 AZA member institutions in the US and Canada. Sponsor: American Zoo and Aquarium Association. For information, contact your local zoo or aquarium. For info: Zoo and Aquarium Assn, 7970 Old Georgetown Rd, Bethesda, MD 20814. Phone: (301) 907-7777. Fax: (301) 907-2980.

BIRTHDAYS TODAY

Karen Wallace, 49, author (*Imagine You Are a Crocodile*), born Ottawa, Canada, Apr 1, 1951.

APRIL 2 — SUNDAY
Day 93 — 273 Remaining

ANDERSEN, HANS CHRISTIAN: BIRTH ANNIVERSARY. Apr 2, 1805. Author chiefly remembered for his more than 150 fairy tales, many of which are regarded as classics of children's literature. Among his tales are "The Princess and the Pea," "The Snow Queen" and "The Ugly Duckling." Andersen was born at Odense, Denmark and died at Copenhagen, Denmark, Aug 4, 1875. See Curriculum Connection.

APRIL 2
HANS CHRISTIAN ANDERSEN'S BIRTHDAY AND INTERNATIONAL CHILDREN'S BOOK DAY

Andersen's fairy tales have delighted generations of children. They capture the attention of young people regardless of grade level. Using illustrated versions of Andersen's tales is a great way to pull in reluctant readers. Because of their relatively short length, the stories are good read-alouds. Perhaps a parent or the principal could be invited to be a guest reader.

Students can read several of Andersen's tales, such as "The Ugly Duckling," "Thumbelina," "The Nightingale" and "The Emperor's New Clothes." Illustrated versions by many different artists are available. Discuss similarities and differences among the stories or compare them with traditional fairy tales.

Encourage students to adapt one of Andersen's stories into a Reader's Theater format. They could also write a short, updated or modern version of a story.

A musical movie about Andersen's life, *Hans Christian Andersen*, made in 1952 and starring Danny Kaye, provides good entertainment. It is two hours long, however, so you might want to suggest it for home entertainment or a class party day.

Exposure to the many wonderful international children's books available is a rewarding first step toward understanding other cultures and giving a worldwide travel experience. *Children's Books from Other Countries*, edited by Carl Tomlinson (Scarecrow, 0-8108-3447-2, $24.50), is an invaluable resource tool for teachers. Books listed are separated into chapters reflecting different genres, each with a short synopsis. Indices list books by subject, country of origin and author or title. Part Two offers many helpful suggestions for sharing international books with children and activities that will help you incorporate them into the curriculum.

International Children's Book Day is sponsored by the International Board on Books for Young People. Each year has a theme and a poster. For more information go to the IBBY website at www.ibby.org/Seiten/04_child.htm.

BARTHOLDI, FREDERIC AUGUSTE: BIRTH ANNIVERSARY. Apr 2, 1834. French sculptor who created *Liberty Enlightening the World* (better known as the Statue of Liberty), which stands in New York Harbor. Also remembered for the *Lion of Belfort* at Belfort, France. Born at Colman, Alsace, France, he died at Paris, France, Oct 4, 1904.

CHECK YOUR BATTERIES DAY. Apr 2. A day set aside for checking the batteries in your smoke detector, carbon monoxide detector, HVAC thermostat, audio/visual remote controls and other electronic devices. This could save your life! Annually, the first Sunday in April.

FIRST WHITE HOUSE EASTER EGG ROLL: ANNIVERSARY. Apr 2, 1877. The first White House Easter Egg Roll took place during the administration of Rutherford B. Hayes. The traditional event was discontinued by President Franklin D. Roosevelt in 1942 and reinstated Apr 6, 1953, by President Dwight D. Eisenhower.

	S	M	T	W	T	F	S
April							1
2000	2	3	4	5	6	7	8
	9	10	11	12	13	14	15
	16	17	18	19	20	21	22
	23	24	25	26	27	28	29
	30						

INTERNATIONAL CHILDREN'S BOOK DAY. Apr 2. Commemorates the international aspects of children's literature and observes Hans Christian Andersen's birthday. Sponsor: International Board on Books for Young People, Nonnenweg 12, Postfach, CH-4003 Basel, Switzerland. For info: USBBY Secretariat, c/o Intl Reading Assn, Box 8139, Newark, DE 19714-8139.

NATIONAL PUBLIC HEALTH WEEK. Apr 2–8. Annually, the first full week in April. For info: American Public Health Assn, 1015 15th St NW, Washington, DC, 20005. Phone: (202) 789-5600.

NICKELODEON CHANNEL PREMIERE: ANNIVERSARY. Apr 2, 1979. Nickelodeon, the cable TV network for kids owned by MTV Networks, premiered. In 1985, Nick at Nite began offering classic TV programs in the evening hours.

PASCUA FLORIDA DAY. Apr 2. Also known as Florida State Day, this holiday commemorates the sighting of Florida by Ponce de Leon in 1513. He named the land Pascua Florida because of its discovery at Easter, the "Feast of the Flowers." Florida also commemorates Pascua Florida Week, Mar 27–Apr 2. When April 2 falls on a weekend, the Governor may declare the preceding Friday or the following Monday as State Day.

PONCE DE LEON DISCOVERS FLORIDA: ANNIVERSARY. Apr 2, 1513. Juan Ponce de Leon discovered Florida, landing at the site that became the city of St. Augustine. He claimed the land for the King of Spain.

RECONCILIATION DAY. Apr 2. Columnist Ann Landers writes, "Since 1989, I have suggested that April 2 be set aside to write that letter or make that phone call and mend a broken relationship. Life is too short to hold grudges. To forgive can be enormously life-enhancing . . . ."

US: DAYLIGHT SAVING TIME BEGINS. Apr 2–Oct 29. Daylight Saving Time begins at 2 AM. The Uniform Time Act of 1966 (as amended in 1986 by Public Law 99–359), administered by the US Dept of Transportation, provides that Standard Time in each zone be advanced one hour from 2 AM on the first Sunday in April until 2 AM on the last Sunday in October (except where state legislatures provide exemption, as in Hawaii and parts of Arizona and Indiana). Many use the popular rule "spring forward, fall back," to remember which way to turn their clocks.

US MINT: ANNIVERSARY. Apr 2, 1792. The first US Mint was established at Philadelphia, PA, as authorized by an act of Congress.

BIRTHDAYS TODAY

Ruth Heller, 76, science author and illustrator (the How to Hide . . . series), born Winnipeg, Manitoba, Canada, Apr 2, 1924.

APRIL 3 — MONDAY
Day 94 — 272 Remaining

ASTRONOMY WEEK. Apr 3–9. To take astronomy to the people. Astronomy Week is observed during the calendar week in which Astronomy Day falls. See also: "Astronomy Day" (Apr 8). See Curriculum Connection.

BLACKS RULED ELIGIBLE TO VOTE: ANNIVERSARY. Apr 3, 1944. The US Supreme Court, in an 8–1 ruling, declared that blacks could not be barred from voting in the Texas Democratic primaries. The high court repudiated the contention that political parties are private associations and held that discrimination against blacks violated the 15th Amendment.

BOSTON PUBLIC LIBRARY: ANNIVERSARY. Apr 3, 1848. The Massachusetts legislature passed legislation enabling Boston

APRIL 3–9
ASTRONOMY WEEK AND
ASTRONOMY DAY (APRIL 8)

People have been fascinated with stars and the sky for thousands of years. The Chinese charted star positions in the 1300s BC. The Babylonians had charted heavenly bodies by 450 BC. Mayan astronomers created an accurate calendar based on the sun about AD 300. Students can find examples of these ancient charts and compare them with today's sky maps and calendars.

Copernicus proposed the theory of a heliocentric (sun-centered) universe in 1543. Later Galileo was tried for heresy when he accepted this theory. Students could debate the issue as it might have occurred at the time, and then present evidence that the planets in our solar system revolve around the sun. This topic lends itself to newspaper editorial stories that students can publish in class.

Studying the moon and its phases is another research project, which extends into two- and three-dimensional art. Representing the planets in our solar system is another art project. A great interactive website on the planets is Nine Planets: Multimedia Tour of the Solar System at seds.lpl.arizona.edu/nineplanets/nineplanets/nineplanets.html. Many students enjoy learning about constellations, and comparing explanations of the night sky's patterns from various cultures. Star gazing can be a fun evening homework assignment.

Books to help you get started include: *The Planets in Our Solar System,* by Franklyn Branley (HarperCollins, 0-06-445178-X, $4.95 Gr. 1–4); *Can You Catch a Falling Star?,* by Sidney Rosen (Carolrhoda, 0-8761-4882-8, $14.95 Gr. 3–6); Seymour Simon's planet series (published by Morrow); *The Planet Hunters,* by Dennis Fradin (Simon & Schuster, 0-689-81323-6, $19.95 Gr. 5–9); *Spacebusters: The Race to the Moon,* by Philip Wilkinson (DK, 0-789-42961-6, $3.95 Gr. 1–4); *One Giant Leap: The Story of Neil Armstrong,* by Don Brown (Houghton Mifflin, 0-395-88401-2, $16 Gr. K–4). Fiction includes the Commander Toad easy readers series by Jane Yolen for ages 5–8 and the Alien Secrets series by Anita Klause for Gr. 4–8.

There are many great astronomy websites; for example, Astronomy for Kids at www.frontiernet.net/~kidpower/astronomy.html and NASA's StarChild site for children at heasarc.gsfc.nasa.gov/docs/StarChild/StarChild.html.

---

to levy a tax for a public library. This created the funding model for public libraries in the US. The Boston Public Library opened its doors in 1854.

IRVING, WASHINGTON: BIRTH ANNIVERSARY. Apr 3, 1783. American author, attorney and one time US Minister to Spain, Irving was born at New York, NY. Creator of *Rip Van Winkle* and *The Legend of Sleepy Hollow,* he was also the author of many historical and biographical works, including *A History of the Life and Voyages of Christopher Columbus* and the *Life of Washington.* Died at Tarrytown, NY, Nov 28, 1859.

MARSHALL PLAN: ANNIVERSARY. Apr 3, 1948. Suggested by Secretary of State George C. Marshall in a speech at Harvard, June 5, 1947, the legislation for the European Recovery Program, popularly known as the Marshall Plan, was signed by President Truman on Apr 3, 1948. After distributing more than $12 billion in war-torn Europe, the program ended in 1952.

WOMAN PRESIDES OVER US SUPREME COURT: 5th ANNIVERSARY. Apr 3, 1995. Supreme Court Justice Sandra Day O'Connor became the first woman to preside over the US high court when she sat in for Chief Justice William H. Rehnquist and second in seniority Justice John Paul Stevens when both were out of town.

BIRTHDAYS TODAY

Jane Goodall, 66, biologist, author (*The Chimpanzee Family Book*), born London, England, Apr 3, 1934.

Eddie Murphy, 39, comedian, actor (*Doctor Dolittle*), born Brooklyn, NY, Apr 3, 1961.

Picabo Street, 29, Olympic skier, born Triumph, ID, Apr 3, 1971.

APRIL 4 — TUESDAY
Day 95 — 271 Remaining

BONZA BOTTLER DAY™. Apr 4. To celebrate when the number of the day is the same as the number of the month. Bonza Bottler Day™ is an excuse to have a party at least once a month. For info: Gail M. Berger, 109 Matthew Ave, Poca, WV 25159. Phone: (304) 776-7746. E-mail: gberger5@aol.com.

DIX, DOROTHEA LYNDE: BIRTH ANNIVERSARY. Apr 4, 1802. American social reformer and author, born at Hampden, ME. She left home at age 10, was teaching at age 14 and founded a home for girls at Boston while still in her teens. In spite of frail health, she was a vigorous crusader for humane conditions in insane asylums, jails and almshouses and for the establishment of state-supported institutions to serve those needs. Named superintendent of women nurses during the Civil War. Died at Trenton, NJ, July 17, 1887.

FLAG ACT OF 1818: ANNIVERSARY. Apr 4, 1818. Congress approved the first flag of the US.

KING, MARTIN LUTHER, JR: ASSASSINATION ANNIVERSARY. Apr 4, 1968. The Reverend Dr. Martin Luther King, Jr, was shot at Memphis, TN. James Earl Ray was serving a 99-year sentence for the crime at the time of his death in 1998. See also: "King, Martin Luther, Jr: Birth Anniversary" (Jan 15).

KING OPPOSES VIETNAM WAR: ANNIVERSARY. Apr 4, 1967. Speaking before the Overseas Press Club at New York City, Reverend Dr. Martin Luther King, Jr, announced his opposition to the Vietnam War. That same day at the Riverside Church, King suggested that those who saw the war as dishonorable and unjust should avoid military service. He proposed that the US take new initiatives to conclude the war.

MOON PHASE: NEW MOON. Apr 4. Moon enters New Moon phase at 2:12 PM, EDT.

NATIONAL READING A ROAD MAP WEEK. Apr 4–10. To promote map reading as an enjoyable pastime and as a survival skill for present and future drivers and all armchair travelers. Motto: Happiness is knowing how to read a road map. For info: RosaLind Schilder, 309 Florence Ave, #225N, Jenkintown, PA 19046. E-mail: mikenroz18@aol.com.

NORTH ATLANTIC TREATY RATIFIED: ANNIVERSARY. Apr 4, 1949. The North Atlantic Treaty Organization was created by this treaty, which was signed by 12 nations, including the US. (Other countries joined later.) The NATO member nations are united for common defense.

SALTER ELECTED FIRST WOMAN MAYOR IN US: ANNIVERSARY. Apr 4, 1887. The first woman elected mayor in the US was Susanna Medora Salter, who was elected mayor of Argonia, KS. Her name had been submitted for election without her knowledge by the Woman's Christian Temperance Union, and she did not know she was a candidate until she went to the polls to vote. She received a two-thirds majority vote and served one year for the salary of $1.

SENEGAL: INDEPENDENCE DAY: 40th ANNIVERSARY. Apr 4. National holiday. Commemorates independence from France in 1960.

TAIWAN: NATIONAL TOMB-SWEEPING DAY. Apr 4. National holiday since 1972. According to Chinese custom, the tombs of ancestors are swept "clear and bright" and rites honoring ancestors are held. Tomb-Sweeping Day is observed Apr 5, except in leap years, when it falls Apr 4.

VITAMIN C ISOLATED: ANNIVERSARY. Apr 4, 1932. Vitamin C was first isolated by C.C. King at the University of Pittsburgh.

BIRTHDAYS TODAY

Richard G. Lugar, 68, US Senator (R, Indiana), born Indianapolis, IN, Apr 4, 1932.

Johanna Reiss, 68, author (*The Upstairs Room*), born Winterswijk, Netherlands, Apr 4, 1932.

APRIL 5 — WEDNESDAY
Day 96 — 270 Remaining

LISTER, JOSEPH: BIRTH ANNIVERSARY. Apr 5, 1827. English physician who was the founder of aseptic surgery, born at Upton, Essex, England. Died at Walmer, England, Feb 10, 1912.

RESNIK, JUDITH A.: BIRTH ANNIVERSARY. Apr 5, 1949. Dr. Judith A. Resnik, the second American woman in space (1984), was born at Akron, OH. The 36-year-old electrical engineer was mission specialist on Space Shuttle *Challenger*. She perished with all others aboard when *Challenger* exploded Jan 28, 1986. See also: "*Challenger* Space Shuttle Explosion: Anniversary" (Jan 28).

WASHINGTON, BOOKER TALLAFERRO: BIRTH ANNIVERSARY. Apr 5, 1856. Black educator and leader born at Franklin County, VA. "No race can prosper," he wrote in *Up from Slavery*, "till it learns that there is as much dignity in tilling a field as in writing a poem." Died at Tuskegee, AL, Nov 14, 1915.

BIRTHDAYS TODAY

Richard Peck, 66, author (*Lost in Cyberspace*), born Decatur, IL, Apr 5, 1934.

Colin Luther Powell, 63, general, former Chairman US Joint Chiefs of Staff, born New York, NY, Apr 5, 1937.

APRIL 6 — THURSDAY
Day 97 — 269 Remaining

"BARNEY & FRIENDS" TV PREMIERE: ANNIVERSARY. Apr 6, 1992. Although most adults find it saccharine, this PBS show is enormously popular with preschoolers. Purple dinosaur Barney, his dinosaur pal, Baby Bop, and a multi-ethnic group of children sing, play games and learn simple lessons about getting along with one another. "Bedtime with Barney" was a 1994 primetime special.

	S	M	T	W	T	F	S
							1
April	2	3	4	5	6	7	8
2000	9	10	11	12	13	14	15
	16	17	18	19	20	21	22
	23	24	25	26	27	28	29
	30						

APRIL 6
FIRST MODERN OLYMPICS DAY

Looking ahead to the summer Olympics in Sydney, Australia, beginning on Sept 15, 2000, students can have fun celebrating the birth of the first modern Olympic Games in Athens, Greece, in 1896, especially if you generate enthusiasm and fact-finding missions before Apr 6.

Students should research the original Olympics and find out what sports were included. (There were only nine, so this isn't a big project.) Compare them with the number of sports included today. Sydney will see the debut of tae kwon do and the triathalon as Olympic sports. Students interested in specific sporting events can seek out winning statistics for their sport at intervals of every three Olympics. Consult *Chronicle of the Olympics* (2nd edition, DK Publishing, 0-789-42312-X, $29.95 All ages) for statistics from the games from 1896 through the winter games in Nagano, Japan, in 1998. Plot the results on graphs and discuss why the results change: better training, better equipment or changes in playing field?

As an art project have students design posters to represent the nine original sports in the first modern Olympics. These can be presented and displayed on the 6th.

Older students can have fun writing proposals for new sports to be added to the Olympics. Students could choose silly events—Sumo Snowboarding—or more realistic ones—skateboarding. Ask them to make a commercial advertising the debut of the new sport. Some students could imagine what a 2096 Olympics might be like.

April is also Youth Sports Safety Month. Tie this into the curriculum by discussing how equipment modifications have made participating in sports safer. Students can examine the school's playground equipment and note safety features or potential problem areas. They can design posters to promote safety on specific apparatus found in their schoolyard and in the gym. Students can gather injury information from schoolmates on what equipment, if any, has led to them being injured. Was the student acting responsibly at the time? The school nurse might also share experiences with playground injuries.

For more information about the Sydney Olympics, visit their website at www.sydney.olympic.org.

FIRST MODERN OLYMPICS: ANNIVERSARY. Apr 6, 1896. The first modern Olympics formally opened at Athens, Greece, after a 1,500-year hiatus. See Curriculum Connection.

ISLAMIC NEW YEAR. Apr 6. Islamic calendar date: Muharram 1, 1421. The first day of the first month of the Islamic calendar. Different methods for "anticipating" the visibility of the new moon crescent at Mecca are used by different groups. US date may vary.

NATIONAL SCIENCE TEACHERS ASSOCIATION NATIONAL CONVENTION. Apr 6–9. Orlando, FL. For info: Natl Science Teachers Assn, 1840 Wilson Blvd, Arlington, VA 22201-3000. Phone: (703) 243-7100. Web: www.nsta.org.

NATIONAL SCIENCE TEACHERS ASSOCIATION ANNUAL CONFERENCE. Apr 6–9. Orlando, FL. For info: Natl Science Teachers Assn, 1840 Wilson Blvd, Arlington, VA 22201-3000. Phone: (703) 243-7100. Web: www.nsta.org.

NORTH POLE DISCOVERED: ANNIVERSARY. Apr 6, 1909. Robert E. Peary reached the North Pole after several failed attempts. The team consisted of Peary, leader of the expedition, Matthew A. Henson, a black man who had served with Peary since

1886 as ship's cook, carpenter and blacksmith, and then as Peary's co-explorer and valuable assistant and four Eskimo guides—Coquesh, Ootah, Eginwah and Seegloo. They sailed July 17, 1908, on the ship *Roosevelt*, wintering on Ellesmere Island. After a grueling trek with dwindling food supplies, Henson and two of the Eskimos were first to reach the Pole. An exhausted Peary arrived 45 minutes later and confirmed their location. Dr. Frederick A. Cook, surgeon on an earlier expedition with Peary, claimed to have reached the Pole first, but that could not be substantiated and the National Geographic Society credited the Peary expedition.

TEFLON INVENTED: ANNIVERSARY. Apr 6, 1938. Polytetrafluoroethylene resin was invented by Roy J. Plunkett while he was employed by E.I. Du Pont de Nemours & Co. Commonly known as Teflon, it revolutionized the cookware industry. This substance or something similar coated three-quarters of the pots and pans in America at the time of Plunkett's death in 1994.

THAILAND: CHAKRI DAY. Apr 6. Commemorates foundation of present dynasty by King Rama I (1782–1809), who also established Bangkok as capital.

US ENTERS WORLD WAR I: ANNIVERSARY. Apr 6, 1917. After Congress approved a declaration of war against Germany, the US entered WWI, which had begun in 1914.

US SENATE ACHIEVES A QUORUM: ANNIVERSARY. Apr 6, 1789. The US Senate was formally organized after achieving a quorum.

BIRTHDAYS TODAY

Graeme Base, 42, author and illustrator (*Animalia, The Sign of the Seahorse*), born Amersham, England, Apr 6, 1958.

Candace Cameron Bure, 24, actress ("Full House"), born Panorama City, CA, Apr 6, 1976.

APRIL 7 — FRIDAY
Day 98 — 268 Remaining

KING, WILLIAM RUFUS DEVANE: BIRTH ANNIVERSARY. Apr 7, 1786. Thirteenth vice president of the US who died on the 46th day after taking the Oath of Office, of tuberculosis, at Cahawba, AL, Apr 18, 1853. The Oath of Office had been administered to King Mar 4, 1853 at Havana, Cuba, as authorized by a special act of Congress (the only presidential or vice presidential oath to be administered outside the US). Born at Sampson County, NY, King was the only vice president of the US who had served in both the House of Representatives and the Senate.

METRIC SYSTEM: ANNIVERSARY. Apr 7, 1795. The metric system was adopted at France, where it had been developed.

NATIONAL GEOGRAPHY BEE, STATE LEVEL. Apr 7. Site is different in each state—many are in state capital. Winners of school-level competitions who scored in the top 100 in their state on a written test compete in the State Geography Bees. The winner of each state bee will go to Washington, DC, for the national level in May. Est attendance: 450. For info: Natl Geography Bee, Natl Geographic Soc, 1145 17th St NW, Washington, DC 20036. Phone: (202) 857-7001.

NO HOUSEWORK DAY. Apr 7. No trash. No dishes. No making of beds or washing of laundry. And no guilt. Give it a rest. [© 1998 by WPL] For info: Tom or Ruth Roy, Wellness Permission League, PO Box 662, Mt Gretna, PA 17064-0662. Phone: (717) 964-1308. Fax: (717) 964-1335. E-mail: wellcat@desupernet.net.

SPOTLIGHT ON BOOKS. Apr 7–8 (tentative). Alexandria, MN. Program designed for parents, teachers, librarians and community leaders who want to promote the satisfaction of reading. Honors authors of children and young adult literature that represent cultural diversity in their books. Sponsors: Bemidji State University and Northern Lights Library Network. For info: Dir, Northern Lights Library Network, PO Box 845, Alexandria, MN 56308. Phone: (320) 762-1032. E-mail: nloffice@northernlights.lib.mn.us.

STUDENT GOVERNMENT DAY IN MASSACHUSETTS. Apr 7. Proclaimed annually by the governor for the first Friday in April.

UNITED NATIONS: WORLD HEALTH DAY. Apr 7. A United Nations observance commemorating the establishment of the World Health Organization in 1948. For more information, visit the UN's website for children at www.un.org/Pubs/CyberSchool Bus/

WORLD HEALTH ORGANIZATION: ANNIVERSARY. Apr 7, 1948. This agency of the UN was founded to coordinate international health systems. It is headquartered at Geneva. Among its achievements is the elimination of smallpox.

WORLD HEALTH DAY. Apr 7. A complete planning kit available. For info: American Assn for World Health, World Health Day, 1825 K St NW, Ste 1208, Washington, DC 20006. Phone: (202) 466-5883. Fax: (202) 466-5896. E-mail: aawhstaff@aol.com. Web: www.aawhworldhealth.org.

BIRTHDAYS TODAY

Jackie Chan, 46, actor, martial arts star, born Hong Kong, Apr 7, 1954.

APRIL 8 — SATURDAY
Day 99 — 267 Remaining

ASTRONOMY DAY. April 8. To take astronomy to the people. International Astronomy Day is observed on a Saturday near the first quarter moon between mid-April and mid-May. Co-sponsored by 15 astronomical organizations. See also: "Astronomy Week" (Apr 3). See Curriculum Connection. For info: Gary E. Tomlinson, Coord, Astronomy Day Headquarters, c/o Chaffee Planetarium, 272 Pearl NW, Grand Rapids, MI 49504. Phone: (616) 456-3532. E-mail: gtomlinson@triton.net. Web: www.mcs.net/~bstevens/al.

BIRTHDAY OF THE BUDDHA: BIRTH ANNIVERSARY. Apr 8. Among Buddhist holidays, this is the most important as it commemorates the birthday of the Buddha. The founder of Buddhism had the given name Siddhartha, the family name Gautama and the clan name Shaka. He is commonly called the Buddha, meaning in Sanskrit "the enlightened one." He is thought to have lived in India from c. 563 BC to 483 BC.

BLACK SENATE PAGE APPOINTED: 35th ANNIVERSARY. Apr 8, 1965. Sixteen-year-old Lawrence Bradford of New York City was the first black page appointed to the US Senate.

CHINA: QING MING FESTIVAL. Apr 8. This Confucian festival is celebrated on the fourth or fifth day of the third month. It is observed by the maintenance of ancestral graves, the presentation of food, wine and flowers as offerings and the burning of paper money at gravesides to help ancestors in the afterworld. People also picnic and gather for family meals. Also observed in Korea and Taiwan.

HOME RUN RECORD SET BY HANK AARON: ANNIVERSARY. Apr 8, 1974. Henry ("Hammerin' Hank") Aaron hit the 715th home run of his career, breaking the record set by Babe Ruth in 1935. Playing for the Atlanta Braves, Aaron broke the record at Atlanta in a game against the Los Angeles Dodgers. He finished his career in 1976 with a total of 755 home runs. This record remains unbroken. At the time of his retirement, Aaron also held records for first in RBIs, second in at-bats and runs scored and third in base hits.

JAPAN: FLOWER FESTIVAL (HANA MATSURI). Apr 8. Commemorates Buddha's birthday. Ceremonies in all temples.

MORRIS, LEWIS: BIRTH ANNIVERSARY. Apr 8, 1726. Signer of the Declaration of Independence, born at Westchester County, NY. Died Jan 22, 1798, at the Morrisania manor at NY.

SEVENTEENTH AMENDMENT TO US CONSTITUTION RATIFIED. Apr 8, 1913. Prior to the 17th Amendment, members of the Senate were elected by each state's respective legislature. The advent and popularity of primary elections during the last decade of the 19th century and the early 20th century and a string of senatorial scandals, most notably a scandal involving William Lorimer, an Illinois political boss in 1909, forced the Senate to end its resistance to a constitutional amendment requiring direct popular election of senators.

WHITE, RYAN: 10th DEATH ANNIVERSARY. Apr 8, 1990. This young man, born Dec 6, 1971, at Kokomo, IN, put the face of a child on AIDS and helped promote greater understanding of the disease. Ryan, a hemophiliac, contracted AIDS from a blood transfusion. Banned from the public school system in Central Indiana in 1984 at the age of 10, he moved with his mother and sister to Cicero, IN, where he was accepted by students and faculty alike. Ryan once stated that he only wanted to be treated as a normal teenager, but that was not to be as media attention made him a celebrity. A few days after attending the Academy Awards in 1990, 18-year-old Ryan was hospitalized and lost his valiant fight, at Indianapolis, IN. His funeral was attended by many celebrities.

WILLIAMS, WILLIAM: BIRTH ANNIVERSARY. Apr 8, 1731. Signer of the Declaration of Independence, born at Lebanon, CT. Died there Aug 2, 1811.

BIRTHDAYS TODAY

Kofi Annan, 62, UN Secretary General, born Kumasi, Ghana, Apr 8, 1938.

Susan Bonners, 53, author (*A Penguin Year*), born Chicago, IL, Apr 8, 1947.

Betty (Elizabeth) Ford, 82, former First Lady, wife of Gerald Ford, 38th president of the US, born Chicago, IL, Apr 8, 1918.

Trina Schart Hyman, 61, illustrator (Caldecott for *Saint George and the Dragon*), born Philadelphia, PA, Apr 8, 1939.

	S	M	T	W	T	F	S
April							1
2000	2	3	4	5	6	7	8
	9	10	11	12	13	14	15
	16	17	18	19	20	21	22
	23	24	25	26	27	28	29
	30						

APRIL 9 — SUNDAY
Day 100 — 266 Remaining

BLACK PAGE APPOINTED TO US HOUSE OF REPRESENTATIVES: 35th ANNIVERSARY. Apr 9, 1965. Fifteen-year-old Frank Mitchell of Springfield, IL, was the first black appointed a page to the US House of Representatives.

CIVIL RIGHTS BILL OF 1866: ANNIVERSARY. Apr 9, 1866. The Civil Rights Bill of 1866, passed by Congress over the veto of President Andrew Johnson, granted blacks the rights and privileges of American citizenship and formed the basis for the Fourteenth Amendment to the US Constitution.

CIVIL WAR ENDING: ANNIVERSARY. Apr 9, 1865. At 1:30 PM, General Robert E. Lee, commander of the Army of Northern Virginia, surrendered to General Ulysses S. Grant, commander-in-chief of the Union Army, ending four years of civil war. The meeting took place in the house of Wilmer McLean at the village of Appomattox Court House, VA. Confederate soldiers were permitted to keep their horses and go free to their homes, while Confederate officers were allowed to retain their swords and side arms as well. Grant wrote the terms of surrender. Formal surrender took place at the Courthouse Apr 12. Death toll for the Civil War is estimated at 500,000 men.

CONGRESS OF RACIAL EQUALITY "FREEDOM RIDERS": ANNIVERSARY. Apr 9, 1947. Testing the US Supreme Court's June 3, 1946, ban against segregation in interstate bus travel, the Congress of Racial Equality (CORE) sent "freedom riders" into the south. Founded by James Farmer in 1942, CORE pioneered the use of passive resistance tactics that were used extensively in the American Civil Rights Movement.

ECKERT, J(OHN) PRESPER, JR: BIRTH ANNIVERSARY. Apr 9, 1919. Co-inventor with John W. Mauchly of ENIAC (Electronic Numerical Integrator and Computer), which was first demonstrated at the Moore School of Electrical Engineering at the University of Pennsylvania at Philadelphia Feb 14, 1946. This is generally considered the birth of the computer age. Originally designed to process artillery calculations for the Army, ENIAC was also used in the Manhattan Project. Eckert and Mauchly formed Electronic Control Company, which later became Unisys Corporation. Eckert was born at Philadelphia and died at Bryn Mawr, PA, June 3, 1995.

KRUMGOLD, JOSEPH: BIRTH ANNIVERSARY. Apr 9, 1908. Author (Newbery for *Onion John* and *. . . And Now Miguel*), born at Jersey City, NJ. Died July 10, 1980.

NATIONAL LIBRARY WEEK. Apr 9–15. A nationwide observance sponsored by the American Library Association. Celebrates libraries and librarians, the pleasures and importance of reading and invites library use and support. For info: American Library Assn, Public Info Office, 50 E Huron St, Chicago, IL 60611. Phone: (312) 280-5044. Fax: (312) 944-8520. E-mail: pio@ala.org. Web: www.ala.org.

NATIONAL WEEK OF THE OCEAN. Apr 9–15. A week focusing on humanity's interdependence with the ocean, asking each of us to appreciate, protect and use the ocean wisely. For info: Pres/Co-Founder, Cynthia Hancock, Natl Week of the Ocean, Inc, PO Box 179, Ft Lauderdale, FL 33302. Phone: (954) 462-5573.

★ **PAN AMERICAN WEEK.** Apr 9–15. Presidential Proclamation customarily issued as "Pan American Day and Pan American Week." Always issued for the week including Apr 14, except in 1965, from 1946 through 1948, 1955 through 1977, and 1979.

PASSION WEEK. Apr 9–15. The week beginning on the fifth Sunday in Lent; the week before Holy Week.

PASSIONTIDE. Apr 9–22. The last two weeks of Lent (Passion Week and Holy Week), beginning with the fifth Sunday of Lent (Passion Sunday) and continuing through the day before Easter (Holy Saturday).

PHILIPPINES: ARAW NG KAGITINGAN. Apr 9, 1942. National observance to commemorate the fall of Bataan. The infamous "Death March" is reenacted at the Mount Samat Shrine, the Dambana ng Kagitingan.

ROBESON, PAUL BUSTILL: BIRTH ANNIVERSARY. Apr 9, 1898. Paul Robeson, born at Princeton, NJ, was an All-American football player at Rutgers University and received his law degree from Columbia University in 1923. After being seen by Eugene O'Neill in an amateur stage production, he was offered a part in O'Neill's play, *The Emperor Jones*. His performance in that play with the Provincetown Players established him as an actor. Without ever having taken a voice lesson, he also became a popular singer. His stage credits include *Show Boat, Porgy and Bess, The Hairy Ape* and *Othello*, which enjoyed the longest Broadway run of a Shakespearean play. In 1950 he was denied a passport by the US for refusing to sign an affidavit stating whether he was or ever had been a member of the Communist Party. The action was overturned by the Supreme Court in 1958. His film credits include *Emperor Jones, Show Boat, King Solomon's Mines* and *Song of Freedom*. Robeson died at Philadelphia, PA, Jan 23, 1976.

TUNISIA: MARTYRS' DAY. Apr 9.

WEEK OF THE YOUNG CHILD. Apr 9–15. To focus on the importance of quality early childhood education. For info: Pat Spahr, Dir of Info Development, Natl Assn for the Educ of Young Children, 1509 16th St, NW, Washington, DC 20036. Phone: (800) 424-2460. Fax: (202) 328-1846. E-mail: naeyc@naeyc.org. Web: www.naeyc.org.

WINSTON CHURCHILL DAY. Apr 9. Anniversary of enactment of legislation in 1963 that made the late British statesman an honorary citizen of the US.

BIRTHDAYS TODAY

Jacques Villeneuve, 29, auto racer, born St. Jean d'Iberville, Quebec, Canada, Apr 9, 1971.

APRIL 10 — MONDAY
Day 101 — 265 Remaining

COMMODORE PERRY DAY. Apr 10, 1794. Matthew Calbraith Perry, commodore in the US Navy, negotiator of first treaty between US and Japan (Mar 31, 1854). Born at South Kingston, RI, he died Mar 4, 1858, at New York, NY.

LIBERATION OF BUCHENWALD CONCENTRATION CAMP: 55th ANNIVERSARY. Apr 10, 1945. Buchenwald, north of Weimar, Germany, was entered by Allied troops. It was the first of the Nazi concentration camps to be liberated. It had been established in 1937 and about 56,000 people died there.

ROBERT GRAY BECOMES FIRST AMERICAN TO CIRCUMNAVIGATE THE EARTH: ANNIVERSARY. Apr 10, 1790. When Robert Gray docked the *Columbia* at Boston Harbor, he became the first American to circumnavigate the earth. He sailed from Boston, MA, in September 1787, to trade with Indians of the Pacific Northwest. From there he sailed to China and then continued around the world. His 42,000-mile journey opened trade between New England and the Pacific Northwest and helped the US establish claims to the Oregon Territory.

SAFETY PIN PATENTED: ANNIVERSARY. Apr 10, 1849. Walter Hunt of New York patented the first safety pin.

SALVATION ARMY FOUNDER'S DAY. Apr 10, 1829. Birth anniversary of William Booth, a Methodist minister who began an evangelical ministry in the East End of London in 1865 and established mission stations to feed and house the poor. In 1878 he changed the name of the organization to the Salvation Army. Booth was born at Nottingham, England; he died at London, Aug 20, 1912.

BIRTHDAYS TODAY

David A. Adler, 53, author (the Cam Jansen mystery series), born New York, NY, Apr 10, 1947.

APRIL 11 — TUESDAY
Day 102 — 264 Remaining

CHILDREN'S DAY IN FLORIDA. Apr 11. A legal holiday on the second Tuesday in April.

CIVIL RIGHTS ACT OF 1968: ANNIVERSARY. Apr 11, 1968. Exactly one week after the assassination of Martin Luther King, Jr, the Civil Rights Act of 1968 (protecting civil rights workers, expanding the rights of Native Americans and providing antidiscrimination measures in housing) was signed into law by President Lyndon B. Johnson, who said: ". . . the proudest moments of my presidency have been times such as this when I have signed into law the promises of a century."

EVERETT, EDWARD: BIRTH ANNIVERSARY. Apr 11, 1794. American statesman and orator, born at Dorcester, MA. It was Edward Everett who delivered the main address at the dedication of Gettysburg National Cemetery, Nov 19, 1863. President Abraham Lincoln also spoke at the dedication, and his brief speech (less than two minutes) has been called one of the most eloquent in the English language. Once a candidate for vice president of the US (1860), Everett died at Boston, MA, Jan 15, 1865.

HUGHES, CHARLES EVANS: BIRTH ANNIVERSARY. Apr 11, 1862. Eleventh chief justice of US Supreme Court. Born at Glens Falls, NY, he died at Osterville, MA, Aug 27, 1948.

MOON PHASE: FIRST QUARTER. Apr 11. Moon enters First Quarter phase at 9:30 AM, EDT.

NATIONAL TEACH CHILDREN TO SAVE DAY. Apr 11. Contact your local bank for materials for grades K-12. For info: American Bankers Assn Education Foundation, 1120 Connecticut Ave NW, Washington, DC 20036. Phone: (202) 663-5000. Web: www.aba.com.

SPACE MILESTONE: *APOLLO 13* **(US): 30th ANNIVERSARY.** Apr 11, 1970. Astronauts Lovell, Haise and Swigert were endangered when an oxygen tank ruptured. The planned moon landing was canceled. Details of the accident were made public and the world shared concern for the crew who splashed down successfully in the Pacific Apr 17. The film *Apollo 13*, starring Tom Hanks, accurately told this story.

UGANDA: LIBERATION DAY: ANNIVERSARY. Apr 11. Republic of Uganda celebrates anniversary of overthrow of Idi Amin's dictatorship in 1979.

BIRTHDAYS TODAY

Josh Server, 21, actor (Nickelodeon's "All That"), born Highland Park, IL, Apr 11, 1979.

APRIL 12 — WEDNESDAY
Day 103 — 263 Remaining

ANNIVERSARY OF THE BIG WIND. Apr 12, 1934. The highest-velocity natural wind ever recorded occurred in the morning at the Mount Washington, NH, Observatory. Three weather observers, Wendell Stephenson, Alexander McKenzie and Salvatore Pagliuca, observed and recorded the phenomenon in which gusts reached 231 miles per hour—"the strongest natural wind ever recorded on the earth's surface."

CLAY, HENRY: BIRTH ANNIVERSARY. Apr 12, 1777. Statesman, born at Hanover County, VA. Was the Speaker of the House of Representatives and later became the leader of the new Whig party. He was defeated for the presidency three times. Clay died at Washington, DC, June 29, 1852.

POLIO VACCINE: 45TH ANNIVERSARY. Apr 12, 1955. Anniversary of announcement that the polio vaccine developed by American physician Dr. Jonas E. Salk was "safe, potent and effective." Incidence of the dreaded infantile paralysis, or poliomyelitis, declined by 95 percent following introduction of preventive vaccines.

ROOSEVELT, FRANKLIN DELANO: 55th DEATH ANNIVERSARY. Apr 12, 1945. With the end of WWII only months away, the nation and the world were stunned by the sudden death of the president shortly into his fourth term of office. Roosevelt, 32nd president of the US (Mar 4, 1933–Apr 12, 1945), was the only president to serve more than two terms—he was elected to four consecutive terms. He died at Warm Springs, GA.

SPACE MILESTONE: *COLUMBIA STS 1* (US) FIRST SHUTTLE FLIGHT. Apr 12, 1981. First flight of Shuttle *Columbia*. Two astronauts (John Young and Robert Crippen), on first manned US space mission since *Apollo-Soyuz* in July 1976, spent 54 hours in space (36 orbits of Earth) before landing at Edwards Air Force Base, CA, Apr 14.

SPACE MILESTONE: *VOSTOK I*, FIRST MAN IN SPACE. Apr 12, 1961. Yuri Gagarin became the first man in space when he made a 108-minute voyage, orbiting Earth in a 10,395-lb vehicle, *Vostok I*, launched by the USSR.

THANK YOU SCHOOL LIBRARIAN DAY. Apr 12. Recognizes the unique contribution made by school librarians who are resource people extraordinaire, supporting the myriad educational needs of faculty, staff, students and parents *all year long*! Three cheers to all the public, private and parochial school info-maniacs whose true love of reading and lifelong learning make them great role models for kids of all ages. To help celebrate, take your school librarian to lunch, donate a book in his/her honor to the library, tell your librarian what a difference he/she has made

	S	M	T	W	T	F	S
April							1
2000	2	3	4	5	6	7	8
	9	10	11	12	13	14	15
	16	17	18	19	20	21	22
	23	24	25	26	27	28	29
	30						

APRIL 12
THANK YOU SCHOOL LIBRARIAN DAY

Honor and recognize the contributions your school librarian makes to the success of the school year.

Primary students can draw a picture showing what they like best about the library. Older students can write thank-you notes to the librarian mentioning a specific way he or she has helped that student. Students can discuss behavior they can use in the library that helps librarians do their job more effectively.

Students of all ages can make hallway posters. "How Ms./Mr. _____ helps me." "Mr./Ms. _____ taught me to _____ with computers in the library." "You can help Ms./Mr. _____ by _____." "Mr./Ms. _____ recommended the book _____ to me. I loved it!" are some prompts you can use. Year-end posters can urge students to return all library books they have borrowed.

Volunteers could clean up the library area. Straightening books, dusting shelves, watering plants and stamping due date cards are a few of the activities that would lighten a librarian's work. Two or three service coupons per classroom could be issued, which would let the librarian redeem them when the need arose.

During library time a student could volunteer to read aloud to his or her class and let the librarian be part of the audience.

in your life. Sponsor: "Carpe Libris" (Seize the Book), a loosely knit group of underappreciated librarians. Press packet available for $5. See Curriculum Connection. For info: Judyth Lessee, Organizer, Carpe Libris, PO Box 40503, Tucson, AZ 85717-0503. Phone: (520) 318-2954. E-mail: rinophyl@rtd.com.

TRUANCY LAW: ANNIVERSARY. Apr 12, 1853. The first truancy law was enacted at New York. A $50 fine was charged against parents whose children between the ages of five and 15 were absent from school.

BIRTHDAYS TODAY

Beverly Cleary, 84, author (Ramona series for children; winner of the Newbery Medal for *Dear Mr Henshaw*), born McMinnville, OR, Apr 12, 1916.
Gary Soto, 48, poet, author (*Neighborhood Odes*, *Too Many Tamales*), born Fresno, CA, Apr 12, 1952.

APRIL 13 — THURSDAY
Day 104 — 262 Remaining

BUTTS, ALFRED M.: BIRTH ANNIVERSARY. Apr 13, 1899. Alfred Butts was a jobless architect in the Depression when he invented the board game Scrabble. The game was just a fad for Butts's friends until a Macy's executive saw the game being played at a resort in 1952, and the world's largest store began carrying it. Manufacturing of the game was turned over to Selchow & Righter when 35 workers were producing 6,000 sets a week. Butts received three cents per set for years. He said, "One-third went to taxes. I gave one-third away, and the other third enabled me to have an enjoyable life." Butts was born at Poughkeepsie, NY. He died Apr 4, 1993, at Rhinebeck, NY.

HENRY, MARGUERITE: BIRTH ANNIVERSARY. Apr 13, 1902. Born at Milwaukee, WI, Henry received the Newbery Medal in 1949 for her book *The King of the Wind*. She also authored *Misty of Chincoteague*, *Brighty of Grand Canyon* and other books about horses. Henry died at Rancho Santa Fe, CA, Nov 26, 1997.

JEFFERSON, THOMAS: BIRTH ANNIVERSARY. Apr 13, 1743. Third president of the US (Mar 4, 1801–Mar 3, 1809), born at Shadwell, VA. He had previously served as vice-president under John Adams. Jefferson, who died at Charlottesville, VA, July 4, 1826, wrote his own epitaph: "Here was buried Thomas Jefferson, author of the Declaration of American Independence, of the statute of Virginia for religious freedom, and father of the University of Virginia." A holiday in Alabama and Oklahoma.

★**JEFFERSON, THOMAS: BIRTH ANNIVERSARY.** Apr 13. Presidential Proclamation 2276, of Mar 21, 1938, covers all succeeding years. (Pub Res No. 60 of Aug 16, 1937.)

NATIONAL COUNCIL OF TEACHERS OF MATHEMATICS ANNUAL MEETING. Apr 13–16. Chicago, IL. For info: Natl Council of Teachers of Mathematics, 1906 Association Dr, Reston, VA 20191-1593. Phone: (703) 620-9840. Fax: (703) 476-2970. E-mail: infocentral@nctm.org. Web: www.nctm.org.

***SILENT SPRING* PUBLICATION: ANNIVERSARY.** Apr 13, 1962. Rachel Carson's *Silent Spring* warned humankind that for the first time in history every person is subjected to contact with dangerous chemicals from conception until death. Carson painted a vivid picture of how chemicals—used in many ways but particularly in pesticides—have upset the balance of nature, undermining the survival of countless species. This enormously popular and influential book was a soft-spoken battle cry to protect our natural surroundings. Its publication signaled the beginning of the environmental movement.

SINGAPORE: SONGKRAN FESTIVAL. Apr 13–15. Public holiday. Thai water festival. To welcome the new year the image of Buddha is bathed with holy or fragrant water and lustral water is sprinkled on celebrants. Joyous event, especially observed at Thai Buddhist temples. (Dates of observance subject to alteration.)

SRI LANKA: SINHALA AND TAMIL NEW YEAR. April 13–14. This New Year festival includes traditional games, the wearing of new clothes in auspicious colors and special foods. Public holiday.

BIRTHDAYS TODAY

Ben Nighthorse Campbell, 67, US Senator (R, Colorado), born Auburn, CA, Apr 13, 1933.
Erik Christian Haugaard, 77, author (*The Rider and His Horse*), born Frederiksberg, Denmark, Apr 13, 1923.
Lee Bennett Hopkins, 62, poet (*Blast Off!: Poems about Space*), born Scranton, PA, Apr 13, 1938.

APRIL 14 — FRIDAY
Day 105 — 261 Remaining

FIRST AMERICAN ABOLITION SOCIETY FOUNDED: 225th ANNIVERSARY. Apr 14, 1775. The first abolition organization formed in the US was The Society for the Relief of Free Negroes Unlawfully Held in Bondage, founded at Philadelphia, PA.

FIRST DICTIONARY OF AMERICAN ENGLISH PUBLISHED: ANNIVERSARY. Apr 14, 1828. Noah Webster published his *American Dictionary of the English Language.*

HONDURAS: DIA DE LAS AMERICAS. Apr 14. Honduras. Pan-American Day, a national holiday.

LINCOLN, ABRAHAM: ASSASSINATION ANNIVERSARY. Apr 14, 1865. President Abraham Lincoln was shot while watching a performance of *Our American Cousin* at Ford's Theatre, Washington, DC. He died the following day. Assassin was John Wilkes Booth, a young actor.

★**PAN AMERICAN DAY.** Apr 14. Presidential Proclamation 1912, of May 28, 1930, covers every Apr 14 (required by Governing Board of Pan American Union). Proclamation issued each year since 1948.

PAN-AMERICAN DAY IN FLORIDA. Apr 14. A holiday to be observed in the public schools of Florida honoring the republics of Latin America. If Apr 14 should fall on a day that is not a school day, then Pan-American Day should be observed on the preceding school day.

SULLIVAN, ANNE: BIRTH ANNIVERSARY. Apr 14, 1866. Anne Sullivan, born at Feeding Hills, MA, became well known for "working miracles" with Helen Keller, who was blind and deaf. Nearly blind herself, Sullivan used a manual alphabet communicated by the sense of touch to teach Keller to read, write and speak and then to help her go on to higher education. Anne Sullivan died Oct 20, 1936, at Forest Hills, NY.

BIRTHDAYS TODAY

Cynthia Cooper, 37, basketball player, born Chicago, IL, Apr 14, 1963.
Sarah Michelle Gellar, 23, actress ("Buffy the Vampire Slayer"), born New York, NY, Apr 14, 1977.
Gregory Alan (Greg) Maddux, 34, baseball player, born San Angelo, TX, Apr 14, 1966.
Pete Rose, 59, former baseball manager and player, born Cincinnati, OH, Apr 14, 1941.

APRIL 15 — SATURDAY
Day 106 — 260 Remaining

ASHURA: TENTH DAY. Apr 15. Islamic calendar date: Muharram 10, 1421. Commemorates death of Muhammad's grandson and the Battle of Karbala. A time of fasting, reflection and meditation. Jews of Medina fasted on the tenth day in remembrance of their salvation from Pharoah. Different methods for "anticipating" the visibility of the new moon crescent at Mecca are used by different groups. US date may vary.

FIRST MCDONALD'S OPENS: 45th ANNIVERSARY. Apr 15, 1955. The first franchised McDonald's was opened at Des Plaines, IL, by Ray Kroc, who had gotten the idea from a hamburger joint at San Bernardino, CA, run by the McDonald brothers. By the mid-1990s, there were more than 15,000 McDonald's in 70 countries.

FIRST SCHOOL FOR DEAF FOUNDED: ANNIVERSARY. Apr 15, 1817. Thomas Hopkins Gallaudet and Laurent Clerc founded the first US public school for the deaf, Connecticut Asylum for the Education and Instruction of Deaf and Dumb Persons (now the American School for the Deaf), at Hartford, CT.

SINKING OF THE *TITANIC* : ANNIVERSARY. Apr 15, 1912. The "unsinkable" luxury liner *Titanic* on its maiden voyage from Southampton, England, to New York, NY struck an iceberg just before midnight Apr 14, and sank at 2:27 AM, Apr 15. The *Titanic* had 2,224 persons aboard. Of these, more than 1,500 were lost. About 700 people were rescued from the icy waters off Newfoundland by the liner *Carpathia*, which reached the scene about two hours after the *Titanic* went down. The sunken *Titanic* was located and photographed in September 1985. In July 1986, an expedition aboard the *Atlantis II* descended to the deck of the *Titanic* in a submersible craft, *Alvin*, and guided a robot named Jason, Jr in a search of the ship. Two memorial bronze plaques were left on the deck of the ship.

YO-YO DAYS. Apr 15–16. Spinning Top Museum, Burlington, WI. Midwest yo-yo convention, Wisconsin State Yo-Yo Contest, classes, demonstrations, collections of yo-yos on exhibit and yo-yo shows for all generations. For info: Spinning Top Museum, 533 Milwaukee Ave (Hwy 36), Burlington, WI 53105. Phone: (414) 763-3946.

BIRTHDAYS TODAY

Evelyn Ashford, 43, Olympic gold medal track athlete, born Shreveport, LA, Apr 15, 1957.

Emma Thompson, 41, actress (*Junior*), born Paddington, England, Apr 15, 1959.

APRIL 16 — SUNDAY
Day 107 — 259 Remaining

DENMARK: QUEEN MARGRETHE'S BIRTHDAY. Apr 16. Thousands of children gather to cheer the queen at Amalienborg Palace and the Royal Guard wears scarlet gala uniforms.

DIEGO, JOSE de: BIRTH ANNIVERSARY. Apr 16, 1866. Puerto Rican patriot and political leader Jose de Diego was born at Aguadilla, PR. His birthday is a holiday in Puerto Rico. He died July 16, 1918, at New York, NY.

GRANGE WEEK. Apr 16–22 (tentative). State and local recognition for Grange's contribution to rural/urban America. Celebrated at National Headquarters at Washington, DC, and in all states with local, county and state Granges. Begun in 1867, the National Grange is the oldest US rural community service, family-oriented organization with a special interest in agriculture. For info: Kermit W. Richardson, Natl Master, The Natl Grange, 1616 H St NW, Washington, DC 20006. Phone: (202) 628-3507 or (888) 4-Grange. Fax: (202) 347-1091. Web: www.grange.org.

GREECE: DUMB WEEK. Apr 16–22. The week preceding Holy Week on the Orthodox calendar is known as Dumb Week, as no services are held in churches throughout this period except on Friday, eve of the Saturday of Lazarus.

HOLY WEEK. Apr 16–22. Christian observance dating from the fourth century, known also as Great Week. The seven days beginning on the sixth and final Sunday in Lent (Palm Sunday), consisting of: Palm Sunday, Monday of Holy Week, Tuesday of Holy Week, Spy Wednesday (or Wednesday of Holy Week), Maundy Thursday, Good Friday and Holy Saturday (or Great Sabbath or Easter Even). A time of solemn devotion to and memorializing of the suffering (passion), death and burial of Christ. Formerly a time of strict fasting.

MASIH, IQBAL: 5th DEATH ANNIVERSARY. Apr 16, 1995. Twelve-year-old Iqbal Masih, born at Pakistan in 1982, who

reportedly had received death threats after speaking out against Pakistan's child labor practices, was shot to death, at Muridke Village, Punjab Province. Masih, who was sold into labor as a carpet weaver at the age of four, spent the next six years of his life shackled to a loom. He began speaking out against child labor after escaping from servitude at the age of ten. In November of 1994 he spoke at an international labor conference in Sweden and he received a $15,000 Reebok Youth in Action Award a month later. There were reports after the shooting that Masih's death was arranged by a "carpet mafia." For more info: *Iqbal Masih and the Crusaders Against Child Slavery*, by Susan Kuklin (Holt, 0-8050-5459-6, $16.95 Gr. 6-12).

NATIONAL COIN WEEK. Apr 16–22. To promote the history and lore of numismatics and the hobby of coin collecting. For info: James Taylor, Dir of Educ, American Numismatic Assn, 818 N Cascade Ave, Colorado Springs, CO 80903. Phone: (719) 632-2646 or 8003679723. Fax: (719) 634-4085. E-mail: anaedu@money.org. Web: www.money.org.

NATIONAL ORGAN AND TISSUE DONOR AWARENESS WEEK. Apr 16–22. To encourage Americans to consider organ and tissue donation and to sign donor cards when getting a driver's license. For info: Natl Kidney Foundation, 30 E 33rd St, New York, NY 10016. Phone: (800) 622-9010 or (212) 889-2210. Web: www.kidney.org or www.organdonor.gov.

NATIONAL PTA EARTH WEEK. Apr 16–22. In 1990, the National PTA recognized the importance of the environment to the health and safety of our children and designated the week in which Earth Day falls (Apr 22) as Earth Week. During Earth Week, PTA members and others work to improve the environment in their homes, schools and communities. For info: Natl PTA Environmental Awareness Program, 330 N Wabash Ave, Ste 2100, Chicago, IL 60611-3690. Phone: (312) 670-6782. Fax: (312) 670-6783. E-mail: info@pta.org. Web: www.pta.org.

NATIONAL SCIENCE AND TECHNOLOGY WEEK. Apr 16–22. National Science and Technology Week is sponsored by the Office of Legislative and Public Affairs of the National Science Foundation to promote awareness of science and technology to the general public and especially to children. Annually, the third full week in April. For info: Mary Bullock, Natl Science Fdtn, 4201 Wilson Blvd, Arlington, VA 22230. E-mail: nstw@nsf.gov. Web: www.nsf.gov/od/lpa/nstw/start.htm.

NATIONAL VOLUNTEER WEEK. Apr 16–22. National Volunteer Week honors those who reach out to others through volunteer community service and calls attention to the need for more community services for individuals, groups and families to help solve serious social problems that affect our communities. For info: Customer Information Center, Points of Light Foundation, 1737 H Street, NW, Washington, DC 20006. Phone: (202) 223-9186. Fax: (202) 223-9256. E-mail: volnet@aol.com. Web: www.pointsoflight.org.

	S	M	T	W	T	F	S
April							1
2000	2	3	4	5	6	7	8
	9	10	11	12	13	14	15
	16	17	18	19	20	21	22
	23	24	25	26	27	28	29
	30						

PALM SUNDAY. Apr 16. Commemorates Christ's last entry into Jerusalem, when His way was covered with palms by the multitudes. Beginning of Holy (or Great) Week in Western Christian churches.

WRIGHT, WILBUR: BIRTH ANNIVERSARY. Apr 16, 1867. Aviation pioneer (with his brother Orville) born at Millville, IN. Died at Dayton, OH, May 30, 1912.

BIRTHDAYS TODAY

Kareem Abdul-Jabbar (born Lewis Ferdinand Alcindor, Jr), 53, former basketball player, born New York, NY, Apr 16, 1947.

APRIL 17 — MONDAY
Day 108 — 258 Remaining

AMERICAN SAMOA: FLAG DAY: 100th ANNIVERSARY. Apr 17. National holiday commemorating first raising of American flag in what was formerly Eastern Samoa in 1900. Public holiday with singing, dancing, costumes and parades.

FAMILIES LAUGHING THROUGH STORIES WEEK. Apr 17–24. By Word of Mouth Storytelling Guild and Teachable Moments Publishing will be distributing educational information to family-oriented and storytelling agencies and organizations, teaching them how to encourage instruction that will enhance the telling of humorous family stories. This activity not only promotes the art of storytelling, but also leaves lasting, laughing memories for family participants. For info: Shirley Trout, Teachable Moments, PO Box 359, Waverly, NE 68462. Phone: (402) 786-3100. Fax: (402) 788-2131. E-mail: strout@teachablemoments.com. Web: www.teachablemoments.com.

INCOME TAX PAY DAY. Apr 17. A day all Americans need to know—the day by which taxpayers are supposed to make their accounting of the previous year and pay their share of the cost of government. Usually Apr 15, but since that date falls on a Saturday this year, taxpayers get an extension until Monday. The US Internal Revenue Service provides free forms.

PATRIOT'S DAY IN MASSACHUSETTS AND MAINE. Apr 17. Commemorates Battles of Lexington and Concord, 1775. Annually, the third Monday in April.

SPACE MILESTONE: *COLUMBIA NEUROLAB*(US). Apr 17, 1998. Seven astronauts and scientists were launched with 2,000 animals (crickets, mice, snails and fish) to study the nervous system in space.

SYRIAN ARAB REPUBLIC: INDEPENDENCE DAY. Apr 17. Official holiday. Proclaimed independence from France in 1946.

TALKING BOOK WEEK. Apr 17–21. This is a national campaign to promote the availability and use of libraries, radio reading services and special-information media services for the visually-disabled community. "Talking Book Week" is now a part of Syracuse University "Living Book Project." For info: Dawn L. Jordan, Outreach Dir, Audio Descriptive Network, Non-Profit Reading Service, 115 Brenton St, Richmond, VA 23222. Phone: (804) 321-2063.

VERRAZANO DAY: ANNIVERSARY. Apr 17, 1524. Celebrates discovery of New York harbor by Giovanni Verrazano, Florentine navigator, 1485–1527.

BIRTHDAYS TODAY

Jane Kurtz, 48, author (*Pulling the Lion's Tale*), born Portland, OR, Apr 17, 1952.

APRIL 18 — TUESDAY
Day 109 — 257 Remaining

CANADA: CONSTITUTION ACT OF 1982: ANNIVERSARY. Apr 18, 1982. Replacing the British North America Act of 1867, the Canadian Constitution Act of 1982 provides Canada with a new set of fundamental laws and civil rights. Signed by Queen Elizabeth II, at Parliament Hill, Ottawa, Canada, it went into effect at 12:01 AM, Sunday, Apr 19, 1982.

THE HOUSE THAT RUTH BUILT: ANNIVERSARY. Apr 18, 1923. More than 74,000 fans attended Opening Day festivities as the New York Yankees inaugurated their new stadium. Babe Ruth christened it with a game-winning three-run homer into the right-field bleachers. In his coverage of the game for the *New York Evening Telegram* sportswriter Fred Lieb described Yankee Stadium as "The House That Ruth Built," and the name stuck.

MOON PHASE: FULL MOON. Apr 18. Moon enters Full Moon phase at 1:41 PM, EDT.

PAUL REVERE'S RIDE: 225th ANNIVERSARY. Apr 18, 1775. The "Midnight Ride" of Paul Revere and William Dawes started at about 10 PM, to warn American patriots between Boston, MA, and Concord, MA of the approaching British.

PET OWNERS INDEPENDENCE DAY. Apr 18. Dog and cat owners take day off from work and the pets go to work in their place, since most pets are jobless, sleep all day and do not even take out the trash. [© 1998 by WPL] For info: Tom or Ruth Roy, Wellness Permission League, PO Box 662, Mt. Gretna, PA 17064-0662. Phone: (717) 964-1308. Fax: (717) 964-1335. E-mail: wellcat@desupernet.net.

SAN FRANCISCO 1906 EARTHQUAKE: ANNIVERSARY. Apr 18, 1906. Business section of San Francisco, some 10,000 acres, destroyed by earthquake. First quake at 5:13 AM, followed by fire. Nearly 4,000 lives lost.

SKY AWARENESS WEEK. Apr 18–24. A celebration of the sky and an opportunity to appreciate its natural beauty, to understand sky and weather processes and to work together to protect the sky as a natural resource (it's the only one we have). Events are held at schools, nature centers, etc, all across the US. Annually, during National Science and Technology Week. For info: Barbara G. Levine, How The Weatherworks, 1522 Baylor Ave, Rockville, MD 20850. Phone: (301) 762-7669 or (301) 251-0242. Fax: (301) 762-7669. E-mail: skyweek@weatherworks.com. Web: www.weatherworks.com.

"THIRD WORLD" DAY: 45th ANNIVERSARY. Apr 18, 1955. Anniversary of the first use of the phrase "third world," which was used by Indonesia's President Sukarno in his opening speech at the Bandung Conference. Representatives of nearly 30 African and Asian countries (2,000 attendees) heard Sukarno praise the American war of independence, "the first successful anticolonial war in history." More than half the world's population, he said, was represented at this "first intercontinental conference of the so-called colored peoples, in the history of mankind." The phrase and the idea of a "third world" rapidly gained currency, generally signifying the aggregate of nonaligned peoples and nations—the nonwhite and underdeveloped portion of the world.

ZIMBABWE: INDEPENDENCE DAY: 20th ANNIVERSARY. Apr 18. National holiday commemorates the recognition by Great Britain of Zimbabwean independence in 1980. Prior to this, the country had been the British colony of Southern Rhodesia.

Melissa Joan Hart, 24, actress ("Sabrina, the Teenage Witch"), born Long Island, NY, Apr 18, 1976.

Rick Moranis, 47, actor (*Honey, I Shrunk the Kids, Honey We Shrunk Ourselves*), born Toronto, Canada, Apr 18, 1953.

APRIL 19 — WEDNESDAY
Day 110 — 256 Remaining

BATTLE OF LEXINGTON AND CONCORD: 225th ANNIVERSARY. Apr 19, 1775. Massachusetts. Start of the American Revolution as the British fired the "shot heard 'round the world."

GARFIELD, LUCRETIA RUDOLPH: BIRTH ANNIVERSARY. Apr 19, 1832. Wife of James Abram Garfield, 20th president of the US, born at Hiram, OH. Died at Pasadena, CA, Mar 14, 1918.

OKLAHOMA CITY BOMBING: 5th ANNIVERSARY. Apr 19, 1995. A car bomb exploded outside the Alfred P. Murrah Federal Building at Oklahoma City, OK, at 9:02 AM, killing 168 people, 19 of them children at a day-care center; a nurse died of head injuries sustained while helping in rescue efforts. The bomb, estimated to have weighed 5,000 pounds, had been placed in a rented truck. The blast ripped off the north face of the nine-story building, leaving a 20-foot-wide crater and debris two stories high. Cost of the damage was estimated at $500 million. Structurally unsound and increasingly dangerous, the bombed building was razed May 23. Timothy J. McVeigh, a decorated Gulf War army vet who is alleged to have been deeply angered by the Bureau of Alcohol, Tobacco and Firearms attack on the Branch Davidian compound at Waco, TX, exactly two years before, has been convicted of the bombing. Terry L. Nicholls, an army buddy of McVeigh, was convicted of lesser charges.

PASSOVER BEGINS AT SUNDOWN. Apr 19. See "Pesach" (Apr 20).

PATRIOT'S DAY IN FLORIDA. Apr 19. A ceremonial day commemorating the first blood shed in the American Revolution at Lexington and Concord in 1775.

SHERMAN, ROGER: BIRTH ANNIVERSARY. Apr 19, 1721. American statesman, member of the Continental Congress (1774–81 and 1783–84), signer of the Declaration of Independence and of the Constitution, was born at Newton, MA. He also calculated astronomical and calendar information for an almanac. Sherman died at New Haven, CT, July 23, 1793.

SIERRA LEONE: NATIONAL HOLIDAY. Apr 19. Sierra Leone became a republic in 1971.

SPACE MILESTONE: *SALYUT* (USSR). Apr 19, 1971. The Soviet Union launched *Salyut*, the first manned orbiting space laboratory. It was replaced in 1986 by *Mir*, a manned space station and laboratory.

Tim Curry, 54, actor (*Muppet Treasure Island, Home Alone 2*), born Cheshire, England, Apr 19, 1946.

April 2000	S	M	T	W	T	F	S
							1
	2	3	4	5	6	7	8
	9	10	11	12	13	14	15
	16	17	18	19	20	21	22
	23	24	25	26	27	28	29
	30						

APRIL 20 — THURSDAY
Day 111 — 255 Remaining

EGYPT: SHAM EL-NESSIM. Apr 20 (tentative date). Sporting Holiday. This feast has been celebrated by all Egyptians since pharaonic time; people go out and spend the day in parks and along the Nile's banks. For info: Egyptian Tourist Authority, 645 N Michigan Ave, Ste 829, Chicago, IL 60611. Phone: (312) 280-4666.

HITLER, ADOLF: BIRTH ANNIVERSARY. Apr 20, 1889. German dictator, frustrated artist, obsessed with superiority of the "Aryan race" and the evil of Marxism (which he saw as a Jewish plot). Hitler was born at Braunau am Inn, Austria. Turning to politics, despite a five-year prison sentence (writing *Mein Kampf* during the nine months he served), his rise was predictable and a German plebiscite vested sole executive power in Führer Adolf Hitler Aug 19, 1934. Facing certain defeat by the Allied Forces, he shot himself Apr 30, 1945 while his mistress, Eva Braun, took poison in a Berlin bunker where they had been hiding for more than three months.

ICELAND: "FIRST DAY OF SUMMER." Apr 20. A national public holiday, *Sumardagurinn fyrsti*, with general festivities, processions and much street dancing, especially at Reykjavik, greets the coming of summer. Flags are flown on this day. Annually, the third Thursday in April.

MAUNDY THURSDAY or HOLY THURSDAY. Apr 20. The Thursday before Easter, originally "dies mandate," celebrates Christ's injunction to love one another, "Mandatus novum do vobis. . . ." ("A new commandment I give to you. . . .")

PESACH or PASSOVER. Apr 20–27. Hebrew calendar dates: Nisan 15–22, 5760. Apr 20, the first day of Passover, begins an eight-day celebration of the delivery of the Jews from slavery in Egypt. Unleavened bread (matzoh) is eaten at this time.

TAURUS, THE BULL. Apr 20–May 20. In the astronomical/astrological zodiac that divides the sun's apparent orbit into 12 segments, the period Apr 20–May 20 is identified, traditionally, as the sun sign of Taurus, the Bull. The ruling planet is Venus.

Mary Hoffman, 55, author (*Amazing Grace*), born Eastleigh, Hampshire, England, Apr 20, 1945.

Joey Lawrence, 24, actor ("Brotherly Love," "Blossom"), born Strawbridge, PA, Apr 20, 1976.

Pat Roberts, 64, US Senator (R, Kansas), born Topeka, KS, Apr 20, 1936.

John Paul Stevens, 80, Associate Justice of the US Supreme Court, born Chicago, IL, Apr 20, 1920.

APRIL 21 — FRIDAY
Day 112 — 254 Remaining

BRAZIL: TIRADENTES DAY. Apr 21. National holiday commemorating execution of national hero, dentist Jose da Silva Xavier, nicknamed Tiradentes (tooth-puller), a conspirator in revolt against the Portuguese in 1789.

FROEBEL, FRIEDRICH: BIRTH ANNIVERSARY. Apr 21, 1782. German educator and author Friedrich Froebel, who believed that play is an important part of a child's education, was born at Oberwiessbach, Thuringia. Froebel invented the kindergarten, founding the first one at Blankenburg, Germany, in 1837. Froebel also invented a series of toys which he intended to stimulate learning. (The American architect Frank Lloyd Wright as a child received these toys [maplewood blocks] from his mother and spoke throughout his life of their value.) Froebel's ideas about the role of directed play, toys and music in children's education had a profound influence in England and the US, where the nursery school became a further extension of his ideas. Froebel died at Marienthal, Germany, June 21, 1852.

GOOD FRIDAY. Apr 21. Observed in commemoration of the crucifixion. Oldest Christian celebration. Possible corruption of "God's Friday." Observed in some manner by most Christian sects and as a public holiday or part holiday in Delaware, Florida, Hawaii, Illinois, Indiana, Kentucky, New Jersey, North Carolina, Pennsylvania and Tennessee.

INDONESIA: KARTINI DAY. Apr 21. Republic of Indonesia. Honors Raden Adjeng Kartini, pioneer in the emancipation of the women of Indonesia.

ITALY: BIRTHDAY OF ROME. Apr 21. Celebration of the founding of Rome, traditionally thought to be in 753 BC.

KINDERGARTEN DAY. Apr 21. A day to recognize the importance of play, games and "creative self-activity" in children's education and to note the history of the kindergarten. Observed on the anniversary of the birth of Friedrich Froebel (Apr 21, 1782) who established the first kindergarten in 1837. German immigrants brought Froebel's ideas to the US in the 1840s. The first kindergarten in a public school in the US was started in 1873, at St. Louis, MO.

SAN JACINTO DAY. Apr 21. Texas. Commemorates Battle of San Jacinto in which Texas won independence from Mexico. A 570-foot monument, dedicated on the 101st anniversary of the battle, marks the site on the banks of the San Jacinto River, about 20 miles from the present city of Houston, TX, where General Sam Houston's Texans decisively defeated the Mexican forces led by Santa Ana in the final battle between Texas and Mexico.

BIRTHDAYS TODAY

Queen Elizabeth II, 74, Queen of the United Kingdom, born London, England, Apr 21, 1926.

Charles Grodin, 65, actor (*Beethoven, Beethoven's 2*), born Pittsburgh, PA, Apr 21, 1935.

Barbara Park, 53, author (the Junie B. Jones series), born Mt Holly, NJ, Apr 21, 1947.

APRIL 22 — SATURDAY
Day 113 — 253 Remaining

BRAZIL: DISCOVERY OF BRAZIL DAY: 500th ANNIVERSARY. Apr 22. Commemorates discovery by Pedro Alvarez Cabral in 1500.

CHILDREN'S READING FESTIVAL. Apr 22–23 (tentative). Ft Lauderdale, FL. Publicizes the importance of reading and reaches out to children through lively arts performances, including puppets, folksingers and storytellers. Books for sale, book illustrations and literary games fill the weekend. Est attendance: 15,000.

For info: Broward County Library, 100 S Andrews Ave, Ft Lauderdale, FL 33301. Phone: (954) 357-7336.

COINS STAMPED "IN GOD WE TRUST": ANNIVERSARY. Apr 22, 1864. By Act of Congress, the phrase "In God We Trust" began to be stamped on all US coins.

EARTH DAY. Apr 22. Earth Day, first observed Apr 22, 1970, with message "Give Earth a Chance" and attention to reclaiming the purity of the air, water and living environment. Earth Day 1990 was a global event with more than 200 million participating in 142 countries. Annually, Apr 22. Note: Earth Day activities are held by many groups on various dates, often on the weekend closest to Apr 22. The vernal equinox (i.e., the first day of Spring) has been chosen by some for this observance. For info: Earth Day Network, PO Box 9827, San Diego, CA 92169. Phone: (619) 272-0347. Fax: (619) 272-2933. E-mail: cdchase@znet.com. Web: www.sdearthtimes.com/edn.

EASTER EVEN. Apr 22. The Saturday before Easter. Last day of Holy Week and of Lent.

FIRST SOLO TRIP TO NORTH POLE: ANNIVERSARY. Apr 22, 1994. Norwegian explorer Borge Ousland became the first person to make the trip to the North Pole alone. The trip took 52 days, during which he pulled a 265-pound sled. Departing from Cape Atkticheskiy at Siberia Mar 2, he averaged about 18½ miles per day over the 630-mile journey. Ousland had traveled to the Pole on skis with Erling Kagge in 1990.

OKLAHOMA DAY. Apr 22. Oklahoma.

OKLAHOMA LAND RUSH: ANNIVERSARY. Apr 22, 1889. At noon a gun shot signaled the start of the Oklahoma land rush as thousands of settlers rushed into the territory to claim land. Under pressure from cattlemen, the federal government opened 1,900,000 acres of central Oklahoma that had been bought from the Creek and Seminole tribes.

BIRTHDAYS TODAY

Paula Fox, 77, author (Newbery for *The Slave Dancer*), born New York, NY, Apr 22, 1923.

APRIL 23 — SUNDAY
Day 114 — 252 Remaining

BERMUDA: PEPPERCORN CEREMONY: ANNIVERSARY. Apr 23. St. George. Commemorates the payment of one peppercorn in 1816 to the governor of Bermuda for rental of Old State House by the Masonic Lodge.

BUCHANAN, JAMES: BIRTH ANNIVERSARY. Apr 23, 1791. Fifteenth president of the US, born near Mercersburg, PA, was the only president who never married. He served one term in office, Mar 4, 1857–Mar 3, 1861, and died at Lancaster, PA, June 1, 1868.

CANADA/US GOODWILL WEEK. Apr 23–29. Celebrates the signing of the Rush-Bagot Agreement in 1817 which resulted in the unfortified US-Canadian border. For info: Kiwanis Intl, 3636 Woodview Trace, Indianapolis, IN 46268. Phone: (800) KIW-ANIS. Web: www.kiwanis.org.

EASTER SUNDAY. Apr 23. Commemorates the Resurrection of Christ. Most joyous festival of the Christian year. The date of Easter, a movable feast, is derived from the lunar calendar: the first Sunday following the first ecclesiastical full moon on or after Mar 21—always between Mar 22 and Apr 25. The Council of Nicaea (AD 325) prescribed that Easter be celebrated on the Sunday after Passover, as that feast's date had been established in

Jesus' time. Orthodox Christians continue to use the Julian calendar, so that Easter can sometimes be as much as five weeks apart in the Western and Eastern churches. An ecumenical group met in 1997 to propose a way that Eastern and Western Christians could set the same date for Easter, starting in 2001 (when the Eastern and Western dates for Easter happen to coincide). Easter in 2001 will be Apr 15; in 2002 it will be Mar 31; in 2003 it will be Apr 20. Many other dates in the Christian year are derived from the date of Easter. See also: "Orthodox Easter Sunday or Pascha." For links to Easter websites, go to: deil.lang.uiuc.edu/web.pages/holidays/easter.html.

FIRST MOVIE THEATER OPENS: ANNIVERSARY. Apr 23, 1896. The first movie theater opened in Koster and Bial's Music Hall at New York City. Up until this time, people viewed movies individually by looking into a Kinetoscope, a box-like "peep show." The first Kinetoscope parlor opened at New York in 1894. But in 1896 Thomas Edison introduced the Vitascope which projected films on a screen. This was the first time in the US that an audience sat in a theater and viewed a movie together.

FIRST PUBLIC SCHOOL IN AMERICA: ANNIVERSARY. Apr 23, 1635. The Boston Latin School opened and is America's oldest public school.

NATIONAL YWCA WEEK. Apr 23–29. To promote the YWCA of the USA nationally. Annually, the last full week in April. For info: YWCA of the USA, Empire State Bldg, Ste 301, 350 Fifth Ave, New York, NY 10118. Phone: (212) 273-7800.

ORTHODOX PALM SUNDAY. Apr 23. Celebration of Christ's entry into Jerusalem, when His way was covered with palms by the multitudes. Beginning of Holy Week in the Orthodox Church.

PEARSON, LESTER B.: BIRTH ANNIVERSARY. Apr 23, 1897. Fourteenth prime minister of Canada, born at Toronto, Canada. He was Canada's chief delegate at the San Francisco conference where the UN charter was drawn up and later served as president of the General Assembly. He wrote the proposal that resulted in the formation of the North Atlantic Treaty Organization (NATO). He was awarded the Nobel Peace Prize. Died at Rockcliffe, Canada, Dec 27, 1972.

PHYSICISTS DISCOVER TOP QUARK: ANNIVERSARY. Apr 23, 1994. Physicists at the Department of Energy's Fermi National Accelerator Laboratory found evidence for the existence of the subatomic particle called the top quark, the last undiscovered quark of the six predicted to exist by current scientific theory. The discovery provides strong support for the quark theory of the structure of matter. Quarks are subatomic particles that make up protons and neutrons found in the nuclei of atoms. The five other quark types that had already been proven to exist are the up quark, down quark, strange quark, charm quark and bottom quark. Further experimentation over many months confirmed the discovery, and it was publicly announced Mar 2, 1995.

READING IS FUN WEEK. Apr 23–29. To highlight the importance and fun of reading. Annually, the last full week of April. For info: Rachael Walker, Reading Is Fundamental, Inc, 600 Maryland Ave SW, Rm 600, Washington, DC 20024-2569. Phone: (202) 287-3371. Fax: (202) 287-3196. Web: www.si.edu/rif.

SAINT GEORGE FEAST DAY. Apr 23. Martyr and patron saint of England, who died Apr 23, AD 303. Hero of the George and the dragon legend. The story says that his faith helped him slay a vicious dragon that demanded daily sacrifice after the king's daughter became the intended victim.

SHAKESPEARE, WILLIAM: BIRTH AND DEATH ANNIVERSARY. Apr 23. England's most famous and most revered poet and playwright. He was born at Stratford-on-Avon, England, Apr 23, 1564 (Old Style), baptized there three days later and died there on his birthday, Apr 23, 1616 (Old Style). Author of at least 36 plays and 154 sonnets, Shakespeare created the most influential and lasting body of work in the English language, an extraordinary exploration of human nature. His epitaph: "Good frend for Jesus sake forbeare, To digg the dust enclosed heare. Blese be ye man that spares thes stones, And curst be he that moves my bones."

SPAIN: BOOK DAY AND LOVER'S DAY. Apr 23. Barcelona. Saint George's Day and the anniversary of the death of Spanish writer Miguel de Cervantes have been observed with special ceremonies in the Palacio de la Disputacion and throughout the city since 1714. Book stands are set up in the plazas and on street corners. This is Spain's equivalent of Valentine's Day. Women give books to men; men give roses to women.

TURKEY: NATIONAL SOVEREIGNTY AND CHILDREN'S DAY. Apr 23, 1923. Commemorates Grand National Assembly's inauguration.

UNITED NATIONS: WORLD BOOK AND COPYRIGHT DAY. Apr 23. Observed throughout the United Nations system.

BIRTHDAYS TODAY

Gabriel Damon, 24, actor (*Newsies*), born Reno, NV, Apr 23, 1976.

APRIL 24 — MONDAY
Day 115 — 251 Remaining

ARMENIA: ARMENIAN MARTYRS DAY: 85th ANNIVERSARY. Apr 24. Commemorates the massacre of Armenians under the Ottoman Turks in 1915 and when deportations from Turkey began. Also called Armenian Genocide Memorial Day. Adolf Hitler, in a speech at Obersalzberg Aug 22, 1939, is reported to have said, "Who today remembers the Armenian extermination?" in an apparent justification of the Nazi's use of genocide.

CANADA: NEWFOUNDLAND: SAINT GEORGE'S DAY. Apr 24. Holiday observed in Newfoundland on Monday nearest Feast Day (Apr 23) of Saint George.

CONFEDERATE MEMORIAL DAY IN MISSISSIPPI. Apr 24. Annually, last Monday in April. Observed on other days in other states.

EASTER MONDAY. Apr 24. Holiday or bank holiday in many places, including England, Northern Ireland, Wales, Canada and North Carolina in the US.

EGG SALAD WEEK. Apr 24–30. Dedicated to the many delicious uses for all of the Easter eggs that have been cooked, colored, hidden and found. Annually, the full week after Easter. For info: Linda Braun, Consumer Serv Dir, American Egg Bd, 1460 Renaissance Dr, Park Ridge, IL 60068. E-mail: aebnet@aol.com. Web: www.aeb.org.

IBM PERSONAL COMPUTER INTRODUCED: ANNIVERSARY. April 24, 1981. Although IBM was one of the pioneers in making mainframe and other large computers, this was the company's first foray into the desktop computer market. Eventually, more IBM-compatible computers were manufactured by IBM's competitors than by IBM itself.

April *2000*	S	M	T	W	T	F	S
							1
	2	3	4	5	6	7	8
	9	10	11	12	13	14	15
	16	17	18	19	20	21	22
	23	24	25	26	27	28	29
	30						

IRELAND: EASTER RISING. Apr 24, 1916. Irish nationalists seized key buildings in Dublin and proclaimed an Irish republic. The rebellion collapsed, however, and it wasn't until 1922 that the Irish Free State, the predecessor of the Republic of Ireland, was established.

LIBRARY OF CONGRESS: 200th ANNIVERSARY. Apr 24, 1800. Congress approved an act providing "for the purchase of such books as may be necessary for the use of Congress . . . and for fitting up a suitable apartment for containing them." Thus began one of the world's greatest libraries. Originally housed in the Capitol, it moved to its own quarters in 1897. For more information about the Library's bicentennial, visit its website at lcweb.loc.gov/bicentennial/bicenweb.html.

NATIONAL PLAYGROUND SAFETY WEEK. Apr 24–28. An opportunity for families, community parks, schools and child-care facilities to focus on preventing public playground-related injuries. Sponsored by the National Program for Playground Safety (NPPS), this event helps educate the public about the more than 200,000 children (that's one child every 2 ½ minutes) that require emergency room treatment for playground-related injuries each year. For info: Natl Program for Playground Safety, School of HPELS, UNI, Cedar Falls, IA 50614-0618. Phone: (800) 554-PLAY. Fax: (319) 273-7308. Web: www.uni.edu/playground.

NESS, EVALINE: BIRTH ANNIVERSARY. Apr 24, 1911. Author and illustrator (Caldecott for *Sam, Bangs & Moonshine*), born at Union City, OH. Died Aug 12, 1986.

NEW ENGLAND CONFERENCE ON STORYTELLING FOR CHILDREN. Apr 24. Arts Center, Keene State College, Keene, NH. Warm, supportive one-day conference for teachers and others interested in learning more about storytelling. Keynote plus two workshops and a performance. Children may attend if capable. Resources will be available. Est attendance: 100. For info: Mary Mayshark-Stavely, Keene State College, Keene, NH 03435-2503. Phone: (603) 358-2218. E-mail: mmayshar@keene.edu.

SOUTH AFRICA: FAMILY DAY. Apr 24. National holiday. Annually, Easter Monday.

TV TURNOFF WEEK. Apr 24–30. For the seventh annual event, more than 7 million Americans will go without TV for 7 days. For info: TV-Free America, Dept P, Ste 3A, 1611 Connecticut Ave NW, Washington, DC 20009. Phone: (800) 939-6737. Web: www.tvfa.org.

WHITE HOUSE EASTER EGG ROLL. Apr 24. Traditionally held on the south lawn of the executive mansion on Easter Monday. Custom is said to have started at the Capitol grounds about 1810. It was transferred to the White House Lawn in the 1870s.

BIRTHDAYS TODAY

A. Paul Cellucci, 52, Governor of Massachusetts (R), born Hudson, MA, Apr 24, 1948.

Jim Geringer, 56, Governor of Wyoming (R), born Wheatland, WY, Apr 24, 1944.

Larry "Chipper" Jones, 28, baseball player, born DeLand, FL, Apr 24, 1972.

APRIL 25 — TUESDAY
Day 116 — 250 Remaining

ANZAC DAY: 85th ANNIVERSARY. Apr 25. Australia, New Zealand and Samoa. Memorial day and veterans' observance, especially to mark WWI Anzac landing at Gallipoli, Turkey, in 1915 (ANZAC: Australia and New Zealand Army Corps).

EGYPT: SINAI DAY. Apr 25. National holiday celebrating the liberation of Sinai in 1982 after the peace treaty between Egypt and Israel. For info: Egyptian Tourist Authority, 645 N Michigan Ave, Ste 829, Chicago, IL 60611. Phone: (312) 280-4666. Fax: (312) 280-4788.

FIRST LICENSE PLATES: ANNIVERSARY. Apr 25, 1901. New York began requiring license plates on automobiles, the first state to do so.

ITALY: LIBERATION DAY: 55th ANNIVERSARY. Apr 25. National holiday. Commemorates the liberation of Italy from German troops in 1945.

LOVELACE, MAUD HART: BIRTH ANNIVERSARY. Apr 25, 1892. Author of the Betsy-Tacy books, born at Mankato, MN. Died at California, Mar 11, 1980.

MARCONI, GUGLIELMO: BIRTH ANNIVERSARY. Apr 25, 1874. Inventor of wireless telegraphy (1895) born at Bologna, Italy. Died at Rome, Italy, July 20, 1937.

NATIONAL CATHOLIC EDUCATIONAL ASSOCIATION CONVENTION AND EXPOSITION. Apr 25–28. Convention Center, Baltimore, MD. Annual meeting for NCEA members and anyone working in, or interested in, the welfare of Catholic education. Est attendance: 11,000. For info: Nancy Brewer, Conv Dir, Natl Catholic Educational Assn, 1077 30th St NW, Ste 100, Washington, DC 20007. Phone: (202) 337-6232. Fax: (202) 333-6706. E-mail: convasst@ncea.org. Web: www.ncea.org.

PORTUGAL: LIBERTY DAY. Apr 25. Portugal. Public holiday. Anniversary of the 1974 revolution.

SPACE MILESTONE: HUBBLE SPACE TELESCOPE DEPLOYED (US): 10th ANNIVERSARY. Apr 25, 1990. Deployed by *Discovery*, the telescope is the largest on-orbit observatory to date and is capable of imaging objects up to 14 billion light-years away. The resolution of images was expected to be seven to 10 times greater than images from Earth-based telescope's, since the Hubble Space Telescope is not hampered by Earth's atmospheric distortion. Launched Apr 12, 1990, from Kennedy Space Center, FL. Unfortunately, the telescope's lenses were defective so that the anticipated high quality of imaging was not possible. In 1993, however, the world watched as a shuttle crew successfully retrieved the Hubble from orbit, executed the needed repair and replacement work and released it into orbit once more.

WALDSEEMULLER, MARTIN: REMEMBRANCE DAY. Apr 25, 1507. Little is known about the obscure scholar now called the "godfather of America," the German geographer and mapmaker Martin Waldseemuller, who gave America its name. In a book titled *Cosmographiae Introductio*, published Apr 25, 1507, Waldseemuller wrote: "Inasmuch as both Europe and Asia received their names from women, I see no reason why any one should justly object to calling this part Amerige, i.e., the land of Amerigo, or America, after Amerigo, its discoverer, a man of great ability." Believing it was the Italian navigator and merchant Amerigo Vespucci who had discovered the new continent, Waldseemuller sought to honor Vespucci by placing his name on his map of the world, published in 1507. First applied only to the South American continent, it soon was used for both the American continents.

Waldseemuller did not learn about the voyage of Christopher Columbus until several years later. Of the thousand copies of his map that were printed, only one is known to have survived. Waldseemuller probably was born at Radolfzell, Germany, about 1470. He died at St. Die, France, about 1517–20. See also: "Vespucci, Amerigo: Birth Anniversary" (Mar 9).

BIRTHDAYS TODAY

Tim Duncan, 24, basketball player, born St. Croix, US Virgin Islands, Apr 25, 1976.

Jon Kyl, 58, US Senator (R, Arizona), born Oakland, NE, Apr 25, 1942.

George Ella Lyon, 51, author (*Come a Tide, Dreamplace*), born Harlan, KY, Apr 25, 1949.

APRIL 26 — WEDNESDAY
Day 117 — 249 Remaining

AUDUBON, JOHN JAMES: BIRTH ANNIVERSARY. Apr 26, 1785. American artist and naturalist, best known for his *Birds of America*, born at Haiti. Died Jan 27, 1851, at New York, NY. For further info: *Capturing Nature: The Writings and Art of John James Audubon*, edited by Peter and Connie Roop (Walker, 0-8027-8205-1, $17.85 Gr. 4–6).

CHERNOBYL NUCLEAR REACTOR DISASTER: ANNIVERSARY. Apr 26, 1986. At 1:23 AM, local time, an explosion occurred at the Chernobyl atomic power station at Pripyat in the Ukraine. The resulting fire burned for days, sending radioactive material into the atmosphere. More than 100,000 persons were evacuated from a 300-square-mile area around the plant. Three months later 31 people were reported to have died and thousands exposed to dangerous levels of radiation. Estimates projected an additional 1,000 cancer cases in nations downwind of the radioactive discharge. The plant was encased in a concrete tomb in an effort to prevent the still-hot reactor from overheating again and to minimize further release of radiation.

CONFEDERATE MEMORIAL DAY IN FLORIDA AND GEORGIA. Apr 26. See also: Confederate Memorial Day entries for May 10, May 31 and June 3.

MOON PHASE: LAST QUARTER. Apr 26. Moon enters Last Quarter phase at 3:30 PM, EDT.

RICHTER SCALE DAY. Apr 26. A day to recognize the importance of Charles Francis Richter's research and his work in development of the earthquake magnitude scale that is known as the Richter scale. Richter, an American author, physicist and seismologist, was born Apr 26, 1900, near Hamilton, OH. An Earthquake Awareness Week was observed in recognition of his work. Richter died at Pasadena, CA, Sept 30, 1985.

SOUTH AFRICAN MULTIRACIAL ELECTIONS: ANNIVERSARY. Apr 26–29, 1994. For the first time in the history of South Africa, the nation's approximately 18 million blacks voted in multiparty elections. This event marked the definitive end of apartheid, the system of racial separation that had kept blacks and other minorities out of the political process. The election resulted in Nelson Mandela of the African National Congress being elected president and F.W. de Klerk (incumbent president) of the National Party vice president.

TANZANIA: UNION DAY. Apr 26. Celebrates union between mainland Tanzania (formerly Tanganyika) and the islands of Zanzibar and Pemba, in 1964.

BIRTHDAYS TODAY

Patricia Reilly Giff, 65, author (*Lily's Crossing*), born Brooklyn, NY, Apr 26, 1935.

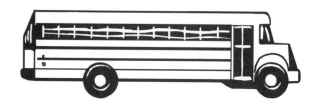

APRIL 27 — THURSDAY
Day 118 — 248 Remaining

BABE RUTH DAY: ANNIVERSARY. Apr 27, 1947. Babe Ruth Day was celebrated in every ballpark in organized baseball in the US as well as Japan. Mortally ill with throat cancer, Ruth appeared at Yankee Stadium to thank his former club for the honor.

BEMELMANS, LUDWIG: BIRTH ANNIVERSARY. Apr 27, 1898. Author, illustrator and artist, born at Austria. Ludwig Bemelmans created the Madeline series, including *Mad About Madeline: The Complete Series*. In 1998, a Madeline film was released. Bemelmans died at New York, NY, Oct 1, 1962.

GRANT, ULYSSES SIMPSON: BIRTH ANNIVERSARY. Apr 27, 1822. Eighteenth president of the US (Mar 4, 1869–Mar 3, 1877), born Hiram Ulysses Grant at Point Pleasant, OH. He graduated from the US Military Academy in 1843. President Lincoln promoted Grant to lieutenant general in command of all the Union armies Mar 9, 1864. On Apr 9, 1865, Grant received General Robert E. Lee's surrender, at Appomattox Court House, VA, which he announced to the Secretary of War as follows: "General Lee surrendered the Army of Northern Virginia this afternoon on terms proposed by myself. The accompanying additional correspondence will show the conditions fully." Nicknamed "Unconditional Surrender Grant," he died at Mount McGregor, NY, July 23, 1885, just four days after completing his memoirs. He was buried at Riverside Park, New York, NY, where Grant's Tomb was dedicated in 1897.

LANTZ, WALTER: 100th BIRTH ANNIVERSARY. Apr 27, 1900. Originator of Universal Studios' animated opening sequence for their first major musical film, *The King of Jazz*. Walter Lantz is best remembered as the creator of Woody Woodpecker, the bird with the wacky laugh and the taunting ways. Lantz received a lifetime achievement Academy Award for his animation in 1979. He was born at New Rochelle, NY, and died Mar 22, 1994, at Burbank, CA.

MAGELLAN, FERDINAND: DEATH ANNIVERSARY. Apr 27, 1521. Portuguese explorer Ferdinand Magellan was probably born near Oporto, Portugal, about 1480, but neither the place nor the date is certain. Usually thought of as the first man to circumnavigate the earth, he died before completing the voyage; thus his co-leader, Basque navigator Juan Sebastian de Elcano, became the world's circumnavigator. The westward, 'round-the-world expedition began Sept 20, 1519, with five ships and about 250 men. Magellan was killed by natives of the Philippine island of Mactan.

April 2000	S	M	T	W	T	F	S
							1
	2	3	4	5	6	7	8
	9	10	11	12	13	14	15
	16	17	18	19	20	21	22
	23	24	25	26	27	28	29
	30						

MORSE, SAMUEL FINLEY BREESE: BIRTH ANNIVERSARY. Apr 27, 1791. American artist and inventor, after whom the Morse code is named, was born at Charlestown, MA, and died at New York, NY, Apr 2, 1872. Graduating from Yale University in 1810, he went to the Royal Academy of London to study painting. After returning to America he achieved success as a portraitist. Morse conceived the idea of an electromagnetic telegraph while on shipboard, returning from art instruction in Europe in 1832, and he proceeded to develop his idea. With financial assistance approved by Congress, the first telegraph line in the US was constructed, between Washington, DC, and Baltimore, MD. The first message tapped out by Morse from the Supreme Court Chamber at the US Capitol building May 24, 1844, was: "What hath God wrought?"

NATIONAL PLAYGROUND SAFETY DAY. Apr 27. An opportunity for families, community parks, schools and childcare facilities to focus on preventing public playground-related injuries. Sponsored by the National Program for Playground Safety (NPPS), this event helps educate the public about the more than 200,000 children (that's one child every 2 ½ minutes) that require emergency room treatment for playground-related injuries each year. Annually, the last Thursday in April. For info: Natl Program for Playground Safety, School of HPELS, UNI, Cedar Falls, IA 50614-0618. Phone: (800) 554-PLAY. Fax: (319) 273-7308. Web: www.uni.edu/playground.

SCHOOL PRINCIPALS' RECOGNITION DAY IN MASSACHUSETTS. Apr 27. Proclaimed annually by the governor.

SIERRA LEONE: INDEPENDENCE DAY. Apr 27. National Day. Commemorates independence from Britain in 1961.

SOUTH AFRICA: FREEDOM DAY. Apr 27. National holiday. Commemorates the day in 1994 when, for the first time, all South Africans had the opportunity to vote.

SPANK OUT DAY USA. Apr 27 (tentative). A day on which all caretakers of children—parents, teachers and daycare workers—are asked not to use corporal punishment as discipline and to become acquainted with positive, effective disciplinary alternatives. For info: Nadine Block, EPOCH-USA, 155 W Main St, Ste 100-B, Columbus, OH 43215. Phone: (614) 221-8829. E-mail: nblock@infinet.com. Web: www.stophitting.com.

TAKE OUR DAUGHTERS TO WORK DAY. Apr 27. A national public education campaign sponsored by the Ms Foundation for Women in which girls aged nine–15 go to work with adult hosts—parents, grandparents, cousins, aunts, uncles, friends. Take Our Daughters to Work Day has succeeded in mobilizing parents, educators, employers and other caring adults to take action to redress the inequalities in girls' lives and focus national attention on the concerns, hopes and dreams of girls. Annually, the fourth Thursday in April. For info: Lauren Wechsler, Natl Media Mgr, Take Our Daughters to Work Day, Ms. Foundation for Women, 120 Wall St, 33rd Fl, New York, NY 10005. Phone: (800) 676-7780 or (212) 742-2300. Fax: (212) 742-1531. E-mail: todtwcom@ms.foundation.org. Web: www.ms.foundation.org.

TOGO: INDEPENDENCE DAY: 40th ANNIVERSARY. Apr 27. National holiday. Gained independence from France in 1960.

YUGOSLAVIA: NATIONAL DAY. Apr 27.

BIRTHDAYS TODAY

Coretta Scott King, 73, lecturer, writer, widow of Dr. Martin Luther King, Jr, born Marion, AL, Apr 27, 1927.

APRIL 28 — FRIDAY
Day 119 — 247 Remaining

BIOLOGICAL CLOCK GENE DISCOVERED: ANNIVERSARY. Apr 28, 1994. Northwestern University announced that the so-called biological clock, that gene governing the daily cycle of waking and sleeping called the circadian rhythm, had been found in mice. Never before pinpointed in a mammal, the biological clock gene was found on mouse chromosome #5.

CONNECTICUT STORYTELLING FESTIVAL. Apr 28–30. Connecticut College, New London, CT. Annual festival features performances for families and adults, plus workshops and story-sharing by Connecticut and nationally renowned storytellers. Annually, the last full weekend in April. Est attendance: 300. For info: Annie Burnham, Adm, Connecticut Storytelling Center, Connecticut College Box 5295, 270 Mohegan Ave, New London, CT 06320. Phone: (860) 439-2764. Fax: (860) 439-2895. E-mail: csc@conncoll.edu.

MARYLAND RATIFIES CONSTITUTION: ANNIVERSARY. Apr 28, 1788. Maryland became the seventh state to ratify the Constitution, by a vote of 63 to 11.

MONROE, JAMES: BIRTH ANNIVERSARY. Apr 28, 1758. The fifth president of the US was born at Westmoreland County, VA, and served two terms in that office (Mar 4, 1817–Mar 3, 1825). Monrovia, the capital city of Liberia, is named after him, as is the Monroe Doctrine, which he enunciated at Washington, DC, Dec 2, 1823. Last of three presidents to die on US Independence Day, Monroe died at New York, NY, July 4, 1831.

MUTINY ON THE *BOUNTY*: ANNIVERSARY. Apr 28, 1789. The most famous of all naval mutinies occurred on board HMS *Bounty*. Captain of the *Bounty* was Lieutenant William Bligh, a mean-tempered disciplinarian. The ship, with a load of breadfruit tree plants from Tahiti, was bound for Jamaica. Fletcher Christian, leader of the mutiny, put Bligh and 18 of his loyal followers adrift in a 23-foot open boat. Miraculously Bligh and all of his supporters survived a 47-day voyage of more than 3,600 miles, before landing on the island of Timor, June 14, 1789. In the meantime, Christian had put all of the remaining crew (excepting eight men and himself) ashore at Tahiti where he picked up 18 Tahitians (six men and 12 women) and set sail again. Landing at Pitcairn Island in 1790 (probably uninhabited at the time), they burned the *Bounty* and remained undiscovered for 18 years, when an American whaler, the *Topaz*, called at the island (1808) and found only one member of the mutinous crew surviving. However, the little colony had thrived and, when counted by the British in 1856, numbered 194 persons.

NATIONAL ARBOR DAY. Apr 28. The Committee for National Arbor Day has as its goal the observance of Arbor Day in all states on the same day, the last Friday in April. This unified Arbor Day date would provide our citizenry with the opportunity to better learn the importance of trees to our way of life. This date is a good planting date for many states throughout the country. National Arbor Day has been observed in 1970, 1972, 1988, 1990, 1991 and 1993 by Presidential Proclamation. More than half the states now observe Arbor Day on the proposed April Friday. Sponsors include: International Society of Arboriculture; Society of Municipal Arborists; American Association of Nurserymen; National Arborist Association; National Recreation and Park Association; Arborists Association of New Jersey. For info: Committee for Natl Arbor Day, 63 Fitzrandolph Rd, West Orange, NJ 07052. Phone: (201) 731-0840. Fax: (201) 731-6020.

NATIONAL CHILD CARE PROFESSIONALS DAY. Apr 28. A day of recognition for child care providers. A day to increase the visibility of the role child care providers play in our society and celebrate the partnership between parents and caregivers to help children develop to their full potential. Sponsored by Child Care Aware and Cheerios®. For info: Anne Nicolai, Child Care Aware, 2116 Campus Dr, SE, Rochester, MN 55904. Phone: (800) 424-2246 or (612) 835-3335.

BIRTHDAYS TODAY

Lois Duncan, 66, author (*The Circus Comes Home, I Know What You Did Last Summer*), born Philadelphia, PA, Apr 28, 1934.

Harper Lee, 74, author (*To Kill A Mockingbird*), 1961 Pulitzer Prize for fiction, born Monroeville, AL, Apr 28, 1926.

Jay Leno, 50, TV talk show host ("Tonight Show"), comedian, born New Rochelle, NY, Apr 28, 1950.

Catherine Reef, 49, writer of history and biography (*John Steinbeck*), born New York, NY, Apr 28, 1951.

Nate Richert, 22, actor ("Sabrina, the Teenage Witch"), born St. Paul, MN, Apr 28, 1978.

APRIL 29 — SATURDAY
Day 120 — 246 Remaining

ELLINGTON, "DUKE" (EDWARD KENNEDY): BIRTH ANNIVERSARY. Apr 29, 1899. "Duke" Ellington, one of the most influential individuals in jazz history, was born at Washington, DC. By 1923 he was leading a small group of musicians at the Kentucky Club at New York City who became the core of his big band. Ellington is credited with being one of the founders of big band jazz. He used his band as an instrument for composition and orchestration to create big band pieces, film scores, operas, ballets, Broadway shows and religious music. Ellington was responsible for more than 1,000 musical pieces. He drew together instruments from different sections of the orchestra to develop unique and haunting sounds such as that of his famous "Mood Indigo." "Duke" Ellington died May 24, 1974, at New York City. For more info: *Duke Ellington: The Piano Prince and His Orchestra*, by Andrea Davis Pinkney (Hyperion, 0-7868-2150-7, $16.49 Gr. K–3).

ELLSWORTH, OLIVER: BIRTH ANNIVERSARY. Apr 29, 1745. Third chief justice of the US Supreme Court, born at Windsor, CT. Died there, Nov 26, 1807.

HIROHITO MICHI-NO-MIYA, EMPEROR: BIRTH ANNIVERSARY. Apr 29, 1901. Former Emperor of Japan, born at Tokyo. Hirohito's death Jan 27, 1989, ended the reign of the world's longest ruling monarch. He became the 124th in a line of monarchs when he ascended to the Chrysanthemum Throne in 1926. Hirohito presided over perhaps the most eventful years in the 2,500 years of recorded Japanese history, including the attempted military conquest of Asia, the attack on the US that brought that country into WWII, leading to Japan's ultimate defeat after the US dropped atomic bombs on Hiroshima and Nagasaki and the amazing economic restoration following the war that led Japan to a preeminent position of economic strength. Although he opposed initiating hostilities with the US, he signed

a declaration of war, allowing Japan's militarist Prime Minister, Hideki Tojo, to begin the fateful campaign. During the war's final days he overruled Tojo and advocated surrender. Hirohito broadcast a taped message to the Japanese people to stop fighting and "endure the unendurable." This radio message was the first time the emperor's voice had ever been heard outside the imperial household and inner circle of government. After the war, Hirohito was allowed to remain on his throne. He denounced his divinity in 1946, bestowed upon him by Japanese law, and became a "symbol of the state" in Japan's new parliamentary democracy. Hirohito turned his energies to his real passion, marine biology, becoming a recognized world authority in the field.

MOMENT OF LAUGHTER DAY. Apr 29. Laughter is a potent and powerful way to deal with the difficulties of modern living. Since the physical, emotional and spiritual benefits of laughter are widely accepted, this day is set aside for everyone to take the necessary time to experience the power of laughter. For info: Izzy Gesell, Head Honcho of Wide Angle Humor, PO Box 962, Northampton, MA 01061. Phone: (413) 586-2634. Fax: (413) 585-0407. E-mail: izzy@izzyg.com. Web: www.izzyg.com.

NATIONAL PUPPETRY DAY. Apr 29. A day to celebrate the lively art of puppetry through performances, seminars, lectures and parades. Sponsored by Puppeteers of America, Inc. Annually, the Saturday of the last full weekend in April. For info: Rick Morse, 3104 Vineyard Ln, Flushing, MI 48433. Phone: (810) 230-0105. E-mail: Rickpuppet@aol.com.

TAIWAN: CHENG CHENG KUNG LANDING DAY. Apr 29. Commemorates landing in Taiwan in 1661 of Ming Dynasty loyalist Cheng Cheng Kung (Koxinga), who ousted Dutch colonists who had occupied Taiwan for 37 years. Main ceremonies held at Tainan, in south Taiwan, where Dutch had their headquarters and where Cheng is buried. Cheng's birthday is also joyously celebrated, but according to the lunar calendar—on the 14th day of the seventh moon.

ZIPPER PATENTED: ANNIVERSARY. Apr 29, 1913. Gideon Sundbach of Hoboken, NJ, received a patent for the zipper.

BIRTHDAYS TODAY

Andre Kirk Agassi, 30, tennis player, born Las Vegas, NV, Apr 29, 1970.

Kate Mulgrew, 45, actress ("Star Trek: Voyager"), born Dubuque, IA, Apr 29, 1955.

Jill Paton Walsh, 63, author (*Fireweed*), born London, England, Apr 29, 1937.

APRIL 30 — SUNDAY
Day 121 — 245 Remaining

HARRISON, MARY SCOTT LORD DIMMICK: BIRTH ANNIVERSARY. Apr 30, 1858. Second wife of Benjamin Harrison, 23rd president of the US, born at Honesdale, PA. Died at New York, NY, Jan 5, 1948.

	S	M	T	W	T	F	S
April							1
2000	2	3	4	5	6	7	8
	9	10	11	12	13	14	15
	16	17	18	19	20	21	22
	23	24	25	26	27	28	29
	30						

INTERNATIONAL READING ASSOCIATION ANNUAL CONVENTION. Apr 30–May 5. Indianapolis, IN. 45th annual convention. For info: Intl Reading Assn, 800 Barksdale Rd, PO Box 8139, Newark, DE 19714-8139. Phone: (302) 731-1600. E-mail: conferences@reading.org. Web: www.ira.org.

INTERNATIONAL SCHOOL SPIRIT SEASON. Apr 30–Sept 30. To recognize everyone who has helped to make school spirit better and to provide time to plan improved spirit ideas for the coming school year. For info: Jim Hawkins, Chairman, Pepsters, Committee for More School Spirit, P.O. Box 122652, San Diego, CA 92112. Phone: (619) 280-0999.

LOUISIANA: ADMISSION DAY: ANNIVERSARY. Apr 30. Became 18th state in 1812.

NATIONAL HONESTY DAY (WITH HONEST ABE AWARDS). Apr 30. To celebrate honesty and those who are honest and honorable in their dealings with others. Nominations accepted for most honest people and companies. Winners to be awarded "Honest Abe" awards and given "Abies" on National Honesty Day. Annually, Apr 30. For info: M. Hirsh Goldberg, Author of *The Book of Lies*, 3103 Szold Dr, Baltimore, MD 21208. Phone: (410) 486-4150.

NETHERLANDS: QUEEN'S BIRTHDAY. Apr 30. A public holiday in celebration of the Queen's birthday and the Dutch National Day. The whole country parties as young and old participate in festivities such as markets, theater, music and games.

ORGANIZATION OF AMERICAN STATES FOUNDED: ANNIVERSARY. Apr 30, 1948. This regional alliance was founded by 21 nations of the Americas at Bogata, Colombia. Its purpose is to further economic development and integration among nations of the Western hemisphere, to promote representative democracy and to help overcome poverty. The Pan-American Union, with offices at Washington, DC, serves as the General Secretariat for the OAS.

ORTHODOX EASTER SUNDAY OR PASCHA. Apr 30. Observed by Eastern Orthodox Churches. See also: "Easter Sunday."

SCHOOLTECH EXPO AND CONFERENCE. Apr 30–May 2. New York, NY. Sponsored by *Technology & Learning* magazine, the conference features training workshops and technology exhibits. Est attendance: 3,000. For info: Miller Freeman Inc, 600 Harrison St, San Francisco, CA 94109. Phone: (888) 857-6883. Web: www.schooltechexpo.com.

SWEDEN: FEAST OF VALBORG. Apr 30. An evening celebration in which Sweden "sings in the spring" by listening to traditional hymns to the spring, often around community bonfires. Also known as Walpurgis Night, the Feast of Valborg occurs annually, Apr 30.

THEATER IN NORTH AMERICA FIRST PERFORMANCE: ANNIVERSARY. Apr 30, 1598. On the banks of the Rio Grande, near present day El Paso, TX, the first North American theatrical performance was acted. The play was a Spanish commedia featuring an expedition of soldiers. On July 10 of the same year, the same group produced *Moros y Los Cristianos* (Moors and Christians), an anonymous play.

WASHINGTON, GEORGE: PRESIDENTIAL INAUGURATION ANNIVERSARY. Apr 30, 1789. George Washington was inaugurated as the first president of the US under the new Constitution at New York, NY. Robert R. Livingston administered the oath of office to Washington on the balcony of Federal Hall, at the corner of Wall and Broad streets.

BIRTHDAYS TODAY

Dorothy Hinshaw Patent, 60, author (*Bold and Bright Black-and-White Animals*), born Rochester, MN, Apr 30, 1940.

MAY 1 — MONDAY

Day 122 — 244 Remaining

★ **ASIAN PACIFIC AMERICAN HERITAGE MONTH.** May 1–31. Presidential Proclamation issued honoring Asian Pacific Americans each year since 1979. Public Law 102-450 of Oct 28, 1992, designated the observance for the month of May each year.

FREEDOM SHRINE MONTH. May 1–31. To bring America's heritage of freedom to public attention through presentations or rededications of Freedom Shrine displays of historic American documents by Exchange Clubs. For info: The Natl Exchange Club, 3050 Central Ave, Toledo, OH 43606-1700. Phone: (419) 535-3232 or (800) 924-2643. Fax: (419) 535-1989. E-mail: nechq@aol.com. Web: www.nationalexchangeclub.com.

GREAT BRITAIN FORMED: ANNIVERSARY. May 1, 1707. A union between England and Scotland resulted in the formation of Great Britain. (Wales had been part of England since the 1500s.) Today's United Kingdom consists of Great Britain and Northern Ireland.

KEEP MASSACHUSETTS BEAUTIFUL MONTH. May 1–31. Proclaimed annually by the governor.

LABOR DAY. May 1. In many countries of the world, May 1 is observed as a workers' holiday. When it falls on a Saturday or Sunday, the following Monday is observed as a holiday. Bermuda, Canada and the US are the only countries that observe Labor Day in September.

★ **LAW DAY.** May 1. Presidential Proclamation issued each year for May 1 since 1958 at request. (PL87–20 of Apr 7, 1961.)

LAW ENFORCEMENT APPRECIATION MONTH IN FLORIDA. May 1–31. A ceremonial observance. May 15 is designated Law Enforcement Memorial Day.

LEI DAY. May 1. Hawaii. On this special day—the Hawaiian version of May Day—leis are made, worn, given, displayed and entered in lei-making contests. One of the most popular Lei Day celebrations takes place in Honolulu at Kapiolani Park in Waikiki. Includes the state's largest lei contest, the crowning of the Lei Day Queen, Hawaiian music, hula and flowers galore.

	S	M	T	W	T	F	S
May		1	2	3	4	5	6
2000	7	8	9	10	11	12	13
	14	15	16	17	18	19	20
	21	22	23	24	25	26	27
	28	28	30	31			

★ **LOYALTY DAY.** May 1. Presidential Proclamation issued annually for May 1 since 1959 at request. (PL85–529 of July 18, 1958.) Note that an earlier proclamation was issued in 1955.

MARSHALL ISLANDS, REPUBLIC OF THE: CONSTITUTION DAY. May 1. National holiday.

MAY DAY. May 1. The first day of May has been observed as a holiday since ancient times. Spring festivals, maypoles and may baskets are still common, but the political importance of May Day has grown since the 1880s, when it became a workers' day. Now widely observed as a workers' holiday or as Labor Day. In most European countries, when May Day falls on Saturday or Sunday, the Monday following is observed as a holiday, with bank and store closings, parades and other festivities.

MOTHER GOOSE DAY. May 1. To re-appreciate the old nursery rhymes. Motto is "Either alone or in sharing, read childhood nursery favorites and feel the warmth of Mother Goose's embrace." Annually, May 1. For info: Gloria T. Delamar, Founder, Mother Goose Soc, 7303 Sharpless Rd, Melrose Park, PA 19027. Phone: (215) 782-1059. E-mail: Mother.Goose.Society@juno.com. Web: www.gbalc.org/MotherGooseSociety.

NATIONAL ALLERGY/ASTHMA AWARENESS MONTH. May 1–31. Kit of materials available for $15 from this nonprofit organization. For info: Frederick S. Mayer, Pres, Pharmacist Planning Services, Inc, c/o Allergy Council of America (ACA), 101 Lucas Valley Rd, #210, San Rafael, CA 94903. Phone: (415) 479-8628. Fax: (415) 479-8608. E-mail: ppsi@aol.com.

NATIONAL BARBECUE MONTH. May 1–31. To encourage people to start enjoying barbecuing early in the season when Daylight Saving Time lengthens the day. Annually, the month of May. Sponsor: Barbecue Industry Association. For info: NBM, DHM Group, Inc, PO Box 767, Dept CC, Holmdel, NJ 07733-0767. Fax: (732) 946-3343.

NATIONAL BIKE MONTH. May 1–31. 43rd annual celebration of bicycling for recreation and transportation. Local activities sponsored by bicycling organizations, environmental groups, PTAs, police departments, health organizations and civic groups. About five million participants nationwide. Annually, the month of May. For info: Donald Tighe, Program Dir, League of American Bicyclists, 1612 K St, Ste 401, Washington, DC 20006. Phone: (202) 822-1333. Fax: (202) 822-1334. E-mail: DWTLAW@aol.com. Web: www.bikeleague.org.

NATIONAL EGG MONTH. May 1–31. Dedicated to the versatility, convenience, economy and good nutrition of "the incredible edible egg." Annually, the month of May. For info: Linda Braun, Consumer Serv Dir, American Egg Board, 1460 Renaissance Dr, Park Ridge, IL 60068. E-mail: aeb@aeb.org. Web: www.aeb.org.

NATIONAL HAMBURGER MONTH. May 1–31. Sponsored by White Castle, the original fast-food hamburger chain, founded in 1921, to pay tribute to one of America's favorite foods. With or without condiments, on or off a bun or bread, hamburgers have grown in popularity since the early 1920s and are now an American meal mainstay. For info: White Castle System, Inc, Marketing Dept, 555 W Goodale St, Columbus, OH 43215-1171. Phone: (614) 228-5781. Fax: (614) 228-8841. Web: www.whitecastle.com.

NATIONAL HEPATITIS AWARENESS MONTH. May 1–31. For info: Hepatitis Foundation Intl, 30 Sunrise Terr, Cedar Grove, NJ 07009. Phone: (800) 891-0707. E-mail: hfi@intac.com. Web: www.hepfi.org.

NATIONAL MENTAL HEALTH MONTH. May 1–31. For info: Natl Mental Health Assn, 1021 Prince St, Alexandria, VA 22314-

MAY 1–31
NATIONAL EGG MONTH

Although National Egg Month focuses on "the incredible edible egg," more specifically chicken eggs, there's no reason you can't expand to other bird and animal species.

Many classrooms have made their own or purchased egg incubators, obtained fertilized chicken or duck eggs and successfully hatched babies. (Local 4-H Clubs or Farm Bureaus may be able to provide informational materials.) If you chose to do this kind of activity, plan well in advance what is to happen to the chicks or ducklings after they hatch. This is also the time of year when frog and caterpillar eggs are available.

Students can research the nutritional benefits of chicken eggs and how they can be judiciously included in our diets. *Everyone Eats Eggs*, by Gillian Powell (Raintree, 0-8172-4759-9, $15.98 Gr. 2–6) contains nutritional information about chicken eggs, a multicultural look at the ways eggs are prepared and lots of egg trivia.

Sea turtles are on the threatened species lists. Their nesting and egg laying habits and how people are working to protect them is a fascinating research topic.

Students may enjoy drawing cross sections of eggs and labeling the parts. If you extend an egg unit to include amphibians, reptiles and mammals, you will have quite a wide range of egg forms to compare. A research topic could be to investigate where the nourishment for different kinds of eggs comes from.

Blowing out the insides of chicken eggs (from the store) and then painting them in patterns inspired by Ukrainian Easter eggs is an imaginative art project.

For further information about eggs and birds, see Lerner Publications series Birder's Bookshelf for grades 4–7. This enjoyable four book series by Dean Spaulding explores feeding, housing, watching and protecting birds. For tadpole information try *Lily Pad Pond*, by Bianca Lavies (Puffin, 0-14-054836-X, $4.99 Gr. K–3).

2971. Phone: (800) 969-6642 or (703) 684-7722. E-mail: nmhainfo @aol.com. Web: www.nmha.org.

NATIONAL MOVING MONTH. May 1–31. Recognizing America's mobile roots and kicking off the busiest moving season of the year. Each year more than 21 million Americans move between Memorial Day and Labor Day, with the average American moving every seven years. During this month moving experts will be educating Americans on how to plan a successful move, to pack efficiently and handle the uncertainties and questions that moving children may have. For info: Allied Van Lines, PO Box 9569, Downers Grove, IL 60515. Phone: (630) 241-2538. Fax: (630) 241-4343. Web: www.alliedvan.com.

NATIONAL SALAD MONTH. May 1–31. Americans celebrate salads and their role in today's healthy lifestyle. Annually, the month of May. For info: The Assn for Dressings and Sauces, 5775-G Peachtree-Dunwoody Rd, Atlanta, GA 30342. Phone: (404) 252-3663. Fax: (404) 252-0774. E-mail: ads@assnhq.com. Web: www.dressings-sauces.org.

NATIONAL SALSA MONTH. May 1–31. Recognizing salsa as America's favorite condiment, used more often than even ketchup as a topping, dip, marinade and to spice up countless recipes. National Salsa Month celebrates more than 50 years of picante sauce, a salsa created in 1947, and celebrates Cinco de Mayo, a major Mexican holiday now recognized across North America. For info: Mary Uhlig, VP, Dublin & Assoc, 111 Soledad, Ste 1600,

San Antonio, TX 78205. Phone: (210) 227-0221. Fax: (210) 226-7097. Web: www.pacefoods.com.

NATIONAL TEACHING AND JOY MONTH. May 1–31. A month of celebrating the joy of great teaching and great learning. Thank a teacher for creating an atmosphere of joy. Notice those students who demonstrate a love of learning. Call or write someone who helped you learn an important life skill. For info: Dr. Jim Scott, Jackson Community College, 2111 Emmons Rd, Jackson, MI 49201. Phone: (517) 796-8488. Fax: (517) 796-8631. E-mail: jim_scott@jackson.cc.mi.us.

★**OLDER AMERICANS MONTH.** May 1–31. Presidential Proclamation; from 1963 through 1973 this was called "Senior Citizens Month." In May 1974 it became Older Americans Month. In 1980 the title included Senior Citizens Day, which was observed May 8, 1980. Always has been issued since 1963.

PEN-FRIENDS WEEK INTERNATIONAL. May 1–7. To encourage everyone to have one or more pen-friends not only in their own country but in other countries. For complete information on how to become a good pen-friend and information about how to write good letters, send $4 to cover expense of printing, handling and postage. Annually, May 1–7. For info: Dr. Stanley J. Drake, Pres, Intl Soc of Friendship and Good Will, 412 Cherry Hills Dr, Bakersfield, CA 93309-7902.

PROJECT SAFE BABY MONTH. May 1–31. Dedicated to raising awareness of correct child safety seat use, to increasing the availability of child safety seats and to educating parents, teachers and health professionals about child safety in the car. Sponsor: Midas International, Inc. For info: Golin/Harris Communications, Inc, Midas Project Safe Baby Team, 111 E Wacker Dr, 10th Fl, Chicago, IL 60601-3704. Phone: (312) 729-4174.

PUBLIC SERVICE RECOGNITION WEEK. May 1–7. Take this opportunity to thank the "Unsung Heroes and Heroines" of the public work force who perform a range of vital services. Public employees are scientists and police officers, teachers and doctors, astronauts and zoologists, engineers and food inspectors, forest rangers and claims representatives, researchers and foreign service agents. Free resource materials to promote the celebration available. Annually, the first Monday–Sunday in May. For info: Nick Nolan, Exec Dir, Public Employees Roundtable, PO Box 44801, Washington, DC 20026-4801. Phone: (202) 401-4344. E-mail: permail@patriot.net. Web: www.theroundtable.org.

READ ME WEEK. May 1–5. National and local celebrities and other volunteers read in classrooms wearing readable clothing with school appropriate messages. For info: Lee Fairbend, Exec Dir, Book'Em!, 2012 21st Ave South, Nashville, TN 37212. Phone: (615) 297-7323.

RUSSIA: INTERNATIONAL LABOR DAY. May 1–2. Public holiday in Russian Federation. "Official May Day demonstrations of working people."

SAVE THE RHINO DAY. May 1. May day! May day! Rhinos still in danger! Help save the world's remaining rhinos on the verge of extinction! Get involved with local, national and international conservation efforts to stop the senseless slaughter of these gentle pachyderms. Call your local zoo or write Really, Rhinos! for a $5 information packet. For info: Judyth Lessee, Founder, Really, Rhinos!, PO Box 40503, Tucson, AZ 85717-0503. Phone: (520) 327-9048. E-mail: rinophyl@rtd.com.

SPRING CLEANING DAY. May 1. A day to begin spring cleaning. For info: Joy Krause, Author, PO Box 22-0173, Hollywood, FL 33022. Phone: (954) 927-3960. Fax: (954) 927-3068. E-mail: sprng clng@aol.com.

VEGETARIAN RESOURCE GROUP'S ESSAY CONTEST FOR KIDS. May 1. Children ages 18 and under are encouraged to submit a two–three-page essay on topics related to vegetarianism. Essays accepted up to May 1. Winners announced Sept 15 and will receive a $50 savings bond. For info: The Vegetarian Resource Group, PO Box 1463, Baltimore, MD 21203. Phone: (410) 366-8343. Fax: (410) 366-8804. E-mail: vrg@vrg.org. Web: www.vrg.org.

WILLIAMS, ARCHIE: 85th BIRTH ANNIVERSARY. May 1, 1915. Archie Williams, along with Jesse Owens and others, debunked Hitler's theory of the superiority of Aryan athletes at the 1936 Berlin Olympics. As a black member of the US team Williams won a gold medal by running the 400-meter in 46.5 seconds (.4 second slower than his own record of earlier that year). Williams, who was born at Oakland, CA, earned a degree in mechanical engineering from the University of California-Berkeley in 1939 but had to dig ditches for a time because they weren't hiring black engineers. In time Williams became an airplane pilot and for 22 years he trained Tuskegee Institute pilots including the black air corp of WWII. He joined the Army Air Corps in 1942. When asked during a 1981 interview about his treatment by the Nazis during the 1936 Olympics, he replied, "Well, over there at least we didn't have to ride in the back of the bus." Archie Williams died June 24, 1993, at Fairfax, CA.

BIRTHDAYS TODAY

Curtis Martin, 27, football player, born Pittsburgh, PA, May 1, 1973.
Elizabeth Marie Pope, 83, author (*The Perilous Gard*), born Washington, DC, May 1, 1917.

MAY 2 — TUESDAY
Day 123 — 243 Remaining

HOLOCAUST DAY (YOM HASHOAH). May 2. Hebrew calendar date: Nisan 27, 5760. A day established by Israel's Knesset as a memorial to the Jewish dead of WWII. Anniversary in Jewish calendar of Nisan 27, 5705 (corresponding to Apr 10, 1945, in the Gregorian calendar), the day on which Allied troops liberated the first Nazi concentration camp, Buchenwald, north of Weimar, Germany, where about 56,000 prisoners, many of them Jewish, perished.

KING JAMES BIBLE PUBLISHED: ANNIVERSARY. May 2, 1611. King James I appointed a committee of learned men to produce a new translation of the Bible in English. This version, popularly called the King James Version, is known in England as the Authorized Version.

LEONARDO DA VINCI: DEATH ANNIVERSARY. May 2, 1519. Italian artist, scientist and inventor. Painter of the famed *Last Supper*, perhaps the first painting of the High Renaissance, and of the *Mona Lisa*. Inventor of the first parachute. Born at Vinci, Italy, in 1452 (exact date unknown), he died at Amboise, France.

ROBERT'S RULES DAY. May 2, 1837. Anniversary of the birth of Henry M. Robert (General, US Army), author of *Robert's Rules of Order*, a standard parliamentary guide. Born at Robertville, SC, he died at Hornell, NY, May 11, 1923.

	S	M	T	W	T	F	S
May 2000		1	2	3	4	5	6
	7	8	9	10	11	12	13
	14	15	16	17	18	19	20
	21	22	23	24	25	26	27
	28	28	30	31			

SPOCK, BENJAMIN: BIRTH ANNIVERSARY. May 2, 1903. Pediatrician and author, born at New Haven, CT. His book on child-rearing, *Common Sense Book of Baby and Child Care* later called *Baby and Child Care*, has sold more than 30 million copies. In 1955 he became professor of child development at Western Reserve University at Cleveland, OH. He resigned from this position in 1967 to devote his time to the pacifism movement. Spock died at San Diego, CA, Mar 15, 1998.

BIRTHDAYS TODAY

Jenna Von Oy, 23, actress (voice on "Pepper Ann," "Blossom"), born Newtown, CT, May 2, 1977.

MAY 3 — WEDNESDAY
Day 124 — 242 Remaining

"CBS EVENING NEWS" TV PREMIERE: ANNIVERSARY. May 3, 1948. The news program began as a 15-minute telecast with Douglas Edwards as anchor. Walter Cronkite succeeded him in 1962 and expanded the show to 30 minutes; Eric Sevareid served as commentator. Dan Rather anchored the newscasts upon Cronkite's retirement in 1981. At one point, to boost sagging ratings, Connie Chung was added to the newscast as Rather's co-anchor, but she left in 1995 in a well-publicized dispute. Rather remains solo, and, as Cronkite would say, ". . . that's the way it is."

JAPAN: CONSTITUTION MEMORIAL DAY. May 3. National holiday commemorating constitution of 1947.

MEXICO: DAY OF THE HOLY CROSS. May 3. Celebrated especially by construction workers and miners, a festive day during which anyone who is building must give a party for the workers. A flower-decorated cross is placed on every piece of new construction in the country.

NATIONAL PUBLIC RADIO FIRST BROADCAST: ANNIVERSARY. May 3, 1971. National noncommercial radio network, financed by Corporation for Public Broadcasting, began programming.

POLAND: CONSTITUTION DAY (SWIETO TRZECIEGO MAJO). May 3. National Day. Celebrates ratification of Poland's first constitution, 1791.

UNITED NATIONS: WORLD PRESS FREEDOM DAY. May 3. A day to recognize that a free, pluralistic and independent press is an essential component of any democratic society and to promote press freedom in the world.

BIRTHDAYS TODAY

Mavis Jukes, 53, author (*Like Jake and Me*), born Nyack, NY, May 3, 1947.
Ron Wyden, 51, US Senator (D, Oregon), born Wichita, KS, May 3, 1949.

MAY 4 — THURSDAY
Day 125 — 241 Remaining

CHINA: YOUTH DAY. May 4. Annual public holiday "recalls the demonstration on May 4, 1919, by thousands of patriotic students in Beijing's Tiananmen Square to protest imperialist aggression in China."

CURACAO: MEMORIAL DAY. May 4. Victims of WWII are honored on this day. Military ceremonies at the War Monument. Not an official public holiday.

DISCOVERY OF JAMAICA BY CHRISTOPHER COLUMBUS: ANNIVERSARY. May 4, 1494. Christopher Columbus discovered Jamaica. The Arawak Indians were its first inhabitants.

MANN, HORACE: BIRTH ANNIVERSARY. May 4, 1796. American educator, author, public servant, known as the "father of public education in the US," was born at Franklin, MA. Founder of Westfield (MA) State College, president of Antioch College and editor of the influential *Common School Journal*. Mann died at Yellow Springs, OH, Aug 2, 1859.

MOON PHASE: NEW MOON. May 4. Moon enters New Moon phase at 12:12 AM, EDT.

★**NATIONAL DAY OF PRAYER.** May 4. Presidential Proclamation always issued for the first Thursday in May since 1981. (PL100–307 of May 5, 1988.) From 1957 to 1981, a day in October was designated, except in 1972 and 1975 through 1977.

NATIONAL WEATHER OBSERVER'S DAY. May 4. For those people, amateurs and professionals alike, who love to follow the everyday phenomenon known as weather. Annually, May 4. For info: Alan W. Brue, 2006 NW 55th Ave, #H-5, Gainesville, FL 32653. E-mail: afn05660@afn.org.

SCHOOL-TO-WORK LAUNCHED: ANNIVERSARY. May 4, 1994. President Clinton signed the School-to-Work Opportunities Act. It provides seed money to states and local partnerships to develop school-to-work systems of education reform, worker preparation and economic development to prepare youth for the high wage, high skill careers of the global economy. For info: Natl School-to-Work Learning & Information Center, 400 Virginia Ave, Rm 150, Washington, DC 20024. Phone: (800) 251-7236. Fax: (202) 401-6211. E-mail: stw-lc@ed.gov. Web: stw.ed.gov/general/general.htm.

SPACE MILESTONE: *ATLANTIS* (US). May 4, 1989. First American planetary expedition in 11 years. Space shuttle *Atlantis* was launched, its major objective to deploy the *Magellan* spacecraft on its way to Venus to map the planet's surface. The shuttle was on its 65th orbit when it landed May 8, mission accomplished.

TYLER, JULIA GARDINER: BIRTH ANNIVERSARY. May 4, 1820. Second wife of John Tyler, 10th president of the US, born at Gardiners Island, NY. Died at Richmond, VA, July 10, 1889.

WHALE AWARENESS DAY IN MASSACHUSETTS. May 4. Proclaimed annually by the governor for the first Thursday in May.

Ben Grieve, 24, baseball player, 1998 American League Rookie of the Year, born Arlington, TX, May 4, 1976.
Dawn Staley, 30, basketball player, born Philadelphia, PA, May 4, 1970.
Don Wood, 55, illustrator (*King Bidgood's in the Bathtub*), born Atwater, CA, May 4, 1945.

MAY 5 — FRIDAY
Day 126 — 240 Remaining

BASEBALL'S FIRST PERFECT GAME: ANNIVERSARY. May 5, 1904. Denton T. "Cy" Young pitched baseball's first perfect game, not allowing a single opposing player to reach first base. Young's outstanding performance led the Boston Americans in a 3–0 victory over Philadelphia in the American League. The Cy Young Award for pitching was named in his honor.

BLY, NELLIE: BIRTH ANNIVERSARY. May 5, 1867. Born at Cochran's Mills, PA, Nellie Bly was the pseudonym used by pioneering American journalist Elizabeth Cochrane Seaman. Like her namesake in a Stephen Foster song, Nellie Bly was a social reformer and human rights advocate. As a journalist, she is best known for her exposé of conditions in what were then known as "insane asylums," where she posed as an "inmate." As an adventurer, she is best known for her 1889–90 tour around-the-world in 72 days, in which she bettered the time of Jules Verne's fictional character Phileas Fogg by eight days. She died at New York, NY, Jan 27, 1922.

BONZA BOTTLER DAY™. May 5. To celebrate when the number of the day is the same as the number of the month. Bonza Bottler Day™ is an excuse to have a party at least once a month. For info: Gail M. Berger, 109 Matthew Ave, Poca, WV 25159. Phone: (304) 776-7746. E-mail: gberger5@aol.com.

HALFWAY POINT OF SPRING. May 5. At 9:48 AM, EDT, May 5, 2000, 47 days, 7 hours and 13 minutes of spring will have elapsed, and the equivalent will remain before June 20, 9:48 PM, EDT, which is the summer solstice and the beginning of summer.

INTERNATIONAL TUBA DAY. May 5. To recognize tubists in musical organizations around the world who have to go through the hassle of handling a tuba in order to make beautiful music. Annually, the first Friday in May. Est attendance: 300. For info: Dr. Sy Brandon, Music Dept, Millersville Univ, PO Box 1002, Millersville, PA 17551-0302. Phone: (717) 872-3439. Fax: (717) 871-2304. E-mail: sbrandon@marander.millersv.edu.

JAPAN: CHILDREN'S DAY. May 5. National holiday. Observed on the fifth day of the fifth month each year.

KOREA: CHILDREN'S DAY. May 5. A time for families to take their children on excursions. Parks and children's centers throughout the country are packed with excited and colorfully dressed children. A national holiday since 1975.

MEXICO: CINCO DE MAYO: ANNIVERSARY. May 5. Mexican national holiday recognizing the anniversary of the Battle of Puebla, May 5, 1862, in which Mexican troops under General Ignacio Zaragoza, outnumbered three to one, defeated invading French forces of Napoleon III. Anniversary is observed by Mexicans everywhere with parades, festivals, dances and speeches.

NETHERLANDS: LIBERATION DAY: 55th ANNIVERSARY. May 5. Marks liberation of the Netherlands from Nazi Germany in 1945.

SPACE MILESTONE: *FREEDOM 7* (US). May 5, 1961. First US astronaut in space, second man in space, Alan Shepard, Jr, projected 115 miles into space in suborbital flight reaching a speed of more than 5,000 miles per hour. This was the first piloted Mercury mission.

THAILAND: CORONATION DAY. May 5. Thailand.

BIRTHDAYS TODAY

Danielle Fishel, 19, actress ("Boy Meets World"), born Mesa, AZ, May 5, 1981.

Leo Lionni, 90, author and illustrator (*Swimmy, Frederick*), born Amsterdam, Netherlands, May 5, 1910.

MAY 6 — SATURDAY
Day 127 — 239 Remaining

EMMETT KELLY CLOWN FESTIVAL. May 5–6 (tentative). Houston, MO. Special appearances by Emmett Kelly, Jr and Joey as well as clowns from across the Midwest. Events include a parade and a huge arts and crafts fair. Est attendance: 10,000. For info: Emmett Kelly Clown Festival, 103 N Grand, Houston, MO 65483. Phone: (417) 967-2220. Fax: (417) 967-3583. E-mail: chamber@train.missouri.org. Web: train.missouri.org/~chamber.

MALTA: CARNIVAL. May 6–7. Valletta. Festival dates from 1535 when Knights of St. John introduced Carnival at Malta. Dancing, bands, decorated trucks and grotesque masks. Annually, the first weekend after May 1.

PEARY, ROBERT E.: BIRTH ANNIVERSARY. May 6, 1856. Born at Cresson, PA. Peary served as a cartographic draftsman in the US Coast and Geodetic Survey for two years, then joined the US Navy's Corps of Civil Engineers in 1881. He first worked as an explorer in tropical climates as he served as subchief of the Inter-Ocean Canal Survey in Nicaragua. After reading of the inland ice of Greenland, Peary became attracted to the Arctic. He organized and led eight Arctic expeditions and is credited with the verification of Greenland's island formation, proving that the polar ice cap extended beyond 82° north latitude, and the discovery of the Melville meteorite on Melville Bay, in addition to his famous discovery of the North Pole, Apr 6, 1909. Peary died Feb 20, 1920, at Washington, DC.

PENN, JOHN: BIRTH ANNIVERSARY. May 6, 1740. Signer of the Declaration of Independence, born at Caroline County, VA. Died Sept 14, 1788.

BIRTHDAYS TODAY

Tony Blair, 47, British prime minister, born Edinburgh, Scotland, May 6, 1953.

George Clooney, 39, actor ("ER," *Batman and Robin*), born Augusta, KY, May 6, 1961.

Ted Lewin, 65, author and illustrator (*The Storytellers*), born Buffalo, NY, May 6, 1935.

Willie Mays, 69, Baseball Hall of Fame outfielder, born Westfield, AL, May 6, 1931.

Richard C. Shelby, 66, US Senator (D, Alabama), born Birmingham, AL, May 6, 1934.

May 2000	S	M	T	W	T	F	S
		1	2	3	4	5	6
	7	8	9	10	11	12	13
	14	15	16	17	18	19	20
	21	22	23	24	25	26	27
	28	28	30	31			

MAY 7 — SUNDAY
Day 128 — 238 Remaining

BARRIER AWARENESS DAY IN KENTUCKY. May 7.

BE KIND TO ANIMALS WEEK®. May 7–13. To promote kindness and humane care toward animals. Annually, the first full week of May. Features "Be Kind to Animals Kid Contest." For info: Joyce Briggs, American Humane Assn, 63 Inverness Dr E, Englewood, CO 80112. Phone: (800) 227-4645 or (303) 792-9900. Fax: (303) 792-5333. E-mail: joyceb@americanhumane.org. Web: www.americanhumane.org.

BEAUFORT SCALE DAY: (FRANCIS BEAUFORT BIRTH ANNIVERSARY). May 7, 1774. A day to honor the British naval officer, Sir Francis Beaufort, who devised in 1805 a scale of wind force from 0 (calm) to 12 (hurricane) that was based on observation, not requiring any special instruments. The scale was adopted for international use in 1874 and has since been enlarged and refined. Beaufort was born at Flower Hill, Meath, Ireland, and died at Brighton, England, Dec 17, 1857.

BEETHOVEN'S NINTH SYMPHONY PREMIERE: ANNIVERSARY. May 7, 1824. Beethoven's Ninth Symphony in D Minor was performed for the first time at Vienna, Austria. Known as the *Choral* because of his use of voices in symphonic form for the first time, the Ninth was his musical interpretation of Schiller's *Ode to Joy*. Beethoven was completely deaf when he composed it, and it was said a soloist had to tug on his sleeve when the performance was over to get him to turn around and see the enthusiastic response he could not hear.

BROWNING, ROBERT: BIRTH ANNIVERSARY. May 7, 1812. English poet and husband of poet Elizabeth Barrett Browning, born at Camberwell, near London. Known for his dramatic monologues. Died at Venice, Italy, Dec 12, 1889.

CONSERVE WATER/DETECT-A-LEAK WEEK. May 7–13 (tentative). To help everyone learn why it is important to conserve our water and how to help accomplish this goal. See Curriculum Connection. For info: American Leak Detection, c/o S&S Public Relations, Inc, 400 Skokie Blvd, Ste 200, Northbrook, IL 60062. Phone: (847) 291-1616. Fax: (847) 291-1758.

DIEN BIEN PHU FALLS: ANNIVERSARY. May 7, 1954. Vietnam's victory over France at Dien Bien Phu ended the Indochina War. This battle is considered one of the greatest victories won by a former colony over a colonial power.

GERMANY'S FIRST SURRENDER: 55th ANNIVERSARY. May 7, 1945. Russian, American, British and French ranking officers crowded into a second-floor recreation room of a small red-brick schoolhouse (which served as Eisenhower's headquarters) at Reims, Germany. Representing Germany, Field Marshall Alfred Jodl signed an unconditional surrender of all German fighting forces. After a signing that took almost 40 minutes, Jodl was ushered into Eisenhower's presence. The American general asked the German if he fully understood what he had signed and informed Jodl that he would be held personally responsible for any deviation from the terms of the surrender, including the requirement that German commanders sign a formal surrender to the USSR at a time and place determined by that government.

NATIONAL ALCOHOL AND OTHER DRUG-RELATED BIRTH DEFECTS WEEK. May 7–13. For info: Natl Council on Alcoholism and Drug Dependence, 12 W 21st St, New York, NY 10010. Phone: (212) 206-6770.

NATIONAL FAMILY WEEK. May 7–13. Traditionally the first Sunday and the first full week in May are observed as National Family Week in many Christian churches.

MAY 7–13
CONSERVE WATER WEEK

Earth is the only planet in our solar system with a large supply of liquid water on its surface. Water gives Earth its distinctive blue color when viewed from outer space. People depend on water for survival. While we can live for weeks with little or no food, it's rare for anyone to survive more than three or four days without water.

Oceans hold 97 percent of the Earth's water. About 2 percent is frozen in glaciers. The remaining amount flows on and inside the land's surface. Water on the Earth's surface absorbs heat from the sun and helps keep temperatures from becoming too hot or too cold. Unless space matter containing frozen water falls into Earth's atmosphere, no new water forms on our planet. The water we have now is all we will ever have. That means it's important for us to use it wisely.

Each person in the US uses about 65 gallons of water per day for drinking, bathing and washing clothes. Industry and agriculture use millions of gallons more. What can your students do to conserve water?

First, ask students to chart their water usage for two or three days. They should include baths, number of toilet flushes, water used for washing hands, brushing teeth, drinking and washing dishes. Have them keep a list of every time they turn on a faucet. Once a record of normal usage has been noted, start discussions about ways to lower usage.

Simple ways that kids can make a difference include: keeping a bottle of water in the refrigerator, turning the water off while brushing teeth and taking showers rather than baths. They can alert adults to leaky faucets and encourage them to be aware of water usage.

Contact your local water department and see if they can provide a speaker who can tell students about your town's water supply, its source area and water usage patterns. You might contact a waste water management representative who can explain water treatment and its importance.

Meredith Hooper's *The Drop in My Drink: The Story of Water on Our Planet* (Viking, 0-670-87618-6, $16.99 Gr. 2–6) is an informative and enjoyable picture book about the life cycle of a drop of water.

NATIONAL PET WEEK. May 7–13. To promote public awareness of veterinary medical service for animal health and care. Annually, the first full week in May. For info: The American Veterinary Medical Assn, 1931 N Meacham Rd, Schaumburg, IL 60173. Phone: (847) 925-8070. Fax: (847) 925-1329. Web: www.avma.org.

NATIONAL POSTCARD WEEK. May 7–13. To advertise use of picture postcards for correspondence and collecting. Annually, the first full week of May since 1984. For info: John H. McClintock, Founder, Postcard History Soc, Box 1765, Manassas, VA 22110. Phone: (703) 368-2757.

NATIONAL PRIVY DIGGERS DAY. May 7. A celebration to honor those individuals who choose to dig up the past in an unconventional way. Many important historical artifacts are found through this exploration of old outhouses. For info: Federation of Historical Bottle Collectors, 88 Sweetbriar Branch, Longwood, FL 32750-2783. Phone: (407) 332-7689. E-mail: glassman.carl@mci2000.com.

NATIONAL PTA TEACHER APPRECIATION WEEK. May 7–13. PTAs across the country conduct activities to strengthen respect and support for teachers and the teaching profession. For info: Natl PTA, 330 N Wabash Ave, Ste 2100, Chicago, IL 60611. Phone: (312) 670-6782. Fax: (312) 670-6783. E-mail: info@pta.org. Web: www.pta.org.

NATIONAL TEACHER APPRECIATION WEEK. May 7–13. A week for elementary through high school students to show appreciation to their teachers. Students are urged to thank their teachers for their care and concerned effort, to be extra cooperative with them. For info: Connie Morris, Natl Education Assn (NEA), 1201 16th St NW, Washington, DC 20036. Phone: (202) 822-7262. Fax: (202) 822-7292. Web: www.nea.org.

NATIONAL TOURISM WEEK. May 7–13. To promote and enhance awareness of travel and tourism's importance to the economic, social and cultural well-being of the US. Annually, beginning the first Sunday in May. For info: Tourism Works for America Council, 1100 New York Ave NW, Ste 450, Washington, DC 20005-3934. Phone: (202) 408-8422. E-mail: ckeefe@tia.org.

TCHAIKOVSKY, PETER ILICH: BIRTH ANNIVERSARY. May 7, 1840. Ranked among the outstanding composers of all time, Peter Ilich Tchaikovsky was born at Vatkinsk, Russia. His musical talent was not encouraged and he embarked upon a career in law, not studying music seriously until 1861. Among his famous works are the three-act ballet *Sleeping Beauty*, two-act ballet *The Nutcracker* and the symphony *Pathetique*. Mystery surrounds Tchaikovsky's death. It was believed he'd caught cholera from contaminated water, but 20th-century scholars believe he probably committed suicide to avoid his homosexuality being revealed. He died at St. Petersburg, Nov 6, 1893.

BIRTHDAYS TODAY

Pete V. Domenici, 68, US Senator (R, New Mexico), born Albuquerque, NM, May 7, 1932.

Nonny Hogrogian, 68, author and illustrator (Caldecott for *One Fine Day*), born New York, NY, May 7, 1932.

MAY 8 — MONDAY
Day 129 — 237 Remaining

CZECH REPUBLIC: LIBERATION DAY: 55th ANNIVERSARY. May 8. Commemorates the liberation of Czechoslovakia from the Germans in 1945.

DUNANT, JEAN HENRI: BIRTH ANNIVERSARY. May 8, 1828. Author and philanthropist, founder of the Red Cross Society, was born at Geneva, Switzerland. Nobel prize winner in 1901. Died at Heiden, Switzerland, Oct 30, 1910.

FRANCE: ARMISTICE DAY: 55th ANNIVERSARY. May 8. Commemorates the surrender of Germany to Allied forces and the cessation of hostilities in 1945.

GERMANY'S SECOND SURRENDER: 55th ANNIVERSARY. May 8, 1945. Stalin refused to recognize the document of unconditional surrender signed at Reims the previous day, so a second signing was held at Berlin. The event was turned into an elaborate formal ceremony by the Soviets who had lost some 10 million lives during the war. As in the Reims document, the end of hostilities was set for 12:01 AM local time on May 9.

LAVOISIER, ANTOINE LAURENT: EXECUTION ANNIVERSARY. May 8, 1794. French chemist and the "father of modern chemistry." Especially noted for having first explained the real nature of combustion and for showing that matter is not destroyed in chemical reactions. Born at Paris, France, Aug 26, 1743, Lavoisier was guillotined at the Place de la Revolution for his former position as a tax collector. The Revolutionary Tribunal is reported to have responded to a plea to spare his life with the statement: "We need no more scientists in France."

NATIONAL ETIQUETTE WEEK. May 8–12. A national recognition of proper etiquette in all areas of American life (business, social, dining, international, wedding, computer, etc.). A national self-assessment on the current status of civility in the US. Annually, the second week in May starting on Monday. For info: Sandra Morisset, Protocol Training Services, PO Box 4981, New York, NY 10185. Phone: (212) 802-9098.

NO SOCKS DAY. May 8. If we give up wearing socks for one day, it will mean a little less laundry, thereby contributing to the betterment of the environment. Besides, we will all feel a bit freer, at least for one day. Annually, May 8. [© 1998 by WPL] For info: Thomas and Ruth Roy, Wellness Permission League, PO Box 662, Mt Gretna, PA 17064-0662. Phone: (717) 964-1308. Fax: (717) 964-1335. E-mail: wellcat@desupernet.net.

SEATTLE INTERNATIONAL CHILDREN'S FESTIVAL. May 8–13 (tentative). Seattle, WA. The largest performing arts festival for families in the US. Artists from Europe, Asia, Africa, Australia and the Americas present theater, dance, music, puppets and acrobatics. Est attendance: 51,000. For info: Seattle Intl Children's Festival, 305 Harrison, Seattle, WA 98109-3944. Phone: (206) 684-7338. E-mail: kidsfest@kidsfest.seanet.com. Web: www.eskimo.com/~kidsfest/info.htm.

SLOVAK REPUBLIC: LIBERATION DAY: 55th ANNIVERSARY. May 8. Commemorates the liberation of Czechoslovakia from the Germans in 1945.

TRUMAN, HARRY S: BIRTH ANNIVERSARY. May 8, 1884. The 33rd president of the US, succeeded to that office upon the death of Franklin D. Roosevelt, Apr 12, 1945, and served until Jan 20, 1953. Born at Lamar, MO, Truman was the last of the nine US presidents who did not attend college. Affectionately nicknamed "Give 'em Hell Harry" by admirers. Truman died at Kansas City, MO, Dec 26, 1972. His birthday is a holiday in Missouri.

V-E DAY: 55th ANNIVERSARY. May 8, 1945. Victory in Europe Day commemorates the unconditional surrender of Germany to Allied Forces. The surrender document was signed by German representatives at General Dwight D. Eisenhower's headquarters at Reims to become effective, and hostilities to end, at one minute past midnight on May 9, 1945, which was 9:01 PM EDT on May 8 in the US. President Harry S Truman on May 8 declared May 9, 1945, to be "V-E Day," but it later came to be observed on May 8 in the US. A separate German surrender to the USSR was signed at Karlshorst, near Berlin, May 8. See also: "Russia: Victory Day: Anniversary" (May 9).

WORLD RED CROSS DAY. May 8. A day for commemorating the birth of Jean Henry Dunant, the Swiss founder of the International Red Cross Movement in 1863, and for recognizing the humanitarian work of the Red Cross around the world. For info on activities in your area, contact your local Red Cross chapter. For info: Ann Stingle, Media Assoc, American Red Cross Natl Headquarters, 8111 Gate House Rd, Falls Church, VA 22042. Phone: (703) 206-7090. Fax: (703) 206-7507.

BIRTHDAYS TODAY

Milton Meltzer, 85, author (*Langston Hughes: A Biography; Brother, Can You Spare a Dime: The Great Depression*), born Worcester, MA, May 8, 1915.

		S	M	T	W	T	F	S
May			1	2	3	4	5	6
2000		7	8	9	10	11	12	13
		14	15	16	17	18	19	20
		21	22	23	24	25	26	27
		28	28	30	31			

MAY 9 — TUESDAY
Day 130 — 236 Remaining

BARRIE, J.M.: BIRTH ANNIVERSARY. May 9, 1860. Author, born at Kirriemuir, Scotland. Wrote the popular children's tale *Peter Pan*, which first became a movie in 1924. Barrie died at London, England, June 19, 1937.

BROWN, JOHN: 200th BIRTH ANNIVERSARY. May 9, 1800. Abolitionist leader born at Torrington, CT, and hanged Dec 2, 1859, at Charles Town, WV. Leader of attack on Harpers Ferry, Oct 16, 1859, which was intended to give impetus to movement for escape and freedom for slaves. His aim was frustrated and in fact resulted in increased polarization and sectional animosity. Legendary martyr of the abolitionist movement.

CHILDHOOD DEPRESSION AWARENESS DAY. May 9. Also known as Green Ribbon Day. Annually on the first Tuesday in the first full week in May. For info: Natl Mental Heath Assn, 1021 Prince St, Alexandria, VA 22314-2971. Phone: (800) 969-6642 or (703) 684-7722. Web: www.nmha.org.

DU BOIS, WILLIAM PENE: BIRTH ANNIVERSARY. May 9, 1916. Illustrator and author of children's books, born at Nutley, NJ. Du Bois was the recipient of the Newbery Medal in 1948 for his book, *The Twenty-One Balloons*. He died at Nice, France, Feb 5, 1993.

EUROPEAN UNION: 50th ANNIVERSARY OBSERVANCE. May 9, 1950. Member countries of the European Union commemorate the announcement by French statesman Robert Schuman of the "Schuman Plan" for establishing a single authority for production of coal, iron and steel in France and Germany. This organization was a forerunner of the European Economic Community, founded in 1957, which later became the European Union.

NATIONAL TEACHER DAY. May 9. To pay tribute to American educators, sponsored by the National Education Association, Teacher Day falls during the National PTA's Teacher Appreciation Week. Local communities and organizations are encouraged to use this opportunity to honor those who influence and inspire the next generation through their work. Annually, the Tuesday of the first full week in May. For info: Natl Education Assn (NEA), 1201 16th St NW, Washington, DC 20036. Phone: (202) 822-7200. Web: www.nea.org.

RUSSIA: VICTORY DAY: 55th ANNIVERSARY. May 9. National holiday observed annually to commemorate the 1945 Allied Forces defeat of Nazi Germany in WWII and to honor the 20 million Soviet people who died in that war. Hostilities ceased and the German surrender became effective at one minute after midnight May 9, 1945. See also: "V-E Day" (May 8).

"VAST WASTELAND" SPEECH: ANNIVERSARY. May 9, 1961. Speaking before the bigwigs of network TV at the annual convention of the National Association of Broadcasters, Newton

Minow, the new chairman of the Federal Communications Commission, exhorted those executives to sit through an entire day of their own programming. He suggested that they "will observe a vast wasteland." Further, he urged them to try for "imagination in programming, not sterility; creativity, not imitation; experimentation, not conformity; excellence, not mediocrity."

BIRTHDAYS TODAY

Richard Adams, 80, author (*Watership Down*), born Newbury, England, May 9, 1920.

John Ashcroft, 58, US Senator (R, Missouri), born Springfield, MO, May 9, 1942.

Candice Bergen, 54, actress ("Murphy Brown"), daughter of ventriloquist Edgar Bergen, born Beverly Hills, CA, May 9, 1946.

Tony Gwynn, 40, baseball player, born Los Angeles, CA, May 9, 1960.

MAY 10 — WEDNESDAY
Day 131 — 235 Remaining

CONFEDERATE MEMORIAL DAY IN SOUTH CAROLINA. May 10. See also Apr 26, May 31 and June 3 for Confederate Memorial Day observances in other southern states.

THE DAY OF THE TEACHER (EL DIA DEL MAESTRO). May 10. California honors its teachers every year on the Day of the Teacher. Patterned after "El Dia Del Maestro" celebrated in Mexico, the Day of the Teacher was originated by the Association of Mexican-American Educators and the California Teachers Association and designated by the California legislature. A tribute to all teachers and their lasting influence on children's lives. Annually, the second Wednesday of May. For info: California Teachers Assn, PO Box 921, Burlingame, CA 94010. Phone: (650) 697-1400. Fax: (650) 697-0786. Web: www.cta.org.

GOLDEN SPIKE DRIVING: ANNIVERSARY. May 10, 1869. Anniversary of the meeting of Union Pacific and Central Pacific railways, at Promontory Point, UT. On that day a golden spike was driven by Leland Stanford, president of the Central Pacific, to celebrate the linkage. The golden spike was promptly removed for preservation. Long called the final link in the ocean-to-ocean railroad, this event cannot be accurately described as completing the transcontinental railroad, but it did complete continuous rail tracks between Omaha and Sacramento. See also: "Transcontinental US Railway Completion: Anniversary" (Aug 15).

ISRAEL: YOM HA'ATZMA'UT (INDEPENDENCE DAY). May 10. Hebrew calendar date: Iyar 5, 5760. Celebrates proclamation of independence from British mandatory rule by Palestinian Jews and establishment of the state of Israel and the provisional government May 14, 1948 (Hebrew calendar date: Iyar 5, 5708). Dates in the Hebrew calendar vary from their Gregorian equivalents from year to year, so, while Iyar 5 in 1948 was May 14, in 2000 it is May 10.

MOON PHASE: FIRST QUARTER. May 10. Moon enters First Quarter phase at 4 PM, EDT.

ROSS, GEORGE: BIRTH ANNIVERSARY. May 10, 1730. Lawyer and signer of the Declaration of Independence, born at New Castle, DE. Died at Philadelphia, PA, July 14, 1779.

SINGAPORE: VESAK DAY. May 10. Public holiday. Monks commemorate their Lord Buddha's entry into Nirvana by chanting holy sutras and freeing captive birds.

TRUST YOUR INTUITION DAY©. May 10. Today is the day we pay homage to the wonderful gift of sixth sense, "gut" feelings or that still small voice that is sometimes the only clue we have to

go on in this ever-changing world. For info: Adrienne Sioux Koopersmith, 1437 W Rosemont, #1W, Chicago, IL 60660-1319. Phone: (773) 743-5341. Fax: (773) 743-5395. E-mail: kooper@interaccess.com.

BIRTHDAYS TODAY

Christopher Paul Curtis, 46, author (*The Watsons Go to Birmingham—1963*), born Flint, MI, May 10, 1954.

Bruce McMillan, 53, author and illustrator (*Jelly Beans for Sale*), born Boston, MA, May 10, 1947.

Rick Santorum, 42, US Senator (R, Pennsylvania), born Winchester, VA, May 10, 1949.

Kenan Thompson, 22, actor ("All That," "Kenan & Kel"), born Atlanta, GA, May 10, 1978.

MAY 11 — THURSDAY
Day 132 — 234 Remaining

EAT WHAT YOU WANT DAY. May 11. Here's a day you may actually enjoy yourself. Ignore all those on-again/off-again warnings. [© 1998 by WPL] For info: Tom and Ruth Roy, Wellness Permission League, PO Box 662, Mt Gretna, PA 17064-0662. Phone: (717) 964-1308. Fax: (717) 964-1335. E-mail: wellcat@desupernet.net.

FAIRBANKS, CHARLES WARREN: BIRTH ANNIVERSARY. May 11, 1852. Twenty-sixth vice president of the US (1905–09) born at Unionville Center, OH. Died at Indianapolis, IN, June 4, 1918.

GLACIER NATIONAL PARK ESTABLISHED: 90th ANNIVERSARY. May 11, 1910. This national park is located in northwest Montana, on the Canadian border. In 1932 Glacier and Waterton Lakes National Park in Alberta were joined together by the governments of the US and Canada as Waterton-Glacier International Peace Park. For further info: www.nps.gov/glac.

GRAHAM, MARTHA: BIRTH ANNIVERSARY. May 11, 1894. Martha Graham was born at Allegheny, PA, and became one of the giants of the modern dance movement in the US. She began her dance career at the comparatively late age of 22 and joined the Greenwich Village Follies in 1923. Her new ideas began to surface in the late '20s and '30s, and by the mid-1930s she was incorporating the rituals of the southwestern American Indians in her work. She is credited with bringing a new psychological depth to modern dance by exploring primal emotions and ancient rituals in her work. She performed until the age of 75, and premiered in her 180th ballet, *The Maple Leaf Rag*, in the fall of 1990. Died Apr 1, 1991, at New York, NY. For more info: *Martha Graham: A Dancer's Life*, by Russell Freedman (Clarion, 0-395-74655-8, $18 Gr. 7-12).

HART, JOHN: DEATH ANNIVERSARY. May 11, 1779. Signer of the Declaration of Independence, farmer and legislator, born about 1711 (exact date unknown), at Stonington, CT, died at Hopewell, NJ.

JAPAN: CORMORANT FISHING FESTIVAL. May 11–Oct 15. Cormorant fishing on the Nagara River, Gifu. "This ancient method of catching Ayu, a troutlike fish, with trained cormorants, takes place nightly under the light of blazing torches."

MINNESOTA: ADMISSION DAY: ANNIVERSARY. May 11. Became 32nd state in 1858.

THE READ IN. May 11. A day-long reading project for students in grades K-12. During the 7th annual Read In, students will chat together online with 22 of the best children's and young adult literature authors. This day is a culmination of several weeks of online participation by teachers and students during which they share information about their schools and communities. For info: Jane Coffey, Program Dir, The Read In Foundation, 6043 Channel Dr, Riverbank, CA 95367. Phone: (209) 869-0713. E-mail: Thereadin@aol.com. Web: www.readin.org.

SPACE DAY. May 11 (tentative). Previous Space Days have included a live broadcast over the Web in which astronauts and scientists answered questions from kids worldwide; a live satellite broadcast about space exploration, and local events in schools and communities. The Space Day website contains lesson plans for teachers and games and puzzles for kids. For info: Web: www.spaceday.com.

BIRTHDAYS TODAY

James Jeffords, 66, US Senator (R, Vermont), born Rutland, VT, May 11, 1934.
Austin O'Brien, 19, actor ("The Baby-Sitters Club," *My Girl 2*), born Eugene, OR, May 11, 1981.
Natasha Richardson, 37, actress (*The Parent Trap*), born London, England, May 11, 1963.
Peter Sis, 51, illustrator and author (*The Starry Messenger*), born Prague, Czechoslovakia, May 11, 1949.
Zilpha Keatley Snyder, 73, author (*The Witches of Worm, The Headless Cupid*), born Lemoore, CA, May 11, 1927.

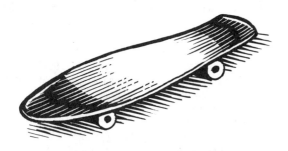

MAY 12 — FRIDAY
Day 133 — 233 Remaining

LIMERICK DAY. May 12. Observed on the birthday of one of its champions, Edward Lear, who was born in 1812. The limerick, which dates from the early 18th century, has been described as the "only fixed verse form indigenous to the English language." It gained its greatest popularity following the publication of Edward Lear's *Book of Nonsense* (and its sequels). Write a limerick today! Example: There was a young poet named Lear/Who said, it is just as I fear/Five lines are enough/For this kind of stuff/Make a limerick each day of the year.

NIGHTINGALE, FLORENCE: BIRTH ANNIVERSARY. May 12, 1820. English nurse and public health activist who contributed perhaps more than any other single person to the development of modern nursing procedures and the dignity of nursing as a profession. During the Crimean War, she supervised nursing care in the British hospital at Scutari, Turkey, where she reduced the death rate dramatically. Returning to England, she reorganized the army medical service. She was the founder of the Nightingale training school for nurses and author of *Notes on Nursing*. Born at Florence, Italy, she died at London, England, Aug 13, 1910.

May 2000	S	M	T	W	T	F	S
		1	2	3	4	5	6
	7	8	9	10	11	12	13
	14	15	16	17	18	19	20
	21	22	23	24	25	26	27
	28	28	30	31			

PORTUGAL: PILGRIMAGE TO FATIMA. May 12–13. Commemorates first appearance of the Virgin of the Rosary to little shepherd children May 13, 1917. Pilgrims come to Cova da Iria religious center for a candlelit procession and Mass for the sick.

BIRTHDAYS TODAY

Yogi Berra, 75, former baseball manager and Baseball Hall of Fame catcher, born Lawrence Peter Berra, St. Louis, MO, May 12, 1925.
Tony Hawk, 31, skateboarder, born Carlsbad, CA, May 12, 1969.

MAY 13 — SATURDAY
Day 134 — 232 Remaining

FEMINIST BOOKSTORE WEEK. May 13–21. Visit your favorite feminist bookstore for author signings and other special events. For info: Feminist Bookstore News, PO Box 882554, San Francisco, CA 94188. Phone: (415) 642-9993. Fax: (414) 642-9995. E-mail: carol@FemBkNews.com.

NETHERLANDS: NATIONAL WINDMILL DAY. May 13. About 950 windmills still survive and some 300 still are used occasionally and have been designated national monuments by the government. As many windmills as possible are in operation on National Windmill Day for the benefit of tourists. Annually, the second Saturday in May.

SPACE MILESTONE: *ENDEAVOUR* (US). May 13, 1992. Three astronauts from the shuttle *Endeavour* simultaneously walked in space for the first time.

BIRTHDAYS TODAY

Francine Pascal, 62, author (the Sweet Valley Twins series), born New York, NY, May 13, 1938.
Dennis Keith ("Worm") Rodman, 39, basketball player, born Trenton, NJ, May 13, 1961.
Stevie Wonder, 49, singer, musician (16 Grammy Awards; "I Just Called to Say I Love You"), born Steveland Morris Hardaway, Saginaw, MI, May 13, 1951.

MAY 14 — SUNDAY
Day 135 — 231 Remaining

FAHRENHEIT, GABRIEL DANIEL: BIRTH ANNIVERSARY. May 14, 1686. German physicist whose name is attached to one of the major temperature measurement scales. He introduced the use of mercury in thermometers and greatly improved their accuracy. Born at Danzig, Germany, he died at Amsterdam, Holland, Sept 16, 1736.

FIRST FEMALE HOUSE PAGE APPOINTMENT: ANNIVERSARY. May 14, 1973. The House of Representatives received formal approval of the appointment of female pages in 1972. In the 93rd Congress, Felda Looper was appointed as the first female page with a regular term. Gene Cox had served as a female page for three hours 34 years earlier.

GIRLS INCORPORATED WEEK. May 14–20. To focus national and local attention on the goals of Girls Incorporated as an organization for the rights and needs of girls. Begins the second Sunday in May. For info: Galia Schechter, Girls Inc, 30 East 33rd St, New York, NY 10016-5394. Phone: (212) 509-2000. E-mail: HN3580@handsnet.org. Web: www.girlsinc.org.

JAMESTOWN, VIRGINIA: FOUNDING ANNIVERSARY. May 14, 1607. The first permanent English settlement in what is now the US took place at Jamestown, VA (named for England's King James I), on this date. Captains John Smith and Christopher

Newport were among the leaders of the group of royally chartered Virginia Company settlers who had traveled from Plymouth, England, in three small ships: *Susan Constant*, *Godspeed* and *Discovery*.

LEWIS AND CLARK EXPEDITION: ANNIVERSARY. May 14, 1804. Charged by President Thomas Jefferson with finding a route to the Pacific, Meriwether Lewis and Captain William Clark left St. Louis May 14. They arrived at the Pacific coast of Oregon in November 1805 and returned to St. Louis, Sept 23, 1806.

MOTHER'S DAY. May 14. Observed first in 1907 at the request of Anna Jarvis of Philadelphia, PA, who asked her church to hold service in memory of all mothers on the anniversary of her mother's death. Annually, the second Sunday in May. For links to Mother's Day sites on the web, go to: deil.lang.uiuc.edu/web.pages/holidays/mother.html.

★**MOTHER'S DAY.** May 14. Presidential Proclamation always issued for the second Sunday in May. (Pub Res No. 2 of May 8, 1914.)

NATIONAL EMERGENCY MEDICAL SERVICES (EMS) WEEK. May 14–20. Honoring EMS providers nationwide who provide life-saving care in a multitude of circumstances. Also a time for the public to learn about injury prevention, safety awareness and emergency preparedness. For info: American College of Emergency Physicians, PO Box 619911, Dallas, TX 75261-9911. Phone: (800) 748-1822. E-mail: emsweek@acep.org. Web: www.acep.org.

NATIONAL FAMILY MONTH™. May 14–June 18. A month-long national observance to celebrate and promote strong, supportive families. Sponsored by KidsPeace®, a private, not-for-profit organization that has been helping kids overcome crisis since 1982. Annually, Mother's Day through Father's Day. For info: Paula Knouse, Kids Peace, 5300 Kidspeace Dr, Orefield, PA 18069. Phone: (610) 799-8325. Web: www.kidspeace.org.

NATIONAL HISTORIC PRESERVATION WEEK. May 14–20. To draw public attention to historic preservation including neighborhoods, districts, landmark buildings, open space and maritime heritage. Annually, the second full week in May. For info: Diana Onorio, Natl Trust for Historic Preservation, 1785 Massachusetts Ave NW, Washington, DC 20036. Phone: (202) 588-6141. Fax: (202) 588-6299. E-mail: pr@nthp.org. Web: www.nationaltrust.org.

NATIONAL POLICE WEEK. May 14–20. See also "Peace Officer Memorial Day" (May 15). For info: American Police Hall of Fame and Museum, 3801 Biscayne Blvd, Miami, FL 33137. Phone: (305) 573-0070.

★**NATIONAL TRANSPORTATION WEEK.** May 14–20. Presidential Proclamation issued for week including third Friday in May since 1960. (PL 86–475 of May 20, 1960, first requested; PL87–449 of May 14, 1962, requested an annual proclamation.)

NORWAY: MIDNIGHT SUN AT NORTH CAPE. May 14–July 30. In the "Land of the Midnight Sun," this is the first day of the season with around-the-clock sunshine. At North Cape and parts of Russia, Alaska, Canada and Greenland surrounding the Arctic Ocean, the sun never dips below the horizon from May 14 to July 30, but the night is bright long before and after these dates. At the equator, on the other hand, the length of day and night never vary.

PARAGUAY: INDEPENDENCE DAY. May 14–15. Commemorates independence from Spain, attained 1811.

★**POLICE WEEK.** May 14–20. Presidential Proclamation 3537 of May 4, 1963, covers all succeeding years. (PL87–726 of Oct 1, 1962.) Always the week including May 15 since 1962.

SMALLPOX VACCINE DISCOVERED: ANNIVERSARY. May 14, 1796. In the 18th century, smallpox was a widespread and often fatal disease. Edward Jenner, a physician in rural England, heard reports of dairy farmers who apparently became immune to smallpox as a result of exposure to cowpox, a related but milder disease. After two decades of studying the phenomenon, Jenner injected cowpox into a healthy eight-year-old boy, who subsequently developed cowpox. Six weeks later, Jenner inoculated the boy with smallpox. He remained healthy. Jenner called this new procedure *vaccination*, from *vaccinia*, another term for cowpox. Within 18 months, 12,000 people in England had been vaccinated and the number of smallpox deaths dropped by two-thirds.

SPACE MILESTONE: *SKYLAB* (US). May 14, 1973. The US launched *Skylab*, its first manned orbiting laboratory.

"THE STARS AND STRIPES FOREVER" DAY: ANNIVERSARY. May 14, 1897. Anniversary of the first public performance of John Philip Sousa's march, "The Stars and Stripes Forever," at Philadelphia, PA. The occasion was the unveiling of a statue of George Washington, and President William McKinley was present.

WAAC: ANNIVERSARY. May 14, 1942. During WWII women became eligible to enlist for noncombat duties in the Women's Auxiliary Army Corps (WAAC) by an act of Congress. Women also served as Women Appointed for Voluntary Emergency Service (WAVES), Women's Auxiliary Ferrying Squadron (WAFS) and Coast Guard or Semper Paratus Always Ready Service (SPARS), the Women's Reserve of the Marine Corp.

★**WORLD TRADE WEEK.** May 14–20. Presidential Proclamation has been issued each year since 1948 for the third week of May with three exceptions: 1949, 1955 and 1966.

BIRTHDAYS TODAY

Byron L. Dorgan, 58, US Senator (D, North Dakota), born Dickinson, ND, May 14, 1942.
George Lucas, 56, filmmaker (*The Empire Strikes Back*, *Star Wars*), born Modesto, CA, May 14, 1944.
George Selden, 71, children's author (*The Cricket in Times Square*), born George Selden Thompson at Hartford, CT, May 14, 1929.
Valerie Still, 39, basketball player, born Lexington, KY, May 14, 1961.

MAY 15 — MONDAY

Day 136 — 230 Remaining

BAUM, L(YMAN) FRANK: BIRTH ANNIVERSARY. May 15, 1856. The American newspaperman who wrote the Wizard of Oz stories was born at Chittenango, NY. Although *The Wonderful Wizard of Oz* is the most famous, Baum also wrote many other books for children, including more than a dozen about Oz. He died at Hollywood, CA, May 6, 1919.

FIRST FLIGHT ATTENDANT: 70th ANNIVERSARY. May 15, 1930. Ellen Church became the first airline stewardess (today's flight attendant), flying on a United Airlines flight from San Francisco to Cheyenne, WY.

GASOLINE RATIONING: ANNIVERSARY. May 15, 1942. Seventeen eastern states initiated gasoline rationing as part of the war effort. By Sept 25, rationing was nationwide. A limit of three gallons a week for nonessential purposes was set and a 35 mph speed limit was imposed.

JAPAN: AOI MATSURI (HOLLYHOCK FESTIVAL). May 15. Kyoto. The festival features a pageant reproducing imperial processions of ancient times that paid homage to the shrine of Shimogamo and Kamigamo.

MEXICO: SAN ISIDRO DAY. May 15. Day of San Isidro Labrador celebrated widely in farming regions to honor St. Isidore, the Plowman. Livestock is gaily decorated with flowers. Celebrations usually begin about May 13 and continue for about a week.

NATIONAL EDUCATIONAL BOSSES WEEK. May 15–19. A special week to honor bosses in the field of education such as principals and school superintendents. Annually, the third week in May. For info: Natl Assn of Educational Office Personnel, PO Box 12619, Wichita, KS 67277. Fax: (316) 942-7100.

NYLON STOCKINGS: 60th ANNIVERSARY. May 15, 1940. Nylon hose went on sale at stores throughout the country. Competing producers bought their nylon yarn from E.J. du Pont de Nemours. W.H. Carothers of Du Pont developed nylon, called "Polymer 66," in 1935. It was the first totally man-made fiber and over time substituted for other materials and came to have widespread application.

★**PEACE OFFICER MEMORIAL DAY.** May 15. Presidential Proclamation 3537, of May 4, 1963, covers all succeeding years. (PL87–726 of Oct 1, 1962.) Always May 15 of each year since 1963; however, first issued in 1962 for May 14.

PEACE OFFICER MEMORIAL DAY. May 15. An event honored by some 21,000 police departments nationwide. Memorial ceremonies at 10 AM in American Police Hall of Fame and Museum, Miami, FL. See also: "National Police Week" (May 9–15). Sponsor: National Association of Chiefs of Police. Est attendance: 1,000. For info: American Police Hall of Fame and Museum, 3801 Biscayne Blvd, Miami, FL 33137. Phone: (305) 573-0070. Web: www.aphf.org.

UNITED NATIONS: INTERNATIONAL DAY OF FAMILIES. May 15. The general assembly (Res 47/237) Sept 20, 1993, voted this as an annual observance beginning in 1994.

WILSON, ELLEN LOUISE AXSON: BIRTH ANNIVERSARY. May 15, 1860. First wife of Woodrow Wilson, 28th president of the US, born at Savannah, GA. She died at Washington, DC, Aug 6, 1914.

BIRTHDAYS TODAY

Madeleine Albright, 63, US Secretary of State (Clinton administration), born Prague, Czechoslovakia, May 15, 1937.

	S	M	T	W	T	F	S
May		1	2	3	4	5	6
2000	7	8	9	10	11	12	13
	14	15	16	17	18	19	20
	21	22	23	24	25	26	27
	28	28	30	31			

George Brett, 47, Baseball Hall of Fame player, born Glen Dale, WV, May 15, 1953.

Norma Fox Mazer, 69, author (*After the Rain*), born New York, NY, May 15, 1931.

Leigh Ann Orsi, 19, actress ("Home Improvement," *Pet Shop*), born Los Angeles, CA, May 15, 1981.

Emmitt Smith, 31, football player, born Escambia, FL, May 15, 1969.

Paul Zindel, 64, author (*The Pigman*), born Staten Island, NY, May 15, 1936.

MAY 16 — TUESDAY
Day 137 — 229 Remaining

BIOGRAPHERS DAY. May 16, 1763. Anniversary of the meeting, at London, England, of James Boswell and Samuel Johnson, beginning history's most famous biographer-biographee relationship. Boswell's *Journal of a Tour to the Hebrides* (1785) and his *Life of Samuel Johnson* (1791) are regarded as models of biographical writing. Thus, this day is recommended as one on which to start reading or writing a biography.

FIRST ACADEMY AWARDS: ANNIVERSARY. May 16, 1929. About 270 people attended a dinner at the Hollywood Roosevelt Hotel at which the first Academy Awards were given in 12 categories for films made in 1928. The silent film *Wings* won Best Picture. A committee of only 20 members selected the winners that year. By the third year, the entire membership of the Academy voted. For links to Academy Awards sites on the web, go to: deil.lang.uiuc.edu/web.pages/holidays/oscars.html.

GWINNETT, BUTTON: DEATH ANNIVERSARY. May 16, 1777. Signer of the Declaration of Independence, born at Down Hatherley, Gloucestershire, England, about 1735 (exact date unknown). Died following a duel at St. Catherine's Island, off of Savannah, GA.

MORTON, LEVI PARSONS: BIRTH ANNIVERSARY. May 16, 1824. Twenty-second vice president of the US (1889–93) born at Shoreham, VT. Died at Rhinebeck, NY, May 16, 1920.

REY, MARGARET: BIRTH ANNIVERSARY. May 16, 1906. Children's author, born at Hamburg, Germany. Together with her illustrator husband, H.A. Rey, she produced the Curious George series. Rey died at Cambridge, MA, Dec 21, 1996.

BIRTHDAYS TODAY

Tracey Gold, 31, actress ("Growing Pains"), born New York, NY, May 16, 1969.

James B. Hunt, Jr, 63, Governor of North Carolina (D), born Greensboro, NC, May 16, 1937.

Gabriela Sabatini, 30, tennis player, born Buenos Aires, Argentina, May 16, 1970.

Joan (Benoit) Samuelson, 43, Olympic gold medal runner, born Cape Elizabeth, ME, May 16, 1957.

MAY 17 — WEDNESDAY
Day 138 — 228 Remaining

BROWN v BOARD OF EDUCATION DECISION: ANNIVERSARY. May 17, 1954. The US Supreme Court ruled unanimously that segregation of public schools "solely on the basis of race" denied black children "equal educational opportunity" even though "physical facilities and other 'tangible' factors may have been equal. Separate educational facilities are inherently unequal." The case was argued before the Court by Thurgood Marshall, who would go on to become the first black appointed to the Supreme Court.

JENNER, EDWARD: BIRTH ANNIVERSARY. May 17, 1749. English physician, born at Berkeley, England. He was the first to establish a scientific basis for vaccination with his work on smallpox. Jenner died at Berkeley, England, Jan 26, 1823.

NEW YORK STOCK EXCHANGE ESTABLISHED: ANNIVERSARY. May 17, 1792. Some two dozen merchants and brokers agreed to establish what is now known as the New York Stock Exchange. In fair weather they operated under a buttonwood tree on Wall Street, at New York, NY. In bad weather they moved to the shelter of a coffeehouse to conduct their business.

NORWAY: CONSTITUTION DAY OR INDEPENDENCE DAY. May 17. National holiday. The constitution was signed in 1814. Parades and children's festivities.

UNITED NATIONS: WORLD TELECOMMUNICATION DAY. May 17. A day to draw attention to the necessity and importance of further development of telecommunications in the global community. For more information, visit the UN's website for children at www.un.org/Pubs/CyberSchoolBus/

BIRTHDAYS TODAY

Eloise Greenfield, 71, author (*Night on Neighborhood Street*), born Parmalee, NC, May 17, 1929.

Mia Hamm, 28, soccer player, born Selma, AL, May 17, 1972.

Gary Paulsen, 61, author (*The Hatchet*), born Minneapolis, MN, May 17, 1939.

Bob Saget, 44, actor ("Full House"), host ("America's Funniest Home Videos"), born Philadelphia, PA, May 17, 1956.

MAY 18 — THURSDAY
Day 139 — 227 Remaining

BUCKLE UP AMERICA! WEEK. May 18–25. An observance to remind Americans of the importance of wearing seat belts. For info: Office of Occupant Protection, Natl Highway Safety Administration, 400 Seventh St SW, Washington, DC 20590. Phone: (202) 366-9550.

HAITI: FLAG AND UNIVERSITY DAY. May 18. Public holiday.

INTERNATIONAL MUSEUM DAY. May 18. To pay tribute to museums of the world. "Museums are an important means of cultural exchange, enrichment of cultures and development of mutual understanding, cooperation and peace among people." Annually, May 18. Sponsor: International Council of Museums, Paris, France. For info: AAM/ICOM, 1575 Eye St NW, 4th Fl, Washington, DC 20005. Phone: (202) 289-1818. Fax: (202) 289-6578.

MOON PHASE: FULL MOON. May 18. Moon enters Full Moon phase at 3:34 AM, EDT.

MOUNT SAINT HELENS ERUPTION: 20th ANNIVERSARY. May 18, 1980. A major eruption of Mount St. Helens volcano, in southwestern Washington, blew steam and ash more than 11 miles into the sky. This was the first major eruption of Mount St. Helens since 1857, though Mar 26, 1980, there had been a warning eruption of smaller magnitude.

NATIONAL BIKE TO WORK DAY. May 18. At the state or local level, Bike to Work events are conducted by small and large businesses, city governments, bicycle clubs and environmental groups. About two million participants nationwide. Annually, the third Tuesday in May. For info: Donald Tighe, Program Dir, League of American Bicyclists, 1612 K St, NW, Ste 401, Washington, DC 20006. Phone: (202) 822-1333. Fax: (202) 822-1334. E-mail: bikeleague@aol.com. Web: www.bikeleague.org.

POPE JOHN PAUL II: 80th BIRTHDAY. May 18, 1920. Karol Wojtyla, 264th pope of the Roman Catholic Church, born at Wadowice, Poland. Elected pope Oct 16, 1978. He was the first non-Italian to be elected pope in 456 years (since the election of Pope Adrian VI, in 1522) and the first Polish pope.

VISIT YOUR RELATIVES DAY. May 18. A day to renew family ties and joys by visiting often-thought-of-seldom-seen relatives. Annually, May 18. For info: A.C. Moeller, Box 71, Clio, MI 48420-1042.

BIRTHDAYS TODAY

Karyn Bye, 29, Olympic ice hockey player, born River Falls, WI, May 18, 1971.

Debra (Debbie) Dadey, 41, author, with Marcia Thornton Jones (The Bailey School Kids series), born Morganfield, KY, May 18, 1959.

Reginald Martinez (Reggie) Jackson, 54, Baseball Hall of Fame outfielder, born Wyncote, PA, May 18, 1946.

MAY 19 — FRIDAY
Day 140 — 226 Remaining

BOYS' CLUBS FOUNDED: ANNIVERSARY. May 19, 1906. The Federated Boys' Clubs, which later became the Boys' Clubs of America, was founded.

DENMARK: COMMON PRAYER DAY. May 19. Public holiday. The fourth Friday after Easter, known as "Store Bededag," is a day for prayer and festivity.

INTERNATIONAL PICKLE WEEK. May 19–29. To give national recognition to the world's most humorous vegetable. Sponsor: Pickle Packers International, Inc. For info: IPW, DHM Group, Inc, PO Box 767, Dept CC, Holmdel, NJ 07733-0767. Fax: (732) 946-3343.

MALCOLM X: 75th BIRTH ANNIVERSARY. May 19, 1925. Black nationalist and civil rights activist Malcolm X was born Malcolm Little at Omaha, NE. While serving a prison term he resolved to transform his life. On his release in 1952 he changed his name to Malcolm X and worked for the Nation of Islam until he was suspended by Black Muslim leader Elijah Muhammed Dec 4, 1963. Malcolm X later made the pilgrimage to Mecca and became an orthodox Muslim. He was assassinated as he spoke to a meeting at the Audubon Ballroom at New York, NY, Feb 21, 1965. For further info: *Malcolm X: By Any Means Necessary*, by Walter Dean Myers (Scholastic, 0-590-46484-1, $10.75 Gr. 6-9).

TEACHER'S DAY IN FLORIDA. May 19. A ceremonial day on the third Friday in May.

TURKEY: YOUTH AND SPORTS DAY. May 19. Public holiday commemorating the beginning of a national movement for independence in 1919, led by Mustafa Kemal Ataturk.

TWENTY-SEVENTH AMENDMENT RATIFIED: ANNIVERSARY. May 19, 1992. The 27th amendment to the Constitution was ratified, prohibiting Congress from giving itself immediate pay raises.

BIRTHDAYS TODAY

Thomas Feelings, 67, author (*The Middle Passage: White Ships, Black Cargo*), born Brooklyn, NY, May 19, 1933.

Kevin Garnett, 24, basketball player, born Mauldin, SC, May 19, 1976.

Eric Lloyd, 14, actor (*Dunston Checks In, The Santa Clause*), born Glendale, CA, May 19, 1986.

MAY 20 — SATURDAY
Day 141 — 225 Remaining

★**ARMED FORCES DAY.** May 20. Presidential Proclamation 5983, of May 17, 1989, covers the third Saturday in May in all succeeding years. Originally proclaimed as "Army Day" for Apr 6, beginning in 1936 (S.Con.Res. 30 of Apr 2, 1936). S.Con.Res. 5 of Mar 16, 1937, requested annual Apr 6 issuance, which was done through 1949. Always the third Saturday in May since 1950. Traditionally issued once by each Administration.

CAMEROON: NATIONAL HOLIDAY. May 20. Republic of Cameroon. Commemorates declaration of the United Republic of Cameroon May 20, 1972. Prior to this, the country had been a federal republic with two states, Eastern Cameroon and Western Cameroon.

COUNCIL OF NICAEA I: ANNIVERSARY. May 20–Aug 25, 325. The first ecumenical council of Christian Church, called by Constantine I, first Christian emperor of the Roman Empire. Nearly 300 bishops are said to have attended this first of 21 ecumenical councils (latest, Vatican II, began Sept 11, 1962), which was held at Nicaea, in Asia Minor (today's Turkey). The council condemned Arianism (which denied the divinity of Christ), formulated the Nicene Creed and fixed the day of Easter—always on a Sunday.

ELIZA DOOLITTLE DAY. May 20. To honor Miss Doolittle (heroine of Bernard Shaw's *Pygmalion*) for demonstrating the importance and the advantage of speaking one's native language properly. For info: H. M. Chase, Doolittle Day Committee, 2460 Devonshire Rd, Ann Arbor, MI 48104-2706.

HOMESTEAD ACT: ANNIVERSARY. May 20, 1862. President Lincoln signed the Homestead Act, opening millions of acres of government-owned land in the West to settlers or "homesteaders," who had to reside on the land and cultivate it for five years.

LINDBERGH FLIGHT: ANNIVERSARY. May 20–21, 1927. Anniversary of the first solo trans-Atlantic flight. Captain Charles Augustus Lindbergh, 25-year-old aviator, departed from muddy Roosevelt Field, Long Island, NY, alone at 7:52 AM, May 20, 1927, in a Ryan monoplane named *Spirit of St. Louis*. He landed at Le Bourget airfield, Paris, at 10:24 PM Paris time (5:24 PM, NY time), May 21, winning a $25,000 prize offered by Raymond Orteig for the first nonstop flight between New York City and Paris, France (3,600 miles). The "flying fool" as he had been dubbed by some doubters became "Lucky Lindy," an instant world hero. See also: "Lindbergh, Charles Augustus: Birth Anniversary" (Feb 4).

MADISON, DOLLY (DOROTHEA) DANDRIDGE PAYNE TODD: BIRTH ANNIVERSARY. May 20, 1768. Wife of

	S	M	T	W	T	F	S
May		1	2	3	4	5	6
2000	7	8	9	10	11	12	13
	14	15	16	17	18	19	20
	21	22	23	24	25	26	27
	28	28	30	31			

James Madison, 4th president of the US, born at Guilford County, NC. Died at Washington, DC, July 12, 1849.

NATIONAL SAFE BOATING WEEK. May 20–26. Brings boating safety to the public's attention, decreases the number of boating fatalities and makes the waterways safer for all boaters. Sponsor: US Coast Guard. For info: Jo Calkin, Commandant (G-OPB-2), US Coast Guard, 2100 Second St SW, Washington, DC 20593. Phone: (800) 368-5647.

★**NATIONAL SAFE BOATING WEEK.** May 20–26. Presidential Proclamation during May since 1995. From 1958 through 1977, issued for a week including July 4 (PL85–445 of June 4, 1958). From 1981 through 1994, issued for the first week in June (PL96–376 of Oct 3, 1980). From 1995, issued for a seven-day period ending on the Friday before Memorial Day. Not issued from 1978 through 1980.

WEIGHTS AND MEASURES DAY: 125th ANNIVERSARY. May 20. Anniversary of international treaty, signed May 20, 1875, providing for the establishment of an International Bureau of Weights and Measures. The bureau was founded on international territory at Sevres, France.

BIRTHDAYS TODAY

Michael Crapo, 49, US Senator (R, Idaho), born Idaho Falls, May 20, 1951.

David Wells, 37, baseball player, born Torrance, CA, May 20, 1963.

MAY 21 — SUNDAY
Day 142 — 224 Remaining

AMERICAN RED CROSS: FOUNDING ANNIVERSARY. May 21, 1881. Commemorates the founding of the American Red Cross by Clara Barton, its first president. The Red Cross had been founded in Switzerland in 1864 by representatives from 16 European nations. The organization is a voluntary, not-for-profit organization governed and directed by volunteers and provides disaster relief at home and abroad. 1.1 million volunteers are involved in community services such as collecting and distributing donated blood and blood products, teaching health and safety classes and acting as a medium for emergency communication between Americans and their armed forces.

GEMINI, THE TWINS. May 21–June 20. In the astronomical/astrological zodiac, which divides the sun's apparent orbit into 12 segments, the period May 21–June 20 is traditionally identified as the sun sign period of Gemini, the Twins. The ruling planet is Mercury.

★**NATIONAL DEFENSE TRANSPORTATION DAY.** May 21. Presidential Proclamation customarily issued as "National Defense Transportation Day and National Transportation Week." Issued each year for the third Friday in May since 1957. (PL85–32 of May 16, 1957.)

BIRTHDAYS TODAY

Judge Reinhold, 44, actor (*The Santa Clause*), born Wilmington, DE, May 21, 1956.

MAY 22 — MONDAY
Day 143 — 223 Remaining

CANADA: VICTORIA DAY. May 22. Commemorates the birth of Queen Victoria, May 24, 1819. Observed annually on the first Monday preceding May 25.

LOBEL, ARNOLD: BIRTH ANNIVERSARY. May 22, 1933. Illustrator and author (The Frog and Toad series, Caldecott for *Fables*), born at Los Angeles, CA. Died Dec 4, 1987, at New York, NY.

"MISTER ROGERS NEIGHBORHOOD" TV PREMIERE: ANNIVERSARY. May 22, 1967. Presbyterian minister Fred Rogers hosts this long-running PBS children's program. Puppets and human characters interact in the neighborhood of make-believe. Rogers plays the voices of many of the puppets and educates young viewers on a variety of important subjects. The human cast members include: Betty Aberlin, Joe Negri, David Newell, Don Brockett, Francois Clemmons, Audrey Roth, Elsie Neal and Yoshi Ito. More than 600 half-hour episodes of the program have aired.

NATIONAL BACKYARD GAMES WEEK. May 22–29. Observance to celebrate the unofficial start of summer by fostering social interaction and family togetherness through backyard games. Explore the history of familiar and not-so familiar games like croquet and volleyball and help preserve the tradition of family and neighbors enjoying pleasant conversation and friendly

MAY 22–29
NATIONAL BACKYARD GAMES WEEK

As the weather gets warmer, summer vacation approaches and attention spans grow shorter, a change of pace during recess is in order. What's more, participating in Backyard Games Week will give students some activities to do when summer boredom sets in. Team sports may be beyond the scope of some neighborhoods, so focusing on smaller group activities may be the route you want to take. These kinds of games foster neighbor involvement and family fun. Students could ask parents and grandparents what games they played as children. These can be shared and played during recess.

Wildly popular years ago, marbles is making a comeback. It's versatile, since it can be played on pavement or dirt. Jacks is another old game now regaining popularity, although for safety's sake it needs to be played on a smooth floor. Hopscotch has never lost its appeal, and chalk, a pebble and pavement are all you need to play. *Jacks Around the World*, by Mary D. Lankford (Morrow, 0-688-13707-5, $16 Gr. K–6) and *Hopscotch Around the World*, also by Lankford (Morrow, 0-688-147453, $5.95 Gr. K–6) contain instructions on how to play international versions of the two games. Jumping rope is still popular, including the elastic around the ankles version, often referred to as Chinese jump rope. *Miss Mary Mack*, by Johanna Cole and Stephanie Calmenson (Morrow, 0-688-09749-9, $6.95 Gr. K–5) contains good jump rope rhymes.

Bocce and horseshoes are games of skill. Ingenuity with materials gets you around purchasing a set. For example, use a golf ball as the "target" and tennis balls marked with Xs and Os as the players' balls. Aluminum foil horseshoes are lightweight, but okay for preschoolers and kindergartners who can only toss a short distance accurately.

A card game or two can be rainy day Backyard Games.

School and public libraries have many game books that explain rules and offer other game and activity suggestions.

competition. See Curriculum Connection. For info: Frank Beres, Patch Products, PO Box 268, Beloit, WI 53511. Phone: (608) 362-6896. Fax: (608) 362-8178. E-mail: patch@patchproducts.com. Web: www.patchproducts.com.

NATIONAL MARITIME DAY. May 22. Anniversary of departure for first steamship crossing of the Atlantic from Savannah, GA, to Liverpool, England, by the steamship *Savannah* in 1819.

★**NATIONAL MARITIME DAY.** May 22. Presidential Proclamation always issued for May 22 since 1933. (Pub Res No. 7 of May 20, 1933.)

SRI LANKA: NATIONAL HEROES DAY. May 22. Commemorates the struggle of the leaders of the National Independence Movement to liberate the country from colonial rule. Public holiday.

YEMEN: NATIONAL DAY: 10th ANNIVERSARY. May 22. Public holiday. Commemorates the reunification of Yemen in 1990.

BIRTHDAYS TODAY

Ann Cusack, 39, actress (*A League of Their Own*, "The Jeff Foxworthy Show"), born Evanston, IL, May 22, 1961.

MAY 23 — TUESDAY
Day 144 — 222 Remaining

BROWN, MARGARET WISE: BIRTH ANNIVERSARY. May 23, 1910. Children's author, born at Brooklyn, NY. Brown wrote *Goodnight Moon* and *The Runaway Bunny*. She died at Nice, France, Nov 13, 1952.

DEBORAH SAMSON DAY IN MASSACHUSETTS. May 23. Proclaimed annually by the governor to commemorate Deborah Samson, a Massachusetts schoolteacher who outfitted herself in men's clothing and fought in the American Revolution.

LAG B'OMER. May 23. Hebrew calendar date: Iyar 18, 5760. Literally, the 33rd day of the omer (harvest time), the 33rd day after the beginning of Passover. Traditionally a joyous day for weddings, picnics and outdoor activities.

MESMER, FRIEDRICH ANTON: BIRTH ANNIVERSARY. May 23, 1734. German physician after whom Mesmerism was named. Magnetism and hypnotism were used by him in treating disease. Born at Iznang, Swabia, Germany, he died Mar 5, 1815, at Meersburg, Swabia, Germany.

NATIONAL GEOGRAPHY BEE: NATIONAL FINALS. May 23–24. National Geographic Society Headquarters, Washington, DC. The first place winner from each state-level competition, Apr 7, advances to the national level. Alex Trebek of "Jeopardy!" fame moderates the finals which are televised on PBS stations. Students compete for scholarships and prizes totaling more than $50,000. Est attendance: 400. For info: Natl Geography Bee, Natl Geographic Soc, 1145 17th St NW, Washington, DC 20036. Phone: (202) 857-7001.

NEW YORK PUBLIC LIBRARY: ANNIVERSARY. May 23, 1895. New York's then-governor Samuel J. Tilden was the driving force that resulted in the combining of the private Astor and Lenox libraries with a $2 million endowment and 15,000 volumes from the Tilden Trust to become the New York Public Library.

O'DELL, SCOTT: BIRTH ANNIVERSARY. May 23, 1898. Born at Los Angeles, CA. Scott O'Dell won the Newbery Medal in 1961 for his book *Island of the Blue Dolphins*. He published more than 26 children's books, including *The Black Pearl*. In 1972, O'Dell was awarded the Hans Christian Andersen International Award for lifetime achievement. He died at Santa Monica, CA, Oct 15, 1989.

SOUTH CAROLINA RATIFIES CONSTITUTION: ANNIVERSARY. May 23, 1788. By a vote of 149 to 73, South Carolina became the eighth state to ratify the Constitution.

SWEDEN: LINNAEUS DAY. May 23. Stenbrohult. Commemorates the birth in 1707, of Carolus Linnaeus (Carl von Linne), Swedish naturalist who died at Uppsala, Sweden, Jan 10, 1778.

BIRTHDAYS TODAY

Susan Cooper, 65, author (Newbery for *The Grey King*), born London, England, May 23, 1935.

Jewel, 26, singer, born Jewel Kilcher, Payson, UT, May 23, 1974.

MAY 24 — WEDNESDAY
Day 145 — 221 Remaining

BASEBALL FIRST PLAYED UNDER LIGHTS: 65th ANNIVERSARY. May 24, 1935. The Cincinnati Reds defeated the Philadelphia Phillies by a score of 2–1, as more than 20,000 fans enjoyed the first night baseball game in the major leagues. The game was played at Crosley Field, Cincinnati, OH.

BELIZE: COMMONWEALTH DAY. May 24. Public holiday.

BROOKLYN BRIDGE OPENED: ANNIVERSARY. May 24, 1883. Nearly 14 years in construction, the $16 million Brooklyn Bridge over the East River connecting Manhattan and Brooklyn opened. Designed by John A. Roebling, the steel suspension bridge has a span of 1,595 feet.

BULGARIA: ENLIGHTENMENT AND CULTURE DAY. May 24. National holiday festively celebrated by schoolchildren, students, people of science and art.

ERITREA: INDEPENDENCE DAY. May 24. National Day. Gained independence from Ethiopia in 1993 after 30-year civil war.

LEUTZE, EMANUEL: BIRTH ANNIVERSARY. May 24, 1816. Itinerant painter, born at Wurttemberg, Germany, who came to the US when he was nine years old and began painting by age 15. He painted some of the most famous of American works, such as *Washington Crossing the Delaware, Washington Rallying the Troops at Monmouth* and *Columbus Before the Queen*. Died July 18, 1868, at Washington, DC.

MORSE OPENS FIRST US TELEGRAPH LINE: ANNIVERSARY. May 24, 1844. The first US telegraph line was formally opened between Baltimore, MD, and Washington, DC. Samuel F.B. Morse sent the first officially telegraphed words "What hath God wrought?" from the Capitol building to Baltimore. Earlier messages had been sent along the historic line during testing, and one, sent May 1, contained the news that Henry Clay had been nominated as president by the Whig party, from a meeting in Baltimore. This message reached Washington one hour prior to a train carrying the same news.

BIRTHDAYS TODAY

John Rowland, 43, Governor of Connecticut (R), born Waterbury, CT, May 24, 1957.

**May
2000**

S	M	T	W	T	F	S
	1	2	3	4	5	6
7	8	9	10	11	12	13
14	15	16	17	18	19	20
21	22	23	24	25	26	27
28	28	30	31			

MAY 25 — THURSDAY
Day 146 — 220 Remaining

AFRICAN FREEDOM DAY: ANNIVERSARY. May 25. Public holiday in Chad, Zambia, Zimbabwe and some other African states. Members of the Organization for African Unity (formed May 25, 1963) commemorate their independence from colonial rule with sports contests, political rallies and tribal dances.

ARGENTINA: NATIONAL HOLIDAY. May 25. Commemoration of the declaration of independence of Argentina in 1810.

CONSTITUTIONAL CONVENTION: ANNIVERSARY. May 25, 1787. At Philadelphia, PA, the delegates from seven states, forming a quorum, opened the Constitutional Convention, which had been proposed by the Annapolis Convention Sept 11–14, 1786. Among those who were in attendance: George Washington, Benjamin Franklin, James Madison, Alexander Hamilton and Elbridge Gerry.

JORDAN: INDEPENDENCE DAY. May 25. National holiday. Commemorates treaty in 1946, proclaiming autonomy (from Britain) and establishing monarchy.

NATIONAL MISSING CHILDREN'S DAY. May 25. To promote awareness of the problem of missing children, to offer a forum for change and to offer safety information for children in school and community. Annually, May 25. For info: Child Find of America, Inc, PO Box 277, New Paltz, NY 12561-0277. Phone: (914) 255-1848. Natl toll-free hotline phone numbers: (800) I-AM-LOST or (800) A-WAY-OUT.

NATIONAL TAP DANCE DAY. May 25. To celebrate this unique American art form that represents a fusion of African and European cultures and to transmit tap to succeeding generations through documentation and archival and performance support. Held on the anniversary of the birth of Bill "Bojangles" Robinson to honor his outstanding contribution to the art of tap dancing on stage and in films through the unification of diverse stylistic and racial elements.

POETRY DAY IN FLORIDA. May 25. In 1947 the Legislature decreed this day to be Poetry Day in all the public schools of Florida.

ROBINSON, BILL "BOJANGLES": BIRTH ANNIVERSARY. May 25, 1878. Born at Richmond, VA, the grandson of a slave, Robinson is considered one of the greatest tap dancers. He is best known for a routine in which he tap-danced up and down a staircase with Shirley Temple. He taught Gene Kelly, Sammy Davis, Jr and others. He died at New York, NY, Nov 25, 1949.

BIRTHDAYS TODAY

Gordon Smith, 48, US Senator (R, Oregon), born Pendleton, OR, May 25, 1952.

Sheryl Swoopes, 29, basketball player, US Olympic Basketball Team, born Brownfield, TX, May 25, 1971.

Joyce Carol Thomas, 62, author (*Marked by Fire*), born Ponca City, OK, May 25, 1938.

MAY 26 — FRIDAY
Day 147 — 219 Remaining

GEORGIA: INDEPENDENCE RESTORATION DAY. May 26. National Day. Commemorates independence from the Soviet Union in 1991.

MOON PHASE: LAST QUARTER. May 26. Moon enters Last Quarter phase at 7:55 AM, EDT.

Brent Musburger, 61, sportscaster, born Portland, OR, May 26, 1939.

Paul E. Patton, 63, Governor of Kentucky (D), born Fallsburg, KY, May 26, 1937.

Sally Kristen Ride, 49, one of the first seven women in the US astronaut program and the first American woman in space, born Encino, CA, May 26, 1951.

MAY 27 — SATURDAY

Day 148 — 218 Remaining

BLOOMER, AMELIA JENKS: BIRTH ANNIVERSARY. May 27, 1818. American social reformer and women's rights advocate, born at Homer, NY. Her name is remembered especially because of her work for more sensible dress for women and her recommendation of a costume that had been introduced about 1849 by Elizabeth Smith Miller but came to be known as the "Bloomer Costume" or "Bloomers." Amelia Bloomer died at Council Bluffs, IA, Dec 30, 1894.

CARSON, RACHEL (LOUISE): BIRTH ANNIVERSARY. May 27, 1907. American scientist and author, born at Springdale, PA. She was the author of *The Sea Around Us* and *Silent Spring* (1962), a book that provoked widespread controversy over the use of pesticides and contributed to the beginning of the environmental movement. She died Apr 14, 1964, at Silver Spring, MD. For further info: *Rachel Carson: A Wonder of Nature*, by Catherine Reef (Twenty-First Century, 0-941477-38-X, $14.95 Gr. 2–5).

CELLOPHANE TAPE PATENTED: 70th ANNIVERSARY. May 27, 1930. Richard Gurley Drew received a patent for his adhesive tape, later manufactured by 3M as Scotch tape.

DUNCAN, ISADORA: BIRTH ANNIVERSARY. May 27, 1878. American-born interpretive dancer who revolutionized the entire concept of dance. Bare-footed, freedom-loving, liberated woman and rebel against tradition, she experienced worldwide professional success and profound personal tragedy (her two children drowned, her marriage failed and she met a bizarre death when the long scarf she was wearing caught in a wheel of the open car in which she was riding, strangling her). Born at San Francisco, CA, she died at Nice, France, Sept 14, 1927.

GOLDEN GATE BRIDGE OPENED: ANNIVERSARY. May 27, 1937. More than 200,000 people crossed San Francisco's Golden Gate Bridge on its first day.

HICKOCK, WILD BILL: BIRTH ANNIVERSARY. May 27, 1837. American frontiersman, legendary marksman, lawman, army scout and gambler, he was born at Troy Grove, IL, and died Aug 2, 1876, at Deadwood, SD. Hickock's end came when he was shot dead at a poker table by a drunk in the Number Ten saloon.

HUMPHREY, HUBERT HORATIO: BIRTH ANNIVERSARY. May 27, 1911. Born at Wallace, SD, he served as 38th vice president of the US and ran for president in 1968 but lost narrowly to Richard Nixon. Humphrey died at Waverly, MN, Jan 13, 1978.

Christopher J. Dodd, 56, US Senator (D, Connecticut), born Willimantic, CT, May 27, 1944.

Frank Thomas, 32, baseball player, born Columbus, GA, May 27, 1968.

MAY 28 — SUNDAY

Day 149 — 217 Remaining

AZERBAIJAN: DAY OF THE REPUBLIC. May 28. Public holiday. Commemorates the declaration of the Azerbaijan Democratic Republic in 1918.

ITALY: PALIO DEI BALESTRIERI. May 28. Gubbio. The last Sunday in May is set aside for a medieval crossbow contest between Gubbio and Sansepolcro; medieval costumes, arms.

RURAL LIFE SUNDAY OR SOIL STEWARDSHIP SUNDAY. May 28. With an increase in ecological and environmental concerns, Rural Life Sunday emphasizes the concept that Earth belongs to God, who has granted humanity the use of it, along with the responsibility of caring for it wisely. Rural Life Sunday was first observed in 1929. The day is observed annually by churches of many Christian denominations and includes pulpit exchanges by rural and urban pastors. Under the auspices of the National Association of Soil and Water Conservation Districts, the week beginning with Rural Life Sunday is now widely observed as Soil Stewardship Week, with the Sunday itself alternatively termed Soil Stewardship Sunday. Traditionally, Rural Life Sunday is Rogation Sunday, the Sunday preceding Ascension Day.

SIERRA CLUB FOUNDED: ANNIVERSARY. May 28, 1892. Founded by famed naturalist John Muir, the Sierra Club promotes conservation of the natural environment by influencing public policy. It has been especially important in the founding of and protection of our national parks. For info: Sierra Club, 85 Second St, 2nd Floor, San Francisco, CA 94105-3441. Phone: (415) 977-5500. Web: www.sierraclub.org.

THORPE, JAMES FRANCIS (JIM): BIRTH ANNIVERSARY. May 28, 1888. This distinguished Native American athlete was the winner of pentathlon and decathlon events at the 1912 Olympic Games and a professional baseball and football player. Born near Prague, OK, he died at Lomita, CA, Mar 28, 1953.

Glen Rice, 33, basketball player, born Flint, MI, May 28, 1967.

MAY 29 — MONDAY

Day 150 — 216 Remaining

AMNESTY ISSUED FOR SOUTHERN REBELS: ANNIVERSARY. May 29, 1865. President Andrew Johnson issued a proclamation giving a general amnesty to all who participated in the rebellion against the US. High ranking members of the Confederate government and military and those who owned more than $20,000 worth of property were excepted and had to apply individually to the President for a pardon. Once an oath of allegiance was taken, all former property rights, except those in slaves, were returned to the former owners.

CONFEDERATE MEMORIAL DAY IN VIRGINIA. May 29. Annually, the last Monday in May. See also Apr 26, May 31 and June 3 for observations in other states.

CONSTANTINOPLE FELL TO THE TURKS: ANNIVERSARY. May 29, 1453. The city of Constantinople was captured by the Turks, who renamed it Istanbul (although the name wasn't officially changed until 1930). This conquest marked the end of the Byzantine Empire; the city became the capital of the Ottoman Empire.

HENRY, PATRICK: BIRTH ANNIVERSARY. May 29, 1736. American revolutionary leader and orator, born at Studley, VA, and died near Brookneal, VA, June 6, 1799. Especially remembered for his speech (Mar 23, 1775) for arming the Virginia militia, at St. Johns Church, Richmond, VA, when he declared: "I know not what course others may take, but as for me, give me liberty or give me death."

KENNEDY, JOHN FITZGERALD: BIRTH ANNIVERSARY. May 29, 1917. Thirty-fifth president of the US, born at Brookline, MA. Kennedy was the youngest man ever elected to the presidency, the first Roman Catholic and the first president to have served in the US Navy. He was assassinated while riding in an open automobile, at Dallas, TX, Nov 22, 1963. (Accused assassin Lee Harvey Oswald was killed at the Dallas police station by a gunman, Jack Ruby, two days later.) He was the fourth US president to be killed by an assassin, and the second to be buried at Arlington National Cemetery (the first was William Howard Taft).

MEMORIAL DAY. May 29. Legal public holiday. Also known as Decoration Day because of the tradition of decorating the graves of servicemen. An occasion for honoring those who have died in battle. Observance dates from Civil War years in US: first documented observance at Waterloo, NY, May 5, 1865. See also: "Confederate Memorial Day" (Apr 26, May 10 and May 31).

★**MEMORIAL DAY, PRAYER FOR PEACE.** May 29. Presidential Proclamation issued each year since 1948. PL81–512 of May 11, 1950, asks President to proclaim annually this day as a day of prayer for permanent peace. PL90–363 of June 28, 1968, requires that beginning in 1971 it will be observed the last Monday in May. Often titled "Prayer for Peace Memorial Day," and traditionally requests the flying of the flag at half-staff "for the customary forenoon period."

MOUNT EVEREST SUMMIT REACHED: ANNIVERSARY. May 29, 1953. New Zealand explorer Sir Edmund Hillary and Tensing Norgay, a Sherpa guide, became the first team to reach the summit of Mount Everest, the world's highest mountain.

RHODE ISLAND: RATIFICATION DAY. May 29. The 13th state to ratify the Constitution in 1790.

SWITZERLAND: PACING THE BOUNDS. May 29. Liestal. Citizens set off at 8 AM and march along boundaries to the beating of drums and firing of pistols and muskets. Occasion for fetes. Annually, the Monday before Ascension Day.

VIRGINIA PLAN PROPOSED: ANNIVERSARY. May 29, 1787. Just five days after the Constitutional Convention met at Philadelphia, PA, the "Virginia Plan" was proposed. It called for establishment of a government consisting of a legislature with two houses, an executive (chosen by the legislature) and a judicial branch.

WISCONSIN: ADMISSION DAY: ANNIVERSARY. May 29, 1848. Became 30th state in 1848.

	S	M	T	W	T	F	S
May		1	2	3	4	5	6
2000	7	8	9	10	11	12	13
	14	15	16	17	18	19	20
	21	22	23	24	25	26	27
	28	28	30	31			

Brock Cole, 62, author and illustrator (*Alpha and the Dirty Baby*), born Charlotte, MI, May 29, 1938.
Blake Foster, 15, actor (*Turbo: A Power Rangers Movie*, "Power Rangers Turbo"), born Northridge, CA, May 29, 1985.

MAY 30 — TUESDAY
Day 151 — 215 Remaining

CROATIA: NATIONAL DAY. May 30. Public holiday commemorating statehood in 1990.

FIRST AMERICAN DAILY NEWSPAPER PUBLISHED: ANNIVERSARY. May 30, 1783. *The Pennsylvania Evening Post* became the first daily newspaper published in the US. The paper was published at Philadelphia, PA, by Benjamin Towne.

LINCOLN MEMORIAL DEDICATION: ANNIVERSARY. May 30, 1922. The memorial is made of marble from Colorado and Tennessee and limestone from Indiana. It stands in West Potomac Park at Washington, DC. The outside columns are Doric, the inside, Ionic. The Memorial was designed by architect Henry Bacon and its cornerstone was laid in 1915. A skylight lets light into the interiors where the compelling statue "Seated Lincoln," by sculptor Daniel Chester French, is situated.

SAINT JOAN OF ARC: FEAST DAY. May 30. French heroine and martyr, known as the Maid of Orleans, led the French against the English invading army. She was captured, found guilty of heresy and burned at the stake in 1431 (at age 19). Her innocence was declared in 1456 and she was canonized in 1920.

SPACE MILESTONE: *MARINER 9* (US). May 30, 1971. Unmanned spacecraft was launched, entering Martian orbit the following Nov 13. The craft relayed temperature and gravitational fields and sent back spectacular photographs of both the surface of Mars and of her two moons. It was the first spacecraft to orbit another planet.

TRINIDAD: INDIAN ARRIVAL DAY. May 30. Port of Spain. Public holiday. About 40 percent of Trinidad's population is descended from immigrants who were brought from India by the British in the 1840s.

Blake Bashoff, 19, actor (*The New Swiss Family Robinson*), born Philadelphia, PA, May 30, 1981.
Omri Katz, 24, actor ("Eerie, Indiana"), born Los Angeles, CA, May 30, 1976.
Manuel "Manny" Ramirez, 28, baseball player, born Santo Domingo, Dominican Republic, May 30, 1972.

MAY 31 — WEDNESDAY
Day 152 — 214 Remaining

COPYRIGHT LAW PASSED: ANNIVERSARY. May 31, 1790. President George Washington signed the first US copyright law. It gave protection for 14 years to books written by US citizens. In 1891, the law was extended to cover books by foreign authors as well.

JOHNSTOWN FLOOD: ANNIVERSARY. May 31, 1889. Heavy rains caused the Connemaugh River Dam to burst. At nearby Johnstown, PA, the resulting flood killed more than 2,300 persons and destroyed the homes of thousands more. Nearly 800 unidentified drowning victims were buried in a common grave at Johnstown's Grandview Cemetery. So devastating was the flood and so widespread the sorrow for its victims that "Johnstown

Flood" entered the language as a phrase to describe a disastrous event. The valley city of Johnstown, in the Allegheny Mountains, has been damaged repeatedly by floods. Floods in 1936 (25 deaths) and 1977 (85 deaths) were the next most destructive.

NATIONAL SPELLING BEE FINALS. May 31–June 1. Washington, DC. Newspapers and other sponsors across the country send 245–255 youngsters to the finals at Washington, DC. Annually, Wednesday and Thursday of Memorial Day week. Est attendance: 1,000. For info: Dir, Natl Spelling Bee, Scripps-Howard, PO Box 5380, Cincinnati, OH 45201. Phone: (513) 977-3040.

WHITMAN, WALT: BIRTH ANNIVERSARY. May 31, 1819. Poet and journalist, born at West Hills, Long Island, NY. Whitman's best known work, *Leaves of Grass* (1855), is a classic of American poetry. His poems celebrated all of modern life, including subjects that were considered taboo at the time. He died Mar 26, 1892, at Camden, NJ.

WORLD NO-TOBACCO DAY. May 31. Intended to discourage tobacco users from consuming tobacco and to encourage governments, communities, groups and individuals to become aware of the challenge and to take action. For info: World No-Tobacco Day, American Assn for World Health, 1825 K St NW, Ste 1208, Washington, DC 20006. Phone: (202) 466-5883. Fax: (202) 466-5896. E-mail: aawhstaff@aol.com. Web: www.aawhworld-health.org.

BIRTHDAYS TODAY

Clint Eastwood, 70, actor, director (Oscar for *Unforgiven*), born San Francisco, CA, May 31, 1930.

Kenny Lofton, 33, baseball player, born East Chicago, IN, May 31, 1967.

JUNE 1 — THURSDAY
Day 153 — 213 Remaining

ASCENSION DAY. June 1. Commemorates Christ's ascension into heaven. Observed since AD 68. Ascension Day is the 40th day after the Resurrection, counting Easter as the first day.

ATLANTIC, CARIBBEAN AND GULF HURRICANE SEASON. June 1–Nov 30. For info: US Dept of Commerce, Natl Oceanic and Atmospheric Admin, Rockville, MD 20852 or www.nws.noaa.gov.

CANADA: YUKON INTERNATIONAL STORYTELLING FESTIVAL. June 1–4. Whitehorse, Yukon. Storytellers from all over Canada and abroad. Est attendance: 5,000. For info: Yukon Intl Storytelling Fest, PO Box 5029, Whitehorse, Yukon, Canada Y1A 4S2. Phone: (867) 633-7550. E-mail: yukonstory@yknet .yk.ca. Web: www.yukonweb.com/special/storytelling/

CANCER FROM THE SUN MONTH. June 1–30. To promote education and awareness of the dangers of skin cancer from too much exposure to the sun. Kit of materials available for $15 from this nonprofit organization. For info: Frederick Mayer, Pres, Pharmacy Council on Dermatology (PCD), 101 Lucas Valley Rd, #210, San Rafael, CA 94903. Phone: (415) 479-8628. Fax: (415) 479-8608. E-mail: ppsi@aol.com.

CHINA, PEOPLE'S REPUBLIC OF: INTERNATIONAL CHILDREN'S DAY. June 1. Shanghai.

CNN DEBUTED: ANNIVERSARY. June 1, 1980. The Cable News Network, TV's first all-news service, went on the air.

FIREWORKS SAFETY MONTH. June 1–July 4. Activities during this month are designed to warn and educate parents and children about the dangers of playing with fireworks. Prevent Blindness America will offer suggestions for safer ways to celebrate the Fourth of July. Materials that can easily be posted or distributed to the community will be provided. For info: Prevent Blindness America®, 500 E Remington Rd, Schaumburg, IL 60173. Phone: (800) 331-2020. Fax: (847) 843-8458. Web: www.prevent blindness.org.

INTERNATIONAL VOLUNTEERS WEEK. June 1–7. To honor men and women throughout the world who serve as volunteers,

rendering valuable service without compensation to the communities in which they live and to honor nonprofit organizations dedicated to making the world a better place in which to live. For complete info, send $4 to cover expense of printing, handling and postage. Annually, the first seven days of June. For info: Dr. Stanley Drake, Pres, Intl Soc of Friendship and Good Will, 412 Cherry Hills Dr, Bakersfield, CA 93309-7902.

JUNE IS TURKEY LOVERS' MONTH. June 1–30. Month-long campaign to promote awareness and increase turkey consumption at a nonholiday time. Annually, the month of June. For info: Natl Turkey Federation, 1225 New York Ave, NW, Ste 400, Washington, DC 20005. Phone: (202) 898-0100. Fax: (202) 898-0203. E-mail: info@turkeyfed.org. Web: www.turkeyfed.org.

KENTUCKY: ADMISSION DAY: ANNIVERSARY. June 1. Became 15th state in 1792.

KENYA: MADARAKA DAY. June 1. Madaraka Day (Self-Rule Day) is observed as a national public holiday.

MARQUETTE, JACQUES: BIRTH ANNIVERSARY. June 1, 1637. Father Jacques Marquette (Père Marquette), Jesuit missionary-explorer of the Great Lakes region. Born at Laon, France, he died at Ludington, MI, May 18, 1675.

NATIONAL ACCORDION AWARENESS MONTH. June 1–30. To increase public awareness of this multicultural instrument and its influence and popularity in today's music. For info: All Things Accordion, 3551 Pierce St, San Francisco, CA 94123. Phone: (415) 440-0800. E-mail: belloblade@aol.com.

NATIONAL BLESS-A-CHILD MONTH. June 1–30. To increase public awareness of the challenges facing at-risk children and promote volunteer as well as community involvement in their lives. For info: Donna Strout, Operation Blessing Intl, 977 Centerville Turnpike, Virginia Beach, VA 23463. Phone: (757) 226-2443. Fax: (757) 226-6183. E-mail: donna.strout@OB.ORG.

NATIONAL CANDY MONTH. June 1–30. Sponsored by *Confectioner Magazine* and manufacturers, wholesalers and retailers to promote candy as a fun food and enhance consumer awareness of products available in the US. Consumer celebrations include chocolate festivals, contests and information on candy making, decorating with candy and the history of chocolate and chewing and bubble gum. For info: Lisbeth Echeandia, Confectioner Magazine, c/o Gavos + Helms, 2811 McKinney Ave, Dallas, TX 75204. Phone: (800) 826-8586. E-mail: Jimwho@hotmail.com.

NATIONAL FROZEN YOGURT MONTH. June 1–30. To inform the public of the benefits and colorful history of frozen yogurt, one of America's new favorite desserts. Annually, the month of June. For info: Stacy Duckett, TCBY, 1200 TCBY Tower, 425 W Capitol Ave, Little Rock, AR 72201. Phone: (501) 688-8229.

NATIONAL ROSE MONTH. June 1–30. To recognize American grown roses, our national floral emblem. America's favorite flower is grown in all 50 states and more than 1.2 billion fresh cut roses are sold at retail each year. For info: Mktg Dir, Roses Inc, Box 99, Haslett, MI 48840. Phone: (517) 339-9544. Web: www.rosesinc .org.

SAMOA: NATIONAL DAY. June 1. Holiday in the country formerly known as Western Samoa.

STAND FOR CHILDREN DAY. June 1. Stand for Children is a national organization that encourages individuals to improve children's lives. Its mission is to identify, train and connect local children's activists engaging in advocacy, awareness-raising and service initiatives as part of Children's Action Teams. On this day each year a special issue, such as quality child care, is highlighted. For more info: *Stand for Children*, by Marian Wright Edelman (Hyperion, 0-7868-0365-7, $15.95 Gr. 5-8). For info: Children's

		S	M	T	W	T	F	S
June							1	2	3
2000		4	5	6	7	8	9	10
		11	12	13	14	15	16	17
		18	19	20	21	22	23	24
		25	26	27	28	29	30	

Defense Fund, Stand for Children, 1834 Connecticut Ave NW, Washington, DC 20009. Phone: (800) 663-4032. Fax: (202) 234-0217. E-mail: tellstand@stand.org. Web: www.stand.org.

TENNESSEE: ADMISSION DAY: ANNIVERSARY. June 1. Became 16th state in 1796. Observed as a holiday in Tennessee.

BIRTHDAYS TODAY

Alexi Lalas, 30, soccer player, born Detroit, MI, June 1, 1970.

JUNE 2 — FRIDAY

Day 154 — 212 Remaining

BAHAMAS: LABOR DAY. June 2. Public holiday. First Friday in June celebrated with parades, displays and picnics.

BULGARIA: HRISTO BOTEV DAY: ANNIVERSARY. June 2. Poet and national hero Hristro Botev fell fighting Turks, 1876.

ITALY: REPUBLIC DAY. June 2. National holiday. Commemorates referendum, in 1946, in which republic status was selected instead of return to monarchy.

MOON PHASE: NEW MOON. June 2. Moon enters New Moon phase at 8:14 AM, EDT.

UNITED KINGDOM: CORONATION DAY. June 2. Commemorates the crowning of Queen Elizabeth II in 1953.

YELL "FUDGE" AT THE COBRAS IN NORTH AMERICA DAY. June 2. Anywhere north of the Panama Canal. In order to keep poisonous cobra snakes out of North America, all citizens are asked to go outdoors at noon, local time, and yell "Fudge." Fudge makes cobras gag and the mere mention of it makes them skeedaddle. Annually, June 2. [© 1998 by WPL] For info: Thomas or Ruth Roy, Wellness Permission League, PO Box 662, Mt Gretna, PA 17064-0662. Phone: (717) 964-1308. Fax: (717) 964-1335. E-mail: wellcat@desupernet.net.

BIRTHDAYS TODAY

Dana Carvey, 45, comedian, actor (*Wayne's World*, "Saturday Night Live"), born Missoula, MT, June 2, 1955.

Norton Juster, 71, author (*The Phantom Tollbooth*), born Brooklyn, NY, June 2, 1929.

Jerry Mathers, 52, actor ("Leave It to Beaver"), born Sioux City, IA, June 2, 1948.

JUNE 3 — SATURDAY

Day 155 — 211 Remaining

CHIMBORAZO DAY. June 3. To bring the shape of the earth into focus by publicizing the fact that Mount Chimborazo, Ecuador, near the equator, pokes farther out into space than any other mountain on earth, including Mount Everest. (The distance from sea level at the equator to the center of the earth is 13 miles greater than the radius to sea level at the north pole. This means that New Orleans is about six miles further from the center of the earth than is Lake Itasca at the headwaters of the Mississippi, so the Mississippi flows uphill.) For info: Robert L. Birch, Puns Corps, Box 2364, Falls Church, VA 22042-0364. Phone: (703) 533-3668.

CONFEDERATE MEMORIAL DAY/JEFFERSON DAVIS DAY IN KENTUCKY. June 3. Commemorated on the birthday of Jefferson Davis.

DAVIS, JEFFERSON: BIRTH ANNIVERSARY. June 3, 1808. American statesman, US senator, only president of the Confederate States of America. Imprisoned May 10, 1865–May 13, 1867, but never brought to trial, deprived of rights of citizenship after the Civil War. Davis was born at Todd County, KY, and died at

JUNE 3
CHARLES DREW'S BIRTHDAY

Charles Drew was an African American doctor who gained fame for his pioneering work on the study of blood plasma. During World War II he directed the Red Cross program to organize blood banks and ship plasma overseas for wounded American soldiers. He was killed in an automobile crash in 1950.

Celebrate Dr. Drew's birthday by drawing students' attention to the importance of your community's blood bank. Invite a hospital employee who can speak about donating blood and its many uses. Specific topics could include trauma and emergency room usage, auto-transfusions, procedures for storing blood and the necessity of maintaining a sufficient on-hand quantity. A representative of the local chapter of the Red Cross could focus on their work in disaster relief and blood supply to war zones. Parents who have donated blood can share their experiences, emphasizing that this is one way students can help the community when they get older. Some high school students have organized blood donor days in their districts.

As part of the science curriculum, students can research blood types, the circulatory system, blood cells and the importance of vitamins and diet for healthy blood. Projects could include making graphs to compare the percentages of people with various blood types, the increase in demand for blood and how much was used during the past ten years. How much blood was used in WWII, the Korean War and the Vietnam War? For a disgusting project, research the use of leeches in early medicine.

Books on these subjects include: *Charles Drew: A Life-Saving Doctor*, by Miles Shapiro (Raintree Steck-Vaughn, 0-8172-4403-4, $18.98 Gr. 5–12); *The Heart*, by Seymour Simon (Morrow, 0-688-11407-5, $16 Gr. 3–6.); *Blood & Gore*, by Vicki Cobb (Scholastic, 0-590-92665-9, $4.99 Gr. 2–6.); *The Circulatory System*, by Darlene R. Stille (Children's Press, 0-516-26261-0, $6.95 Gr. 2–5).

New Orleans, LA, Dec 6, 1889. His citizenship was restored, posthumously, Oct 17, 1978, when President Carter signed an Amnesty Bill. This bill, he said, "officially completes the long process of reconciliation that has reunited our people following the tragic conflict between the states." Davis's birth anniversary is observed in Florida, Kentucky and South Carolina on this day, in Alabama on the first Monday in June and in Mississippi on the last Monday in May. Davis's birth anniversary is observed as Confederate Memorial Day in Kentucky and Tennessee.

DREW, CHARLES RICHARD: BIRTH ANNIVERSARY. June 3, 1904. African American physician who discovered how to store blood plasma and who organized the blood bank system in the US and UK during WWII. Born at Washington, DC, he was killed in an automobile accident near Burlington, NC, Apr 1, 1950. See Curriculum Connection.

FIRST WOMAN RABBI IN US: ANNIVERSARY. June 3, 1972. Sally Jan Priesand was ordained the first woman rabbi in the US. She became assistant rabbi at the Stephen Wise Free Synagogue, New York City, Aug 1, 1972 .

HOBART, GARRET AUGUSTUS: BIRTH ANNIVERSARY. June 3, 1844. Twenty-fourth vice president of the US (1897–99), born at Long Branch, NJ. Died at Paterson, NJ, Nov 21, 1899.

RABI'I: THE MONTH OF THE MIGRATION. June 3. Begins on Islamic calendar date Rabi'I 1, 1421. The month of the migration or Hegira of the Prophet Muhammad from Mecca to Medina in AD 622 the event that was used as the starting year of the Islamic era. Different methods for "anticipating" the visibility of the new moon crescent at Mecca are used by different Muslim groups. US date may vary.

SPACE MILESTONE: *GEMINI 4* (US): 35th ANNIVERSARY. June 3, 1965. James McDivitt and Edward White made 66 orbits of Earth. White took the first space walk by an American and maneuvered 20 minutes outside the capsule.

BIRTHDAYS TODAY

Anita Lobel, 66, author and illustrator (*Away From Home*), born Krakow, Poland, June 3, 1934.

JUNE 4 — SUNDAY
Day 156 — 210 Remaining

CHINA: TIANANMEN SQUARE MASSACRE: ANNIVERSARY. June 4, 1989. After almost a month and a half of student demonstrations for democracy, the Chinese government ordered its troops to open fire on the unarmed protestors at Tiananmen Square at Beijing. The demonstrations began Apr 18 as several thousand students marched to mourn the death of Hu Yaobang, a pro-reform leader within the Chinese government. A ban was imposed on such demonstrations; Apr 22, 100,000 gathered in Tiananmen Square in defiance of the ban. On May 13, 2,000 of the students began a hunger strike and May 20, the government imposed martial law and began to bring in troops. On June 2, the demonstrators turned back an advance of unarmed troops in the first clash with the People's Army. Under the cover of darkness, early June 4, troops opened fire on the assembled crowds and armored personnel carriers rolled into the square crushing many of the students as they lay sleeping in their tents. Although the government claimed that few died in the attack, estimates range from several hundred to several thousand casualties. In the following months thousands of demonstrators were rounded up and jailed.

FINLAND: FLAG DAY. June 4. Finland's armed forces honor the birth anniversary of Carl Gustaf Mannerheim, born in 1867.

GHANA: REVOLUTION DAY. June 4. National holiday.

ITALY: WEDDING OF THE SEA. June 4. Venice. The feast of the Ascension is the occasion of the ceremony recalling the "Wedding of the Sea" performed by Venice's Doge, who cast his ring into the sea from the ceremonial ship known as the *Bucintoro*, to symbolize eternal dominion. Annually, on the Sunday following Ascension.

JAPAN: DAY OF THE RICE GOD. June 4. Chiyoda. Annual rice-transplanting festival observed on first Sunday in June. Centuries-old rural folk ritual revived in 1930s and celebrated with colorful costumes, parades, music, dancing and prayers to the Shinto rice god Wbai-sama.

★ **SMALL BUSINESS WEEK.** June 4–10. To honor the 22 million small businesses in the US. Annually, the first full week in June. For info: Small Business Administration, Info Services, 409 3rd St SW, 7th Fl, Washington, DC 20416. Phone: (202) 205-6606 or (202) 205-6531. Web: www.sba.gov.

		S	M	T	W	T	F	S
June						1	2	3
2000		4	5	6	7	8	9	10
		11	12	13	14	15	16	17
		18	19	20	21	22	23	24
		25	26	27	28	29	30	

TEACHER'S DAY IN MASSACHUSETTS. June 4. Proclaimed annually by the governor for the first Sunday in June.

TONGA: EMANCIPATION DAY: 30th ANNIVERSARY. June 4. National holiday. Commemorates independence from Britain in 1970.

UNITED NATIONS: INTERNATIONAL DAY OF INNOCENT CHILDREN VICTIMS OF AGGRESSION. June 4. On Aug 19, 1982, the General Assembly decided to commemorate June 4 of each year as the International Day of Innocent Children Victims of Aggression.

BIRTHDAYS TODAY

Andrea Jaeger, 35, former tennis player, born Chicago, IL, June 4, 1965.

JUNE 5 — MONDAY
Day 157 — 209 Remaining

APPLE II COMPUTER RELEASED: ANNIVERSARY. June 5, 1977. The Apple II computer, with 4K of memory, went on sale for $1,298. Its predecessor, the Apple I, was sold largely to electronic hobbyists the previous year. Apple released the Macintosh computer Jan 24, 1984.

DENMARK: CONSTITUTION DAY: ANNIVERSARY. June 5. National holiday. Commemorates Denmark's becoming a constitutional monarchy in 1849.

FIRST BALLOON FLIGHT: ANNIVERSARY. June 5, 1783. The first public demonstration of a hot-air balloon flight took place at Annonay, France, where the co-inventor brothers, Joseph and Jacques Montgolfier, succeeded in launching their 33-foot-diameter *globe aerostatique*. It rose an estimated 1,500 feet and traveled, windborne, about 7,500 feet before landing after the 10-minute flight—the first sustained flight of any object achieved by man.

SCARRY, RICHARD McCLURE: BIRTH ANNIVERSARY. June 5, 1919. Author and illustrator of children's books was born at Boston, MA. Two widely known books of the more than 250 Scarry authored are *Richard Scarry's Best Word Book Ever* (1965) and *Richard Scarry's Please & Thank You* (1973). The pages are crowded with small animal characters who live like humans. More than 100 million copies of his books sold worldwide. Died Apr 30, 1994, at Gstaad, Switzerland.

UNITED NATIONS: WORLD ENVIRONMENT DAY. June 5. Observed annually on the anniversary of the opening of the UN Conference on the Human Environment held in Stockholm in 1972, which led to establishment of UN Environment Programme, based in Nairobi. The General Assembly has urged marking the day with activities reaffirming concern for the preservation and enhancement of the environment. For more information, visit the UN's website for children at www.un.org/Pubs/CyberSchool Bus/

Allan Ahlberg, 62, author (*The Jolly Postman*), born Croydon, England, June 5, 1938.

Joe Clark, 61, Canada's 16th prime minister, 1979–80, born High River, Alberta, Canada, June 5, 1939.

Mark Wahlberg, 29, singer (Marky Mark), host ("AIXN"), born Dorchester, MA, June 5, 1971.

JUNE 6 — TUESDAY

Day 158 — 208 Remaining

BONZA BOTTLER DAY™. June 6. To celebrate when the number of the day is the same as the number of the month. Bonza Bottler Day™ is an excuse to have a party at least once a month. For info: Gail M. Berger, 109 Matthew Ave, Poca, WV 25159. Phone: (304) 776-7746. E-mail: gberger5@aol.com.

CHINA: DRAGON BOAT FESTIVAL. June 6. An important Chinese observance, the Dragon Boat Festival commemorates a hero of ancient China, poet Qu Yuan, who drowned himself in protest against injustice and corruption. It is said that rice dumplings were cast into the water to lure fish away from the body of the martyr, and this is remembered by the eating of zhong zi, glutinous rice dumplings filled with meat and wrapped in bamboo leaves. Dragon boat races are held on rivers. The Dragon Boat Festival is observed in many countries by their Chinese populations. Also called Fifth Month Festival or Summer Festival. Annually, the fifth day of the fifth lunar month.

D-DAY: ANNIVERSARY. June 6, 1944. In the early-morning hours Allied forces landed in Normandy on the north coast of France. In an operation that took months of planning, a fleet of 2,727 ships of every description converged from British ports from Wales to the North Sea. Operation *Overlord* involved 2,000,000 tons of war materials, including more than 50,000 tanks, armored cars, jeeps, trucks and half-tracks. The US alone sent 1,700,000 fighting men. The Germans believed the invasion would not take place under the adverse weather conditions of this early June day. But as the sun came up the village of Saint Mèere Eglise was liberated by American parachutists and by nightfall the landing of 155,000 Allies attested to the success of D-Day. The long-awaited second front of WWII had at last materialized.

HALE, NATHAN: BIRTH ANNIVERSARY. June 6, 1755. American patriot Nathan Hale was born at Coventry, CT. During the battles for New York in the American Revolution, he volunteered to seek military intelligence behind enemy lines and was captured on the night of Sept 21, 1776. In an audience before General William Howe, Hale admitted he was an American officer and was ordered hanged the following morning. Although some question them, his dying words, "I only regret that I have but one life to lose for my country," have become a symbol of American patriotism. He was hanged Sept 22, 1776, at Manhattan, NY.

KOREA: MEMORIAL DAY. June 6. Nation pays tribute to the war dead and memorial services are held at the National Cemetery at Seoul. Legally recognized Korean holiday.

KOREA: TANO DAY. June 6. Fifth day of fifth lunar month. Summer food offered at the household shrine of the ancestors. Also known as Swing Day, since girls, dressed in their prettiest clothes, often compete in swinging matches. The Tano Festival usually lasts from the third through eighth day of the fifth lunar month: June 4–9.

SPACE MILESTONE: *SOYUZ 11* (USSR). June 6, 1971. Launched with cosmonauts G.T. Dobrovolsky, V.N. Volkov and V.I. Patsayev, who died during the return landing June 30, 1971, after a 24-day space flight. *Soyuz 11* had docked at *Salyut* orbital space station June 7–29; the cosmonauts entered the space station for the first time and conducted scientific experiments. First humans to die in space.

SUSAN B. ANTHONY FINED FOR VOTING: ANNIVERSARY. June 6, 1872. Seeking to test for women the citizenship and voting rights extended to black males under the 14th and 15th Amendments, Susan B. Anthony led a group of women who registered and voted at a Rochester, NY, election. She was arrested, tried and sentenced to pay a fine. She refused to do so and was allowed to go free by a judge who feared she would appeal to a higher court.

SWEDEN: FLAG DAY. June 6. Commemorates the day upon which Gustavus I (Gustavus Vasa) ascended the throne of Sweden in 1523.

Verna Aardema, 89, author (*Anansi Does the Impossible: An Ashanti Tale*), born New Era, MI, June 6, 1911.

Dalai Lama, 65, Tibet's spiritual leader and Nobel Peace Prize winner, born Taktser, China, June 6, 1935.

Marian Wright Edelman, 61, president of Children's Defense Fund, civil rights activist, born Bennettsville, SC, June 6, 1939.

Staci Keanan, 25, actress ("Step By Step"), born Devon, PA, June 6, 1975.

Cynthia Rylant, 46, author (Newbery for *Missing May*), born Hopewell, VA, June 6, 1954.

Peter Spier, 73, illustrator and author (Caldecott for *Noah's Ark*), born Amsterdam, Netherlands, June 6, 1927.

JUNE 7 — WEDNESDAY

Day 159 — 207 Remaining

APGAR, VIRGINIA: BIRTH ANNIVERSARY. June 7, 1909. Dr. Apgar developed the simple assessment method that permits doctors and nurses to evaluate newborns while they are still in the delivery room to identify those in need of immediate medical care. The Apgar score was first published in 1953, and the Perinatal Section of the American Academy of Pediatrics is named for Dr. Apgar. Born at Westfield, NJ, Apgar died Aug 7, 1974, at New York, NY.

GAUGUIN, PAUL: BIRTH ANNIVERSARY. June 7, 1848. French painter born at Paris. He became a painter in middle age and renounced his life at Paris and moved to Tahiti. He is remembered for his broad, flat tones and use of color. He died on the island of Hiva Oa in the Marquesas, May 8, 1903.

VCR INTRODUCED: 25th ANNIVERSARY. June 7, 1975. The Sony Corporation released its videocassette recorder, the Betamax, which sold for $995. Eventually, another VCR format, VHS, proved more successful and Sony stopped making the Betamax.

Anna Kournikova, 19, tennis player, born Moscow, Russia, June 7, 1981.

Mike Modano, 30, hockey player, born Livonia, MI, June 7, 1970.

Larisa Oleynik, 19, actress ("The Secret World of Alex Mack"), born San Francisco, CA, June 7, 1981.

JUNE 8 — THURSDAY
Day 160 — 206 Remaining

BILL OF RIGHTS PROPOSED: ANNIVERSARY. June 8, 1789. The Bill of Rights, which led to the first 10 amendments to the US Constitution, was first proposed by James Madison.

COCHISE: DEATH ANNIVERSARY. June 8, 1874. Born around 1810 in the Chiricahua Mountains of Arizona, Cochise became a fierce and courageous leader of the Apache. After his arrest in 1861, he escaped and launched the Apache Wars, which lasted for 25 years. He died 13 years later near his stronghold in southeastern Arizona.

McKINLEY, IDA SAXTON: BIRTH ANNIVERSARY. June 8, 1847. Wife of William McKinley, 25th president of the US, born at Canton, OH. Died at Canton, May 26, 1907.

MOON PHASE: FIRST QUARTER. June 8. Moon enters First Quarter phase at 11:29 PM, EDT.

ORTHODOX ASCENSION DAY. June 8. Observed by Eastern Orthodox Churches.

WHITE, BYRON RAYMOND: BIRTHDAY. June 8, 1917. Retired associate justice of the Supreme Court of the US, nominated by President Kennedy Apr 3, 1962. (Oath of office, Apr 16, 1962.) Justice White was born at Fort Collins, CO.

WRIGHT, FRANK LLOYD: BIRTH ANNIVERSARY. June 8, 1867. American architect born at Richland Center, WI. In his autobiography Wright wrote: "No house should ever be *on* any hill or on anything. It should be *of* the hill, belonging to it, so hill and house could live together each the happier for the other." Wright died at Phoenix, AZ, Apr 9, 1959.

WYTHE, GEORGE: DEATH ANNIVERSARY. June 8, 1806. Signer of the Declaration of Independence. Born at Elizabeth County, VA, about 1726 (exact date unknown). Died at Richmond, VA.

BIRTHDAYS TODAY

Barbara Pierce Bush, 75, former First Lady, wife of George Bush, 41st president of the US, born Rye, NY, June 8, 1925.

Lindsay Davenport, 24, tennis player, born Palos Verdes, CA, June 8, 1976.

JUNE 9 — FRIDAY
Day 161 — 205 Remaining

DONALD DUCK: BIRTHDAY. June 9, 1934. Donald Duck was "born," introduced in the Disney short, *Orphans' Benefit.*

HOORAY FOR YEAR-ROUND SCHOOL DAY. June 9. To promote the benefits of a year-round school calendar which makes learning a continuous process and better suits the demanding educational needs of today's world. Annually, the second Friday in June. For more info, send 9½" SASE to: Hooray for Year-Round School Day, Horace Mann Choice School, 3530-38th Ave, Rock

	S	M	T	W	T	F	S
					1	2	3
June	4	5	6	7	8	9	10
2000	11	12	13	14	15	16	17
	18	19	20	21	22	23	24
	25	26	27	28	29	30	

Island, IL 61201. Web: www.augustana.edu:80/library/horace mann/HMCS_Principal.html.

SHAVUOT or FEAST OF WEEKS. June 9. Jewish Pentecost holy day. Hebrew date, Sivan 6, 5760. Celebrates giving of Torah (the Law) to Moses on Mount Sinai.

BIRTHDAYS TODAY

Michael J. Fox, 39, actor ("Family Ties," *Back to the Future* films), born Edmonton, Alberta, Canada, June 9, 1961.

JUNE 10 — SATURDAY
Day 162 — 204 Remaining

BALL-POINT PEN PATENTED: ANNIVERSARY. June 10, 1943. Hungarian Laszlo Biro patented the ball-point pen, which he had been developing since the 1930s. He was living at Argentina, where he had gone to escape the Nazis. In many languages, the word for ball-point pen is "biro."

JORDAN: GREAT ARAB REVOLT AND ARMY DAY: ANNIVERSARY. June 10. Commemorates the beginning of the Great Arab Revolt in 1916. National holiday.

PORTUGAL: DAY OF PORTUGAL. June 10, 1580. National holiday. Anniversary of the death of Portugal's national poet, Luis Vas de Camoes (Camoens), born in 1524 (exact date unknown) at either Lisbon or possibly Coimbra. Died at Lisbon, Portugal.

TAKE A KID FISHING WEEKEND. June 10–11. St. Paul, MN. Resident adults may fish without a license on these days when fishing with a child under age 16. For info: Jack Skrypek, Fisheries Chief, DNR, Box 12, 500 Lafayette Rd, St. Paul, MN 55155. Phone: (612) 296-0792 or (612) 296-3325. Fax: (612) 297-4916. Web: www.dnr.state.mn.us/

UNITED KINGDOM: TROOPING THE COLOUR—QUEEN'S OFFICIAL BIRTHDAY PARADE. June 10 (tentative). National holiday in the United Kingdom. Horse Guards Parade, Whitehall, London. Colorful ceremony with music and pageantry during which Her Majesty The Queen takes the salute. Starts at 11 AM. When requesting info, send stamped, self-addressed envelope. [Final date not set at press time.] Trooping the Colour is always on a Saturday in June; the Queen's real birthday is Apr 21. Est attendance: 10,000. For info: The Ticket Office, HQ Household Division, 1 Chelsea Barracks, London, England SW1H 8RF. Phone: (44) (171) 414-2357.

BIRTHDAYS TODAY

John Edwards, 47, US Senator (D, North Carolina), born Seneca, SC, June 10, 1953.

Tara Lipinski, 18, figure skater, born Philadelphia, PA, June 10, 1982.

Maurice Sendak, 72, author, illustrator (*Chicken Soup with Rice*, Caldecott for *Where the Wild Things Are*), born Brooklyn, NY, June 10, 1928.

Leelee Sobieski, 18, actress (*Deep Impact*), born Liliane Sobieski, New York, NY, June 10, 1982.

JUNE 11 — SUNDAY
Day 163 — 203 Remaining

CHILDREN'S SUNDAY. June 11. Traditionally the second Sunday in June is observed as Children's Sunday in many Christian churches.

COUSTEAU, JACQUES: 90th BIRTH ANNIVERSARY. June 11, 1910. French undersea explorer, writer and filmmaker born at St. Andre-de-Cubzac, France. He invented the Aqualung, which allowed him and his colleagues to produce more than 80 documentary films about undersea life, two of which won Oscars. This scientist and explorer was awarded the French Legion of Honor for his work in the Resistance in WWII. He died June 25, 1997 at Paris, France.

KING KAMEHAMEHA I DAY. June 11. Designated state holiday in Hawaii honors memory of Hawaiian monarch (1737–1819). Governor appoints state commission to plan annual celebration.

MOUNT PINATUBO ERUPTS IN PHILIPPINES: ANNIVERSARY. June 11, 1991. Long-dormant volcano Mount Pinatubo erupted with a violent explosion, spewing ash and gases that could be seen for more than 60 miles, into the air. The surrounding areas were covered with ash and mud created by rainstorms. US Military bases Clark and Subic Bay were also damaged. On July 6, 1992, Ellsworth Dutton of the National Oceanic and Atmospheric Administration's Climate Monitoring and Diagnostics Laboratory announced that a layer of sulfuric acid droplets released into the Earth's atmosphere by the eruption had cooled the planet's average temperature by about 1 degree Fahrenheit. The greatest difference was noted in the Northern Hemisphere with a drop of 1.5 degrees. Although the temperature drop was temporary, the climate trend made determining the effect of greenhouse warming on the Earth more difficult.

★**NATIONAL FLAG WEEK.** June 11–17. Presidential Proclamation issued each year since 1966 for the week including June 14. (PL89–443 of June 9, 1966.) In addition, the president often calls upon the American people to participate in public ceremonies in which the Pledge of Allegiance is recited. See Curriculum Connection.

PENTECOST. June 11. The Christian feast of Pentecost commemorates descent of the Holy Spirit unto the Apostles, 50 days after Easter. Observed on the seventh Sunday after Easter. Recognized since the third century. See also: "Whitsunday" (below).

RANKIN, JEANNETTE: BIRTH ANNIVERSARY. June 11, 1880. First woman elected to the US Congress, a reformer, feminist and pacifist, was born at Missoula, MT. She was the only member of Congress to vote against a declaration of war against Japan in December 1941. Died May 18, 1973, at Carmel, CA.

WHITSUNDAY. June 11. Whitsunday, the seventh Sunday after Easter, is a popular time for baptism. "White Sunday" is named for the white garments formerly worn by the candidates for baptism and occurs at the Christian feast of Pentecost. See also: "Pentecost" (above).

BIRTHDAYS TODAY

Parris Glendening, 58, Governor of Maryland (D), born Bronx, NY, June 11, 1942.

Joe Montana, 44, former sportscaster and football player, born New Eagle, PA, June 11, 1956.

JUNE 11–17
NATIONAL FLAG WEEK AND FLAG DAY (JUNE 14)

There are many flag-oriented projects that will help students understand and appreciate the American flag. This is a good week to write out and discuss the Pledge of Allegiance. Put poor "Richard Stands" to rest in the minds of primary students. Discussion of ways to honor and display the flag are appropriate this week. See books about flags or encyclopedias.

All students will recognize today's flag, but many will be unfamiliar with historic American flags. Research projects could include locating pictures of early versions of the flag. Discuss the significance of the 13 stripes, the stars, and why the colors red, white and blue were chosen. The Continental Congress left no record of why they chose these colors, but if students investigate the creation of the Great Seal of the US in 1782, they will find that the Congress of Confederation passed a resolution stating the choice of red, white and blue for the Great Seal and their significance. Students might wish to draw and display early versions of the flag.

Students may wish to read about Frances Hopkinson, a signer of the Declaration of Independence, and the man most scholars credit with designing the first flag. They may also want to learn about Betsy Ross, who may or may not have sewn the first flag.

Flag etiquette-under what conditions the flag should be flown, how to dispose of an old flag and other issues-could be a discussion topic. Older students could research and debate flag desecration (burning, hanging upside down) and freedom of speech, a hotly debated current events issue. Research and discussion will help students decide where they stand on this issue.

For a musical tie-in, play a recording of John Philip Sousa's march "The Stars and Stripes Forever."

The website at www.usflag.org has information on every aspect of our flag and on Flag Day.

JUNE 12 — MONDAY
Day 164 — 202 Remaining

FRANK, ANNE: BIRTH ANNIVERSARY. June 12, 1929. Born at Frankfurt, Germany. Anne Frank moved with her family to Amsterdam to escape the Nazis but after Holland was invaded by Germany, they had to go into hiding. In 1942, Anne began to keep a diary. She died at Bergen-Belsen concentration camp in 1945. After the war, her father published her diary, on which a stage play and movie were later based. See also "Diary of Anne Frank: Last Entry" (Aug 1).

LOVING v VIRGINIA : **ANNIVERSARY.** June 12, 1967. The US Supreme Court decision in *Loving v Virginia* swept away all 16 remaining state laws prohibiting interracial marriages.

NATIONAL BASEBALL HALL OF FAME: ANNIVERSARY. June 12, 1939. The National Baseball Hall of Fame and Museum, Inc, was dedicated at Cooperstown, NY. More than 200 individuals have been honored for their contributions to the game of baseball by induction into the Baseball Hall of Fame. The first players chosen for membership (1936) were Ty Cobb, Honus Wagner, Babe Ruth, Christy Mathewson and Walter Johnson. Relics and memorabilia from the history of baseball are housed at this shrine of America's national sport.

★**NATIONAL LITTLE LEAGUE BASEBALL WEEK.** June 12–18. Presidential Proclamation 3296, of June 4, 1959, covers all succeeding years. Always the week beginning with the second Monday in June. (H.Con.Res. 17 of June 1, 1959.)

PHILIPPINES: INDEPENDENCE DAY. June 12. National holiday. Declared independence from Spain in 1898.

RUSSIA: INDEPENDENCE DAY. June 12. National holiday. Commemorates the election in 1991 of the first popularly elected leader (Gorbachev) in the 1,000-year history of the Russian state.

WHITMONDAY. June 12. The day after Whitsunday is observed as a public holiday in many European countries.

BIRTHDAYS TODAY

Spencer Abraham, 48, US Senator (R, Michigan), born Lansing, MI, June 12, 1952.

George Herbert Walker Bush, 76, 41st US president, born Milton, MA, June 12, 1924.

Helen Lester, 64, author (*Tacky the Penguin*), born Evanston, IL, June 12, 1936.

Hillary McKay, 41, author (*The Amber Cat*), born the Midlands, England, June 12, 1959.

JUNE 13 — TUESDAY

Day 165 — 201 Remaining

MIRANDA DECISION: ANNIVERSARY. June 13, 1966. The US Supreme Court rendered a 5–4 decision in the case of *Miranda v Arizona*, holding that the Fifth Amendment of the Constitution "required warnings before valid statements could be taken by police." The decision has been described as "providing basic legal protections to persons who might otherwise not be aware of their rights." Ernesto Miranda, the 23-year-old whose name became nationally known, was retried after the Miranda Decision, convicted and sent back to prison. Miranda was stabbed to death in a card game dispute at Phoenix, AZ, in 1976. A suspect in the killing was released by police after he had been read his "Miranda rights." Police procedures now routinely require the reading of a prisoner's constitutional rights ("Miranda") before questioning.

SCOTT, WINFIELD: BIRTH ANNIVERSARY. June 13, 1786. American army general, negotiator of peace treaties with the Indians and twice nominated for president (1848 and 1852). Leader of brilliant military campaign in Mexican War in 1847. Scott was born at Petersburg, VA and died at West Point, NY, May 29, 1866.

BIRTHDAYS TODAY

Tim Allen, 47, comedian, actor ("Home Improvement"), born Denver, CO, June 13, 1953.

Ashley Olsen, 13, actress ("Full House," "Two of a Kind"), born Los Angeles, CA, June 13, 1987.

Mary-Kate Olsen, 13, actress ("Full House," "Two of a Kind"), born Los Angeles, CA, June 13, 1987.

JUNE 14 — WEDNESDAY

Day 166 — 200 Remaining

BARTLETT, JOHN: BIRTH ANNIVERSARY. June 14, 1820. American editor and compiler of Bartlett's *Familiar Quotations* [1855] was born at Plymouth, MA. Though he had little formal education, he created one of the most-used reference works of the English language. No quotation of his own is among the more than 22,000 listed today, but in the preface to the first edition he wrote that the object of this work "originally made without any view of publication" was to show "the obligation our language owes to various authors for numerous phrases and familiar quotations which have become 'household words.' " Bartlett died at Cambridge, MA, Dec 3, 1905. His book remains in print today in the 16th edition.

FIRST NONSTOP TRANSATLANTIC FLIGHT: ANNIVERSARY. June 14–15, 1919. Captain John Alcock and Lieutenant Arthur W. Brown flew a Vickers Vimy bomber 1,900 miles nonstop from St. Johns, Newfoundland, to Clifden, County Galway, Ireland. In spite of their crash landing in an Irish peat bog, their flight inspired public interest in aviation. See also: "Lindbergh Flight: Anniversary" (May 20).

★**FLAG DAY.** June 14. Presidential Proclamation issued each year for June 14. Proclamation 1335, of May 30, 1916, covers all succeeding years. Has been issued annually since 1941. (PL81–203 of Aug 3, 1949.) Customarily issued as "Flag Day and National Flag Week," as in 1986; the president usually mentions "a time to honor America," Flag Day to Independence Day (89 Stat. 211). See also: "National Flag Day USA: Pause for the Pledge" (this date).

FLAG DAY: ANNIVERSARY OF THE STARS AND STRIPES. June 14, 1777. John Adams introduced the following resolution before the Continental Congress, meeting at Philadelphia, PA: "Resolved, That the flag of the thirteen United States shall be thirteen stripes, alternate red and white; that the union be thirteen stars, white on a blue field, representing a new constellation." Legal holiday in Pennsylvania.

JAPAN: RICE PLANTING FESTIVAL. June 14. Osaka. Ceremonial transplanting of rice seedlings in paddy field at Sumiyashi Shrine, Osaka.

MAWLID AL NABI: THE BIRTHDAY OF THE PROPHET MUHAMMAD. June 14. Mawlid al-Nabi (Birth of the Prophet Muhammad) is observed on Muslim calendar date Rabi al-Awal 12, 1421. Different methods for calculating the visibility of the new moon crescent at Mecca are used by different Muslim groups.

NATIONAL FLAG DAY USA: PAUSE FOR THE PLEDGE. June 14. Held simultaneously across the country at 7 PM, EDT. Public law 99–54 recognizes the Pause for the Pledge as part of National Flag Day ceremonies. The concept of the Pause for the Pledge of Allegiance was conceived as a way for all citizens to share a patriotic moment. National ceremony at Fort McHenry National Monument and Historic Shrine. See Curriculum Connection.

STOWE, HARRIET BEECHER: BIRTH ANNIVERSARY. June 14, 1811. American writer Harriet Beecher Stowe, daughter of the Reverend Lyman Beecher and sister of Henry Ward Beecher. Author of *Uncle Tom's Cabin*, an antislavery novel that provoked a storm of protest and resulted in fame for its author. Two characters in the novel attained such importance that their names became part of the English language—the Negro slave,

June *2000*	S	M	T	W	T	F	S
					1	2	3
	4	5	6	7	8	9	10
	11	12	13	14	15	16	17
	18	19	20	21	22	23	24
	25	26	27	28	29	30	

Uncle Tom, and the villainous slaveowner, Simon Legree. The reaction to *Uncle Tom's Cabin* and its profound political impact are without parallel in American literature. It is said that during the Civil War, when Harriet Beecher Stowe was introduced to President Abraham Lincoln, his words to her were, "So you're the little woman who wrote the book that made this great war." Stowe was born at Litchfield, CT and died at Hartford, CT, July 1, 1896.

TAIWAN: BIRTHDAY OF CHENG HUANG. June 14. Thirteenth day of fifth moon. Celebrated with a procession of actors on stilts doing dragon and lion dances.

UNIVAC COMPUTER: ANNIVERSARY. June 14, 1951. Univac 1, the world's first commercial computer, designed for the US Bureau of the Census, was unveiled, demonstrated and dedicated at Philadelphia, PA. Though this milestone of the computer age was the first commercial electronic computer, it had been preceded by ENIAC (Electronic Numeric Integrator and Computer), completed under the supervision of J. Presper Eckert, Jr and John W. Mauchly, at the University of Pennsylvania, in 1946.

US ARMY ESTABLISHED BY CONGRESS: 225th ANNIVERSARY. June 14, 1775. Anniversary of Resolution of the Continental Congress establishing the army as the first US military service.

WARREN G. HARDING BECOMES FIRST PRESIDENT TO BROADCAST ON RADIO: ANNIVERSARY. June 14, 1922. Warren G. Harding became the first president to broadcast a message over the radio. The event was the dedication of the Francis Scott Key Memorial at Baltimore, MD. The first official government message was broadcast Dec 6, 1923.

BIRTHDAYS TODAY

Stephanie Maria (Steffi) Graf, 31, tennis player, born Bruhl, West Germany, June 14, 1969.
James Gurney, 42, author and illustrator (*Dinotopia*), born Glendale, CA, June 14, 1958.
Laurence Yep, 52, author (*Dragon's Gate, Child of the Owl*), born San Francisco, CA, June 14, 1948.

JUNE 15 — THURSDAY
Day 167 — 199 Remaining

ARKANSAS: ADMISSION DAY: ANNIVERSARY. June 15. Became the 25th state in 1836.

JACKSON, RACHEL DONELSON ROBARDS: BIRTH ANNIVERSARY. June 15, 1767. Wife of Andrew Jackson, 7th president of the US, born at Halifax County, NC. Died at Nashville, TN, Dec 22, 1828.

MAGNA CARTA DAY: ANNIVERSARY. June 15. Anniversary of King John's sealing, in 1215, of the Magna Carta "in the meadow called Ronimed between Windsor and Staines on the fifteenth day of June in the seventeenth year of our reign." This document is regarded as the first charter of English liberties and one of the most important documents in the history of political and human freedom. Four original copies of the 1215 charter survive.

TWELFTH AMENDMENT TO US CONSTITUTION RATIFIED: ANNIVERSARY. June 15, 1804. The 12th Amendment to the Constitution was ratified. It changed the method of electing the president and vice president after a tie in the electoral college during the election of 1800. Rather than each elector voting for two candidates with the candidate receiving the most votes elected president and the second-place candidate elected vice president, each elector was now required to designate his choice for president and vice president, respectively.

BIRTHDAYS TODAY

Wade Boggs, 42, baseball player, born Omaha, NE, June 15, 1958.
Christopher Castile, 20, actor ("Step By Step," *Beethoven*), born Los Alamitos, CA, June 15, 1980.
Brian Jacques, 61, author (the Redwall series), born Liverpool, England, June 15, 1939.
Justin Leonard, 28, golfer, born Dallas, TX, June 15, 1972.

JUNE 16 — FRIDAY
Day 168 — 198 Remaining

MOON PHASE: FULL MOON. June 16. Moon enters Full Moon phase at 6:27 PM, EDT.

SOUTH AFRICA: YOUTH DAY. June 16, 1976. National holiday. Commemorates a student uprising in Soweto against "Bantu Education" and the enforced teaching of the Afrikaans language.

SPACE MILESTONE: FIRST WOMAN IN SPACE, *VOSTOK 6* (USSR). June 16, 1963. Valentina Tereshkova, 26, former cotton-mill worker, born on collective farm near Yaroslavl, USSR, became the first woman in space when her spacecraft, *Vostok 6*, took off from the Tyuratam launch site. She manually controlled *Vostok 6* during the 70.8-hour flight through 48 orbits of Earth and landed by parachute (separate from her cabin) June 19, 1963. In November 1963 she married cosmonaut Andrian Nikolayev, who had piloted *Vostok 3* through 64 earth orbits, Aug 11–15, 1962. Their child Yelena (1964) was the first born to space-traveler parents.

BIRTHDAYS TODAY

Lincoln Almond, 64, Governor of Rhode Island (R), born Central Falls, RI, June 16, 1936.
Cobi Jones, 30, soccer player, played in 1994 World's Cup, born Westlake Village, CA, June 16, 1970.
Kerry Wood, 23, baseball player, born Irving, TX, June 16, 1977.

JUNE 17 — SATURDAY
Day 169 — 197 Remaining

BUNKER HILL DAY IN MASSACHUSETTS. June 17. Legal holiday in the county in commemoration of the Battle of Bunker Hill that took place in 1775. Proclaimed annually by the governor.

HOOPER, WILLIAM: BIRTH ANNIVERSARY. June 17, 1742. Signer of the Declaration of Independence, born at Boston, MA. Died Oct 14, 1790, at Hillsboro, NC.

ICELAND: INDEPENDENCE DAY. June 17. Anniversary of founding of republic in 1944 and independence from Denmark is major festival, especially in Reykjavik. Parades, competitions, street dancing.

SOUTH AFRICA REPEALS LAST APARTHEID LAW: ANNIVERSARY. June 17, 1991. The Parliament of South Africa repealed the Population Registration Act, removing the law that was the foundation of apartheid. The law, first enacted in 1950, required the classification by race of all South Africans at birth. It established four compulsory racial categories: white, mixed race, Asian and black. Although this marked the removal of the last of the apartheid laws, blacks in South Africa still could not vote.

UNITED NATIONS: WORLD DAY TO COMBAT DESERTIFICATION AND DROUGHT. June 17. Proclaimed by the General Assembly Dec 19, 1994 (Res 49/115). States were invited to devote the World Day to promoting public awareness of the need for international cooperation to combat desertification and the effects of drought and on the implementation of the UN Convention to Combat Desertification. For info: United Nations, Dept of Public Info, New York, NY 10017.

WORLD JUGGLING DAY. June 17. Juggling clubs affiliated with the International Jugglers Association in cities all over the world hold local festivals to demonstrate, teach and celebrate their art. For info: Intl Jugglers' Assn, PO Box 218, Montague, MA 01351. Phone: (413) 367-2401. Fax: (413) 367-0259. E-mail: IJugglersA@aol.com. Web: www.juggle.org/wjd/

BIRTHDAYS TODAY

Venus Williams, 20, tennis player, born Lynwood, CA, June 17, 1980.

JUNE 18 — SUNDAY

Day 170 — 196 Remaining

★**FATHER'S DAY.** June 18. Presidential Proclamation issued for third Sunday in June in 1966 and annually since 1971. (PL 92–278 of Apr 24, 1972.)

FATHER'S DAY. June 18. Recognition of the third Sunday in June as Father's Day occurred first at the request of Mrs John B. Dodd of Spokane, WA, on June 19, 1910. It was proclaimed for that date by the mayor of Spokane and recognized by the governor of Washington. The idea was publicly supported by President Calvin Coolidge in 1924, but not presidentially proclaimed until 1966. It was assured of annual recognition by Public Law 92–278 of April 1972.

FIRST AMERICAN WOMAN IN SPACE: ANNIVERSARY. June 18, 1983. Dr. Sally Ride, 32-year-old physicist and pilot, functioned as a "mission specialist" and became the first American woman in space when she began a six-day mission aboard the space shuttle *Challenger*. The "near-perfect" mission was launched from Cape Canaveral, FL, and landed, June 24, 1983, at Edwards Air Force Base, CA.

NATIONAL SPLURGE DAY©. June 18. Today is the day to go out and do something indulgent. Have fun! For info: Adrienne Sioux Koopersmith, 1437 W Rosemont, #1W, Chicago, IL 60660-1319. Phone: (773) 743-5341. Fax: (773) 743-5395. E-mail: kooper@interaccess.com.

ORTHODOX PENTECOST. June 18. Observed by Eastern Orthodox churches.

SEYCHELLES: CONSTITUTION DAY. June 18. National holiday commemorating 1993 constitution.

SPACE MILESTONE: *CHALLENGER STS-7* (US). June 18, 1983. Shuttle *Challenger*, launched from Kennedy Space Center,

FL, with crew of five, including Sally K. Ride (first American woman in space), Robert Crippen, Norman Thagard, John Fabian and Frederick Houck. Landed at Edwards Air Force Base, CA, on June 24 after near-perfect six-day mission.

TRINITY SUNDAY. June 18. Christian Holy Day on the Sunday after Pentecost commemorates the Holy Trinity, the three divine persons—Father, Son and Holy Spirit—in one God. See also: "Pentecost" (June 11).

WAR OF 1812: DECLARATION ANNIVERSARY. June 18, 1812. After much debate in Congress between "hawks" such as Henry Clay and John Calhoun, and "doves" such as John Randolph, Congress issued a declaration of war on Great Britain. The action was prompted primarily by Britain's violation of America's rights on the high seas and British incitement of Indian warfare on the frontier. War was seen by some as a way to acquire Florida and Canada. The hostilities ended with the signing of the Treaty of Ghent on Dec 24, 1814, at Ghent, Belgium.

BIRTHDAYS TODAY

Pam Conrad, 53, author (*Prairie Songs*), born New York, NY, June 18, 1947.
Paul McCartney, 58, singer, songwriter (The Beatles), born Liverpool, England, June 18, 1942.
John D. Rockefeller IV, 63, US Senator (D, West Virginia), born New York, NY, June 18, 1937.
Chris Van Allsburg, 51, illustrator and author (Caldecott for *The Polar Express, Jumanji*), born Grand Rapids, MI, June 18, 1949.

JUNE 19 — MONDAY

Day 171 — 195 Remaining

EMANCIPATION DAY IN TEXAS. June 19, 1865. In honor of the emancipation of the slaves in Texas.

FORTAS, ABE: 90th BIRTH ANNIVERSARY. June 19, 1910. Abe Fortas was born at Memphis, TN. He was appointed to the Supreme Court by President Lyndon Johnson in 1965. Prior to his appointment he was known as a civil libertarian, having argued cases for government employees and other individuals accused by Senator Joe McCarthy of having communist affiliations. He argued the 1963 landmark Supreme Court case of *Gideon v Wainwright*, which established the right of indigent defendants to free legal aid in criminal prosecutions. In 1968, he was nominated by Johnson to succeed Chief Justice Earl Warren, but his nomination was withdrawn after much conservative opposition in the Senate. In 1969 Fortas became the first Supreme Court Justice to be forced to resign after revelations about questionable financial dealings were made public. He died Apr 5, 1982, at Washington, DC.

GARFIELD: BIRTHDAY. June 19, 1978. America's favorite lasagna-loving cat is 22. *Garfield*, a modern classic comic strip created by Jim Davis, first appeared in 1978, and has brought laughter to millions. For info: Paws, Inc, Kim Campbell, 5440 E Co Rd 450 N, Albany, IN 47320.

GEHRIG, LOU: BIRTH ANNIVERSARY. June 19, 1903. Henry Louis Gehrig, Baseball Hall of Fame first baseman born Ludwig Heinrich Gehrig, at New York, NY. Gehrig, known as the "Iron Horse," played in 2,130 consecutive games, a record not surpassed until Cal Ripken did in 1995. He played 17 years with the Yankees, hit .340 and slugged 493 home runs, 23 of them grand slams. Gehrig retired in 1939 and was diagnosed with the degenerative muscle disease amyotrophic lateral sclerosis, later known as Lou Gehrig's disease. Died at New York, NY, June 2, 1941.

June *2000*	S	M	T	W	T	F	S
					1	2	3
	4	5	6	7	8	9	10
	11	12	13	14	15	16	17
	18	19	20	21	22	23	24
	25	26	27	28	29	30	

JUNETEENTH. June 19. Celebrated in Texas to commemorate the day when Union General Granger proclaimed the slaves of Texas free. This is also a ceremonial holiday in Florida, commemorating the day slaves in Florida were notified of the Emancipation Proclamation.

VIRGIN ISLANDS: ORGANIC ACT DAY: ANNIVERSARY. June 19. Commemorates the enactment by the US Congress, July 22, 1954, of the Revised Organic Act, under which the government of the Virgin Islands is organized. Observed annually on the third Monday in June.

BIRTHDAYS TODAY

Andrew Lauer, 35, actor (*I'll Be Home for Christmas*), born Santa Monica, CA, June 19, 1965.

Brian McBride, 28, soccer player, born Arlington Heights, IL, June 19, 1972.

JUNE 20 — TUESDAY
Day 172 — 194 Remaining

CHESNUTT, CHARLES W.: BIRTH ANNIVERSARY. June 20, 1858. Born at Cleveland, OH, Chesnutt was considered by many as the first important black novelist. His collections of short stories included *The Conjure Woman* (1899) and *The Wife of His Youth and Other Stories of the Color Line* (1899). *The Colonel's Dream* (1905) dealt with the struggles of the freed slave. His work has been compared to later writers such as William Faulkner, Richard Wright and James Baldwin. He died Nov 15, 1932, at Cleveland.

CHICAGO BULLS WIN THIRD CONSECUTIVE NBA CHAMPIONSHIP: ANNIVERSARY. June 20, 1993. With a four-games-to-two victory over the Phoenix Suns in the National Basketball Association (NBA) finals the Chicago Bulls earned their third straight NBA title. The Bulls became the first team to win three in a row since 1966, when the Boston Celtics won their eighth in a row. In 1996 they won the NBA title for a fourth time, in 1997 for a fifth and in 1998 for a sixth, for another three-in-a-row sweep.

SUMMER. June 20–Sept 22. In the Northern Hemisphere summer begins today with the summer solstice, at 9:48 PM, EDT. Note that in the Southern Hemisphere today is the beginning of winter. Anywhere between the Equator and Arctic Circle, the sun rises and sets farthest north on the horizon for the year and length of daylight is maximum (12 hours, 8 minutes at equator, increasing to 24 hours at Arctic Circle).

WEST VIRGINIA: ADMISSION DAY: ANNIVERSARY. June 20. Became 35th state in 1863. Observed as a holiday in West Virginia. The state of West Virginia is a product of the Civil War. Originally part of Virginia, West Virginia became a separate state when Virginia seceded from the Union.

BIRTHDAYS TODAY

John Goodman, 48, actor (*Arachnophobia*, *The Flintstones*), born Afton, MO, June 20, 1952.

JUNE 21 — WEDNESDAY
Day 173 — 193 Remaining

CANCER, THE CRAB. June 21–July 22. In the astronomical/astrological zodiac, which divides the sun's apparent orbit into 12 segments, the period June 21–July 22 is identified, traditionally, as the sun sign of Cancer, the Crab. The ruling planet is the moon.

NEW HAMPSHIRE RATIFIES CONSTITUTION: ANNIVERSARY. June 21, 1788. By a vote of 57 to 47, New Hampshire became the ninth state to ratify the Constitution.

SMITHSONIAN INSTITUTION FESTIVAL OF AMERICAN FOLKLIFE. June 21–25. (Also June 30–July 4.) National Mall, Washington, DC. The 34th annual festival features programs on California. Est attendance: 1,500,000. For info: Smithsonian Institution, 900 Jefferson Dr SW, Washington, DC 20560. Phone: (202) 357-2700.

TOMPKINS, DANIEL D.: BIRTH ANNIVERSARY. June 21, 1774. Sixth vice president of the US (1817–25), born at Fox Meadows, NY. Died at Staten Island, NY, June 11, 1825.

WASHINGTON, MARTHA DANDRIDGE CUSTIS: BIRTH ANNIVERSARY. June 21, 1731. Wife of George Washington, first president of the US, born at New Kent County, VA. Died at Mount Vernon, VA, May 22, 1802.

BIRTHDAYS TODAY

Togo D. West, 58, US Secretary of Veterans Affairs (Clinton administration), born Winston-Salem, NC, June 21, 1942.

Prince William, 18, son of Prince Charles and Princess Diana, born London, England, June 21, 1982.

JUNE 22 — THURSDAY
Day 174 — 192 Remaining

SWITZERLAND: MORAT BATTLE ANNIVERSARY. June 22, 1476. The little, walled town of Morat played a decisive part in Swiss history. There, the Confederates were victorious over Charles the Bold of Burgundy, laying the basis for French-speaking areas to become Swiss. Now an annual children's festival.

US DEPARTMENT OF JUSTICE: ANNIVERSARY. June 22. Established by an act of Congress, the Department of Justice is headed by the attorney general. Prior to 1870, the attorney general (whose office had been created Sept 24, 1789) had been a member of the president's cabinet but had not been the head of a department.

BIRTHDAYS TODAY

Dianne Feinstein, 67, US Senator (D, California), born San Francisco, CA, June 22, 1933.

Lindsay Ridgeway, 15, actress ("Boy Meets World"), born Loma Linda, CA, June 22, 1985.

JUNE 23 — FRIDAY
Day 175 — 191 Remaining

DENMARK: MIDSUMMER EVE. June 23. Celebrated all over the country with bonfires and merrymaking.

FIRST TYPEWRITER: ANNIVERSARY. June 23, 1868. First US typewriter was patented by Luther Sholes.

LAURA INGALLS WILDER PAGEANT. June 23–25. (Also June 30–July 2 and July 7–9.) De Smet, SD. An outdoor pageant on the natural prairie stage depicting "Medley of Memories," historically based on Laura Ingalls Wilder's life. Est attendance: 10,000. For info: The Laura Ingalls Wilder Pageant, PO Box 154, De Smet, SD 57231. Phone: (605) 692-2108.

LUXEMBOURG: NATIONAL HOLIDAY. June 23. Commemorating birth of His Royal Highness Grand Duke Jean in 1921. Luxembourg's independence is also celebrated.

MIDSUMMER DAY/EVE CELEBRATIONS. June 23. Celebrates the beginning of summer with maypoles, music, dancing and bonfires. Observed mainly in northern Europe, including Finland, Latvia and Sweden. Day of observance is sometimes St. John's Day (June 24), with celebration on St. John's Eve (June 23) as well, or June 19. Time approximates the summer solstice. See also: "Summer" (June 20).

BIRTHDAYS TODAY

Theodore Taylor, 79, author (*The Cay*), born Statesville, NC, June 23, 1921.

Clarence Thomas, 52, Associate Justice of the Supreme Court, born Pinpoint, GA, June 23, 1948.

JUNE 24 — SATURDAY
Day 176 — 190 Remaining

BERLIN AIRLIFT: ANNIVERSARY. June 24, 1948. In the early days of the Cold War the Soviet Union challenged the West's right of access to Berlin. The Soviets created a blockade and an airlift to supply some 2,250,000 people at West Berlin resulted. The airlift lasted a total of 321 days and brought into Berlin 1,592,787 tons of supplies. Joseph Stalin finally backed down and the blockade ended May 12, 1949.

CANADA: NEWFOUNDLAND DISCOVERY DAY. June 24. Commemorates the discovery of Newfoundland by John Cabot in 1497.

CANADA: QUEBEC FÊTE NATIONALE. June 24. Saint Jean Baptiste Day.

CIARDI, JOHN: BIRTH ANNIVERSARY. June 24, 1916. Poet for adults and children (*You Read to Me, I'll Read to You*), born at Boston, MA. Died Mar 30, 1986, at Edison, NJ.

LATVIA: JOHN'S DAY (MIDSUMMER NIGHT DAY). June 24. The festival of Jani, which commemorates the summer solstice and the name day of (Janis) John, is one of Latvia's most ancient as well as joyous rituals. This festival is traditionally celebrated in the countryside, as it emphasizes fertility and the beginning of summer. Festivities begin June 23. For info: Embassy of Latvia, 4325 17th St, NW, Washington DC, 20011. Phone: (202) 726-8213.

MOON PHASE: LAST QUARTER. June 24. Moon enters Last Quarter phase at 9 PM, EDT.

BIRTHDAYS TODAY

Kathryn Lasky, 56, author (*Sugaring Time*), born Indianapolis, IN, June 24, 1944.

June *2000*	S	M	T	W	T	F	S
					1	2	3
	4	5	6	7	8	9	10
	11	12	13	14	15	16	17
	18	19	20	21	22	23	24
	25	26	27	28	29	30	

George Pataki, 55, Governor of New York (R), born Peekskill, NY, June 24, 1945.

Predrag "Preki" Radosavljevic, 37, soccer player, born Belgrade, Yugoslavia, June 24, 1963.

JUNE 25 — SUNDAY
Day 177 — 189 Remaining

BATTLE OF LITTLE BIGHORN: ANNIVERSARY. June 25, 1876. Lieutenant Colonel George Armstrong Custer, leading military forces of more than 200 men, attacked an encampment of Sioux Indians led by Chiefs Sitting Bull and Crazy Horse near Little Bighorn River, MT. Custer and all men in his immediate command were killed in the brief battle (about two hours) of Little Bighorn. For more info: *It Is a Good Day to Die: Indian Eyewitnesses Tell the Story of the Battle of Little Bighorn*, by Herman Viola (Crown, 0-517-70913-9, $19.99 Gr. 5-8).

CBS SENDS FIRST COLOR TV BROADCAST OVER THE AIR: ANNIVERSARY. June 25, 1951. Columbia Broadcast System broadcast the first color television program. The four-hour program was carried by stations in New York City, Baltimore, Philadelphia, Boston and Washington, DC, although no color sets were owned by the public. At the time CBS, itself, owned fewer than 40 color receivers.

CIVIL WAR IN YUGOSLAVIA: ANNIVERSARY. June 25, 1991. In an Eastern Europe freed from the iron rule of communism and the USSR, separatist and nationalist tensions suppressed for decades rose to a violent boiling point. The republics of Croatia and Slovenia declared their independence, sparking a fractious and bitter war that spread throughout what was formerly Yugoslavia. Ethnic rivalries between Serbians and Croatians began the military conflicts that spread to Slovenia, and in 1992 fighting began in Bosnia-Herzegovina between Serbians and ethnic Muslims. Although the new republics were recognized by the UN and sanctions passed to stop the fighting, it raged on through 1995 despite the efforts of UN peacekeeping forces.

CORPUS CHRISTI (US OBSERVANCE). June 25. A movable Roman Catholic celebration commemorating the institution of the Holy Eucharist. The solemnity has been observed on the Thursday following Trinity Sunday since 1246, except in the US, where it is observed on the Sunday following Trinity Sunday.

DEAF-BLINDNESS AWARENESS WEEK. June 25–July 1. A week to observe the birth anniversary of Helen Keller who was born June 27, 1880. Annually, the full week that includes Helen Keller's birthday. See Curriculum Connection. Library Kit is available for $3.95. For info: FOLDA Inc, 2930 Craiglawn Rd, Silver Spring, MD 20904-1816. Phone: (301) 572-5168. Fax: (301) 572-4134. E-mail: alhagemeyer@juno.com.

JOHN CARVER DAY IN MASSACHUSETTS. June 25. Proclaimed annually by the governor on the fourth Sunday in June to commemorate the first governor of the Plymouth Colony, John Carver, who served from 1620 to 1621.

KIM CAMPBELL SWORN IN AS CANADIAN PRIME MINISTER: ANNIVERSARY. June 25, 1993. After winning the June 13 election to the leadership of the ruling Progressive-Conservative Party, Kim Campbell became Canada's 19th prime minister and its first woman prime minister. However, in the general election held Oct 25, 1993, the Liberal Party routed the Progressive-Conservatives in the worst defeat for a governing political party in Canada's 126-year history, reducing the former government's seats in the House of Commons from 154 to 2. Campbell was among those who lost their seats.

JUNE 25–JULY 1
DEAF-BLINDNESS AWARENESS WEEK

Deaf-Blindness Awareness Week incorporates Helen Keller's birthday on the 27th of June, so you might wish to make her story the focal point of the week.

There are a number of books about Helen Keller, including her adult level autobiography. Children's books include: *A Picture Book of Helen Keller*, by David Adler (Holiday House, 0-8234-0818-3, $15.95 Gr. PreS–3.); *A Girl Named Helen Keller*, by Margo Lundell (Scholastic, 0-590-47963-6, $3.99 Gr. 1–3.); *Helen Keller*, by Johanna Hurwitz (Random House, 0-679-87705-3, $3.99 Gr. 2–4); and *Helen Keller*, by Lois Nicholson (Chelsea House, 0-7910-2086-X, $19.95 Gr. 5 & up).

Students can first be asked to imagine that they are blind. Have them list ways they could communicate. Then, ask them to do the same activity as though they are deaf. Finally, compare the lists and strike out ways of possible communication if they were both blind and deaf. Now how would they communicate?

Older students could research how, in the last hundred years, educating blind and deaf people has changed. Key figures include Louis Braille and Thomas Gallaudet and his two sons Thomas and Edward.

Local groups that promote awareness of and sensitivity to people with physical disabilities are often willing to provide a classroom speaker. Many school districts have staff members who specialize in working with deaf or hearing-impaired children. They may be able to address the added challenges of working with a person who is deaf and blind.

Students can look for improvements in your community to make life easier for a blind or deaf person. Braille numbering in elevators and closed captioned TV are two examples. Telephone services for the hearing impaired are also available. Software with an audio component makes it possible for blind people to use computers. There are many books about the Braille alphabet and American Sign Language. Students can learn some words and phrases.

Videos available about Helen Keller's life include two versions of *The Miracle Worker*. The 1962 movie, starring Anne Bancroft and Patty Duke, is in black and white. The 1979 TV remake stars Patty Duke and Melissa Gilbert.

KOREAN WAR BEGAN: 50th ANNIVERSARY. June 25, 1950. Forces from northern Korea invaded southern Korea, beginning a civil war. US ground forces entered the conflict June 30. An armistice was signed at Panmunjom July 27, 1953, formally dividing the country into two—North Korea and South Korea.

LAST GREAT BUFFALO HUNT: ANNIVERSARY. June 25–27, 1882. By 1882 most of the estimated 60–75 million buffalo had been killed by white hide hunters, the meat left to rot. Buffalo numbered only about 50,000 when "The Last Great Buffalo Hunt" took place on Indian reservation lands near Hettinger, ND. Some 2,000 Teton Sioux Indians in full hunting regalia killed about 5,000 buffalo. The occasion is also referred to as "The Last Stand of the American Buffalo" as within 16 months the last of the free-ranging buffalo were gone. For info: Wendy Hehn, Dir Community Promotions, Box 1323, Hettinger, ND 58639. Phone: (701) 567-2531. Fax: (701) 567-2690. E-mail: adamsdv@hettinger.ctctel.com. Web: hettingernd.com.

MONTSERRAT: VOLCANO ERUPTS: ANNIVERSARY. June 25, 1997. After lying dormant for 400 years, the Soufriere Hills volcano began to come to life in July, 1995. It erupted in 1997, cov-ering Plymouth, Montserrat's capital city, and two-thirds of the rest of the lush Caribbean island with a heavy layer of ash. Two-thirds of the population relocated to other islands or to Great Britain.

MOZAMBIQUE: INDEPENDENCE DAY: 25th ANNIVERSARY. June 25. National holiday. Commemorates independence from Portugal in 1975.

ORTHODOX FESTIVAL OF ALL SAINTS. June 25. Observed by Eastern Orthodox churches on the Sunday following Orthodox Pentecost (June 18 in 2000). Marks the end of the 18-week Triodion cycle.

SLOVENIA: NATIONAL DAY. June 25. Public holiday. Commemorates independence from the former Yugoslavia in 1991.

SUPREME COURT BANS OFFICIAL PRAYER: ANNIVERSARY. June 25, 1962. The US Supreme Court ruled that a prayer read aloud in public schools violated the 1st Amendment's separation of church and state. The court again struck down a law pertaining to the First Amendment when it disallowed an Alabama law that permitted a daily one-minute period of silent meditation or prayer in public schools June 1, 1985. (Vote 6–3.)

TWO YUGOSLAV REPUBLICS DECLARE INDEPENDENCE: ANNIVERSARY. June 25, 1991. The republics of Slovenia and Croatia formally declared independence from Yugoslavia. The two northwestern republics did not, however, secede outright.

VIRGINIA: RATIFICATION DAY. June 25. Became the 10th state to ratify the Constitution in 1788.

BIRTHDAYS TODAY

Dikembe Mutombo, 34, basketball player, born Kinshasa, Zaire, June 25, 1966.

JUNE 26 — MONDAY
Day 178 — 188 Remaining

BORDEN, SIR ROBERT LAIRD: BIRTH ANNIVERSARY. June 26, 1854. Canadian statesman and prime minister, born at Grand Pre, Nova Scotia. Died at Ottawa, June 10, 1937.

CN TOWER: OPENING ANNIVERSARY. June 26, 1976. Birthday of the world's tallest building and freestanding structure, the CN Tower, 1,815 feet, 5 inches high, at Toronto, Ontario, Canada. For info: CN Tower, 301 Front St W, Toronto, Ont, Canada M5V 2T6. Phone: (416) 360-8500. Fax: (416) 601-4713.

FARLEY, WALTER: BIRTH ANNIVERSARY. June 26, 1922. Children's author, born at New York, NY. He wrote the tale of the famous horse, *The Black Stallion* and later wrote the prequel, *The Young Black Stallion* with his son in 1989. Farley died at Sarasota, FL, Oct 16, 1989.

FLAG AMENDMENT DEFEATED: 10th ANNIVERSARY. June 26, 1990. The Senate rejected a proposed constitutional amendment that would have permitted states to prosecute those who destroyed or desecrated American flags.

MADAGASCAR: INDEPENDENCE DAY: 40th ANNIVERSARY. June 26. National holiday. Commemorates independence from France in 1960.

MIDDLETON, ARTHUR: BIRTH ANNIVERSARY. June 26, 1742. American Revolutionary leader and signer of the Declaration of Independence, born near Charleston, SC. Died at Goose Creek, SC, Jan 1, 1787.

PIZARRO, FRANCESCO: DEATH ANNIVERSARY. June 26, 1541. Spanish conqueror of Peru, born at Extremadura, Spain, ca 1471. Pizarro died at Lima, Peru.

SAINT LAWRENCE SEAWAY DEDICATION: ANNIVERSARY. June 26, 1959. President Dwight D. Eisenhower and Queen Elizabeth II jointly dedicated the St. Lawrence Seaway in formal ceremonies held at St. Lambert, Quebec, Canada. A project undertaken jointly by Canada and the US, the waterway (which provides access between the Atlantic Ocean and the Great Lakes) had been opened to traffic Apr 25, 1959.

UNITED NATIONS CHARTER SIGNED: 55th ANNIVERSARY. June 26, 1945. The UN Charter was signed at San Francisco by 50 nations.

UNITED NATIONS: INTERNATIONAL DAY AGAINST DRUG ABUSE AND ILLICIT TRAFFICKING. June 26, 1987. Following a recommendation of the 1987 International Conference on Drug Abuse and Illicit Trafficking, the United Nations General Assembly (Res 42/112), expressed its determination to strengthen action and cooperation for an international society free of drug abuse and proclaimed June 26 as an annual observance to raise public awareness. For info: UN, Dept of Public Info, Public Inquiries Unit, RM GA-57, New York, NY 10017. Phone: (212) 963-4475. Fax: (212) 963-0071. E-mail: inquiries@un.org.

ZAHARIAS, MILDRED "BABE" DIDRIKSON: BIRTH ANNIVERSARY. June 26, 1914. Born Mildred Ella Didrikson at Port Arthur, TX, the great athlete was nicknamed "Babe" after legendary baseball player Babe Ruth. She was named to the women's All-America basketball team when she was 16. At the 1932 Olympic Games, she won two gold medals and also set world records in the javelin throw and the 80-meter high hurdles; only a technicality prevented her from obtaining the gold in the high jump. Didrikson married professional wrestler George Zaharias in 1938, six years after she began playing golf casually. In 1946 Babe won the US Women's Amateur tournament, and in 1947 she won 17 straight golf championships and became the first American winner of the British Ladies' Amateur Tournament. Turning professional in 1948, she won the US Women's Open in 1950 and 1954, the same year she won the All-American Open. Babe also excelled in softball, baseball, swimming, figure skating, billiards—even football. In a 1950 Associated Press poll she was named the woman athlete of the first half of the 20th century. She died of cancer, Sept 27, 1956, at Galveston, TX.

BIRTHDAYS TODAY

Robert Burch, 75, author (*Christmas with Ida Early*), born Inman, GA, June 26, 1925.

Chris O'Donnell, 30, actor (*Dead Poet's Society, Batman & Robin*), born Winnetka, IL, June 26, 1970.

Charles Robb, 61, US Senator (D, Virginia), born Phoenix, AZ, June 26, 1939.

Nancy Willard, 64, author (Newbery for *A Visit to William Blake's Inn: Poems for Innocent and Experienced Travelers*), born Ann Arbor, MI, June 26, 1936.

Charlotte Zolotow, 85, author (*The Moon Was the Best, Peter and the Pigeons*), born Norfolk, VA, June 26, 1915.

	S	M	T	W	T	F	S
June					1	2	3
2000	4	5	6	7	8	9	10
	11	12	13	14	15	16	17
	18	19	20	21	22	23	24
	25	26	27	28	29	30	

JUNE 27 — TUESDAY

Day 179 — 187 Remaining

DJIBOUTI: INDEPENDENCE DAY. June 27. National day. Commemorates independence from France in 1977.

HAPPY BIRTHDAY TO "HAPPY BIRTHDAY TO YOU." June 27, 1859. The melody of probably the most often sung song in the world, "Happy Birthday to You," was composed by Mildred J. Hill, a schoolteacher born at Louisville, KY. Her younger sister, Patty Smith Hill, was the author of the lyrics which were first published in 1893 as "Good Morning to All," a classroom greeting published in the book *Song Stories for the Sunday School*. The lyrics were amended in 1924 to include a stanza beginning "Happy Birthday to You." Now it is sung somewhere in the world every minute of the day. Although the authors are believed to have earned very little from the song, reportedly it later generated about $1 million a year for its copyright owner. The song is expected to enter public domain upon expiration of copyright in 2010. Mildred Hill died at Chicago, IL, June 5, 1916 without knowing that her melody would become the world's most popular song. Patty Hill, born Mar 27, 1868 at Louisville, KY, died at New York, NY, May 25, 1946. See Curriculum Connection.

KELLER, HELEN: BIRTH ANNIVERSARY. June 27, 1880. Born at Tuscumbia, AL, Helen Keller was left deaf and blind by a disease she contracted at 18 months of age. With the help of

JUNE 27
HAPPY BIRTHDAY TO "HAPPY BIRTHDAY TO YOU"

When Mildred Hill composed the melody for the song that would become "Happy Birthday to You," she had no idea how popular it would become. The song is sung every day all over the world. June 27, the birthday of Mildred Hill, is also likely to be a student's birthday. Since many schools hold group birthday sing-a-longs during assembly times, here is a good opportunity to teach children about the song's origins.

In class, students can write short essays about the way they celebrate birthdays in their family. Some celebrate with large parties, others observe the special day in a more subdued manner. Special meals and a birthday cake are often part of the occasion. Some families include the birthday person's mother as an honoree. Students can write about a particular birthday moment, not necessarily their own, but one that sticks out in their memory. Students can share silly variations on the "Happy Birthday" song, or make up new verses, perhaps one that tells something about themselves.

It's fun to learn how birthdays are celebrated elsewhere. The book *Happy Birthday Everywhere*, by Arlene Erlbach (Millbrook, 0-761-30346-4, $8.95 Gr. K–3) presents birthday celebrations from around the world. *Birthday Surprises: Ten Great Stories to Unwrap*, edited by Johanna Hurwitz (Morrow, 0-688-13194-8, $16 Gr. 3–7) is a collection of stories by ten top children's book authors. It's a great prompt for creative writing.

A discussion about creative and economical gift-giving might provide students with useful ideas. Coupons redeemable for chores around the home, a back rub or a meal prepared by the student are several gift ideas. Many elderly people prefer gifts of time rather than purchased items. Students might also discuss gifts for their peers that do not involve spending money.

If nothing else, the class can sing "Happy Birthday to You" and know that chances are excellent that someone else—maybe far away—is singing the same song at that very same moment.

her teacher, Anne Sullivan, she graduated from college and had a career as an author and lecturer. She died June 1, 1968, at Westport, CT.

BIRTHDAYS TODAY

Bruce Babbitt, 62, US Secretary of Interior (Clinton administration), born Los Angeles, CA, June 27, 1938.

Lucille Clifton, 64, author (*Everett Anderson's Goodbye*), born Depew, NY, June 27, 1936.

James Lincoln Collier, 72, author of historical fiction, with his brother Christopher Collier (*My Brother Sam Is Dead*), born New York, NY, June 27, 1928.

Captain Kangaroo (Bob Keeshan), 73, TV personality, born Lynbrook, NY, June 27, 1927.

JUNE 28 — WEDNESDAY
Day 180 — 186 Remaining

FORBES, ESTHER: BIRTH ANNIVERSARY. June 28, 1891. Author and illustrator, born at Westborough, MA. She won the Pulitzer Prize for history in 1943 for her book *Paul Revere and the World He Lived In*. Her children's book, *Johnny Tremain*, was awarded the 1944 Newbery Medal. Forbes died at Worcester, MA, Aug 12, 1967.

MONDAY HOLIDAY LAW: ANNIVERSARY. June 28, 1968. President Lyndon B. Johnson approved Public Law 90–363, which amended section 6103(a) of title 5, United States Code, establishing Monday observance of Washington's Birthday, Memorial Day, Labor Day, Columbus Day and Veterans Day. The new holiday law took effect Jan 1, 1971. Veterans Day observance subsequently reverted to its former observance date, Nov 11. See individual holidays for further details.

TREATY OF VERSAILLES: ANNIVERSARY. June 28, 1919. The signing of the Treaty of Versailles at Versailles, France formally ended World War I.

BIRTHDAYS TODAY

John Elway, 40, football player, born Port Angeles, WA, June 28, 1960.

Mark Eugene Grace, 36, baseball player, born Winston-Salem, NC, June 28, 1964.

Bette Greene, 66, author (*Philip Hall Likes Me, I Reckon Maybe*), born Memphis, TN, June 28, 1934.

Carl Levin, 66, US Senator (D, Michigan), born Detroit, MI, June 28, 1934.

JUNE 29 — THURSDAY
Day 181 — 185 Remaining

LATHROP, JULIA C.: BIRTH ANNIVERSARY. June 29, 1858. A pioneer in the battle to establish child-labor laws, Julia C. Lathrop was the first woman member of the Illinois State Board of

Charities and in 1900 was instrumental in establishing the first juvenile court in the US. In 1912, President Taft named Lathrop chief of the newly created Children's Bureau, then part of the US Dept of Commerce and Labor. In 1925 she became a member of the Child Welfare Committee of the League of Nations. Born at Rockford, IL, she died there Apr 15, 1932.

PETER AND PAUL DAY. June 29. Feast day for Saint Peter and Saint Paul. Commemorates dual martyrdom of Christian apostles Peter (by crucifixion) and Paul (by beheading) during persecution by Roman Emperor Nero. Observed since third century.

SAINT-EXUPERY, ANTOINE DE: BIRTH ANNIVERSARY. June 29, 1900. French aviator and children's author, born at Lyons, France. Saint-Exupery is best known for *The Little Prince*. Other books include *Wind, Sand and Stars* and *Night Flight*. Saint-Exupery died at sea, July 31, 1944.

BIRTHDAYS TODAY

Theo Fleury, 32, hockey player, born Oxbow, Saskatchewan, Canada, June 29, 1968.

JUNE 30 — FRIDAY
Day 182 — 184 Remaining

CHARLES BLONDIN'S CONQUEST OF NIAGARA FALLS: ANNIVERSARY. June 30, 1859. Charles Blondin, a French acrobat and aerialist (whose real name was Jean François Gravelet), in view of a crowd estimated at more than 25,000 persons, walked across Niagara Falls on a tightrope. The walk required only about five minutes. On separate occasions he crossed blindfolded, pushing a wheelbarrow, carrying a man on his back and even on stilts. Blondin was born Feb 28, 1824, at St. Omer, France, and died at London, England, Feb 19, 1897.

CONGO (DEMOCRATIC REPUBLIC): INDEPENDENCE DAY: 40th ANNIVERSARY. June 30. National holiday. The Democratic Republic of Congo was previously known as Zaire. Commemorates independence from Belgium in 1960.

GUATEMALA: ARMED FORCES DAY. June 30. Guatemala observes public holiday.

LAST HURRAH FOR BRITISH HONG KONG: ANNIVERSARY. June 30, 1997. The crested flag of the British Crown Colony was officially lowered at midnight and replaced by a new flag (marked by the bauhinia flower) representing China's sovereignty over Hong Kong and the official transfer of power. Though Britain owned Hong Kong in perpetuity, the land areas surrounding the city were leased from China and the lease expired July 1, 1997. Rather than renegotiate a new lease, Britain ceded its claim to Hong Kong.

LEAP SECOND ADJUSTMENT TIME. June 30. June 30 is one of the times that has been favored for the addition or subtraction of a second from our clock time (to coordinate atomic and astronomical time). The determination to adjust is made by the Central Bureau of the International Earth Rotation Service, at Paris, France.

MONROE, ELIZABETH KORTRIGHT: BIRTH ANNIVERSARY. June 30, 1768. Wife of James Monroe, fifth president of the US, born at New York, NY. Died at their Oak Hill estate at Loudon County, VA, Sept 23, 1830.

NATIONAL TOM SAWYER DAYS (WITH FENCE PAINTING CONTEST). June 30–July 2. Hannibal, MO. Frog jumping, mud volleyball, Tom and Becky Contest, parade, Tomboy Sawyer Contest, 10K run, arts & crafts show and fireworks launched from the banks of the Mississippi River. Highlight is the National Fence

Painting Contest. Sponsor: Hannibal Jaycees. Est attendance: 100,000. For info: Hannibal Visitors Bureau, 505 N 3rd St, Hannibal, MO 63401. Phone: (573) 221-2477.

NOW FOUNDED: ANNIVERSARY. June 30, 1966. The National Organization for Women was founded at Washington, DC, by people attending the Third National Conference on the Commission on the Status of Women. NOW's purpose is to take action to take women into full partnership in the mainstream of American society, exercising all privileges and responsibilities in equal partnership with men. For info: Natl Organization for Women, 1000 16th St NW, Washington, DC 20036. Phone: (202) 331-0066.

TWENTY-SIXTH AMENDMENT RATIFIED: ANNIVERSARY. June 30, 1971. The 26th Amendment to the Constitution granted the right to vote in all federal, state and local elections to all persons 18 years or older. On the date of ratification the US gained an additional 11 million voters. Up until this time, the minimum voting age was set by the states; in most states it was 21.

WHEELER, WILLIAM ALMON: BIRTH ANNIVERSARY. June 30, 1819. Nineteenth vice president of the US (1877–81), born at Malone, NY. Died there June 4, 1887.

BIRTHDAYS TODAY

Mollie Hunter, 78, author (*A Sound of Chariots*), born Longniddry, Scotland, June 30, 1922.

David McPhail, 60, author and illustrator (*Pigs Ahoy!*), born Newburyport, MA, June 30, 1940.

Mitchell "Mitch" Richmond, 35, basketball player, born Ft Lauderdale, FL, June 30, 1965.

JULY 1 — SATURDAY

Day 183 — 183 Remaining

AMERICAN FEDERATION OF TEACHERS CONVENTION. July 1–6. Pennsylvania Convention Center, Philadelphia, PA. For info: American Federation of Teachers, 555 New Jersey Ave NW, Washington, DC 20001. Phone: (202) 879-4587. Web: www.aft.org.

BATTLE OF GETTYSBURG: ANNIVERSARY. July 1, 1863. After the Southern success at Chancellorsville, VA, Confederate General Robert E. Lee led his forces on an invasion of the North, initially targeting Harrisburg, PA. As Union forces moved to counter the invasion, the battle lines were eventually formed at Gettysburg, PA, in one of the Civil War's most crucial battles, beginning July 1, 1863. On the climactic third day of the battle (July 3), Lee ordered an attack on the center of the Union line, later to be known as Pickett's Charge. The 15,000 rebels were repulsed, ending the Battle of Gettysburg. After the defeat, Lee's forces retreated back to Virginia, listing more than one-third of the troops as casualties in the failed invasion. Union General George Meade initially failed to pursue the retreating rebels, allowing Lee's army to escape across the rain-swollen Potomac River.

BURUNDI: INDEPENDENCE DAY. July 1. National holiday. Anniversary of establishment of independence in 1962. Had been under Belgian administration as part of Ruanda-Urundi.

CANADA: CANADA DAY. July 1. National holiday. Canada's national day, formerly known as Dominion Day. Observed on following day when July 1 is a Sunday. Commemorates the confederation of Upper and Lower Canada and some of the Maritime Provinces into the Dominion of Canada in 1867.

CHILDREN'S COLONIAL FAIR. July 1–2. Yorktown Victory Center, Yorktown, VA. 18th-century games and entertainment and crafts to make and take home are among a variety of activities planned for young people. Est attendance: 1,500. For info: Jamestown-Yorktown Foundation, PO Box 1607, Williamsburg, VA 23187. Phone: (757) 253-4838. Fax: (757) 253-5299. Web: www.historyisfun.org.

DIANA, PRINCESS OF WALES: BIRTH ANNIVERSARY. July 1, 1961. Former wife of Charles, Prince of Wales, and mother of Prince William and Prince Harry. Born Lady Diana Spencer at Sandringham, England, she died in an automobile accident at Paris, France, Aug 31, 1997.

DORSEY, THOMAS A.: BIRTH ANNIVERSARY. July 1, 1899. Thomas A. Dorsey, the father of gospel music, was born at Villa Rica, GA. Originally a blues composer, Dorsey eventually combined blues and sacred music to develop gospel music. It was Dorsey's composition "Take My Hand, Precious Lord" that Reverend Dr. Martin Luther King, Jr, had asked to have performed just moments before his assassination. Dorsey, who composed more than 1,000 gospel songs and hundreds of blues songs in his lifetime, died Jan 23, 1993, at Chicago, IL.

FIRST ADHESIVE US POSTAGE STAMPS ISSUED: ANNIVERSARY. July 1, 1847. The first adhesive US postage stamps were issued by the US Postal Service.

FIRST US ZOO: ANNIVERSARY. July 1, 1874. The Philadelphia Zoological Society, the first US zoo, opened. Three thousand visitors traveled by foot, horse and carriage and steamboat to visit the exhibits. Price of admission was 25 cents for adults and 10 cents for children. There were 1,000 animals in the zoo on opening day.

GHANA: REPUBLIC DAY: 40th ANNIVERSARY. July 1. National holiday. Commemorates the inauguration of the Republic in 1960.

HALFWAY POINT OF 2000. July 1. At midnight, July 1, 2000, 183 days of the year will have elapsed and 183 will remain before Jan 1, 2001.

MOON PHASE: NEW MOON. July 1. Moon enters New Moon phase at 3:20 PM, EDT.

NATIONAL BAKED BEAN MONTH. July 1–31. To pay tribute to one of America's favorite and most healthful and nutritious foods, baked beans, made with dry or canned beans. For info: Gwen DeVries, Bean Education & Awareness Network, 303 E Wacker Dr, Ste 440, Chicago, IL 60601. Phone: (312) 861-5200. Fax: (312) 861-5252.

NATIONAL EDUCATION ASSOCIATION MEETING. July 1–6. Chicago, IL. More than 9,000 delegates from the local and state level debate issues and set NEA policy at the Representative Assembly. Est attendance: 10,000. For info: National Education Assn, 1201 16th St NW, Washington, DC 20036-3290. Phone: (202) 822-7769. Web: www.nea.org.

NATIONAL HOT DOG MONTH. July 1–31. Celebrates one of America's favorite hand–held foods with fun facts and new topping ideas. More than 16 billion hot dogs per year are sold in the US. Sponsor: National Hot Dog and Sausage Council. For info: Natl Hot Dog & Sausage Council, 1700 N Moore St, Ste 1600, Arlington, VA 22209. Phone: (703) 841-2400. Web: www.hotdog.org.

NATIONAL JULY BELONGS TO BLUEBERRIES MONTH. July 1–31. To make the public aware that this is the peak month for fresh blueberries. For info: North American Blueberry Council, 4995 Golden Foothill Parkway, Ste #2, El Dorado Hills, CA 95762.

NATIONAL POSTAL WORKER DAY. July 1. To express appreciation to all past and present postal employees for their service and dedication in serving the American people. Annually, July 1. For info: Connie Totten-Oldham, 475 L'Enfant Plaza SW, Rm 10546, HQ US Postal Service, Washington, DC 20260-3100.

NATIONAL RECREATION AND PARKS MONTH. July 1–31. To showcase and invite community participation in quality leisure activities for all segments of the population. For info: Natl Recreation and Park Assn, 22377 Belmont Ridge Rd, Ashburn, VA 20148. Phone: (703) 858-0784. Fax: (703) 858-0794. E-mail: info@nrpa.org. Web: www.nrpa.org.

NICK AT NITE PREMIERE: 15th ANNIVERSARY. July 1, 1985. The first broadcast of Nick at Nite, the creation of the kids' network Nickelodeon, occurred. Owned and operated by MTV Networks, Nick at Nite presents many of the old classic television series.

PERIGEAN SPRING TIDES. July 1. Spring tides, the highest possible tides, occur when New Moon or Full Moon falls within 24 hours of the moment the Moon is nearest Earth (perigee) in its monthly orbit July 1, at 6 PM, EDT. Spring refers not to the season but to the German word *springen*, "to rise up."

RWANDESE REPUBLIC: INDEPENDENCE DAY. July 1. National holiday. Commemorates independence from Belgium in 1962.

SOLAR ECLIPSE. July 1. Partial eclipse of the sun. Eclipse begins at 2:07 PM, EDT, reaches greatest eclipse at 3:32 PM and ends at 4:57 PM. Visible in central southern Pacific Ocean, southern part of Chile and Argentina.

SPACE MILESTONE: *KOSMOS 1383* (USSR). July 1, 1982. First search and rescue satellite—equipped to hear distress calls from aircraft and ships—launched in cooperative project with the US and France.

UNITED NATIONS: INTERNATIONAL DAY OF COOPERATIVES. July 1. On Dec 16, 1992, the General Assembly proclaimed this observance for the first Saturday of July 1995 (Res 47/60). On Dec 23, 1994, recognizing that cooperatives are becoming an indispensable factor of economic and social development, the Assembly invited governments, international organizations, specialized agencies and national and international cooperative organizations to observe this day annually (Res 49/155). For info: United Nations, Dept of Public Info, New York, NY 10017.

BIRTHDAYS TODAY

Carl Lewis, 39, Olympic gold medal sprinter and long jumper, born Birmingham, AL, July 1, 1961.

Emily Arnold McCully, 61, author and illustrator (Caldecott for *Mirette on the High Wire*), born Galesburg, IL, July 1, 1939.

JULY 2 — SUNDAY

Day 184 — 182 Remaining

CIVIL RIGHTS ACT OF 1964: ANNIVERSARY. July 2, 1964. President Lyndon Johnson signed the Voting Rights Act of 1964 into law, prohibiting discrimination on the basis of race in public accommodations, in publicly owned or operated facilities, in employment and union membership and in the registration of voters. The bill included Title VI, which allowed for the cutoff of federal funding in areas where discrimination persisted.

CONSTITUTION OF THE US TAKES EFFECT: ANNIVERSARY. July 2, 1788. Cyrus Griffin of Virginia, the president of the Congress, announced that the Constitution had been ratified by the required nine states (the ninth being New Hampshire June 21, 1788), and a committee was appointed to make preparations for the change of government.

July 2000

S	M	T	W	T	F	S
						1
2	3	4	5	6	7	8
9	10	11	12	13	14	15
16	17	18	19	20	21	22
23	24	25	26	27	28	29
30	31					

DECLARATION OF INDEPENDENCE RESOLUTION: ANNIVERSARY. July 2, 1776. Anniversary of adoption by the Continental Congress, Philadelphia, PA, of a resolution introduced June 7, 1776, by Richard Henry Lee of Virginia: "Resolved, That these United Colonies are, and of right ought to be, free and independent States, that they are absolved from all allegiance to the British Crown, and that all political connection between them and the State of Great Britain is, and ought to be, totally dissolved. That it is expedient forthwith to take the most effectual measures for forming foreign Alliances. That a plan of confederation be prepared and transmitted to the respective Colonies for their consideration and approbation." This resolution prepared the way for adoption, July 4, 1776, of the Declaration of Independence. See also: "Declaration of Independence: Anniversary" (July 4).

MARSHALL, THURGOOD: BIRTH ANNIVERSARY. July 2, 1908. Thurgood Marshall, the first African American on the US Supreme Court, was born at Baltimore, MD. For more than 20 years, he served as director-counsel of the NAACP Legal Defense and Educational Fund. He experienced his greatest legal victory May 17, 1954, when the Supreme Court decision on *Brown v Board of Education* declared an end to the "separate but equal" system of racial segregation in public schools in 21 states. Marshall argued 32 cases before the Supreme Court, winning 29 of them, before becoming a member of the high court himself. Nominated by President Lyndon Johnson, he began his 24-year career on the high court Oct 2, 1967, becoming a voice of dissent in an increasingly conservative court. Marshall announced his retirement June 27, 1991, and he died Jan 24, 1993, at Washington, DC.

VESEY, DENMARK: DEATH ANNIVERSARY. July 2, 1822. Planner of what would have been the biggest slave revolt in US history, Denmark Vesey was executed at Charleston, SC. He had been born around 1767, probably in the West Indies, where he was sold at around age 14 to Joseph Vesey, captain of a slave ship. He purchased his freedom in 1800. In 1818 Vesey and others began to plot an uprising; he held secret meetings, collected disguises and firearms and chose a date in June 1822. But authorities were warned, and police and the military were out in full force. Over the next two months 130 blacks were taken into custody; 35, including Vesey, were hanged and 31 were exiled. As a result of the plot Southern legislatures passed more rigorous slave codes.

BIRTHDAYS TODAY

Jose Canseco, Jr, 36, baseball player, born Havana, Cuba, July 2, 1964.

Jack Gantos, 49, author (the Rotten Ralph series), born Mt Pleasant, PA, July 2, 1951.

Jean Craighead George, 81, author (Newbery for *Julie of the Wolves*), born Washington, DC, July 2, 1919.

Lindsay Lohan, 14, actress (*The Parent Trap*), born New York, NY, July 2, 1986.

JULY 3 — MONDAY

Day 185 — 181 Remaining

AIR CONDITIONING APPRECIATION DAYS. July 3–Aug 15. Northern Hemisphere. During Dog Days, the hottest time of the year in the Northern Hemisphere, to acknowledge the contribution of air conditioning to a better way of life. Annually, July 3–Aug 15. For info: Air-Conditioning and Refrig Institute, 4301 N Fairfax Dr, Ste 425, Arlington, VA 22203. Phone: (703) 524-8800. Fax: (703) 528-3816. E-mail: ari@ari.org. Web: www.ari.org.

BELARUS: INDEPENDENCE DAY. July 3. National holiday. A former republic of the Soviet Union, it became independent in 1991.

BENNETT, RICHARD BEDFORD: BIRTH ANNIVERSARY. July 3, 1870. Former Canadian prime minister, born at Hopewell Hill, NB. Died at Mickelham, England, June 26, 1947.

CANADA: NEWFOUNDLAND MEMORIAL DAY. July 3.

CARIBBEAN OR CARICOM DAY. July 3. The anniversary of the treaty establishing the Caribbean Community (also called the Treaty of Chaguaramas), signed by the prime ministers of Barbados, Guyana, Jamaica and Trinidad and Tobago July 4, 1973. Observed as a public holiday by the participating nations. Annually, the first Monday in July.

DOG DAYS. July 3–Aug 15. Hottest days of the year in Northern Hemisphere. Usually about 40 days, but variously reckoned at 30–54 days. Popularly believed to be an evil time "when the sea boiled, wine turned sour, dogs grew mad, and all creatures became languid, causing to man burning fevers, hysterics and phrensies" (from Brady's *Clavis Calendarium*, 1813). Originally the days when Sirius, the Dog Star, rose just before or at about the same time as sunrise (no longer true owing to precession of the equinoxes). Ancients sacrificed a brown dog at beginning of Dog Days to appease the rage of Sirius, believing that star was the cause of the hot, sultry weather.

EARTH AT APHELION. July 3. At approximately 8 PM, EDT, planet Earth will reach aphelion, that point in its orbit when it is farthest from the sun (about 94,510,000 miles). The Earth's mean distance from the sun (mean radius of its orbit) is reached early in the months of April and October. Note that Earth is farthest from the sun during Northern Hemisphere summer. See also: "Earth at Perihelion" (Jan 3).

HUNTINGTON, SAMUEL: BIRTH ANNIVERSARY. July 3, 1731. President of the Continental Congress, Governor of Connecticut, signer of the Declaration of Independence, born at Windham, CT, died at Norwich, CT, Jan 5, 1796.

IDAHO: ADMISSION DAY: ANNIVERSARY. July 3. Became 43rd state in 1890.

STAY OUT OF THE SUN DAY. July 3. For health's sake, give your skin a break today. [© 1998 by WPL] For info: Tom and Ruth Roy, Wellness Permission League, PO Box 662, Mt. Gretna, PA 17064-0662. Phone: (717) 964-1308. Fax: (717) 964-1335. E-mail: well cat@desupernet.net.

VIRGIN ISLANDS: DANISH WEST INDIES EMANCIPATION DAY: ANNIVERSARY. July 3, 1848. Commemorates freeing of slaves in the Danish West Indies. Ceremony at Frederiksted, St. Croix, where actual proclamation was first read by Governor-General Peter Von Scholten.

BIRTHDAYS TODAY

Tom Cruise, 38, actor (*Rain Man, Born on the Fourth of July*), born Syracuse, NY, July 3, 1962.

Teemu Selanne, 30, hockey player, born Helsinki, Finland, July 3, 1970.

JULY 4 — TUESDAY

Day 186 — 180 Remaining

AMERICA THE BEAUTIFUL PUBLISHED: ANNIVERSARY. July 4, 1895. The poem "America the Beautiful" by Katherine Lee Bates, a Wellesley College professor, was first published in the *Congregationalist*, a church publication. Later it was set to music. For more info: *Purple Mountain Majesties: The Story of Katherine Lee Bates and "America the Beautiful"*, by Barbara Younger (Dutton, 0-525-45653-8, $15.99 Gr. 3-5). In *America the Beautiful* 16 landscape paintings by Neil Waldman help bring the lyrics alive for children (0-689-31861-8, Atheneum, $16 All ages).

COOLIDGE, CALVIN: BIRTH ANNIVERSARY. July 4, 1872. The 30th president of the US was born John Calvin Coolidge at Plymouth, VT. He succeeded to the presidency Aug 3, 1923, following the death of Warren G. Harding. Coolidge was elected president once, in 1924, but did "not choose to run for president in 1928." Nicknamed Silent Cal, he is reported to have said, "If you don't say anything, you won't be called on to repeat it." Coolidge died at Northampton, MA, Jan 5, 1933.

DECLARATION OF INDEPENDENCE APPROVAL AND SIGNING: ANNIVERSARY. July 4, 1776. The Declaration of Independence was approved by the Continental Congress: "Signed by Order and in Behalf of the Congress, John Hancock, President, Attest, Charles Thomson, Secretary." The official signing occurred Aug 2, 1776. The manuscript journals of the Congress for that date state: "The declaration of independence being engrossed and compared at the table was signed by the members."

FOSTER, STEPHEN: BIRTH ANNIVERSARY. July 4, 1826. Stephen Collins Foster, one of America's most famous and best-loved songwriters, was born at Lawrenceville, PA. Among his nearly 200 songs: "Oh! Susanna," "Camptown Races," "Old Folks at Home" ("Swanee River"), "Jeanie with the Light Brown Hair," "Old Black Joe" and "Beautiful Dreamer." Foster died in poverty at Bellevue Hospital at New York, NY, Jan 13, 1864. The anniversary of his death has been observed as Stephen Foster Memorial Day by Presidential Proclamation since 1952.

INDEPENDENCE DAY (FOURTH OF JULY): ANNIVERSARY. July 4, 1776. The US commemorates adoption of the Declaration of Independence by the Continental Congress. The nation's birthday. Legal holiday in all states and territories. For links to websites about the Fourth of July, go to: deil.lang.uiuc .edu/web.pages/holidays/fourth.html.

PHILIPPINES: FIL-AMERICAN FRIENDSHIP DAY. July 4. Formerly National Independence Day, when the Philippines were a colony of the US, now celebrated as Fil-American Friendship Day.

SPACE MILESTONE: *MARS PATHFINDER* (US). July 4, 1997. Unmanned spacecraft landed on Mars after a seven-month flight.

Carried *Sojourner*, a roving robotic explorer that sent back photographs of the landscape. One of its missions was to find if life ever existed on Mars. See also: "Space Milestone: *Mars Global Surveyor*" (Sept 11).

SPACE MILESTONE: *NOZOMI* (JAPAN). July 4, 1998. Japan launched this mission to Mars, making it the third country (after the US and Russia) to try an interplanetary space mission. *Nozomi*, which means "Hope," will orbit 84 miles above Mars and beam images back to Earth.

ZAMBIA: UNITY DAY. July 4. Memorial day for Zambians who died in the struggle for independence. Political rallies stressing solidarity throughout country. Annually, the first Tuesday in July.

BIRTHDAYS TODAY

Harvey Grant, 35, basketball player, born Augusta, GA, July 4, 1965.
Horace Grant, 35, basketball player, born Augusta, GA, July 4, 1965.

JULY 5 — WEDNESDAY
Day 187 — 179 Remaining

ALGERIA: INDEPENDENCE DAY. July 5. National holiday. Commemorates the day in 1962 when Algeria gained independence from France, after more than 100 years as a colony.

BARNUM, PHINEAS TAYLOR: BIRTH ANNIVERSARY. July 5, 1810. Promoter of the bizarre and unusual. Barnum's American Museum opened in 1842, promoting unusual acts including the Feejee Mermaid, Chang and Eng (the original Siamese Twins) and General Tom Thumb. In 1850 he began his promotion of Jenny Lind, "The Swedish Nightingale," and parlayed her singing talents into a major financial success. Barnum also cultivated a keen interest in politics. As a founder of the newspaper *Herald of Freedom*, his outspoken editorials resulted not only in lawsuits but also in at least one jail sentence. In 1852 he declined the Democratic nomination for governor of Connecticut but did serve two terms in the Connecticut legislature beginning in 1865. He was defeated in a bid for US Congress in 1866 but served as mayor of Bridgeport, CT, from 1875 to 1876. In 1871 "The Greatest Show on Earth" opened at Brooklyn, NY; Barnum merged with his rival J.A. Bailey in 1881 to form the Barnum and Bailey Circus. P.T. Barnum was born at Bethel, CT, and died at Bridgeport, CT, Apr 7, 1891.

CAPE VERDE: NATIONAL DAY. July 5. Commemorates independence from Portugal in 1975.

SLOVAKIA: SAINT CYRIL AND METHODIUS DAY. July 5. This day is dedicated to the Greek priests and scholars from Thessalonniki, who were invited by Prince Rastislav of Great Moravia to introduce Christianity and the first Slavic alphabet to the pagan people of the kingdom in AD 863.

VENEZUELA: INDEPENDENCE DAY. July 5. National holiday. Commemorates Proclamation of Independence from Spain in 1811. Independence achieved in 1821.

ZAMBIA: HEROES DAY. July 5. First Monday in July is Zambian national holiday—memorial day for Zambians who died in the struggle for independence. Political rallies stress solidarity.

July 2000	S	M	T	W	T	F	S
							1
	2	3	4	5	6	7	8
	9	10	11	12	13	14	15
	16	17	18	19	20	21	22
	23	24	25	26	27	28	29
	30	31					

BIRTHDAYS TODAY

Meredith Ann Pierce, 42, fantasy author (*The Darkangel*), born Seattle, WA, July 5, 1958.

JULY 6 — THURSDAY
Day 188 — 178 Remaining

AMERICAN LIBRARY ASSOCIATION ANNUAL CONFERENCE. July 6–13. Chicago, IL. Est attendance: 20,000. For info: Public Information Office, American Library Assn, 50 E Huron St, Chicago, IL 60611. Phone: (312) 280-5044. Fax: (312) 944-8520. E-mail: pro@ala.org. Web: www.ala.org.

COMOROS: INDEPENDENCE DAY: 25th ANNIVERSARY. July 6. Federal and Islamic Republic of Comoros commemorates Declaration of Independence from France in 1975.

CZECH REPUBLIC: COMMEMORATION DAY OF BURNING OF JOHN HUS. July 6. In honor of Bohemian religious reformer John Hus, who was condemned as a heretic and burned at the stake in 1415.

FIRST SUCCESSFUL ANTIRABIES INOCULATION: ANNIVERSARY. July 6, 1885. Louis Pasteur gave the first successful antirabies inoculation to a boy who had been bitten by an infected dog.

LUXEMBOURG: ETTELBRUCK REMEMBRANCE DAY. July 6. In honor of US General George Patton, Jr, liberator of the Grand-Duchy of Luxembourg in 1945, who is buried at the American Military Cemetery at Hamm, Germany, among 5,100 soldiers of his famous Third Army.

MAJOR LEAGUE BASEBALL HOLDS FIRST ALL-STAR GAME: ANNIVERSARY. July 6, 1933. The first midsummer All-Star Game was held at Comiskey Park, Chicago, IL. Babe Ruth led the American League with a home run, as they defeated the National League 4–2. Prior to the summer of 1933, All-Star contests consisted of pre- and postseason exhibitions that often found teams made up of a few stars playing beside journeymen and even minor leaguers.

MALAWI: REPUBLIC DAY. July 6. National holiday. Commemorates independence of the former Nyasaland from Britain in 1964 and Malawi's becoming a republic in 1966.

MICHIGAN STORYTELLERS FESTIVAL. July 6–8. Flint, MI. Storytelling performances, workshops and swaps come together for family fun and professional support at this 20th annual event. Annually, the weekend after July 4th. Est attendance: 1,500. For info: Cynthia Stilley, Flint Public Library, 1026 E Kearsley, Flint, MI 48502. Phone: (810) 232-7111. Fax: (810) 232-8360. E-mail: cstilley@flint.lib.mi.us.

BIRTHDAYS TODAY

George W. Bush, 54, Governor of Texas (R), born Midland, TX, July 6, 1946.

Tamera Mowry, 22, actress ("Sister, Sister"), born West Germany, July 6, 1978.

Tia Mowry, 22, actress ("Sister, Sister"), born West Germany, July 6, 1978.

Nancy Davis Reagan, 79, former First Lady, wife of Ronald Reagan, 40th president of the US, born New York, NY, July 6, 1921.

JULY 7 — FRIDAY

Day 189 — 177 Remaining

BONZA BOTTLER DAY™. July 7. To celebrate when the number of the day is the same as the number of the month. Bonza Bottler Day™ is an excuse to have a party at least once a month. For info: Gail M. Berger, 109 Matthew Ave, Poca, WV 25159. Phone: (304) 776-7746. E-mail: gberger5@aol.com.

FATHER-DAUGHTER TAKE A WALK TOGETHER DAY. July 7. A special time in the summer for fathers and daughters of all ages to spend time together in the beautiful weather. Annually, July 7. For info: Janet Dellaria, 202 N Bennett St, Geneva, IL 60134. Phone: (630) 232-0425.

HAWAII ANNEXED BY US: ANNIVERSARY. July 7, 1898. President William McKinley signed a resolution annexing Hawaii. No change in government took place until 1900, when Congress passed an act making Hawaii an "incorporated" territory of the US. This act remained in effect until Hawaii became a state in 1959.

JAPAN: TANABATA (STAR FESTIVAL). July 7. As an offering to the stars, children set up bamboo branches to which colorful strips of paper bearing poems are tied.

PAIGE, LEROY ROBERT (SATCHEL): BIRTH ANNIVERSARY. July 7, 1906. Baseball Hall of Fame pitcher born at Mobile, AL. Paige was the greatest attraction in the Negro Leagues and was also, at age 42, the first black pitcher in the American League. Inducted into the Hall of Fame in 1971. Died at Kansas City, MO, June 8, 1982.

SOLOMON ISLANDS: INDEPENDENCE DAY. July 7. National holiday. Commemorates independence from Britain in 1978.

TANZANIA: SABA SABA DAY. July 7. Tanzania's mainland ruling party, TANU, was formed in 1954.

BIRTHDAYS TODAY

Michelle Kwan, 20, figure skater, born Torrance, CA, July 7, 1980.

Joe Sakic, 31, hockey player, born Burnaby, British Columbia, Canada, July 7, 1969.

JULY 8 — SATURDAY

Day 190 — 176 Remaining

DECLARATION OF INDEPENDENCE FIRST PUBLIC READING: ANNIVERSARY. July 8, 1776. Colonel John Nixon read the Declaration of Independence to the assembled residents at Philadelphia's Independence Square.

MOON PHASE: FIRST QUARTER. July 8. Moon enters First Quarter phase at 8:53 AM, EDT.

ROCKEFELLER, NELSON ALDRICH: BIRTH ANNIVERSARY. July 8, 1908. Forty-first vice-president of the US (1974–77), born at Bar Harbor, ME. Rockefeller was nominated for vice-president by President Ford when Ford assumed the presidency after the resignation of Richard Nixon. Rockefeller was the second person to have become vice-president without being elected (Gerald Ford was the first). Rockefeller died Jan 26, 1979, at New York, NY.

BIRTHDAYS TODAY

Raffi Cavoukian, 52, children's singer and songwriter, born Cairo, Egypt, July 8, 1948.

James Cross Giblin, 67, author (*Chimney Sweep*), born Cleveland, OH, July 8, 1933.

Phil Gramm, 58, US Senator (R, Texas), born Fort Benning, GA, July 8, 1942.

JULY 9 — SUNDAY

Day 191 — 175 Remaining

ARGENTINA: INDEPENDENCE DAY. July 9. Anniversary of establishment of independent republic, with the declaration of independence from Spain in 1816.

FOURTEENTH AMENDMENT TO US CONSTITUTION RATIFIED: ANNIVERSARY. July 9, 1868. The 14th Amendment defined US citizenship and provided that no State shall have the right to abridge the rights of any citizen without due process and equal protection under the law. Coming three years after the Civil War, the 14th Amendment also included provisions for barring individuals who assisted in any rebellion or insurrection against the US from holding public office and releasing federal and state governments from any financial liability incurred in the assistance of rebellion or insurrection against the US.

BIRTHDAYS TODAY

Nancy Farmer, 59, author (*A Girl Named Disaster, The Ear, the Eye and the Arm*), born Phoenix, AZ, July 9, 1941.

Tom Hanks, 44, actor (*Big, Sleepless in Seattle*; Oscars for *Philadelphia, Forrest Gump*), born Concord, CA, July 9, 1956.

Fred Savage, 24, actor ("The Wonder Years," *The Princess Bride*), born Highland Park, IL, July 9, 1976.

JULY 10 — MONDAY

Day 192 — 174 Remaining

ASHE, ARTHUR: BIRTH ANNIVERSARY. July 10, 1943. Born at Richmond, VA, Arthur Ashe became a legend for his list of firsts as a black tennis player. He was chosen for the US Davis Cup team in 1963 and became captain in 1980. He won the US men's singles championship and US Open in 1968 and in 1975 the men's singles at Wimbledon. Ashe won a total of 33 career titles. In 1985 he was inducted into the International Tennis Hall of Fame. A social activist, Ashe worked to eliminate racism and stereotyping. He helped create inner-city tennis programs for youth and wrote the three-volume *A Hard Road to Glory: A History of the African-American Athlete*. Aware that *USA Today* intended to publish an article revealing that he was infected with the AIDS virus, Ashe announced Apr 8, 1992, that he probably contracted HIV through a transfusion during bypass surgery in 1983. He began a $5 million fundraising effort on behalf of the Arthur Ashe Foundation for the Defeat of AIDS and during his last year campaigned for public awareness of the AIDS epidemic. He died at New York, NY, Feb 6, 1993.

BAHAMAS: INDEPENDENCE DAY. July 10. Public holiday. At 12:01 AM in 1973, the Bahamas gained their independence after 250 years as a British Crown Colony.

BORIS YELTSIN INAUGURATED AS RUSSIAN PRESIDENT: ANNIVERSARY. July 10, 1991. Boris Yeltsin took the oath of office as the first popularly elected president in Russia's 1,000-year history. He defeated the Communist Party candidate resoundingly, establishing himself as a powerful political counterpoint to Mikhail Gorbachev, the president of the Soviet Union, of which Russia was the largest republic. Yeltsin had been dismissed from the Politburo in 1987 and resigned from the Communist Party in 1989. His popularity forced Gorbachev to make concessions to the republics in the new union treaty forming the Confederation of Independent States.

CLERIHEW DAY. July 10. A day recognized in remembrance of Edmund Clerihew Bentley, journalist and author of the celebrated detective thriller *Trent's Last Case* (1912), but perhaps best known for his invention of a popular humorous verse form, the clerihew, consisting of two rhymed couplets of unequal length:/Edmund's middle name was Clerihew/A name possessed by very few,/But verses by Mr Bentley/Succeeded eminently./ Bentley was born at London, July 10, 1875, and died there, Mar 30, 1956.

DALLAS, GEORGE MIFFLIN: BIRTH ANNIVERSARY. July 10, 1792. Eleventh vice president of the US (1845–49), born at Philadelphia, PA. Died there, Dec 31, 1864.

DON'T STEP ON A BEE DAY. July 10. Nine-year-old Michael Roy of the Wellness Permission League reminds kids and grown-ups that now is the time of year when going barefoot can mean getting stung by a bee. If you get stung tell Mom. [© 1998 by WPL] For info: Michael Roy, Wellness Permission League, PO Box 662, Mt Gretna, PA 17064-0662. Phone: (717) 964-1308. Fax: (717) 964-1335. E-mail: wellcat@desupernet.net.

O'HARA, MARY: BIRTH ANNIVERSARY. July 10, 1885. Born at Cape May, NJ, Mary O'Hara Alsop wrote the children's horse tale *My Friend Flicka*. She died at Chevy Chase, MD, Oct 15, 1980.

SPACE MILESTONE: *TELSTAR* (US). July 10, 1962. First privately owned satellite (American Telephone and Telegraph Company) and first satellite to relay live TV pictures across the Atlantic was launched.

US LIFTS SANCTIONS AGAINST SOUTH AFRICA: ANNIVERSARY. July 10, 1991. President George Bush lifted US trade and investment sanctions against South Africa. The sanctions had been imposed through the Comprehensive Anti-Apartheid Act of 1986, which Congress had passed to punish South Africa for policies of racial separation.

WYOMING: ADMISSION DAY: ANNIVERSARY. July 10. Became 44th state in 1890.

BIRTHDAYS TODAY

Candice F. Ransom, 48, author (*The Big Green Pocketbook*), born Washington, DC, July 10, 1952.

JULY 11 — TUESDAY

Day 193 — 173 Remaining

ADAMS, JOHN QUINCY: BIRTH ANNIVERSARY. July 11, 1767. Sixth president of the US and the son of the second president, John Quincy Adams was born at Braintree, MA. After his single term as president, he served 17 years as a member of Congress from Plymouth, MA. He died Feb 23, 1848, at the House of Representatives (in the same room in which he had taken the presidential Oath of Office Mar 4, 1825). John Quincy Adams was the only president whose father had also been president of the US.

	S	M	T	W	T	F	S
July							1
2000	2	3	4	5	6	7	8
	9	10	11	12	13	14	15
	16	17	18	19	20	21	22
	23	24	25	26	27	28	29
	30	31					

JULY 11
E.B. WHITE'S BIRTHDAY

Charlotte's Web is one of the best loved of all children's books. But E.B. White has other books to his credit that are also children's favorites. Celebrate his birthday by introducing students to *Stuart Little* and *The Trumpet of the Swan*.

Although *Charlotte's Web* is often used as a wonderful read aloud in primary classrooms, we seldom use it with older students. However, a revisit with *Charlotte's Web* at the upper middle school or junior high level is one way to familiarize students with the elements of literature. *Charlotte's Web* has easily identifiable foreshadowing, character types and development, irony, setting and a linear plot that make a literature group discussion of these elements interesting and fun. Students love seeing the story in a new, adult light. Teachers may also want to introduce older students to his classic book on writing, Strunk and White's *The Elements of Style* (3rd edition, Allyn & Bacon, 0-0241-8190-0, $11.95 Gr. 6 & up). For 40 years, this slender volume has been helping Americans become better writers.

Extend Charlotte into the science curriculum with a unit on spiders. Books and articles about spiders will help your students overcome their fears and learn to appreciate the spider's role in the ecosystem. The same can be done with Stuart Little and Wilbur using units on mice and pigs.

Stuart Little, like *Charlotte's Web*, explores the theme of friendship. Students will appreciate these novels by drawing comparisons between Stuart and Wilbur, who lend themselves well to character development study.

Children who want to read other books with animal protagonists can look for the Miss Spider books by David Kirk (PreS–2), Beverly Cleary's Ralph Mouse novels (Gr. 2–5), *The School Mouse*, by Dick King-Smith (Little, Brown, 0-786-81156-0, $4.40 Gr. 2–5), and Cynthia Rylant's Poppleton Pig series (Gr. K–2).

DAY OF THE FIVE BILLION: ANNIVERSARY. July 11, 1987. An eight-pound baby boy, Matej Gaspar, born at 1:35 AM, EST, at Zagreb, Yugoslavia, was proclaimed the five billionth inhabitant of Earth. The United Nations Fund for Population Activities, hoping to draw attention to population growth, proclaimed July 11 as "Day of the Five Billion," noting that 150 babies are born each minute. The US Census Bureau has estimated that the world's population will reach 6.2 billion by the year 2000.

MONGOLIA: NAADAM NATIONAL HOLIDAY. July 11. Public holiday. Commemorates overthrow of the feudal monarch in 1921.

SMITH, JAMES: DEATH ANNIVERSARY. July 11, 1806. Signer of the Declaration of Independence, born at Ireland about 1719 (exact date unknown). Died at York, PA.

SPACE MILESTONE: *SKYLAB* (US): FALLS TO EARTH. July 11, 1979. The 82-ton spacecraft launched May 14, 1973, re-entered Earth's atmosphere. Expectation was that 20–25 tons probably would survive to hit Earth, including one piece of about 5,000 pounds. This generated intense international public interest in where it would fall. The chance that some person would be hit by a piece of *Skylab* was calculated at one in 152. Targets were drawn and *Skylab* parties were held but *Skylab* broke up and fell to Earth in a shower of pieces over the Indian Ocean and Australia, with no known casualties.

UNITED NATIONS: WORLD POPULATION DAY. July 11. In June 1989, the Governing Council of the United Nations Development Programme recommended that July 11 be observed by the international community as World Population Day. An outgrowth of the Day of Five Billion (July 11, 1987), the Day seeks to focus public attention on the urgency and importance of population issues, particularly in the context of overall development plans and programs and the need to create solutions to these problems. For info: United Nations, Dept of Public Info, Public Inquiries Unit, RM GA-57, New York, NY 10017. Phone: (212) 963-4475. Fax: (212) 963-0071. E-mail: inquiries@un.org.

WHITE, E.B.: BIRTH ANNIVERSARY. July 11, 1899. Author of books for adults and children (*Charlotte's Web, Trumpet of the Swan*) and *New Yorker* editor. Born at Mount Vernon, NY, White died at North Brooklyn, ME, Oct 1, 1985. See Curriculum Connection.

WORLD CONGRESS ON READING. July 11–14. Auckland, New Zealand. The International Reading Association stages a world congress every two years at various locales around the globe. This is the 18th congress. For info: Conferences Division, Intl Reading Assn, 800 Barksdale Rd, PO Box 8139, Newark, DE 19714-8139. Phone: (302) 731-1600. E-mail: conferences@reading.org. Web: www.reading.org.

BIRTHDAYS TODAY

Helen Cresswell, 66, author (*The Night Watchmen*), born Nottinghamshire, England, July 11, 1934.
Mike Foster, 70, Governor of Louisiana (R), born Shreveport, LA, July 11, 1930.
Jane Gardam, 72, author (*A Long Way from Verona*), born Coatham, England, July 11, 1928.
Patricia Polacco, 56, author (*Chicken Sunday, Pink and Say*), born Lansing, MI, July 11, 1944.
James Stevenson, 71, author and illustrator (*I Meant to Tell You*), born New York, NY, July 11, 1929.

JULY 12 — WEDNESDAY
Day 194 — 172 Remaining

ETCH-A-SKETCH INTRODUCED: 40th ANNIVERSARY. July 12, 1960. In 1958 a French garage mechanic named Arthur Granjean developed a drawing toy he called The Magic Screen. In 1959 he exhibited his toy at a toy fair at Nuremberg, West Germany where it was seen by a representative of the Ohio Art Company, a toy company at Bryan, OH. The rights were purchased and the product was renamed and released in 1960. More than 100 million have been sold.

KIRIBATI: INDEPENDENCE DAY. July 12. Republic of Kiribati attained independence from Britain in 1979. Formerly known as the Gilbert Islands.

NORTHERN IRELAND: ORANGEMEN'S DAY. July 12. National holiday commemorates Battle of Boyne, July 1 (Old Style), 1690, in which the forces of King William III of England, Prince of Orange, defeated those of James II, at Boyne River in Ireland. Ordinarily observed July 12. If July 12 is a Saturday or a Sunday the holiday observance is on the following Monday.

SAO TOME AND PRINCIPE: NATIONAL DAY: 25th ANNIVERSARY. July 12. National holiday observed. Commemorates independence from Portugal in 1975.

SPYRI, JOHANNA: BIRTH ANNIVERSARY. July 12, 1827. Children's author, born at Hirzel, Switzerland. Her book *Heidi* is the story of an orphan girl who goes to live with her grandfather in the mountains. *Heidi* was made into a movie in 1920. Spyri wrote several other books, including *Heidi Grows Up* and *Heidi's Children*. She died at Zurich, Switzerland, July 7, 1901.

THOREAU, HENRY DAVID: BIRTH ANNIVERSARY. July 12, 1817. American author and philosopher, born at Concord, MA. Died there May 6, 1862. In *Walden* he wrote, "I frequently tramped eight or ten miles through the deepest snow to keep an appointment with a beechtree, or a yellow birch, or an old acquaintance among the pines." For further info: *Into the Deep Forest with Henry David Thoreau*, by Jim Murphy (Clarion, 0-395-60522-9, $14.95 Gr. 5–8).

BIRTHDAYS TODAY

Bill Cosby, 62, comedian, actor (Emmys for "I Spy," "The Cosby Show"), born Philadelphia, PA, July 12, 1938.
Kristi Tsuya Yamaguchi, 29, Olympic gold medal figure skater, born Hayward, CA, July 12, 1971.

JULY 13 — THURSDAY
Day 195 — 171 Remaining

JAPAN: BON FESTIVAL (FEAST OF LANTERNS). July 13–15. Religious rites throughout Japan in memory of the dead, who, according to Buddhist belief, revisit Earth during this period. Lanterns are lighted for the souls. Spectacular bonfires in the shape of the character *dai* are burned on hillsides on the last day of the Bon or O-Bon Festival, bidding farewell to the spirits of the dead.

NORTHWEST ORDINANCE: ANNIVERSARY. July 13, 1787. The Northwest Ordinance, providing for government of the territory north of the Ohio River, became law. The ordinance guaranteed freedom of worship and the right to trial by jury, and it prohibited slavery.

WORLD CUP INAUGURATED: 70th ANNIVERSARY. July 13, 1930. The first World Cup soccer competition was held at Montevideo, Uruguay, with 14 countries participating. The host country had the winning team. The next World Cup competition will be in Japan and Korea in 2002.

BIRTHDAYS TODAY

Marcia Brown, 82, illustrator and author (Caldecott for *Shadow, Once a Mouse, Cinderella*), born Rochester, NY, July 13, 1918.
Ashley Bryan, 77, author and illustrator (*Lion and the Ostrich: And Other African Folk Tales*), born Bronx, NY, July 13, 1923.
Harrison Ford, 58, actor (*American Graffiti, Star Wars* and *Indiana Jones* films), born Chicago, IL, July 13, 1942.
Patrick Stewart, 60, actor ("Star Trek: The Next Generation," *Excalibur, LA Story*), born Mirfield, England, July 13, 1940.

JULY 14 — FRIDAY

Day 196 — 170 Remaining

CHILDREN'S PARTY AT GREEN ANIMALS. July 14. Green Animals Topiary Gardens, Portsmouth, RI. Annual party for children and adults at Green Animals, a delightful topiary garden and children's toy museum. Party includes pony rides, merry-go-round, games, clowns, refreshments, hot dogs, hamburgers and more. Annually, July 14. Est attendance: 200. For info: The Preservation Soc of Newport County, 424 Bellevue Ave, Newport, RI 02840. Phone: (401) 847-1000. Fax: (401) 847-1361. Web: www.NewportMansions.org.

FRANCE: BASTILLE DAY OR FETE NATIONAL. July 14. Public holiday commemorating the fall of the Bastille at the beginning of the French Revolution in 1789. Also celebrated or observed in many other countries. For further info: www.premier-ministre.gouv.fr/GB/HIST/FETNAT.HTM.

GARFIELD, LEON: BIRTH ANNIVERSARY. July 14, 1921. Author of children's books (*Smith*), born at Brighton, England. Died at London, England, June 2, 1996.

SINGER, ISAAC BASHEVIS: BIRTH ANNIVERSARY. July 14, 1904. Author who wrote in Yiddish and won the Nobel Prize for literature in 1978. His books for children include *The Fearsome Inn* and *When Shlemiel Went to Warsaw and Other Stories*. Born at Radzymin, Poland, I.B. Singer died at Surfside, FL, July 24, 1991.

BIRTHDAYS TODAY

Gerald Rudolph Ford, 87, 38th US President (1974-77), born Leslie King, Omaha, NE, July 14, 1913.
Laura Numeroff, 47, author (*If You Give a Mouse a Cookie*), born Brooklyn, NY, July 14, 1953.
Peggy Parish, 73, author (the Amelia Bedelia series), born Manning, SC, July 14, 1927.

JULY 15 — SATURDAY

Day 197 — 169 Remaining

BATTLE OF THE MARNE: ANNIVERSARY. July 15, 1918. General Erich Ludendorff launched Germany's fifth, and last, offensive to break through the Chateau-Thierry salient during WWI. This all-out effort involved three armies branching out from Rheims to cross the Marne River. The Germans were successful in crossing the Marne near Chateau-Thierry before American, British and Italian divisions stopped their progress. On July 18 General Foch, Commander-in-Chief of the Allied troops, launched a massive counteroffensive that resulted in a German retreat that continued for four months until they sued for peace in November.

HIGHLIGHTS FOUNDATION WRITERS WORKSHOP AT CHAUTAUQUA. July 15–22. Chautauqua, NY. A seven-day immersion in study, peer exchange and individual professional guidance for those interested in writing for children. Est attendance: 125. For info: Kent Brown, Exec Dir, Highlights Fdtn, Inc, 814 Court St, Honesdale, PA 18431. Phone: (717) 253-1192. Fax: (717) 253-0179.

July 2000

S	M	T	W	T	F	S
						1
2	3	4	5	6	7	8
9	10	11	12	13	14	15
16	17	18	19	20	21	22
23	24	25	26	27	28	29
30	31					

MAXWELL, GAVIN: BIRTH ANNIVERSARY. July 15, 1914. Born at Elrig, Scotland. Children's author and illustrator, known for *Ring of Bright Water* and *The Rocks Remain*. Maxwell died at Inverness, Scotland, Sept 6, 1969.

MOORE, CLEMENT CLARKE: BIRTH ANNIVERSARY. July 15, 1779. American author and teacher, best remembered for his popular verse, "A Visit from Saint Nicholas" ("'Twas the Night Before Christmas"), which was first published anonymously and without Moore's knowledge in a newspaper, Dec 23, 1823. Moore was born at New York, NY, and died at Newport, RI, July 10, 1863.

REMBRANDT: BIRTH ANNIVERSARY. July 15, 1606. Dutch painter and etcher, born at Leiden, Holland. Known for *The Night Watch* and many portraits and self-portraits, he died at Amsterdam, Holland, Oct 4, 1669.

SAINT FRANCES XAVIER CABRINI: 150th BIRTH ANNIVERSARY. July 15, 1850. First American saint, founder of schools, orphanages, convents and hospitals, born at Lombardy, Italy. Died of malaria at Chicago, IL, Dec 22, 1917. Canonized July 7, 1946.

SAINT SWITHIN'S DAY. July 15. Swithun (Swithin), Bishop of Winchester (AD 852–862), died July 2, 862. Little is known of his life, but his relics were transferred into Winchester Cathedral July 15, 971, a day on which there was a heavy rainfall. According to old English belief, it will rain for 40 days thereafter when it rains on this day. "St. Swithin's Day, if thou dost rain, for 40 days it will remain; St. Swithin's Day, if thou be fair, for 40 days, –will rain nea mair."

BIRTHDAYS TODAY

Marcia Thornton Jones, 42, author, with Debbie Dadey (the Bailey School Kids series), born Joliet, IL, July 15, 1958.
Jesse Ventura, 49, Governor of Minnesota (I), born Minneapolis, MN, July 15, 1951.
George V. Voinovich, 64, US Senator (R, Ohio), born Cleveland, OH, July 15, 1936.

JULY 16 — SUNDAY

Day 198 — 168 Remaining

AMUNDSEN, ROALD: BIRTH ANNIVERSARY. July 16, 1872. Norwegian explorer born near Oslo, Roald Amundsen was the first man to sail from the Atlantic to the Pacific Ocean via the Northwest Passage (1903–05). He discovered the South Pole (Dec 14, 1911) and flew over the North Pole in a dirigible in 1926. He flew, with five companions, from Norway, June 18, 1928, in a daring effort to rescue survivors of an Italian Arctic expedition. No trace of the rescue party or the airplane was ever located. See also: "South Pole: Discovery Anniversary" (Dec 14). See Curriculum Connection.

ATOMIC BOMB TESTED: 55th ANNIVERSARY. July 16, 1945. In the New Mexican desert at Alamogordo Air Base, 125

JULY 16
ROALD AMUNDSEN'S BIRTHDAY

Cool off during warm summer days by spending some time with Roald Amundsen (born in 1872) and other Antarctic explorers. Amundsen, a Norwegian explorer, turned his sights South when he found out that the North Pole had been reached by Robert Peary. At about the same time, Robert Scott put together a British Antarctic expedition. Students could compare and contrast the routes and transportation methods of the two groups. (Scott's ill-fated mission relied on ponies rather than sled dogs.) How do present day expeditions differ from early Antarctic explorations? How have new equipment and technology like satellite positioning changed the life of the explorer?

It was big news when Amundsen's expedition reached the South Pole on Dec 14, 1911. Have your students write and publish an Antarctic newspaper reporting the momentous occasion. Columns might include a cooking section (what they ate), weather reports, transportation (the latest in sleds), a column featuring the Amundsen/Scott race Letters to the Editor and feature articles.

Amundsen also made history in 1926 when he flew in an airship over the North Pole. He and his crew vanished while on an Arctic rescue mission in 1928. Students interested in researching what may have happened to them can explore other famous disappearances, like Amelia Earhart's.

There are many ways to expand the Antarctic exploration theme. A creative writing focus is *Black Whiteness*, by Robert Burleigh (Atheneum, 0-689-81299-X, $16 Gr. 4 & up), a lyrical journal-like account of Richard Byrd's six-month period alone in the Antarctic. *Shipwreck at the Bottom of the World*, by Jennifer Armstrong (Crown, 0-517-80013-6, $18 Gr. 5 & up), is a don't-miss, riveting survival story about Ernest Shackleton's expedition to cross Antarctica in 1914. This intense story will stimulate a number of classroom discussions and raise some interesting moral issues.

An additional exploration theme might be modern-day explorers and the places they go. The ocean floor and space are two examples.

miles southeast of Albuquerque, the experimental atomic bomb was set off at 5:30 AM. Dubbed "Fat Boy" by its creator, the plutonium bomb vaporized the steel scaffolding holding it as the immense fireball rose 8,000 ft in a fraction of a second—ultimately creating a mushroom cloud to a height of 41,000 ft. At ground zero the bomb emitted heat three times the temperature of the interior of the sun. All plant and animal life for a mile around ceased to exist. When informed by President Truman at Potsdam of the successful experiment, Winston Churchill responded, "It's the Second Coming in wrath!"

★ **CAPTIVE NATIONS WEEK.** July 16–22. Presidential proclamation issued each year since 1959 for the third week of July. (PL86–90 of July 17, 1959.)

COMET CRASHES INTO JUPITER: ANNIVERSARY. July 16, 1994. The first fragment of the comet Shoemaker-Levy crashed into the planet Jupiter, beginning a series of spectacular collisions, each unleashing more energy than the combined effect of an explosion of all our world's nuclear arsenal. Video imagery from earthbound telescopes as well as the Hubble telescope provided vivid records of the explosions and their aftereffects. In 1993 the comet had shattered into a series of about a dozen large chunks that resembled "pearls on a string" after its orbit brought it within the gravitational effects of our solar system's largest planet.

DISTRICT OF COLUMBIA: ESTABLISHING LEGISLATION ANNIVERSARY. July 16, 1790. George Washington signed legislation that selected the District of Columbia as the permanent capital of the US. Boundaries of the district were established in 1792. Plans called for the government to remain housed at Philadelphia, PA, until 1800, when the new national capital would be ready for occupancy.

LUNAR ECLIPSE. July 16. Total eclipse of the Moon. Moon enters penumbra 6:46 AM, EDT, middle of eclipse 9:55 AM, Moon leaves penumbra 1:04 PM. The beginning of the umbral phase is visible in the western US, Hawaii, the southern half of Alaska, the west coast of Canada, most of Mexico, extreme southern South America, Australia, New Zealand, the east coast of Asia, Antartica, the Pacific Ocean and the southeastern Indian Ocean; the end visible in Asia except the extreme western portion and the north coast, Australia, New Zealand, Hawaii, the extreme western Aleutian Islands, the east coast of Africa, Antartica, the Indian Ocean and the western Pacific Ocean.

MOON PHASE: FULL MOON. July 16. Moon enters Full Moon phase at 9:55 AM, EDT.

NATIONAL FARRIER'S WEEK. July 16–22. A salute from horse owners to the men and women who keep their horses shod and equine feet and legs in top-notch condition. Annually, the third week in July. For info: Frank Lessiter, American Farriers Journal, PO Box 624, Brookfield, WI 53008-0624. Phone: (414) 782-4480. Fax: (414) 782-1252. E-mail: Lesspub@aol.com.

SPACE MILESTONE: *APOLLO 11* (US): MAN SENT TO THE MOON: ANNIVERSARY. July 16, 1969. This launch resulted in man's first moon landing, the first landing on any extraterrestrial body. See also: "Space Milestone: Moon Day" (July 20).

SPACE WEEK. July 16–22. The calendar week containing July 20 has been observed in a number of communities and states as Space Week, commemorating the July 20, 1969, landing on the moon by two US astronauts, Neil Alden Armstrong and Edwin Eugene Aldrin, Jr. See also: "Space Milestone: Moon Day" (July 20).

WELLS, IDA B.: BIRTH ANNIVERSARY. July 16, 1862. African American journalist and anti-lynching crusader Ida B. Wells was born the daughter of slaves at Holly Springs, MS and grew up as Jim Crow and lynching were becoming prevalent. Wells argued that lynchings occurred not to defend white women but because of whites' fear of economic competition from blacks. She traveled extensively, founding anti-lynching societies and black women's clubs. Wells's *Red Record* (1895) was one of the first accounts of lynchings in the South. She died Mar 25, 1931, at Chicago, IL.

BIRTHDAYS TODAY

Arnold Adoff, 65, poet (*Black Is Brown Is Tan*), born Bronx, NY, July 16, 1935.

Richard H. Bryan, 63, US Senator (D, Nevada), born Washington, DC, July 16, 1937.

Alexis Herman, 53, Secretary of Labor (Clinton administration), born Mobile, AL, July 16, 1947.

Barry Sanders, 32, football player, born Wichita, KS, July 16, 1968.

Eve Titus, 78, author (the Franklin series), born New York, NY, July 16, 1922.

JULY 17 — MONDAY
Day 199 — 167 Remaining

DISNEYLAND OPENED: 45th ANNIVERSARY. July 17, 1955. Disneyland, America's first theme park, opened at Anaheim, CA.

GERRY, ELBRIDGE: BIRTH ANNIVERSARY. July 17, 1744. Fifth vice president of the US (1813–14), born at Marblehead, MA. Died at Washington, DC, Nov 23, 1814. His name became part of the language (gerrymander) after he signed a redistricting bill while governor of Massachusetts in 1812.

IRAQ: NATIONAL DAY. July 17. National holiday commemorating the 1968 revolution.

KOREA: CONSTITUTION DAY. July 17. Legal national holiday. Commemorates the proclamation of the constitution of the republic of Korea in 1948. Ceremonies at Seoul's capitol plaza and all major cities.

PUERTO RICO: MUÑOZ-RIVERA DAY. July 17. Public holiday on the anniversary of the birth of Luis Muñoz-Rivera. The Puerto Rican patriot, poet and journalist was born at Barranquitas, Puerto Rico in 1859. He died at Santurce, a suburb of San Juan, Puerto Rico, Nov 15, 1916.

SPACE MILESTONE: *APOLLO-SOYUZ* LINKUP (US, USSR): 25th ANNIVERSARY. July 17, 1975. After three years of planning, negotiation and preparation, the first US–USSR joint space project reached fruition with the linkup in space of *Apollo 18* (crew: T. Stafford, V. Brand, D. Slayton; landed in Pacific Ocean July 24, during 136th orbit) and *Soyuz 19* (crew: A.A. Leonov, V.N. Kubasov; landed July 21, after 96 orbits). *Apollo 18* and *Soyuz 19* were linked for 47 hours (July 17–19) while joint experiments and transfer of personnel and materials back and forth between craft took place. Launch date was July 15, 1975.

SPACE MILESTONE: *SOYUZ T-12* (USSR). July 17, 1984. Cosmonaut Svetlana Savitskaya became the first woman to walk in space (July 25) and the first woman to make more than one space voyage. With cosmonauts V. Dzhanibekov and I. Volk. Docked at *Salyut 7* July 18 and returned to Earth July 29.

BIRTHDAYS TODAY

Karla Kuskin, 68, author and illustrator (*The Philharmonic Gets Dressed, City Dog*), born New York, NY, July 17, 1932.

JULY 18 — TUESDAY
Day 200 — 166 Remaining

PRESIDENTIAL SUCCESSION ACT: ANNIVERSARY. July 18, 1947. President Harry S Truman signed an Executive Order determining the line of succession should the president be temporarily incapacitated or die in office. The speaker of the house and president pro tem of the senate are next in succession after the vice president. This line of succession became the 25th Amendment to the Constitution, which was ratified Feb 10, 1967.

RUTLEDGE, JOHN: 200th DEATH ANNIVERSARY. July 18, 1800. American statesman, associate justice on the Supreme Court, born at Charleston, SC, in September 1739. Nominated second Chief Justice of the Supreme Court to succeed John Jay and

	S	M	T	W	T	F	S
July							1
2000	2	3	4	5	6	7	8
	9	10	11	12	13	14	15
	16	17	18	19	20	21	22
	23	24	25	26	27	28	29
	30	31					

---

served as Acting Chief Justice until his confirmation was denied because of his opposition to the Jay Treaty. He died at Charleston, SC.

BIRTHDAYS TODAY

John Glenn, 79, astronaut, first American to orbit Earth, former US Senator (D, Ohio), born Cambridge, OH, July 18, 1921.
Anfernee "Penny" Hardaway, 28, basketball player, born Memphis, TN, July 18, 1972.
Nelson Mandela, 82, President of South Africa, born Transkei, South Africa, July 18, 1918.
Jerry Stanley, 59, author of nonfiction (*Children of the Dust Bowl*), born Highland Park, MI, July 18, 1941.

JULY 19 — WEDNESDAY
Day 201 — 165 Remaining

DEGAS, EDGAR: BIRTH ANNIVERSARY. July 19, 1834. French Impressionist painter, especially noted for his paintings of ballet dancers and horse races, was born at Paris, France. He died at Paris, Sept 26, 1917.

NEWBERY, JOHN: BIRTH ANNIVERSARY. July 19, 1713. The first bookseller and publisher to make a specialty of children's books. Born at Waltham St. Lawrence, England, he died Dec 22, 1767, at London, England. The American Library Association awards the Newbery Medal annually for the most distinguished contribution to American literature for children.

NICARAGUA: NATIONAL LIBERATION DAY. July 19. Following the National Day of Joy (July 17—anniversary of date in 1979 when dictator Anastasio Somoza Debayle fled Nicaragua) is annual July 19 observance of National Liberation Day, anniversary of day the National Liberation Army claimed victory over the Somoza dictatorship.

WOMEN'S RIGHTS CONVENTION AT SENECA FALLS: ANNIVERSARY. July 19, 1848. A convention concerning the rights of women, called by Lucretia Mott and Elizabeth Cady Stanton, was held at Seneca Falls, NY, July 19–20, 1848. The issues discussed included voting, property rights and divorce. The convention drafted a "Declaration of Sentiments" that paraphrased the Declaration of Independence, addressing man instead of King George, and called for women's "immediate admission to all the rights and privileges which belong to them as citizens of the United States." This convention was the beginning of an organized women's rights movement in the US. The most controversial issue was Stanton's demand for women's right to vote.

BIRTHDAYS TODAY

Teresa Edwards, 36, basketball player, born Cairo, GA, July 19, 1964.
Chris Kratt, 31, biologist, co-host with his brother Martin of "Kratts' Creatures," born Summit, NJ, July 19, 1969.

JULY 20 — THURSDAY
Day 202 — 164 Remaining

COLOMBIA: INDEPENDENCE DAY. July 20. National holiday. Commemorates the beginning of the independence movement with an uprising against Spanish officials in 1810 at Bogota. Colombia gained independence from Spain in 1819 when Simon Bolivar decisively defeated the Spanish.

DELAWARE STATE FAIR. July 20–29. Harrington, DE. Fireworks, country, gospel and pop talent, rodeos, demolition derby, amusement rides and harness racing. Plenty of food and entertainment.

Est attendance: 216,000. For info: Delaware State Fair, PO Box 28, Harrington, DE 19952. Phone: (302) 398-3269. Fax: (302) 398-5030. Web: www.delawarestatefair.com.

FAST OF TAMMUZ. July 20. Jewish holiday. Hebrew calendar date: Tammuz 17, 5760. Shiva Asar B'Tammuz begins at first light of day and commemorates the first-century Roman siege that breached the walls of Jerusalem. Begins a three-week time of mourning.

FIRST SPECIAL OLYMPICS: ANNIVERSARY. July 20, 1968. One thousand mentally retarded athletes from the US and Canada competed in the first Special Olympics at Soldier Field, Chicago, IL. Today more than one million athletes from 146 countries compete in local, national and international games.

PROVENSEN, MARTIN: BIRTH ANNIVERSARY. July 20, 1916. Author and illustrator, with his wife Alice (Caldecott for *The Glorious Flight: Across the Channel with Louis Bleriot*), born at Chicago, IL. Died Mar 27, 1987, at New York, NY.

SPACE MILESTONE: MOON DAY: ANNIVERSARY. July 20, 1969. Anniversary of man's first landing on moon. Two US astronauts (Neil Alden Armstrong and Edwin Eugene Aldrin, Jr) landed lunar module *Eagle* at 4:17 PM, EDT and remained on lunar surface 21 hours, 36 minutes and 16 seconds. The landing was made from the *Apollo XI*'s orbiting command and service module, code named *Columbia*, whose pilot, Michael Collins, remained aboard. Armstrong was first to set foot on the moon. Armstrong and Aldrin were outside the spacecraft, walking on the moon's surface, approximately 2¼ hours. The astronauts returned to Earth July 24, bringing photograph and rock samples.

BIRTHDAYS TODAY

Larry E. Craig, 55, US Senator (R, Idaho), born Council, ID, July 20, 1945.

Peter Forsberg, 27, hockey player, born Ornskoldvik, Sweden, July 20, 1973.

Charles Johnson, Jr, 29, baseball player, born Ft Pierce, FL, July 20, 1971.

Barbara Ann Mikulski, 64, US Senator (D, Maryland), born Baltimore, MD, July 20, 1936.

JULY 21 — FRIDAY
Day 203 — 163 Remaining

BELGIUM: NATIONAL HOLIDAY. July 21. Marks accession of first Belgian king, Leopold I, in 1831 after independence from the Netherlands

CLEVELAND, FRANCES FOLSOM: BIRTH ANNIVERSARY. July 21, 1864. Wife of Grover Cleveland, 22nd and 24th president of the US, born at Buffalo, NY. She was the youngest First Lady at age 22, and the first to marry a president in the White House. Died at Princeton, NJ, Oct 29, 1947.

GUAM: LIBERATION DAY. July 21. US forces returned to Guam in 1944.

NORTH DAKOTA STATE FAIR. July 21–29. Minot, ND. For nine days the State Fair features the best in big-name entertainment, farm and home exhibits, displays, the Midway and NPRA rodeo. Est attendance: 250,000. For info: North Dakota State Fair, Box 1796, Minot, ND 58702. Phone: (701) 857-7620. Fax: (701) 857-7622. E-mail: ndsf@minot.com.

BIRTHDAYS TODAY

Hatty Jones, 12, actress (*Madeline*), born London, England, July 21, 1988.

Janet Reno, 62, US Attorney General (Clinton administration), born Miami, FL, July 21, 1938.

Paul D. Wellstone, 56, US Senator (D, Minnesota), born Washington, DC, July 21, 1944.

Robin Williams, 48, actor (*Flubber, Mrs Doubtfire*), born Chicago, IL, July 21, 1952.

JULY 22 — SATURDAY
Day 204 — 162 Remaining

BIANCO, MARGERY WILLIAMS: BIRTH ANNIVERSARY. July 22, 1881. Author of children's books (*The Velveteen Rabbit*, written under the name Margery Williams). Born at London, England, she died at New York, NY, Sept 4, 1944.

PIED PIPER OF HAMELIN: ANNIVERSARY—MAYBE. July 22, 1376. According to legend, the German town of Hamelin, plagued with rats, bargained with a piper who promised to, and did, pipe the rats out of town and into the Weser River. Refused payment for his work, the piper then piped the children out of town and into a hole in a hill, never to be seen again. More recent historians suggest that the event occurred in 1284 when young men of Hamelin left the city on colonizing adventures.

SPOONER'S DAY (*WILLIAM SPOONER BIRTH ANNIVERSARY*). July 22. A day named for the Reverend William Archibald Spooner (born at London, England, July 22, 1844), whose frequent slips of the tongue led to coinage of the term *spoonerism* to describe them. A day to remember the scholarly man whose accidental transpositions gave us blushing crow (for crushing blow), tons of soil (for sons of toil), queer old dean (for dear old queen), swell foop (for fell swoop) and half-warmed fish (for half-formed wish). Warden of New College, Oxford, 1903–24, Spooner died at Oxford, England, Aug 29, 1930.

BIRTHDAYS TODAY

Tim Brown, 34, football player, born Dallas, TX, July 22, 1966.

Kay Bailey Hutchison, 57, US Senator (R, Texas), born Galveston, TX, July 22, 1943.

William V. Roth, 79, US Senator (R, Delaware), born Great Falls, MT, July 22, 1921.

JULY 23 — SUNDAY
Day 205 — 161 Remaining

EGYPT, ARAB REPUBLIC OF: ANNIVERSARY NATIONAL DAY. July 23, 1952. Anniversary of the Revolution in 1952, which was launched by army officers and changed Egypt from a monarchy to a republic.

FIRST US SWIMMING SCHOOL: OPENING ANNIVERSARY. July 23, 1827. The first swimming school in the US opened at Boston, MA. Its pupils included John Quincy Adams and James Audubon.

LEO, THE LION. July 23–Aug 22. In the astronomical/astrological zodiac, which divides the sun's apparent orbit into 12 segments, the period July 23–Aug 22 is identified, traditionally, as the sun sign of Leo, the Lion. The ruling planet is the sun.

SPACE MILESTONE: *SOYUZ 37* (USSR): 20th ANNIVERSARY. July 23, 1980. Cosmonauts Viktor Gorbatko and, the first non-Caucasian in space, Lieutenant Colonel Pham Tuan (Vietnam), docked at *Salyut 6* July 24. Returned to Earth July 31.

BIRTHDAYS TODAY

Anthony M. Kennedy, 64, Supreme Court Justice, born Sacramento, CA, July 23, 1936.
Gary Payton, 32, basketball player, born Oakland, CA, July 23, 1968.

JULY 24 — MONDAY
Day 206 — 160 Remaining

BOLIVAR, SIMON: BIRTH ANNIVERSARY. July 24, 1783. "The Liberator," born at Caracas, Venezuela. Commemorated in Venezuela and other Latin American countries. Died Dec 17, 1830, at Santa Marta, Colombia. Bolivia is named after him.

MOON PHASE: LAST QUARTER. July 24. Moon enters Last Quarter phase at 7:02 AM, EDT.

PIONEER DAY: ANNIVERSARY. July 24. Utah. Commemorates the first settlement in the Salt Lake Valley in 1847 by Brigham Young.

VIRGIN ISLANDS: HURRICANE SUPPLICATION DAY. July 24. Legal holiday. Population attends churches to pray for protection from hurricanes. Annually, the fourth Monday in July.

BIRTHDAYS TODAY

Barry Bonds, 36, baseball player, born Riverside, CA, July 24, 1964.
Karl Malone, 37, basketball player, born Summerfield, LA, July 24, 1963.
Albert Marrin, 64, author of military history (*Commander in Chief Abraham Lincoln and the Civil War*), born New York, NY, July 24, 1936.
Anna Paquin, 18, actress (*Fly Away Home*), born Wellington, New Zealand, July 24, 1982.
Marc Racicot, 52, Governor of Montana (R), born Thompson Falls, MT, July 24, 1948.
Mara Wilson, 13, actress (*Mrs Doubtfire, Matilda*), born Burbank, CA, July 24, 1987.

JULY 25 — TUESDAY
Day 207 — 159 Remaining

HARRISON, ANNA SYMMES: 225th BIRTH ANNIVERSARY. July 25, 1775. Wife of William Henry Harrison, ninth president of the US, born at Morristown, NJ. Died at North Bend, IN, Feb 25, 1864.

PUERTO RICO: CONSTITUTION DAY ANNIVERSARY. July 25. Also called Commonwealth Day or Occupation Day. Commemorates proclamation of constitution in 1952.

July 2000	S	M	T	W	T	F	S
							1
	2	3	4	5	6	7	8
	9	10	11	12	13	14	15
	16	17	18	19	20	21	22
	23	24	25	26	27	28	29
	30	31					

TEST-TUBE BABY: BIRTHDAY. July 25, 1978. Anniversary of the birth of Louise Brown at Oldham, England. First documented birth of a baby conceived outside the body of a woman. Parents: Gilbert John and Lesley Brown, of Bristol, England. Physicians: Patrick Christopher Steptoe and Robert Geoffrey Edwards.

BIRTHDAYS TODAY

Clyde Watson, 53, author (*Applebet: An ABC*), born New York, NY, July 25, 1947.

JULY 26 — WEDNESDAY
Day 208 — 158 Remaining

AMERICANS WITH DISABILITIES ACT SIGNED: 10th ANNIVERSARY. July 26, 1990. President Bush signed the Americans with Disabilities Act, which went into effect two years later. It required that public facilities be made accessible to the disabled.

CATLIN, GEORGE: BIRTH ANNIVERSARY. July 26, 1796. American artist known for his paintings of Native American life, born at Wilkes-Barre, PA. He toured the West, painting more than 500 portraits. He died Dec 23, 1872, at Jersey City, NJ. See Curriculum Connection.

CHINCOTEAGUE PONY PENNING. July 26–27. Chincoteague Island, VA. To round up the 150 wild ponies living on Assateague Island and swim them across the inlet to Chincoteague, where about 50–60 of them are sold. Annually, the last Wednesday and Thursday of July. Marguerite Henry's *Misty of Chincoteague* is a fictional account of this event. Est attendance: 50,000. For info: Jacklyn Russell, Chamber of Commerce, Box 258, Chincoteague, VA 23336. Phone: (757) 336-6161. Fax: (757) 336-1242. E-mail: pony@shore.intercom.net. Web: www.intercom.net/local/chincoteague.

CLINTON, GEORGE: BIRTH ANNIVERSARY. July 26, 1739. Fourth vice president of the US (1805–12), born at Little Britain, NY. Died at Washington, DC, Apr 20, 1812.

CUBA: NATIONAL HOLIDAY: ANNIVERSARY OF REVOLUTION. July 26. Anniversary of 1953 beginning of Fidel Castro's revolutionary "26th of July Movement."

CURACAO: CURACAO DAY. July 26. "Although not officially recognized by the government as a holiday, various social entities commemorate the fact that on this day Alonso de Ojeda, a companion of Christopher Columbus, discovered the Island of Curaçao in 1499, sailing into Santa Ana Bay, the entrance of the harbor of Willemstad."

LIBERIA: INDEPENDENCE DAY. July 26. National holiday. Became republic in 1847, under aegis of the US societies for repatriating former slaves in Africa.

MALDIVES: INDEPENDENCE DAY: 35th ANNIVERSARY. July 26. National holiday. Commemorates the independence of this group of 200 islands in the Indian Ocean from Britain in 1965.

NEW YORK RATIFIES CONSTITUTION: ANNIVERSARY. July 26. Eleventh state to ratify Constitution in 1788.

US ARMY FIRST DESEGREGATION: ANNIVERSARY. July 26, 1944. During WWII the US Army ordered desegregation of its training camp facilities. Later the same year black platoons were assigned to white companies in a tentative step toward integration of the battlefield. However, it was not until after the War—July 26, 1948—that President Harry Truman signed an order officially integrating the armed forces.

JULY 26
GEORGE CATLIN'S BIRTHDAY

Born in 1796, Catlin's first career was in law but his expertise as a portrait painter led to a career change in 1823. After meeting a group of Indians visiting Washington, DC, Catlin decided to focus his painting on Native Americans and their culture. During the years 1830–1836, Catlin spent his summers touring the West, where he painted close to 500 portraits of Indians from many different tribes. These paintings hang in many famous museums.

Incorporate Catlin's work into units on Indian life and the effects of westward expansion. Adult art books about Catlin contain reproductions of his paintings. For young readers, you can find *George Catlin: Painter of the Indian West*, by Mark Sufrin (Simon & Schuster, Gr. 5–9). Although out of print, many libraries own a copy. Ask students to notice how different clothing, hair styles and home construction are shown in Catlin's paintings. What similarities, if any, do they share?

Compare Catlin's portraits with early photographs. For example, about 70 years after Catlin did his paintings, Edward S. Curtis set out to photograph Native Americans. For 30 years, he traveled through the Western US and Canada and took more than 2,000 photos. Laurie Lawlor's *Shadow Catcher: The Life and Work of Edward S. Curtis*, (Walker, 0-8027-8288-4, $19.95 Gr. 6 & up) contains many examples of Curtis's photographs. Russell Freedman's *Indian Chiefs* (Holiday House, 0-8234-0971-6, $9.95 Gr. 4 & up) is another source of photographs. What changes can students find—clothing is one starting point—as a result of contact with white settlers? Be aware that photographers sometimes staged their pictures, dressing Indians in clothing they no longer wore in order to appeal to people in the East and in Europe. Some Americans have romanticized Indians. How realistically do you think these paintings and photographs reflect Indian life of their day? The National Museum of American Art at the Smithsonian Institution offers a free teaching guide, "The West As America," for grades 5–12. It discusses how artists created a Western mythology by drawing a less-than-objective history of the westward movement. Write the Office of Educational Programs at the Museum at MRC 210, Washington, DC 20560 or go to its website at www.nmaa.si.edu.

Also compare Catlin's work with that of Charles Marion Russell and Frederic Remington, two other famous frontier artists.

BIRTHDAYS TODAY

Jan Berenstain, 77, author and illustrator, with her husband Stan (the Berenstain Bears series), born Philadelphia, PA, July 26, 1923.

JULY 27 — THURSDAY
Day 209 — 157 Remaining

BARBOSA, JOSÉ CELSO: BIRTH ANNIVERSARY. July 27, 1857. Puerto Rican physician and patriot, born at Bayamon, PR. His birthday is a holiday at Puerto Rico. He died at San Juan, PR, Sept 21, 1921.

INSULIN FIRST ISOLATED: ANNIVERSARY. July 27, 1921. Dr. Frederick Banting and his assistant at the University of Toronto Medical School, Charles Best, gave insulin to a dog whose pancreas had been removed. In 1922 insulin was first administered to a diabetic, a 14-year-old boy.

KOREAN WAR ARMISTICE: ANNIVERSARY. July 27, 1953. Armistice agreement ending war that had lasted three years and 32 days was signed at Panmunjom, Korea (July 26, US time), by US and North Korean delegates. Both sides claimed victory at conclusion of two years, 17 days of truce negotiations.

US DEPARTMENT OF STATE FOUNDED: ANNIVERSARY. July 27, 1789. The first presidential cabinet department, called the Department of Foreign Affairs, was established by the Congress. Later the name was changed to Department of State.

BIRTHDAYS TODAY

Paul Janeczko, 55, poet (*Home on the Range: Cowboy Poetry*), born Passaic, NJ, July 27, 1945.
Alex Rodriguez, 25, baseball player, born New York, NY, July 27, 1975.

JULY 28 — FRIDAY
Day 210 — 156 Remaining

FOR ALL WHO LOVE STORIES CONFERENCE. July 28. Columbus State Community College, Columbus, OH. Sponsored by the Creative Arts Institute, Columbus State Community College and the Ohio Arts Council. Annually, the last Friday in July. Est attendance: 200. For info: Donna Foster, Creative Arts, 8021 Kennedy Rd, Blacklick, OH 43004. Phone: (614) 759-9407. Fax: (614) 759-8480. E-mail: dfoster@freenet.columbus.oh.us.

HEYWARD, THOMAS: BIRTH ANNIVERSARY. July 28, 1746. American Revolutionary soldier, signer of the Declaration of Independence. Died Mar 6, 1809.

IOWA STORYTELLING FESTIVAL. July 28–29. City Park, Clear Lake, IA. This annual storytelling event is held in a scenic lakeside setting. Friday evening "Stories After Dark." Two performances Saturday plus story exchange for novice tellers. Annually, the last Friday and Saturday in July. Est attendance: 800. For info: Jean Casey, Dir, Clear Lake Public Library, 200 N 4th St, Clear Lake, IA 50428. Phone: (515) 357-6133. Fax: (515) 357-4645.

ONASSIS, JACQUELINE LEE BOUVIER KENNEDY: BIRTH ANNIVERSARY. July 28, 1929. Editor, widow of John Fitzgerald Kennedy (35th president of the US), born at Southampton, NY. Later married (Oct 20, 1968) Greek shipping magnate Aristotle Socrates Onassis, who died Mar 15, 1975. The widely admired and respected former First Lady died May 19, 1994, at New York City.

PERU: INDEPENDENCE DAY. July 28. San Martin declared independence in 1821. After the final defeat of Spanish troops by Simon Bolivar in 1824, Spanish rule ended.

POTTER, (HELEN) BEATRIX: BIRTH ANNIVERSARY. July 28, 1866. Author and illustrator of the Peter Rabbit stories for children, born at London, England. Died at Sawrey, Lancashire, Dec 22, 1943. For further info: *Beatrix Potter*, by Alexandra Wallner (Holiday House, 0-8234-1181-8, $15.95 Gr. K-2).

WORLD WAR I BEGINS: ANNIVERSARY. July 28, 1914. Archduke Francis Ferdinand of Austria-Hungary and his wife were assassinated at Sarajevo, Bosnia, by a Serbian nationalist June 28, 1914, touching off the conflict that became WWI. Austria-Hungary declared war on Serbia July 28, the formal beginning of the war. Within weeks, Germany entered the war on the side of Austria-Hungary and Russia, France and Great Britain on the side of Serbia.

BIRTHDAYS TODAY

Natalie Babbitt, 68, author (*Tuck Everlasting*), born Dayton, OH, July 28, 1932.

Jim Davis, 55, creator of "Garfield," born Marion, IN, July 28, 1945.

JULY 29 — SATURDAY

Day 211 — 155 Remaining

ALLEGANY COUNTY INVITATIONAL DRUM AND BUGLE CORPS CHAMPIONSHIPS. July 29. Cumberland, MD. Eastern Regional Senior Drum and Bugle Corps Championship featuring 10 drum and bugle corps competing for top honors. Annually, the last Saturday in July. Est attendance: 7,000. For info: Drumfest, PO Box 3571, LaVale, MD 21504. Phone: (301) 777-8325.

MONTANA STATE FAIR. July 29–Aug 6. Great Falls, MT. Horse racing, petting zoo, carnival, discount days, nightly entertainment and plenty of food. Est attendance: 200,000. For info: Kelly Michel, State Fair, Box 1888, Great Falls, MT 59403. Phone: (406) 727-8900. Fax: (406) 452-8955.

ROOSEVELT, ALICE HATHAWAY LEE: BIRTH ANNIVERSARY. July 29, 1861. First wife of Theodore Roosevelt, 26th President of the US, whom she married in 1880. Born at Chestnut Hill, MA, she died at New York, NY, Feb 14, 1884.

SPACE MILESTONE: NASA ESTABLISHED. July 29, 1958. President Eisenhower signed a bill creating the National Aeronautics and Space Administration to direct US space policy.

BIRTHDAYS TODAY

Debbie Black, 34, basketball player, born Philadelphia, PA, July 29, 1966.

Sharon Creech, 55, author (Newbery for *Walk Two Moons*), born Cleveland, OH, July 29, 1945.

Elizabeth Hanford Dole, 64, former president, American Red Cross, former secretary of transportation and secretary of labor, born Salisbury, NC, July 29, 1936.

Peter Jennings, 62, journalist (anchorman for "ABC Evening News"), born Toronto, Ontario, Canada, July 29, 1938.

Kathleen Krull, 48, author of nonfiction (*Wilma Unlimited: How Wilma Rudolph Became the World's Fastest Woman*), born Ft Leonard Wood, MO, July 29, 1952.

JULY 30 — SUNDAY

Day 212 — 154 Remaining

MOON PHASE: NEW MOON. July 30. Moon enters New Moon phase at 10:25 PM, EDT.

PAPERBACK BOOKS INTRODUCED: 65th ANNIVERSARY. July 30, 1935. Although books bound in soft covers were first introduced in 1841 at Leipzig, Germany, by Christian Bernhard Tauchnitz, the modern paperback revolution dates to the publication of the first Penguin paperback by Sir Allen Lane at London in 1935. Penguin Number 1 was *Ariel*, a life of Shelley by Andre Maurois.

PERIGEAN SPRING TIDES. July 30. Spring tides, the highest possible tides, occur when New Moon or Full Moon falls within 24 hours of the moment the Moon is nearest Earth (perigee) in its monthly orbit at 4 AM, EDT.

SOLAR ECLIPSE. July 30. Partial eclipse of the sun. Eclipse begins at 8:37 PM, EDT, reaches greatest eclipse at 10:13 PM and ends at 11:48 PM. Visible in west Russia, northern parts of Scandinavia and Greenland, north Russia, Arctic Ocean, north-west North America.

VANUATU: INDEPENDENCE DAY: 20th ANNIVERSARY. July 30. Vanuatu became an independent republic in 1980, breaking ties with France and the UK, and observes its national holiday.

BIRTHDAYS TODAY

Irene Ng, 26, actress ("Mystery Files of Shelby Woo"), born Malaysia, July 30, 1974.

Arnold Schwarzenegger, 53, bodybuilder, actor (*The Terminator, Twins, True Lies*), born Graz, Austria, July 30, 1947.

JULY 31 — MONDAY

Day 213 — 153 Remaining

US PATENT OFFICE OPENS: ANNIVERSARY. July 31, 1790. The first US Patent Office opened its doors and the first US patent was issued to Samuel Hopkins of Vermont for a new method of making pearlash and potash. The patent was signed by George Washington and Thomas Jefferson.

BIRTHDAYS TODAY

Dean Cain, 34, actor ("Lois & Clark"), born Mt Clemens, MI, July 31, 1966.

Lynn Reid Banks, 71, author (*The Indian in the Cupboard*), born London, England, July 31, 1929.

☆ *The Teacher's Calendar, 1999–2000* ☆

CALENDAR INFORMATION FOR THE YEAR 1999
Time shown is Eastern Standard Time. All dates are given in terms of the Gregorian calendar.
(Based in part on information prepared by the Nautical Almanac Office, US Naval Observatory.)

ERAS	YEAR	BEGINS
Jewish*	5760	Sept 10
Chinese (Year of the Hare)	4697	Feb 16
Japanese (Heisei)	11	Jan 1
Indian (Saka)	1921	Mar 22
Islamic (Hegira)**	1420	Apr 17

*Year begins at sunset.   **Year begins at moon crescent.

RELIGIOUS CALENDARS—1999

Christian Holy Days
Epiphany .... Jan 6
Shrove Tuesday .... Feb 16
Ash Wednesday .... Feb 17
Lent.. Feb 17–Apr 3
Palm Sunday.. Mar 28
Good Friday .... Apr 2
Easter Day.. Apr 4
Ascension Day .... May 13
Whit Sunday (Pentecost) .... May 23
Trinity Sunday .... May 30
First Sunday in Advent .... Nov 28
Christmas Day (Saturday)............................. Dec 25

Eastern Orthodox Church Observances
Great Lent begins .... Feb 22
Pascha (Easter) .... Apr 11
Ascension... May 20
Pentecost .... May 30

Jewish Holy Days
Purim .... Mar 2
Passover (1st day) .... Apr 1
Shavuot.. May 21
Tisha B'av .... July 22
Rosh Hashanah (New Year) .... Sept 11–12
Yom Kippur .... Sept 20
Succoth .... Sept 25–Oct 3
Chanukah .... Dec 4–11

Islamic Holy Days
Eid-Al-Fitr (1419) .... Jan 19
Islamic New Year (1420) .... Apr 17
First Day of Ramadan (1420) .... Dec 9

CIVIL CALENDAR—USA—1999
New Year's Day.. Jan 1
Martin Luther King's Birthday (obsvd) .... Jan 18
Lincoln's Birthday .... Feb 12
Washington's Birthday (obsvd)/Presidents' Day .... Feb 15
Memorial Day (obsvd)................................ May 31
Independence Day...................................... July 4
Labor Day.. Sept 6
Columbus Day (obsvd) .... Oct 11
General Election Day .... Nov 2
Veterans Day .... Nov 11
Thanksgiving Day .... Nov 25

Other Days Widely Observed in US—1999
Groundhog Day (Candlemas) .... Feb 2
St. Valentine's Day.................................... Feb 14
St. Patrick's Day .... Mar 17
Mother's Day .... May 9
Flag Day .... June 14
Father's Day .... June 20
National Grandparents Day............................ Sept 12
Hallowe'en .... Oct 31

CIVIL CALENDAR—CANADA—1999
Victoria Day.. May 24
Canada Day... July 1
Labor Day.. Sept 6
Thanksgiving Day .... Oct 11
Remembrance Day .... Nov 11
Boxing Day .... Dec 27

CIVIL CALENDAR—MEXICO—1999
New Year's Day.. Jan 1
Constitution Day .... Feb 5
Benito Juarez Birthday .... Mar 21
Labor Day.. May 1
Battle of Puebla Day (Cinco de Mayo) .... May 5
Independence Day* .... Sept 16
Dia de La Raza.. Oct 12
Mexican Revolution Day .... Nov 20
Guadalupe Day .... Dec 12

*Celebration begins Sept 15 at 11:00 P.M.

ECLIPSES—1999
Penumbral eclipse of the Moon........................ Jan 31
Annular eclipse of the Sun .... Feb 16
Partial eclipse of the Moon........................... July 28
Total eclipse of the Sun .... Aug 11

SEASONS—1999
Spring (Vernal Equinox)................. Mar 20, 8:46 PM, EST
Summer (Summer Solstice).............. June 21, 3:49 PM, EDT
Autumn (Autumnal Equinox) .... Sept 23, 7:31 AM, EDT
Winter (Winter Solstice) .... Dec 22, 2:44 AM, EST

DAYLIGHT SAVING TIME SCHEDULE—1999
Sunday, Apr 4, 2:00 AM–Sunday, Oct 31, 2:00 AM—in all time zones.

CALENDAR INFORMATION FOR THE YEAR 2000

Time shown is Eastern Standard Time. All dates are given in terms of the Gregorian calendar.
(Based in part on information prepared by the Nautical Almanac Office, US Naval Observatory.)

ERAS	YEAR	BEGINS
Jewish*	5761	Sept 29
Chinese (Year of the Dragon)	4698	Feb 5
Japanese (Heisei)	12	Jan 1
Indian (Saka)	1922	Mar 21
Islamic (Hegira)**	1421	Apr 6

*Year begins at sunset.   **Year begins at moon crescent.

RELIGIOUS CALENDARS—2000

Christian Holy Days

Epiphany .... Jan 6
Shrove Tuesday .... Mar 7
Ash Wednesday .... Mar 8
Lent .... Mar 8–Apr 22
Palm Sunday .... Apr 16
Good Friday .... Apr 21
Easter Day .... Apr 23
Ascension Day .... June 1
Whit Sunday (Pentecost) .... June 11
Trinity Sunday .... June 18
First Sunday in Advent .... Dec 3
Christmas Day (Monday) .... Dec 25

Eastern Orthodox Church Observances

Great Lent begins .... Mar 13
Pascha (Easter) .... Apr 30
Ascension .... June 8
Pentecost .... June 18

Jewish Holy Days

Purim .... Mar 21
Passover (1st day) .... Apr 20
Shavuot .... June 9
Tisha B'av .... Aug 10
Rosh Hashanah (New Year) .... Sept 30–Oct 1
Yom Kippur .... Oct 9
Succoth .... Oct 14–22
Chanukah .... Dec 22–29

Islamic Holy Days

Eid-Al-Fitr (1420) .... Jan 8
Islamic New Year (1421) .... Apr 6
First Day of Ramadan (1421) .... Nov 27
Eid-Al-Fitr (1421) .... Dec 27

CIVIL CALENDAR—USA—2000

New Year's Day .... Jan 1
Martin Luther King's Birthday (obsvd) .... Jan 17
Lincoln's Birthday .... Feb 12
Washington's Birthday (obsvd)/Presidents' Day .... Feb 21
Memorial Day (obsvd) .... May 29
Independence Day .... July 4
Labor Day .... Sept 4
Columbus Day (obsvd) .... Oct 9
General Election Day .... Nov 7
Veterans Day .... Nov 11
Thanksgiving Day .... Nov 23

Other Days Widely Observed in US—2000

Groundhog Day (Candlemas) .... Feb 2
St. Valentine's Day .... Feb 14
St. Patrick's Day .... Mar 17
Mother's Day .... May 14
Flag Day .... June 14
Father's Day .... June 18
National Grandparents Day .... Sept 10
Hallowe'en .... Oct 31

CIVIL CALENDAR—CANADA—2000

Victoria Day .... May 22
Canada Day .... July 1
Labor Day .... Sept 4
Thanksgiving Day .... Oct 9
Remembrance Day .... Nov 11
Boxing Day .... Dec 26

CIVIL CALENDAR—MEXICO—2000

New Year's Day .... Jan 1
Constitution Day .... Feb 5
Benito Juarez Birthday .... Mar 21
Labor Day .... May 1
Battle of Puebla Day (Cinco de Mayo) .... May 5
Independence Day* .... Sept 16
Dia de La Raza .... Oct 12
Mexican Revolution Day .... Nov 20
Guadalupe Day .... Dec 12

*Celebration begins Sept 15 at 11:00 P.M.

ECLIPSES—2000

Total eclipse of the Moon .... Jan 21
Partial eclipse of the Sun .... Feb 5
Partial eclipse of the Sun .... July 1
Total eclipse of the Moon .... July 16
Partial eclipse of the Sun .... July 31
Partial eclipse of the Sun .... Dec 25

SEASONS—2000

Spring (Vernal Equinox) .... Mar 20, 2:35 AM, EST
Summer (Summer Solstice) .... June 20, 9:48 PM, EDT
Autumn (Autumnal Equinox) .... Sept 22, 1:27 PM, EDT
Winter (Winter Solstice) .... Dec 21, 8:37 AM, EST

DAYLIGHT SAVING TIME SCHEDULE—2000

Sunday, Apr 2, 2:00 AM–Sunday, Oct 29, 2:00 AM—in all time zones.

Perpetual Calendar, 1753–2100

A perpetual calendar lets you find the day of the week for any date in any year. Since January 1 may fall on any of the seven days of the week, and may be a leap or non-leap year, 14 different calendars are possible. The number next to each year corresponds to one of the 14 calendars. Calendar 6 will be used in 1999; calendar 14 will be used in 2000.

Year	No.	Year	No.	Year	No.	Year	No.	Year	No.	Year	No.	Year	No.	Year	No.	Year	No.
1753	2	1792	8	1831	7	1870	7	1909	6	1948	12	1987	5	2026	5	2065	5
1754	3	1793	3	1832	8	1871	1	1910	7	1949	7	1988	13	2027	6	2066	6
1755	4	1794	4	1833	3	1872	9	1911	1	1950	1	1989	1	2028	14	2067	7
1756	12	1795	5	1834	4	1873	4	1912	9	1951	2	1990	2	2029	2	2068	8
1757	7	1796	13	1835	5	1874	5	1913	4	1952	10	1991	3	2030	3	2069	3
1758	1	1797	1	1836	13	1875	6	1914	5	1953	5	1992	11	2031	4	2070	4
1759	2	1798	2	1837	1	1876	14	1915	6	1954	6	1993	6	2032	12	2071	5
1760	10	1799	3	1838	2	1877	2	1916	14	1955	7	1994	7	2033	7	2072	13
1761	5	1800	4	1839	3	1878	3	1917	2	1956	8	1995	1	2034	1	2073	1
1762	6	1801	5	1840	11	1879	4	1918	3	1957	3	1996	9	2035	2	2074	2
1763	7	1802	6	1841	6	1880	12	1919	4	1958	4	1997	4	2036	10	2075	3
1764	8	1803	7	1842	7	1881	7	1920	12	1959	5	1998	5	2037	5	2076	11
1765	3	1804	8	1843	1	1882	1	1921	7	1960	13	1999	6	2038	6	2077	6
1766	4	1805	3	1844	9	1883	2	1922	1	1961	1	2000	14	2039	7	2078	7
1767	5	1806	4	1845	4	1884	10	1923	2	1962	2	2001	2	2040	8	2079	1
1768	13	1807	5	1846	5	1885	5	1924	10	1963	3	2002	3	2041	3	2080	9
1769	1	1808	13	1847	6	1886	6	1925	5	1964	11	2003	4	2042	4	2081	4
1770	2	1809	1	1848	14	1887	7	1926	6	1965	6	2004	12	2043	5	2082	5
1771	3	1810	2	1849	2	1888	8	1927	7	1966	7	2005	7	2044	13	2083	6
1772	11	1811	3	1850	3	1889	3	1928	8	1967	1	2006	1	2045	1	2084	14
1773	6	1812	11	1851	4	1890	4	1929	3	1968	9	2007	2	2046	2	2085	2
1774	7	1813	6	1852	12	1891	5	1930	4	1969	4	2008	10	2047	3	2086	3
1775	1	1814	7	1853	7	1892	13	1931	5	1970	5	2009	5	2048	11	2087	4
1776	9	1815	1	1854	1	1893	1	1932	13	1971	6	2010	6	2049	6	2088	12
1777	4	1816	9	1855	2	1894	2	1933	1	1972	14	2011	7	2050	7	2089	7
1778	5	1817	4	1856	10	1895	3	1934	2	1973	2	2012	8	2051	1	2090	1
1779	6	1818	5	1857	5	1896	11	1935	3	1974	3	2013	3	2052	9	2091	2
1780	14	1819	6	1858	6	1897	6	1936	11	1975	4	2014	4	2053	4	2092	10
1781	2	1820	14	1859	7	1898	7	1937	6	1976	12	2015	5	2054	5	2093	5
1782	3	1821	2	1860	8	1899	1	1938	7	1977	7	2016	13	2055	6	2094	6
1783	4	1822	3	1861	3	1900	2	1939	1	1978	1	2017	1	2056	14	2095	7
1784	12	1823	4	1862	4	1901	3	1940	9	1979	2	2018	2	2057	2	2096	8
1785	7	1824	12	1863	5	1902	4	1941	4	1980	10	2019	3	2058	3	2097	3
1786	1	1825	7	1864	13	1903	5	1942	5	1981	5	2020	11	2059	4	2098	4
1787	2	1826	1	1865	1	1904	13	1943	6	1982	6	2021	6	2060	12	2099	5
1788	10	1827	2	1866	2	1905	1	1944	14	1983	7	2022	7	2061	7	2100	6
1789	5	1828	10	1867	3	1906	2	1945	2	1984	8	2023	1	2062	1		
1790	6	1829	5	1868	11	1907	3	1946	3	1985	3	2024	9	2063	2		
1791	7	1830	6	1869	6	1908	11	1947	4	1986	4	2025	4	2064	10		

Calendar 1

```
JAN                          APR                          JULY                         OCT
 S  M  T  W  T  F  S          S  M  T  W  T  F  S          S  M  T  W  T  F  S          S  M  T  W  T  F  S
 1  2  3  4  5  6  7                            1                            1          1  2  3  4  5  6  7
 8  9 10 11 12 13 14          2  3  4  5  6  7  8          2  3  4  5  6  7  8          8  9 10 11 12 13 14
15 16 17 18 19 20 21          9 10 11 12 13 14 15          9 10 11 12 13 14 15         15 16 17 18 19 20 21
22 23 24 25 26 27 28         16 17 18 19 20 21 22         16 17 18 19 20 21 22         22 23 24 25 26 27 28
29 30 31                     23 24 25 26 27 28 29         23 24 25 26 27 28 29         29 30 31
                             30                           30 31

FEB                          MAY                          AUG                          NOV
 S  M  T  W  T  F  S          S  M  T  W  T  F  S          S  M  T  W  T  F  S          S  M  T  W  T  F  S
          1  2  3  4             1  2  3  4  5  6             1  2  3  4  5                      1  2  3  4
 5  6  7  8  9 10 11          7  8  9 10 11 12 13          6  7  8  9 10 11 12          5  6  7  8  9 10 11
12 13 14 15 16 17 18         14 15 16 17 18 19 20         13 14 15 16 17 18 19         12 13 14 15 16 17 18
19 20 21 22 23 24 25         21 22 23 24 25 26 27         20 21 22 23 24 25 26         19 20 21 22 23 24 25
26 27 28                     28 29 30 31                  27 28 29 30 31               26 27 28 29 30

MAR                          JUNE                         SEPT                         DEC
 S  M  T  W  T  F  S          S  M  T  W  T  F  S          S  M  T  W  T  F  S          S  M  T  W  T  F  S
          1  2  3  4                         1  2  3                   1  2  3                      1  2
 5  6  7  8  9 10 11          4  5  6  7  8  9 10          4  5  6  7  8  9 10          3  4  5  6  7  8  9
12 13 14 15 16 17 18         11 12 13 14 15 16 17         11 12 13 14 15 16 17         10 11 12 13 14 15 16
19 20 21 22 23 24 25         18 19 20 21 22 23 24         18 19 20 21 22 23 24         17 18 19 20 21 22 23
26 27 28 29 30 31            25 26 27 28 29 30            24 25 26 27 28 29 30         24 25 26 27 28 29 30
                                                                                       31
```

Calendar 2

```
JAN                          APR                          JULY                         OCT
 S  M  T  W  T  F  S          S  M  T  W  T  F  S          S  M  T  W  T  F  S          S  M  T  W  T  F  S
    1  2  3  4  5  6          1  2  3  4  5  6  7          1  2  3  4  5  6  7             1  2  3  4  5  6
 7  8  9 10 11 12 13          8  9 10 11 12 13 14          8  9 10 11 12 13 14          7  8  9 10 11 12 13
14 15 16 17 18 19 20         15 16 17 18 19 20 21         15 16 17 18 19 20 21         14 15 16 17 18 19 20
21 22 23 24 25 26 27         22 23 24 25 26 27 28         22 23 24 25 26 27 28         21 22 23 24 25 26 27
28 29 30 31                  29 30                        29 30 31                     28 29 30 31

FEB                          MAY                          AUG                          NOV
 S  M  T  W  T  F  S          S  M  T  W  T  F  S          S  M  T  W  T  F  S          S  M  T  W  T  F  S
          1  2  3                1  2  3  4  5             1  2  3  4                         1  2  3
 4  5  6  7  8  9 10          6  7  8  9 10 11 12          5  6  7  8  9 10 11          4  5  6  7  8  9 10
11 12 13 14 15 16 17         13 14 15 16 17 18 19         12 13 14 15 16 17 18         11 12 13 14 15 16 17
18 19 20 21 22 23 24         20 21 22 23 24 25 26         19 20 21 22 23 24 25         18 19 20 21 22 23 24
25 26 27 28                  27 28 29 30 31               26 27 28 29 30 31            25 26 27 28 29 30

MAR                          JUNE                         SEPT                         DEC
 S  M  T  W  T  F  S          S  M  T  W  T  F  S          S  M  T  W  T  F  S          S  M  T  W  T  F  S
          1  2  3                            1  2                            1                            1
 4  5  6  7  8  9 10          3  4  5  6  7  8  9          2  3  4  5  6  7  8          2  3  4  5  6  7  8
11 12 13 14 15 16 17         10 11 12 13 14 15 16          9 10 11 12 13 14 15          9 10 11 12 13 14 15
18 19 20 21 22 23 24         17 18 19 20 21 22 23         16 17 18 19 20 21 22         16 17 18 19 20 21 22
25 26 27 28 29 30 31         24 25 26 27 28 29 30         23 24 25 26 27 28 29         23 24 25 26 27 28 29
                                                          30                           30 31
```

(2001 uses calendar 2)

3

JAN

S	M	T	W	T	F	S
		1	2	3	4	5
6	7	8	9	10	11	12
13	14	15	16	17	18	19
20	21	22	23	24	25	26
27	28	29	30	31		

FEB

S	M	T	W	T	F	S
					1	2
3	4	5	6	7	8	9
10	11	12	13	14	15	16
17	18	19	20	21	22	23
24	25	26	27	28		

MAR

S	M	T	W	T	F	S
					1	2
3	4	5	6	7	8	9
10	11	12	13	14	15	16
17	18	19	20	21	22	23
24	25	26	27	28	29	30
31						

APR

S	M	T	W	T	F	S
	1	2	3	4	5	6
7	8	9	10	11	12	13
14	15	16	17	18	19	20
21	22	23	24	25	26	27
28	29	30				

MAY

S	M	T	W	T	F	S
			1	2	3	4
5	6	7	8	9	10	11
12	13	14	15	16	17	18
19	20	21	22	23	24	25
26	27	28	29	30	31	

JUNE

S	M	T	W	T	F	S
						1
2	3	4	5	6	7	8
9	10	11	12	13	14	15
16	17	18	19	20	21	22
23	24	25	26	27	28	29
30						

JULY

S	M	T	W	T	F	S
	1	2	3	4	5	6
7	8	9	10	11	12	13
14	15	16	17	18	19	20
21	22	23	24	25	26	27
28	29	30	31			

AUG

S	M	T	W	T	F	S
				1	2	3
4	5	6	7	8	9	10
11	12	13	14	15	16	17
18	19	20	21	22	23	24
25	26	27	28	29	30	31

SEPT

S	M	T	W	T	F	S
1	2	3	4	5	6	7
8	9	10	11	12	13	14
15	16	17	18	19	20	21
22	23	24	25	26	27	28
29	30					

OCT

S	M	T	W	T	F	S
		1	2	3	4	5
6	7	8	9	10	11	12
13	14	15	16	17	18	19
20	21	22	23	24	25	26
27	28	29	30	31		

NOV

S	M	T	W	T	F	S
					1	2
3	4	5	6	7	8	9
10	11	12	13	14	15	16
17	18	19	20	21	22	23
24	25	26	27	28	29	30

DEC

S	M	T	W	T	F	S
1	2	3	4	5	6	7
8	9	10	11	12	13	14
15	16	17	18	19	20	21
22	23	24	25	26	27	28
29	30	31				

4

JAN

S	M	T	W	T	F	S
			1	2	3	4
5	6	7	8	9	10	11
12	13	14	15	16	17	18
19	20	21	22	23	24	25
26	27	28	29	30	31	

FEB

S	M	T	W	T	F	S
						1
2	3	4	5	6	7	8
9	10	11	12	13	14	15
16	17	18	19	20	21	22
23	24	25	26	27	28	

MAR

S	M	T	W	T	F	S
						1
2	3	4	5	6	7	8
9	10	11	12	13	14	15
16	17	18	19	20	21	22
23	24	25	26	27	28	29
30	31					

APR

S	M	T	W	T	F	S
		1	2	3	4	5
6	7	8	9	10	11	12
13	14	15	16	17	18	19
20	21	22	23	24	25	26
27	28	29	30			

MAY

S	M	T	W	T	F	S
				1	2	3
4	5	6	7	8	9	10
11	12	13	14	15	16	17
18	19	20	21	22	23	24
25	26	27	28	29	30	31

JUNE

S	M	T	W	T	F	S
1	2	3	4	5	6	7
8	9	10	11	12	13	14
15	16	17	18	19	20	21
22	23	24	25	26	27	28
29	30					

JULY

S	M	T	W	T	F	S
		1	2	3	4	5
6	7	8	9	10	11	12
13	14	15	16	17	18	19
20	21	22	23	24	25	26
27	28	29	30	31		

AUG

S	M	T	W	T	F	S
					1	2
3	4	5	6	7	8	9
10	11	12	13	14	15	16
17	18	19	20	21	22	23
24	25	26	27	28	29	30
31						

SEPT

S	M	T	W	T	F	S
	1	2	3	4	5	6
7	8	9	10	11	12	13
14	15	16	17	18	19	20
21	22	23	24	25	26	27
28	29	30				

OCT

S	M	T	W	T	F	S
			1	2	3	4
5	6	7	8	9	10	11
12	13	14	15	16	17	18
19	20	21	22	23	24	25
26	27	28	29	30	31	

NOV

S	M	T	W	T	F	S
						1
2	3	4	5	6	7	8
9	10	11	12	13	14	15
16	17	18	19	20	21	22
23	24	25	26	27	28	29
30						

DEC

S	M	T	W	T	F	S
	1	2	3	4	5	6
7	8	9	10	11	12	13
14	15	16	17	18	19	20
21	22	23	24	25	26	27
28	29	30	31			

5 — 1998

JAN

S	M	T	W	T	F	S
				1	2	3
4	5	6	7	8	9	10
11	12	13	14	15	16	17
18	19	20	21	22	23	24
25	26	27	28	29	30	31

FEB

S	M	T	W	T	F	S
1	2	3	4	5	6	7
8	9	10	11	12	13	14
15	16	17	18	19	20	21
22	23	24	25	26	27	28

MAR

S	M	T	W	T	F	S
1	2	3	4	5	6	7
8	9	10	11	12	13	14
15	16	17	18	19	20	21
22	23	24	25	26	27	28
29	30	31				

APR

S	M	T	W	T	F	S
			1	2	3	4
5	6	7	8	9	10	11
12	13	14	15	16	17	18
19	20	21	22	23	24	25
26	27	28	29	30		

MAY

S	M	T	W	T	F	S
					1	2
3	4	5	6	7	8	9
10	11	12	13	14	15	16
17	18	19	20	21	22	23
24	25	26	27	28	29	30
31						

JUNE

S	M	T	W	T	F	S
	1	2	3	4	5	6
7	8	9	10	11	12	13
14	15	16	17	18	19	20
21	22	23	24	25	26	27
28	29	30				

JULY

S	M	T	W	T	F	S
			1	2	3	4
5	6	7	8	9	10	11
12	13	14	15	16	17	18
19	20	21	22	23	24	25
26	27	28	29	30	31	

AUG

S	M	T	W	T	F	S
						1
2	3	4	5	6	7	8
9	10	11	12	13	14	15
16	17	18	19	20	21	22
23	24	25	26	27	28	29
30	31					

SEPT

S	M	T	W	T	F	S
		1	2	3	4	5
6	7	8	9	10	11	12
13	14	15	16	17	18	19
20	21	22	23	24	25	26
27	28	29	30			

OCT

S	M	T	W	T	F	S
				1	2	3
4	5	6	7	8	9	10
11	12	13	14	15	16	17
18	19	20	21	22	23	24
25	26	27	28	29	30	31

NOV

S	M	T	W	T	F	S
1	2	3	4	5	6	7
8	9	10	11	12	13	14
15	16	17	18	19	20	21
22	23	24	25	26	27	28
29	30					

DEC

S	M	T	W	T	F	S
		1	2	3	4	5
6	7	8	9	10	11	12
13	14	15	16	17	18	19
20	21	22	23	24	25	26
27	28	29	30	31		

6 — 1999

JAN

S	M	T	W	T	F	S
					1	2
3	4	5	6	7	8	9
10	11	12	13	14	15	16
17	18	19	20	21	22	23
24	25	26	27	28	29	30
31						

FEB

S	M	T	W	T	F	S
	1	2	3	4	5	6
7	8	9	10	11	12	13
14	15	16	17	18	19	20
21	22	23	24	25	26	27
28						

MAR

S	M	T	W	T	F	S
	1	2	3	4	5	6
7	8	9	10	11	12	13
14	15	16	17	18	19	20
21	22	23	24	25	26	27
28	29	30	31			

APR

S	M	T	W	T	F	S
				1	2	3
4	5	6	7	8	9	10
11	12	13	14	15	16	17
18	19	20	21	22	23	24
25	26	27	28	29	30	

MAY

S	M	T	W	T	F	S
						1
2	3	4	5	6	7	8
9	10	11	12	13	14	15
16	17	18	19	20	21	22
23	24	25	26	27	28	29
30	31					

JUNE

S	M	T	W	T	F	S
		1	2	3	4	5
6	7	8	9	10	11	12
13	14	15	16	17	18	19
20	21	22	23	24	25	26
27	28	29	30			

JULY

S	M	T	W	T	F	S
				1	2	3
4	5	6	7	8	9	10
11	12	13	14	15	16	17
18	19	20	21	22	23	24
25	26	27	28	29	30	31

AUG

S	M	T	W	T	F	S
1	2	3	4	5	6	7
8	9	10	11	12	13	14
15	16	17	18	19	20	21
22	23	24	25	26	27	28
29	30	31				

SEPT

S	M	T	W	T	F	S
			1	2	3	4
5	6	7	8	9	10	11
12	13	14	15	16	17	18
19	20	21	22	23	24	25
26	27	28	29	30		

OCT

S	M	T	W	T	F	S
					1	2
3	4	5	6	7	8	9
10	11	12	13	14	15	16
17	18	19	20	21	22	23
24	25	26	27	28	29	30
31						

NOV

S	M	T	W	T	F	S
	1	2	3	4	5	6
7	8	9	10	11	12	13
14	15	16	17	18	19	20
21	22	23	24	25	26	27
28	29	30				

DEC

S	M	T	W	T	F	S
			1	2	3	4
5	6	7	8	9	10	11
12	13	14	15	16	17	18
19	20	21	22	23	24	25
26	27	28	29	30	31	

7

JAN

S	M	T	W	T	F	S
						1
2	3	4	5	6	7	8
9	10	11	12	13	14	15
16	17	18	19	20	21	22
23	24	25	26	27	28	29
30	31					

APR

S	M	T	W	T	F	S
					1	2
3	4	5	6	7	8	9
10	11	12	13	14	15	16
17	18	19	20	21	22	23
24	25	26	27	28	29	30

JULY

S	M	T	W	T	F	S
					1	2
3	4	5	6	7	8	9
10	11	12	13	14	15	16
17	18	19	20	21	22	23
24	25	26	27	28	29	30
31						

OCT

S	M	T	W	T	F	S
						1
2	3	4	5	6	7	8
9	10	11	12	13	14	15
16	17	18	19	20	21	22
23	24	25	26	27	28	29
30	31					

FEB

S	M	T	W	T	F	S
		1	2	3	4	5
6	7	8	9	10	11	12
13	14	15	16	17	18	19
20	21	22	23	24	25	26
27	28					

MAY

S	M	T	W	T	F	S
1	2	3	4	5	6	7
8	9	10	11	12	13	14
15	16	17	18	19	20	21
22	23	24	25	26	27	28
29	30	31				

AUG

S	M	T	W	T	F	S
	1	2	3	4	5	6
7	8	9	10	11	12	13
14	15	16	17	18	19	20
21	22	23	24	25	26	27
28	29	30	31			

NOV

S	M	T	W	T	F	S
		1	2	3	4	5
6	7	8	9	10	11	12
13	14	15	16	17	18	19
20	21	22	23	24	25	26
27	28	29	30			

MAR

S	M	T	W	T	F	S
		1	2	3	4	5
6	7	8	9	10	11	12
13	14	15	16	17	18	19
20	21	22	23	24	25	26
27	28	29	30	31		

JUNE

S	M	T	W	T	F	S
			1	2	3	4
5	6	7	8	9	10	11
12	13	14	15	16	17	18
19	20	21	22	23	24	25
26	27	28	29	30		

SEPT

S	M	T	W	T	F	S
				1	2	3
4	5	6	7	8	9	10
11	12	13	14	15	16	17
18	19	20	21	22	23	24
25	26	27	28	29	30	

DEC

S	M	T	W	T	F	S
				1	2	3
4	5	6	7	8	9	10
11	12	13	14	15	16	17
18	19	20	21	22	23	24
25	26	27	28	29	30	31

8

JAN

S	M	T	W	T	F	S
1	2	3	4	5	6	7
8	9	10	11	12	13	14
15	16	17	18	19	20	21
22	23	24	25	26	27	28
29	30	31				

APR

S	M	T	W	T	F	S
1	2	3	4	5	6	7
8	9	10	11	12	13	14
15	16	17	18	19	20	21
22	23	24	25	26	27	28
29	30					

JULY

S	M	T	W	T	F	S
1	2	3	4	5	6	7
8	9	10	11	12	13	14
15	16	17	18	19	20	21
22	23	24	25	26	27	28
29	30	31				

OCT

S	M	T	W	T	F	S
	1	2	3	4	5	6
7	8	9	10	11	12	13
14	15	16	17	18	19	20
21	22	23	24	25	26	27
28	29	30	31			

FEB

S	M	T	W	T	F	S
			1	2	3	4
5	6	7	8	9	10	11
12	13	14	15	16	17	18
19	20	21	22	23	24	25
26	27	28	29			

MAY

S	M	T	W	T	F	S
		1	2	3	4	5
6	7	8	9	10	11	12
13	14	15	16	17	18	19
20	21	22	23	24	25	26
27	28	29	30	31		

AUG

S	M	T	W	T	F	S
			1	2	3	4
5	6	7	8	9	10	11
12	13	14	15	16	17	18
19	20	21	22	23	24	25
26	27	28	29	30	31	

NOV

S	M	T	W	T	F	S
				1	2	3
4	5	6	7	8	9	10
11	12	13	14	15	16	17
18	19	20	21	22	23	24
25	26	27	28	29	30	

MAR

S	M	T	W	T	F	S
				1	2	3
4	5	6	7	8	9	10
11	12	13	14	15	16	17
18	19	20	21	22	23	24
25	26	27	28	29	30	31

JUNE

S	M	T	W	T	F	S
					1	2
3	4	5	6	7	8	9
10	11	12	13	14	15	16
17	18	19	20	21	22	23
24	25	26	27	28	29	30

SEPT

S	M	T	W	T	F	S
						1
2	3	4	5	6	7	8
9	10	11	12	13	14	15
16	17	18	19	20	21	22
23	24	25	26	27	28	29
30						

DEC

S	M	T	W	T	F	S
						1
2	3	4	5	6	7	8
9	10	11	12	13	14	15
16	17	18	19	20	21	22
23	24	25	26	27	28	29
30	31					

9

JAN

S	M	T	W	T	F	S
	1	2	3	4	5	6
7	8	9	10	11	12	13
14	15	16	17	18	19	20
21	22	23	24	25	26	27
28	29	30	31			

APR

S	M	T	W	T	F	S
	1	2	3	4	5	6
7	8	9	10	11	12	13
14	15	16	17	18	19	20
21	22	23	24	25	26	27
28	29	30				

JULY

S	M	T	W	T	F	S
	1	2	3	4	5	6
7	8	9	10	11	12	13
14	15	16	17	18	19	20
21	22	23	24	25	26	27
28	29	30	31			

OCT

S	M	T	W	T	F	S
		1	2	3	4	5
6	7	8	9	10	11	12
13	14	15	16	17	18	19
20	21	22	23	24	25	26
27	28	29	30	31		

FEB

S	M	T	W	T	F	S
				1	2	3
4	5	6	7	8	9	10
11	12	13	14	15	16	17
18	19	20	21	22	23	24
25	26	27	28	29		

MAY

S	M	T	W	T	F	S
			1	2	3	4
5	6	7	8	9	10	11
12	13	14	15	16	17	18
19	20	21	22	23	24	25
26	27	28	29	30	31	

AUG

S	M	T	W	T	F	S
				1	2	3
4	5	6	7	8	9	10
11	12	13	14	15	16	17
18	19	20	21	22	23	24
25	26	27	28	29	30	31

NOV

S	M	T	W	T	F	S
					1	2
3	4	5	6	7	8	9
10	11	12	13	14	15	16
17	18	19	20	21	22	23
24	25	26	27	28	29	30

MAR

S	M	T	W	T	F	S
					1	2
3	4	5	6	7	8	9
10	11	12	13	14	15	16
17	18	19	20	21	22	23
24	25	26	27	28	29	30
31						

JUNE

S	M	T	W	T	F	S
						1
2	3	4	5	6	7	8
9	10	11	12	13	14	15
16	17	18	19	20	21	22
23	24	25	26	27	28	29
30						

SEPT

S	M	T	W	T	F	S
1	2	3	4	5	6	7
8	9	10	11	12	13	14
15	16	17	18	19	20	21
22	23	24	25	26	27	28
29	30					

DEC

S	M	T	W	T	F	S
1	2	3	4	5	6	7
8	9	10	11	12	13	14
15	16	17	18	19	20	21
22	23	24	25	26	27	28
29	30	31				

10

JAN

S	M	T	W	T	F	S
		1	2	3	4	5
6	7	8	9	10	11	12
13	14	15	16	17	18	19
20	21	22	23	24	25	26
27	28	29	30	31		

APR

S	M	T	W	T	F	S
		1	2	3	4	5
6	7	8	9	10	11	12
13	14	15	16	17	18	19
20	21	22	23	24	25	26
27	28	29	30			

JULY

S	M	T	W	T	F	S
		1	2	3	4	5
6	7	8	9	10	11	12
13	14	15	16	17	18	19
20	21	22	23	24	25	26
27	28	29	30	31		

OCT

S	M	T	W	T	F	S
			1	2	3	4
5	6	7	8	9	10	11
12	13	14	15	16	17	18
19	20	21	22	23	24	25
26	27	28	29	30	31	

FEB

S	M	T	W	T	F	S
					1	2
3	4	5	6	7	8	9
10	11	12	13	14	15	16
17	18	19	20	21	22	23
24	25	26	27	28	29	

MAY

S	M	T	W	T	F	S
				1	2	3
4	5	6	7	8	9	10
11	12	13	14	15	16	17
18	19	20	21	22	23	24
25	26	27	28	29	30	31

AUG

S	M	T	W	T	F	S
					1	2
3	4	5	6	7	8	9
10	11	12	13	14	15	16
17	18	19	20	21	22	23
24	25	26	27	28	29	30
31						

NOV

S	M	T	W	T	F	S
						1
2	3	4	5	6	7	8
9	10	11	12	13	14	15
16	17	18	19	20	21	22
23	24	25	26	27	28	29
30						

MAR

S	M	T	W	T	F	S
						1
2	3	4	5	6	7	8
9	10	11	12	13	14	15
16	17	18	19	20	21	22
23	24	25	26	27	28	29
30	31					

JUNE

S	M	T	W	T	F	S
1	2	3	4	5	6	7
8	9	10	11	12	13	14
15	16	17	18	19	20	21
22	23	24	25	26	27	28
29	30					

SEPT

S	M	T	W	T	F	S
	1	2	3	4	5	6
7	8	9	10	11	12	13
14	15	16	17	18	19	20
21	22	23	24	25	26	27
28	29	30				

DEC

S	M	T	W	T	F	S
	1	2	3	4	5	6
7	8	9	10	11	12	13
14	15	16	17	18	19	20
21	22	23	24	25	26	27
28	29	30	31			

11

JAN
S	M	T	W	T	F	S
			1	2	3	4
5	6	7	8	9	10	11
12	13	14	15	16	17	18
19	20	21	22	23	24	25
26	27	28	29	30	31	

FEB
S	M	T	W	T	F	S
						1
2	3	4	5	6	7	8
9	10	11	12	13	14	15
16	17	18	19	20	21	22
23	24	25	26	27	28	29

MAR
S	M	T	W	T	F	S
1	2	3	4	5	6	7
8	9	10	11	12	13	14
15	16	17	18	19	20	21
22	23	24	25	26	27	28
29	30	31				

APR
S	M	T	W	T	F	S
			1	2	3	4
5	6	7	8	9	10	11
12	13	14	15	16	17	18
19	20	21	22	23	24	25
26	27	28	29	30		

MAY
S	M	T	W	T	F	S
					1	2
3	4	5	6	7	8	9
10	11	12	13	14	15	16
17	18	19	20	21	22	23
24	25	26	27	28	29	30
31						

JUNE
S	M	T	W	T	F	S
	1	2	3	4	5	6
7	8	9	10	11	12	13
14	15	16	17	18	19	20
21	22	23	24	25	26	27
28	29	30				

JULY
S	M	T	W	T	F	S
			1	2	3	4
5	6	7	8	9	10	11
12	13	14	15	16	17	18
19	20	21	22	23	24	25
26	27	28	29	30	31	

AUG
S	M	T	W	T	F	S
						1
2	3	4	5	6	7	8
9	10	11	12	13	14	15
16	17	18	19	20	21	22
23	24	25	26	27	28	29
30	31					

SEPT
S	M	T	W	T	F	S
		1	2	3	4	5
6	7	8	9	10	11	12
13	14	15	16	17	18	19
20	21	22	23	24	25	26
27	28	29	30			

OCT
S	M	T	W	T	F	S
				1	2	3
4	5	6	7	8	9	10
11	12	13	14	15	16	17
18	19	20	21	22	23	24
25	26	27	28	29	30	31

NOV
S	M	T	W	T	F	S
1	2	3	4	5	6	7
8	9	10	11	12	13	14
15	16	17	18	19	20	21
22	23	24	25	26	27	28
29	30					

DEC
S	M	T	W	T	F	S
		1	2	3	4	5
6	7	8	9	10	11	12
13	14	15	16	17	18	19
20	21	22	23	24	25	26
27	28	29	30	31		

12

JAN
S	M	T	W	T	F	S
				1	2	3
4	5	6	7	8	9	10
11	12	13	14	15	16	17
18	19	20	21	22	23	24
25	26	27	28	29	30	31

FEB
S	M	T	W	T	F	S
1	2	3	4	5	6	7
8	9	10	11	12	13	14
15	16	17	18	19	20	21
22	23	24	25	26	27	28
29						

MAR
S	M	T	W	T	F	S
	1	2	3	4	5	6
7	8	9	10	11	12	13
14	15	16	17	18	19	20
21	22	23	24	25	26	27
28	29	30	31			

APR
S	M	T	W	T	F	S
				1	2	3
4	5	6	7	8	9	10
11	12	13	14	15	16	17
18	19	20	21	22	23	24
25	26	27	28	29	30	

MAY
S	M	T	W	T	F	S
						1
2	3	4	5	6	7	8
9	10	11	12	13	14	15
16	17	18	19	20	21	22
23	24	25	26	27	28	29
30	31					

JUNE
S	M	T	W	T	F	S
		1	2	3	4	5
6	7	8	9	10	11	12
13	14	15	16	17	18	19
20	21	22	23	24	25	26
27	28	29	30			

JULY
S	M	T	W	T	F	S
				1	2	3
4	5	6	7	8	9	10
11	12	13	14	15	16	17
18	19	20	21	22	23	24
25	26	27	28	29	30	31

AUG
S	M	T	W	T	F	S
1	2	3	4	5	6	7
8	9	10	11	12	13	14
15	16	17	18	19	20	21
22	23	24	25	26	27	28
29	30	31				

SEPT
S	M	T	W	T	F	S
			1	2	3	4
5	6	7	8	9	10	11
12	13	14	15	16	17	18
19	20	21	22	23	24	25
26	27	28	30			

OCT
S	M	T	W	T	F	S
					1	2
3	4	5	6	7	8	9
10	11	12	13	14	15	16
17	18	19	20	21	22	23
24	25	26	27	28	29	30
31						

NOV
S	M	T	W	T	F	S
	1	2	3	4	5	6
7	8	9	10	11	12	13
14	15	16	17	18	19	20
21	22	23	24	25	26	27
28	29	30				

DEC
S	M	T	W	T	F	S
			1	2	3	4
5	6	7	8	9	10	11
12	13	14	15	16	17	18
19	20	21	22	23	24	25
26	27	28	29	30	31	

13

JAN
S	M	T	W	T	F	S
					1	2
3	4	5	6	7	8	9
10	11	12	13	14	15	16
17	18	19	20	21	22	23
24	25	26	27	28	29	30
31						

FEB
S	M	T	W	T	F	S
	1	2	3	4	5	6
7	8	9	10	11	12	13
14	15	16	17	18	19	20
21	22	23	24	25	26	27
28	29					

MAR
S	M	T	W	T	F	S
		1	2	3	4	5
6	7	8	9	10	11	12
13	14	15	16	17	18	19
20	21	22	23	24	25	26
27	28	29	30	31		

APR
S	M	T	W	T	F	S
					1	2
3	4	5	6	7	8	9
10	11	12	13	14	15	16
17	18	19	20	21	22	23
24	25	26	27	28	29	30

MAY
S	M	T	W	T	F	S
1	2	3	4	5	6	7
8	9	10	11	12	13	14
15	16	17	18	19	20	21
22	23	24	25	26	27	28
29	30	31				

JUNE
S	M	T	W	T	F	S
			1	2	3	4
5	6	7	8	9	10	11
12	13	14	15	16	17	18
19	20	21	22	23	24	25
26	27	28	29	30		

JULY
S	M	T	W	T	F	S
					1	2
3	4	5	6	7	8	9
10	11	12	13	14	15	16
17	18	19	20	21	22	23
24	25	26	27	28	29	30
31						

AUG
S	M	T	W	T	F	S
	1	2	3	4	5	6
7	8	9	10	11	12	13
14	15	16	17	18	19	20
21	22	23	24	25	26	27
28	29	30	31			

SEPT
S	M	T	W	T	F	S
				1	2	3
4	5	6	7	8	9	10
11	12	13	14	15	16	17
18	19	20	21	22	23	24
25	26	27	28	29	30	

OCT
S	M	T	W	T	F	S
						1
2	3	4	5	6	7	8
9	10	11	12	13	14	15
16	17	18	19	20	21	22
23	24	25	26	27	28	29
30	31					

NOV
S	M	T	W	T	F	S
		1	2	3	4	5
6	7	8	9	10	11	12
13	14	15	16	17	18	19
20	21	22	23	24	25	26
27	28	29	30			

DEC
S	M	T	W	T	F	S
				1	2	3
4	5	6	7	8	9	10
11	12	13	14	15	16	17
18	19	20	21	22	23	24
25	26	27	28	29	30	31

14 — 2000

JAN
S	M	T	W	T	F	S
						1
2	3	4	5	6	7	8
9	10	11	12	13	14	15
16	17	18	19	20	21	22
23	24	25	26	27	28	29
30	31					

FEB
S	M	T	W	T	F	S
		1	2	3	4	5
6	7	8	9	10	11	12
13	14	15	16	17	18	19
20	21	22	23	24	25	26
27	28	29				

MAR
S	M	T	W	T	F	S
			1	2	3	4
5	6	7	8	9	10	11
12	13	14	15	16	17	18
19	20	21	22	23	24	25
26	27	28	29	30	31	

APR
S	M	T	W	T	F	S
						1
2	3	4	5	6	7	8
9	10	11	12	13	14	15
16	17	18	19	20	21	22
23	24	25	26	27	28	29
30						

MAY
S	M	T	W	T	F	S
	1	2	3	4	5	6
7	8	9	10	11	12	13
14	15	16	17	18	19	20
21	22	23	24	25	26	27
28	29	30	31			

JUNE
S	M	T	W	T	F	S
				1	2	3
4	5	6	7	8	9	10
11	12	13	14	15	16	17
18	19	20	21	22	23	24
25	26	27	28	29	30	

JULY
S	M	T	W	T	F	S
						1
2	3	4	5	6	7	8
9	10	11	12	13	14	15
16	17	18	19	20	21	22
23	24	25	26	27	28	29
30	31					

AUG
S	M	T	W	T	F	S
		1	2	3	4	5
6	7	8	9	10	11	12
13	14	15	16	17	18	19
20	21	22	23	24	25	26
27	28	29	30	31		

SEPT
S	M	T	W	T	F	S
					1	2
3	4	5	6	7	8	9
10	11	12	13	14	15	16
17	18	19	20	21	22	23
24	25	26	27	28	29	30

OCT
S	M	T	W	T	F	S
1	2	3	4	5	6	7
8	9	10	11	12	13	14
15	16	17	18	19	20	21
22	23	24	25	26	27	28
29	30	31				

NOV
S	M	T	W	T	F	S
			1	2	3	4
5	6	7	8	9	10	11
12	13	14	15	16	17	18
19	20	21	22	23	24	25
26	27	28	29	30		

DEC
S	M	T	W	T	F	S
					1	2
3	4	5	6	7	8	9
10	11	12	13	14	15	16
17	18	19	20	21	22	23
24	25	26	27	28	29	30
31						

☆ *The Teacher's Calendar, 1999–2000* ☆

SELECTED SPECIAL YEARS: 1957–1999

Intl Geophysical Year: July 1957-Dec 1958
World Refugee Year: July 1959-June 1960
Intl Cooperation Year: 1965
Intl Book Year: 1972
World Population Year: 1974
Intl Women's Year: 1975
Intl Year of the Child: 1979
Intl Year for Disabled Persons: 1981
World Communications Year: 1983
Intl Youth Year: 1985
Intl Year of Peace: 1986
Intl Year of Shelter for the Homeless: 1987
Year of the Reader: 1987
Year of the Young Reader: 1989
Intl Literacy Year: 1990
US Decade of the Brain: 1990-99
Intl Space Year: 1992
Intl Year for World's Indigenous Peoples: 1993
Intl Year of the Family: 1994
Year for Tolerance: 1995
Intl Year for Eradication of Poverty: 1996
Intl Year of the Ocean: 1998
Intl Year of Older Persons: 1999

CHINESE CALENDAR

The Chinese lunar year is divided into 12 months of 29 or 30 days. The calendar is adjusted to the length of the solar year by the addition of extra months at regular intervals. The years are arranged in major cycles of 60 years. Each successive year is named after one of 12 animals. These 12-year cycles are continuously repeated.

1996	Rat
1997	Ox
1998	Tiger
1999	Hare
2000	Dragon
2001	Snake
2002	Horse
2003	Sheep (Goat)
2004	Monkey
2005	Rooster
2006	Dog
2007	Pig

LOOKING FORWARD

2000
- Leap Year
- California Statehood Sesquicentennial
- US presidential election
- Holy Year for Roman Catholic Church—Great Jubilee
- Summer Olympics (Sydney, Australia)
- Expo 2000—world's fair in Hannover, Germany
- 22nd Decennial Census of the US
- US population projected to be 275,000,000

2001
- 21st Century and Third Millennium of the Christian Era
- Centennial of Australian Federation
- James Madison's birth, 250th anniversary

2002
- Winter Olympics (Salt Lake City)

2003
- Ohio Statehood Bicentennial
- Wright Brothers' first flight, 100th anniversary

2004
- First successful newspaper in America, 300th anniversary
- US presidential election
- Summer Olympics (Athens, Greece)

2006
- Benjamin Franklin's birth, 300th anniversary
- Woodrow Wilson's birth, 150th anniversary

2007
- Oklahoma Statehood Centennial
- Jamestown Colony, 400th anniversary
- Sputnik launched by USSR, 50th anniversary
- William H. Taft's birth, 150th anniversary

2008
- James Monroe's birth, 250th anniversary
- Andrew Johnson's birth, 200th anniversary
- Theodore Roosevelt's birth, 150th anniversary
- Lyndon Johnson's birth, 100th anniversary
- US presidential election

2009
- Abraham Lincoln's birth, 200th anniversary

2010
- US population projected to be 298,000,000

2011
- Ronald Reagan's birth, 100th anniversary

2012
- Arizona Statehood Centennial
- Louisiana Statehood Bicentennial
- New Mexico Statehood Centennial
- US presidential election

2013
- Richard Nixon's birth, 100th anniversary
- Gerald Ford's birth, 100th anniversary

2015
- US population projected to be 310,000,000

2016
- Indiana Statehood Bicentennial
- US presidential election

2017
- Mississippi Statehood Bicentennial
- John Q. Adams's birth, 250th anniversary
- Andrew Jackson's birth, 250th anniversary
- John F. Kennedy's birth, 100th anniversary

2018
- Illinois Statehood Bicentennial

2019
- Alabama Statehood Bicentennial
- Apollo 11 astronauts walk on moon, 50th anniversary

2020
- US population projected to be 323,000,000
- Maine State Bicentennial
- US presidential election

2050
- US population projected to be 394,000,000
- World population of 9 billion predicted

2061
- Halley's comet returns

SOME FACTS ABOUT THE STATES

State	Capital	Popular name	Area (sq. mi.)	State bird	State flower	State tree	Admitted to the Union	Order of Admission
Alabama	Montgomery	Cotton or Yellowhammer State; or Heart of Dixie	51,609	Yellowhammer	Camellia	Southern pine (Longleaf pine)	1819	22
Alaska	Juneau	Last Frontier	591,004	Willow ptarmigan	Forget-me-not	Sitka spruce	1959	49
Arizona	Phoenix	Grand Canyon State	114,000	Cactus wren	Saguaro (giant cactus)	Palo Verde	1912	48
Arkansas	Little Rock	The Natural State	53,187	Mockingbird	Apple blossom	Pine	1836	25
California	Sacramento	Golden State	158,706	California valley quail	Golden poppy	California redwood	1850	31
Colorado	Denver	Centennial State	104,091	Lark bunting	Rocky Mountain columbine	Blue spruce	1876	38
Connecticut	Hartford	Constitution State	5,018	Robin	Mountain laurel	White oak	1788	5
Delaware	Dover	First State	2,044	Blue hen chicken	Peach blossom	American holly	1787	1
Florida	Tallahassee	Sunshine State	58,664	Mockingbird	Orange blossom	Cabbage (sabal) palm	1845	27
Georgia	Atlanta	Empire State of the South	58,910	Brown thrasher	Cherokee rose	Live oak	1788	4
Hawaii	Honolulu	Aloha State	6,471	Nene (Hawaiian goose)	Hibiscus	Kukui	1959	50
Idaho	Boise	Gem State	83,564	Mountain bluebird	Syringa (mock orange)	Western white pine	1890	43
Illinois	Springfield	Prairie State	56,345	Cardinal	Native violet	White oak	1818	21
Indiana	Indianapolis	Hoosier State	36,185	Cardinal	Peony	Tulip tree or yellow poplar	1816	19
Iowa	Des Moines	Hawkeye State	56,275	Eastern goldfinch	Wild rose	Oak	1846	29
Kansas	Topeka	Sunflower State	82,277	Western meadowlark	Sunflower	Cottonwood	1861	34
Kentucky	Frankfort	Bluegrass State	40,409	Kentucky cardinal	Goldenrod	Kentucky coffeetree	1792	15
Louisiana	Baton Rouge	Pelican State	47,752	Pelican	Magnolia	Bald cypress	1812	18
Maine	Augusta	Pine Tree State	33,265	Chickadee	White pine cone and tassel	White pine	1820	23
Maryland	Annapolis	Old Line State	10,577	Baltimore oriole	Black-eyed Susan	White oak	1788	7
Massachusetts	Boston	Bay State	8,284	Chickadee	Mayflower	American elm	1788	6
Michigan	Lansing	Wolverine State	58,527	Robin	Apple blossom	White pine	1837	26
Minnesota	St. Paul	North Star State	84,402	Common loon	Pink and white lady's-slipper	Norway, or red, pine	1858	32
Mississippi	Jackson	Magnolia State	47,689	Mockingbird	Magnolia	Magnolia	1817	20
Missouri	Jefferson City	Show Me State	69,697	Bluebird	Hawthorn	Flowering dogwood	1821	24
Montana	Helena	Treasure State	147,046	Western meadowlark	Bitterroot	Ponderosa pine	1889	41
Nebraska	Lincoln	Cornhusker State	77,355	Western meadowlark	Goldenrod	Cottonwood	1867	37
Nevada	Carson City	Silver State	110,540	Mountain bluebird	Sagebrush	Single-leaf piñon	1864	36
New Hampshire	Concord	Granite State	9,304	Purple finch	Purple lilac	White birch	1788	9
New Jersey	Trenton	Garden State	7,787	Eastern goldfinch	Purple violet	Red oak	1787	3
New Mexico	Santa Fe	Land of Enchantment	121,593	Roadrunner	Yucca flower	Piñon, or nut pine	1912	47
New York	Albany	Empire State	49,108	Bluebird	Rose	Sugar maple	1788	11
North Carolina	Raleigh	Tar Heel State or Old North State	52,669	Cardinal	Dogwood	Pine	1789	12
North Dakota	Bismarck	Peace Garden State	70,702	Western meadowlark	Wild prairie rose	American elm	1889	39

☆ *The Teacher's Calendar, 1999–2000* ☆

State	Capital	Popular name	Area (sq. mi.)	State bird	State flower	State tree	Admitted to the Union	Order of Admission
Ohio	Columbus	Buckeye State	41,330	Cardinal	Scarlet carnation	Buckeye	1803	17
Oklahoma	Oklahoma City	Sooner State	69,956	Scissortail flycatcher	Mistletoe	Redbud	1907	46
Oregon	Salem	Beaver State	97,073	Western meadowlark	Oregon grape	Douglas fir	1859	33
Pennsylvania	Harrisburg	Keystone State	45,308	Ruffed grouse	Mountain laurel	Hemlock	1787	2
Rhode Island	Providence	Ocean State	1,212	Rhode Island Red	Violet	Red maple	1790	13
South Carolina	Columbia	Palmetto State	31,113	Carolina wren	Carolina jessamine	Palmetto	1788	8
South Dakota	Pierre	Sunshine State	77,116	Ring-necked pheasant	American pasqueflower	Black Hills spruce	1889	40
Tennessee	Nashville	Volunteer State	42,114	Mockingbird	Iris	Tulip poplar	1796	16
Texas	Austin	Lone Star State	266,807	Mockingbird	Bluebonnet	Pecan	1845	28
Utah	Salt Lake City	Beehive State	84,899	Sea Gull	Sego lily	Blue spruce	1896	45
Vermont	Montpelier	Green Mountain State	9,614	Hermit thrush	Red clover	Sugar maple	1791	14
Virginia	Richmond	Old Dominion	40,767	Cardinal	Dogwood	Dogwood	1788	10
Washington	Olympia	Evergreen State	68,139	Willow goldfinch	Coast rhododendron	Western hemlock	1889	42
West Virginia	Charleston	Mountain State	24,231	Cardinal	Rhododendron	Sugar maple	1863	35
Wisconsin	Madison	Badger State	56,153	Robin	Wood violet	Sugar maple	1848	30
Wyoming	Cheyenne	Equality State	97,809	Meadowlark	Indian paintbrush	Cottonwood	1890	44

STATE & TERRITORY ABBREVIATIONS: UNITED STATES

Alabama . . . . AL
Alaska . . . . AK
Arizona . . . . AZ
Arkansas . . . . AR
American Samoa . . . . AS
California . . . . CA
Canal Zone . . . . CZ
Colorado . . . . CO
Connecticut . . . . CT
Delaware . . . . DE
District of Columbia . . . . DC
Florida . . . . FL
Georgia . . . . GA
Guam . . . . GU
Hawaii . . . . HI
Idaho . . . . ID
Illinois IL
Indiana . . . . IN
Iowa . . . . IA

Kansas . . . . KS
Kentucky . . . . KY
Louisiana . . . . LA
Maine . . . . ME
Maryland . . . . MD
Massachusetts . . . . MA
Michigan . . . . MI
Minnesota . . . . MN
Mississippi . . . . MS
Missouri . . . . MO
Montana . . . . MT
Nebraska . . . . NE
Nevada . . . . NV
New Hampshire . . . . NH
New Jersey . . . . NJ
New Mexico . . . . NM
New York . . . . NY
North Carolina . . . . NC
North Dakota . . . . ND

Ohio . . . . OH
Oklahoma . . . . OK
Oregon . . . . OR
Pennsylvania . . . . PA
Puerto Rico . . . . PR
Rhode Island . . . . RI
South Carolina . . . . SC
South Dakota . . . . SD
Tennessee . . . . TN
Trust Territories . . . . TT
Texas . . . . TX
Utah . . . . UT
Vermont . . . . VT
Virginia . . . . VA
Virgin Islands VI
Washington . . . . WA
West Virginia . . . . WV
Wisconsin . . . . WI
Wyoming . . . . WY

PROVINCE & TERRITORY ABBREVIATIONS: CANADA

Alberta . . . . AB
British Columbia . . . . BC
Manitoba . . . . MB
New Brunswick . . . . NB

Newfoundland . . . . NFLD
Nova Scotia . . . . NS
Ontario . . . . ON
Prince Edward Island . . . . PEI

Quebec . . . . QC
Saskatchewan . . . . SK
Yukon Territory . . . . YK
Northwest Territories . . . . NWT

☆ *The Teacher's Calendar, 1999–2000* ☆

SOME FACTS ABOUT CANADA

Province/Territory	Capital	Population*	Flower	Land/Fresh Water (sq. mi.)	Total Area
Alberta	Edmonton	2,774,512	Wild rose	400,423/10,437	410,860
British Columbia	Victoria	3,835,748	Pacific dogwood	578,230/11,227	589,458
Manitoba	Winnipeg	1,141,727	Prairie crocus	340,834/63,129	403,964
New Brunswick	Fredericton	761,873	Purple violet	44,797/835	45,633
Newfoundland	St. John's	571,192	Pitcher plant	230,219/21,147	251,367
Northwest Territories	Yellowknife	66,164	Mountain avens	2,017,306/82,829	2,100,136
Nova Scotia	Halifax	941,235	Mayflower	32,835/1,647	34,482
Ontario	Toronto	11,209,474	White trillium	553,788/110,229	664,012
Prince Edward Island	Charlottetown	137,316	Lady's-slipper	3,515/0	3,515
Quebec	Quebec City	7,366,883	White garden lily	843,109/114,269	957,379
Saskatchewan	Regina	1,020,138	Red lily	354,365/51,347	405,712
Yukon Territory	Whitehorse	31,107	Fireweed	297,050/2,784	299,835

*1996

SOME FACTS ABOUT THE PRESIDENTS

	Name	Birthdate, Place	Party	Tenure	Died	First Lady	Vice President
1.	George Washington	2/22/1732, Westmoreland Cnty, VA	Federalist	1789–1797	12/14/1799	Martha Dandridge Custis	John Adams
2.	John Adams	10/30/1735, Braintree (Quincy), MA	Federalist	1797–1801	7/4/1826	Abigail Smith	Thomas Jefferson
3.	Thomas Jefferson	4/13/1743, Shadwell, VA	Democratic-Republican	1801–1809	7/4/1826	Martha Wayles Skelton	Aaron Burr, 1801–05 George Clinton, 1805–09
4.	James Madison	3/16/1751, Port Conway, VA	Democratic-Republican	1809–1817	6/28/1836	Dolley Payne Todd	George Clinton, 1809–12 Elbridge Gerry, 1813–14(?)
5.	James Monroe	4/28/1758, Westmoreland Cnty, VA	Democratic-Republican	1817–1825	7/4/1831	Elizabeth Kortright	Daniel D. Tompkins
6.	John Q. Adams	7/11/1767, Braintree (Quincy), MA	Democratic-Republican	1825–1829	2/23/1848	Louisa Catherine Johnson	John C. Calhoun
7.	Andrew Jackson	3/15/1767, Waxhaw Settlement, SC	Democrat	1829–1837	6/8/1845	Mrs. Rachel Donelson Robards	John C. Calhoun, 1829–32 Martin Van Buren, 1833–37
8.	Martin Van Buren	12/5/1782, Kinderhook, NY	Democrat	1837–1841	7/24/1862	Hannah Hoes	Richard M. Johnson
9.	William H. Harrison	2/9/1773, Charles City Cnty, VA	Whig	1841	4/4/1841†	Anna Symmes	John Tyler
10.	John Tyler	3/29/1790, Charles City Cnty, VA	Whig	1841–1845	1/18/1862	Letitia Christian Julia Gardiner	
11.	James K. Polk	11/2/1795, near Pineville, NC	Democrat	1845–1849	6/15/1849	Sarah Childress	George M. Dallas
12.	Zachary Taylor	11/24/1784, Barboursville, VA	Whig	1849–1850	7/9/1850†	Margaret Mackall Smith	Millard Fillmore
13.	Millard Fillmore	1/7/1800, Locke, NY	Whig	1850–1853	3/8/1874	Abigail Powers Mrs. Caroline Carmichael McIntosh	
14.	Franklin Pierce	11/23/1804, Hillsboro, NH	Democrat	1853–1857	10/8/1869	Jane Means Appleton	William R. D. King
15.	James Buchanan	4/23/1791, near Mercersburg, PA	Democrat	1857–1861	6/1/1868		John C. Breckinridge

16. Abraham Lincoln	2/12/1809, near Hodgenville, KY	Republican	1861–1865	4/15/1865*	Mary Todd	Hannibal Hamlin, 1861–65 Andrew Johnson, 1865
17. Andrew Johnson	12/29/1808, Raleigh, NC	Democrat	1865–1869	7/31/1875	Eliza McCardle	
18. Ulysses S. Grant	4/27/1822, Point Pleasant, OH	Republican	1869–1877	7/23/1885	Julia Boggs Dent	Schuyler Colfax, 1869–73 Henry Wilson, 1873–75
19. Rutherford B. Hayes	10/4/1822, Delaware, OH	Republican	1877–1881	1/17/1893	Lucy Ware Webb	William A. Wheeler
20. James A. Garfield	11/19/1831, Orange, OH	Republican	1881	9/19/1881*	Lucretia Rudolph	Chester A. Arthur
21. Chester A. Arthur	10/5/1829, Fairfield, VT	Republican	1881–1885	11/18/1886	Ellen Lewis Herndon	
22. Grover Cleveland	3/18/1837, Caldwell, NJ	Democrat	1885–1889	6/24/1908	Frances Folsom	Thomas A. Hendricks, 1885
23. Benjamin Harrison	8/20/1833, North Bend, OH	Republican	1889–1893	3/13/1901	Caroline Lavinia Scott Mrs. Mary Dimmick	Levi P. Morton
24. Grover Cleveland	3/18/1837, Caldwell, NJ	Democrat	1893–1897	6/24/1908	Frances Folsom	Adlai Stevenson, 1893–97
25. William McKinley	1/29/1843, Niles, OH	Republican	1897–1901	9/14/1901*	Ida Saxton	Garret A. Hobart, 1897–99 Theodore Roosevelt, 1901
26. Theodore Roosevelt	10/27/1858, New York, NY	Republican	1901–1909	1/6/1919	Alice Hathaway Lee Edith Kermit Carow	Charles W. Fairbanks
27. William H. Taft	9/15/1857, Cincinnati, OH	Republican	1909–1913	3/8/1930	Helen Herron	James S. Sherman
28. Woodrow Wilson	12/28/1856, Staunton, VA	Democrat	1913–1921	2/3/1924	Ellen Louise Axson Edith Bolling Galt	Thomas R. Marshall
29. Warren G. Harding	11/2/1865, near Corsica, OH	Republican	1921–1923	8/2/1923†	Florence Kling DeWolfe	Calvin Coolidge
30. Calvin Coolidge	7/4/1872, Plymouth Notch, VT	Republican	1923–1929	1/5/1933	Grace Anna Goodhue	Charles G. Dawes
31. Herbert C. Hoover	8/10/1874, West Branch, IA	Republican	1929–1933	10/20/1964	Lou Henry	Charles Curtis
32. Franklin D. Roosevelt	1/30/1882, Hyde Park, NY	Democrat	1933–1945	4/12/1945†	Eleanor Roosevelt	John N. Garner, 1933–41 Henry A. Wallace, 1941–45 Harry S. Truman, 1945
33. Harry S. Truman	5/8/1884, Lamar, MO	Democrat	1945–1953	12/26/1972	Elizabeth Virginia (Bess) Wallace	Alben W. Barkley
34. Dwight D. Eisenhower	10/14/1890, Denison, TX	Republican	1953–1961	3/28/1969	Mamie Geneva Doud	Richard M. Nixon
35. John F. Kennedy	5/29/1917, Brookline, MA	Democrat	1961–1963	11/22/1963*	Jacqueline Lee Bouvier	Lyndon B. Johnson
36. Lyndon B. Johnson	8/27/1908, near Stonewall, TX	Democrat	1963–1969	1/22/1973	Claudia Alta (Lady Bird) Taylor	Hubert H. Humphrey
37. Richard M. Nixon	1/9/1913, Yorba Linda, CA	Republican	1969–1974**	4/22/1994	Thelma Catherine (Pat) Ryan	Spiro T. Agnew, 1969–73 Gerald R. Ford, 1973–74
38. Gerald R. Ford	7/14/1913, Omaha, NE	Republican	1974–1977		Elizabeth (Betty) Bloomer	Nelson A. Rockefeller
39. James E. Carter, Jr	10/1/1924, Plains, GA	Democrat	1977–1981		Rosalynn Smith	Walter F. Mondale
40. Ronald W. Reagan	2/6/1911, Tampico, IL	Republican	1981–1989		Nancy Davis	George H. W. Bush
41. George H. W. Bush	6/12/1924, Milton, MA	Republican	1989–1993		Barbara Pierce	J. Danforth Quayle
42. William J. Clinton	8/19/1946, Hope, AR	Democrat	1993–2001		Hillary Rodham	Albert Gore, Jr.

* assassinated while in office
** resigned Aug 9, 1974
† died while in office—nonviolently

Sources: *World Book*, 1991 Edition; *Encyclopedia Americana*, 1990 Edition; *Collier's Encyclopedia*, 1994 Edition

1999 AMERICAN LIBRARY ASSOCIATION AWARDS FOR CHILDREN'S BOOKS

NEWBERY MEDAL

For most distinguished contribution to American literature for children published in 1998:

Louis Sachar, author, *Holes*

Honor Book

Richard Peck, author, *A Long Way From Chicago*

CALDECOTT MEDAL

For most distinguished American picture book for children published in 1998:

Mary Azarian, illustrator, *Snowflake Bentley*

Honor Books

Brian Pinkney, illustrator, *Duke Ellington: The Piano Prince and His Orchestra*
David Shannon, illustrator, *No, David!*
Uri Shulevitz, illustrator, *Snow*
Peter Sís, illustrator, *Tibet Through the Red Box*

CORETTA SCOTT KING AWARD

For outstanding books by African-American authors and illustrators:

Angela Johnson, author, *Heaven*
Michele Wood, illustrator, *i see the rhythm*

Honor Books-Authors

Nikki Grimes, *Jazmin's Notebook*
Joyce Hansen and Gary McGowan, *Breaking Ground, Breaking Silence: The Story of New York's African Burial Ground*
Angela Johnson, *The Other Side: Shorter Poems*

Honor Books-Illustrators

Floyd Cooper, *I Have Heard of a Land*
E.B. Lewis, *The Bat Boy & His Violin*
Brian Pinkney, *Duke Ellington: The Piano Prince and His Orchestra*

MARGARET A. EDWARDS AWARD

For lifetime achievement in writing books for young adults:
Anne McCaffrey, recipient

MILDRED L. BATCHELDER AWARD

For the best children's book first published in a foreign language in a foreign country and subsequently translated into English for publication in the US:

Dial Books for Young Readers, publisher, *Thanks To My Mother*

Honor Book

Viking, *Secret Letters From 0 to 10*

ANDREW CARNEGIE MEDAL FOR EXCELLENCE IN CHILDREN'S VIDEO

Frank Moynihan, *The First Christmas*

MAY HILL ARBUTHNOT LECTURE AWARD

Hazel Rochman, recipient

RESOURCES

PROFESSIONAL READING

Financial Tips for Teachers, by Alan Jay Weiss and Larry Strauss. 6th edition. Lowell House, 1-56565-941-4, $13.95.

The Teacher's Almanac: The Professional Teacher's Handbook, by Pat Woodward. 2nd edition. Lowell House, 0-7373-0025-6, $15.

Unbelievably Good Deals That You Absolutely Can't Get Unless You're a Teacher, by Barry Harrington and Beth Christensen. 2nd edition. Contemporary Books, 0-8092-2877-7, $12.95.

BIBLIOGRAPHIES

Literature Connection to American History, K-6: Resources to Enhance and Entice, by Lynda G. Adamson. Libraries Unlimited, 1-56308-502-X, $33.50. A similar volume by Adamson covers books appropriate for grades 7-12.

Great Books for African American Children, by Pamela Toussaint. Plume, 0-45-228044-3, $12.95.

Great Books for Boys: More Than 600 Books for Boys 2 to 14, by Kathleen Odean. Ballantine, 0-34-542083-7, $12.95.

Great Books for Girls: More Than 600 Books to Inspire Today's Girls and Tomorrow's Women, by Kathleen Odean. Ballantine, 0-34-540484-X, $12.95.

Once Upon a Heroine: 450 Books for Girls to Love, by Alison Cooper-Mullin and Jennifer Marmaduke Coye. Contemporary Books, 0-8092-3020-8, $16.95.

PERIODICALS

Both these publications suggest books and electronic products related to specific themes for grades K–8.

Book Links: Connecting Books, Libraries, and Classrooms. 6/year at $24.95. American Library Association, 50 E Huron St, Chicago, IL 60611. Web: www.ala.org/BookLinks.

Online/Offline: Themes and Resources. 9/year at $66.50. Rock Hill Press, 14 Rock Hill Rd, Bala Cynwyd, PA 19004. Web: www.rockhillpress.com/products.htm.

WEBSITES

CIA World Factbook: www.odci.gov/cia/publications/factbook/index.html. Detailed information about every country of the world.

United Nations Infonation: www.un.org/Pubs/CyberSchoolBus/infonation/e_infonation.htm. Statistical information on 185 nations.

Consumer Information Center: www.pueblo.gsa.gov. Many helpful government pamphlets available online.

Libraries: sunsite.berkeley.edu/Libweb. Links to the catalogs of more than 2,000 libraries in 70 countries can be found here.

The American Memory Project at the Library of Congress: memory.loc.gov/ammen. Thousands of photographs and the text of documents and pamphlets suitable for upper elementary and middle school students.

Ask ERIC: www.askeric.org. The Virtual Library section of this site contains lesson plans, links to the companion study guides to TV series and access to the journal literature and research

reports in the ERIC (Education Resources Information Center) system.

PBS site: www.pbs.org. This site has information on kids' favorite TV shows, such as "Arthur" and "Kratts' Creatures." "Reading Rainbow" is also found here. Bill Nye, the Science Guy, has his own website at nyelabs.kcts.org.

Author Sites

Many children's authors and illustrators have websites. Dav Pikey, Virginia Hamilton and Jan Brett, for example, have interesting ones. For links to these sites, go to the Children's Literature Web Guide at www.acs.ucalgary.ca/~dkbrown/authors.html or Kay Vandergrift's Learning about the Author and Illustrator Pages at www.scils.rutgers.edu/special.kay/author.html.

Corporate Websites

These sites sometimes have useful stuff for teachers. For example, look at www.crayola.com.

UNIVERSAL, STANDARD AND DAYLIGHT TIMES

Universal Time (UT) is also known as Greenwich Mean Time (GMT) and is the standard time of the Greenwich meridian (0° of longitude). A time given in UT may be converted to local mean time by the addition of east longitude (or the subtraction of west longitude), where the longitude of the place is expressed in time-measure at the rate of one hour for every 15°. Local clock times may differ from standard times, especially in summer when clocks are often advanced by one hour ("daylight saving" or "summer" time).

The time used in this book is Eastern Standard Time. The following table provides conversion between Universal Time and all Time Zones in the United States. An asterisk denotes that the time is on the preceding day.

Universal Time	Eastern Daylight Time	Eastern Standard Time and Central Daylight Time	Central Standard Time and Mountain Daylight Time	Mountain Standard Time and Pacific Daylight Time	Pacific Standard Time
0^h	* 8 P. M.	* 7 P. M.	* 6 P. M.	* 5 P. M.	* 4 P. M.
1	* 9	* 8	* 7	* 6	* 5
2	*10	* 9	* 8	* 7	* 6
3	*11 P. M.	*10	* 9	* 8	* 7
4	0 Midnight	*11 P. M.	*10	* 9	* 8
5	1 A. M.	0 Midnight	*11 P. M.	*10	* 9
6	2	1 A. M.	0 Midnight	*11 P. M.	*10
7	3	2	1 A. M.	0 Midnight	*11 P. M.
8	4	3	2	1 A. M.	0 Midnight
9	5	4	3	2	1 A. M.
10	6	5	4	3	2
11	7	6	5	4	3
12	8	7	6	5	4
13	9	8	7	6	5
14	10	9	8	7	6
15	11 A. M.	10	9	8	7
16	12 Noon	11 A. M.	10	9	8
17	1 P. M.	12 Noon	11 A. M.	10	9
18	2	1 P. M.	12 Noon	11 A. M.	10
19	3	2	1 P. M.	12 Noon	11 A. M.
20	4	3	2	1 P. M.	12 Noon
21	5	4	3	2	1 P. M.
22	6	5	4	3	2
23	7 P. M.	6 P. M.	5 P. M.	4 P. M.	3 P. M.

The longitudes of the standard meridians for the standard time zones are:

Eastern . . . . . 75° West   Central . . . . . 90° West   Mountain . . . . . 105° West   Pacific . . . . . 120° West

LEAP SECONDS

The information below is developed by the editors from data supplied by the International Earth Rotation Service.

Because of Earth's slightly erratic rotation and the need for greater precision in time measurement it has become necessary to add a "leap second" from time to time to our clocks to coordinate them with astronomical time. Rotation of the Earth has been slowing since 1900, making an astronomical second longer than an atomic second. Since 1972, by international agreement, adjustments have been made to keep astronomical and atomic clocks within 0.9 second of each other. The determination to add (or subtract) seconds is made by the Central Bureau of the International Earth Rotation Service, in Paris. Preferred times for adjustment have been June 30 and December 31, but any time may be designated by the International Earth Rotation Service. The first such adjustment was made in 1972, and as of Dec 31, 1998, a total of 22 leap seconds had been added. The additions have been made at 23:59:60 UTC (Coordinated Universal Time) = 6:59:60 EST (Eastern Standard Time). Leap seconds have been inserted into the UTC time scale on the following dates:

June 30, 1972	Dec 31, 1976	June 30, 1982	Dec 31, 1990
Dec 31, 1972	Dec 31, 1977	June 30, 1983	June 30, 1992
Dec 31, 1973	Dec 31, 1978	June 30, 1985	June 30, 1993
Dec 31, 1974	Dec 31, 1979	Dec 31, 1987	June 30, 1994
Dec 31, 1975	June 30, 1981	Dec 31, 1989	Dec 31, 1995
			June 30, 1997
			Dec 31, 1998

ALPHABETICAL INDEX

Events are generally listed under key words; events that can be attended are also listed under the states or countries where they are to be held. Many broad categories have been created, including African American, Agriculture, Animals, Aviation, Books, Civil Rights, Civil War, Computer, Constitution, Disabled, Earthquakes, Education, Employment, Environment, Ethnic Observances, Fire, Food and Beverages, Health and Welfare, Human Relations, Library/Librarians, Literature, Music, Native American, Parades, Poetry, Reading, Revolution (American), Safety, Science/Technology, Space Milestones, Storytelling, Television, Time/Calendars, United Nations, United States, World War I, World War II, Women, names of sports, etc. The index indicates only the initial date for each event.

See the chronology for inclusive dates of events lasting more than one day.

Aardema, Verna: Birth, June 6
Aaron, Hank: Birth, Feb 5
Aaron, Hank: Home Run Record: Anniv, Apr 8
Abbott and Costello Show TV Premiere: Anniv, Dec 5
Abdul-Jabbar, Kareem: Birth, Apr 16
Abolition Soc Founded, First American: Anniv, Apr 14
Abraham, Spencer: Birth, June 12
Absolutely Incredible Kid Day, Mar 16
Academy Awards, First: Anniv, May 16
Accession of Queen Elizabeth II: Anniv, Feb 6
Accordion Awareness Month, Natl, June 1
Ada, Alma Flor: Birth, Jan 3
Adams, Abigail: Birth Anniv, Nov 22
Adams, Ansel: Birth Anniv, Feb 20
Adams, John: Birth Anniv, Oct 30
Adams, John Quincy: Birth Anniv, July 11
Adams, John Quincy: Returns to Congress, Mar 4
Adams, Louisa Catherine Johnson: Birth Anniv, Feb 12
Adams, Richard: Birth, May 9
Adams, Samuel: Birth Anniv, Sept 27
Addams Family TV Premiere: Anniv, Sept 18
Addams, Jane: Birth Anniv, Sept 6
Adler, David A.: Birth, Apr 10
Adoff, Arnold: Birth, July 16
Adopt-a-Shelter-Animal Month, Oct 1
Adoption Month, Natl, Nov 1
Adoption Week, Natl, Nov 21
Advent, First Sunday of, Nov 28
Afghanistan,
  Independence Day, Aug 19
AFL Founded: Anniv, Dec 8
AFL-CIO Founded: Anniv, Dec 5
African Natl Congress Ban Lifted, Feb 2
African American,
  African American History Month, Natl, Feb 1
  African American Read-In, Feb 6
  Amistad Seized: Anniv, Aug 29
  Black History Month, Feb 1
  Black Page Appointed US House: Anniv, Apr 9
  Black Poetry Day, Oct 18
  Black Press Day: Anniv of First Black Newspaper in US, Mar 16
  Black Senate Page Appointed: Anniv, Apr 8
  Blacks Ruled Eligible to Vote: Anniv, Apr 3
  Brown, Jesse Leroy: Birth Anniv, Oct 13
  Bud Billiken Parade (Chicago, IL), Aug 14
  Civil Rights Act of 1964: Anniv, July 2
  Civil Rights Act of 1968: Anniv, Apr 11
  Civil Rights Bill of 1866: Anniv, Apr 9
  CORE Freedom Rides: Anniv, Apr 9
  Desegregation, US Army First: Anniv, July 26
  Drew, Charles: Birth Anniv, June 3
  Emancipation of 500: Anniv, Aug 1
  Escape to Freedom (F. Douglass): Anniv, Sept 3
  First American Abolition Soc Founded: Anniv, Apr 14
  First Black Governor Elected: Anniv, Nov 7

First Black Plays in NBA Game: Anniv, Oct 31
First Black Serves in US House Reps: Anniv, Dec 12
First Black US Cabinet Member: Anniv, Jan 18
First Natl Conv for Blacks: Anniv, Sept 15
Forten, James: Birth Anniv, Sept 2
Foster, Andrew: Birth Anniv, Sept 17
Frederick Douglass Speaks: Anniv, Aug 11
Juneteenth, June 19
King Awarded Nobel Peace Prize: Anniv, Oct 14
King, Martin Luther, Jr: Birth Anniv, Jan 15
Kwanzaa Fest, Dec 26
Loving v Virginia: Anniv, June 12
Meredith (James) Enrolls at Ole Miss: Anniv, Sept 30
Million Man March: Anniv, Oct 16
Minority Enterprise Development Week (Pres Proc), Oct 3
Minority Scientists Showcase (St. Louis, MO), Jan 15
Montgomery Boycott Arrests: Anniv, Feb 22
Montgomery Bus Boycott Begins: Anniv, Dec 5
NAACP Founded: Anniv, Feb 12
Ralph Bunche Awarded Nobel Peace Prize: Anniv, Dec 10
Robinson Named First Black Manager: Anniv, Oct 3
Rosa Parks Day, Dec 1
Stokes Becomes First Black Mayor in US: Anniv, Nov 13
Truth, Sojourner: Death Anniv, Nov 26
Agassi, Andre: Birth, Apr 29
Agnew, Spiro: Birth Anniv, Nov 9
Agriculture,
  Agriculture Day, Natl, Mar 20
  Agriculture Week, Natl, Mar 19
  Alabama State Fair, South (Montgomery, AL), Oct 8
  Alaska State Fair (Palmer, AK), Aug 27
  Arizona State Fair (Phoenix, AZ), Oct 21
  Arkansas State Fair (Little Rock, AR), Oct 8
  Big E (West Springfield, MA), Sept 17
  California State Fair (Sacramento, CA), Aug 20
  Colorado State Fair (Pueblo, CO), Aug 20
  Delaware State Fair (Harrington, DE), July 20
  Farm Animals Awareness Week, Natl, Sept 19
  Farm Safety Week, Natl (Pres Proc), Sept 19
  FFA Conv, Natl, Oct 27
  Florida State Fair (Tampa, FL), Feb 3
  Georgia National Fair (Perry, GA), Oct 8
  Grange Week, Apr 16
  Indiana State Fair (Indianapolis, IN), Aug 11
  Iowa State Fair (Des Moines, IA), Aug 12
  Kansas State Fair (Hutchinson, KS), Sept 10
  Kentucky State Fair (Louisville, KY), Aug 19
  Louisiana, State Fair of (Shreveport, LA), Oct 22
  Maryland State Fair (Timonium, MD), Aug 29
  Michigan State Fair (Detroit, MI), Aug 24

Minnesota State Fair (St. Paul, MN), Aug 26
Mississippi State Fair (Jackson, MS), Oct 6
Missouri State Fair (Sedalia, MO), Aug 12
Montana State Fair (Great Falls, MT), July 29
MontanaFair (Billings, MT), Aug 8
Nebraska State Fair (Lincoln, NE), Aug 27
Nevada State Fair (Reno, NV), Aug 25
New Jersey State Fair (Cherry Hill, NJ), Aug 3
New Mexico State Fair (Albuquerque, NM), Sept 11
New York State Fair (Syracuse, NY), Aug 26
North Carolina State Fair (Raleigh, NC), Oct 15
North Dakota State Fair (Minot, ND), July 21
Ohio State Fair (Columbus, OH), Aug 6
Oklahoma, State Fair of (Oklahoma City, OK), Sept 17
Oregon State Fair (Salem, OR), Aug 26
Rural Life Sunday, May 28
South Carolina State Fair (Columbia, SC), Oct 7
South Dakota State Fair (Huron, SD), Sept 1
Texas, State Fair of (Dallas, TX), Sept 24
Utah State Fair (Salt Lake City, UT), Sept 9
Vermont State Fair (Rutland, VT), Sept 3
Virginia on Strawberry Hill, State Fair of (Richmond, VA), Sept 23
Wisconsin State Fair (Milwaukee, WI), Aug 5
Wyoming State Fair (Douglas, WY), Aug 16
Ahlberg, Allan: Birth, June 5
Ahlberg, Janet: Birth, Oct 21
AIDS Day, World (UN), Dec 1
AIDS: White, Ryan, Apr 8
Aiken, Joan: Birth, Sept 4
Aikman, Troy: Birth, Nov 21
Ailey, Alvin: Birth Anniv, Jan 5
Air Conditioning Appreciation Days, July 3
Akaka, Daniel: Birth, Sept 11
Akihito: Birth, Dec 23
Alabama,
  Admission Day, Dec 14
  American Assn of School Librarians Conference (Birmingham), Nov 10
  Battle of Mobile Bay: Anniv, Aug 5
  South Alabama State Fair (Montgomery), Oct 8
Alamo: Anniv of the Fall, Mar 6
Alaska,
  Admission Day, Jan 3
  Alaska Day, Oct 18
  Alaska Day Celebration (Sitka), Oct 14
  Earthquake Strikes Alaska: Anniv, Mar 27
  Seward's Day, Mar 27
  State Fair (Palmer), Aug 27
Albania,
  Independence Day, Nov 28
Albright, Madeleine: Birth, May 15
Alcohol and Other Drug-Related Birth Defects Week, Natl, May 7
Alcohol Awareness Month, Natl, Apr 1
Alcott, Louisa May: Birth Anniv, Nov 29
Aldrin, Edwin "Buzz": Birth, Jan 20
Alexander, Lloyd: Birth, Jan 30
Alger, Horatio, Jr: Birth Anniv, Jan 13

Children's Day in Florida, **Apr 11**
Children's Eye Health and Safety Month, **Sept 1**
Children's Good Manners Month, **Sept 1**
Children's Lawn Party (Woodstock, CT), **Aug 7**
Children's Literature 2000, **Feb 10**
Children's Literature Festival (Keene, NH), **Oct 23**
Children's Literature Festival (Warrensburg, MO), **Mar 23**
Children's Literature New England, **Aug 15**
Children's Memorial Day, Natl, **Dec 12**
Children's Reading Fest (Ft Lauderdale, FL), **Apr 22**
Children's Sunday, **June 11**
Children's Vision and Learning Month, **Aug 1**
Chile,
  Independence Day, **Sept 18**
  National Month, **Sept 1**
Chimborazo Day, **June 3**
China, People's Republic of,
  Double 10th Day, **Oct 10**
  Dragon Boat Fest, **June 6**
  Fest of Hungry Ghosts, **Aug 25**
  International Children's Day, **June 1**
  Lantern Fest, **Feb 19**
  Mid-Autumn Fest, **Sept 24**
  National Day, **Oct 1**
  Qing Ming Fest, **Apr 8**
  Sun Yat-Sen Birth Anniv, **Nov 12**
  Tiananmen Square Massacre: Anniv, **June 4**
  Youth Day, **May 4**
Chinese Nationalists Move to Formosa: Anniv, **Dec 8**
Chinese New Year, **Feb 5**
Chirac, Jacques Rene: Birth, **Nov 29**
Chlumsky, Anna: Birth, **Dec 3**
Chou En-Lai: Death Anniv, **Jan 8**
Chretien, Jean: Birth, **Jan 11**
Christmas,
  Armenian Christmas, **Jan 6**
  Black Friday, **Nov 26**
  Christmas, **Dec 25**
  Christmas at the Top Museum (Burlington, WI), **Dec 26**
  Christmas Eve, **Dec 24**
  Christmas Greetings from Space: Anniv, **Dec 19**
  Christmas Tree/Rockefeller Center (New York, NY), **Dec 1**
  Humbug Day, **Dec 21**
  Macy's Thanksgiving Day Parade (New York, NY), **Nov 25**
  Navidades (Puerto Rico), **Dec 15**
  Old Calendar Orthodox Christmas, **Jan 7**
  Russia: Christmas Day, **Jan 7**
  Saint Nicholas Day, **Dec 6**
  Shopping Reminder Day, **Nov 25**
  Silent Night, Holy Night Celebrations (Austria), **Dec 24**
  Whiner's Day, Natl, **Dec 26**
Christopher, Matt: Birth, **Aug 16**
Chung Yeung Fest (Hong Kong), **Oct 17**
Churchill, Winston: Day, **Apr 9**
Ciardi, John: Birth Anniv, **June 24**
Cigarettes Reported Hazardous: Anniv, **Jan 11**
Cinco de Mayo (Mexico), **May 5**
Circle K Service Day, Intl, **Nov 13**
Circus: Greatest Show on Earth: Anniv, **Mar 28**
Citizenship Day (Pres Proc), **Sept 17**
Civil Aviation Day, Intl, **Dec 7**
Civil Rights,
  24th Amendment (Eliminated Poll Taxes), **Jan 23**
  Brown v Board of Education: Anniv, **May 17**
  Civil Rights Act of 1968: Anniv, **Apr 11**
  Civil Rights Act of 1964: Anniv, **July 2**

  Civil Rights Bill of 1866: Anniv, **Apr 9**
  Civil Rights Week (MA), **Dec 8**
  CORE Freedom Riders: Anniv, **Apr 9**
  March on Washington: Anniv, **Aug 28**
  Montgomery Bus Boycott: Anniv, **Dec 5**
  Rosa Parks Day, **Dec 1**
Civil War, American,
  Amnesty Issued for Southern Rebels: Anniv, **May 29**
  Battle of Antietam: Anniv, **Sept 17**
  Battle of Gettysburg: Anniv, **July 1**
  Battle of Mobile Bay: Anniv, **Aug 5**
  Civil War Ending: Anniv, **Apr 9**
  Davis, Jefferson: Inauguration: Anniv, **Feb 18**
  Fort Sumter Shelled by North: Anniv, **Aug 17**
  Grant Commissioned Commander: Anniv, **Mar 9**
  Lincoln Approves 13th Amendment (Freedom Day), **Feb 1**
  Lincoln Assassination Anniv, **Apr 14**
  Lincoln's Gettysburg Address: Anniv, **Nov 19**
  Sherman Enters Atlanta: Anniv, **Sept 2**
  Tubman, Harriet: Death Anniv, **Mar 10**
  U.S. Grant Put in Charge of Mississippi: Anniv, **Oct 16**
  Vote to Impeach Pres Andrew Johnson: Anniv, **Feb 24**
Clark, Abraham: Birth Anniv, **Feb 15**
Clark, Barney: Artificial Heart Transplant: Anniv, **Dec 2**
Clark, Joe: Birth, **June 5**
Clay (Muhammad Ali) Becomes Heavyweight Champ: Anniv, **Feb 25**
Clay, Cassius, Jr (Muhammad Ali): Birth, **Jan 17**
Clay, Henry: Birth Anniv, **Apr 12**
Clean-Off-Your-Desk Day, Natl, **Jan 10**
Cleary, Beverly: Birth, **Apr 12**
Cleland, Max: Birth, **Aug 24**
Clemens, Roger: Birth, **Aug 4**
Clemens, Samuel (Mark Twain): Birth Anniv, **Nov 30**
Clemente, Roberto: Birth Anniv, **Aug 18**
Clerc, Laurent: Birth Anniv, **Dec 26**
Clerc-Gallaudet Week, **Dec 5**
Clerihew Day (Edmund Bentley Clerihew Birth Anniv), **July 10**
Cleveland, Esther: First White House Presidential Baby, **Aug 30**
Cleveland, Frances: Birth Anniv, **July 21**
Cleveland, Grover: Birth Anniv, **Mar 18**
Cleveland, Grover: Second Pres Inauguration: Anniv, **Mar 4**
Clifton, Lucille: Birth, **June 27**
Clinton, George: Birth Anniv, **July 26**
Clinton, Hillary Rodham: Birth, **Oct 26**
Clinton, President, Impeached: Anniv, **Dec 20**
Clinton, William Jefferson: Birth, **Aug 19**
Cloning of an Adult Animal, First: Anniv, **Feb 23**
Clooney, George: Birth, **May 6**
Close, Glenn: Birth, **Mar 19**
Clown Fest, Emmett Kelly (Houston, MO), **May 6**
Clymer, George: Birth Anniv, **Mar 16**
CN Tower: Anniv, **June 26**
CNN Debuted: Anniv, **June 1**
Coast Guard Day, **Aug 4**
Cochise: Death Anniv, **June 8**
Cochran, Jacqueline: Death Anniv, **Aug 9**
Cochran, Thad: Birth, **Dec 7**
Cody, William F. "Buffalo Bill": Birth Anniv, **Feb 26**
Cohen, William S.: Birth, **Aug 28**
Coin Week, Natl, **Apr 16**
Coins Stamped "In God We Trust": Anniv, **Apr 22**
Cold War: Treaty Signed to Mark End: Anniv, **Nov 19**
Cole, Brock: Birth, **May 29**

Cole, Joanna: Birth, **Aug 11**
Coleman, Bessie: Birth Anniv, **Jan 26**
Colfax, Schuyler: Birth Anniv, **Mar 23**
Collier, Christopher: Birth, **Jan 29**
Collier, James Lincoln: Birth, **June 27**
Collins, David R.: Birth, **Feb 29**
Collins, Susan M.: Birth, **Dec 7**
Colombia: Independence Day, **July 20**
Color TV Broadcast, First: Anniv, **June 25**
Colorado,
  Admission Day, **Aug 2**
  Colorado Day, **Aug 2**
  State Fair (Pueblo), **Aug 20**
Columbus, Christopher,
  Columbus Day (Observed), **Oct 11**
  Columbus Day (Traditional), **Oct 12**
  Columbus Day, Natl (Pres Proc), **Oct 11**
  Columbus Sails for New World: Anniv, **Aug 3**
  Discovery of Jamaica By: Anniv, **May 4**
Comics: Funky Winkerbean: Anniv, **Mar 27**
Commodore Perry Day, **Apr 10**
Common Prayer Day (Denmark), **May 19**
Commonwealth Day (United Kingdom), **Mar 13**
Commonwealth Day, Belize, **May 24**
Communication Week, World, **Nov 1**
Communications: UN World Telecommunication Day, **May 17**
Communist Party Suspended, Soviet: Anniv, **Aug 29**
Community Education Day, Natl, **Nov 16**
Comoros: Independence Day, **July 6**
Compliment Day, Natl, **Jan 26**
Computer,
  Apple II Computer Released: Anniv, **June 5**
  Computer Learning Month, **Oct 1**
  Eckert, J. Presper, Jr: Birth Anniv, **Apr 9**
  IBM PC Introduced: Anniv, **Apr 24**
  Microsoft Releases Windows: Anniv, **Nov 10**
  Mouse Developed: Anniv, **Dec 9**
  Shareware Day, Intl, **Dec 12**
Concorde Flight, First: Anniv, **Jan 21**
Cone, David: Birth, **Jan 2**
Confederate Heroes Day, **Jan 19**
Confederate Memorial Day (FL, GA), **Apr 26**
Confederate Memorial Day (MS), **Apr 24**
Confederate Memorial Day (SC), **May 10**
Confederate Memorial Day (VA), **May 29**
Confederate Memorial Day/Jefferson Davis Day in Kentucky, **June 3**
Confederation, Articles of: Ratification Anniv, **Mar 1**
Confucius: Birthday and Teacher's Day (Taiwan), **Sept 28**
Confucius: Birthday Observance (Hong Kong), **Oct 6**
Congo (Brazzaville): National Holiday, **Aug 15**
Congo (Democratic Republic): Independence Day, **June 30**
Congress (House of Reps) First Quorum: Anniv, **Apr 1**
Congress Assembles (US), **Jan 3**
Congress: First Meeting Anniv, **Mar 4**
Congress First Meets in Washington: Anniv, **Nov 21**
Connecticut,
  Children's Lawn Party (Woodstock), **Aug 7**
  Connecticut Storytelling Fest (New London), **Apr 28**
  Constitution Ratification: Anniv, **Jan 9**
  Kid'rific (Hartford), **Sept 11**
  Kids After Christmas (Mystic), **Dec 26**
Connery, Sean: Birth, **Aug 25**
Conrad, Kent: Birth, **Mar 12**
Conrad, Pam: Birth, **June 18**
Conserve Water/Detect-a-Leak Week, **May 7**
Constantinople Fell to the Turks: Anniv, **May 29**

Reading (cont'd)——Safety

☆ *The Teacher's Calendar, 1999–2000* ☆ Index

Virgin (cont'd)——Women

Yes! Please send me additional copies of *The Teacher's Calendar, 1999–2000*.

Ship to _____

Address _____

_____

City, State, Zip _____

Phone (____) _____

Please send me _____ copies of *The Teacher's Calendar, 1999–2000*
at $19.95 each $_____

Add applicable sales tax in AL, CA, FL, IL, NC, NJ, NY, OH, PA, TX, WA $_____

Shipping & Handling: Add $5.00 for the first copy,
$3.50 for each additional copy $_____

                                          Total $_____

☐ Check or money order enclosed payable to: NTC/Contemporary Publishing Group

Charge my   ☐ Visa   ☐ MasterCard   ☐ American Express   ☐ Discover Card

Acct. #_____ Exp. Date ____ / ____

X _____

                     Signature (if charging to bankcard)

Name (please print) _____

GUARANTEE: Any book you order is unconditionally guaranteed and may be returned
within 10 days of receipt for full refund.

Prices subject to change without notice.

Mail to: **NTC/Contemporary Publishing Group, Inc.**
                  4255 W Touhy Ave
                  Lincolnwood, IL 60646-1975

<table>
<tr><td>┌─────────────────┐
│ **HOW TO SUBMIT**
│ **AN ENTRY**
└─────────────────┘</td><td>There is no charge for being listed in *The Teacher's Calendar*. Use the form below to submit new entries for forthcoming editions of *The Teacher's Calendar*. Background information about your entry is also appreciated. Please be sure your dates are confirmed for 2000–2001, or clearly indicate if dates are tentative. Use a separate sheet for each entry submitted. Information selected by the editors may</td></tr>
</table>

be used and publicized through their books, electronic formats, syndicated services and/or other related products and services. The editors reserve the right to select and edit information received. Please mail all information to: Editor, The Teacher's Calendar, NTC/Contemporary Publishing Group, 4255 W Touhy Ave, Lincolnwood, IL 60646-1975.

☞DEADLINE FOR 2000–2001 EDITION: DEC 15, 1999.   PLEASE TYPE OR PRINT VERY CLEARLY.

---

1. Exact name of entry:
2. Exact INCLUSIVE DATES for 2000/2001:
3. If applicable, estimated attendance (one figure—grand total all days):
4. Location (site [not address], city and state):
5. Brief description:

6. Formula—ONLY if used to set date(s) each year (Example: Annually, the third Monday in May):

7. For public use, complete contact info to be printed in book—name, address, phone, fax, e-mail, web.

8. For Teacher's Calendar staff use, complete address info we can use to mail our update form to you next year—name, title or department, organization name, address:

9. For Teacher's Calendar staff use, name, dept and phone and fax numbers of person we can call with questions about your entry:

10. Person furnishing information: (print) _____ (sign) _____
11. PLEASE CIRCLE THE EXACT INCLUSIVE DATES FOR YOUR 2000/2001 EVENT ON THE CALENDAR BELOW.

2000 – 2001

AUG 2000
S	M	T	W	T	F	S
		1	2	3	4	5
6	7	8	9	10	11	12
13	14	15	16	17	18	19
20	21	22	23	24	25	26
27	28	29	30	31		

NOV 2000
S	M	T	W	T	F	S
			1	2	3	4
5	6	7	8	9	10	11
12	13	14	15	16	17	18
19	20	21	22	23	24	25
26	27	28	29	30		

FEB 2001
S	M	T	W	T	F	S
				1	2	3
4	5	6	7	8	9	10
11	12	13	14	15	16	17
18	19	20	21	22	23	24
25	26	27	28			

MAY 2001
S	M	T	W	T	F	S
		1	2	3	4	5
6	7	8	9	10	11	12
13	14	15	16	17	18	19
20	21	22	23	24	25	26
27	28	29	30	31		

SEPT 2000
S	M	T	W	T	F	S
					1	2
3	4	5	6	7	8	9
10	11	12	13	14	15	16
17	18	19	20	21	22	23
24	25	26	27	28	29	30

DEC 2000
S	M	T	W	T	F	S
					1	2
3	4	5	6	7	8	9
10	11	12	13	14	15	16
17	18	19	20	21	22	23
24	25	26	27	28	29	30
31						

MAR 2001
S	M	T	W	T	F	S
				1	2	3
4	5	6	7	8	9	10
11	12	13	14	15	16	17
18	19	20	21	22	23	24
25	26	27	28	29	30	31

JUNE 2001
S	M	T	W	T	F	S
					1	2
3	4	5	6	7	8	9
10	11	12	13	14	15	16
17	18	19	20	21	22	23
24	25	26	27	28	29	30

OCT 2000
S	M	T	W	T	F	S
1	2	3	4	5	6	7
8	9	10	11	12	13	14
15	16	17	18	19	20	21
22	23	24	25	26	27	28
29	30	31				

JAN 2001
S	M	T	W	T	F	S
	1	2	3	4	5	6
7	8	9	10	11	12	13
14	15	16	17	18	19	20
21	22	23	24	25	26	27
28	29	30	31			

APR 2001
S	M	T	W	T	F	S
1	2	3	4	5	6	7
8	9	10	11	12	13	14
15	16	17	18	19	20	21
22	23	24	25	26	27	28
29	30					

JULY 2001
S	M	T	W	T	F	S
1	2	3	4	5	6	7
8	9	10	11	12	13	14
15	16	17	18	19	20	21
22	23	24	25	26	27	28
29	30	31				

Note: This page may be photocopied in order to submit additional event entries to *The Teacher's Calendar*

4255 W Touhy Ave, Lincolnwood, IL 60646-1975 • Phone (847) 679-5500 • Fax (847) 679-6388